D0074879

Zionism and Religion

ZIONISM
AND
RELIGION

Shmuel Almog,

Jehuda Reinharz, and

Anita Shapira, editors

BRANDEIS UNIVERSITY PRESS

in association with the Zalman Shazar Center for Jewish History

Published by University Press of New England ‖ Hanover and London

Brandeis University Press

Published by University Press of New England, Hanover, NH 03755

© 1998 by the Trustees of Brandeis University

All rights reserved

Printed in the United States of America   5 4 3 2 1

CIP data appear at the end of the book

Published with the support of the Jacob and Libby Goodman Institute for the Study of Zionism and Israel.

THE TAUBER INSTITUTE FOR THE STUDY OF EUROPEAN JEWRY SERIES

Jehuda Reinharz, General Editor

Michael Brenner, Associate Editor

The Tauber Institute for the Study of European Jewry, established by a gift to Brandeis University from Dr. Laszlo N. Tauber, is dedicated to the memory of the victims of Nazi persecutions between 1933 and 1945. The Institute seeks to study the history and culture of European Jewry in the modern period. The Institute has a special interest in studying the causes, nature, and consequences of the European Jewish catastrophe within the contexts of modern European diplomatic, intellectual, political, and social history.

The Jacob and Libby Goodman Institute for the Study of Zionism and Israel was founded through a gift to Brandeis University by Mrs. Libby Goodman and is organized under the auspices of the Tauber Institute. The Goodman Institute seeks to promote an understanding of the historical and ideological development of the Zionist movement through an exploration of the seminal issues in the history of Zionism and the State of Israel.

Gerhard L. Weinberg
World in the Balance: Behind the Scenes of World War II 1

Richard Cobb
French and Germans, Germans and French: A Personal Interpretation of France under Two Occupations, 1914–1918/1940–1944 2

Eberhard Jäckel
Hitler in History 3

Frances Malino and Bernard Wasserstein, editors
The Jews in Modern France 4

Jacob Katz
The Darker Side of Genius: Richard Wagner's Anti-Semitism 5

Jehuda Reinharz, editor
Living with Antisemitism: Modern Jewish Responses 6

Michael R. Marrus
The Holocaust in History 7

Paul Mendes-Flohr, editor
The Philosophy of Franz Rosenzweig 8

Joan G. Roland
Jews in British India: Identity in a Colonial Era 9

Yisrael Gutman, Ezra Mendelsohn, Jehuda Reinharz, and Chone Shmeruk, editors
The Jews of Poland Between Two World Wars 10

Avraham Barkai
From Boycott to Annihilation: The Economic Struggle of German Jews, 1933–1943 11

Alexander Altmann
The Meaning of Jewish Existence: Theological Essays 1930–1939 12

Magdalena Opalski and Israel Bartal
Poles and Jews: A Failed Brotherhood 13

Richard Breitman
The Architect of Genocide: Himmler and the Final Solution 14

Jehuda Reinharz and
Walter Schatzberg, editors
*The Jewish Response to German Culture:
From the Enlightenment to the Second
World War* 15

George L. Mosse
*Confronting the Nation:
Jewish and Western Nationalism* 16

Daniel Carpi
*Between Mussolini and Hitler:
The Jews and the Italian Authorities in
France and Tunisia* 17

Walter Laqueur and Richard Breitman
*Breaking the Silence: The German Who
Exposed the Final Solution* 18

Ismar Schorsch
*From Text to Context: The Turn
to History in Modern Judaism* 19

Jacob Katz
*With My Own Eyes:
The Autobiography of an Historian* 20

Gideon Shimoni
The Zionist Ideology 21

Moshe Prywes and Haim Chertok
Prisoner of Hope 22

János Nyiri
Battlefields and Playgrounds 23

Alan Mintz, editor
The Boom in Contemporary Israeli Fiction 24

Samuel Bak, paintings
Lawrence L. Langer, essay and commentary
Landscapes of Jewish Experience 25

Simon Rawidowicz
*State of Israel, Diaspora, and Jewish Contin-
uity: Essays on the "Ever-Dying People"* 26

Jacob Katz
*A House Divided: Orthodoxy and Schism
in Nineteenth Century Central European
Jewry* 27

Jeffrey Shandler and Beth S. Wenger, editors
*Encounters with the "Holy Land":
Place, Past and Future in American
Jewish Culture* 28

Elisheva Carlebach, John M. Efron, and
David N. Myers, editors
*Jewish History and Jewish Memory: Essays
in Honor of Yosef Hayim Yerushalmi* 29

Shmuel Almog, Jehuda Reinharz, and
Anita Shapira, editors
Zionism and Religion 30

The publication of these essays has been assisted by the Arnold Spicehandler Fund. This book is dedicated to the memory of Arnold Spicehandler, a life-long student of Jewish history who had unwavering faith in the promise of Zionism and its unfolding future.

Contents

Preface   xi

SHLOMO AVINERI
    Zionism and the Jewish Religious Tradition: The Dialectics   1
    of Redemption and Secularization

Tradition and Modernity in Eastern Europe

ISRAEL BARTAL
    Responses to Modernity: Haskalah, Orthodoxy, and   13
    Nationalism in Eastern Europe

YOSEF SALMON
    Zionism and Anti-Zionism in Traditional Judaism in   25
    Eastern Europe

EHUD LUZ
    The Limits of Toleration: The Challenge of Cooperation   44
    between the Observant and the Nonobservant during the
    Hibbat Zion Period, 1822–1895

STEVEN J. ZIPPERSTEIN
    Symbolic Politics, Religion, and the Emergence of   55
    Ahad Haam

AVIEZER RAVITZKY
    Munkács and Jerusalem: Ultra-Orthodox Opposition to   67
    Zionism and Agudaism

Orthodoxy, Liberalism, and Zionism in Western Europe

MICHAEL A. MEYER
    Liberal Judaism and Zionism in Germany   93

YAAKOV ZUR
    German Jewish Orthodoxy's Attitude toward Zionism   107

JEHUDA REINHARZ
    Zionism and Orthodoxy: A Marriage of Convenience   116

ROBERT S. WISTRICH
   Zionism and Its Religious Critics in Fin-de-Siècle Vienna   140

STUART A. COHEN
   Religious Motives and Motifs in Anglo-Jewish Opposition   159
   to Political Zionism, 1895–1920

Reform, Conservative, and Orthodox Judaism: Zionism in the United States

EVYATAR FRIESEL
   The Meaning of Zionism and Its Influence among the   175
   American Jewish Religious Movements

JONATHAN D. SARNA
   Converts to Zionism in the American Reform Movement   188

LLOYD P. GARTNER
   Conservative Judaism and Zionism: Scholars, Preachers,   204
   and Philanthropists

JEFFREY S. GUROCK
   American Orthodox Organizations in Support of Zionism,   219
   1880–1930

Tradition and Zionism in the Yishuv

SHMUEL ALMOG
   The Role of Religious Values in the Second Aliyah   237

ANITA SHAPIRA
   The Religious Motifs of the Labor Movement   251

ISRAEL KOLATT
   Religion, Society, and State during the Period of the   273
   National Home

CHAIM SCHATZKER
   Confronting the Religious Question within the Zionist   302
   Youth Movement

YARON TSUR
   The Religious Factor in the Encounter between Zionism and   312
   the Rural Atlas Jews

   List of Contributors   331
   Index   333

Preface

The link between nationalism and religion is undoubtedly a universal phenomenon. It emerges within the history of diverse national movements and has a formative influence on national consciousness and the various paths taken by nationalism.

This nexus is sometimes explained in terms of the opposition between nationalism and religion, or to be more precise, the antagonisms between the national movement and the official representatives of established religion. At times, it is religion that sustains nationalism, imbuing it with content and legitimacy. Moreover, this linkage is not fortuitous: perhaps there is indeed some mutual interdependence between religion and nationalism, which in the course of time acts to exacerbate the contrasts and antinomies between the two. The permutations in the dynamic interaction between nationalism and religion are not confined to the plane of historical events but are also evident in society and the intellectual sphere. National movements are far from homogeneous. They exhibit a range of nuances in their multifarious relations to religion; and various groups within the nation each tend to develop their own particular stance toward religion. It would appear that all national movements find themselves constrained to take some position in regard to religion and to reinterpret that relation anew from time to time.

That is all the more true in the case of Jewish nationalism, which lacks some of the distinguishing marks of nationalism more generally. On the eve of the era of modern nationalism, the ligature linking the Jews to past generations was universally conceived as a religious bond, not a national one. The very representation of Judaism as a national identity harbored a challenge to both the modern religious leaders in the West and the traditional Jewish leadership in Eastern Europe, despite the profound gulf that existed between them.

More than all other nationalist currents in Judaism, Zionism felt the need to define its specific position on religion and Jewish tradition. Zionism chose the historical homeland, the Holy Land, and Hebrew, the Holy Language, thus linking its fate to a sanctified and binding patrimony. Right from the beginning of the Zionist movement, its supporters were divided over the meaning of the obligation they had taken upon themselves by their embrace of the historical heritage. From the days of Hibbat Zion to the establishment of the State of Israel, the relation to religion was a source of repeated ideological and political dispute. Some saw religion as the essential foundation for Zionism, while others viewed it as a traditional component amenable to modern interpretation. Still others wished to wrench Zionism from the arms of religion. And some rejected Zionism out of hand, regarding it as the antithesis of traditional Judaism.

These quarrels formed part of the legacy of Zionist history, but debate developed in new directions within the Jewish state as a result of constraints engendered by time and, in particular, place. The establishment of the state marks the *terminus ad quem* of the era the essays gathered together here seek to examine. The volume is the product of a joint venture by scholars from Israel and the United States in a number of disciplines—history, sociology, Jewish philosophy, law, and other fields—who came together at Brandeis University for an international conference on Zionism and religion.

The conference aimed to shed light on various facets of the differing significations, particularly in regard to designations such as observant, Orthodox, Ultra-Orthodox, secular, nonobservant, and radical. Rather than attempt to impose a uniform terminology on the book, we have chosen to respect the wishes of the individual contributors and have thus left these terms open to multiple interpretations as they stand. We are confident that the reader will be able to grasp the author's intended purport on the basis of context.

The Brandeis conference on Zionism and religion was organized in cooperation with the Zalman Shazar Center for Jewish History and made possible through the generous support of Edgar Bronfman and the Samuel Bronfman Foundation, Frank Green, Betty and Max Ratner, Abram Sachar, Valya and Robert Shapiro and the Valya and Robert Shapiro Endowment, and Cyrene and Andrew Weiner. We acknowledge with thanks the assistance of Michael Brenner, Sylvia Fuks Fried, Ann Hofstra Grogg, Susan Jacobowitz, Mark Raider, and Janet Webber in the preparation of this volume for publication, as well as Maayan Avineri-Rebhun and Zvi Yekutiel of the Zalman Shazar Center for their cooperation and collegiality.

The Editors

Zionism and Religion

Zionism and the Jewish Religious Tradition

The Dialectics of Redemption and Secularization

I

In a letter to Walter Benjamin of August 1, 1933, Gershom Scholem says that Franz Kafka's "linguistic world . . . with its affinity to the Last Judgment, represents the prosaic in its most canonical." Not all the hidden ironies of this sentence will be obvious to an observer not familiar with the hermetic world of Scholem's complex relationship to Benjamin, but in the triangle of such disparate spirits as Kafka, Scholem, and Benjamin, it certainly brings out the complexity of the relationship to the Jewish religious traditions of three such major stars in the firmament of Jewish European culture.

In trying to delineate the boundaries of the complex relationships between Zionism and religion in modern Jewish life, I do not intend to supplement the meticulous historical studies recently published by Ehud Luz, Israel Bartal, Yosef Salmon, and—last and not least—Jacob Katz, whose breadth of vision fuses the historical and the sociological, the traditionally Jewish and the comparatively universal. My aim will be to suggest that beyond this complexity lies a much wider problem, one that also goes beyond the borders between religion and secularization in modern Jewish life. It is the question of the adequacy of the conventional answers given to the problem of the rise of modern nationalism in general. As such, this question relates to the general problem of the genesis and legitimization processes of transformative ideologies and movements.

Conventional historical writing has it that secularization is at the root of modern nationalism. It is true that Hans Kohn in his seminal study on nationalism goes back to the roots of ideas about nations to both classical Hellas and ancient Israel, but he, like practically everyone else who deals with the issues, attributed the rise of nationalism to the disintegration of the traditional modes of legitimacy implied in the old religious order. With the breakup of the *gens Christian* begins the quest for ethnicity, historicity, language, and national culture. The thesis I would like to propose in dealing with the question of Zionism and religion is that there exists a much more dialectical relationship between religion and nationalism. The secularization thesis, to my mind, has to be tested, and in testing it I suggest that it will be found wanting.

We know that historians invent the past and describe the future. The same can be said of political movements, and especially of revolutionary movements—and nationalism is one of these movements. But far from being a clear break with the past, national movements are essays in reinterpretations of the past and its retrieval. And since one element of this past has to deal with religion, every national movement has to deal in an innovative and transformative way with the religious dimension of its past. Far from being imagined communities, national communities relate to a past made usable, reinterpreted and retrieved.

Thus Irish nationalism, despite the fact that it was initiated mainly by people hailing from the Protestant ascendancy, became inextricably linked to the Catholic ingredient in Irish history; Polish nationalism, while inspired by the French Revolution, could not sever Polish history from its Catholic setting; Hungarian and German nationalism, despite the religious pluralism involved, did in one way or another get linked to some of the Protestant elements in their respective histories; and even Czech nationalism, for all its secular bent, did eventually identify a religious reformer, Jan Hus, as the first Czech patriot. How much Russian and Arab nationalism are linked with Orthodoxy and Islam, respectively, is incontestable, even if in the Arab case the origin of modern Arab nationalism derives from the specific problematic of an identifiable Christian Arab community (the Greek Orthodox, to be precise). And Greek nationalism—almost the paradigm of modern nationalism—had its strong attachment to the dream of the reconquest of Constantinople that some Western supporters of Greek independence, like Lord Byron, could hardly comprehend: they were intoxicated with the *Iliad*, while the Greeks fighting for their independence were inspired much more by the vision of cleansing Hagia Sophia from its Islamic abominations.

On the other hand, there is no doubt that the quest for a national symbol of political integration does attest to the attenuation of the traditional, religious bonds of allegiance. But is secularization to be seen as a total dismantling of religious attachment and its symbols, or is it an appropriation of these symbols? Paradoxically, the only political culture truly based on the principle of the separation of state and church—the American experience—presents, on the other side, a political realm imbued with a degree of a civil religion that is almost unprecedented in any other instance. The American experience may suggest that when a secular political belief system totally supplants religious alliance, then this new political ideology will become endowed with the trappings of a faith. As both François Furet and Simon Schama have recently shown,[1] this investment of the secular occurred in the

French Revolution and, as hinted above, in practically every modern national movement. The same applies to Zionism.

II

Let us start with what are the obvious truisms about Zionism. Zionism is not a linear continuation of the Jewish religious messianic quest. It is a modern and revolutionary ideology, signifying a clear break with the quietism of the religious belief in messianic redemption that should occur only through divine intercession in the mundane cycles of world history. Moses Hess and Leon Pinsker, Theodor Herzl and Max Nordau, Ber Borochov, and Vladimir Jabotinsky, all came from the secularized—and sometimes assimilated—Jewish intelligentsia, imbued with European ideas, sometimes driven by a feverish attempt to "make it" in the non-Jewish milieu of nineteenth- and twentieth-century Europe.

Because their names are occasionally cited as a refutation to this theory, one should add that Judah Solomon Hai Alkalai and Zvi Hirsch Kalischer, for all their traditionalism, are equally imbued with ideas derived from the general European experience and cannot be seen as acquiring their proto-Zionism merely from their religious background.

Impressed by the linguistic revival of Magyar and Slavonic languages, Alkalai suggests purely instrumental, and not sacral, arguments for the revival of the Hebrew language. While sticking to the traditionalist view about the divine provenance of ultimate redemption, he asks a very modern and instrumentalist question:

If the Almighty should indeed show us his miraculous favor and gather us into our land, we should not be able to speak to each other and such a divided community will not succeed. . . . We are alas so scattered and divided today, because each Jewish community speaks a different language and has different customs. These divisions are an obstacle to Redemption. . . . But one should not despair, but try with all our might to re-establish our language and make it central; and God Almighty will inspire the teachers and the students, *the boys and the girls*, to speak Hebrew fluently.[2]

Similarly, Alkalai reinterprets the traditional view of the preceding of the ultimate messiah, son of David, by a temporal messiah, son of Joseph, by suggesting that this terrestrial messianic forerunner should be understood not in terms of an individual but as a constituent assembly which would lay down the institutional framework for the social organization that could carry out the political work of the redemption:

The Redemption will begin by the efforts of the Jews themselves; they must organize and unite, choose leaders, and leave the land of exile. Since no community can exist without a governing body, the very first ordinance must be the appointment of the elders of each district to oversee all the affairs of the community. I humbly suggest that this chosen assembly—the Assembly of Elders—is what is meant by the promise to us of the Messiah, the Son of Joseph.

These elders should be chosen by our greatest magnates. . . . The organization of an international Jewish body is in itself the first step to the Redemption, for out of this organization there will come a fully authorized Assembly of Elders, and from the Elders, the Messiah, Son of Joseph, will appear.[3]

While still cloaked within the normative language of traditional religiosity, the idea of general education for boys and girls, as well as the idea of a representative assembly, are modern and revolutionary. They could not appear before 1789.

Similarly Kalischer, when exhorting his fellow Jews to make sacrifices for their homeland and remember it not only in their prayers but in their daily praxis, draws on the experience of his contemporary European world:

Why do the people of Italy and of other countries sacrifice their lives for the land of their fathers, while we, like men bereft of strength and courage, do nothing? Are we inferior to all other peoples, who have no regard for life and fortune as compared with the love of their land and nation? Let us take to heart the examples of the Italians, Poles, and Hungarians, who laid down their lives and possessions in the struggles for national independence, while we, the children of Israel, who have the most glorious and holiest of lands as our inheritance, are spiritless and silent. Should we not be ashamed of ourselves?[4]

While these modern ingredients are clear in the thoughts of Alkalai and Kalischer, Samuel Mohilever's address to the First Zionist Congress is replete with circumlocutions and admonitions, suggesting the difficulties faced by a religious leader calling for a movement that is basically political. While praying for the success of the deliberations of the congress, he also offers a prayer that members "not stumble with their tongues, God forbid, to speak against our Holy Law or in opposition to the secular governments that rule over us. . . . Allow them to find favor in the eyes of Kings, Princes and Rulers before whom they may stand to plead for Thy people and Thy land." Mohilever clearly circumscribes the aims of the movement by suggesting that it should "intercede . . . with the Turkish government to permit our people to purchase land and to build houses without hindrance." But then he goes on to suggest that *mitzvat yishuv haaretz* (the commandment to settle the Land of Israel) is a fundamental commandment, and "some say is equivalent to all of the Torah."[5] Starting from rather timid premises, it is Mohilever himself who lays the halakhic foundations for what would only later appear as the unusual amalgam of religiosity and Zionism in the thought of Rabbi Abraham Isaac Kook.

III

Paradoxically, Zionism is not the only movement in the modern Jewish world that could be understood by some of its adherents as a reinterpretation of the messianic belief. It is today almost totally forgotten that emancipation—sometimes personified by the appearance of Napoleon and his armies—was greeted by many Jews as the modern realization, in terrestrial terms, of the messianic dream. And much of the spiritual *élan* of the Reform movement grew out of the intellectual ability of interpreting such a secular phenomenon as political emancipation in messianic terms. But even before that, the Declaration of the Rights of Man and the Citizen and its enactment as the law of the land in the wake of French military victories in the Netherlands and the Rhineland produced numerous Hebrew odes to liberty composed by members of the Jewish communities in Amsterdam and Cologne, who welcomed the French armies as the troops of the Lord of Hosts liberating the Israelites and leading them to the Promised Land of Liberty, Equality, and Fraternity. Similarly, Samson Raphael Hirsch and Zacharias Fränkel tried to redefine Jewish religion within the context of emancipation, balancing civic duties with adherence to the Torah and thus incorporating some universalistic elements into what eventually appeared as normative Neo-Orthodoxy. Not only Reform Judaism but also the articulate spokesmen of Western Neo-Orthodoxy incorporated this interpretation of modernity as somewhat approaching the end of times and, in any case, a break in the jeremiad of Jewish history. Out of all these conflicting reinterpretations of Judaism, the context became ripe for the specific Zionist reinterpretation.

How much even that most secularized, if not assimilated, vision of Zionism heralded by Theodor Herzl brings out these elements of continuity should not be overlooked. The accusation against Herzl that his vision of Zion lacked a cultural context has become a commonplace since it was first voiced by Ahad Haam, and it is basically correct. His contention that Hebrew cannot be revived and that the cultural life of the New Zion will be dominated by German literature, French theater, and Italian opera hardly appears to address the questions of culture involved in nationalism. Yet in his *Altneuland* (1902), a Temple of Peace stands at the center of Jerusalem (though not suggesting it would replace the mosques on the Temple Mount), and the last word in the novel is "God," as if to answer the numerous explanations offered by the various participants, about the origins of the "Old-New Land." These intimations may be no more than the minimal piety of the Austro-Hungarian subject who recognizes religion as an ingredient of the political order, yet they are still there.

The real paradox is that the one movement within Zionism more successful than others in reinterpreting the redemptive language of normative Judaism and adapting it to the political aims of Zionism has been the Labor Zionist movement. For all its militant atheism in the formative years of the Yishuv, this movement created a universe of discourse that, while revolutionary and innovative, was deeply steeped in the symbolical language of the Judaic tradition. Not only were land, language, and people given a modern reinterpretation. The revival of Hebrew was seen as a triumph not for a sacral language but for the historical language. Yet the texts thus raised to a normative and symbolical level were deeply imbued with a religious tradition. The return to the study of the Bible—basically neglected by exilic Judaism, which was much more talmudo-centric than biblio-centric—gave to the Bible a new meaning as the source for the historical knowledge of the past of the Jewish people. Its poetry was made into the poetry of literature, not of a religious vision, while the prophets were reinterpreted as the forerunners and advocates of social justice and universal human—if not socialist—redemption. The jubilee year and the fallow year became another example of this socially oriented vision of Zionism grounded in a reinterpretation of a religious tradition. And no one ever doubted that the Sabbath would be the day of rest in the Jewish land, even if shorn of its religious observance. And in most *kibbutzim, oneg shabbat* became the substitute for the prayer and prayer-meals connected with the traditional Sabbath.

One has to look carefully at the language used by Zionist institutions to realize the force of this reinterpretation of tradition. Buying land from Arab proprietors for Jewish settlement became *geulat haaretz*—the redemption of the land—not just a matter of sometimes shady real estate transactions. The Jewish National Fund was called in Hebrew *Keren Kayemet*, with all the necessary associations with the permanence of proprietary rights involved in this Jewish rabbinical legal term. Hanukah was interpreted as a triumph in a war of national liberation, and the three main festivals, while shorn of their strict religious observance, were retained as festivals of nature, with the additional twist that Passover became a symbol for both national liberation and the first successful revolt of slaves in history. Even in the depth of their Stalinist infatuation in the 1950s, Hashomer Hazair *kibbutzim* celebrated Passover with *haggadot* in which odes to Stalin, "who pulled us out from the house of slavery," alternated with rites of spring associated with Passover—all in the eclectic nature of the traditional *haggadah*.

A. D. Gordon's "religion of labor" clearly viewed itself as a substitute for traditional religion, and his language clearly attests to this. And on another symbolical level, Berl Katznelson insisted that workers' soup kitchens in the 1920s not serve pork—not because of religious observance but because not eating pork had become a historical Jewish symbol ("since we have been martyred for it"). This restriction is another example of how a revolutionary movement is legitimized by a language that is historical and replete with a reinterpretation of a religious tradition. Similarly, the Tel Hai Memorial Day on 11th Adar became an evocative moment in the new Palestinian calendar because, in part, of Katznelson's powerful memorial, "Yizkor Am Israel," consciously modeled on the *yizkor* prayer while omitting any reference to the divinity. Hundreds of similar examples could be cited as evidence of reinterpretation through a powerful synthesis of creativity and conservation.

The Labor Zionist movement was more successful in reinterpreting tradition than other movements within Zionism. The so-called general Zionists lacked that *élan* and ideological richness, and the Revisionist movement, with its cult of personality and power, paradoxically introduced the most un-Jewish elements to be found within the modern Jewish national movement. Not only was Jabotinsky himself far from an attachment to any form of Jewish culture; his choice of Samson as his heroic figure suggests a Dionysian element integral to some strong currents in early twentieth-century European culture. It should also come as no surprise that the founders of the Canaanite movement—Adaya Horon, Yonatan Ratosh, and Aharon Amir—came from a Revisionist background.[6] That the social origins of most Labor Zionists were the Jewish *shtetlekh*, while the general Zionists as well as the Revisionists initially tended to come from the more urban, and therefore more assimilated, milieus, adds a sociological dimension to the cultural context in which this reinterpretation took place.

Seen in this context, the historical alliance between the Labor Zionist movement and the National Religious Party appears thus as more than merely a marriage of convenience—much as the details of this historical coalition were dictated by the politics of the day. Paradoxically, the erstwhile atheists of the Labor movement and the moderate religious Zionists were moving within parallel discourses relating to the same tradition, and while the interpretations varied and conflicted, they were not strangers to the same language that was their common heritage.

The current rupture of this traditional alliance of Labor and religious Zionists may then portend more than a mere breakdown of a mutually rewarding political coalition. Similarly, the current decline of Labor may also suggest more than a mere weakening of electoral appeal and a failure of leadership. Since 1948, the Labor Party has hardly been successful in continuing its work of historical reinterpretations. Perhaps *kibbutz galuyot* (the ingathering of the exiles) was the last attempt of linking a modern political agenda with traditional symbolism as reinterpreted by the Labor movement. Currently, the Labor Party lacks the sources of its historical appeal—a transformative ideology that nonetheless draws on a reinterpretation of historical, traditional, and religious symbols and discourse.

If Zionism is, then, a transformative revolution that reinterprets the traditions of the past, its future equally hinges on a reemergence of such a historical synthesis between memory and political praxis, for it is only those revolutions that were able to integrate historical memory into their future-oriented praxis which proved to be successful.

In a surprising way, some of these dilemmas have been prefigured in the thoughts of Moses Hess, the first secular proto-Zionist thinker. Coming from the socialist tradition, Hess nonetheless admitted that one had to recognize the role of the religious Jewish tradition in preserving Jewish national self-consciousness. Consequently he castigated Reform Judaism, as then practiced in Germany and Hungary, as denuding the Jews of their national identity, and in his *Rome and Jerusalem* (1862) there is much more sympathy for the role—not the normative content—of Orthodoxy than for Reform. Equally, Hess was the first to reinterpret the Judaic legislation about the fallow year and the jubilee year as "social democratic."

But the most poignant confrontation appears in the last part of *Rome and Jerusalem*. There Hess responds to the comments of one of his correspondents. Hess admits that the reestablishment of a Jewish commonwealth in Palestine may give birth to voices calling for the rebuilding of the Temple of Solomon and the reintroduction of animal sacrifices there. How could he, a secular socialist, acquiesce in such consequences of his call for the rebirth of a Jewish commonwealth?

Hess's response is classical, though not well known in the current debates about state and religion in Israel. First he presents a lengthy historical excursus on the origins and legitimacy of animal sacrifices in biblical Judaism, following Maimonides' line of argument that the sacrifices were never central to Judaism and were historically a compromise measure intended to help legitimize a monotheistic, invisible god in a society permeated with paganism and indiscriminate sacrifices, including human sacrifices. Hess hopes that modern Judaism, on returning to the Land of Israel, would be enlightened enough to realize that in the contemporary world such defense measures against residual paganism would no longer be necessary. But, he then reluctantly admits, even if the rabbis will not been enlightened enough, and will insist on reinstituting animal sacrifices, such an obvious barbarity should not be used to undermine the whole enterprise of the rebirth of the Jewish people as a modern nation in its historical homeland. In the romantic vein that sometimes underlines his rhetoric, Hess then likens his own attachment to the historical Jewish people to a lover's sentiment toward his beloved:

Real love . . . is in actuality blind. It is blind because it does not aim, philosophically or aesthetically, at the perfect qualities of the beloved creature, but loves it as it is, with its faults and its perfections; it does not try to gloss them over, but it loves the undivided individuality of the object of its love.

The scar on the face of my beloved does not diminish my love for her one bit. On the contrary, it may even be more dear to me—who knows?—than her beautiful eyes, which can be found in other beautiful women as well, while this scar is characteristic of the individuality of my beloved.[7]

"The scar on the face of my beloved": no idealization of the past, no romanticized nostalgia. Neither is the scar viewed as a norm, to be revered in its distinctiveness. It is, and remains, a scar—but it is the scar on the face of the beloved one. Such is the dialectics of history and transformation, of memory and renewal in all historical national movements, and the Zionist example is a classic case.

Notes

1. François Furet, *Revolutionary France, 1770–1880* (Oxford, 1992); Simon Schama, *Citizens: A Chronicle of the French Revolution* (New York, 1989).

2. Judah Solomon Hai Alkalai, *Minhat Yehuda*, 1945, in *The Zionist Idea,* ed. Arthur Hertzberg (New York, 1969), p. 106 (italics added).

3. Ibid., pp. 106–7.

4. Zvi Hirsch Kalischer, *Derishat Zion,* 1862, in ibid., p. 114.

5. Samuel Mohilever, Address to the First Zionist Congress, 1897, in ibid., pp. 402–4.

6. Yehoshua Porath's *Shelah veet beyado: Sipur hayav shel Uriel Shelah* (Tel-Aviv, 1989), a study of Yonatan Ratosh, brings out this connection between Revisionist "goyish" power cult and Canaanite ideology.

7. Moses Hess, *Ausgewählte Schriften,* ed. Horst Lademacher (Cologne, 1962), p. 274. See also my *Moses Hess: Prophet of Communism and Zionism* (New York, 1985), p. 236.

TRADITION AND MODERNITY IN EASTERN EUROPE

Responses to Modernity

Haskalah, Orthodoxy, and Nationalism in Eastern Europe

The challenge of modernity first penetrated the consciousness of Eastern European Jewry during the waning years of the independent Polish Commonwealth. The ideas of social and political reform that influenced statesmen and administrators in the Polish state before it was partitioned among its neighbors were not foreign to the Jews, and as slices of Poland were annexed to the Russian and Austrian Empires and Prussian kingdom, the influence of these ideas seemed increasingly crucial for the survival of the traditional Jewish way of life. But the ideals of the European Enlightenment were not yet threatening to supplant the fundamentals of the Jewish heritage, although the former were already known in Eastern Europe. Nor was there a sense that religious and cultural values were being lost. The menace of the Haskalah was not felt in Eastern Europe until the passing of Napoleon: in Galicia not before the second and third decades of the nineteenth century; in Lithuania not until the 1840s. But what did threaten Jewish society and traditional Jewish life as it had been lived in the Polish Commonwealth for centuries was above all the institutional revolution: the alteration in the authority of the Jewish community and the powers of the autonomous Jewish institutions.

Within a few years, the exposure of Polish Jewry to the administrative reforms that had been promulgated in the states of Central and Eastern Europe undermined the authority of the internal Jewish governing institutions and set off a sociological restructuring that has yet to be adequately studied. It has been shown that the Austrian and Russian regimes, while partially or totally abolishing the competence of the autonomous Jewish institutions, coopted the social elites of Eastern Europe into the changing political systems. An examination of the leadership of the Jewish community of Brody during the first half of the nineteenth century, for example, reveals that scions of the families that had held leadership posts in the eighteenth century continued to play a central role well into the Austrian period. In Vilna, the leadership stratum survived without modification from the Polish into the Russian period. Nevertheless, the administrative reforms, accompanied by the change in regimes, did lead to significant developments.

First, the age-old link between the Jewish elite and the Polish nobility grew ever more tenuous—or at least lost its political significance. Whereas the rabbis and wealthy community leaders of prepartition Poland had intimate contacts with the social and political networks of the Polish aristocracy and sometimes even owed their posts to a Polish patron with political influence, in postpartition Poland this relationship grew less and less significant. It was replaced by strengthening ties between the state bureaucracy and the Jewish community, accompanied by a gradual depreciation of the latter's authority that culminated in the formal abolition of the *kahal*, or governing body. One must not forget, of course, that in Lithuania this significant change in the relations between Jews and Poles was delayed until after the failure of the Polish insurrection of 1831 and was not reflected in any major way in Congress Poland until 1863. Nevertheless, the parting of ways between the Polish aristocracy and Jewish autonomy was already on the horizon at the time of the first partition in 1772.

Second, the administrative reforms that affected the Jews were ultimately aimed at integrating them into the polity of the estates as part of the bourgeoisie (although there were exceptions in both Austria and Russia), since they were a distinctly urban group. Specifically, the reforms meant the abrogation of Jewish society as a self-sufficient corporate body and its merger into broader corporate groupings. For example, the reforms of Catherine the Great integrated the Jews into the municipal administrations in Belorussia, even though the *kahal* continued to be recognized. Integration can be traced even more clearly in Russian legislation affecting Jews in the first half of the nineteenth century that divided the Jews into classes and subclasses. Fundamentally, the transition was from a view of the Jews as a separate "nation," with their own corporate institutions, as had been the situation in the Polish Commonwealth, to a view of them as subjects professing a different faith, who fit into one corporate framework or another in accordance with their economic status and occupation.

But a series of factors hindered this transformation of the Jews from a medieval "nation" into subjects professing another religion; these factors shaped the differing influence of modernity in Eastern Europe as opposed to Western and Central Europe. First, we should note the power of the social structures that sustained the collective Jewish existence even in the absence of the *kahal* in its traditional format. Jewish society maintained well-developed social structures that, in the course of the nineteenth century, came to provide an almost total alternative to the old corporate structure. Even though the state bent the autonomous organizations to its yoke and supervised their activities, the Jews of Eastern Europe managed to preserve a significant portion of their traditional way of life alongside the old corporation and later even without it. These social structures were: (1) the hasidic movement, which spread throughout Eastern Europe precisely during the years when the absolutist regimes threatened Jewish collective existence; (2)

the supracommunal *yeshivot*, of which the first was Volozhin in nineteenth-century Lithuania; (3) various types of associations or societies that took over some of the *kahal*'s roles within the community and later replaced it. These three sociological phenomena, which perpetuated movements, organizations, and institutions that predated the dismantling of Jewish autonomy, were certainly not the only social factors that helped preserve the unity of Eastern European Jewish society. But an analysis of their influence on Jewish society's capacity to withstand the external threats can teach us something about the influence of similar factors not mentioned here. The secret of these bodies' power certainly lay in their religious underpinnings: they drew their authority from faith in the power of the *zaddik* or *rebbe*; from the Torah-derived authority of the great sages of Lithuania; or from the "sanctity" attributed to Jewish society as a whole in the premodern era. The authority of the *kahal*, too, had sprung from religious sources, and the traditional community was a corporation founded on holiness. When the *kahal* withered, the bodies and organizations that performed its functions were able to stand in for it without any crisis of secularization or revolutionary change to an organization with a modern character. The hasidic sects, the supracommunal *yeshivot*, and the various societies ensured the total and continuous domination of life by religion. Whereas Eastern European authorities wanted to reform traditional Jewish society by separating the religious element from civil life, the "confessional" from the "political"—a central tenet of the European Enlightenment, adopted both by the *maskilim* and the Orthodox in Germany—membership in these groups permitted an almost autarkic existence "alongside" the state, with no conscious concession of the integrity of the old way of life. In short, even in the era that sought to break down the traditional social frameworks, an alternative way was found to channel traditional life into new paths over which the state had no direct influence or power. It is no coincidence that the Eastern European *maskilim* saw the despised *hasidim* as the political foes of the state and took great pains to convince Austrian and Russian authorities of this. Haskalah literature is replete with negative descriptions of ways the *hasidim* impede the integration of the Jews into their social environment, display rampant hostility to the political and social order, and carry out their activities far from the watchful eye of the government administration.

Another reason why Eastern European Jewish society sustained its unique nature despite the political changes has to do with the ethnic and demographic structure of Eastern Europe. Significant factors include the large number of Jews and their concentration in the cities and towns, where they sometimes constituted an almost absolute majority; the dispersion of Jewish communities over large districts; the ongoing contacts among the various population centers (in the nineteenth century hundreds of thousands of Jews flocked from Lithuania to central and western Poland and from Galicia to New Russia); and the lack of a significant social stratum

among the surrounding gentiles who could serve as a model for acculturation. For all of these reasons, the large Jewish population acquired by the
powers that partitioned Poland underwent almost no change during the next
two generations. True, a wafer-thin economic elite adopted one of the dominant cultures in the region—Polish, Russian, or German. But the vast majority of Jewish society preserved its unique nature. As the first buds of
modern nationalism were sprouting in Eastern Europe, one could still speak
of the Jews as a distinct group. Even those who desired the disappearance of
the Jews as a separate entity, like the radical *maskilim* of the 1860s and
1870s, or the first Jewish socialists, like A. S. Liebermann, recognized the
unique lineaments of Eastern European Jewish society.

Thus the Eastern European Jews' awareness of their separate and unique
identity was drawn both from the unbroken existence of voluntary corporate social frameworks and from their geographic and demographic situation. Haskalah literature has many detailed descriptions of Jewish society as
a separate entity closed off from its surroundings, having almost nothing in
common with the outside world. Its affairs were settled by internal bodies
and organizations, and "foreigners" had no foothold within its domain.
The reader of this literature gets the impression that, so far as the *maskilim*
were concerned, the massive intervention by the centralized state worked
no significant changes in traditional society. A similar impression is con-
veyed by Polish and Russian writings of the mid-nineteenth century. There
the Jews appear as a large block of strange and alien people who show no
real inclination to change, over whom the state has no control worthy of the
name, and who manage their own internal affairs as if the *kahal* had never
been abolished. Such arguments were sounded with increasing frequency
following the birth of modern antisemitism in Eastern Europe. The "invisible" *kahal* was associated, *inter alia*, with the solidarity of Jewish society
and identified as a single limb of the large body of a nation living throughout the western provinces of the Russian Empire. The influence of modernity, as expressed through the bureaucratic apparatus of the state, was extremely limited in Eastern Europe. In the final analysis, the government
schools for Jews that were established in Austrian Galicia and the Pale of
Settlement did not generate significant changes; nor did the compulsory
military service, with which the Jews contended with relative success
through the selective induction of members of the lower classes. Three
decades of autocratic rule by Nicholas I (1825–55) left no measurable imprint on the unique nature of Jewish society. It was rather during the reign
of Alexander II (1855–81), when a relaxation of legal restrictions accompanied major economic developments, that the massive changes worked by
the modern age became a central issue of conscious concern.

The 1860s and 1870s wrought a major demographic, economic, and
social upheaval among the Jewish communities of Eastern Europe. The
accelerated rise of the capitalist economy, the growth of the large cities

and improvement of means of transportation, the abolition of serfdom and sundering of the Jews from the estate system—all severely impinged on the institutions of traditional society and eradicated what all the Russian and Austrian decrees had failed to budge. Massive emigration from the less-developed regions to the new centers of industrialization changed the map of Jewish population dispersal. Cities such as Odessa and Warsaw that had almost no Jews at the beginning of the nineteenth century became important communities with tens and even hundreds of thousands of members. At the same time, the social forces that held Jewish society together during the first half of the century lost some of their potency and were no longer able to cope with new and unfamiliar challenges. Simultaneously, some segments of Jewish society redoubled their efforts to integrate into the dominant cultures and began writing and speaking Russian, Polish, or German. New organizational patterns and vehicles of communication appeared in Eastern Europe that had been hitherto practically unknown—in Russia, the Hebrew-, Yiddish-, Russian-, and Polish-language press, for example, and Hevrat Marbei Haskalah, the Society for the Promotion of Enlightenment among the Jews. The disintegrative forces of urbanization and industrialization undid social frameworks that had survived so tenaciously despite the onslaught of government policy. It was precisely now, in an age when the conservative faction in Jewish society had entered into an alliance with the authorities, that its ability to stand in the breach against new developments was weakened. It is true that the influence of Hasidism did not abate in the second half of the nineteenth century; on the contrary, it gained strength even in the densely populated Jewish districts of the metropolises. The Lithuanian *yeshivot*, too, grew and increased in number. But unlike the situation in the first half of the century, there was also an accelerated mass disintegration of traditional society, reflected, *inter alia*, in the tradition's loss of authority for broad segments of the population. Another change, with profound implications for the growth of new political movements within Jewish society, was the increasing consolidation of a significant social stratum that to a large extent cut itself off from the traditional way of life. Within the span of a single generation Eastern European Jewry became much more heterogeneous, and the distance between its various segments widened. In the 1860s and 1870s some Jews of Warsaw—the Polonized branch of the family—grew further apart from their Russian cousins in St. Petersburg. Both, of course, were vastly different from the "German" Jew of Posen and Breslau. But the quickening of the processes of modernity also had a dialectic influence that reinforced the bonds within Jewish society: the Jewish press, mentioned above, linked Vienna with Odessa and Warsaw with Vilna; the mounting tide of westward migration filled Warsaw with Litvaks and Vienna with Galitsianers; the disintegration of the old forms of life and the rush to urban centers brought extremes together and made the massive presence of Jews as a distinct and different element even more conspicuous.

The two major responses of the Ashkenazi diaspora to the encounter with modernity were the Haskalah movement and Orthodoxy. Both flourished in Central Europe, inexorably intertwined. As early as the 1780s the Berlin-Königsberg Haskalah spawned an Orthodox reaction. The German Haskalah united within itself two vastly different social elements: the economic elite, which had close ties with the government bureaucracy, and the circle of Jewish intellectuals, many of them from Eastern Europe, who congregated in Berlin. The two groups shared the idea that Jewish society ought to adapt itself to the new age in philosophy, political and social behavior, and life-style. Quite soon, however, the members of the second group recoiled from the rapid changes taking place all around them and ultimately adopted a far more moderate stance on reforms in Jewish society.

It was this retreat that enabled the Haskalah movement to continue after the Berlin period. The "moderate" *maskilim* did not see the Haskalah as a transitional phenomenon between traditional Jewish society and full integration into the host culture, but imagined instead a reformed Jewish society that would maintain its own language and culture. Paradoxically, one could even say that even at its inception the Haskalah movement contained an element of Orthodox reaction—defensiveness alongside controlled adaptation—to modernity. Orthodoxy, a phenomenon unique to the new age, also bloomed while merging various trends. It combined an element of adaptation, dictated by a positive attitude toward German society and the state, with an element of rejection and self-protection. In different regions and times, some version of one or the other element was dominant. But certain fundamentals of the moderate Haskalah could always be accepted by members of German Neo-Orthodoxy. The ideas of Naftali Herz Wessely, for example, were quite compatible with the Orthodox conception that blended scrupulous observance of religious commandments with civil and cultural assimilation into the German milieu.

This approach was not appropriate for the cultural and social situation of Eastern European Jewry, where the Jews maintained social frameworks with a distinctly corporate nature. Even though it is common to speak of an Eastern European Orthodox reaction to the political and social changes, that reaction does not at all resemble its German counterpart. In Germany, Orthodoxy was fundamentally a matter of making the religious element of life fit in with the demands of the state and the spirit of the age, while leaving behind the total immersion that had typified life in the tradition community. In Eastern Europe this total immersion continued, with no separation of religion and life. In Germany new organizations sprang up, many of which seceded from the existing community. In Eastern Europe the social reorganization preceded the challenge of modernity—or at least was not a response to it. Another difference, which has major significance for the intensity of the reaction to the changes wrought by modernity, was that German Orthodoxy was born as a reaction to the attempts to reform religious ritual and modify the liturgy. In Eastern Europe, however, the *maskilim* took on all of traditional society with their aim to modify social and economic activity, their desire to reform language and behavior, and their revision of attitude toward the state and neighboring peoples—but hardly touched matters of ritual and liturgy.

The Eastern European Haskalah also differed from its Berlin antecedent in its attitude toward Jewish autonomy. The *maskilim* did indeed speak of removing the barriers that separated the Jews from other peoples, but they never imagined a total abrogation of the distinct Jewish identity and transformation of the Jews into a merely confessional community. Such stances are much more visible when the radical Haskalah makes its appearance in the 1860s and 1870s. In the controversy with radicals like Abraham Uri Kovner, who foresaw the total elimination of a separate Jewish existence, veteran *maskilim* adopted positions that favored the clear perpetuation of this existence. Men like Abraham Dov Gottlober and Abraham Mapu, members of the older generation of *maskilim*, thought of the integration of Jewish society into the Russian state as rapprochement rather than assimilation. Their religious and cultural outlook corresponded with their expectations of enlightened autocracy, which was supposed to perpetuate Jewish existence as an estate or nation within the fabric of the hierarchical state.

Given the above, we should not be astonished that the first blossoms of modern Jewish nationalism in Eastern Europe were connected with the moderate Haskalah, which could meld loyalty to the regime and expectations of changes in the legal status of Jews with an awareness of ethnic uniqueness and a sense of identification with Jewish culture, past, and aspirations for the future. Indeed, if nationalism means identifying with some political body, the Eastern European *maskilim*, from the beginning of the nineteenth century until the 1880s, identified with the Russian Empire or the Austrian throne. But this identification was based on the premise that such a large empire, which does not demand total assimilation on the part of the Jews (unlike Polish nationalism of the same era), would leave the Jews enough elbow room for their separate existence. It was the radical *maskilim* who preached assimilation into every host society and argued for the elimination of every sign of uniqueness.

Thus we see in Eastern Europe in the 1860s and 1870s two fundamental ideas concerning the survival of the Jewish identity. On the one hand was a broad population who perpetuated the alternative frameworks that had taken the place of the traditional community; on the other hand was the moderate Haskalah, which argued for a controlled integration into the state while preserving Jewish linguistic and cultural identity. The first idea was "Orthodox," since by this time the mere existence of the frameworks represented a distinctly defensive position against changes in life-style. The second idea was indeed maskilic, but it, too, contained a strong element of defensiveness and rejection of all that was implied by a more consistent

adoption of the ideals of the European Enlightenment in its more radical av-
atars. Between these two trends there was clearly an historic rivalry, already
decades old. While some individuals established points of contact, and in
the cases of Yehiel Michal Pines and Zeev Jawitz, enlightened Orthodoxy
overlapped moderate Haskalah, the tension was most pronounced when
similar arguments were based on different principles and parallel goals
sought through different methods.

But the two trends had one thing in common: both were anachronistic.
The quasi-corporate frameworks of the Orthodox could no longer solve the
central existential problems of Jewish society; neither could the moderate
maskilic vision, based on the enlightened autocratic state of the eighteenth
century, satisfy the dilemmas of the second half of the nineteenth century. It
is true that both offered an answer to the challenge posed by modernity, but
the concrete challenge was already quite different from that for which the
answers were appropriate. This challenge involved a number of threats to
the survival of a separate Jewish society: (1) the disintegration of Jewish society consequent on the undermining of the authority of tradition; (2) severe
economic hardship and the vast gaps between the social classes, which increased the feeling of estrangement among the various segments of Jewish
society; (3) the lack of contact among the different sectors of Eastern European Jewry who were ruled by different powers and the integration of the
Jews into one of the nations among whom they lived (particularly significant in the case of the Polish insurrection of 1863); (4) the physical threat to
the Jews as a result of the lifting of government protection (a peril first
brought home in the Odessa pogrom of 1871); and (5) the mass migrations,
which tore society apart (first felt in the mass emigration from Lithuania
following the famine of the 1860s).

Neither Orthodoxy nor the *maskilim* adequately addressed these threats.
For example Orthodoxy, crystallizing in Lithuania in the 1860s and 1870s,
concentrated on the struggle against religious reform (in the wake of the articles by Moshe Leib Lilienblum), while Haskalah literature counterat-
tacked against rabbinic stringencies or continued to produce antihasidic
satires. The radical *maskilim* attacked the moderate Haskalah for its preoccupation with irrelevant matters and clearly sketched out the great questions that required answers; but their responses led in the direction of the
total abrogation of a distinct Jewish existence. The appearance on the
scene, in these years, of the harbingers of modern Jewish nationalism was
connected—and not by coincidence—with the juxtaposition of the criticism
by the radical Haskalah with the nationalist ideas that were latent in the
moderate Haskalah. Peretz Smolenskin, Eliezer Ben-Yehuda, Judah Leib
Levin, and, a few years later, Moshe Leib Lilienblum all expressed in their
writing both their affinity for the Eastern European Jewish social milieu,
with its culture and languages, as well as their reservations about the anachronistic nature of the Haskalah. What was special about them is that they

underwent a conscious transformation that the *maskilim* of the previous generation had not fully experienced: a transmutation of religious values into secular symbols and concepts. Only for them could the Hebrew language become a national language and virtually lose its religious value (a phenomenon that was not so clear-cut with Gottlober and Mapu). Only for them could the collective Jewish identity be considered in historical terms, utterly devoid of a religious burden. Only for them, at this or any stage in the evolution of Jewish national thought, could Eretz Israel be thought of in political terms and viewed through the glass of romantic nationalism, while the Orthodox attitude toward it was set aside.

This synthesis between the moderate Haskalah and important elements of the radical Haskalah made possible, for the first time in the 1870s, the consolidations of a national awareness that claimed a place, albeit modest, alongside the other two trends for maintaining Jewish existence. This third trend argued that its answers were relevant for the questions of the day. It divorced itself from the anachronism of Orthodoxy as well as from the "suicidal" aspect of the radical Haskalah. At the same time, there appeared in Eastern Europe the first notions of nationalist Orthodoxy, which accepted some of the maskilic positions or dealt with them through a process of partial internationalization. Jewish nationalism as a third avenue for preserving Jewish existence in Eastern Europe antedated the pogroms of 1881 by several years, offering its own answers to the question of continued Jewish collective existence. Its stands and emphases differed from both the Orthodox and maskilic positions. Thus, for example, it viewed Jewish autonomy as a positive manifestation of inner strength but echoed the maskilic criticism of its shape and forms. The new nationalism stressed independent Jewish activity, as against the passivity for which the traditional society was criticized, and thereby opened the way for the politicization of Jewish society. It also created country-wide networks of associations that had at first sprung up quite of their own accord in various cities and towns and represented a new matrix for social identification, one with a clearly modern character. The new nationalism made extensive use of traditional symbols that had been consciously and sometimes unconsciously expropriated from their traditional religious context. In this way the new movement spoke to the masses of traditional society, who did not always discern the novelty hiding behind the seemingly familiar words. But this appropriation of traditional symbols also fanned the flames of Orthodox antagonism to the new movement in Eastern Europe. When the moderate Haskalah joined forces with one wing of the radical Haskalah and with the nationalist Orthodox, a fierce struggle against it was launched by the more extreme Orthodoxy, which viewed the new nationalism as Haskalah in disguise. This time the confrontation was particularly bitter because of the feeling that nationalism was bent on conquering the heartland of Orthodoxy by offering an alternative formula for Jewish survival and even a new meaning for the bond between the Jewish people and the Land of Israel.

The relatively late disintegration of traditional Jewish society in Eastern Europe and the weight of the massive Jewish presence there thus explain the fact that Jewish nationalism was inaugurated in Eastern Europe at a time when the social frameworks were still fairly strong. Both the Eastern European Haskalah and Orthodoxy were active in a context where collective Jewish existence seemed to be resilient and likely to continue. The modern nationalist movement was conceived by the encounter between social radicalism and a Haskalah with a nationalist tinge on the one hand and, on the other, Orthodoxy as it crystallized in the late nineteenth century. Both were active in similar social and cultural settings. Firm foundations of autonomous life and a clear awareness of a separate identity characterized the various movements that were active in Eastern Europe at the end of the nineteenth century. Some of the similarities and links between the movements, which at first sight seem to have been hostile and antagonistic, were undoubtedly connected through a common language in modern Jewish nationalism and through the social structures that had survived in Eastern Europe right up to the birth of the modern political movements.

The vitality of Eastern European Jewish society and preservation of its unique character until the appearance of modern Jewish nationalism determined the role of the religious component in modern nationalist thinking and political activity of various currents within the Zionist movement. The idea of the separation of the religious component in Jewish society from the political, in the spirit of the European Enlightenment and the tendencies of the centralized state, did not strike deep roots in Eastern Europe. Unlike Central Europe, the idea of the Jews as a confessional community devoid of any political character was not widely held. While it is true that such ideas stirred the hearts of Jews who identified with the Polish nation in the middle of the nineteenth century and were held by proponents of Russification at the beginning of the reign of Alexander II, they never gave rise to broad-based social movements such as Neo-Orthodoxy and Reform in Germany. In any event, since the beginning of Hibbat Zion in the 1880s, it was clear to both the *haredim* and the *maskilim* in the movement that there was no separation between religion and nationalism. However, while the former believed that the religion of Israel encompassed what the innovators termed "nation," the latter insisted that religion was an essential component of the nation's history and culture. The strife-ridden controversy between proponents of the Haskalah and Orthodoxy was now refocused on a question to which neither side had paid much attention, having considered it resolved in another manner altogether. The *maskilim*, including the more moderate among them, regarded as the political "nation" the state to which they belonged, that is, where they lived, and they cultivated a notion of cultural nationalism in their writings. The Orthodox in Eastern Europe tended to steer clear of the definition "nation"; as an idea promoted by other peoples, it undermined the notion of the uniqueness of the Jewish people. Hence, proponents of each camp came to modern nationalism debating whose "nationalism" was preferable: that which posited a unity, religious in essence, encompassing all of Jewish existence in all its complexity, or that which defined the Jewish religion as a central but not sole tenet of Jewish existence. Moreover, both sides became partners in one movement, each carrying forward its particular vision of the people's future. However, while one group, fearful of change, sought to impart to the emerging society in Palestine a traditional cast, its counterpart strove to create an innovative, even revolutionary, national culture. Not only did the two sides not agree on the role of religion in national life, but both sought to eliminate the other. The Orthodox, interpreting the expressions of secular nationalism as heresy, hoped for the ultimate repentance of its proponents, whereas the *maskilim* hoped the Orthodox would eventually recognize the national values embodied in their faith and ritual practices and would relent in their opposition. And yet, the appearance of modern nationalism drew together two currents, between which any cooperation would have been heretofore inconceivable, into movements that explained Jewish existence in terms of religion as spirituality. Orthodoxy's willingness to cooperate with those who, according to Jewish law, were sinners, constituted an unprecedented compromise. The nationalist *maskilim* were likewise prepared to make considerable concessions on religious observance in Palestine settlements in the name of cooperation. Conflicts over matters of education and culture, however, in which neither was willing to concede, found both parties realigned according to earlier Orthodox and maskilic positions. The bitter dispute over the character of the Jaffa School in the mid-1890s revealed yet again the extent to which the tensions prevalent in Eastern European society several decades prior to Hibbat Zion still lay at the heart of the modern nationalist movement.

Modern nationalism, as noted earlier, arose as a "third alternative" response to modern challenges to the survival of the Jewish people. It incorporated, however, elements of the two other responses, Orthodoxy and Haskalah. These three responses to modernity, which competed with one another even as they were intertwined, developed within a society that had preserved through the ages a separate identity based on "national" traits that made it possible for modern nationalism to take root and develop. But it was not the voluntary bodies and organizations that had maintained traditional Jewish existence until the end of the nineteenth century that provided the foundation for the nationalist movement; rather, it was organizations and parties bearing a blatantly modern character. Even the *haredi* arm of Hovevei Zion, not to mention those who moved on directly into the Zionist movement, organized in a modern fashion. Neither religious authority nor the remnants of the corporate structures set the tone for the new political alignment. Even religion, *per se*, was transformed, perhaps unconsciously among some, into an ideological and political factor within a broader social and political framework and was presented as such in party platforms and political activity. The forces that had preserved Jewish society until the appearance of modern nationalism fell victim to modernization, which, in turn, played itself out in a national context. The Jewish religion, likewise, lost its all-encompassing nature, grew politicized, and was reduced to an ideological current within the national movement. What the centralized powers in Russia and Austria, the proponents of the Haskalah, and reverberations of religious movements in Germany were unable to achieve was wrought by the integration of the Jewish religion into Eastern European Jewry's "third alternative."

Zionism and Anti-Zionism in Traditional Judaism in Eastern Europe

In the course of the modern era, traditional Jewry in Europe experienced several far-reaching religious crises that forced it to reconsider its basic values and its society. These include the rise of Hasidism, the Haskalah and Reform movements, and Zionism. The conflict with Hasidism was concerned primarily with nuances of religious ritual and the nature of leadership, while the Reform movement challenged the very foundations of Halakhah as well.

But it was the Zionist threat that offered the gravest danger, for it sought to rob the traditional community of its very birthright, both in the diaspora and in Eretz Israel, the object of its messianic hopes. Zionism challenged all the aspects of traditional Judaism: in its proposal of a modern, national, Jewish identity; in the subordination of traditional society to new life-styles; and in its attitude to the religious concepts of diaspora and redemption. The Zionist threat reached every Jewish community. It was unrelenting and comprehensive, and therefore it met with uncompromising opposition. Unlike the other threats, which could be warded off by self-isolation in separate communities, Zionism, which aspired to political sovereignty, blocked the way to the sectarian isolationism possible under a non-Jewish government. The position was aptly put by Rabbi Alexander Moses Lapidot of Rossiyeny, a leading Russian rabbi of his time, who was an enthusiastic supporter of the Hovevei Zion movement before changing his mind in the summer of 1894:

We thought that this sacred sapling would be a sapling true to the Lord and to His people, and that it would restore our souls. . . . But O weariness! While still in its infancy it sent forth weeds and its evil odor is wafted afar. . . . Indeed, it is useless to cry over spilt milk, and wherever there is profanation of the Lord, His Torah and the Holy Land, far be it from us to stand on our honor, but we say, "Indeed, we have committed a grievous error." . . . If they [the Zionists] repudiate this advice of ours, we withdraw our support and shall stand aside and oppose them to the best of our ability, for we muster our forces in the name of the Lord.[1]

The controversy over Zionism that shook traditional Jewry in Eastern Europe put the final stamp on two types of Eastern European Orthodoxy that I call *haredim* and neo-*haredim*. The *haredim* rejected Zionism every step of the way, ultimately becoming its bitterest opponents, while the neo-*haredim* embraced it. These different positions stemmed not so much from their respective attitudes to the concept of redemption—miraculous or natural—but rather from their approach to modernity and consequently to nonreligious Jews.

The split in traditional Jewish society on this question, which paved the way for separate organizations and sometimes even separate communities, only intensified the disagreement over modernity in general. The time-honored methods of excommunication were no longer effective in dealing with dissidents in a society more or less dominated by religious pluralism. The struggle with Zionism was even more complicated because its borderlines, internal and external, were difficult to delineate. The *haredim* and neo-*haredim* both took up arms against secular Zionism, fighting one another at the same time.[2] The *haredim* accused Zionism in general of the gravest offenses—heresy and apostasy—arguing that the Zionists were no better than the Karaites or the Sabbateans, falling into the same category of "those who lead many astray."[3]

These two types of Eastern European Orthodox Jewry—the *haredim* led by such figures as Rabbi Hayim Soloveichik of Brest-Litovsk (in Yiddish, Brisk), and the neo-*haredim* headed by, among others, Rabbi Samuel Mohilever of Białystok—were not new. Similar positions had been formulated in relation to the Haskalah movement and modernity, in Hungary as early as the 1860s and in Russia-Poland in the early 1870s. In Russia-Poland, however, they lacked social coherence until the 1890s, when Zionism came to be seen as a rallying point for all the elements threatening traditional Jewish society,[4] especially modernity in the sense of secular education and nationalism. The developments that led to this situation form the subject of this essay.

When Zionist ideas were first aired in the 1860s and 1870s, they met with very little real opposition in traditional Jewish society in Eastern Europe. What opposition there was came from Orthodoxy and particularly Neo-Orthodoxy in Western Europe, which feared that a nationalist definition of the Jewish people might hinder demands for integration in the German states and the Austro-Hungarian Empire. Coupled with this fear was the sense that adoption of a national identity might provide for an escape route for those desiring to repudiate religious observance. Such arguments were presented to Rabbi Zvi Hirsch Kalischer by Rabbi Samson Raphael Hirsch,[5] by Dr. Marcus Lehmann, the editor of *Der Israelit*, and even by Rabbi Azriel Hildesheimer, rabbi of the separatist Orthodox community of Berlin.[6]

In Russia-Poland, the question of religious reform had been raised in a moderate form by various *maskilim*, including Moshe Leib Lilienblum and Judah Leib Gordon, but these leaders were not at the time identified as committed nationalists. Paradoxically, it was their opponents from the traditional camp, such as Yehiel Michal Pines and Mordecai Eliasberg, who began to express nationalist ideas. In this regard they may have been influenced by the opponents of religious reform in the West, who took up nationalism as the antithesis of reform and assimilation. Only during the 1870s did the Eastern European Jewish nationalist outlook begin to take shape, a development reflected mainly in the Hebrew journalism of the time. Hebrew journalism received new impetus in the early 1880s, in reaction to the pogroms, which "converted" many radical *maskilim* to nationalism. But this conversion did not yet have the effect of prompting traditional circles to reject Zionist nationalism out of hand. On the contrary, in the wake of the pogroms the leaders of the traditional camp in Russia-Poland, Rabbis Elijah Hayim of Łódź and Joseph Dov-Baer Soloveichik of Brisk, agreed to issue a manifesto calling for emigration from Russia to Palestine.[7]

The first reservations were voiced only in 1883, when it became clear that the immigrants to Palestine included coherent groups, such as the Biluim, who were not observant at all. While the first attempts were being made to combine the various local Hovevei Zion associations into a single, national movement, it turned out that prominent Lithuanian rabbis were opposed to organized cooperation between traditional and secular circles, like that in which Rabbi Soloveichik was involved. Others, headed by Rabbi Mohilever, saw nothing wrong with such common initiatives and associated themselves with the plans to convene the Katowice Conference of Hovevei Zion in late 1884. One result of the conference, however, was to place the leadership of the movement in the hands of secular figures such as Dr. Leon Pinsker and Lilienblum. As a result, some rabbis who had been willing to take part in Hovevei Zion activities left the movement *en masse*. Among them were such prominent personalities as Eleazar Waks of Piotrków, Eliezer Gordon of Telšiai (in Yiddish, Telz), and, somewhat later, also David Friedman of Karlin.[8]

Efforts on the part of traditional elements in Hovevei Zion to transform the character of the leadership bore fruit in the second conference of the movement at Druzkieniki in the summer of 1887, at which they were awarded a disproportionate representation in the movement's institutions. Although Mohilever was disappointed at his failure to be elected to a leading position, he made his peace with the results, taking the opportunity to clarify his view that, in principle, the leadership of the movement, as well as its pioneers, should come from the ranks of the observant.[9] After the Druzkieniki Conference, some important religious leaders were successfully persuaded to support the movement; the most prominent of these were Rabbi Isaac Elchanan Spektor of Kowno and in particular Rabbi Naphtali Zevi Judah Berlin (known as the Neziv) of Volozhin. Their support was by no means unconditional, however. The Neziv, who took an active part in the day-to-day business of the movement, threatened to resign whenever rumors were heard of the irreligious behavior of settlers in Palestine.[10]

Still, traditionally minded leaders did not make sufficient efforts to attract their own followers to Hovevei Zion. Attempts by Menahem Ussishkin in the summer of 1887 and Meir Dizengoff to enlist the Habad *admor* (title of hasidic rabbi) Zalman Schneersohn of Kopys and Rabbi Isaac Friedman of Buhusi met with no success. In the 1880s, just as in the 1870s, no prominent hasidic leader was willing to support the initiatives to settle Jews in Palestine.[11] A turning point was the Hovevei Zion conference at Vilna in August 1889, where three of the traditional leaders, headed by Mohilever, were elected to the leadership. They thus had an opportunity to impose their will on the movement and try to attract their own support. These achievements came to nought, however, following the establishment of the Odessa Committee in spring 1890, which restored the reins of leadership to the secularists from Odessa.[12]

By the end of the 1880s opposition to Hovevei Zion among religious leaders was beginning to crystallize against the background of disagreements within the movement about the impious behavior of the settlers of Gederah and the question of working the land during the sabbatical year.[13] The position of the religious leadership in Russia *vis-à-vis* Hovevei Zion was influenced in no small measure by the people of the Old Yishuv in Jerusalem (the original, Ultra-Orthodox inhabitants of the Jewish Quarter), who watched the development of the new settlements closely and were quick, for obvious reasons, to pounce on their shortcomings. Even before the Katowice Conference, at the end of 1883, they had sent a letter to the Russian rabbis accusing the settlers in the new colonies of laxity in religious observance: "They do not walk in the path of Torah and fear of God . . . and their purpose is not to bring the redemption close but to delay it, God forbid."[14] The campaign against the new settlers in Palestine continued through the 1880s, although at this time even the nonreligious leaders of Hovevei Zion agreed that the settlers should be observant;[15] the argument was only whether they should conduct themselves with exceptional piety or behave as was normal for "simple Jews." The rabbinical supporters of Hovevei Zion generally wanted the settlers in Palestine to provide a model of pious Judaism, a position which *inter alia* prompted some of them to oppose the rabbinical disposition permitting agricultural work during the sabbatical year. But such expectations were absolutely unrealistic. Secularization had set in not only among young people who had abandoned traditional society and its way of life before immigrating to the Holy Land; it was also making headway among the youth in the colonies whose parents had been observant Jews.

Even those in traditional Jewish society who responded favorably to Zionist modernity did not relinquish their ideal of a scrupulously observant Jewish society in Eretz Israel. The bone of contention between them and the traditionalist opponents of Zionism concerned the means to that end, their evaluation of the present situation, and the length of time they were willing to allot for the realization of this religious Zionist utopia. Mohilever, on his return in 1890 from a successful trip to Palestine as an emissary of the Odessa Committee, published a bold article in which he proposed a topical interpretation of the rabbinic saying, "The settlement of Eretz Israel outweighs all the commandments of the Torah" (Sifrei, Reeh, 80): "The Holy One, Blessed be He, prefers that His sons should settle in His land, even if they do not observe the Torah properly."[16] Such an extreme declaration from a religious Zionist had not been heard before Mohilever and indeed was never equaled later. Nevertheless, it did not immediately arouse negative reactions from traditional society, even when published in the book *Shivat Zion* (1891–92).

By the early 1890s, it seemed that the traditional opposition to Hovevei Zion in regard to these issues was dying down. The establishment of the Odessa Committee, with official government sanction, raised hopes for legal immigration of Jews to Palestine. Yet these hopes were dashed shortly thereafter, when the institutions set up by the committee in Palestine failed in their task of absorbing the wave of immigration of 1890–91 and the Ottoman authorities renewed the legal restrictions on entering Palestine.

A new storm broke out in the years 1893–95, when an *avante-garde* element—Ahad Haam's Bnei Moshe—appeared on the scene and sought to take over the leadership of the Odessa Committee, the Hovevei Zion movement, and the Jewish national revolution in general. The only achievements of these pretentious aspirations were the establishment of educational institutions in Jaffa, the publication of a few books and textbooks, and the attempt to establish educational institutions in some major Russian cities.[17] Ahad Haam's thesis that religion was only one of the national institutions and that the dominant power was the "national spirit," from which all commitments of the national society were to be derived, was of course diametrically opposed to traditional viewpoints. For the traditionally minded, Jewish tradition, with its basic tenets of belief and halakhic way of life, was absolutely sovereign, deriving its authority from the divine revelation at Mount Sinai, and national identity could not but be subordinate to it. This was the first time that the conflict came up for public discussion, not in connection with the personal behavior of some specific leader or group of settlers but as a question of principle, a clash between two mutually contradictory ideologies.[18]

In the present context, suffice it to say that this phase of the conflict gave rise to the first clear definition of both parties' positions; it was to become the cornerstone of all later manifestations of the dispute. Statements of principles were also made within the movement, by adherents of both camps, and these statements were later taken up by the opponents from without. Ahad Haam claimed, "Peace between these two groups cannot be based on ideological unanimity—a goal that can never be achieved—but only on that sacred virtue . . . , the virtue of toleration in all matters of beliefs and opinions."[19] For Ahad Haam, however, the "virtue of toleration" did not mean individual freedom, but the right to wage a *Kulturkampf*.[20] On the other hand, several young rabbis such as Jonathan Eliasberg and Joshua Joseph Preil, hitherto avid supporters of Hovevei Zion, made it clear that they would not be willing to compromise beyond certain limits. Writing to Ahad Haam, Eliasberg asserted:

We hoped that the settlement of Eretz Israel would be the linchpin that would hold together the separate parts of the house of Israel. We thought that one commandment would lead to another, that the "commandment of the settlement of Eretz Israel" would restore the hearts of the Children of Israel to the Torah and worship of God, and that the *maskilim* too would return to the camp of Israel.[21]

But if Ahad Haam insisted on his position, wrote Eliasberg, "it is inevitable that all leaders of Israel and God-fearing folk will oppose it."[22] And Preil added that the uniqueness of the Jewish people consisted in "its Torah and the observance of the laws through which the God of Israel set his people apart" rather than in the mere territory of Eretz Israel and the Hebrew language. The Jewish people had refused to assimilate, not because of their national "will to exist" but by virtue of the "spirit of Torah which animates and inspires them, not the national spirit in which every [other] nation takes pride."[23] This precise definition of the borderline between the two camps made cooperation between the traditionalists and their opponents quite impossible.

The advent of Theodor Herzl, with the publication of *Der Judenstaat* in 1896, the convening of the First Zionist Congress, and the establishment of the Zionist Organization in 1897 offered prospects for a resolution of the deadlock. The key was the shift in the Zionist rationale, from culture and ideology to a program of practical action, which was supposed to solve the crucial problems of the Jewish nation in context of the general emergence of nationalism in European society. The goal was normalization of the Jewish nation in its own state, whether in its historic homeland or elsewhere.

The program was accepted enthusiastically by traditional Jewish society in Eastern Europe, as the traditional elements could do without having to compromise their own values. Unlike the secular Zionists in Eastern Europe, who suspected that Herzl was neglecting their hopes for cultural and ideological reform of Jewish society, advocating instead a Jewish political entity (which was not at all to their taste), the traditional elements were immediately taken with the Basle Program. The new course of the Zionist movement raised hopes that it would be possible to enlist the support of the masses of religiously observant Jews in Eastern Europe. And Herzl, for his part, repeatedly stressed that he was addressing himself primarily to that audience. His appeal for support to the hasidic *admor* David Moses Friedman of Czortków only emphasized his willingness to make efforts to win over the traditional camp.[24]

These hopes were quickly dashed, however. During the First Zionist Congress itself, and even more so at Zionist gatherings held in Russia, Zionists were loath to give up their cultural goals. Moreover, Herzl, in his negotiations with traditional circles, increasingly revealed his Western-liberal inclinations, which finally tipped the scales against the traditional cause. Already in *Der Judenstaat*, and later in *Altneuland*, Herzl had not concealed his conception of the Jewish state of his desires.[25] In this respect he was quite adamant, and at the Second Zionist Congress, in response to pressure, he made his famous call to "conquer the communities." Similar sentiments were expressed by Herzl's colleagues in the leadership of the movement, from both Eastern and Western Europe.[26] This appeal was immediately seen as a challenge to the traditional leadership.[27]

Both before and after the Second Zionist Congress, right up to the Third Congress, attempts were made to secure a compromise and institute a rabbinical committee alongside the Zionist Actions Committee, but to no avail.[28] Rabbis who had supported the Zionist Organization up to this time, such as Elijah Akiva Rabinowitz of Poltava and Judah Zirelson of Priluki, crossed the lines and began to organize traditional Jews in Russia-Poland against Zionism.[29] Those rabbis who continued actively to support Zionism after the Second Congress were in the minority. After the Second Congress it became clear that Mohilever's appeal to the First Congress—"that our Torah, which is the mainspring of our life, shall be the foundation of our revival in the land of our fathers"—originally received with tumultuous applause, had fallen on deaf ears as far as the official institutions of the new Zionist Organization were concerned.[30]

Those traditional leaders who tried to remain within the Zionist Organization faced a dilemma. On the one hand, they could agree to divide up the cultural activity between the two camps, each going its own way within the various local Zionist organizations. This was the proposal of Rabbi Jacob Samuel Rabinowitz of Sopotskin immediately after the Second Congress, and it was actually adopted by the conference of Russian Zionists at Minsk in 1902. On the other hand, they could take cultural activities out of the hands of the Zionist movement, laying the emphasis on political Zionism. This was the approach of Rabbi Isaac Jacob Reines and one of the foundations for the establishment of the Mizrahi movement. Reines's initiative, however, though supported by other political Zionists including Herzl, had no chance of acceptance among most Eastern European Zionists, and it in fact broke up a few months after its proposal.[31] The deathblow came at the Tenth Zionist Congress in 1911, which adopted the cultural program of the Cultural Committee, charging the Zionist Actions Committee with carrying out educational activities in Palestine and in Eastern Europe. This resolution caused a split in the Mizrahi: the minority broke away and ultimately, together with other groups, became the nucleus of Agudat Israel in 1912.[32]

The two rabbinical figures most active in organizing the anti-Zionist *ha-*

redi movement in 1898–99 were joined by a public figure and writer, Jacob Lipschitz of Kowno, and by the Habad *admor* Shalom Dov-Baer Schneersohn of Lubavich, both of whom already entertained firmly *haredi* positions.[33] The outcome of the initiative was the book *Or layesharim* (1900), an anthology of anti-Zionist tracts by leading rabbis. The publication of this book put an end to discussions between the two sides. At this point, traditional Jewry split into two factions. At the one extreme was the majority, which was opposed to Zionism and thus clearly defined the *haredi* stand (rejection of modernity in both cultural and national senses); at the other was the neo-*haredi* minority, which did not leave the Zionist Organization and by remaining cast its vote for modernity, although it did not give up its ideals of Torah and observance.

The publishers of *Or layesharim* had intended to collect the viewpoints of the traditional Jewry in Russia-Poland, both *mitnagdim* and *hasidim*. The book was largely successful in presenting the views of the most prominent leaders of the *mitnagdim*, and in addition it carried a piece by British Chief Rabbi Hermann Adler, representing Neo-Orthodoxy in Great Britain.[34] The only hasidic luminary appearing in its pages was the Habad *admor* Shalom Dov-Baer Schneersohn. From Eretz Israel it brought the view of J. D. Frumkin, editor of *Havazelet*, representing the Old Yishuv, and of Eleazar Atlas, a writer and journalist.[35] There were, of course, variations in the *haredi* opposition to Zionism. Put briefly, the general *haredi* conception of Zionism was of a secularizing force in Jewish society, following in the footsteps of its predecessor, the Haskalah movement. Since its major programs were associated with the Holy Land—the object of traditional messianic hopes—it was infinitely more dangerous than any other secularizing force in Judaism and, accordingly, it had to be attacked. Alongside this argument of principle, the book also cited various secondary arguments that challenged the Zionist rationale and belittled the chances of its realization. None of the contributions, except that of Schneersohn, viewed Zionism as conflicting with traditional messianic conceptions.[36] Nevertheless, even Schneersohn, whose tone was the most extreme of all, did not cite the messianic question as his central argument: "The commandment of settling Eretz Israel is contingent upon its sanctity . . . , on condition that they be of those who observe each and every detail of the Torah and the commandments."[37] In Schneersohn's view, the Zionists were violating the sanctity of the land, and there was therefore not only no religious duty to settle there but those who were already there were permitted to leave.[38]

The summer and winter of 1899 and spring of 1900 marked the turning point in the attitude of traditional Jewish society to Zionism. As early as July 1899, a group of laymen in Kowno published a kind of manifesto proclaiming that most traditional elements were opposed to Zionism, some "out of conviction and awareness," others "out of an inner religious feeling born of ancestral tradition." The writers claimed that their position was not adequately known to the public since the press was controlled by the Zionists, "the evil men of this generation." Zionism was more dangerous than all the false messiahs that had appeared in the course of Jewish history, because it alone was determined "to uproot all the laws of the Torah and the commandments."[39]

The Zionist press, in particular *Hamelitz*, was full of letters from rabbis trying to influence public opinion in favor of Zionism, but none of these came from the first rank of rabbinical leaders in Russia. The year 1902 saw the publication in Poland of two books, *Orah leZion* and *Daat rabbanim*,[40] containing *haredi* anti-Zionist statements of Polish rabbis, probably mostly hasidic. None, however, was a leading member of the *haredi* leadership of Polish Jewry, and many relied explicitly on *Or layesharim*.

The impression given by the sources is that in Poland, unlike Russia, the leadership of the Jews was mostly in the hands of the hasidic *admorim*, who were unable to agree. Hasidic society was based on a system of individual leaders, each acting independently. Each hasidic court was basically a closed society, so that one cannot speak of a hasidic society parallel to that of the *mitnagdim*. Hasidism was dominant in the regions of Galicia and Congress Poland, northeast Hungary, Transylvania, and Bukovina.

Generally speaking, although the *hasidim* preceded the *mitnagdim* in organized immigration to Palestine, the wave of 1777 was exceptional and was not followed by other waves; it did not lay the ideological foundations for hasidic immigration, and the hasidic leaders in Palestine were not of the first rank. The situation was different among the *mitnagdim* who immigrated to Palestine and were known there as *perushim*. Not surprisingly, the major leaders of the Ashkenazi community in Palestine before the First World War were *perushim*. It is difficult to say whether Hasidism had a consistently anti-Zionist outlook, for there was in fact no one hasidic position. All we can say is that some hasidic circles expressed opposition to the very idea of immigration to Palestine even prior to Zionism; there is no parallel to this view among the *mitnagdim* in Eastern Europe.[41] In fact, hasidic symbolism contains the seeds of a neutralization of the physical Palestine in favor of Eretz Israel as a spiritual concept. The *zaddik* and his court were the symbolic embodiment of Eretz Israel and Jerusalem.[42] The other aspect of the hasidic attitude to Palestine was an implacable opposition to modernity. The *hasidim* were the harbingers of Ultra-Orthodoxy in Galicia and Poland, and they brought it with them to Hungary.[43]

When the freethinking life-styles of the Biluim came up for public debate, hasidic rabbis from Russia joined the attackers of Hovevei Zion. It was reported that Rabbi Aaron Perlow of Koidanov told his followers: "Whoever gives money to Hovevei Zion forfeits his reward in the world to come, despite all the charitable deeds that he may have performed and may yet perform throughout his life."[44]

Still, hasidic opposition to Zionism was not without its exceptions.

There were undoubtedly followers of Hasidism and even rabbis who supported Zionism during or even after the period of Hovevei Zion; but none of them were members of the hasidic leadership.[45] One who expressed pro-Zionist views was Rabbi Israel Morgenstern of Pilov-Kotsk; another was Rabbi David Moses Friedman of Czortków. Did their positions follow from the views in the hasidic dynasties to which they belonged (Kotsk and Ruzhin, respectively)? Or were they exceptions in their own circles, too? Students of Hasidism have tried to detect pro–Eretz Israel tendencies, though not nationalist ones, in both dynasties, but their attempts are unconvincing.[46]

Rabbi Israel Morgenstern of Pilov, Central Poland, was the third *admor* of the Kotsk dynasty. He wrote his pamphlet *Shelom Yerushalayim* as early as 1886. It would appear from reactions to the pamphlet that he sought to secure *haskamot* (rabbinic approval) for his work in 1890–91, probably against the background of the renewed wave of immigration to Palestine and the temporary relaxation of Ottoman government policy on purchase of land by Eastern European Jews. There are no specifically hasidic elements in Morgenstern's arguments. In his introduction he explains that he was publishing the pamphlet on his own initiative, with an eye to publicizing his ideas about the purchase of land for colonization in Palestine in the early 1890s.[47] His practical plan was to establish a colony of *hasidim*, along the lines of the Agudat Haelef associations founded at the time throughout Russia in order to buy land and establish colonies. Morgenstern received enthusiastic reactions from leaders of the *mitnagdim* such as Rabbi Isaac Elchanan Spektor and Rabbi Israel Joshua of Kutno, but the hasidic response was far more reserved; among the hasidic leaders who reacted to his plan were Rabbi Abraham Bornstein of Sochaczew and Rabbi Judah Leib of Gur.[48] Both stressed marginal elements of Morgenstern's initiative, pointing out the difficulties of making a living in Palestine and ruling that observance of the commandment of settling the land was contingent on the consent of the would-be settler's family.[49] In fact, Morgenstern's initiative met with considerable opposition among the hasidic leaders of Poland, who even blamed it for various tragedies in his family. His son, Rabbi Isaac Zelig of Sokołów, was considerably less enthusiastic than his father and, at any rate, claimed that after Herzl's appearance Morgenstern had abandoned his plans.[50] Morgenstern had proposed a new and interesting principle, according to which God had chosen to bring about the redemption through unobservant Jews: "Even though those who are occupying themselves [with settling the land] are not so righteous, we have already learned that the Holy One Blessed be He derives pleasure from the simple people of the Children of Israel, sometimes more than from completely righteous people."[51]

Another prominent Polish supporter of Hovevei Zion was Rabbi Isaac Feigenbaum, chief justice of the Warsaw *bet din* (rabbinical court) and a close associate of the greatest hasidic leaders in Poland, Rabbi Isaac Meir of Gur and Rabbi Hanoch Henich of Alexander. Feigenbaum supported the association Menuhah Venahalah, which founded the colony of Rehovot.[52] His son reports that he was the only traditional leader in Warsaw to support the Zionist movement. He made a point of drinking only wines from Palestine and preferred books written in Jerusalem. He agreed with Rabbi Kalischer's theory of gradual stages, "that before the advent of the messiah the Jews will be settled on their land." As to the participation of nonreligious Jews in the movement, he replied that "if the religious were to take part, everything would undoubtedly go forward according to the way of the Torah."[53]

In Galicia, the hasidic *admorim* had been extremely hostile to any initiative connected with Palestine since the early years of the nineteenth century.[54] In this respect they differed from the Polish *hasidim*, whose attitude had always been more favorable.[55] Nevertheless, when the first Hovevei Zion associations appeared, one of them was in Cracow, founded by Rabbi Simon Sofer, the rabbi of Cracow and one of the foremost leaders of Galician Jewry at the time.[56] Some time before, in 1879, Sofer had cooperated with Rabbi Joshua of Belz, leader of the largest hasidic dynasty in Galicia, in founding an organization entitled Mahzikei Hadas, to combat the influence of the Haskalah movement.[57] It was not till the late 1880s, however, that Hovevei Zion came to be associated particularly with the Haskalah. For example, a Hovevei Zion association was founded in Borislav with the participation of both *hasidim* and *maskilim*. Toward the end of the 1880s, however, a report arrived from Palestine that the settlers in the new colonies were not observing the Torah; one of the *admorim* reacted with an injunction "not to render aid to sinners . . . and not to make common cause with the wicked," and the association was disbanded.[58] It follows that the turning point in attitudes to Hovevei Zion in Galicia occurred at the same time as in Russia, following the dispute about the Biluim and the sabbatical year.[59]

Nevertheless, Galicia differed from Russia-Poland in that attempts were made there to set up *haredi* Hovevei Zion associations. These refused to cooperate with the central institutions and apparently tried to establish an alternative movement. The most prominent manifestation of this trend was the Ahavat Zion association in Tarnov founded in December 1896, which was headed by such hasidic figures as Rabbi Asher Isaiah Horowitz of Rymanow, Rabbi Feibush Shreier of Bohorodczany, Rabbi Aaron Marcus of Cracow, and Rabbi Zechariah Mendel Avardam of Sieniawa.[60] One of the association's greatest successes was to enlist one of the most renowned hasidic leaders in Galicia, Rabbi David Moses Friedman of Czortków, as well as the rabbi of Lwów, Rabbi Isaac Schmelkes.[61] In Russia at that time, on the eve of the establishment of the Zionist Organization, no traditional leader of the first rank could be counted among the supporters of Zionism.

Even before the First Zionist Congress, however, a demand to disband Ahavat Zion was published by Rabbi Ezekiel Schraga Halberstam of Sieniawa, leader of the Zanz dynasty and its oldest living *admor*. Rabbi Ezekiel presented two arguments. The first was Mohilever's article in *Shivat Zion,*

expressing preference for secular Jews living in Palestine over the most scrupulously observant Jews abroad. This statement now boomeranged against
the Hovevei Zion movement: "May boiling gold be poured on their lips."
In addition, claimed Rabbi Ezekiel, the immigrants to the Holy Land "have
in them not one spark of righteousness and some of them publicly desecrate
the Sabbath."[62] The rivalry between the hasidic courts of Zanz and Sadgora
undoubtedly played a part in the dispute. Although the traditional leadership was not yet institutionalized, there is no similar instance in Lithuania,
with its *mitnagdim*, of one leader attacking another publicly for his pro-
Zionist views. But hasidic society, as we have seen, was split into several
subsocieties that had no commitments to one another. Thus the Rabbi of
Czortków could come out in favor of Zionism and the Rabbi of Zanz
against it—even before the First Zionist Congress. In the wake of the Rabbi
of Zanz's appeal, many members left Ahavat Zion, which nevertheless did
not cease operations and even founded the colony of Mahanayim. It had
originally tried to work independently of the Zionist Organization, but
after losing its principal supporters, it became a local association within the
larger body.[63]

Another hasidic leader who did not adopt a wholly negative attitude to
Hovevei Zion was Rabbi Isaac Friedman of Buhusi, the greatest hasidic
leader in Rumania, of the Ruzhin dynasty.[64] An association named Doresh
Zion, founded in Jassy in 1887, appealed to Rabbi Friedman to instruct his
followers to support the association, whose goal was "to support Rumanian Jews who wish to immigrate to Eretz Israel and cultivate the land
there." In his first response Friedman sidestepped the main issue and explained that he was willing to give preference to *etrogim* (citrons) from Palestine; he even added advice as to how the fruit could be prevented from
rotting on the way. The association repeated its appeal to him, and this time
he addressed the real question, explaining that in his view, for practical reasons, Palestine could not provide a solution to the present plight of Rumanian Jews. At the same time, he did not object to the idea of settlement but
requested that a charter first be procured from the Ottoman authorities for
immigration to Palestine; otherwise, he feared that the Zionists might be
tempted to mislead the people. Rabbi Isaac Friedman's son, Rabbi Jacob of
Husyatin, explained later that his father had supported the establishment of
Rosh Pina but had made his support contingent on the settlers maintaining
a traditional life-style—probably in the wake of rumors about the behavior
of the settlers in the new colonies.[65] From then on Rabbi Friedman's attitude was more reserved.

Yet another hasidic leader who favored the Zionist ideas was Rabbi
David Moses Friedman of Czortków. The extensive influence of Czortków
Hasidism (an offshoot of the Ruzhin dynasty) in Galicia, the Ukraine, and
Rumania and statements by the previous *admor*, before and during Herzl's
activities, in favor of attempts to settle Jews on the land in Palestine,[66] made

Friedman a natural candidate for Herzl's solicitations. The contact between the two was set up by the Rabbi of Botosani, Rabbi Leibush Mendel, and the *hasid* and former *maskil* Aaron Marcus, an affiliate of Czortków Hasidism.[67] The go-betweens spread the impression that Friedman's attitude was positive, and indeed it would seem that at first the *admor* was not troubled by cooperation with secular-minded Jews: "We, the *hasidim*, will maintain the inner strength of the house, establishing *yeshivot* to spread Torah and fear of God, while they [the secularists] will deal with external matters."[68] Rabbi David Moses Friedman's son Israel also supported the Zionist movement and expressed his willingness to take an active part, provided assurances were made that the movement would not harm the interests of the traditional community.[69]

Aaron Marcus, who regarded hasidic support for Zionism as his own personal responsibility, persuaded Herzl to travel to Czortków in January 1900 to obtain Rabbi David Moses Friedman's agreement to convene a conference of sympathetic rabbis. Friedman agreed to Marcus's request that he ask Rabbi Benjamin Weiss, chief rabbi of Chernovtsy, to lend a hand in convening a conference of rabbis in support of Ozar Hahityashvut.[70] Friedman proposed to bring the question before a conference of rabbis that was scheduled to take place at the time in Słonim. He believed that if the rabbis of Russia and Galicia agreed, the support of traditional Jewish society would be secured even if the Hungarian rabbis were to object.[71] However, it appears that when the matter was discussed by rabbis from Russia and Galicia, the latter demanded clarifications from the Zionist Actions Committee in connection with religious questions. By March there had been no response. Marcus, in a bitter letter to Herzl, wrote that the contempt of the Zionist leaders "for their opponents is now an old legacy of our young intelligentsia."[72] With this letter Marcus dealt the deathblow to the last chance of convincing traditional leaders in Galicia and Poland to join the Zionist movement. This also marked the end of Marcus's Zionist "career." His initiative thus came to an end approximately at the same time as the publication of *Or layesharim* in Russia, which, as we have seen, marked the turning point in traditional attitudes against Zionism.

From this time on traditional Jewry in Eastern Europe (Russia-Poland, Hungary, Rumania, and Galicia) split into two camps. The *haredi* majority adopted an anti-Zionist line, the organizational expression of which in Russia was an association named Mahzikei Hadas; the minority ultimately formed the Mizrahi movement. These two organizations, established in Russia in 1902, both had earlier historical roots. Mahzikei Hadas was created to combat the forces threatening traditional society, and its activities were necessarily of a reactionary nature. The Mizrahi movement, on the other hand, was determined to take up the nationalist challenge while at the same time maintaining a religious way of life. Of course, it is self-evident that even a reactionary movement does not simply stagnate but creates, albeit unintentionally, a new social reality with its own particular rationale. On the other hand, a movement aiming at responding to modernity will also fight to preserve its old traditions. This tension between tradition and innovation was typical of both movements.

As mentioned above, an organization named Mahzikei Hadas had been established in Galicia in 1879 by Rabbi Joshua of Belz and Rabbi Simon Sofer of Cracow, to cope with the threat of the Haskalah movement and the *maskilim*. The *maskilim* had already set up their own organization in Galicia, called Shomer Israel, which now dominated some major communities.[73] The bitter struggle between Galician *maskilim* and the traditional circles for control of the communities and Jewish representation in the Austrian parliament, coming ten years after a similar conflict in Hungary, anticipated the crystallization of the *haredi* attitude in Russia-Poland by twenty-five years. Sofer's attempt to establish a Hovevei Zion association in Cracow in 1883 only illustrates the hopes that the Ultra-Orthodox had originally put in the idea that the colonization of Eretz Israel would stem the tides of modernization and assimilation.[74] More than two hundred communities were affiliated with Mahzikei Hadas in Galicia; among its members were leading rabbis, the heads of the hasidic dynasties of Belz, Vizhnitz, Sadgora, and Dzykow.[75] Only toward the late 1880s were the first reservations expressed about the activities of Hovevei Zion, and these were relatively moderate until 1892. The general trend was to accept the idea of settlement in Palestine without the secularist programs that rejected religious commitment in favor of national attachment or messianic redemption in favor of agricultural settlement.[76]

Besides arguments of principle, criticism of the Zionist program was voiced in view of the rising Arab enmity, and doubts were expressed about the ability of the Zionist leaders to realize their goals. But during the various discussions in 1892 the mask was thrown off. In view of the circumstances, it was said, "it is better to dwell on foreign soil in America than to usurp the divine prerogative and settle in a colony in the holy land which is not pleasing to the pure-minded."[77] With the advent of Herzl, Mahzikei Hadas laid special emphasis on the more practical arguments, claiming that the Herzlian program was unrealistic. In its response to the First Zionist Congress, the newspaper *Kol mahzikei hadas* admitted that Galician rabbis did not support political Zionism. By the summer of 1899 the critical tone was becoming more prominent, in Galicia as in Russia.[78] A perusal of this newspaper reveals great interest in events within the Zionist movement but also numerous pessimistic evaluations: the sultan would never agree; even if a charter were granted, few Jews would be willing to immigrate to Palestine; and so on. The explanation for this critical and pessimistic attitude, characteristic of *haredi* Jews of all factions, was primarily religious: since those who desired to lead the reconstruction of Eretz Israel came from the ranks of the nonobservant, it was self-evident, said the *haredim*, that they could not succeed. Redemption and the Holy Land were basically incompatible with secularism; such a combination ran counter to God's will; hence it could not survive: "Any gathering that is not for the sake of heaven is doomed to failure."[79]

The first attempts to establish a *haredi* anti-Zionist organization in Russia date from 1890.[80] Behind the initiative stood the writer Jacob Lipschitz of Kowno, who had tried to organize traditional Jewry in Eastern Europe against the Haskalah movement as far back as the 1870s.[81] The cornerstone of the organization was laid by the publication of *Or layesharim* and the first appearance of an anti-Zionist *haredi* periodical named *Hapeles* (1901), published in Poltava by E. A. Rabinowitz. Its platform covered all *haredi* interests, such as control of the communities, educational institutions, and *haredi* literature. It adopted a defensive stance against the attempt to base the entire Torah on the study of Hebrew and Jewish history.[82] Despite the deep and bitter feelings of the Russian *haredim* against those who were threatening them, at no time was there any suggestion of establishing separatist communities, as had occurred in Germany and Hungary.[83] The organization attracted both *hasidim* and *mitnagdim* from all over Russia and Poland, among them such leaders as Rabbi Elijah Hayyim Meisel of Łódź, Rabbi Samuel of Słonim, Rabbi Shalom Dov-Baer Schneersohn of Lubavich, and now also Rabbi David Moses Friedman of Czortków, Rabbi Abraham Bornstein of Sochaczew and others.[84]

In sum, by the spring of 1900, *haredi* and neo-*haredi* attitudes to Zionism had crystallized. Two more years were needed before these attitudes were translated into social, organizational terms. The development of the two groupings, the relations between them, and the dynamics prevailing within each form a different chapter in the drama of Zionism and tradition.

Notes

1. Alexander Lapidot to Mordecai Eliasberg, 4 Elul 5654 [1894], Central Zionist Archives, Jerusalem, 35/4/10. The present paper is based on a historiographic conception that sees the different shades of Jewish Orthodoxy in Western, Central, and Eastern Europe as a response to modernity. See "Shinnui umasoret," *Encyclopaedia Hebraica*, vol. 32, cols. 193–99. To the present, scholarly research has distinguished three trends in Western and Central European Orthodoxy: Orthodoxy, Neo-Orthodoxy and Ultra-Orthodoxy. It is my thesis in this paper that in Eastern Europe Orthodoxy—which I designate mainly by the adjective "traditional"—should be treated differently; it consisted essentially of two groups, now commonly referred to as *haredim*, more or less parallel but *not* identical to Orthodoxy; and neo-*haredim*, parallel to Neo-Orthodoxy. The distinction between these groups depends on their attitude to modernity: whereas the *haredim* rejected modernity in general, the neo-*haredim* were willing to meet it halfway, accepting modernity at least in the guise of Jewish nationality.

2. Jacob Lipschitz, "Mahzikei hadas," *Hapeles* (Poltava), 1902, p. 475.

3. Yosef Salmon, "Hamaavak al daat hakahal haharedit bemizrah Eropah beyahas latenuah haleumit," in *Perakim betoledot hahevrah hayehudit biyeme habenayim uva et hahadashah mukdashim leprofessor Yaakov Katz* (Jerusalem, 1980), p. 352. See also Yosef Salmon, "Hasefer *Shivat Zion* veriko hahistori," *Eshel Beer-Sheva* 2 (1980): 331–32.

4. Salmon, "Hamaavak al daat hakahal haharedit bemizrah Eropah beyahas latenuah haleumit."

5. Samson Raphael Hirsch to Jacob Lipschitz, 1886, in Jacob Lipschitz, *Mahzikei Hadas* (Piotrków, 1903), pp. 35–36.

6. Azriel Hildesheimer to Hovevei Zion association in Warsaw, in *Igrot R. Azriel Hildesheimer,* ed. Mordechai Eliav (Jerusalem, 1966), no. 35, p. 70 and n. 299. See also Zvi Hirsch Kalischer to Azriel Hildesheimer, November 11, 1862 and May 16, 1867, in Meier Hildesheimer, "Aus dem Briefwechsel Israel Hildesheimers," *Festschrift für Salomon Carlebach* (Berlin, 1910), pp. 294–95, 299.

7. Y. L. Fishman, ed., *Sefer Shmuel* (Jerusalem, 1923), pp. 20–21.

8. On the secession of Eliezer Gordon of Telz, see B. Z. Dinur, *Olam sheshaka* (Jerusalem, 1958), p. 87; E. E. Friedman, *Sefer hazikhronot* (Tel-Aviv, 1926), p. 170; Gordon to Hovevei Zion in Poswol, Tammuz 5649 (1889), in Z. A. Rabbiner, *Hagaon R. Eliezer Gordon z"l* (Tel-Aviv, 1928), p. 130; Yosef Salmon, "Haimut bein haharedim lamaskilim bitenuat Hibbat Zion," *Hazionut* 5 (1978): 46–48.

9. Salmon, "Haimut bein haharedim lamaskilim bitenuat Hibbat Zion," p. 49.

10. Ibid., pp. 50, 60. See also R. N. Z. Berlin to R. S. Y. Fuehn, Av 5649 (1889), in *Ketavim letoldot Hibbat Zion veyishuv Eretz Israel,* ed. Alter Druyanov, vol. 2 (Tel-Aviv, 1925), no. 924, p. 727.

11. Salmon, "Haimut bein haharedim lamaskilim bitenuat Hibbat Zion," p. 50. See also *Ketavim letoldot Hibbat Zion veyishuv Eretz Israel,* vol. 5, rev. Shulamit Laskov (Tel-Aviv, 1988), pp. 17, 251, 256–57, 327–28, 398–90. On Jacob Lipschitz's measures to enlist the support of the *admor* of Kopys for his efforts to establish Mahzikei Hadas in 1893, see Lipschitz, *Mahzikei Hadas,* p. 41.

12. Salmon, "Heimut bein haharedim lamaskilim bitenuat Hibbat Zion," pp. 53–54.

13. Ibid., pp. 56–77.

14. Circular letter from heads of the *kollelim* and rabbinical court in Jerusalem to Russian rabbis, Kislev 5644 (1884), in *Ketavim,* no. 1186, p. 580; see also Salmon, "Haimut bein haharedim lamaskilim bitenuat Hibbat Zion,", pp. 57–59.

15. See *Ketavim letoldot Hibbat Zion veyishuv Eretz Israel,* 5:442–43.

16. Fishman, ed., *Sefer Shmuel,* pp. 38–39.

17. Salmon, "Hamaavak al daat hakahal haharedit bemizrah Eropah beyahas latenuah haleumit," pp. 330–68.

18. Ibid. See also Salmon, "Hakituv bayishuv hayehudi beEretz Israel bishnot ha-90," *Cathedra* 12 (1979): 4–30.

19. Ahad Haam, "El haorekh hehadash," *Hamelitz,* 1894, no. 2, pp. 1–3. The statement was written on January 7, 1894.

20. Salmon, "Hamaavak al daat hakahal haharedit bemizrah Eropah beyahas latenuah haleumit," pp. 337–39.

21. Jonathan Eliasberg to Ahad Haam, 5655 (1894/95), Jewish National University Library, Ahad Haam Archives, Jerusalem, E-1.

22. Ibid.

23. Joshua Joseph Preil, "Davar lameshiv," *Hamelitz,* 1894, no. 183, pp. 1–2, and no. 184, pp. 1–2.

24. J. J. Rapaport, "Mikhtav meet Theodor Herzl el harabbi miCzortkow," *Zion* 4 (1939): 351–52.

25. See Yosef Salmon, "Teguvat haharedim bemizrah Eropah lazionut hamedinit," in Salmon, *Dat vezionut: Imutim rishonim* (Jerusalem, 1990), p. 320.

26 See Geulah Bat-Yehudah, "Sheelat hakulturah vehaMizrahi," in *Sefer Shragai,* vol. 1 (Jerusalem, 1981), pp. 66–73.

27. Salmon, *Dat vezionut,* p. 328.

28. Bat-Yehudah, "Sheelat hakulturah vehaMizrahi," pp. 68–69.

29. Salmon, *Dat vezionut,* p. 329.

30. Ibid., pp. 279–83.

31. Voting at the Fourth and Fifth Zionist Congresses on the so-called cultural question and the formation of the Democratic Faction proved beyond a doubt that the idea of purely political Zionism was simply not feasible. See Bat-Yehudah, "Sheelat hakulturah vehaMizrahi," pp. 69–80. However, Bat-Yehudah does not make the necessary distinctions among the three formulas appearing in Rabbi Isaac Jacob Reines's works: Zionism and religion; Zionism and culture; Zionism and messianism. By the very definition of Judaism as a "total" religion, no Eastern European traditional rabbi could possibly have proposed the separation of Zionism and religion. Reines did not believe in divorcing the return of Jews to Eretz Israel from its religious aspect. The formula separating Zionism from messianism was intended to appease the *haredim,* who suspected Zionism of false messianism. The separation of Zionism and culture, on the other hand, was meant to appease the political Zionists in Eastern and Western Europe, who feared that the cultural question would impede realization of the Basle Program, and to calm the *haredim,* who accused Zionism of trying to conceal their real aim—the secularization of Jewish society—behind the banner of relief for the Jewish plight. A misunderstanding of the broader context of the dispute has prompted many scholars to ascribe to Reines a spiritually anemic religious Zionist outlook. See ibid., p. 70, who confuses "Zionism and religion" with "Zionism and messianism." Compare M. Z. Nehorai, "Lemahutah shel hazionut hadatit: Iyun bemishnoteihem shel harav Reines veharav Kook," *Bishvilei hatehiyah,* vol. 3 (Ramat Gan, 1899), pp. 25–38; Yosef Salmon, review of *Makbilim nifgashim* by Ehud Luz, in *Zmanim,* nos. 30–31 (1989): 185–87.

32. Bat-Yehudah, "Sheelat hakulturah vehaMizrahi," pp. 83–85.

33. Yosef Salmon, "Emdatah shel hahevrah haharedit beRusyah-Polin lazionut bashanim 1898–1900," *Eshel Beer-Sheva,* 1 (1976): 377–438.

34. The second edition of *Or layesharim,* published in New York in 1917, apparently on the initiative of Ultra-Orthodox circles, omitted the contributions of nonrabbinical figures and of Rabbi Hermann Adler.

35. For more on the position of each participant, see Salmon, "Emdatah shel hahevrah haharedit beRusyah-Polin lazionut bashanim 1898–1900," pp. 394–430.

36. Ibid., p. 430.

37. S. D. Schneersohn, *Igeret bidvar hamosad hakadosh kupat harambahn* (1907), p. 21.

38. Ibid., p. 31. See also *Or layesharim* (1900 ed.), pp. 57–58; E. E. Friedman, *Karyena deigarta* (Warsaw, 1900); *Haktav vehamikhtav* (New York, 1917). And see "Hilufei hadevarim bein R. Shalom Duber miLubavich ve R. Shalom Hakohen Aharonson miKiyov bead veneged hazionut," in Isaac Alfasi, *Hahasidut veshivat Zion* (Tel-Aviv, 1986), pp. 115–21.

39. See *Or layesharim* (1900 ed.), pp. 50–52; Doberush Tursh, *Stirat zekenim,* Jewish National University Library, 854. See also Israel Klausner, "Hatenuah hazionit beLita," in *Yahadut Lita,* vol. 1 (Jerusalem, 1959), p. 513.

40. E. S. Z. Vingott, *Orah leZion* (Warsaw, 1902); Abraham Steinberg, *Daat rabbanim* (Warsaw, 1902).

41. Alfasi, *Hahasidut veshivat Zion,* pp. 9–12.

42. Ibid.

43. Ibid., pp. 17–19.

44. H. Z. Maccabee to Ussishkin, *Ketavim,* vol. 2, no. 819, p. 570.

45. Alfasi, *Hahasidut veshivat Zion,* pp. 22–23.

46. Yitzhak Rafael, "R.Hayim Israel miPilov—admor zioni," in *Sefer Shragai,* vol. 1 (Jerusalem, 1981), pp. 40–50. The fact is that Rabbi Israel Morgenstern did not publish his pamphlet even after obtaining *haskamot;* see also Alfasi, *Hahasidut veshivat Zion,* pp. 23–24. He claimed that as renowned an authority as Rabbi Simhah Bunem of Przysucha had stated that should Palestine fall into Jewish hands, that would be the beginning of the redemption. Israel Morgenstern, *Shelom Yerushalayim* (Piotrków, 1925), pp. 7–8.

47. Morgenstern, *Shelom Yerushalayim,* first introd. (probably 1886), and second introd. (probably 1890–91), pp. 3–4.

48. Alfasi, *Hahasidut veshivat Zion,* pp. 25–26; Rafael, "R. Hayim Israel miPilov—admor zioni," pp. 47–50.

49. Rafael, "R. Hayim Israel miPilov—admor zioni," p. 48.

50. Ibid., pp. 49–50; Alfasi, *Hahasidut veshivat Zion,* p. 28.

51. Morgenstern, *Shelom Yerushalayim,* p. 7.

52. I. I. Feigenbaum, *Or pnei Yitzhak* (Warsaw, 1939; reprint, Jerusalem, 1966), p. 30.

53. Ibid.

54. B. B. Dienstag, *Titen emet leYaakov* (New York, 1957), pp. 61–64.

55. Ibid., pp. 91–92, 95, statements cited in the name of Rabbi Simhah Bunem of Przysucha, Rabbi Abraham of Ciechanow, Solomon Leib of Leczna, and Rabbi Meir Alter of Gur.

56. See *Hamagid,* 1883, no. 3, pp. 20–21.

57. For Mahzikei Hadas support of Hibbat Zion in 1883, see Alfasi, *Hahasidut veshivat Zion,* p. 28.

58. *Hamagid,* 1890, no. 35, p. 285; according to Alfasi, *Hahasidut veshivat Zion,* the reference is to the *admor* of Belz.

59. See Alfasi, *Hahasidut veshivat Zion,* p. 28.

60. Ibid, p. 29.

61. Dienstag, *Titen emet leYaakov,* p. 86.

62. N. M. Gelber, *Hatenuah hazionit beGalizyah* (Jerusalem, 1958), 1:337–39 n. 16.

63. Ibid., pp. 332–426.

64. According to Dienstag, *Titen emet leYaakov,* p. 95, the Ruzhin dynasty traditionally had a positive attitude to Palestine.

65. Alfasi, *Hahasidut veshivat Zion,* pp. 32–33.

66. These positions were confirmed by Rabbi David Moses Friedman's son, Rabbi Israel, himself a bitter opponent of Zionism who later became a supporter, probably after the Balfour Declaration. See Yosef Sternberg, Rabbi Israel's secretary, to Rabbi Zalman Halperin, summer 1931, in M. Z. Fogel, *Sefer zimrat haaretz* (Jerusalem, 1941), p. 7. Dienstag, *Titen emet leYaakov,* pp. 78, 87; Alfasi, *Hahasidut veshivat Zion,* pp. 35–36; Gelber, *Hatenuah hazionit beGalizyah,* 2:782.

67. Yitzhak Rafael, *Rishonim veaharonim* (Tel-Aviv, 1957), p. 381; Gelber, *Hatenuah hazionit beGalizyah,* 2:782–83.

68. Dienstag, *Titen emet leYaakov,* pp. 78, 96.

69. Gelber, *Hatnuah hazionit beGalizyah,* 2:783.

70. Ibid., p. 784.

71. Ibid., p. 786.

72. Ibid., pp. 786–87.

73. Meir Bosak, "Yehudei Kraka bemahazit hashniyah shel hameah ha-19," in *Sefer Kraka* (Jerusalem, 1959), pp. 104–6. See also Simon Sofer to leaders of Galician communities, 5638 (1878), in Shlomo Sofer, ed., *Igrot sofrim* (Tel-Aviv, 1970), pp. 70–72; Joshusa Rokeah of Belz to Simon Sofer, 5639 (1879), ibid., p. 75. See also Salmon, "Hamaavak al daat hakahal haharedit bemizrah Eropah beyahas latenuah haleumit," pp. 347ff.

74. Bosak, "Yehudei Kraka bemahazit hashniyah shel hameah ha-19," pp. 106–7.

75. Alfasi, *Hahasidut veshivat Zion,* pp. 68–69.

76. Ibid., p. 71.

77. Salmon, "Hamaavak al daat hakahal haharedit bemizrah Eropah beyahas latenuah haleumit," p. 350.

78. Alfasi, *Hahasidut veshivat Zion,* p. 72.

79. Ibid., p. 73.

80. See Salmon, "Hamaavak al daat hakahal haharedit bemizrah Eropah beyahas latenuah

haleumit," pp. 349–63; Salmon, "Hasefer *Shivat Zion* veriko hahistori," pp. 337–40. For the attempt of 1893, see Lipschitz, *Mahzikei Hadas,* p. 41.

81. Jacob Lipschitz, *Zikhron Yaakov,* vol. 2 (Kowno-Sloboda, 1924) (reprint 1968), pp. 104–6. See also Lipschitz, *Mahzikei Hadas,* letters from the early 1880s, pp. 21ff.

82. See Lipschitz, "Mahzikei Hadas," *Hapeles,* 1902, pp. 465–76; quoted passage in ibid., p. 470; see also pp. 533–49.

83. Lipschitz, *Mahzikei Hadas,* p. 13 n.

84. Ibid. Among those who contributed *haskamot* were such undoubted Zionists as Rabbi Elijah Klatzkin of Mariampol, Isaac Jacob Rabinovich of Ponevezh and Hayim Meir Noah Levin of Vilna. Had they changed their minds, or were they dissembling? See ibid., pp. 7–11. Klatzkin's text, at least, implies that in his understanding the pamphlet was acceptable to all the religious "parties."

E H U D   L U Z

The Limits of Toleration

The Challenge of Cooperation between the Observant and the Nonobservant during the Hibbat Zion Period, 1882–1895

The Impact of Modernization

The development of pluralism and patterns of toleration within a traditional community is one outcome of modernization and secularization. These processes, tending to dissolve cohesiveness and homogeneity, undermine the authority of the traditional leadership. Gradually, a new leadership develops to challenge the old one. The new leadership fosters fresh ideologies that strive to establish a new social order, increasing flexibility and pluralism in defining the personal identity of community members.

Facing this situation, the traditional leadership has two main options: either to secede from the community to defend its old values, or to acknowledge the power of reality and adapt. In the latter case, this leadership would also develop a new ideology granting "traditional" legitimacy to the idea of toleration. Henceforth, such an ideology would be based on integrated pragmatic and theological arguments.

This process has characterized the Jewish community in the modern age, with a certain qualification. In Christian Europe, where most of the Jews were settled, various social and intellectual movements such as humanism and the Reformation had prepared the ground for the gradual development of patterns of tolerant thought and co-existence within common political systems. In Judaism, however, such movements did not arise before the nineteenth century. Due to the special situation of the Jews as a minority in the diaspora, the traditional leadership experienced the process of modernization as a trauma that threatened the very existence of the Jewish community. This experience was one of the sources of the powerful opposition to modernity, especially in Eastern Europe.

However, the traditional leadership lost its exclusive power and authority within the community. New forms of Jewish identity had emerged, and they challenged the traditionalists to define their position in the face of Jewish pluralism. Sometimes the challenge led the leadership to take a more flexible halakhic stance toward deviants. Elsewhere, especially in Central Europe, the leadership's response was secession and the creation of separate communities based on the argument that cooperation with sinners would imply a recognition of their Jewish legitimacy. Such a response showed that the traditional leadership of Central Europe had perceived the Jewish people as a purely halakhic community, a view implied that those who did not accept the Halakhah in its Orthodox interpretation automatically excluded themselves from the bond of the community.

Due to demographic and political conditions, the situation in Eastern Europe was different: although the antagonism between traditionalist and modernist, prior to the emergence of Zionism, had become acute, strong ethnic solidarity served as a major restraint to the creation of separate communities, even where the traditionalists had become a minority. There was no place for a movement of secession. Yet due to the national idea, a new theology of toleration developed, legitimizing cooperation between observant and nonobservant Jews.[1] This theology was developed by religious Zionists in Eastern Europe during the period of Hibbat Zion (Love of Zion), 1882–95.

Nationalism as a Basis for Toleration

The main innovation in this theology is the emphasis on the idea that Judaism is not merely a religion or a halakhic community. It is also a covenant of fate. In this sense, it contains a "neutral" dimension, beyond the formal Halakhah, that makes cooperation between the observant and nonobservant possible. Values such as the attachment to Zion as the symbol of national redemption, the care for the Jewish people and its traditional culture, and certain economic and social values are common concerns for all Jews, irrespective of personal behavior. Thus the national idea was the main drive for unity and religious toleration.

The crucial importance of nationalism in shaping the new tolerant ideology is proved by the dominant place given now to the concept of *klal Israel* (the entire Jewish people), which implies the unity of the people of Israel in spite of its inner division. Certainly the concept itself was not new, but what was new was the decisive role it assumed in shaping the ideological position of each side. This concept is obviously not an empirical but a metaphysical idea whose roots are irrational or, better, historical feeling, and in this sense it reflects a new historical consciousness shaped by the great changes within the Jewish community. The social diagnosis of the condition of the Jewish people in the *galut* (exile) is common to both camps: The "Jewish people as an entity is in a process of disintegration on the one hand, and it suffers from political and economic distress on the other. The attachment to the Torah by itself cannot sustain the existence and unity of the people, so it is necessary to establish an additional factor. This is the national idea. In spite of the rift within the community, between observant and nonobservant, the national idea can restore harmony, since it can serve as a basis for the synthesis between tradition and modernity, a goal that cannot be achieved in the *galut*. Hence all those who fight against assimilation can join together. Thus, for example, Moshe Leib Lilienblum, one of the leading exponents of the nonobservant, stated that should the Jews be reestablished in their homeland, an ethical and religious revival would follow as a matter of course and "the political life will cure everything." On the other hand, rabbis such as Naphtali Zevi Judah Berlin and Mordecai Eliasberg stated that the greatest value of the Zionist idea was in "uniting many opinions into one center." They made a historical analogy between the old return to Zion (in the time of Ezra, the fifth century B.C.) and the new one: as much as Ezra had let "nonpure" Jews to return to Zion, trusting the power of the Land of Israel to rectify them, we, too, have to trust that the nonobservant would return to the Torah as a consequence of their life in that land.

From this perspective one can understand the decidedly different attitudes of leading rabbis to the nonobservant Zionists and to the Reform Jews. Orthodox rabbis were unequivocally negative toward Reform Jews, but they were ambivalent about nonobservant Zionists.[2] The idea of the unity of Israel enabled the rabbis to demonstrate a certain halakhic flexibility toward those who deviated from the Torah, so long as they identified themselves with the "entire Jewish people." As Rabbi Alexander Moses Lapidot wrote, "The people have grown wiser and come to understand that we do not save the individual but rather the community and in affairs that affect the community we do not watch over individual deeds."[3]

Obviously the idea of unity could not obliterate the basic controversy over the aims of the partnership and the identity of *klal Israel*. Here we have to recall again the peculiar nature of Judaism as a dialectical unity of religion and nation. For the observant, *klal Israel* is a concept that includes all who are obliged to observe the Torah in its Orthodox interpretation. Hence there is no legitimate place in *klal Israel* for any trend that is not Orthodox. Regarding this issue, there was no difference between Zionist and anti-Zionist observant. The controversy concerned the evaluation of nationalism in the present historical situation and the operative conclusions stemming from it. Conversely, for the nonobservant, *klal Israel* is a concept that denotes all those who identify with the Jewish fate and with the cultural heritage of Judaism, while their personal way of life is a private matter. This controversy over the definition of *klal Israel* has determined the limits of tolerance from the time of Hibbat Zion until the present. The issues that emerged in this period are still of concern today.

The Focuses of the Conflict

The focuses of the practical friction between the two camps can be classified according to two main issues: first, the dissemination of the Zionist idea among the Jewish masses, either through direct propaganda or through the channel of education; and, second, the way of life of the colonists in Palestine and the nature of the new Jewish publicity created there.

Regarding the first issue, the main problem was how the Zionist idea should be presented to the public in order to recruit as many adherents as possible. Although the majority of the Jewish masses were still traditionalist, the best candidates for fulfilling Zionist aims were those who had been alienated from the tradition, namely the Jewish youth and intelligentsia, for whom the question of identity had been extremely urgent. Precisely because they became uprooted, they could constitute the most dynamic element of the movement. To appeal to those circles, the Zionist intelligentsia had to present them with an attractive goal in a form and language that did not conform to Orthodoxy. Naturally, the observant were antagonized, claiming that such a presentation could seduce even perfect believers and lead them astray from the Torah. This dilemma was ironically formulated in a saying of one of the greatest opponents of Zionism, Rabbi Shalom Dov Baer Schneersohn. "Zionism," he said, "is like the red heifer. It purifies the impure, but it defiles the pure."[4]

The dilemma of the formal propaganda was even more acute regarding education. Education was always the central concern of the traditional leadership. Prior to the rise of Zionism, this leadership had succeeded in defeating all attempts to modernize traditional education in Eastern Europe. But it is obvious that without modernization one could not foster the national idea.[5] The Zionist observant knew this, but they hesitated either because they were afraid of their observant opponents or because they were afraid that modernization would accelerate the process of secularization and deviation from the Torah. Their apprehension was all the greater regarding the Holy Land. Hence they insisted on control over propaganda and education, and they denied the right of the nonobservant to disseminate their opinions and establish a secular education program. There is no wonder that the dispute in 1894 over the Jaffa School founded by Ahad Haam's followers almost triggered the disintegration of cooperation.

The second issue—the colonists' way of life—was no less problematic. At the beginning of the period, there was a tacit agreement between the observant and the nonobservant that settlement in the Land of Israel bound the settlers to observe the commandments and to maintain a Jewish public life. The observant leaders demanded control over the way of life in the new colonies. The nonobservant accepted this demand for tactical reasons, probably believing that time would inevitably make the observant position more flexible. But the character of the settlers in the Land of Israel depended on more than the goodwill of Hibbat Zion. Many who went to Palestine, especially during the 1890s, though influenced by the national idea, were not a part of Hibbat Zion, and they were not ready to accept control of the observant. Thus the New Yishuv had evolved to be much more secular in appearance than the observant leaders had expected.

The debate over the sabbatical year in 1889 publicly exposed the problem of shaping Jewish public life in the Holy Land. For the nonobservant it was a test case for the ability of the Jewish religion to adapt itself to the new reality of establishing a modern settlement on a rational basis. For the observant, however, it was a test case of the nonobservants' readiness to agree that the observant should have the final word in every public issue that had halakhic ramification. Later I shall discuss the question whether more goodwill and tact on the part of the nonobservant could have prevented the rift.

Before I move to the detailed analysis of the positions of both sides, let me emphasize two other points that seem important for understanding the nature of the confrontation. First, for most of the period, the actual leadership of the movement was in the hands of the nonobservant. Yet although the Zionist movement was not based on democratic principles at this time, the observant demanded spiritual hegemony, claiming that they represented the majority of the Jewish masses. Second, right from the beginning the observant asserted that the conflict between the two camps was asymmetrical: the issue that was immaterial for the nonobservant—the religious nature of Zionist settlement—was crucial for the observant. Therefore, they claimed the nonobservant were obliged to make more concessions.[6]

The Observant Position

Indeed, both camps lacked any democratic tradition; there is no doubt, however, that the problem of toleration was much more difficult for the observant. The Halakhah clearly condemned those who maliciously deviated from the way of the Torah and prescribed that the Jewish community remove them from the Jewish fold. In certain extreme cases, as with the Karaites, it permitted the forceful oppression of the sinners, or even their extermination.[7] Hence the observant leaders had to develop a new theology and to search for new halakhic concepts that would enable them to ascribe a positive halakhic status to the nonobservant. From a theological point of view, the most serious problem was what I would call the paradox of "redemption by heretics." Eretz Israel was the Holy Land, and the rise of a secular settlement there implied a shattering and denial of a dream fostered by religious Jews for many generations. Could the Orthodox agree to such a move and yet remain innocent? As for the halakhic perspective, we may say that the old concepts for defining the status of the deviants could hardly be appropriate for the new reality in which deviation from the Torah became more and more common. Those concepts, such as *poshim* (sinners), *avaryanim* (offenders), or *reshaim* (evildoers), all had negative connotations, sometimes very extreme, and they appeared to be in deep contradiction to the strong spirit of national solidarity that moved the observant Zionists to include within *klal Israel* everyone who identified himself or herself as a Jew, irrespective of practice.[8]

The obstacles were not only theological and legal but also emotional. Rabbi Kook vividly and candidly described the bitter inner conflict in the heart of observant leaders.[9] If those leaders could overcome their instinctive response of revulsion, it was only due to a new theology of a clearly dialectical nature.

This theology was founded on two main assumptions. First, the deviation of the nonobservant from the Torah was a temporary phase only ("a transient malady" according to Rabbi Isaac Jacob Reines[10]) in the process of redemption. This assumption derived from the belief in the mystical power of the people of Israel, which can never be totally defiled, and in the therapeutic power of the Holy Land. Accordingly, unbelief can never strike roots in the people of Israel. Its only source is external—the exile with its negative effects. Thus a return to the homeland should redeem the sinners. The Zionist project is the channel through which they would finally make repentance. On the basis of this belief, there is room for halakhic flexibility, which permits cooperation with sinners in building the land. This position also opens the way for fostering common concerns without recognition of the Jewish legitimacy of the nonobservant.

The second assumption, which goes even further, ascribes to the phenomenon of nonobservance a positive theological function. Nonobservance is a tool in the hands of providence itself—something like the Hegelian concept of "the cunning of reason"—for the attainment of the historical goal of redemption. The nonobservant are distinguished by certain talents and qualifications that grant them certain advantages over the observant in everything which concerns the material side of the Zionist enterprise. Therefore they have some priority in accomplishing the first stage of redemption. However, they should not have a dominant place in shaping the spiritual image of Zionism. Here they must accept the authority of the traditional leadership.

These two assumptions lead to the conclusion that toleration on the part of the observant is conditional: the nonobservant are permitted to be partners on condition that they not have any impact on the spiritual nature of Zionism and that ultimately they find their way back to the bosom of the Torah.[11] As I have said, this optimistic view was nourished by the assumption that the main source of secularization among the Jewish people had been the impact of exile, and consequently a return to the homeland would put an end to this phenomenon. In any case, such a position reflects a certain paradox: it acknowledges the fact that secular nationalism is the only road open for secular Jews to be committed to Judaism at the same time that it denies the equal right of secular Zionism within the movement.

The Nonobservant Position

Among the nonobservant we may note a process of radicalization. As long as they had a feeling of dependence on the Orthodox leadership, they were ready to make long-range concessions to the observant in order to attract Orthodox Jews to the movement. Leaders such as Leon Pinsker and Moshe Leib Lilienblum, and later Theodor Herzl, believed that the great reserves of the Zionist movement were among Orthodox Jews, and consequently they preferred to postpone every ideological division to the unseen future, assuming that political reality itself would force the observant to adapt themselves to modernization. In this sense their position conformed to that of the observant. But gradually it became obvious that modernization was the precondition for Zionist fulfillment rather than its outcome. That was the argument of Ahad Haam and his followers: without educational work, there was no chance for Zionism. The revolutionary spirit of that age and the struggle of Zionism with other modern movements for the hearts of Jewish youth and the intelligentsia led the Zionist intelligentsia to be less tolerant toward the observant and more radical in their demands. It is no wonder that their educational and cultural activity among the Jewish masses appeared to be the main reason for the secession of the major part of the observant, who in 1900–1901 became bitter opponents of Zionism.

At this point I would like to present a speculative question: Was the rift with the majority of Orthodox inevitable, or would it have been possible to create some *modus vivendi*? Perhaps we can answer this question by examining the pattern of toleration offered by Ahad Haam, which was tested in the society of Bnei Moshe. The history of this society (1889–96) clearly presents the difficulty of creating a consensus on a basis of compromise. I think that Ahad Haam was the only person in this period who really tried to shape a true pattern of toleration, and therefore his failure is instructive. The very man who himself was so far from any extremism triggered the eruption of the most fierceful *Kulturkamp* during this period.

What did he conceive? On the one hand, Ahad Haam was a man of integrity. In contrast to many other Zionists, he never tried to hide or to obliterate the conflict of opinions since he believed that a genuine partnership could not be built on a lack of honesty. He sharply criticized the rabbis who had tried to enforce their authority on the nonobservant in matters of both opinion and behavior. He considered freedom of expression as the *sine qua non* for cooperation. Being an agnostic freethinker, he became the first Zionist thinker who outspokenly declared that it was possible to be an authentic Jew out of secular motives. In this sense, he was the first to define an ideology that granted legitimacy to secular nationalism. On the other hand, Ahad Haam tried very hard to avoid any intentional injury to the feelings of the observant so that, in spite of the divisive opinions, the two camps could cooperate in practical matters. Each side could freely work and express its opinions without constraint, in the hope that its views would eventually triumph. In other words, he believed in free competition with mutual respect and opposed any kind of public aggression. For Ahad Haam, tolerance was a matter of prudence.

Yet when Ahad Haam came to define the ideological basis for the partnership, he used the term "national spirit." This was a historicist concept that could be interpreted in different ways, and Ahad Haam believed that its very vagueness would open the way for cooperation. For Ahad Haam himself, the concept meant most of all the feeling of historical continuity built on historical knowledge and the crucial importance of certain national symbols common to all Jews, even though for different reasons.

We know that this approach was rejected by both camps, and the reasons are obvious. The nonobservant rejected it since they were of the opinion that Ahad Haam was not sufficiently consistent. You cannot be a historicist and at the same time try to limit, or define ahead, what should be included in the national spirit. The radicals among Ahad Haam's followers, who were also members in Bnei Moshe, were not ready to be so considerate of the feelings of the observant and to adopt traditional customs out of "national" reasons only, namely, in order to appease the observant. The concept of Jewish culture was much more obscure for them. Furthermore, they came to the conclusion that there was a need for a deep spiritual revolution without which Zionism had no chance to compete with the other movements within the Jewish pale. Hence they strove for complete separation between religion and nationality.

The observant rejected Ahad Haam's position since it implied a formal acknowledgment of the supremacy of nationalism over religion and the granting of legitimacy to secular Zionism. Practically, they refused to accept Ahad Haam's demand for freedom of expression and education since they were afraid that the freethinkers, by their dynamic initiative, would take over all the influence within the movement. Thus, for example, even the observant members of Bnei Moshe had not only opposed secular education but even demanded their nonobservant colleagues take upon themselves a certain minimum of commandments or, at least, give respect to Jewish religion publicly. The fact that the bylaws of the society, and especially the religious clause, were changed frequently demonstrated that the gap in religious matters was unbridgeable.[12]

The only one of the observant Zionists who was ready to draw operative conclusions from the failure of Bnei Moshe's experiment was Yehiel Michal Pines. Pines was the first who called for a separate religious Zionist organization to struggle against secular Zionism. But Pines was well acquainted with observant indolence, namely its passiveness and its lack of initiative, which would leave the nonobservant to conquer the entire field of Zionism. Indeed, there was no response to his views at that time.

Conclusion

The lesson we can extract from the analysis of the relationships during the Hibbat Zion period is obvious: as long as the ideological divisions had been masked behind the vague idea of settling the Land of Israel, the observant could believe that they would be able to guide the movement according to their spirit even though the leadership was practically in the hands of the nonobservant. But once the nonobservant disclosed publicly their ideological position and acted accordingly, the rift with Orthodoxy became inevitable and only a small minority of observant remained ready to continue cooperation. In this sense, nothing changed in Herzl's time (1897–1904). In contrast to the majority of observant who condemned Zionism as a secular, heretical movement, this minority persisted in its belief that Zionism would serve as a forerunner of the return to tradition and eventually as a preparation for redemption. Therefore they participated in all the activities of the Zionist organization and supported the building of the Land of Israel and the creating there of an independent Jewish polity.

Generally speaking, we may say that whenever a certain issue is invested with a symbolic or ideological aura, it immediately touches the whole meaning of Zionism and consequently shakes the foundations of cooperation. There is no wonder that whenever the issue of "who is a Jew" is raised in Israel it creates a political storm and the observant threaten to break off cooperation. On the other hand, it can be proved that the observant leaders never welcomed historical changes until those changes to some extent were forced on them. No one would refute the fact that gradually the observant adapted themselves to the democratic principles of the Zionist movement, and they have learned to take advantage of it. This process began at the Minsk Conference in 1902, where the equal rights of secular and religious education were first acknowledged by the leaders of Mizrahi, the observant Zionist organization founded in 1902. Not until ten years later was this acknowledgment formally approved by the Zionist Congress. On the other hand, the nonobservant complied with the demand of the observant to keep a minimum of Jewish public behavior within the institutions of the Zionist organization. Thus Ahad Haam's approach has not completely failed. Yet the Jewish characteristics of the New Yishuv remained an open issue for the future.

In the light of such deeply divided opinions one may wonder how the cooperation between the two camps could be achieved at all. The answer, I believe, is to be found in the combination of pragmatic and ideological motives. At first, reality forced the two camps to make mutual concessions. That "reality" encompassed the enormous pressure of Jewish distress that constantly became worse and the common feeling, sometimes intuitively sensed, that there was a mutual dependence between the two sides. The second motive for toleration was the ideological source of Zionist vision, namely the mystical belief in the therapeutic power of Eretz Israel on the one hand and the utopian nature of the Zionist idea, which had left the future open for each group to foster its own dream, on the other hand.[13] It was the combination of these two factors that propelled the two sides to emphasize their common practical goals and to postpone, as far as possible, the principal decisions of an undefined future, believing that time would work out some kind of a compromise. Perhaps, this postponement was one of the reasons for the success of the Zionist idea, but it has also been the source of its many faults today. The problems that were present during that formative period became more acute within the state. The observant face the problem of creating new theological-halakhic concepts that will enable them to accept the democratic principles of the State of Israel and to recognize secular Zionism *de jure* and not only *de facto*. The nonobservant are forced to define the meaning of secular Jewish culture and its relation to the past. It seems that both sides are still far from genuine toleration. Genuine toleration is something more than a pragmatic arrangement based on mutual benefit. It is mutual respect built on human solidarity and on the recognition of the right of existence for each group to search for the truth in its own way.

Notes

1. I prefer the terms "observant" and "nonobservant" since I believe they are more appropriate for the division than the common Hebrew terms *dati* (religious) and *hiloni* (secular) describe. The terms "observant" and "nonobservant" have a much more objective meaning. In the periodicals of the Hibbat Zion period, the usual terms are *hared* and *hofshi*. *Hared* is the Hebrew equivalent of "Orthodox." Literally it means someone who strictly obeys God and observes his Torah. *Hofshi* means one who perceives himself free from the yoke of the Torah. In this sense, these terms are close to those I use. The "observant" were divided between those who supported Zionism (later called religious Zionists) and those who rejected it (later called anti-Zionist Orthodox).

2. Rabbi Abraham Isaac Hacohen Kook made this distinction very clearly. Rejecting the idea of excluding the secular Zionists from *klal Israel,* he stated that the main reason for excluding the Reform Jews was that they intended to destroy the foundations of the nation by establishing a special religious sect. "But to exclude those sinners, who maintain that Israel is one nation and we should preserve the nature of the nation as a special and united one . . . this is a way of heresy." "Kuntres yishuv mishpat," quoted in *Morasha* 10 (Winter 1976): 48–49.

3. Discussion of the halakhic and theological problems of cooperation with "sinners" can be found in my *Parallels Meet* (Philadelphia, 1988), pp. 46–58.

4. Shalom Dov Baer Schneersohn, quoted in my *Parallels Meet*, p. 214.

5. On the importance of secular education for nationalist movements, see A. D. Smith, *Nationalism in the Twentieth Century* (New York, 1979), p. 37.

6. Luz, *Parallels Meet*, p. 59.

7. *Perush haRambam lamishnah*, Hullin 1:1. Compare his *Mishneh torah*, Hilkhot mamrim, chap. 3.

8. This statement is applied even to the most moderate concept of *tinok shenishbah* (infant taken prisoner by gentiles). Jews defined by the concept of *tinok shenishbah*, namely, those raised by non-Jews, should be forgiven for their deviance from the Torah since it is inadvertent.

9. See Luz, *Parallels Meet*, p. 55.

10. Ibid., p. 53.

11. This theory, later developed extensively by Rabbi Kook, is similar to the tolerant theory of the Catholic theolgian Karl Rahner concerning "the Anonymous Christian." Rahner's argument is that the non-Christian believer is influenced unconsciously by a spirit whose source is the revelation of God through Christ. Those who oppose Christianity are people who have not yet acknowledged that they are already under the spell of the spirit, despite that they outwardly reject it. In other words, they are Christians who have not yet reached self-consciousness. See Karl Rahner, "Christianity and the Non-Christian Religions" in *Christianity and Other Religions,* ed. John Hick and Brian Hebblethwaite (Philadelphia, 1980), pp. 52–79.

12. On Ahad Haam's position and the controversy over Bnei Moshe, compare Luz, *Parallels Meet*, pp. 77–97, 160–63; S[hmuel] Tchernowich, *Bnei Moshe utekufatam* (Warsaw, 1914).

13. Compare: "For a practical ideology like nationalism the 'messianic' element is contained in its vision of ethnic fraternity for which it strives. Nationalists believe that a 'messianic age' will arrive only when men and women come to share common values and sentiments, as in a close-knit family. The nation is such a 'family' writ large." Smith, *Nationalism*, p. 41.

Symbolic Politics, Religion, and the Emergence of Ahad Haam

I

Zionist historiography has characteristically viewed the Bnei Moshe as a bizarre interlude in the movement's prehistory, as a strangely contentious and mysterious group that accomplished little and, mercifully, was allowed to die a quiet death when Theodor Herzl appeared on the scene. Its Masonic-like symbolism and secrecy, its code names and ritualized salutations, above all, its grand design to constitute itself as the core of a new Yavneh—all appeared rather pathetic in view of its tiny size (about two hundred members) and its tumultuous, inconclusive record. It was unable to resolve something so basic as its attitude toward religious Judaism (nor was this issue resolved, of course, by the Zionist movement, which nonetheless finessed it with greater dexterity); its claim to be the pioneer of a reconstructed Judaism fell flat when it proved unable to persuade its minuscule constituency to live in peace with one another.[1]

In retrospect the Bnei Moshe appeared exotic, excessively quarrelsome, self-important, and very quickly dated. Even those most closely associated with it gave it, at best, mixed reviews: Ahad Haam (pen name for Asher Ginzberg, 1856–1927) distanced himself from it, claiming that he led it for only a short period and declaring flatly that it constituted an "experiment that failed."[2] No important sector of the Zionist movement saw the Bnei Moshe as its imagined ancestor as, for instance, the Second Aliyah viewed Bilu. The fact that Chaim Weizmann, Leo Motzkin, or Menahem Mendel Ussishkin had joined it was, or so it seemed in retrospect, of little more than passing biographical interest. There were no Zionist institutions committed to sustaining its memory or relevance, and its erstwhile members went on to pursue more pressing priorities than those set down in its strangely lyrical declarations. When there was a desultory attempt to revive the Bnei Moshe in Tel Aviv in the 1920s, it quickly showed itself as little more than an esoteric discussion group of aging, nostalgic men.[3]

This tendency, however, to view the Bnei Moshe as a curious anachronism, even in its lifetime, ignores its considerable achievements—political as well as cultural—which, as Yossi Goldstein has shown, were downplayed or distorted because of the group's secrecy.[4] It also obscures one of the central features of maskilic nationalism as best represented by it, namely, the way in which it drew upon, and transmuted, traditional (and in its case specifically hasidic) leadership patterns and imagery. The Bnei Moshe's goals, and the role assumed in it by Ahad Haam, translated into modern Jewish political idiom methods used to inspire and rule the hasidic sector of traditional Jewry that Ahad Haam and his immediate followers knew intimately. Ahad Haam's leadership, it was believed, represented proof of the viability of the secularization of spiritual politics, the central goal of the Bnei Moshe.

When, in 1891, Bnei Moshe activist Ben-Avigdor (pen name for Abraham Leib Shalkovich) fantasized in a published booklet about Moses, who descended Mount Sinai and preached the teachings of Ahad Haam—"Sons of Isaiah, if your thoughts are good but your deeds bad, this is not the way!"—he was merely airing publicly views characteristic of the Bnei Moshe since its inception.[5] Ben-Avigdor's adulation embarrassed him, Ahad Haam claimed; yet it was precisely such adulation that constituted the group's linchpin. If there was much that was uncannily familiar about the way in which Ahad Haam conducted himself as its leader, it was because he was able, at least in the first few years of his public activity, to secularize hasidic leadership patterns more effectively than any other modern Jewish figure. His effectiveness was predicated upon the degree to which his constituency retained an allegiance, often instinctual and frequently despite strongly felt secularist commitments, for such religious imagery and strategy. The Bnei Moshe sought to transform the central teachings of Judaism from religious to national-cultural ones and attempted to do so through techniques associated with Ashkenazi Jewry. Its ideology is what has interested most of those who have studied the group. My primary interest is its symbolic politics, and particularly the role assumed by its leader, Ahad Haam, whose actions, mannerisms, and style of leadership served, at least at the outset, to reassure its constituency that past and present, religion and secularism could be bridged. This essay will study the origins of the Bnei Moshe and the first stages of its development before relations between its religious and irreligious members broke down in 1893–94.

II

That the Bnei Moshe sought out as members both religious and irreligious Jews is well known. During his trips, its first recruiter Yehoshua Barzilai attempted to attract the pious by relating "legendlike tales" (according to one source) of Ahad Haam's commitment to the revival of Jewish spiritual impulses. (More secular Jews were told that Ahad Haam was a Europeanized master; Barzilai, a pious Palestinian pioneer, believed him to be both.)[6] Eventually, as Ehud Luz has shown, the delicate compromise fashioned in the Bnei Moshe between the religious and nonreligious was under severe, even irreparable attack from both within and outside the organization.[7] And not surprisingly so, since Ahad Haam sought to rebuild Judaism on national-cultural foundations while alienating the sensibilities of neither the assimilated nor the religiously inclined. When, in 1893, this endeavor proved impossible, the group dropped the clause in its bylaws that asked members to respect the religious dictates of Judaism even if these conflicted with their personal inclinations. In effect, the Bnei Moshe now discarded efforts to court religious Jewry and set its sights, without great success, on the recruitment of Russified and secular Jews.[8]

The core of its membership, primarily its original Odessa constituency along with the most prominent members of its Warsaw branch, were, as described in Ahad Haam's first major published article, "Lo zeh haderekh" (This Is Not the Way, 1889), those who have "halted half-way . . . whose [religious] faith has weakened and who have no longer the patience to wait for miracles, but who, on the other hand, are still attached to their people by bonds which have lost none of their strength."[9] Nearly all of the original nine members of Odessa's *lishkah alef* (lodge number one) were underemployed Hebrew tutors, bookkeepers working for the Hovevei Zion, or journalists who eked out a living by writing for what was then a small cluster of Hebrew, Yiddish, or Russian-language Jewish periodicals. None had secular training; only one, Yehoshua Hana Rawnitzky, was born in Odessa. Nearly all were drawn to the city from Ukrainian, hasidic-dominated townlets; they came because of Odessa's reputation for freedom, culture, and wealth. Self-consciously "modern" though they were, their pious backgrounds, poverty, and lack of formal European education set them apart from the vast majority of Odessa's Jewish intelligentsia, who were secularly sophisticated, fluent in Russian, cultivated in ways that such newcomers would never be, and considerably more distant from the rhythm of traditional Jewish life. They were, according to Chaim Tchernowitz, who knew them well and felt great affection for them, a bunch of *batlanim* and *melamdim* (idlers and tutors).[10]

Theirs was only one of several overlapping local maskilic circles. The men who frequented Ginzberg's also on occasion met on Friday evenings at the Yiddish writer Mendele Mokher Seforim's or at Moshe Leib Lilienblum's. Mendele entertained guests in his spartan home adjacent to the *talmud torah* (a communally funded school for indigent children) that he ran in Moldavanka, one of the city's poor neighborhoods. Lilienblum, who himself was very poor and lived in a series of wretched apartments, nonetheless maintained an occasional salon.

Each stamped evenings at his home with a particular style: Mendele entertained guests with long, elaborate monologues (sometimes lasting four or five hours at one sitting) in which he related in humorous detail conversations that he had overheard on the streets of Odessa. In contrast, Lilienblum was uncommunicative, but those who sat at his feet had great respect for his skill as a publicist demonstrated in his autobiography, *Hataot neurim* (1876), one of the most influential Hebrew books of the 1870s and which had inspired a generation of *maskilim*. Relations between the heads of these circles were strained. Both Lilienblum and Mendele found Ginzberg overbearing; once the Bnei Moshe was established with Ginzberg as its totem, the mordant Mendele referred to its members as "the ten lost tribes." Both found the veneration by local maskilic nationalists of the otherwise unknown, unpublished, and untested Ginzberg to be all but inexplicable.[11]

What distinguished Ginzberg was his wealth, his *yihus* (former *hasidim* could not but be impressed with his relations to two hasidic dynasties, including the distinguished Schneersohns), the range of his learning, and his coveted membership on the Hovevei Zion executive. There were other reasons, as well: his Victorian-like rigidity—the same rigidity that Mendele found so jarring—impressed his circle who saw it as a sign of European sophistication. They spoke admiringly of his exceptionally rigid schedule, the way in which he divided his time between the business office that he maintained with his father where he spent his mornings—they ran a liquor distillery in Odessa and, later, an olive oil factory—and his study, where he would not permit himself to be disturbed, except on Friday evenings and Saturdays when he entertained guests. Chaim Tchernowitz wrote of his first encounter with Ginzberg, who told him on his doorstep that he hadn't the time to speak with him but would set an appointment: "Jews talk even when they don't have the time; he seemed like a gentile [*goy lehavdil*]." Simon Dubnov recalled in his autobiography that Ginzberg's personal demeanor was severe, his movements spare and deliberate.[12]

For Ginzberg's admirers this self-discipline was inspiring. Even his coolness and apparent lack of intimacy was seen by them as indicative of the sensibility of a European free from the burdens of Russian tempestuousness and impracticality. In contrast, Ginzberg was viewed as both realistic and intellectually expansive, a sober visionary, an authentic Jew who eschewed all parochialism. This perspective on him as a European was influenced by the fact that he was the only one of his circle seen by local Russified Jewish intellectuals, who dominated the Jewish cultural scene in Odessa, as worldly, unparochial, and an uncharacteristically cultivated Hebraist. Even before meeting him, Dubnov, a regular writer for the St. Petersburg Russian Jewish monthly *Voskhod*, heard things about him and intended to seek him out. The view of Ginzberg as a European originated, at least in part, because of his Hebraist circle's need for an emblem, a source of legitimization, and Ginzberg fit the bill.[13]

The publication of "Lo zeh haderekh" in 1889 was engineered behind the scenes by Abraham Elijah Lubarsky. Lubarsky had persuaded *Hamelitz*'s haughty editor Alexander Zederbaum, during a visit to Odessa in the fall of 1888, to see Ginzberg and urge him to publish in his newspaper. Lubarsky told the Hebrew editor that Ginzberg was a *nistar* (literally, a hidden holy man), and Zederbaum, who usually expected authors to court him, set out in pursuit of the talented newcomer. Ginzberg agreed to write the article, and Zederbaum, with considerable persistence and some finesse, managed to extract it from him.[14]

In his correspondence with Zederbaum, Ginzberg already spoke with surprising authority and with the self-possession of the mature Ahad Haam. For instance, in an effusive letter, Zederbaum urged Ginzberg to send his article quickly: "I am certain that one article written by you will attract many readers to you," perhaps alluding to the article's political goals. In response, Ginzberg admitted that he had nearly despaired of writing the piece:

Despite the fact that it is my custom to guard my tongue, I will nonetheless admit that various difficulties that I have faced in my personal affairs, coupled with my recent frame of mind and fear of the reactions of the community and of writers . . . caused me to nearly abandon hope of writing anything for *Hamelitz*, as I had promised, Sir, when you were here.[15]

In this exchange of letters, which continued for several months, Ginzberg showed himself alternatively to be carping, imperial, touchy, and apologetic. He complained frequently of lack of time (a lifelong complaint), apologized when his suspicions proved unwarranted, and demanded repeatedly special treatment. Apparently Zederbaum did not feel such demands excessive. His first letter to Ginzberg was addressed: "Beloved one of my soul, man of wisdom and might, man of great knowledge, modest one with numerous followers [*hasidim*], Mr. A. Ginzberg."[16] Even by the typically florid standards of contemporary Hebrew salutations, this was obsequious in a letter written by a well-established editor to a literary unknown. It bordered on prostration.

III

For his immediate entourage, the regimen of the Bnei Moshe—and its veneration for Ginzberg—represented something of a substitute for the rigors of traditional Jewish life. In this respect, the ornate and ritualistic demands made on them by the Bnei Moshe were both unsurprising and familiar. Ahad Haam's followers spoke of him in terms that were, at once, paternal and religious, describing him as a *zaddik*, as a man of genius, charisma, and unmatched moral authority. The launching of his public career and, indeed, the role played by Lubarsky in the publication of "Lo zeh haderekh" involved many of the same pious, backdoor manipulations that existed in the hasidic communities of their pasts.

A vivid description of how these activities looked even before the establishment of the Bnei Moshe in February–March 1889 may be found in a letter written to the Hebrew journalist Reuven Brainin by Jehuda Leib Dawidowicz in 1888. Dawidowicz (also known by his pen name Ben David) gained entry into this circle and observed it as neither a follower nor one with a vested interest in undermining it. He would, in fact, soon embrace Ginzberg's teachings with much the same fervor that he mocks in his letter.[17] His comments reflect the condescension of a Vilna-born Jew for the excesses of former *hasidim*. More important, they show Ginzberg as having moved his followers to a rare state of devotion:

Not long ago the metropolis Odessa was chosen as the home of a fine young gentleman, Asher Ginzberg is his name. Together with his father he settled here and opened up an olive oil factory, and the owners themselves are both fine fellows, like pure olive oil. The father is a *hasid* and the only son is the son-in-law of the *Admor*, the Lubavitcher Rebbe. [In fact, the *rebbe* was his wife's uncle.] The bridegroom himself actually resembles the *Admor*, in that he too is a *rebbe* of another sort, of a European kind, a *rebbe* of the Left. . . . He came from some village, as it were, and there, in splendid isolation, he prepared himself for the redemption that he, as *rebbe*, would bring about for the Jewish people—all this in the style of the Baal Shem Tov. The light of this new *rebbe* was revealed suddenly in our sinful Odessa, by his new devotees among our writers. And to this new *rebbe* (in these truly messianic days) were attributed coronets and legends. They associated him with miracles and great deeds: that he has mastered the seven wisdoms, that he has learned seventy languages, that he is a man of mighty wisdom (with money in his purse) and a fine character.

And this *rebbe*, Reb Asherl Ginzberg, oversees a hasidic-like table, just like a real hasidic master and on Sabbath eve his followers gather at his home, Hebrew writers and just plain *maskilim*, the chosen ones.

I am one of those who merited on several occasions an invitation (not all do—not a single one of my friends has been invited), and I don't know what good deed of mine might have caused this to happen, and I was permitted to sit at the table of Asherl on Sabbath eve. The *rebbe* sits surrounded by a "congregation" of *hasidim*, drinking boiling tea, treating him with fervent devotion and respect. The *rebbe* lights Sabbath cigarettes, and his *hasidim* follow suit. For if this is permissible for the *rebbe*, all the more so for his followers. His "assembly" is silent, endeavoring to hear what his holy mouth utters. But this *rebbe* of ours is a real quiet one, whose very silence is golden [paraphrasing an Aramaic saying]. The *rebbe*, Gospodin [Mr.] Ginzberg, a red-headed man, short, modest, with a sharp and complex mind, gesticulates with the use of his bony hands in a manner that is vaguely hostile. . . . And his followers search his remarks eagerly for his hints and intimations. The *rebbe*, may he live a long life, is stingy, careful with words. . . . Not so his *hasidim*. The "assembly" devours tea, smokes cigarettes, slowly gets more and more heated, and then words begin to flow. . . . The *rebbe* maintains his distance, cool, chilly, and, like a real *mitnaged* [opponent of Hasidism], not an unbecoming word passes his lips.[18]

In creating the Bnei Moshe, Ahad Haam attempted to translate into Jewish political idiom methods used to inspire and rule traditional Jewry. The group was to serve as a fulcrum, a focal point—comparable to that of a hasidic court—that would inspire Jews elsewhere by virtue of the austere and exemplary behavior of its members and especially its leaders. This method explains why Ahad Haam would later dismiss the criticisms of members who insisted on knowing what they were expected to do, what activities they should perform as members of this elite group. If, Ahad Haam felt, they did not appreciate what was expected of an elite in times of cultural crisis and were unable to understand that their service to the community had less to do with concrete activity than with inspiration, they were unworthy of membership.[19]

It is within this context that Ginzberg's choice of the pen name Ahad Haam (literally, "One of the People") must be understood. It was first used by him in "Lo zeh haderekh," and he claimed that he selected it to highlight his unprofessional standing, to explain that the essay was for him simply a casual excursion into literature: "The idea of this pen name was to make it clear that I was not a writer, and had no intention of becoming one, but was just incidentally expressing my opinion on the subject about which I wrote as 'one of the people' interested in his people's affairs."[20]

In fact, Ginzberg was not "just incidentally expressing" his opinions; rather his essay encapsulated, as we have seen, many months of discussions and sought to serve as the public manifesto of a politically ambitious group of men. His explanation for the choice of the pen name is also less than frank. Here, too, what was visible mirrored (and only rather vaguely) a hidden, and immeasurably more significant, reality. The choice of his pen name was made for reasons different from the one he gave.

In a culture where humility (in the right hands) implied greatness, a stated disdain for power was something of a prerequisite for it, and the pursuit of anonymity characterized true saintliness, someone who called himself "One of the People" did not necessarily intend to be seen in quite the way that the name might imply. A clue as to why Ahad Haam chose it may be gleaned from its use in the Pentateuch, where it appears only once, in Genesis 26:10: "And Abimelech said, 'What is this that you have done to us? One of the people [ahad haam] might easily have lain with your wife and you would have brought guilt upon us.'" Rashi comments, "'One of the people': The special one of the people, namely the King." [Ahad haam: hameyuhad baam, zeh hamelekh]. Here Rashi draws on the second-century exegete Onkelos, whose Aramaic translation is identical.

Ahad Haam's choice of pen name was, then, at the very least, ambiguous, combining, as it did, claims of modesty and ambition, anonymity and greatness, the pretense to blend into the folk and an affirmation that this was impossible. It is unlikely that Ahad Haam, a Bible scholar, was unaware of the passage and its midrashic implications, particularly in view of the extensive notes that he took (much later, to be sure, in England) on nearly every passage of the Bible in preparation for the writing of a never-completed book on biblical literary style. Interestingly, the index card devoted to Genesis 26 skips the passage.[21]

IV

Critics of the Bnei Moshe typically credited its ornate and secret ritualism to Masonic influences. Members were required, among other things, to swear absolute allegiance to *Maleh* (abbreviation for *manhig lishkah alef*, or "leader of lodge number one," i.e., Ahad Haam), and they were provided with code names for themselves and their branches. Masonic influences were, without doubt, felt in a milieu where the Bnei Moshe's secrecy was also a by-product of its illegality and its leaders' circumspection. But no less apparent was the influence of Hasidism and, in Ahad Haam's own case, of the Sadgora dynasty, whose influence on him, as he acknowledged, was abiding.

Ginzberg was raised in the Sadgora *kloyz* in Skvira, and he begins one version of his reminiscences: "As I have indicated elsewhere, I received the beginnings of my education from 'Hasidism,' upon whose knees I was born and lived for first years of my childhood." The Sadgora Rebbe, as Ahad Haam and his sister Esther (whose memoirs are also an invaluable source) both make clear, dominated their family's life. "I learned to respect the Sadgora Rebbe with the reverence of God," Ahad Haam recalls. Once his father Isaiah Ginzberg acquired riches, an estate, and a sizable number of servitors, he conducted himself in a style resembling that of his *rebbe*. Often more than fifty guests at a time gathered around his Sabbath or festival table—many of them visiting Sadgora *hasidim*—as Isaiah sternly guided them through the meal with Asher sitting on his right. The connection between the dynasty's founder Israel Ruzhin and Asher's mother's father—who had served as an interpreter for the charismatic, organizationally adept leader—was the family's single greatest distinction. Isaiah Ginzberg made the move to the Gopchitse estate upon his *rebbe*'s advice and against the wishes of his wife and her family; he spent Sukkot in the *rebbe*'s presence, and it was at the sect's imposing Italian, neo-Gothic Bukovina center that he negotiated the terms of his twelve-year-old son's betrothal to the daughter of another Sagdora *hasid*.[22]

And it was also at the *rebbe*'s court, and at the age of twelve, that Asher Ginzberg, then a conventionally pious prodigy, was suddenly transformed into a critic of Hasidism and soon of traditional Judaism in general. Interestingly, his veneration for the *rebbe* himself would remain secure, and he would still, when writing his memoirs nearly half a century later, recall vividly the salutary impressions that the *rebbe* made on him. What the prudish, cloistered adolescent found troubling was the coarseness and indelicacy of the *rebbe*'s entourage. But the *rebbe* himself, Avraham Yaakov ben haZaddik miRuzhin, writes Ahad Haam, was thoroughly impressive, both in terms of his "splendid appearance, and his actions and teachings." Indeed, throughout his life those whom he perceived as great men moved Ginzberg to rare moments of effusiveness: Charles Netter, whom he spotted in Brody surrounded by Russian Jewish emigrants; Leon Pinsker, whom he claimed had bequeathed his legacy to him in deathbed declarations repeated to no one else, and even Zadoc Kahn. If only French Jewry could produce someone else like the chief rabbi who would devote himself to Jewish nationalism, he wrote in an 1893 diary, the entire Jewish scene in Western Europe would be transformed.[23]

Ginzberg, then, was particularly well situated to emulate models of religious leadership, as inspired by the austere examples of both his father and the Sadgora Rebbe. He, along with the rest of his family, were treated like nobility on their estate, and, once the family had amassed a small fortune, also back in Skvira. Ahad Haam's sister recalls how their return visits would be accompanied by calls throughout the *shtetl*: "Golda Ginzberg from Gopchitsa is coming!" as if a Rothchild had stumbled into the Kiev district town.[24] By the time he settled in Odessa, at the age of thirty, Ginzberg had learned the prerequisites of leadership: that a leader must not seek honors (irrespective of how hungry he is for them) and must not seem eager to assume power (thrust upon him by others and accepted, only then, grudgingly). Indeed, he showed himself to be a master of these skills. He managed to leave his immediate Odessa entourage (and Zionist historiography) with the impression of utter disinterest in either power or leadership, though for some three years before the formal establishment of the Bnei Moshe those who would form the core of the group met weekly, and eventually daily, at his home, with Ginzberg serving as their leading figure. He nonetheless claimed that he was shocked when asked to lead the Bnei Moshe and did everything he could to decline. Frequently he admitted in letters how pleased he was that others made arrangements for him—arranging for the publication of his first article "Lo zeh haderekh," for example, and finding him employment after he lost his small fortune—without his even having to ask.[25] In short, he was launched like a hugely promising prodigy—with the same pious, backdoor machinations, the same overpowering regard for youthful brilliance, the same beliefs that those best suited to lead were those least likely to do so. Judging from the responses of his circle, the way he carried himself—distant, disapproving, cerebral, reclusive—represented for them, as much as did the arguments made in his essays, proof of his authenticity as a leader of Israel.

In a semiautobiographical essay written sometime between 1881 and 1884, entitled "Ketavim balim" (A Tattered Manuscript), Ahad Haam described the anguish and beauty of abiding religious attachments in a transitional maskilic figure caught between conflicting worlds:

But what am I now? A *maskil*? I cannot say that with certainty. Still now, in the moments before the end of the Sabbath, between the time that the sun sets and one begins lighting candles once again, I love to sit in a corner in the dark to examine the range of my feelings. In such moments I feel my soul rising heavenward, as if my spiritual elation has emerged from within me to the sound of heavenly voices, and I recall various memories from the days of my youth, memories that make me laugh, pleasant recollections—recollections that please me very much. . . . Sometimes my lips will open as if by themselves, and I find myself chanting some well-known melody in a hushed voice. . . . During those long winter evenings, at times when I'm sitting in the company of enlightened men and women, sitting at a table with *treyf* food and cards, and my heart is glad and my face bright, suddenly then—I don't know how this happens—suddenly before me is a very old table with broken legs, full of tattered books [*sefarim balim*], torn and dusty books of genuine value and I'm sitting alone in their midst, reading them by the light of a dim candle, opening up one and closing another, not even bothering to look at their tiny print . . . and the entire world is like the Garden of Eden.[26]

The Bnei Moshe represented for Ahad Haam—and the core of his constituency—an attempt to bridge the awful gap that divided "modern" and "traditional" Jewry, to cut across artificial barriers and affirm Judaism's fundamental unity. As he wrote in one of the addenda to the group's credo, "Derekh hehayim" (The Way of Life): "If you understand—and this is not easy—if you sense all of this, with all your heart, with all your soul, and throughout your life until your last drop of blood, then you are ours! Then, give us your hands and be blessed. And know today, as you stand here before us, that great and holy are such moments in one's life."[27]

Ahad Haam's political career would be devoted to cultivating an appreciation of *ruhaniyut*, or spirituality. True, the term was understood in the inner circle of the Bnei Moshe to imply a cultural, not religious, transformation. But such distinctions would soon be rendered irrelevant and anachronistic, Ahad Haam believed, as Jewry moved toward redefining itself along national rather than theological lines. To accomplish this would take more than the mobilization of ideas and demanded that Ahad Haam himself set a personal example as the man who integrated harmoniously Jewry's seemingly disparate characteristics: *zaddik* and European, Torah master and enlightened Jew.

The Bnei Moshe was intended to constitute a Garden of Eden of sorts—one that transcended distinctions between religious and irreligious in a way that embodied true Jewish authenticity. In light of the backgrounds of its leader and original membership, it is hardly surprising that it took on some of the features of a hasidic *kloyz*. Descriptions of it in this vein represented more than the linguistic conventions of the ex-*hasidim* who made up its first members. Rather, they reflected the existential commitments of those who, like their *manhig lishkah alef*, conceived of politics along lines shaped by traditional influences that proved to be abiding and also served to mark them off as maskilic and transitional. Like the narrator of Ahad Haam's "Ketavim balim," they felt comfortable neither in a larger secular world nor in the cloistered confines of the *batei midrash*. The latter might serve as the object of nostalgic longing, but only because they had already escaped its constraints. The Bnei Moshe was as a congenial way station, an attempt at reconciling equally unsatisfactory extremes. Its failure was the product of more than the administrative ineptitude of Ahad Haam or the political immaturity of its members. Quite simply, it failed because its task was impossible: it attempted to salvage out of the wreckage of traditional Eastern European Jewish life a thoroughly integrated Jewish identity, to reconstruct

Judaism on the basis of cultural-national foundations. Hence, its resurrection of "national" holidays (such as Hanukah) and the veneration of its leader Ahad Haam. Both were central to the new ritual that the Bnei Moshe sought to introduce. Neither represented an adequate substitute for the religious regimen that its core constituency had only recently discarded. It is little surprise that they were so insistent upon demanding from Ahad Haam that the group provide them with more tasks, with a clear direction as to what he required of them. They sought to fill the void described so movingly by their leader in "Ketavim balim," one that, as he would eventually learn, could never be satisfied.

Notes

I wish to thank Tony Judt, Hans Rogger, and Anita Shapira for their helpful comments. For a suggestive discussion of symbolic politics—by which I mean the use of ritual to affirm power, legitimacy, and group cohesion—see David I. Kertzer, *Ritual, Politics, and Power* (New Haven, 1988).

1. Typical is the characterization by Walter Laqueur in *A History of Zionism* (New York, 1972), p. 82: "Ahad Ha'am established a little semi-conspiratorial *corps d'elite*, called Bnei Moshe. . . . Its immediate political importance was not very great, nor was it meant to be." Ahad Haam's biographer, Leon Simon, he adds, observed "that Milton's 'They also serve who only stand and wait' could well have been its motto." For Simon's comments, see Leon Simon and Yosef Eliyahu Heller, *Ahad Haam: Haish, poalo vetorato* (Jerusalem, 1955), pp. 22–23; Yitzhak Maor, *Hatenuah hazionit beRusyah* (Jerusalem, 1974–75), pp. 91–95. The best survey of the group is still S[hmuel] Tchernowitz, *Bnei Moshe utekufatam* (Warsaw, 1914). Good accounts of the group may be found in Yossi Goldstein, "The Zionist Movement in Russia (1897–1904)" (Ph.D. diss., Hebrew University, Jerusalem), pp. 107–13; Ehud Luz, *Parallels Meet*, trans. Lenn J. Schramm (Philadelphia, 1988), pp. 78–85; Joseph Salmon, "Ahad Ha-am and the Benei Moshe: An 'Unsuccessful Experiment'?" in *At the Crossroads: Essays on Ahad Ha-am*, ed. Jacques Kornberg (Albany, N.Y., 1983), pp. 98–105.

2. Ahad Haam, "Nisayon shelo hizliah," in *Kol kitvei Ahad Haam* (Tel Aviv, 1956), p. 437.

3. Mordecai Ben Hillel Hacohen, *Olami* vol. iv (Jerusalem, 1928), pp. 158–59.

4. Yossi Goldstein has produced several excellent essays on Ahad Haam and his political activities. See, for instance, "Maamado shel Ahad Haam ad bo Herzl berei 'mishpat dibah' neged Margalit," *Zion* 52, no. 4 (1987): 471–87.

5. Ben-Avigdor, *Shnei hezyonot* (Warsaw, 1891), p. 29.

6. Tchernowitz, *Bnei Moshe utekufatam*, p. 26.

7. Ehud Luz, *Parallels Meet* (Philadelphia, 1988).

8. Tchernowitz, *Bnei Moshe utekufatam*, pp. 95–98.

9. Ahad Haam, "Lo zeh haderekh," in *Kol kitvei*, p. 11.

10. Yehoshua Barzilai, "Eikh naasah Asher Ginzberg leAhad Haam?" *Hashiloah* 30 (March 1914): 302–5; Simon Dubnov, *Kniga zhizni*, vol. 1 (Riga, 1934); Chaim Tchernowitz (Rav Tsair), *Masekhet zikhronot* (New York, 1945), p. 88. See also Abraham Elijah Lubarsky's recollections in *Hashiloah* 6, no. 5 (November 1899): 476–78.

11. A vivid sketch of this circle may be found in Chaim Tchernowitz, *Masekhet zikhronot*, pp. 87–93.

12. Ibid., p. 74; Dubnov's *Kniga zhizni*, 1:149–50.

13. Dubnov, *Kniga zhizni*, 1:247–48. For more extensive discussion, see Steven J. Zipperstein, *Elusive Prophet: Ahad Ha'am and the Origins of Zionism* (Berkeley, 1993), chap. 2.

14. Barzilai, "Eikh naasah," pp. 302–3.

15. See this exchange in *Pirkei zikhronot veigrot* (Tel Aviv, 1931), pp. 177–78.

16. Ibid., p. 177.

17. Even before his move to Odessa, Dawidowicz was closely connected with the Ginzberg family. As Ahad Haam relates in his memoirs, Dawidowicz spent several years at Gopchitse as a Russian tutor for one of his sisters, probably Chana. See *Pirkei zikhronot*, pp. 66-67. In a portion of his letter not cited in the text above he tells Brainin that he sought out Ahad Haam because, as a recent convert to Hebraism, he was concerned by rumors that Ginzberg was engaged in writing an attack on the Palestine-based Hebrew advocate Eliezer Ben-Yehuda. Whether Ahad Haam had ever intended to write such a piece is unknown; perhaps the rumor referred to his work on "Lo zeh haderekh," which made no mention of Eliezer Ben-Yehuda's efforts on behalf of the revival of Hebrew.

18. The document was published in Reuven Brainin, *Ketavim nivharim* (Merhavia, 1965), pp. 499–501.

19. See, for instance, Ahad Haam's letter of 1892–93 to the heads of the Warsaw branch of Bnei Moshe, in *Igrot Ahad Haam* (Jerusalem, 1925), 6:102.

20. *Pirkei zikhronot*, p. 11.

21. Ahad Haam Archives, Jewish National and University Library, Department of Manuscripts and Archives, Jerusalem, no. 1876.

22. Much information about the hasidic character of the Ginzberg household can be found in Esther Ginzberg-Shimkin, "Akhad Ga'am v dome ego roditelei v derevne Gopchitse," Central Zionist Archives, Jerusalem, no. 4 791, 1917, esp. pp. 8–14, 26–28. For Ahad Haam's recollections, see *Pirkei zikhronot*, pp. 42–43.

23. *Pirkei zikhronot*, pp. 43, 21.

24. Ginzberg-Shimkin, "Akhad Ga'am," p. 17.

25. See, for instance, *Igrot*, 3:84. Here, in describing how his employment at the Wissotzky tea firm came about—after he had vigorously lobbied his friends for precisely such a job—he told Simon Bernfeld that it all "seemed to materialize as if by itself, without the need for any intervention on my part." He records how pleased he was by the firm's respectful treatment of him and mentions, in passing, that he knew that A. E. Lubarsky played an important role in arranging the offer.

26. Ahad Haam, *Kol kitvei*, p. 115.

27. Quoted in S[hmuel] Tchernowitz, *Bnei Moshe utekufatam*, p. 71.

Munkács and Jerusalem

Ultra-Orthodox Opposition to Zionism and Agudaism

Sixty-eight years ago Rabbi Hayim Elazar Shapira, the Munkaczer Rebbe, took a brief, mysterious trip to Palestine. Upon returning home, he dispatched a message to his faithful followers in Jerusalem—"the fervent God-fearing inhabitants of the holy city"—offering guidance and encouragement for the struggle against their wicked contemporaries. Shapira's message included an illustrative parable (attributed to "our elders"), which he used in an especially ironic, acerbic fashion.

When I journeyed to the Holy Land I said to the Adversary before embarking at Istanbul, "A berth costs a great deal of money. . . . You decide: either you go to the Holy Land and I stay here . . . or you stay here and I go alone to the Holy Land. . . ." And he chose to stay there. . . . And I rejoiced in my voyage. But when I reached the Holy Land, I immediately caught sight of the Adversary standing in the port, and I cried out in anguish, "What are you doing here? Did I not leave you in Istanbul with the understanding that you would stay there?" And he answered, saying, "You ask me what I am doing here? 'The fellow came here as an alien, and already he acts as the ruler' (Gen. 19:9). Why, this is my regular abode, and the one with whom you spoke in Istanbul was. . . . just my overseas emissary."[1]

Readers familiar with the writings of Shmuel Yosef Agnon, including the work entitled "A Whole Loaf," will easily recognize that both Shapira's parable and Agnon's story emerge from one and the same tradition. Yet, unlike Agnon, Shapira goes on to spell out the meaning of his parable. Today's Satan, who makes his home in the Holy Land, is none other than the new Zionist settlement movement. Zion (Shapira argued) has always been the focus of a great struggle between light and darkness, between God, on the one hand, and the Evil Impulse on the other. So it remains in our own time with its dreadful events. It is not only God who delights to dwell in the Holy Land and the Holy City, but also the new ones, who came but lately (Deut. 32:17), those who seek to subjugate Zion by making it the center of their sacrilegious "national" enterprise. In this spirit, Shapira goes on to interpret the sense of the verse in Zechariah 3:2. It is not "May the Lord who has chosen Jerusalem rebuke you, O Satan" but rather "May the Lord rebuke you, O Satan who chooses Jerusalem."[2]

Rabbi Hayim Elazar Shapira of Munkács (1872–1937) was among the most prominent hasidic leaders of Hungarian Jewry in his era. He was famous both for his halakhic erudition and his mastery of kabbalistic doctrine. In many respects, he represents the prototypical teacher of the most conservative, radical wing of Ultra-Orthodoxy. Shapira conducted a merciless battle against the new settlement movement in Palestine. He developed an original ideological stance against the Zionists and their Ultra-Orthodox "collaborators," basing it upon both halakhic and theological arguments. In fact, he formulated a distinctly demonological conception of the Holy Land and of the forces nesting within it. Indeed, Shapira carried his protests against the Zionist settlement further than all his predecessors (and apparently even his successors) in the Ultra-Orthodox camp.

The Religious Retreat from the Land of Israel

Let us first clarify the fundamental approach underlying all of Rabbi Shapira's sermons and writings about the settlement of the Land of Israel. Naturally, Shapira takes a stand against development of the Holy Land by secular means at the hands of sinners. Accordingly, he seeks to deprive the licentious Zionists of any foothold in the Land of Israel.[3] But he insists that Eretz Israel is no place for ordinary Jews either. Here he is elaborating on a much earlier tradition, dating back to the medieval era, which sought—on halakhic and ideological grounds—to discourage people from settling in the Holy Land. This trend of thought emphasizes the awesome holiness and dangerous uniqueness of the Land of Israel and points to the prodigious religious demands that the land makes upon its inhabitants: the extra degree of spirituality required and the extra punishment for those who violate the commandments there. Accordingly, the Munkaczer Rebbe often cited the warning issued by the twelfth-century Rabbi of Rothenburg to every God-fearing Jew who wished to travel to the Land of Israel:

> Let him be abstinent in the Land and beware of any transgression, for if he sins there, he will be punished most severely. For God supervises the Land and watches over its inhabitants [see Deut. 11:12]. He who rebels against the kingdom from within the king's palace is not the same as he who rebels outside it. This is the meaning of "a land that consumes its inhabitants" [Num. 13:32]. As for those who go there and think they can get away with levity and reckless contentiousness, I would invoke the verses, "But you came and defiled my Land" [Jer. 2:7] and "Who asked of you to trample my courts?" [Isa. 1:2].[4]

The Munkaczer Rebbe sought to develop this view and add to its sting. He explicitly depicted the Holy Land as fraught with religious danger warning his followers of the terrible spiritual decline that would befall unworthy Jews who moved there. In fact, Shapira regarded the Land of Israel as the abode of the ideal Jew, not of the real, average Jew.[5] It is a place reserved for righteous zealots, for those who will sacrifice themselves in the service of God, not for ordinary run-of-the-mill persons. How much less should the new Zionist heretics and sinners, who unabashedly portray their undertaking as a revolt against God and his Torah, be permitted to set foot in the Land of Israel!

Moreover, the physical rebuilding of the Land of Israel entails, by definition, spiritual decay and destruction. Shapira vehemently denied the very legitimacy of agricultural work and any other form of manual labor in the Holy Land. He therefore forbade Jews, even God-fearing and observant ones, to devote themselves to material concerns in Palestine. "For, those who travel to the Holy Land for this-worldly purposes, rather than to study Torah and to worship God, place themselves 'in the seat of the scornful' [Ps. 1:1]. It is written of such persons: 'but you came and you defiled my land' [Jer. 2:7]."[6] That is to say, the Land of Israel demands one's whole being and shapes one's entire life. The land was designed solely for prayer and spiritual activity. Therefore, "We must follow in the footsteps of our old rabbis and forefathers, by supporting only those residents of the Land who devote themselves to the study of Torah and the worship of God. . . . [Indeed,] the evil forces have become stronger in our Holy Land and they undermine its very foundation through their plowshares and agricultural colonies."[7]

It should be noted that the Lubavitcher Rebbe, Joseph Isaac Schneersohn, adopted a similar stance in those days. He, too, castigated those who "contaminate the Land with all types of material things, stores, workshops, and factories!"[8] These hasidic leaders thus carried the idea of the Land of Israel as a religious object to its most radical and dichotomous conclusion: The Holy Land sustains its holiness (during the period of exile) only by denying its very "materiality."

These ideas were also in keeping with Shapira's messianic outlook. He argued that any merely human attempt to bring the Jews collectively to the Land of Israel represents a usurpation of the messiah's role and an attempt to force the end of days. The very effort to settle the land with human hands implies an abandonment of "faith in miraculous redemption from heaven."[9] Likewise, Shapira completely dismissed the Zionist hope to achieve diplomatic and political progress through the help of other nations, and he vehemently dismissed the Balfour Declaration and its implications.[10] Like many other Ultra-Orthodox leaders, he upheld the value of Jewish political passivity and made it an ultimate religious norm of the exilic era: "One may not rely on any natural effort or on material salvation by human labor. One should not expect redemption from any source other than God."[11] Accordingly, Shapira often cited Rabbi Jonathan Eibeschütz's sharp formulation of the path taken by Israel (according to the Midrash) not to hasten the end of days prematurely:

The congregation of Israel shouted out their vow, "Ye awaken not, nor excite my love" [Song of Songs 2:7]; for even if the whole people of Israel is prepared to go to Jerusalem, and even if all the nations consent, it is absolutely forbidden to go there. Because the End is unknown and perhaps this is the wrong time.[12]

The inevitable result of the new settlers' activity is thus not physical construction, but spiritual destruction. They threaten to bring upon the people of Israel a new exile, even harsher than the preceding ones.[13]

But what of the commandment to settle Eretz Israel? In his volume of halakhic responsa, *Minhat Elazar*, the Munkaczer Rebbe argued first, that this precept applies only to the messianic era, not to our own time, and, second, that even in the days to come, the responsibility for bringing about the return to Zion will be entirely in the hands of the messiah. That is to say: the Jewish people are to play no active role, either collectively or as individuals, in the process of return, "For it will not be up to them to conquer [the land]; they will come rather from a commandment and an order imposed upon the holy king messiah, who alone will do it. . . . It will not come to pass by natural means, but through strange and marvelous signs and wonders."[14] The question of settling in Eretz Israel is thus removed from the normative realm altogether, and there is no possible historical situation in which the Jewish people as a collectivity would be called upon to go there.[15] On the contrary, any merely human effort in this direction, even if undertaken by pious Jews, would inevitably betray a lack of faith and the beginning of heresy.

To summarize: Shapira distances the real Jewish people from the Holy Land, both by emphasizing its awesome spiritual demands and by depicting it exclusively in the most ultimate messianic categories. We shall subsequently examine his penultimate effort to drive a wedge between the people and the land, which finds expression in his demonology of Eretz Israel.

Denunciation and Isolation

It should come as no surprise that Shapira's wrath was directed not only toward the Zionists but also—and perhaps primarily—toward Agudat Israel, the more middle-of-the-road *haredi* [Ultra-Orthodox] group that settled strictly observant Jews in Eretz Israel. Such Jews might take pride in their beards and piety, but they were, in effect, tacit partners of the Zionists, and "in their hypocrisy they have done us more harm than all the wicked of the earth."[16] Accordingly, Shapira waged a vigorous struggle against them all his life.

The struggle reached its height in 1922 at a protest meeting of *haredi* leaders held in Csap, Slovakia. Those in attendance, the leaders of the radical Ultra-Orthodox wing of Hungarian Jewry, sought to stem the tide of secularization and "sacrilege" that seemed to threaten religious education in Eastern Europe and Jewish life in the Holy Land. But on this occasion, their criticism was not aimed directly at the *maskilim* (proponents of the Enlightenment), the Zionists, or the Reform movement; it was primarily aimed at Agudat Israel, whose rabbis and leaders the *haredim* perceived as compromisers, accommodations, and, ultimately, collaborators with the secular adversary. The Munkaczer Rebbe, who had called the meeting and chaired it, rose to enumerate, one by one, the sins of the Agudah and its leaders: from the way they conducted *yeshivah* education, through their approach to the Land of Israel, and to messianism.[17]

First, Shapira charged, the Agudists were allowing themselves to be influenced by the new, suspect currents of thought sweeping West European Orthodoxy. In their schools, they were permitting the purity of genuine sacred study to be tainted with "admixtures of secular learning," combining Torah and worldly knowledge. (It should be noted that many Agudah supporters in Western Slovakia, who had been educated in the *yeshivah* of Pressburg [Bratislava], had indeed been exposed to the influence of German Neo-Orthodoxy; Rabbi Shapira feared that this line of influence would eventually penetrate his own circles.) Thus the *yeshivah* newly established in Warsaw by the Gerer Rebbe [Góra Kalwarja] deviated gravely, in Shapira's view, from what was acceptable: it was nothing more than an imitation of the misguided modern rabbinical seminaries set up by the German "doctor-rabbis" (university-trained rabbis) and *ra-banim* (literally "evil sons"—a play on the Hebrew word *rabanim*, or "rabbis," used to designate the errant reformers). This development might spread to other places, including the Holy City of Jerusalem, where these people might presume to establish a world rabbinical seminary, a technical school, and the like: "a stock sprouting poisonous weed and wormwood (Deut. 29:17)."[18]

Second, although the Agudists pretended to fight the Zionists, the two groups increasingly revealed a similarity of thought and action. Like the Zionists, the Agudah was developing Eretz Israel physically and preaching settlement "through [the tilling of] fields and vineyards." Such actions were contrary to the traditional view that the Holy Land is intended only for prayer and sacred study.[19] In the final analysis, the Agudists were collaborating with the Zionists and even infecting innocent schoolchildren with the Zionist ethos and style. "They are defiling the children's minds and hearts with foolishness that leads to levity and heresy, God forbid, and with songs that speak of the settlement of the Land, the fields and the vineyards of Eretz Israel—just like [those of] the Zionist poets."[20] Moreover, the Agudists were sabotaging the economic basis of Torah study in the Holy Land, because their words and deeds were causing the diversion of funds from the academies and *yeshivot* of Eretz Israel to agricultural settlement and material development. In this way, they were taking food from the mouths of the students of Torah. "Sages and saints who were spending their lives in holiness and purity in our Holy Land have now suddenly and unaccountably fallen prey to the wickedness of the Zionists, the Mizrahi [religious Zionists], and the Agudists."[21]

Third, Shapira found that the Agudah literature contained statements that could be construed as directly challenging the traditional belief in the messiah and subverting the traditional Jew's simple, passive yearning for divine salvation. He cited expressions that allegedly echoed the false Zionist doctrine that Israel would inherit the land through its own physical efforts—aided by the other nations—rather than through profound penitence and exclusive devotion to the study of Torah. According to Shapira, the spokesmen of Agudah even place messianic faith in the actions of what they call "the exalted government of England."[22] Thus, in this area as well, the Agudists had adopted the Zionist myth and ethos.

In conclusion: the Agudists had deviated from the correct path in their approach to education, the Land of Israel, and messianism. Therefore, the Agudists, decreed Shapira, "are for all practical purposes Zionists. . . . They pour fuel on the fire, claiming they are trying to put it out, but in the end the Agudists and the Zionists will be joined arm in arm."[23]

Of course, Shapira's formulation was not an objective reflection of the views or activity of Agudat Israel at the time. In fact, the Agudah came into being through its struggle against the Zionist movement; from the outset, it declared all-out war on secular Jewish nationalism and the new Zionist ideas about revival and redemption. Although Agudah ideologues did approve of settling the land, they believed that only the faithful should undertake such activity, under conditions conducive to piety, and they forbade any collaboration with the Zionist enterprise. Likewise, although they sometimes allowed the limited introduction of secular studies into the curriculum of their schools, they did so merely to meet their students' practical needs as future jobholders; the Agudists had no enthusiasm for the ideal of a secular national revival.

Nevertheless, the dispute between the Munkaczer Rebbe and his camp, on the one hand, and Agudat Israel, on the other, must be taken seriously. Although the depiction of Agudah voiced at the rabbinic meeting was inaccurate, it amply illustrated the self-image of the radical *haredi* camp. This camp sensed that it was at odds with the great majority of Ultra-Orthodox Jews in Poland and Lithuania and, of course, Western Europe.[24] Indeed, other speakers on that occasion supported the views expressed by the Munkaczer Rebbe, and the meeting ended with a unanimous ban on any association with Agudat Israel.[25]

The first name on the list of signatories to the ban was that of a young rabbi, scion of one of the hasidic dynasties, who was presiding at that time over the small community of Orsova. Of all the speakers, he was the most vehement in his support of Shapira's separatist, antisettlement views. This man, Rabbi Yoel Teitelbaum, was destined to become the Satmarer Rebbe (of Szatmár [Satu-Mare]), the adored leader of tens of thousands of *hasidim* and the most vigorous opponent that Zionism and the State of Israel were ever to know in the *haredi* camp.[26] Fundamental ideas and principles developed within the Munkaczer school were transformed by the Satmarer Rebbe into a detailed, full-fledged theory, which he elaborated in numerous writings and speeches. This theory was concretized in reaction to dramatic historical events—the Holocaust and the establishment of the State of Israel—and eventually came to guide the political (or, rather, antipolitical) reactions of a large *haredi* community.

Thus, the opposition to mass *aliyah* and settlement that had existed all along grew over the years into an uncompromising struggle led by Teitelbaum against the sovereign Jewish state and all its works. Under his guidance, the time-honored call for the establishment of separate "holy communities" turned into an insistence on total self-segregation by the new "remnant of Israel" and the delegitimation of all those who continued to falsely consider themselves part of the Jewish people—from the secularists to Agudat Israel. Moreover, the fear of prematurely hastening the messianic end of days ("forcing the end") and undermining faith in divine redemption—a fear that had emerged at the turn of the century—grew in Teitelbaum's doctrine into a metahistorical demonization of the Zionist enterprise as the ongoing antimessianic work of Satan himself.

Teitelbaum echoed the Munkaczer Rebbe's reading of the verse from Zechariah ("May the Lord rebuke you, O Satan who chooses Jerusalem"), which he interpreted in relation to actual events in the Land of Israel:

May the Lord rebuke Satan, for the [the latter] has chosen Jerusalem in order better to overcome those who dwell there . . . to seduce and corrupt the entire world wrapped in the mantle of Jerusalem's glory. . . . And "outrages [have been] committed by the enemy against the Sanctuary" [Ps. 74:3] in the hallowed land . . . for vicious people have come there and defiled it with their heretical government, may God protect us.[27]

In Teitelbaum's view, the Holocaust and the establishment of the State of Israel were not contrary developments—destruction and reconstruction—but a single continuous process: the final eruption of the forces of evil as a prelude to redemption.

A detailed comparison of the writings of Rabbis Shapira and Teitelbaum reveals the manifest and decisive influence of the former upon the latter, and consequently, upon the entire school of radical Ultra-Orthodoxy in our time. Were it not for the severe personal dispute that later erupted between the two figures concerning the territorial boundaries of their rabbinical jurisdiction, and were it not for the breakdown in relations ensuing from this dispute, then the intense conceptual affinity between the two rabbis might have become common knowledge. To be sure, both Shapira and Teitelbaum were following their respective family traditions, which rejected emigration to and physical settlement of Eretz Israel. (The Teitelbaum tradition can be traced back at least four generations!) Yet only now, in response to the Zionist movement, was this tradition bolstered theoretically and made paramount in the consciousness of this radical, separatist community.

The Demonology of the Land of Israel

In his sermons from the late 1920s and 1930s, the Munkaczer Rebbe developed a bold new idea—in truth, he made a mythic breakthrough—which even his most radical successors did not dare to embrace in both letter and spirit.

Earlier we discussed Shapira's "religious retreat" from the Land of Israel, which he based upon the land's holiness and its severe spiritual demands. His attitude illustrates the inner tension that characterizes the religious consciousness *per se*: the believer is attracted to the holy, he or she is fascinated by it, but at the same time the believer withdraws from the holy in awe and fear.[28] This same dialectic also applies to the holy place and the Holy Land: the religious person is intensely attracted to them, seeking to partake intimately in their metaphysical power; but simultaneously he or she is likely to retreat from the holy and to keep a distance from its threatening metaphysical forces.[29] No doubt the Munkaczer Rebbe upset the delicate equilibrium between these conflicting poles because of his direct confrontation with Zionism, which—in his eyes—threatened to secularize and desecrate the Holy Land.

Interestingly enough, Shapira sought to add a distinctly mystical, indeed demonic dimension to this spiritual fear of the Land of Israel. In this context, he adopted extremely polarizing formulations, unparalleled in Jewish literature.

The Land of Israel's impurity is tantamount to its holiness. The land concentrates and expresses the ultimate manifestations of both direct divine revelation and satanic evil; these two influences are locked in direct confrontation. On the one hand, Shapira emphasizes and amplifies the divine presence in the land. Not only is the land subject to God's direct providence, unmediated by natural laws or supernatural forces[30] ("the Land of the Hart [biblical Israel] was not subjected to the rule of ministers, to the laws of the celestial spheres, or to the reign of heaven"), but also it is directly supervised "under the governance of the *ein sof*, may His name be blessed, without the mediation of any minister or celestial sphere, and without any contraction [zimzum]."[31] The *ein sof*, the supreme hidden face of God (according to kabbalistic theory), is manifested in the land without any mediation or limitation and, so to speak, without the gradual contraction of God's abundant emanation through spheres and vessels! This manner of expression is quite unique in kabbalistic literature. Even mystics like Nahmanides and Joseph Karo, who elevated the spiritual status of the Land of Israel and depicted it as a mystical gateway to the highest stages of the divine world (from *tiferet* up to *binah* and *hokhmah*, God's mystical qualities according to Jewish mysticism),[32] did not blaze a path all the way to the hidden Divine One. Even if one reads Shapira's words as rhetorical hyperbole, one cannot simply ignore such expressions when they are produced by the pen of an authentic kabbalist. In any case, Shapira's position raises a pressing question: Who is worthy of living in the land, and who would dare to do so?

The Land of Israel—the palace of a king—is, on the other hand, also a gateway to hell. There, in the Holy Land itself, "where the Canaanite of Palestine dwells, lies the source and inspiration of defilement."[33] Shapira makes liberal use of the traditional myth about the evil forces that attach themselves to holiness and try to transform and displace it. He intensifies this idea sevenfold in relation to the Holy Land. The Zionists' new foothold in the Land of Israel is interpreted entirely within this sinister framework: it is nothing but the external manifestation of the destructive forces that have always inhered in the inner sanctum of holiness; it demonstrates "that the adversary himself chose his dwelling in Jerusalem."[34] It follows that any God-fearing Jew who goes to the Land of Israel, inevitably plunges into the arena of a struggle: immigration to Palestine means, by definition, declaration of war against "the evil side" and against its concrete social manifestation, or alternatively, exposure to their detrimental influence. And who is worthy or willing to face such danger? As the Munkaczer Rebbe warned his followers in the diaspora several months before his death in 1937:

Only our forefather, Abraham, was holy enough to withstand the ordeal [of going to the Land of Israel], but as for us, the present ordeals and conflicts are quite sufficient. Thus, Abraham demanded that "thou shalt not take a wife from the daughters of the Canaanites" (Gen. 24:3), so that his descendants would not, God forbid, fall under the influence of the Canaanites in Palestine. . . . [As if Abraham was saying:] "I alone can fight the forces of defilement and conquer them entirely, but I do not wish my children to engage in such a fight, for the journey there poses a great danger to them."[35]

And as Shapira warned his followers, the denizens of Jerusalem, who resided in the place of danger itself:

May the Lord rebuke you, O Satan, who seeks to overcome the righteous men of Jerusalem! . . . This is the secret of the verse: "For to excite my anger and my fury hath been unto me this city [of Jerusalem]" (Jer. 32:31). The evil forces excite God's anger and fury; they are most powerful in the Land of Israel, particularly in Jerusalem. For Satan has his foothold in this very place. Yet he desists from tormenting those who seek to eliminate him through [holy] deeds and studies; thus, the residents of Jerusalem must bolster and strengthen themselves with Torah.[36]

The Evil Impulse that festers in the Holy Land was endowed by Shapira with an autonomous ontological status: this force came into existence long before it was concretely manifested through the new settlers of the land.

Shapira thus took great pains to depict the Land of Israel as an arena of conflict, as a mystic and social battlefield, not as an abode or a homestead. The Land of Israel was suited to the spiritual strengths and qualities of the ancient forefathers, and in the future, after the final messianic victory in the battle, it would also become the residence of the redeemed sons: "Only when the blessed God will appear 'to judge the mountain of Esau' [to root out the forces of evil], and when 'the kingdom shall be the Lord's' [Ob. 21]—we will then walk [to the Land] together with the righteous messiah."[37] But at the present time, the land is designed only for warriors, for "zealous fearers of God" who set out "to fight the just war for the residue of God's heritage in the holy mount of Jerusalem." (Shapira consistently used such language in the messages he sent to his followers in the Land of Israel.)[38] We have already seen that the land was designed for the truly righteous, not for ordinary people: it is these righteous ones who were now depicted as "valiant men of war."[39] This characterization also applied to their concrete religious-social struggle.

It is apparent how far things have gone these days, when the Land of Israel is full of defilement. . . . The religious ordeals are especially difficult there, and it is extremely dangerous to dwell in the Land since the new immigrants, who pretend to "ascend" to the land, are in fact descending to the depths of hell. When they lived herein the diaspora they were already ruined by false ideas; but when they arrive in the Land of Israel, they lose all contact with Judaism, by violating the holy Sabbath and the Torah as a whole.[40]

It is now mortally dangerous to reside in the Land. With all those who are defiling the land, the God-fearing Jews will be forced against their will to fight difficult battles.[41]

In conclusion, Shapira greatly intensified the spiritual fear of the land by emphasizing, on the one hand, the land's heightened holiness "under the governance of the *ein sof*" and, on the other hand, by stressing the heightened impurity that festers "where the Canaanite of Palestine dwells." The original ideological rejection of the Zionist enterprise was thus transformed into a religious-existential terror focusing upon the land's awesome powers. Truly, the Munkaczer Rebbe skillfully integrated his teaching with sayings of some later kabbalists, but it is difficult to find parallels in Jewish literature to Shapira's overall, semignostic approach to the Land of Israel.

This daring approach later left its mark on the most radical, separatist stream of Ultra-Orthodoxy. But it appears that even a figure like Rabbi Teitelbaum, the great zealot who carried his predecessor's views to extremes in other areas, adopted a more moderate position than his predecessor on this issue. It is true that Teitelbaum also spoke of "Satan's strong hand in the holy realm."[42] But Teitelbaum did not use this idea to instill fear of the Land of Israel itself. Instead, he demonized the historical process, that is, the Zionist enterprise and its achievements in the Land of Israel.

The Guardians of the Walls

The extreme anti-Zionists and anti-Agudists in the diaspora who chose to split off from the rest of the *haredi* camp found faithful allies in the Holy City itself. (This alliance has endured for two generations.)

The old Ashkenazi Yishuv (the pre-Zionist Jewish community) in Jerusalem had long been a stronghold of the most conservative attitudes on education and religious practice. It served as a kind of refuge, particularly for Hungarian Jews, from the winds of change sweeping Europe. But at the turn of the century, this stronghold itself seemed to be threatened by the new waves of *aliyah*. The latter brought together in Jerusalem people of widely diverse beliefs and practices. More than in any other place, it was at this crossroads of the Jewish world that one could find the full spectrum of secularists, traditionalists, moderate Orthodox, Ultra-Orthodox, and self-styled zealots—and all had to live together in close quarters. What is more, they had to deal with the question of institutional cooperation, a matter that was particularly troublesome for the non-Zionist Ultra-Orthodox and which came up repeatedly in a variety of settings: the city council, the Jewish Agency, the National Council (that among other things, collected voluntary taxes), the Chief Rabbinate, the prestate militia, and, later, the Israeli Knesset, government, and army.

It is no wonder that the conservative forces in the face of this social and political reality should feel the need to barricade themselves behind an ideology that would permit them to attack the mounting threat at its root. And, of course, the extremists kept a close watch on their own camp for any signs of cooperation with the enemy institutions—cooperation that, if exposed, was promptly vilified. The most zealous would enter into conflict with the rabbinic leadership of the Ultra-Orthodox community itself whenever it seemed insufficiently resolute in pursuit of its own stated values and goals.[43] It was thus natural that Munkács and Satmar should find allies in these circles in Jerusalem.

With the death in 1932 of Joseph Hayim Sonnenfeld, rabbi of the Edah Haredit (Jerusalem's organized Ultra-Orthodox community), the radicals pressed for the election of Teitelbaum (who had not yet become the Satmarer Rebbe) as his successor. The leaders of the community were frightened by Teitelbaum's close ties to the zealots, however, and the effort came to naught.[44] Three years later, in the wake of severe disagreements over matters of education and self-segregation, a group of radicals led by Rabbi Amram Blau and Rabbi Aharon Katzenellenbogen split off from the Edah Haredit and formed a separate group, later to become the Natorei Karta (Guardians of the City). In 1945, this group obtained a majority in the Edah Haredit council and thus took control. The circle was closed in 1953 when the Satmarer Rebbe was chosen as the rabbi of the Edah. To be sure, the Rebbe continued to live in Williamsburg, Brooklyn, where tens of thousands of his followers were concentrated, and he never exercised direct control over the lives of the Jerusalem zealots. Nevertheless, he placed his distinctive stamp on their emerging ideology along with his halakhic backing. Thus all three interlocking groups—the Satmarer *hasidim*, the Natorei Karta, and the Edah Haredit—could henceforth be considered one ideological camp despite the obvious differences among them, though in recent years, since the Satmarer Rebbe's death, disputes have arisen.

It was only after the Holocaust and the founding of the State of Israel that the worldview of this group was fully crystallized in written form. Nevertheless, note should be taken of a significant contribution made to this process by the Jerusalem community in the preceding period. This contribution is well represented in the works of Rabbi Yeshayahu Asher Zelig Margolis, "one of the leaders of the hosts of the zealous *hasidim* in Jerusalem,"[45] who wrote in the 1920s and 1930s.[46]

Margolis, more than any other figure, represents the alliance between the zealots in Jerusalem and those in Hungary and Slovakia. He was one of the ardent followers of the Munkaczer Rebbe in Jerusalem. He corresponded regularly with the Munkaczer Rebbe, and in 1930 he arranged for Shapira to visit Jerusalem.[47] He was less successful in his efforts two years later to have the Satmarer Rebbe appointed Rabbi of this group. But he kept up contact with Teitelbaum over a period of years,[48] and after the State of Israel was established, it was Rabbi Margolis who encouraged Teitelbaum to publish a comprehensive tract explaining his opposition to the state and the boycott of the Knesset elections.[49] It was at this time that Teitelbaum's major work, *Vayoel Moshe*, began to take shape.

Margolis, a rabbinic scholar well versed in the Kabbalah, sought to give depth to the ideology—one might even call it a theology—of zealotry and self-segregation and to ground this doctrine in early sources. A creative thinker in his own right, he also had a gift for anthologizing, editing and polemics, and he knew how to tap the potential for radicalism long dormant in his comrades. Indeed, Teitelbaum was later to eulogize Margolis as "the great luminary who fought the Lord's battle and was zealous for the faith, [the man] who was long close to my soul."[50]

What follows is a summary of the principal components of the Jerusalem separatists' ideology, as formulated by Margolis:

1. *Conservatism.* An extremely conservative attitude is taken toward all aspects of the Jewish way of life. Innovation is forbidden in all areas, from education and study to the details of dress, the cut of the beard, and the "impurity of waving the hair."[51] Seemingly external details take on a deep, inner, and often symbolic and mystical significance. Thus the slightest departure from accepted patterns is forbidden: "Care should be taken that the right lapel overlaps the left, so that the right hand of the most High, 'the right hand of the Lord uplifted' in its exalted Love, predominates over the left

side, which represents Power, the strength of the Evil Impulse." Whoever makes changes is presumed guilty; better that there be fewer *yeshivah* students than that boys be admitted whose "dress and deportment" deviate in the slightest from the established custom.[52]

2. *An embattled minority.* According to the worldview of the Jews as an embattled minority, it is the zealot, he who fights the Lord's battles, who is the normative Jew. Those who are prepared to step into the breach and stand fast against the tide are the bulwark of Jewish survival down through the ages. Thus Jewish history is not mainly the story of the people of Israel as such but rather that of the repeated encounters between the "guardians of the walls" and the benighted masses. Similarly, the true leader is portrayed not as one who leads the people but rather as one who is prepared to oppose them without fear. In other words, Margolis's is a kind of counterhistory pivoted entirely on the heroism of the zealous minority fighting for its Torah. It is noteworthy that, according to the Munkaczer Rebbe, the Land of Israel was destined for such warriors and zealots only.

For example, the true distinction of the tribe of Levi was not its service in the Temple but rather its zeal in the Lord's cause—slaying the multitudes of sinners—after the making of the Golden Calf.[53] Moses was first and foremost the one who stood up to his fellow Hebrews—the one who intervened in the fight between the two Jews ("And he said to the offender, 'Why do you strike your fellow?'" [Exod. 2:13]) and who met single-handedly the challenge of Korah, Dathan and Abiram. Even Aaron, portrayed in rabbinic sources as the archetypal "lover of peace and pursuer of peace," is seen by Margolis in a new light. To "pursue" does not necessarily mean to seek; rather, "sometimes [Aaron] would drive peace away, for 'pursue' peace [Ps. 34:15] can also mean to drive something away." Similarly, to say that Aaron was a "lover of peace" does not necessarily mean that he would make peace among his fellow men. On the contrary, he would reprove Israel for its sins and thus "make peace between Israel and its Heavenly Father."

Thus zealotry, protest, and controversy for the sake of heaven are not particular or exceptional responses but rather the perennial Jewish norm. Moses and Phinehas Ben Eleazar, the leader and the zealot, respectively, are no longer viewed as contrasting models of Jewish behavior; they belong to the same end of a continuum.[54] Moreover, it makes no difference whether the battle must be fought against the Jews who violate the Covenant, and thus bear falsely the name of Israel, or against the gentile enemies of the Jewish people: it is all one battle.

Thus all those "who have not taken a false oath by My life" [Ps. 24:4] or indulged in deceit should go forth like the tribe of Levi. Moses our Teacher, of blessed memory, did not praise the Levites for the holiness and exaltation of their singing in the Temple but for "[slaying] of [their] fathers and mothers, 'I consider them not'" [Deut. 33:9], at the time of the sin of the [Golden] Calf, when they gave their full devotion to the sanctification of the Divine Name, may it be blessed. . . . From this we conclude that the Holy One, blessed be He, considers [such devotion] more important and precious even than the Temple service.

And thus would our forefathers always act when the wicked arose in the land. . . . At the time of the Hasmoneans, the blessed Lord came to [their] aid, "delivering the mighty into the hands of the weak and the many into the hands of the few.". . . [in the words of the prayer book], Even if there be but one [righteous person] in the city, the Tanna says, "let him be strong as a tiger and light as an eagle, swift as a deer and courageous as a lion" [Abot 5:23]; this is the true heroism that every God-fearing person should display. And indeed Phinehas stood up against Omri, although the latter was the leader of Israel, and his tribe defended him. "Thou shalt not be affrighted at them for the Lord thy God is in the midst of thee, a God mighty and terrible" [Deut. 7:21]. Thus did Elijah stand up to Ahab and the 450 prophets of Baal and the whole generation that followed them. And Hananiah, Mishael, and Azariah stood up to the wicked Nebuchadnezzar, a tyrant who made the great powers of the world tremble. And thus did the righteous Mordecai stand up to the evil Haman without quavering. . . . It is therefore a sacred obligation for every Israelite to take up this holy war, as it is written, "The Lord will be at war with Amalek throughout the generations" [Exod. 17:16].[55]

3. *Social and metaphysical separation.* Margolis's ideology demands that the "remnant of Israel" separate itself completely from the community of nonobservant and (in his view) incompletely observant; he considered all those outside his own camp as lacking in religiosity! This demand, one that originally arose out of the purely pragmatic need to protect the faithful and shelter their children from the "evil winds" of the time, now takes on greater depth and is given a mystical grounding.

By joining forces with evil, the Jewish heretic proclaims that he is "not rooted in the soul of Israel" but rather belongs to the "the external souls, the Amalekite spirits. . . . These are descended from the mixed multitude [who came with Israel] out of Egypt."[56] The way such people end up proves their origins. Thus one must define boundaries to separate the sacred and profane, light and darkness, Israel and so-called Israel.

Nor, in fact, can these Jewish infidels be expected to repent and truly change their ways. A Jew who transgresses as a result of momentary transgression can, of course, atone for his transgression. But the wicked have made sin a positive ideology rather than just a lapse; their heresy is a faith in its own right. Thus, their very personality and inner being are bound up with evil and impurity and, as a result, the gates of penitence are utterly closed to them.[57] (This distinction, it should be noted, does have a sound basis in halakhic and philosophical sources.) As for Zionism, then, "none who go to her can return" (Prov. 2:19).[58] The rebel who throws off the yoke can never go back. "If the Lord is God, follow Him; and if Baal, follow him!" (1 Kings 18:21). An ontological gulf has opened between those who continue to keep the embers of the faith glowing, on the one hand, and the apostate seducers and corrupters on the other, "the mixed multitude who mingled with the people of Israel. . . . These, the offspring of Pharaoh, arise in every generation and every age in a different guise and with different names, seeking to undo us."[59] Any attempt to win these renegades back into the fold can only result in a blurring of boundaries and a confusion of values. Let them rather carry on as before, and let this lead to the final parting of ways between good and evil, pure and impure, on the eve of the ultimate redemption. "For the pruning of deadwood improves the tree"; and "When Israel is rid of these people, the Son of David will come."[60] Hence, social self-segregation comes to symbolize, at bottom, a metaphysical separation. As in so many other instances in the history of religions, the embattled few come to see themselves as the "children of light," the elect, who take their stand against a fallen society that is fundamentally debased.

Of course, such sharp formulations result at times from the heat of debate as the speaker gets carried away with his own rhetoric. However, as Yehuda Liebes has pointed out, these particular ideas do have a basis in the kabbalistic tradition, including the polemics of that self-styled "zealot and son of a zealot," Rabbi Jacob Emden (1697–1796), against the Sabbatians.[61]

4. *Redemption and its false substitutes.* Margolis repeatedly stressed the profoundly subversive effect of Zionism on traditional messianic beliefs, replacing as it does the supernatural with the natural, the religious with the secular, the passive with the active. In this, he added little of substance to the views of the Munkaczer and Lubavitcher schools; he was only more sharply polemical. Like them, he warned against "forcing the end" by mass *aliyah* in advance of the final redemption, and he, too, went to great lengths in his demonization of Zionism:

Samael [Satan] himself and all his host have come down to mislead and intoxicate the whole of Israel throughout the world. . . . And this is the substitute they offer for [true] Redemption: false idolatry, *zarat Ba'al Pe'or* [literally, the "troubles of *Ba'al Pe'or*"—a play on *hazharat Balfour* (Balfour Declaration)] that, through our sins, has darkened the vision of Israel; and blind [*iverim*] Hebrews [*ivrim*] have arisen . . . saying "Redemption is coming," . . . and verily, since the time of the first Golden Calf, Satan has never had such an opportunity to blind Israel (God forbid) as he has now.[62]

Most noteworthy in this context is that in Jerusalem at this time (the interwar period) a doctrine of redemptive religious Zionism was being developed by Rabbi Abraham Isaac Hacohen Kook. Margolis took note of this development and damned it in the strongest terms. His principal grievance was with Kook's defense of the secular Zionists, his readiness to accord the contemporary return to Zion a religious meaning:

He takes the Lord's sanctuary and recasts it in the idolatrous image of their national revival. . . . He accords [the latter] all the traditional [*mesorsi* (Ashkenazi transliteration)], albeit emasculated [*mesorasi*] splendor and depth. . . . "And he dreamed a dream" [Gen. 37:5] and "prophesied to you delusion and folly" [Lam. 2:14], [a vision] in which the angels of Redemption—"wicked people called angels were ascending and descending upon it" [Gen. 28:12].[63]

This criticism is undoubtedly directed against Rabbi Kook's letter to the Mizrahi movement, in which he wrote: "The source of Zionism is the most supreme source of holiness, the Bible, which affords all of the tradition's splendor and depth.[64] Margolis was well acquainted with Rabbi Kook's innovative theory of Jewish religious nationalism, the gist of which is, according to Margolis, that what was taking place was neither redemption nor "the beginning of redemption," but the work of Satan, pure and simple.

Thus far we have been examining the radical *haredi* viewpoint as articulated by Asher Zelig Margolis of Jerusalem. His major contribution, it appears, lies in his development of the separatist zealot ideology (historically rooted in Hungarian Jewry).[65] These ideas were crystallized in accord with Rabbi Shapira's approach to messianism and the Land of Israel. The two trends were later integrated in the doctrines of the Satmarer Rebbe into a detailed full-fledged theory and thus left a decisive imprint upon the radical *haredi* circles to this day.

Epilogue

Margolis was a close disciple of the elderly Sephardi sage Rabbi Solomon Eliezer Alfandari, known as "the Holy Grandfather," who lived to be more than a hundred years old.[66] Margolis attributed special mystical qualities to this sage. He often quoted Alfandari and received the latter's *haskamah* (imprimatur) for his book. He also cared for him personally on his sickbed. Margolis was certainly more extreme than his mentor, but Alfandari, too, adopted a radical approach to the issue of self-segregation. He wrote a tract attacking Rav Kook, and the Jerusalemite zealots attributed to him such acerbic sayings as, "The Mizrahi and the Agudah differ in name alone, and what binds them all together is money and power rather than [concern for] the honor of Heaven."[67]

The Munkaczer Rebbe also looked to Rabbi Alfandari for guidance. Of all the sages of the Land of Israel, it was Alfandari whom Shapira revered as the leading saint of his generation. Various documents indicate that Margolis played a decisive role in mediating between his two mentors and in engendering Rabbi Shapira's great admiration for Alfandari.[68]

In 1930 Shapira set out for the Holy Land, after many years during which he refused—"for great and secret reasons"[69]—to do so. His whole mysterious pilgrimage to Palestine, attended by a considerable entourage, centered around Alfandari. Shapira insistently claimed: "My main concern is to meet and honor the Holy Grandfather . . . because the commandment to settle the Land of Israel is not applicable in our era."[70] Indeed, it seemed as though it was on this man's stature and mystical virtues that Shapira pinned his hopes for a speedy redemption. Those of his companions who were privy to his meeting with Alfandari later reported it as follows. Basing himself on the rabbinic dictum, "What the righteous decree, the Holy One, blessed be He, fulfills," the Rebbe pleaded with the Holy Grandfather, as the leading saint of his generation, that he decree irrevocably, for the glory of the *shekhinah* and the well-being of all Israel, that the messiah, son of David, come quickly in our own time, for we could no longer bear our plight. . . . And the Holy Grandfather, in his humility said, "I am not a righteous man." And our Rebbe stayed and pleaded with him for a long time.[71]

It was as if the Holy Grandfather were the very antithesis of the "Satan who chooses Jerusalem." Rabbi Shapira's scribe recorded his own impression of this meeting in the following words: "From behind the curtains we heard them dealing with the issue of our total redemption, in the manner of the council of the holy angels. We who stood outside were seized with dread and horror, and to this day my pen trembles as I recall the great awe that gripped us on that day."[72]

A few days later, Alfandari was afflicted with illness. The next day he was summoned to heaven while Shapira and his followers were standing by his bedside.[73]

Let us recall a marvelous story that Shapira used to tell his disciples: Rebbe Menahem Mendel of Rymanów once came to visit Rabbi Jacob, the Seer of Lublin, in order to work with him to hasten the redemption. But the demonic "counterforces" overcame them. Rebbe Menahem Mendel took ill, and "he did not have the strength to stay and fight the adversaries who were forcing him to leave. They thus sensed that this was a decree from heaven preventing them from doing anything [for the sake of redemption]."[74]

Did the counterforces also gain the upper hand over the forces of holiness emanating from Alfandari and Shapira? In any case, on the very next day the Munkaczer Rebbe and his followers left the Holy Land.[75] Upon returning to Munkács, Shapira refused to attend the festive homecoming ceremony organized on his behalf. "Nor did he allow his disciples to dance and sing."[76] Years later, his followers were said to decipher the hidden reason for the Rebbe's unusual behavior on that day, the second day of the month of Sivan. "The heart knows its own bitterness" (Prov. 14:10): they calculated that exactly seven years later, on the second of Sivan, the Munkaczer Rebbe died, his soul departing for the world to come; after exactly seven more years had transpired, on that very same day, the grim reaper came to Munkács and sent its last sons to Auschwitz.[77]

Shapira's only daughter and his son-in-law were spared, for they had left for the Land of Israel before the Holocaust.[78] The son-in-law, Rabbi Baruch Rabinowitz, strayed from the path charted by his father-in-law and was later appointed as the chief rabbi of the town of Holon in Israel. But the wheel continues to turn. His own son, Rabbi Moshe Leib, left Israel for the United States, placing himself under the tutelage of the Satmarer Rebbe and thereby attained the title of the Munkaczer Rebbe (while his father was still living!). In this way the loyal remnants of the Munkács tradition have attempted to restore the crown to its former glory.

Notes

1. Hayim Elazar Shapira, *Divrei torah,* vol. 6 (Munkács, 1938), sec. 25; Moshe Goldstein, ed., *Tikun olam* (Munkács, 1933), p. 151.

2. The source of this interpretation is to be found in Azariah of Pano's *Hakor din: Asarah maamarot,* 2:7.

3. Hayim Elazar Shapira, *Hayim veshalom* (Munkács), 1940), 2:99; Shapira, *Divrei torah,* vol. 1 (Bratislava, 1922), sec. 113, and vol. 9 (Munkács, 1936), sec. 27; Shapira, *Hamishah maamarot* (Bergsas, 1922), p. 94; Shapira, *Olat tamid* (Bratislava, 1922), p. 6; Shapira, *Shaar Yissakhar* (Jerusalem, 1968), 1:120, 2;375; Shapira, *Kuntres divrei kodesh* (Munkács, 1934), p. 3; Itzhak Adler, ed., *Seder shanah haaharonah,* vol. 1 (Munkács, 1937), p. 8.

4. Meir Ben-Baruch of Rothenburg, *Sheelot uteshuvot Maharam* (Berlin, 1891), pp. 14–15. See also Hayim Elazar Shapira, *Minhat Elazar* (Bratislava, 1922; Bnei Brak, 1968), vol. 5, sec. 16; Shapira, *Hayim veshalom,* 2:61; Shapira, *Divrei torah,* vol. 4 (Munkács, 1930), sec. 17, and vol. 9, secs. 10, 28; Berish Weinberger, ed., *Igrot shapirin* (Brooklyn, N.Y., 1983), p. 271. Shapira cites Rabbi Meir, who adds, "But whoever goes for the sake of heaven and lives there in holiness and purity shall enjoy unlimited reward, provided he can make a living there." See Ephraim Urbach, *Al zionut veyahadut* (Jerusalem, 1985), p. 151; Elhanan Reiner, "Aliyah vaaliyah laregel leEretz Israel: 1517–1909" (Ph.D. diss., Hebrew University, Jerusalem, 1988), pp. 100–108. For additional sources, see Eliezer Azkari, *Sefer haredim* (Venice, 1971), pp. 57–60; Nahmanides, "Sermon for Rosh Hashanah," in *Kitvei haRamban,* ed. H. D. Shavel (Jerusalem, 1963), p. 250.

5. Shapira, *Minhat Elazar,* vol. 5, sec. 16; Goldstein, ed., *Tikun olam,* p. 134; Itzhak Adler, ed., *Seder shanah haaharonah,* vol. 5 (Munkács, 1940), pp. 79–80; Shapira, *Shaar Yissakhar,* 1:239.

6. Compare Shapira, *Olat tamid,* p. 7: "Settling the Land of Israel in this period of exile means worshiping in the Holy Land, not engaging in mundane follies, such as agricultural work, industry, artisanship, or socialist labor."

7. Shapira, *Shaar Yissakhar,* 2:373; Shapira, *Kezat rishumei devarim veimrot tehorot* (Jerusalem, 1931), p. 1.

8. Goldstein, ed., *Tikun olam,* p. 51.

9. Shapira, *Hayim veshalom,* 1:42, 70, 77–78, 2:25, 36–37, 41–42, 59, 68, 75; Shapira, *Hamishah maamarot,* p. 91; Shapira, *Shaar Yissakhar,* 1:244, 291, 2:376; Shapira, *Divrei torah,* vol. 4, secs. 8, 11–12; Shapira, *Maamar milei dehespedyah* (Bratislava, 1922), p. 8; Shapira, *Kuntres yemot hamashiah* (Jerusalem, 1970), pp. 14–47.

10. Shapira, *Hayim veshalom,* 1:41, 71, 2:58, 88, 98–99; Shapira, *Shaar Yissakhar,* 2:375; Shapira, *Divrei torah,* vol. 6, sec. 16, and vol. 9, sec. 82; Shapira, *Minhat Elazar,* vol. 5, sec. 16; Shapira, *Kuntres divrei kodesh,* p. 4.

11. Shapira, *Kuntres divrei kodesh,* p. 6.

12. Rabbi Jonathan Eibeschütz, *Ahavat Yehonatan* (Warsaw, 1872), p. 74a. See Shapira, *Hayim veshalom,* 2:55; Shapira, *Minhat Elazar,* vol. 5, sec. 16; Shapira, *Divrei haigeret* (Jerusalem, 1932), p. 5; Weinberger, ed., *Igrot shapirin,* p. 272; Goldstein, ed., *Tikun olam,* p. 136; For a discussion of Eibeschütz's words, see Samuel Hacohen Weingarten, *Hishbeati etkhem* (Jerusalem, 1966), pp. 11–12; Aviezer Ravitzky, "Hazivi lakh ziunim lezion: Gilgulo shel raayon," *Eretz Israel bahagut hayehudit bimei habeinayim,* ed. Moshe Halamish and Aviezer Ravitzky (Jerusalem, 1991), pp. 1–39.

13. Shapira, *Hayim veshalom,* 1:1, 2:37, 71; Shapira, *Divrei torah,* vol. 4, sec. 22; Goldstein, ed., *Tikun olam,* p. 3, and sec. 85, p. 147. See also Shapira, *Minhat Elazar,* vol. 3, secs. 46, 77.

14. Shapira, *Minhat Elazar,* vol. 5, sec. 16; Goldstein, ed., *Tikun olam,* p. 184. Note the disagreement with Rabbi Avraham of Sochaczew, the author of *Avnei nezer.* (In Shapira's view,

the commandment to settle the land applied to all Jews only during the first Jewish conquest—in the era of Joshua—and therefore Maimonides did not include this obligation in his list of commandments. See Shapira, *Hayim veshalom*, 2:37, 84; Shapira, *Divrei torah*, vol. 4, sec. 17; Shapira, *Maamar adon kol* (Munkács, 1936), p. 14.

15. According to Shapira, the commandments that apply specifically to the Land of Israel are, by definition, contingent upon full redemption. See Shapira, *Hayim veshalom*, 2:43, 95, 105–6.

16. Goldstein, ed., *Tikun olam*, p. 32. See also Hayim Elazar Shapira, *Zavaah* (Arad, 1937), p. 3; Shapira, *Hamishah maamarot*, p. 170.

17. Goldstein, ed., *Tikun olam*, pp. 34–35.

18. Ibid., p. 32. See the correspondence with the Gerer Rebbe, pp. 7–17. See also Shapira, *Divrei torah*, vol. 5, sec. 82.

19. Goldstein, ed., *Tikun olam*, p. 34, see also p. 146; and see Shapira, *Divrei torah*, vol. 6, sec., 82. The first general convention of Agudat Israel (1923) and the Gerer Rebbe's visit to Eretz Israel prepared the ground for the *haredi* agricultural settlement. See also Shapira's remarks about the Gerer Rebbe: "How can I keep silent when I see . . . that he has written there [that it is praiseworthy] to engage in labor and material pursuits in all the trades in Eretz Israel, which is the Zionist way of building the land by human means and contrary to what we have learned [in the holy books]." Goldstein, ed., *Tikun olam*, p. 18. See also Shapira's speech in Jerusalem (1930), in Moshe Goldstein, ed., *Sefer masot Yerushalayim* (Munkács, 1931), p. 105.

20. Goldstein, ed., *Tikun olam*, p. 32. The text was probably slightly edited.

21. Ibid., p. 36. See Rivka Shatz, "Imut hasifrut haharedit im hazionut," *Nativ* 5 (1989): 48–52. Interestingly enough, in the late 1880s, Rabbi Isaac Jacob Reines, founder of the Mizrahi (religious Zionist) movement, was already trying to prevent such a conflict of interests. As Reines says, "I saw fit to warn members of the Hovevei Zion group, which supports the settlements in the land, not to neglect—God forbid—the need to contribute to the traditional charities, which distribute money to the old religious community in Palestine. It would be a terrible sin to touch these funds, for we must not deprive food from thousands of our brothers." See Moshe Reines, *Nezah Israel* (Cracow, 1890), p. 49.

22. Goldstein, ed., *Tikun olam*, p. 34. See also Shapira, *Shaar Yissakhar*, p. 376; Shapira, *Kuntres yemot hamashiah*, p. 69.

23. Goldstein, ed., *Tikun olam*, pp. 6, 34–35. Shapira attacked the Agudah on countless occasions. See, for example, Shapira, *Divrei haigeret;* Shapira, *Divrei hayim veshalom* (Munkács, 1940), p. 221; Shapira, *Shaar Yissakhar*, 1:123, 125; 2:375, 385, 394, 457; Shapira, *Hayim veshalom*, 1:1, 3, 43, 63, 104, 2:24, 36, 40, 47, 64, 83, 99; Shapira, *Divrei torah*, vol. 4, sec. 17, and vol. 9, sec. 82; Shapira, *Divrei kodesh* (Jerusalem, 1934), pp. 4–5; Shapira, *Kuntres yemot hamashiah*, p. 69. The Lubavitcher Rebbe, like many rabbis in Galicia, also opposed Agudat Israel in those days. See: Yitzhak Alfasi, *Hahasidut veshivat zion* (Tel-Aviv, 1986), pp. 86–89; Mendel Piekarz, *Hasidut Polin* (Jerusalem, 1990), pp. 25–31, 115.

24. B. B. Wilson, *Religious Sects* (New York and Toronto, 1970); Wilson, "An Analysis of Sect Development," in his *Patterns of Sectarianism* (London, 1967), pp. 244–86. Shapira and his followers were the most militant of the Ultra-Orthodox. (The Lubavitch school, which held similar views, refrained from such extreme and strident polemics.) At this time, their circle included the martyred Rabbi Issakhar Shlomo Teichtal, one of those whose letters appears in Goldstein, ed., *Tikun olam*, sec. 80: "No human action or deed can help in the slightest to cause the horn of Zion and Jerusalem to be raised to the point where the Lord looks down from on high and pours over us a heavenly spirit of purity." During the Holocaust, in which Rabbi Teichtal perished, he wrote a book, *Em habanim semehah* (Budapest, 1943), that reflects a change of heart.

25. See Goldstein, ed., *Tikun olam*, p. 38; Weinberger, ed., *Igrot shapirin*, p. 286; Shapira, *Kuntres divrei kodesh*, p. 13.

26. See also the open letter signed by Hayim Elazar Shapira, Yoel Teitelbaum, and others

in the 1925 tract *Shimu devar Hashem*, published in *Hakol kol Yaakov* (Jerusalem, 1980), p. 2; the 1924 tract against the Zionists by Teitelbaum and others, published in Abraham Fuchs, *Haadmor miSatmar* (Jerusalem, 1980), p. 228; Teitelbaum's 1927 broadside against Zionism, published in *Divrei Yoel* (Brooklyn, N.Y., 1980), vol. 1, secs. 62–63; and Teitelbaum's responsum condemning Agudat Israel in his tract *Shomer emunim* (Budapest, 1939). The fact that Teitelbaum's views were nurtured in radical circles that even then had broken away from the Ultra-Orthodox mainstream contradicts the thesis—put forth, for example, in A. L. Nadler, "Piety and Politics," *Judaism* 31, no. 2 (1982): 135–52—that his position was in line with then-current Ultra-Orthodox rabbinic opinion. On Teitelbaum's biography, see Fuchs, *Haadmor miSatmar;* Aaron Rosmarin, *Der Satmarer Rebbe* (New York, 1967); I. Z. Rubin, *Satmar: An Island in the City* (New York, 1972), pp. 34–40.

27. Yoel Teitelbaum, "Yishuv Eretz Israel," in his *Vayoel Moshe* (Jerusalem, 1978), sec. 149, see also sec. 68.

28. See Rudolf Otto, *The Idea of the Holy* (Oxford, 1969), pp. 12–40.

29. See Mircea Eliade, *Patterns of Comparative Religion* (New York, 1972), p. 384.

30. This conception is commonplace in kabbalistic literature. See, for example, Nahmanides' *Commentary on the Torah,* Leviticus 18:25; Nahmanides, "Sermon for Rosh Hashanah," p. 250; *Sefer hazohar* 1:108b, and 3:209a. See also Berakhah Zack, "Eretz veeretz Israel bazohar," *Jerusalem Studies in Jewish Thought* 8 (1989): 246–48. See also *Tanhuma,* Reen, 88; *Babylonian Talmud,* Taanit, 10a.

31. Hayim Elazar Shapira, *Maamar zikhron zadikim* (Munkács, 1925), p. 7. Compare Shapira, *Hayim veshalom,* 1:24.

32. See Haviva Pedaya, "Eretz-shel-ruah veeretz-mamash: R. Ezra, R. Azriel vehaRamban," and Mordechai Pechter, "Eretz Israel besifrut haderush vehamusar shel hakhmei Tzfat bameah ha-16," both in *Eretz Israel behagut hayehudit bimei habeinayim,* ed. Halamish and Ravitzky, pp. 233–89, 290–319.

33. Adler, ed., *Seder shanah haaharonah,* 5:80. See also Shapira, *Divrei torah,* vol. 4, secs. 22, 30; Shapira, *Hamishah maamarot,* p. 94. On the Evil Impulse's extra powers in the Holy Land, see also Rabbi Yehezkel Rabinowitz of Radomsk, *Knesset Yehezkel* (Bunden, 1913), p. 52; Peikarz, *Hasidut Polin,* p. 72.

34. Shapira, *Divrei torah,* vol. 6, sec. 25. The question of the Evil Impulse's control of Eretz Israel is discussed at length in kabbalistic literature. See, for example, *Sefer hazohar,* 1:75b, 2:141a, 3:25b. See also Moshe Halamish "Kavim lehaarkhatah shel Eretz Israel basifrut hahalakhah," in *Eretz Israel behagut hayehudit beyemei habeinayim,* ed. Halamish and Ravitzky, pp. 215–32; Yoram Yaakobson, "Torat hageulah shel rabi mordechai dato" (Ph.D. diss., Hebrew University, Jerusalem, 1982), p. 431.

35. Adler, ed., *Seder shanah haaharonah,* 5:80, see also p. 73. And see Shapira, *Hayim veshalom,* 1:13; Shapira, *Shaarei Yissakhar,* 2:377. Abraham symbolizes the *sefirah* of *hesed,* which guards the Land of Israel against the forces of defilement. See also Menahem Recannati, "Lekh lekha," *Perush al hatorah* (Lwów, 1930), p. 21d.

36. Shapira, *Divrei torah,* vol. 6, sec. 25; Goldstein, ed., *Tikun olam,* sec. 97, pp. 153–54. Shapira incorporated into his sermon quotations from Rabbi Azariah of Pano's *Asarah maamarot* and from Rabbi Yaakov Shealtiel Ninio's *Emet leyaakov* (Lvorno, 1853), p. 100. For Pano's passive ideology and his objection to emigration, see Shalom Rosenberg, "Exile and Redemption in Jewish Thought in the Sixteenth Century: Contending Conceptions," in *Jewish Thought in the Sixteenth Century,* ed. B. D. Cooperman (Cambridge, Mass., 1983), pp. 419–21.

37. Adler, ed., *Seder shanah haaharonah,* 5:80. See also Shapira, *Kezat rishumei devarim veimrot tehorot,* p. 2.

38. Shapira, *Divrei torah,* vol. 6, sec. 25; Weinberger, ed., *Igrot shapirin,* pp. 236–38; Goldstein, ed., *Tikun olam,* pp. 147, 152. See also Shapira, *Hayim veshalom,* 1:7, 53; 2:56, 104; Shapira, *Divrei torah,* vol. 4, sec. 65; Goldstein, ed., *Sefer masot Yerushalayim,* pp. 134, 238–40, 247.

39. Weinberger, ed., *Igrot shapirin*, p. 237.

40. Adler, ed., *Seder shanah haaharonah*, 5:80.

41. Shapira, *Divrei torah*, vol. 5 (Munkács, 1934), sec. 24. See also Shapira, *Hayim ve-shalom*, 2:88, 99.

42. Yoel Teitelbaum, "Yishuv Eretz Israel," *Vayoel Moshe*, sec. 149.

43. For a sociological perspective on this subject, see Menahem Friedman, *Hevrah vedat: haortodoksyah halo-zionit beEretz Israel, 1918–1936* (Jerusalem: 1978), and especially on zealotry, see pp. 19–22; Yehoshua Kaniel, *Hemshekh utemurah* (Jerusalem, 1982), pp. 190–210; Netanel Katzburg, "Hapulmus haruhani baolam hayehudi vehayishuv birushalayim bameah hatesha-esreh," in *Yerushalayim: Mishivat zion ad layeziah min hahomot* (Jerusalem, 1980), pp. 168–72; Menahem Friedman, "Religious Zealotry in Israeli Society," in *On Ethnic and Religious Diversity in Israel*, ed. Solomon Poll and Ernest Krausz (Ramat Gan, 1975), pp. 99–111; Charles S. Liebman, "Extremism as a Religious Norm," *Journal of the Scientific Study of Religion* 2 (1983): 75–86. On changes in the Jerusalem Jewish community, see Shmuel Ravitzky, "Lekorot hayishuv hayehudi birushalayim," *Measef yavneh* 1 (1939): 154–72; Uziel O. Schmelz, "The Development of the Jewish Population of Jerusalem during the Past Hundred Years," *Jewish Journal of Sociology* 2 (1960): 57–73. On typical defenses against secularization and change, see Erich Voegelin, *The New Science of Politics* (Chicago, 1952), p. 122.

44. Friedman, *Hevrah vedat*, pp. 345, 134–35, 141. In a handbill issued in the fall of 1933, the city's Ultra-Orthodox people were asked to sign a manifesto in support of Teitelbaum. Fuchs, *Haadmor miSatmar*, p. 154.

45. The language is that of Moshe Goldstein, a Munkaczer *hasid*, in his *Maamar hayut esh* (Munkács, 1931). A Jerusalem handbill (1933) condemning the excitement in Agudat Israel over the Balfour Declaration bears the stamp of Margolis's thinking. And indeed, in *Tikun olam*, also edited by Goldstein, these words are attributed to "God-fearing people, the leaders of the zealots in the cause of the Lord of Hosts and His Torah" (sec. 85).

46. See Yehuda Leibes, "Haedah haharedit birushalayim vekat midbar Yehudah," *Jerusalem Studies in Jewish Thought* 1 (1982): 137–52.

47. See Weinberger, ed., *Igrot shapirin*, p. 264; Goldstein, ed., *Sefer masot Yerushalayim*, pp. 27–31, 319; Yeshayahu A. Z. Margolis, *Amudei arazim* (Jerusalem, 1932), pp. 30, 53, 64. Margolis also wrote a commentary on *Beer lahai roi*, which was written by Rabbi Zeev Hirsh Shapira of Munkács, the father of Hayim Elazar Shapira. For a discussion of Margolis's relation to Shapira, see Weinberger, ed., *Igrot shapirin*, pp. 234, 238, 262–64.

48. See also the reproduction of a letter from Teitelbaum to Margolis that is included in the latter's *Sefer midot rashbi* (Meron, 1979).

49. See Teitelbaum, *Divrei Yoel*, vol. 1, sec. 88. The discussion here of the question of the elections was afterward expanded into the main body of Teitelbaum's *Vayoel Moshe*. See the introduction to the Jerusalem edition of 1978, p. ii, *Mishmeret homatenu* 2, no. 41 (1959): 393.

50. See the beginning of Margolis's work, *Beur hashir bar yohai* (Meron, 1974).

51. Margolis, *Amudei arazim*, pp. 38–47.

52. Ibid., pp. 31, 35. Dozens of pages are devoted to demonstrating the halakhic and kabbalistic importance of the style of dress that is customary in the author's circle. See also Yeshayahu A. Z. Margolis, *Ashrei haish* (Jerusalem, 1925), p. 71. Compare with the words of the Rabbi of Rymanów as quoted by Shapira in *Kuntres yemot hamashiah*, p. 70.

53. Yeshayahu A. Z. Margolis, *Kumi ori* (Jerusalem, 1925), p. 24, cited in Friedman, *Hevrah vedat*, p. 135; Yeshayahu A. Z. Margolis, *Kumi roni* (Jerusalem, 1925), p. 44: Margolis, *Ashrei haish*, p. 34.

54. Margolis, *Ashrei haish*, p. 10. The author also suggests classical sources for these ideas.

55. Ibid., pp. 61–64. Numerous examples are found throughout the book, e.g., pp. 5, 24, 32, 69, 75. See also Margolis, *Kumi roni*, pp. 44–45 and elsewhere.

56. Margolis, *Ashrei haish*, p. 65.

57. Ibid., pp. 23–25.

58. Compare with Shapira's words in *Hayim veshalom*, 2:26; Shapira, *Divrei torah*, vol. 9, sec. 10; Shapira, *Kungres yemot hamashiah*, p. 43.

59. Margolis, *Kum roni*, p. 39.

60. Margolis, *Ashrei haish*, p. 25; Margolis, *Maamarei rabi Elazar* (Jerusalem, 1930), p. 22.

61. Yehuda Liebes, "Haedah haharedit," p. 143. See also Liebes, "Meshihiyuto shel rabi Yaakov Emden veyahaso lashabtaut," *Tarbiz* 49 (1980): 125.

62. Margolis, *Amudei arazim*, p. 6. The question of messianism and Zionism is treated at length in Margolis, *Kumi roni*, pp. 38–41; Margolis, *Ashrei haish*, pp. 41–50; and throughout Margolis's *Kumi ori*.

63. Margolis, *Ashrei haish*, p. 56 (the book lambasts Rav Kook); Margolis, *Amudei arazim*, p. 5. See Liebes, "Haedah haharedit," p. 148; Rivka Shatz, "Reshit hamasa neged harav kook," *Molad*, n.s., 6, no. 32 (1974): 25–262.

64. See Abraham Isaac Kook, *Hazon hageulah* (New York, 1974), p. 195.

65. See. I. I. Gruenwald, *Liflagot Israel beHungaryah* (New York, 1929); Michael Silver, "Shorshei hapilug bayahadut Hungaryah" (Ph.D. diss., Hebrew University, Jerusalem, 1985); Moshe Samet, "The Beginnings of Orthodoxy," *Modern Judaism* 8 (1988): 258–63; Netanel Katzburg, "The Jewish Congress in Hungary," *Hungarian Jewish Studies* 2 (1969): pp. 1–35.

66. Rabbi Solomon Eliezer Alfandari, a halakhic and kabbalistic sage, taught in Turkey, Safed, and Jerusalem. Margolis was influenced by him (see Margolis, *Ashrei haish*, pp. 14, 35, 38; Margolis, *Amudei arazim*, pp. 37, 68); he received Alfandari's imprimatur for his book *Kumi roni* (most of his books were written after Alfandari's death); and he tried to publish some of Alfandari's halakhic responsa (Goldstein, ed., *Sefer masot Yerushalayim*, p. 321). Margolis complained that "strangers have trespassed upon [Alfandari's] patrimony, plundering his holy writings and the treasures of his teachings." Margolis, *Amudei arazim*, p. 53. On Alfandari, see Pinhas Grayevsky, *Miginzei Yerushalayim* 19 (1931); Meir Benayahu, introduction to Raphael Bitran, *Midot tovot* (Jerusalem, 1988); and Goldstein, *Maamar hayut esh*. See also R. Y. Nissim, ed., *Sheelot uteshuvot Maharsha* (Jerusalem, 1932), vol. 1; and D. Y. Weiss, ed., *Sheelot uteshuvot saba kadisha* (Jerusalem, 1973–74). On the nature of the Weiss edition, see the above-mentioned introduction by Benayahu to Bitran's *Midot tovot*.

67. Goldstein, ed., *Sefer masot Yerushalayim*, p. 308. See remarks attributed to Alfandari criticizing rabbis who "flatter the wicked" (p. 302) and praising the Munkaczer Rebbe for knowing how to "tell the House of Jacob of its iniquities" (p. 313). See also Alfandari's letter concerning the chief rabbinate (p. 308), in which he writes: "Rav Kook, may God preserve and protect him, must disavow the things he has written in his pamphlets, things that are not in accordance with the Torah, for this is the cause of the bitterness against him on the part of the God-fearing, because it is against our holy Torah, as I have shown clearly in a pamphlet especially devoted to this subject." (However harsh his criticism, Alfandari's style is far more moderate than that of Margolis's calumnies). See also Alfandari's responsum concerning prayer in the company of sinners as quoted in Goldstein, ed., *Sefer masot Yerushalayim*, "Now, in these latter days, we are not dealing with Jewish transgressors [in general], but with emissaries and witnesses [of the Evil Impulse], and [the latter] seek only to overwhelm the God-fearing, using tokens of purity that make it [appear to be] the will of God." (There can be little doubt that it is the religious Zionists who are the objects of this attack.) This observation is relevant to Yosef Toby's article "Shorshei yahasah shel yahadut hamizrah el hatenuah hazionit," in *Temurot bahistoryah hayehudit hahadashah* (Jerusalem, 1988), pp. 169–92, esp. pp. 189–92.

68. See Weinberger, ed., *Igrot shapirin*, p. 264; Goldstein, ed., *Sefer masot Yerushalayim*, pp. 27–31: Solomon Eliezer Alfandari, "Teshuvah meahavah" in H. Y. D. Azulai, *Eyn zokher* (Jerusalem, 1962).

69. Weinberger, ed., *Igrot shapirin*, p. 262. See also Goldstein, ed., *Sefer masot Yerushalayim*, p. 20.

70. Goldstein, ed., *Sefer masot Yerushalayim*, p. 121. The Rebbe's "Jerusalem journeys" of

the 1930s, as described in this book, revolved around the charismatic personality of Alfandari. It was on the basis of the latter's explicit invitation and blessing that Shapira conditioned the trip, and he actually had to postpone the trip several times, because of the latter's evasive replies. Ibid., p. 20. See also his characterization of Alfandari as the leading saint of his generation. Ibid., p. 24. Hayim Beer has portrayed the episode in literary form in his *Et hazamir* (Tel Aviv, 1987), pp. 200–225.

71. Goldstein, ed., *Sefer masot Yerushalayim*, p. 121.

72. Ibid.

73. Ibid, p. 240.

74. Shapira, *Kuntres yemot hamashiah*, p. 33. Shapira goes on to say that Rabbi Menahem Mendel recovered immediately upon returning home.

75. Shapira later compared the thirteen days he spent in the Land of Israel to the thirteen years that—according to tradition—Rabbi Simeon Bar Yohai spent in a cave. Goldstein, ed., *Tikun olam*, p. 152. Shapira also cited halakhic reasons for his decision to leave the Land of Israel before the festival of Shavuot. "And also for secret reasons I did not remain in Israel during the festival." Goldstein, ed., *Sefer masot Yerushalayim*, p. 365.

76. Goldstein, *Sefer masot Yerushalayim*, p. 358.

77. Ibid.

78. See also Pinhas Miller, *Olamo shel abba* (Jerusalem, 1984), p. 228.

Portions of this essay appeared in my book *Messianism, Zionism, and Religious Radicalism* (Chicago: University of Chicago Press, 1996) and are reprinted here by permission.

ORTHODOXY, LIBERALISM, AND ZIONISM IN WESTERN EUROPE

Liberal Judaism and Zionism in Germany

It is customary in German Jewish historiography to speak of the opposition between Zionists and Liberal Jews, the former represented by the Zionistische Vereinigung für Deutschland (German Zionist Association), the latter by the Centralverein deutscher Staatsbürger jüdischen Glaubens (Central Association of German Citizens of the Jewish Faith). Indeed, the Centralverein was the most significant non-Zionist, and sometimes anti-Zionist organization of German Jewry, and its members tended to be both political liberals and non-Orthodox Jews. Yet its basic goal was the quest for harmonization between good German citizenship and a certain *Stammesbewusstsein* (awareness of lineage). It did not posit an alternative religious interpretation of Jewish tradition and destiny. On religious matters the Centralverein, like its foe the Zionistische Vereinigung, remained neutral. Their differences were political and cultural.

Yet it was on the grounds of religion that Zionism could be and was opposed, not pragmatically but dogmatically, by both Orthodox and Liberal Jews. When the latter did so they were speaking not as political liberals but as part of the Reform movement, which, to differentiate itself from its radical wing, by the late nineteenth century had taken on the designation "Liberal." It was these Liberals who presented the most formidable intellectual, if not political, counterforce to German Zionism. The theoretical struggle between the two in Germany has received far less attention than the practical conflicts between Zionists and their political opponents, the liberal political factions they vied with for control of the German communities, and the Centralverein. My purpose therefore will be to look at the representatives of Liberal Judaism as a religious philosophy, examine their religious justifications for varying attitudes to Zionism, and at the same time investigate the changing Zionist attitude toward Liberal Judaism. I shall begin with the Second Reich, focus on the Weimar period, and conclude with some comments about the Hitler years.

I

The opposition to international Zionism in Germany began with rabbis. In June 1897 two Liberals, Heinemann Vogelstein of Stettin and Sigmund

Maybaum of Berlin, expressed their opposition to the First Zionist Congress. A few weeks later, the Executive Committee of the Rabbiner-Verband in Deutschland (the general rabbinical association that included Conservatives as well as Liberals) issued a formal protest, which was endorsed the following year by a nearly unanimous voice vote of its plenum.[1] As far as we know, no German rabbi present at that meeting voted against the resolution. Only two, the Liberal Leo Baeck and the Conservative Saul Kaatz, chose to abstain.[2]

In the years that followed, religious Liberals, with few exceptions, remained adamant in their opposition to the new movement. Some of their arguments had little to do with religion: Zionism was a danger to Jewish political status in Germany, a spur to antisemitism.[3] But especially among the rabbis, other contentions appear as well, whose main purpose is to declare the Jewish illegitimacy of Zionism—not because it was "forcing the messianic end" (the reason why Orthodox opponents often castigated it) but because it was a misunderstanding of Jewish history and destiny.

Among the Liberals the chief spokesmen for the religious critique of Zionism were Rabbis Heinemann Vogelstein of Stettin and Felix Goldmann of Oppeln (and later Leipzig). Of the two, Vogelstein was older and less compromising, Goldmann more profound and less dogmatic. Though organizationally a leader of Liberal Judaism, Vogelstein was not an original thinker. His generation within the Reform movement had received the heritage of Abraham Geiger and his contemporaries intact and added little to it themselves. Vogelstein's reaction to Zionism was therefore basically an attempt to point out where the new movement contradicted the accepted heritage. He put it very directly: Judaism means the religion of the Prophets of Israel understood as faith in a universal, moral God and the Jewish mission to bring its tiding to humanity. Since Zionism undermined that faith, especially among the young, it constituted a serious danger to the future of Judaism no less than to the political future of German Jews.[4]

Goldmann, who considered himself a non-Zionist rather than an anti-Zionist, drove to the heart of the matter: Zionism represented a fundamentally different and contradictory understanding of Jewishness. It held that one could be an atheist and at the same time a perfectly good Jew. The Zionists could afford to be neutral and even indifferent to religion, but Liberal Judaism could not adopt that position. While there were indeed Jews who called themselves Liberal and cared little about religion, Goldmann saw them on that account as Jewishly inadequate. Their Jewishness was simply an *Abwehrjudentum* (Judaism defined in terms of defense), and, despite Zionist claims, that was not what Liberal Judaism was all about. Assimilated Jews were indeed the norm, but they stood outside both camps, the common prey of Liberals no less than Zionists. Like the Zionists, Goldmann's goal was to win them over to a more content-rich Jewishness. But that basic content had to be religion, not nationhood, for, as he argued, only Judaism as a religion was historically authentic. And because Judaism, unlike Jewish nationalism, was eternal and not temporal, it alone could assure Jewish survival.[5]

For the most part, Liberal rabbis and laity in Germany continued to see Liberal Judaism and Zionism as fundamentally contradictory. Theoretical nuances were generally lost in the midst of vigorously fought community elections and persistent outcroppings of antisemitism that kept anxieties at a high pitch. Increasingly, Liberal Jews sensed that the Zionists were successfully alienating some of their own offspring, "dripping the Zionist poison into the souls of the children," as one of them put it. In 1912, lay leaders of Liberal Judaism were instrumental in forming an Antizionistisches Komitee (Anti-Zionist Committee),[6] and most of them continued throughout the Weimar period to regard the practical fight against Zionism as a basic imperative of their Liberalism.[7] However, by the early Weimar years, the Liberal rabbinate was neither consistently nor unambiguously anti-Zionist.

In 1918 even Goldmann acknowledged that Jewish nationalism was unobjectionable, provided only that it would recognize the primacy of Judaism as a religion.[8] Religious Jews could legitimately be members of the Zionist organization, according to Goldmann, as long as they did not share the prevalent national view that religion was a dispensable manifestation of Jewishness—as long as they continued to consider religion its essence. Rabbi Caesar Seligmann went further. Although he never joined the ranks of the Zionists and, like Goldmann, continued to insist upon the primacy of religion, Seligmann paid early tribute to its beneficent effect in restoring Jewish self-consciousness to alienated Jews, and by 1918 he could regard their roles as complementary. Both were striving to preserve Judaism, "we through preservation of the Jewish religion, they through preservation of the community."[9] In Martin Buber, a Zionist and a non-Orthodox believer, Seligmann found points of contact with Liberal Judaism.[10]

Although Hermann Cohen did not associate himself organizationally with Liberal Judaism, he was widely regarded as its most respected spokesman. His position on Zionism was similar to that of the more moderate among the Liberal rabbis and laity. Like them he could not conceive of a Jewishness that did not have ethical monotheism as its essence and did not strive for a universal messianic fulfillment. But like them also, he realized that the religious definition was not exhaustive. Judaism, he held in 1916, was not, as the Zionists believed, a nation, but it was a "nationality." As such, and not as a religion alone, it could co-exist within the German state. That, of course, did not make Cohen a Zionist. On the contrary, like the rabbis mentioned above, he continued to see Liberal Judaism and Zionism as struggling against one another for the minds and hearts of German Jewry.[11]

Yet even in the first decade of the century a few intrepid souls had set out to combine the two. The case of Rabbi Emil Cohn is for the most part well known.[12] On account of his Zionism, it is generally noted, he lost his job as a Liberal rabbi in the Berlin Jewish community in 1907, the governing body being unwilling to tolerate his views. However, the Cohn affair was not quite so simple. Cohn had not suddenly become a Zionist. He was a graduate of the Liberal seminary in Berlin, the Lehranstalt für die Wissenschaft des Judentums (Educational Institute for the Scientific Study of Judaism), where he had been the co-founder of a Zionist student society that was quickly suppressed by the administration. Nonetheless, the Berlin Jewish community had hired him, albeit with the proviso that he keep his views out of the pulpit and classroom. Although Cohn did not entirely abide by his promise, it was only when complaint was made against him by the director of a prominent *Gymnasium* that the community board felt compelled to take action.[13] Moreover, his Zionism did not prevent Cohn from thereafter getting a rabbinical position in Kiel, where no conditions were made about keeping his views private. In fact, while he was the rabbi in Kiel, he delivered an unpublished lecture to the Königsberg Zionist Association on religiosity and Judaism in which he combined Liberal religious views with Zionist ones. He called for a full-scale reformation of Judaism that would bring it religious renewal by "cleansing it of foreign rubble and the withered foliage of . . . suffocating forms." But that renewal, he argued, required genuine religious experience (*Erlebnis*), which was possible only through a historical sense of peoplehood. Zionism was essential if Judaism were to regain its fluidity and religious creativity.[14] Cohn went on to obtain pulpits in Essen, Bonn,[15] and finally again in Berlin, though by that time his religious views had become distinctly conservative and he no longer wholeheartedly affirmed Zionism.[16]

The first German Liberal rabbi to remain true to both Liberalism and Zionism was Max Joseph, the rabbi of Stolp in Pomerania. Like Cohn, he was a graduate of the Liberal Lehranstalt in Berlin, but during the period before political Zionism. Joseph gained public attention with a pro-Zionist work that he published in 1908 entitled *Das Judentum am Scheidewege* (Judaism at the Crossroads).[17] Eschewing both the political and cultural arguments for Zionism, Joseph took a new tack: The Jewish religion will not survive without Jewish nationalism. Or as he put it, "Judaism will either be Zionist or it will not be at all." Joseph went on to show that the Jewish religion, as it developed historically, was inextricably intertwined with national elements without which it could not hope to survive. They appeared both in concepts such as ethical monotheism and practices such as celebration of the holidays. Even the mission of Israel idea, so cherished by Liberal Judaism, he believed, must arouse "a sense of national exultation." The Zionism that is necessary for Jewish religious survival is not essentially secular in Joseph's view—though that was regularly claimed by his Liberal colleagues. Quite the contrary, it fostered moral idealism and from there the path was short to religious enthusiasm. In Joseph's words: "The great struggle for the rebirth of the people, which stirs the soul to its depths, is one in which a Jew can scarcely participate without being seized by religious sentiments."[18] Joseph's program entailed the abandonment of what he considered the antinational course of Liberal Judaism. His own religious Liberalism was especially evident in his approach to the Bible, to which he applied the radical High Criticism of his day. But Joseph addressed his book to Liberal Jews almost as if he were not one of them. He did not try to speak as an insider within both traditions, and he did not rise to a position of prominence in Liberal Judaism.[19] In contrast to its counterpart in the United States, German Liberal Jewry failed to produce religious figures like Stephen Wise, Max and James Heller, and Abba Hillel Silver, who were prominent both in their rabbinical roles and in the leadership of organized Zionism.[20]

II

The early failure to establish a shared identity must also be explained in terms of Zionist attitudes toward Liberal Judaism. For the Zionist leadership in Germany, Liberalism represented the ideological enemy as well as the political enemy in community elections. The enthusiasm that Zionism drew from its adherents, especially the young, was in no small measure dependent upon a sense of generational revolt against the bourgeois establishment, whose ideology was Liberalism. The tactics of the Zionists were less restrained than those of their opponents, and their polemics were peppered with sarcasm. They attacked the *sancta* of Liberal Judaism—religious reform, the mission idea—with utmost irreverence. They were unwilling to acknowledge Liberal Judaism as a serious form of Jewish identity, except—in an occasional grudging admission—for a very few, mostly the rabbis. They stereotyped it as nothing more than assimilationism, repeatedly showing through beneath a thin layer of Jewish religion. They aroused anxiety by claiming they had won over the youth, that they represented true progress, while Liberal Judaism stood for the past. They even claimed their opponents had no right to the term "liberalism," for true liberalism referred only to the general political movement that had led to emancipation in Germany. The religious Liberals' self-designation was therefore nothing but a smoke screen for a Judaism of convenience, a way station on the road to Christianity. In short, from the Zionist side too, Liberal Judaism and Jewish nationalism were initially seen as incompatible.[21]

Despite a declared policy of religious neutrality, German Zionists often allied themselves politically with the Orthodox, justifying the alliance—seen as cynical by the Liberals—by their claim that Orthodoxy was better able to preserve Jewish distinctiveness. They opposed liturgical reforms that removed national elements from the prayer book.[22]

In the same period that the Anti-Zionist Committee engaged in its propaganda on the eve of the First World War, the Zionist movement was likewise undergoing a radicalization that set it further apart from the Liberals.[23] Still, the Zionists could not resist noting that among the younger religious leadership of the Liberals a turn to Zionism was increasingly apparent.[24] Following the war, they evolved a new strategy with regard to Liberal Judaism: they would try to use those religious leaders that were sympathetic to Zionism for their own purposes. In 1918 the chief Zionist propagandist in Germany, Alfred Klee, turned to Rabbi Max Joseph, asking him to distribute some Zionist literature and seeking his assistance in enlisting other sympathetic rabbis for active participation in the Zionist cause. For his part, Joseph was not so sure that the ploy would work. "My dear doctor," he replied, "*Golus* [exile] does not make one manly, and the Prussian rabbi is doubly in *Golus*. He trembles quicker than the leaf on a tree. But," he added, "the younger generation of rabbis seems to be somewhat braver."[25]

During the Weimar period that "younger generation" was increasingly occupying rabbinical positions of prominence. Although most were not outspoken Zionists, they were considerably more friendly to the movement than their elders. A number of them were now teaching at the Lehranstalt (during the Weimar years once again raised to the rank of *Hochschule* [college]) in Berlin. Could these men be persuaded to express themselves on Zionism in a manner that would be helpful to the movement? In the mid-1920s, German Zionism changed its course with regard to religious Liberalism. No longer did it see the religious Liberals as the enemy. Now at least some of them became potential recruits for the cause.

A rapprochement between Zionists and Liberals had been in the making as early as 1920 when both groups joined in support of the Palestine Foundation Fund, the Keren Hayesod. Even Rabbi Felix Goldmann signed the declaration, principally, as he wrote in justification, because it was not political and because "building up the land of Israel is an eternal religious obligation that no one can cavalierly remove from the store of our religious commandments."[26] Goldmann also explicitly dissociated himself from Max Naumann's Verband nationaldeutscher Juden (League of German Nationalist Jews), formed in 1921, which regarded Jewish pro-Palestine activity as virtual treason. The views of that group, he suggested, rested on a misunderstanding of the Jewish religion.[27] It is not unlikely that the Verband, many of whose members were also associated with the radical Reform Congregation in Berlin, may have removed from Liberal circles some of the more extreme anti-Zionists.

From the Liberal side the rapprochement proceeded with unanimous adoption of a neutrality resolution on the subject of Zionism by the Vereinigung der Liberalen Rabbiner Deutschlands (Association of Liberal Rabbis in Germany) in 1927—fully eight years before a similar position was adopted by the parallel organization in America, the Central Conference of American Rabbis.[28] However, the Liberal laity did not go along. Meeting six weeks later, the governing body of the Vereinigung für das liberale Judentum in Deutschland (Association for Liberal Judaism in Germany) unanimously adopted a resolution stating that since religion was the foundation and essence of Judaism, it altogether rejected the idea that it develops out of Jewish nationalism.[29] The split between Liberal rabbis and Liberal laity, which as early as 1912 had manifested itself bitterly on the question of ritual religious obligation, now became increasingly apparent on the issue of Zionism as well.[30]

The German Zionists, for their part, were quick to exploit this split in Liberal Judaism. In October 1927 the governing body of the Zionistische Vereinigung decided on a new policy, which the protocol of their meeting formulated as follows:

Liberal Association: The crisis currently existing within its ranks demands the sharpest attack against the Association. It is our task to influence and win over the younger generation of rabbis and to harness for our propaganda (for example, lectures on "Zionism and Liberalism") individual organized Liberals who are also Zionists. The intellectual analysis must present the opposition between Zionism and Liberalism in such a way as to urge attack upon the antinational reforming tendency, but to allow that the Jewish conception, borne by a national Jewish way of thinking, which is based on the idea of [religious] development, has its place within the Zionist movement.[31]

Shortly thereafter, the German Zionist Central Committee affirmed the new strategy even more specifically. No longer would opponents simply be branded assimilationists. Instead, it called for "penetration of the historical development of liberalism and, together with all necessary critique, an acknowledgment of the lines of connection between it and us ([recognition of] changes within Liberalism)."[32]

This new Zionist line of the mid-1920s had already been put into effect before the official bodies gave it sanction. In the June 23, 1925, issue of the Zionist paper, the *Jüdische Rundschau*, Zionist activist Hans Kohn had published an article entitled "Liberal Judaism" in which he argued that Zionism and Liberal Judaism were similar in their eclecticism and in their view of Judaism as an ongoing spiritual process. He was careful to distinguish between the "old" and the "new" Liberalism, the former associated with assimilationism, the latter a worthy partner for the Zionists. He even went so far as to acknowledge that Liberal Judaism was of "major significance in our history" because it had broken down the rigidity produced by the preceding centuries of ghetto life. Citing Abraham Geiger's view of an organically developing Jewish tradition, Kohn added: "In this respect we stand on the shoulders of this early Liberal Judaism." But Kohn's rapprochement was limited to a common understanding of Jewish religious history; it did not extend to the future. Here he thought Liberal Judaism lacked a sense of direction, and he did not suggest common goals.[33]

The following year an unprecedented event gave the Zionists further cause for reflection. In the summer of 1926 Liberal Jews from various European countries and the United States gathered in London to form the World Union for Progressive Judaism. Almost thirty years after the Zionists, Liberal Jews had finally succeeded in creating their own international organization. Henceforth it was no longer possible to accuse them of fearing anti-semitic charges about "international Jewry." Nor could their movement be regarded as somnolent.[34] Moreover, the London meeting had refrained from taking any stance with regard to Zionism. Thus when the first official conference of the World Union was scheduled for Berlin in 1928, the German Zionists saw this new challenge as a providential opportunity. They would try to win the delegates over to Zionism.

In anticipation of the conference, Robert Weltsch, editor of the *Jüdische Rundschau*, invited a number of leading Liberal Jews to express their views on the relation between Liberal Judaism and Zionism. Their replies, together with essays by prominent Zionists, then appeared in a special double issue of the paper that was distributed at the conference. Shortly thereafter, they were gathered into a pamphlet for wider circulation together with a foreword by Kurt Blumenfeld, the president of the German Zionist Association.[35] On the front page of the special issue Weltsch declared that there could be no antagonism between Liberalism as a religious world view and Zionism, and he added his own appreciation for the work of both Hermann Cohen and Claude Montefiore, the leader of English Liberal Jewry and president of the World Union. "The opposition between religious Liberalism and Jewish nationalism has no internal basis," he concluded. However, remembering that there were also Zionists who were religiously Orthodox, he hastily added, that, of course, the *Jüdische Rundschau* did not therefore identify itself with religious Liberalism. Politically its stance remained neutral.[36]

The most important spiritual and intellectual leaders of Liberal Judaism responded to the Zionist invitation with brief, balanced statements. Leo Baeck, who enjoyed the widest respect of all the Liberal rabbis, was neither a Zionist nor an anti-Zionist. But in his advocacy of a more serious, inner-directed Liberal Judaism, he set himself clearly apart from the assimilationist tendency that Zionists had so long condemned.[37] Self-criticism was also the tone of Ismar Elbogen's response. Flexibility, the historian and one of the chief organizers of the Berlin Conference noted, was of the essence of Liberalism, and the present demanded a shift from national adaptation toward a return to Jewish roots and toward building bridges to the mass of the Jewish people. Max Wiener used the occasion to make a theological point: Because Liberal Jews recognized a human component in revelation, they—more than the Orthodox—needed to acknowledge the important religious role of the national spirit as a source for the ongoing process of interpretation and reinterpretation of God's will.[38]

Less well-known Liberal rabbis were more explicitly Zionist. Malwin Warschauer was a rabbi of the Berlin community who, like the men just mentioned, also taught at the *Hochschule*. His contribution was unique in offering an internal critique of the Zionist attitude toward Liberal Judaism. Unlike Weltsch and the other Zionist participants, whose smooth words were largely motivated by tactical considerations, who never suggested that Zionism had hitherto erred in its attitude to religious Liberalism, and who certainly did not identify themselves as Liberal Jews, Warschauer chastised his fellow Zionists for failing to recognize that Liberal Judaism contained indispensable religious values and qualities that represented "the most profound and noble aspects of our national spirit." Warschauer called for an alliance of the Liberal and national ideas to bring about religious revival. Max Elk, who would later found the first school in Palestine that drew upon Liberal Judaism, the Leo Baeck School in Haifa, even shared the controversial Zionist assumption that Jewish life in the diaspora would always remain deficient. Only in the Jews' own land could the Liberal Jewish idea reach fruition. When the national movement would physically establish its "old-new land," Elk maintained, Liberal Judaism would be its soul.

The conference itself did not raise the Zionist issue, choosing to concentrate on strictly religious matters instead.[39] However, in the following years the drift toward Zionism among German Liberal Jews continued. Although there was still be opposition to Jewish nationalism among some Liberal lay leaders—and especially within the circle of the Berlin Reform Congregation—well into the Hitler years,[40] the broadened Jewish Agency after 1928 provided another basis for cooperation alongside the Keren Hayesod. During the Nazi period even Heinrich Stern, the lay head of organized Liberal Judaism in Germany, who had long been an avowed opponent of Zionism, attested that the two movements had grown much closer.[41] The youngest generation of Liberal rabbis, men like Joachim Prinz[42] and Max Nussbaum, were clearly committed to Zionism from the beginning of their careers. Some older men, like Paul Lazarus, became converts in the early 1930s.[43]

As more and more German Jews immigrated to Palestine, Liberal Judaism looked increasingly toward its self-perpetuation there.[44] Caesar Seligmann even suggested that forming a Liberal version of Mizrahi, the Orthodox Zionist organization, might be the best way to achieve that end.[45] In the mid-1930s German Liberal rabbis established congregations in Haifa, Tel-Aviv, and Jerusalem.[46] On a visit to Palestine in 1934, shortly before his own *aliyah*, the once anti-Zionist Liberal rabbi Max Dienemann wrote in his diary: "The remarkable thing about Palestine is that here one works for the future, while in Europe today one lives only for each day and for the liquidation of the past."[47] Liberal Judaism in Germany had come a long way: from the virulent opposition to Zionism in Heinemann Vogelstein's generation, through various forms of acknowledgment and rapprochement, finally to the realization—forced upon it by history—that, without Zion, a Jewish future was not possible.

Notes

1. *Allgemeine Zeitung des Judentums* 61 (1897): 277, 338; *Verhandlungen und Beschlüsse der Generalversammlung des Rabbiner-Verbandes in Deutschland zu Berlin am 1. und 2. Juni 1898* (Berlin, 1898), pp. 30–32. It is not evident from these protocols that Rabbi Selig Gronemann of Hannover voted against the declaration, as maintained in the article in *Enclyclopedia Judaica*, s.v. *Protestrabbiner*. At the meeting he said explicitly that he was not opposed to it as such. When the declaraction had been issued a year ago, it had pleased him and he had considered it a "manly deed." However, he now favored a new, more moderately phrased resolution rather than merely an endorsement of the old one.

2. Kurt Wilhelm, "Der zionistische Rabbiner," in *In zwei Welten: Siegfried Moses zum fünfundsiebzigsten Geburtstag,* ed. Hans Tramer (Tel-Aviv, 1962), pp. 55–56.

3. See, for example, the principally nonreligious arguments by the son of Abraham Geiger, Ludwig Geiger, in his "Zionismus und Deutschtum," *Die Stimme der Wahrheit* 1 (1905): 165–69; and in Werner Sombert, *Judentaufen* (Munich, 1912), pp. 44–48. Because of his lineage, his editorship of the *Allgemeine Zeitung des Judentums,* and his active role in the Berlin community, combined with his extreme views explicitly favoring virtually complete assimilation, Geiger served the Zionists as a convenient symbol for their stereotype of Liberal Judaism. On Geiger's anti-Zionism, see Yehuda Eloni, *Zionismus in Deutschland: Von den Anfängen bis 1914* (Gerlingen, 1987), pp. 194–200.

4. Heinemann Vogelstein, *Der Zionismus: Eine Gefahr für die gedeihliche Entwickelung des Judentums* (Berlin, 1906). That the diaspora was providential, and hence meant by God to be permanent, continued to be the dominant position of German Liberal Judaism. See, for example, Max Dienemann, *Galuth* (Berlin, 1929).

5. Felix Goldmann, *Zionismus oder Liberalismus: Atheismus oder Religion* (Frankfurt a.M., 1911). Originally appearing as a series of articles in *Liberales Judentum* in 1911, in pamphlet form it was widely distributed, even handed out at large public meetings. *Liberales Judentum* 3 (1911): 263.

6. It is not true, however, as has been repeatedly claimed, that the Vereinigung für das liberale Judentum in Deutschland (Association for Liberal Judaism in Germany) and the Antizionistisches Komitee shared the same address, although on one occasion a meeting of the committee was held in the former's office. Moreover, unlike the Centralverein, the committee did not seek the open participation of Liberal rabbis. No rabbis signed their declarations. See the material on the committee in the Leo Wolff Collection in the archives of the Leo Baeck Institute, New York. The reference to poison appears in the protocol for May 2, 1914. The committee's second pamphlet, *Der Zionismus: Seine Theorien Aussichten und Wirkungen* (Berlin, n.d.) noted that it was based on the writings not only of the Liberal rabbis Vogelstein and Goldmann but also of the Orthodox rabbi Raphael Breuer and the Conservative Moritz Guedemann.

7. *Caesar Seligmann Erinnerungen,* ed. Erwin Seligmann (Frankfurt a.M., 1975), pp. 159–60.

8. Felix Goldmann, *Warum sind und bleiben wir Juden?* (Leipzig, 1918), p. 24; Goldmann, *Das liberale Judentum* (Berlin, 1919), 11. Despite his increasing appreciation for Zionist activities, Goldmann continued to view Liberal Judaism and Zionism as two fundamentally opposed conceptions of Jewish existence that were engaged in a contest for the souls of young Jews. See his *Der Jude im deutschen Kulturkreise: Ein Beitrag zum Wesen des Nationalismus* (Berlin, 1930).

9. *Liberales Judentum* 1 (1908–09): 7–8; 10 (1918): 3.

10. Caesar Seligmann, *Geschichte der jüdischen Reformbewegung* (Frankfurt a.M., 1922), pp. 31–33. Seligmann's final position on Zionism before the Holocaust was still more appreciative: "The Jewish national self-consciousness, which revived in Zionism with unparalleled force, was a curative bath in which the Jewish soul of the bloodless masses regained its health."

Cesar Seligmann, "Religiös-Liberales Judentum: Rückschau und Ausblick" (mimeo) (N.p. 1938), 16. On Seligmann's role within Liberal Judaism, see Michael A. Meyer, "Caesar Seligmann and the Development of Liberal Judaism in Germany at the Beginning of the Twentieth Century," *Hebrew Union College Annual* 40–41 (1969–70): 529–54.

11. Hermann Cohen, *Jüdische Schriften*, 3 vols. (Berlin, 1924), 2:319–40.

12. The most recent treatment is in Eloni, *Zionismus in Deutschland*, pp. 475–83, 508–15.

13. The director of the Mommsen Gymnasium gave the notes from his conversation with Emil Cohn to four Jewish teachers who taught there—and who must have felt threatened that Cohn's position (Jewish identification takes precedence over German) would cast suspicion on their own views. They, in turn, reported the matter to the governing body of the community.

14. Emil Cohn, "Religiosität und Judentum: Vortrag gehalten am 20 März 1909 in der Königsberger Zionistischen Vereinigung" (mimeo.), in my possession.

15. In Bonn, where he was elected unanimously, Cohn did agree not to make public speeches on Zionism in the immediate area. See Eloni, *Zionismus in Deutschland*, p. 515.

16. The new religious conservatism is evident in his *Judentum: Ein Aufruf an die Zeit* (Munich, 1923). Here Cohn, describing himself as filled with remorse, forsakes both religious Liberalism and Zionism. He now criticizes Liberal Judaism for insufficient attention to religious forms and Zionism for having become a substitute religion. Franz Rosenzweig wrote a review of Cohn's book in *Der Jude* (8 [1923]: 237–40) that was highly critical of Cohn's preachy tone and assumed self-importance, but sympathetic to some of his views.

17. Max Joseph, *Das Judentum am Scheidewege: Ein Wort zur Schicksalsfrage an die Starken und Edlen des jüdischen Volkes* (Berlin, 1908). The title was obviously influenced by the collection of Ahad Haam's essays, which had appeared in German translation bearing the title *Am Scheidewege* (Berlin, 1904).

18. Joseph, *Judentum am Scheidewege*, p. 90.

19. Joseph's book received no attention in the general press. In Jewish periodicals he was assailed for his critique of Liberal Judaism by Liberal rabbis and for his biblical criticism by traditional ones. Joseph responded to his critics in *Ist das alles? Eine Antwort an die Kritiker und Nichtkritiker meines Buches* (Berlin, 1910). The volume was issued by the publishing house of the Zionist newspaper *Jüdische Rundschau*. As far as I can determine, not until 1926 did an article appear in which both Liberalism and Zionism are affirmed equally. The October 26 issue of the *Jüdische Rundschau* for that year contains a piece by a recently deceased Hans Norden (apparently not a rabbi) entitled "Liberalismus und Zionismus." Norden notes that he had long believed the two were irreconcilable polar opposites and that he had to choose one or the other. At length he had come to the conclusion that they could exist together not only intellectually but also emotionally. He concluded: "Also and above all in feeling, in my sense of closest connection in terms of destiny and race [*Stamm*], I affirm both poles, Liberalism and Zionism." Hans Norden may have been a relative of Joseph Norden, the Liberal rabbi in Elberfeld. The latter made reference to the article in his *Grundlagen und Ziele des religiös-liberalen Judentums*, 2d ed. (Berlin, 1926), p. 27n. Joseph Norden's own position, expressed in this pamphlet, was to assign Liberalism and Zionism to two separate realms and then argue that they did not conflict. The former, being an interpretation of the Jewish religion, had Orthodoxy as its opponent; the latter was strictly political. Neither should regard itself as a sufficient content of Jewishness or seek to impinge upon the realm of the other. Rabbi Norden's toleration for Zionism in principle did not, however, make him a Zionist, since Zionism, he believed, in fact did impinge on the religious realm, for example by pressing Judaism wholly into a national framework.

20. A similar point is made by Wilhelm, "Der zionistische Rabbiner," p. 70, with regard to German rabbis in general in contrast to rabbis elsewhere in Europe.

21. See esp. Heinrich Sachse [Loewe], *Dr. Vogelsteins Propaganda für den Zionismus* (Berlin, 1906). The publisher was the *Jüdische Rundschau;* the title is to be taken ironically. See

also Arthur Ruppin, *The Jews of To-Day* (London, 1913), p. 154; Ruppin, *Soziologie der Juden*, 2 vols. (Berlin, 1931) 2:187, 189.

22. *Dokumente zur Geschichte des deutschen Zionismus 1882–1933*, ed. Jehuda Reinharz (Tübingen, 1981), p. 83.

23. Marjorie Lamberti, "From Coexistence to Conflict: Zionism and the Jewish Community in Germany, 1897–1914," *Leo Baeck Institute Year Book* 27 (1982): 84–86; Lamberti, "The Centralverein and the Anti-Zionists: Setting the Record Straight," *Leo Baeck Institute Year Book* 33 (1988): 127–28; Jehuda Reinharz, "Advocacy and History: The Case of the Centralverein and the Zionists," *Leo Baeck Institute Year Book* 33 (1988): 121.

24. As early as 1906 Heinemann Vogelstein had remarked that there were "several instances" of anti-Zionistic communities appointing Zionistic rabbis and teachers who openly espoused their own views and that Zionism was especially prevalent among rabbinical students. *Der Zionismus: Eine Gefahr*, pp. 10–12. See also Sachse, *Dr. Vogelsteins Propaganda*, p. 7.

25. Max Joseph to Alfred Klee, May 28, 1918, Alfred Klee Collection, Central Zionist Archives, Jerusalem, A142/58/3. The individuals Joseph was apparently supposed to approach were the biblical scholar and rabbi Sigmund Jampel in Schwedt on the Oder; Rabbi Abraham Schlesinger, a graduate of the Breslau seminary; and a Rabbi Bernstein, who may be the Hungarian Jewish historian, Béla Bernstein, a graduate of the Neologue seminary in Budapest who held various rabbinical positions in Hungary. Joseph hoped that Klee would help him publish another pro-Zionist work, then in preparation. But nothing seems to have come either of Joseph's propaganda efforts or of his projected volume.

26. Felix Goldmann, *Eine ewige religiöse Pflicht: Warum ich den Keren-Hayessod-Aufruf unterschrieb* (Berlin, 1922), p. 5. The piece first appeared in the April 16, 1992, issue of the *Jüdische Zeitung* of Leipzig, where Goldmann was then serving as rabbi, and was later reprinted as a pamphlet by the Keren Hayesod. A copy is to be found under Goldmann's name in the Central Zionist Archives.

27. Felix Goldmann, *Warum sind und bleiben wir Juden?* 2d ed. (Berlin, 1924), pp. 28–29. See also *Dokumente*, ed. Reinharz, p. 319.

28. The text of the resolution was as follows: "The Association of Liberal Rabbis in Germany declares that the basic character of Judaism is religious and must remain so. It decisively rejects every attempt to interpret Judaism as an exclusively national structure. It leaves to the personal sense of responsibility of each individual what position to take in relation to Zionism. It hopes that the settlement of Palestine will proceed in a spirit that will assure a revival of Jewish religiosity." *Jüdische Rundschau*, April 1, 1927.

29. Hermann Vogelstein, *Report on Liberal Judaism in Germany to the World Union for Progressive Judaism Conference* (Berlin, 1928), pp. 1–2. However, the "Guidelines of a Program for Liberal Judaism," adopted by the Liberal lay organization (with reservation as to its binding character) in 1912, did not specifically negate Zionism.

30. *Caesar Seligmann Erinnerungen*, pp. 159–60.

31. *Dokumente*, ed. Reinharz, p. 392.

32. Ibid, p. 398.

33. Hans Kohn, "Liberales Judentum," *Jüdische Rundschau*, June 23, 1925. The article was reprinted in *Zionistische Politik*, ed. Hans Kohn and Robert Weltsch (Mährisch-Ostrau, Czechoslovakia, 1927), pp. 84–96. An otherwise critical editorial in the *Jüdische Rundschau*, February 10, 1925, entitled "Die Lehren der Wahlen," had noted: "Religious Liberalism does not stand in opposition to Zionism or to the Jewish national idea. A large portion of prominent Zionists, in respect of religion, have been Liberal."

34. Robert Weltsch, "Zur liberalen Weltkonferenz," in *Zionistische Politik*, ed. Kohn and Weltsch, 97–106.

35. *Jüdische Rundschau*, August 17, 1928; *Die jüdische Religion und ihre Träger: Beiträge zur Frage des jüdischen Liberalismus und Nationalismus* (Berlin, 1928). The pamphlet also contained a report on the conference by a rather critical Zionist observer who nonetheless re-

marked on the "Jewish energy" displayed there, an energy he could only call "national." The particiants in the symposium, in the order in which their essays appeared in the pamphlet, were Leo Baeck (Berlin), Ismar Elbogen (Berlin), Robert Weltsch (Berlin), Malwin Warschauer (Berlin), Felix Weltsch (Prague), Max Wiener (Berlin), Max Elk (Stettin), Max Grünwald (Mannheim), Maurice L. Perlzweig (London), Max Joseph (Stolp), Ignaz Ziegler (Carlsbad), David Baumgardt (Berlin), Ernst Simon (Jerusalem), and Martin Buber (Heppenheim).

36. Still, Weltsch's wooing of the Liberals did not sit well with the Mizrahi in Germany. At a meeting of the Zionist governing body shortly thereafter, Oscar Wolfsberg, head of the Orthodox Zionists, strenuously objected to what he regarded as a wasteful expression of sympathy. Kurt Blumenfeld was thereupon forced to defend the new policy of trying to win over the Liberals. See *Dokumente,* ed. Reinharz, pp. 408–11.

37. Baeck's piece was printed in large type on the front page of the special issue of the *Jüdische Rundschau.* Still before the rise of Nazism, Baeck had said in a speech on behalf of the Keren Hayesod, delivered in Königsberg: "Perhaps your children or grandchildren will have need for the Land of Israel in order to find shelter there from the anger of the oppressor." Cited by Ernst Simon, "Mashehu al Leo Baeck habilti yadua," Central Zionist Archives, A198/1, kindly called to my attention by Esther Herlitz.

38. Two years earlier, in a speech at the organizing conference of the World Union in London, Max Wiener had expressed a similar view when he concluded his remarks by saying to his fellow Liberal Jews: "If, therefore, tradition does not mean for us that unqualified authority which it constitutes for Conservatism, then we must all be guided by a strong conscious life in common with the Jewish world community and its destiny, by work on the great tasks of preserving and gathering our people, and certainly not least, by concern for the new home in the old ancestral land." *International Conference of Liberal Jews* (London, 1926), p. 38. However, when Wiener was later requested to do active Zionist propaganda, he responded that, as a rabbi, he would not get involved in party disputes. Rather he believed that he best served the cause of "a genuinely Jewish program," Jewish education, and the work for Palestine by freely and individually expressing himself on the issues. Wiener thus continued to follow Baeck's lead in avoiding open partisanship. Max Wiener to Alfred Klee, November 14, 1930, Klee Collection, Central Zionist Archives.

39. Curiously, the German Liberals were suspect of Zionism among at least some American Reform Jews. On March 10, 1928, a leading Reform layman from Pittsburgh, A. Leo Weil, wrote to the secretary of the World Union for Progressive Judaism, Lily H. Montagu, that he considered it possible "our German members wanted to have this meeting in Berlin so that they could obtain a large enough attendance of delegates affiliated with Zionism to commit our organization to that movement. . . .You will recall that Dr. [Stephen S.] Wise, at our London conference, made an effort in that direction, and it would not surprise me at all if a similar movement was being carefully planned and prepared for by Zionists in Germany." World Union for Progressive Judaism, American Jewish Archives, Cincinnati, Ohio, 16/1.

40. Max Dienemann, *Liberales Judentum* (Berlin, 1935), p. 19.

41. Heinrich Stern, *Ernst Machen! Ein Wort an die religiös-liberalen Juden* (Berlin, 1935), p. 11.

42. In *Wir Juden* (Berlin, 1934), Joachim Prinz argued that the triumph of nationalism over political liberalism should now drive the Jews to the only possible solution of the Jewish question: the acceptance of their own status as a nation. And the Jews could not develop culturally and religiously as a nation except by mass migration to Palestine. Prinz also preached Zionism from Berlin pulpits, apparently without backlash. The reprimand (*Maßregelung*) he received for a brief sermon delivered in 1935 seems to have been not on account of its Zionism but because he challenged the established practice of moving rabbis around from one synagogue to another, thus preventing the establishment of lasting ties between rabbi and congregants. See *Jüdische Rundschau,* May 28, 1935, pp. 3, 8. Prinz continued to serve as rabbi in Berlin until his emigration in 1937. It is therefore necessary to correct Eloni, *Zionismus in Deutschland,* p. 204, n. 98.

43. *Paul Lazarus Gedenkbuch: Beiträge zur Würdigung der letzten Rabbinergeneration in Deutschland* (Jerusalem, 1961), pp. 19–20.

44. Max Dienemann, "Das Gesicht des religiösen Liberalismus in Palästina," *Der Morgen* 12 (1936): 157–63.

45. Seligmann, "Religiös-Liberales Judentum," p. 22.

46. See the reports on their work by Max Elk (Haifa) and Kurt Wilhelm (Jerusalem) in ibid., pp. 23–33.

47. *Max Dienemann: Ein Gedenkbuch* (London, 1946), p. 51.

German Jewish Orthodoxy's Attitude toward Zionism

The Orthodox segment constituted but a minority—15 percent—of German Jewry. Like Orthodox groups elsewhere, it was loyal to the precepts of the Jewish tradition and meticulous in the observance of the *mitzvot* (commandments). Its observance did not prevent it from being integrated in its German gentile environment, and indeed the Orthodox shared a sense of identification with German values and heritage, such as homeland, government, language, art, and literature. German Jewish Orthodoxy was proud of its country's political, scientific, and technological achievements.

Most German Jews opposed the Zionist movement at the end of the nineteenth century. They were apprehensive about this captivating new movement that had hoisted the banner of Jewish nationalism. Zionist activities and emphasis on national aims threatened to harm the civic cause of the Jews in Germany. Resistance to Zionism, in fact, united all strains of German Jewry, from Reform to extreme Orthodoxy. The *Israelit*, the organ of the Orthodox that regularly stressed the differences among the strains of German Jewry declared, "On the issues of love for the Kaiser and the Reich, for the state and the fatherland, all parties of Jewry are of one mind, Orthodox as well as Reform, the most devout as the most liberal."[1]

The Zionist movement was attacked on all fronts—in newspapers, speeches, and even in homiletics from synagogue pulpits. German Jews across the spectrum were apprehensive about the specter of "dual loyalty." They unanimously opposed utopian ideas that could only produce trouble and end in failure. Arguments were heard from all sides about the futility of the Zionist plans because of the inevitable opposition of state and the church. They even conjured up the possibility of missionary zeal coming to the aid of Zionism. Insuperable economic problems, too, they believed would perforce bring all plans to nought. The notion that Zionism incited antisemitism was not ignored, either. While Zionists held that antisemitism was a consequence of the diaspora, anti-Zionists saw it as annoying and disturbing but, nevertheless, temporary. Those who opposed Zionism argued that deserting Germany in response to antisemitism would only assure its victory.[2]

In the view of its opponents Zionism was not only a response to antisemitism but its very catalyst and stimulus. Zionism and antisemitism were seen to share three fundamental views: Jews were not a religious community but a nationality; Jews could not integrate in their host countries; the solution to the Jewish problem must be based on a radical program of exodus by the Jews.[3] Yet another contention, strange sounding to our contemporary ears, was raised against Zionism from both the Liberal-Reform and the Orthodox wings: How could one expect Jews from Central and Western Europe to live in a state in which the Eastern Europe Jews *(Ostjuden)* would doubtlessly form the majority?[4]

German Jewish Orthodox reaction to Zionism were not, however, limited to these arguments. In this essay I will concentrate on two salient aspects: first, the collaboration between observant and nonobservant Jews, and second, the debate about the secular nature of Zionism that saw in Jewish nationalism the main vehicle of Judaism. In addition, I shall make some observations on an ambivalence toward Zionism that crystallized in Orthodoxy.

Collaboration between Orthodox and Non-Orthodox

The dispute between Orthodoxy and Zionism stirred anew the principal question of whether organizational collaboration was possible between observant and nonobservant Jews. On this issue three different positions had evolved in German Jewish Orthodoxy in the course of the nineteenth century. The first denied that any collaboration with the religious Reform movement was possible. The proponents of this policy had succeeded in various *Länder* (semiautonomous provinces of the German Reich) to enact a law of secession from the city community that enabled them to establish separate congregations in Germany. This movement was headed by Rabbi Samson Raphael Hirsch and his successors, the rabbis and leaders of the *Austrittsgemeinde* (seceding congregation) in Frankfurt am Main.[5] A more accommodating attitude was espoused by Rabbi Azriel Hildesheimer, a well-known leader with an influential congregation in Berlin. Although he advocated congregational separation, he nonetheless supported cooperation with other organizations such as Hovevei Zion (Lovers of Zion) and Jewish social and philanthropic umbrella organizations.[6] Those who opposed severing relations with Reform communities and organizations operated within organizations such as *Einheitsgemeinden* (United Congregations) and the *Gemeindeorthodoxie* (Orthodox congregation within United Congregations). The foremost leader of the latter group was Rabbi Mordechai Halevi Horovitz, the spiritual head of the Orthodox community in Frankfurt am Main.[7] Cooperation with all Jewish people was, in the view of this sector, not merely desirable but imperative.[8]

All three groups initially opposed Zionism. Over the years, however, those willing to cooperate in common Jewish causes grew more willing to recognize, and even support, Zionism. Eventually some even joined Zionist organizations, particularly the Mizrahi. Thus, while the first group described above did not waver in its opposition to Zionism, nor did some among the second, others in the second group and all in the third saw no obstacle to joining the Zionists. Most of the Mizrahi members and the other religious Zionists hailed from this camp.

Reaction to the First Zionist Congress helped consolidate a principal position in this respect. Criticizing the Zionists' comparison of their own times to the times of Ezra and Nehemiah, a writer in the *Israelit* observed that even if the events in the earlier era appeared to be the outcome of natural developments, they had been foretold by the prophets of Israel. The comparison was therefore not valid, and the writer argued that the response to the Zionists should be like that to the Samaritans, who had been told, "It is not for you to build a house of God together with us" (Ezra 4:3). The writer explained that the sages were aware of the dangers that could result from a refusal to cooperate, but he surmised, "We also know they would have abandoned Temple and land rather than permit their [the Samaritans'] participation in the Temple construction." Cooperation in itself was banned even when the goal was sacred. Thus, he concluded that, under the circumstances, "to waive the Temple and the land was preferable."[9]

During the following years the debate over Zionism continued. Not until 1904, however, did the Freie Vereinigung für die Interessen des orthodoxen Judentums (Free Association of Orthodox Rabbis) pass a resolution stating: "The precepts of the Mizrahi, as a party within Zionism, are irreconcilable with the fundamental principles of masoretic Judaism."[10] The timing of the resolution and its publication were no coincidence. The Zionist movement had taken roots, notwithstanding Theodor Herzl's death, and become an established fact. Moreover, after the Pressburg Convention of 1904, the Mizrahi became a worldwide movement, and its regional center for Central and Western Europe had been established in, of all places, Frankfurt. Ultra-Orthodoxy led by Rabbi Isaac Breuer, the rabbi of the *Austrittsgemeinde* in Frankfurt, perceived this development as an outright provocation.

Once the Mizrahi became a religious party within Zionism, one might have expected opposition to Zionism to relent. Quite the opposite occurred. The Mizrahi was perceived as another, even more dangerous incarnation of Orthodox cooperation with non-Orthodox bodies. It was thus no coincidence that the anti-Zionist resolution was aimed at the "collaborators," the Mizrahi, and was amended by detailed "clarifying comments" that pertain to the topic of our discussion.[11] The author saw the Mizrahi as another endeavor seeking common ground for unity and peace by compromise, an endeavor he believed was tantamount to heresy. While Orthodoxy was locked in a protracted struggle to prove that separatism was the only road to peace within Jewry, the Mizrahi, by joining the Zionist movement, made of itself a kind of alternative strand of Judaism. Herein this author finds lay the crux and fundamental difference between Orthodoxy and the Zionist movement.

The common characteristic of both movements was their bid to exclusivity. Both claimed to be the sole representative of authentic Judaism. Each refused to be a mere party within Judaism.[12] Each presented its development as continuing the struggle of Orthodoxy against non-Orthodox organizations in general and "Orthodox collaborators" in particular. The Mizrahi, for its part, perceived the resolution as nothing more than a reapplication of the old weapon, of "separation" from the sphere of community and organization, against Zionism and the Mizrahi.[13]

History fated a revealing affirmation to the respective attitudes of the adversaries. Two Orthodox congregations existed side by side in Frankfurt, though often with strained relations—the *Austrittsgemeinde* and the congregation that remained an integral part of the greater Frankfurt Jewish community.[14] The *Austrittsgemeinde* (Adath Jeschurun) became the stronghold of Agudat Israel, while the other Orthodox congregation became the stronghold of religious Zionism in Germany.

The Secular Character of Zionist Nationalism

On the surface it seemed, the attitudes of Orthodoxy and Liberal-Reform Jewry toward Germany and life in Germany appeared to be similar. Orthodoxy, too, was very eager to merge with the surrounding society, though mindful of guarding its religious uniqueness. Beneath this common façade, however, their difference of life-style produced quite different situations.

In the wake of emancipation and its consequences, Orthodoxy, like Reform, perceived Judaism as possessing a solely religious character. But it must be remembered that for the Orthodox religious laws shaped all aspects of everyday life, which was not the case for the Liberal-Reform sector. For Orthodoxy, Halakhah was the binding norm of conduct for the individual and the community alike. Practice of *mitzvot* and study of Torah, observance of the Sabbath and adherence to dietary laws, and, of course, refusal to enter into mixed marriages placed formidable barriers to social intercourse with the gentile environment. Orthodox Jews were therefore not very sensitive to the isolation foisted upon them by antisemitism. Sabbath observance precluded, *a priori*, advancement to higher civil or military ranks. Orthodox Jews were not merely inured to this condition, they were strengthened by it because it enabled them to derive deeply satisfying spiritual sustenance from their traditional environment at home and in their congregations, in their personal as well as public life.[15]

The Orthodox also drew the line at assimilation. Influenced by Rabbi Samson Raphael Hirsch's thinking, the Orthodox transformed Jewish nationalism into a transcendental idea. This kind of nationalism did not depend on physical possession of land or political sovereignty. In the view of Hirsch and his successors, the Jewish people were not destined to return to

Zion to attain political or national independence. The true return to Zion would be the creation of conditions that would enable the Jewish people to fulfill their noble destiny—living a life dedicated to Torah and *mitzvot*. In other words, statehood is not an end in itself but only a means to a loftier goal. The Torah does not exist for the state but the state for the Torah. The Torah, and the Torah only, makes the Jews a nation.

Important practical consequences result from these beliefs. Orthodox Jews were thus compelled to be loyal citizens of the state in which they reside until called upon by divine providence to fulfill their mission. This attitude served their civic and religious need well. It eased their adaptation to the prevailing political order and fortified them against the vagaries of the regime and its unstable attitude to the Jews.[16]

This attitude toward the state did not totally negate the idea of Jewish nationality. The concepts of "people" and "nation" were simply infused with meanings different from those accepted by the world around them. These meanings, which acknowledged identity as existing on two different levels, helped Orthodoxy come to terms with the specter of "dual loyalty."

Against this background we can understand how the secular nationalism of Zionism was perceived as the very antithesis of Orthodoxy's view. To Orthodoxy, civic responsibilities and patriotic feelings were rooted in the religious world; they were fundamental principles. Nationalism was secondary, whereas to Zionists it was the essence and foundation of Judaism. Jacob Rosenheim explained Zionism as follows: "In this manner a total inversion of traditional values takes place: what until now was regarded as mere means to an end becomes the object, and that which was formerly the object becomes the means."[17] Or, in Isaac Breuer's stinging language: "Zionism is the most terrible enemy that has ever arisen to the Jewish Nation. The antinationalistic Reform engages it [the Jewish nation] at least in an open fight, but Zionism kills the nation and then elevates the corpse to the throne."[18]

Herein lies the reason why Orthodoxy's fight against Zionism was at times more bitter than that against Liberal-Reform Jewry. To Orthodoxy, the debate with Zionism concerned the fundamental nature of Judaism. Both camps recognized the same values, but their interpretations and emphases were diametrically opposed. Orthodoxy understood such terms as "Jerusalem," "Zion," "Land of Israel," "Hebrew language," "redemption," "ingathering of exiles" as sanctified, often prefixing them with "holy," while Zionism used the terms literally, as pertaining to action in this world.

The dialectic confrontation with national Zionism brought about a consolidation of Orthodox national religious ideology. As far back as 1910 Isaac Breuer proudly proclaimed: "Jawohl, ich bin ein Nationaljude" (Yes, I am a national Jew).[19] He stunned his listeners with this provocative declaration, which was in fact a denouncement of the Zionists' right to carry the banner of Jewish nationalism. There was, in Breuer's view, an irreconcilable paradox embedded in Zionist ideology that defied the very laws of the

Torah, which made the Jewish nation what it was and thanks to which it continued to exist. "Thus Zionism is self-contradictory; it affirms and denies the nation at the same time."[20]

Against this background, we can understand the anti-Zionist notion that Zionism was a movement not so much denying religion as indifferent to it.[21] The "clarifying comments" to the resolution against Mizrahi asserted, "Zionism is a purely nationalist-racist movement without the least commonality with religion."[22] The logical conclusion was that the struggle against Zionism was more important than the conflict with Reform Judaism. The latter was by its own definition at least a religious movement, acknowledging the Jewish religion as central to its existence. Zionism however, was making it possible for a Jew to declare himself a heretic and still be "a good Jew."[23]

But in real life things were not that simple. When Orthodoxy opposed the Reform's assimilatory leanings regarding the Hebrew language, Jewish nationalism, and affiliation with Eretz Israel, it found itself allied with Zionism against the Reform.[24] A marked example of Orthodox-Zionist cooperation was demonstrated during 1905–08 in the South German province of Baden in the debate on the revision of the prayer book, mainly concerning the prayer on Return to Zion.[25]

The establishment of the Agudat Israel world movement was primarily designed to counter the Mizrahi. In this German Orthodoxy took a leading role. Jacob Rosenheim of Frankfurt, who until the end of his life served as president of Agudat Israel, stated in his inaugural speech that Agudat Israel was not a new movement but a resumption of the historical continuity interrupted during the emancipation. It was "a correction to Jewish history." Agudat Israel was not just a movement but "rather the revival of the ancient concept of *klal Israel*" (communality of the Jewish people).[26] Isaac Breuer, too, saw in Agudat Israel "*klal Israel* organized in the diaspora."[27] These and similar pronouncements contested the Zionist presumption that it represented the whole nation, in Herzl's words: "Zionism is not a party, . . . Zionism is the Jewish people on its way."[28]

As can be seen, even in its early years Zion was depicted not only as a secular movement because of its general character, its leaders, and supporters, but as a movement whose secular nature was an integral part of its ideology. Orthodoxy, on the other hand, did not denounce Jewish nationalism *per se*, provided it was accorded the appropriate place in time (by divine providence) and was instilled with the right religious spirit. Here Orthodoxy clashed with Zionism on all counts.

Ambivalence

The vigor of Orthodoxy's opposition to Zionism on both ideological and practical levels notwithstanding, voices supporting some positive aspects of

Zionism were not entirely absent. Approval was usually embedded in severe criticism, but the fact it was possible at all indicated a certain ambivalence. Zionism's positive contributions were said to be that it helped stem the tide of assimilation, it was an ally in the battle against Reform, and it was a step toward the return to Judaism. Let me give some examples.

Mendel Hirsch, the son of Samson Raphael Hirsch, concluded a fiery speech against Zionism by wondering whether it should not be regarded, after all, as a symptom of the longed-for change. Young Jews who had sought a distance from Judaism were suddenly proudly calling themselves Jews. This consciousness of Judaism could lead to a redemptive return. Hirsch concluded that the Orthodox should welcome the movement "through which the Almighty, in His ways beyond human grasp, leads His people to His purpose."[29]

The other example is furnished by Isaac Breuer, the grandson of Samson Raphael Hirsch. Breuer did not spare Zionism and the Mizrahi the sharpest criticism. But in eulogizing Herzl, Breuer revealed a warm esteem. He concluded his eulogy by exclaiming, "What a great Jew he could have been."[30]

Following the Balfour Declaration, Breuer's position underwent a significant change. In 1921 he wrote, "Agudaism assigns to the land of the Lord the status it deserves, because not only the people but also the land of the Lord should be ready for His awakening call."[31] Here he was expressing an attempt by the Agudah strain of Zionism to meet the challenge posed by the general Zionist movement. Not without reason did Jacob Levinger call Breuer the "Zionist fighting Zionism."[32] More important, Breuer's call for a historical activism for Eretz Israel constituted a radical departure from the accepted theories of Orthodoxy.

A more poignant expression was to be heard after the Nazis came to power in Germany in 1933. Returning from a visit to Palestine, Breuer declared in a public address that "Zionism was an instrument of God who used Zionism and Sabbath desecrators to start a historical process. It was up to Orthodox Jewry to channel the process in the right direction."[33] But Breuer worked in splendid isolation. His fellow leaders in Agudat Israel misunderstood and pitied him.[34] Yet his young Agudah followers revered him, and in him are the antecedents to the idea of the "third Yishuv" (generation of pioneering settlers) that began to take root among Orthodox youth under the Noar Agudati (Youth Organization). They negated the New and the Old Yishuv. True, the latter had the study of Torah to their credit, but it suffered from three important shortcomings. It did not constitute a socioterritorial entity, it was not productive in economic terms, and it took no part in the leading economic professions. The "third Yishuv" was to be the answer that was to combine the dynamism of the New Yishuv with the devoutness of the Old.[35]

At first the idea appeared to be unrealistic, but it triggered an important development. It opened the possibility of *aliyah* for observant youth, brought up on the ideology of Agudat Israel. This generation, following the generation that staunchly opposed Zionism, turned its energies toward the pioneering ideals of Zionism par excellence, the *kibbutz* movement. German Orthodoxy, which originated the *Torah im derekh eretz* (Torah way of life combined with worldly occupation) ideal, brought forth two Orthodox *kibbutz* movements: Hakibbutz Hadati and Poalei Agudat Israel.[36] This unexpected phenomenon seems worthy of a separate inquiry.

The tension between Orthodoxy's initial, relentlessly uncompromising opposition to Zionism on the one hand, and, on the other, the emergence of an ambivalent attitude, the daring reinterpretation of historio-philosophical processes that acknowledged secular Zionism's historical role as an instrument of divine providence, and finally the participation in the rebuilding of the Land of Israel are the stuff of which the mosaic of Zionism and Orthodoxy in Germany is made. Despite the space and time that distance us from the developments of German Orthodoxy reviewed here, the debate continues to reverberate with each succeeding generation.

Notes

1. *Israelit* 39 (October 11, 1898): 1460.

2. For the political arguments against Zionism commonly used by all Jewish strains in Germany, see Yaakov Zur, "Haortodoksyah hayehudit beGermanyah veyahasah lehitargenut yehudit velazionut (1896–1911)" (Ph.D. diss., Tel-Aviv University, 1982), pp. 336–50.

3. Ibid. pp. 343–48.

4. For examples, see Mendel Hirsch, *Der Zionismus* (Frankfurt a.M., 1898), p. 16; *Allgemeine Zeitung des Judentums* 61 (September 24, 1897): 461; and, in its most scathing form, Martin Philippson, *Neueste Geschichte de jüdischen Volkes* (Leipzig, 1910), 2:154.

5. On the *Austrittsgemeinde,* see Zur, "Haortodoksyah hayehudit beGermanyah," pp. 63–73 and the bibliographical comments, pp. 480, 342. See also the articles in English of three different opinions: Samy Japhet, "The Secession from the Frankfurt Jewish Community under Samson Raphael Hirsch," Isaac Heinemann, "Supplementary Remarks on the Secession from the Frankfurt Jewish Community under Samson Raphael Hirsch," and Jacob Rosenheim, "The Historical Significance of the Struggle for Secession from the Frankfurt Jewish Community," *Historia Judaica* 10, no. 2 (1948): pp. 99–146.

6. For Rabbi Azriel Hildesheimer and his public career, see the entry by Isaac Unna in *Jewish Leaders, 1750–1940,* ed. Leo Jung (Jerusalem, 1964), pp. 215–31. See also *Rabbi Esriel Hildesheimer: Briefe,* ed. Mordechai Eliav (Jerusalem, 1965).

7. See the entry on Marcus Horovitz by Unna in *Jewish Leaders,* pp. 249–72.

8. Zur, "Haortodoksyah hayehudit beGermanyah," esp. pp. 36–40, esp. p. 455. For a comprehensive view that idealizes the *Einheitsgemeinde,* see Alexander Adler, "Gemeindearbeit," *Zion: Monatsblätter für Lehre, Volk, Land* (Berlin) 4 (1932): p. 97: "But the *Einheitsgemeinde* is for us a Jewish religious goal . . . One God, one law, one people, and also one community."

9. *Israelit* (September 23, 1897): 1483–84.

10. The resolution was not published until 1905. Freie Vereinigung für die Interessen des orthodoxen Judentums, *Mitteilungen,* May 18, 1905, p. 3. See also Jehuda Reinharz, *Dokumente zur Geschichte des deutschen Zionismus, 1882–1933* (Tübingen, 1981), pp. 73ff.

11. Erläuternde Anmerkungen zu der von der Rabbiner-Kommission der "Freien Vereini-

gung" gegen den Zionismus angenommenen Resolution, Freie Vereinigung, *Mitteilungen,* May 18, 1905, pp. 4–29.

12. Ibid., p. 29.

13. Jacob Feuchtwanger to Ephraim Adler, June 23, 1905, in the private collection of Adler's grandson, Ephraim Adler, in Tirat Zvi.

14. In 1938 Nazi legislation forced the unification of the two communities. See *Dokumente zur Geschichte der Frankfurter Juden, 1933–1945,* ed. Kommission zur Erforschung der Geschichte der Frankfurter Juden (Frankfurt, 1963), pp. 256–57.

15. Moses Auerbach, in *Jeschurun* 4 (1917): 626–28.

16. Mendel Hirsch, *Der Zionismus* (Frankfurt a.M., 1898), p. 15.

17. Jacob Rosenheim, *Augsewählte Aufsätze und Ansprachen* (Frankfurt a.M., 1930), 2:104.

18. Isaac Breuer, *Judenproblem* (Halle, 1918), p. 89.

19. Isaac Breuer, *Lehre, Gesetz und Nation* (Frankfurt a.M. [1910?]), p. 37.

20. Ibid. p. 38.

21. Ibid., p. 39. See also *Jüdische Presse* 34 (January 30, 1903): 49.

22. Erläuternde Anmerkungen, p. 13.

23. Ibid. pp. 13ff.

24. Zur, "Haortodoksyah hayehudit beGermanyah," p. 352; see also p. 585, nn. 352–54.

25. See Moshe Unna, *Lemaan ahdut veyihud* (Jerusalem, 1975), pp. 31–37.

26. Agudas Jisroel, *Berichte und Materialien* (Frankfurt a.M., [1912 ?]), pp. 18, 63. On the reciprocal effects on Zionism and the Mizrahi following the founding of Agudat Israel, see Yacov Zur, "HaMizrahi veAgudat Israel bashanim 1911–1914: Zikot gomlim veimutim," in *Bishvilei hatehiyah C,* ed. Mordechai Eliav (Ramat-Gan, 1988), pp. 59–78.

27. Isaac Breuer, in *Jüdische Monatschefte* (Frankfurt a.M.,) 1 (December 1913): 29.

28. Theodor Herzl, "Protestrabbiner," *Die Welt* 1, no. 7 (July 16, 1897).

29. Hirsch, *Zionismus,* pp. 27ff.

30. *Israelit* 45 (August 1, 1904): 1294–96. Modechai Breuer, Isaac Breuer's son, attributed the eulogy to his father.

31. Isaac Breuer, *Die Idee des Agudismus* (Frankfurt a.M., 1921), p. 5.

32. Jacov Levinger, "Hazioni halohem bezionut," in *Sefer Barukh Kurzweil,* ed. A. Saltman, M. Z. Kaddarj, and M. Schwartz (Ramat-Gan, 1975), pp. 151–68.

33. Isaac Breuer, *Jacob Rosenheim, Erez Jisroel und die Orthodoxie* (Frankfurt a.M., 1934), p. 5.

34. Isaac Breuer, *Weltwende,* ed. Mordechai Breuer (Jerusalem, 1979), pp. 31–32.

35. *Hajischuw Haschlischi, Bundesleitung Noar Agudati* (Frankfurt a.M., March 1934), p. 11.

36. Yacob Zur, "Tenuot hanoar hadatiyot beGermanyah bashanim 1933–1939," paper presented June 7–10, 1987, Lohamei Hagetaot, Haifa University, pp. 6ff.

Zionism and Orthodoxy

A Marriage of Convenience

I

When Jewish nationalism arose, rival ideologies did not succumb to it. They engaged instead in a sharp polemic through which their own positions became more fully elaborated and well defined. Nor did the whole nationalist movement concentrate upon the primary objective of national sovereignty. Numerous nationalist factions emerged, each insisting that its goal was most important and all others secondary.

As no party enjoyed unquestioned, continuous, and universal dominance in the Jewish community, each was forced to compromise with others. The Zionists, for example, bore primary responsibility for building the Jewish national home in Palestine. But they were able to rely on substantial assistance from many non-Zionist factions in the community, and they were ready, within limits, to define their specific, immediate objectives in a way that made such cooperation possible. On the other hand, the Chief Rabbinate and Israel's plantation settlements were institutions derived primarily from non-Zionist sources, to which Zionists lent conditional support and cooperation.

Competing ideologies *within* the Zionist movement also had to cooperate with one another. The difficulties of achieving national sovereignty for Jews in a country where they were at first a tiny minority made even the most extreme political Zionists regard sovereignty as an *ultimate* goal, to be approached by stages. This plan opened the way for other Zionists, concentrating on nationalist cultural or social and economic aims, to enlist general *immediate* support for these objectives.

Cultural, social, and economic aims, usually subordinate in national liberation movements, are the primary concern for humanitarians, social reformers, and social revolutionaries. Owing to the anomalies of the Jewish position, *all* Jewish ideologies since the eighteenth-century Enlightenment had to define cultural, social, and economic as well as purely political aims and adopt humanitarian reform or revolutionary rather than purely civil, political methods. This necessity caused not only Zionism but all modern Jewish ideologies to assume a character distinctly different from comparable movements among other peoples.

For most of the nineteenth century, Jewish responsiveness to a nationalist solution of the Jewish problem was effectively blocked. Pious traditionalists regarded the history of Jewish suffering as a penance to be lovingly borne until the messiah brought redemption, and they suspected any proposal for active efforts by Jews to end the exile as heretical. Modernists who favored action to end Jewish disabilities and improve the social and economic positions of Jews had other reasons to reject nationalist ideas: the contention that Jews were a separate nation was used as an argument against their emancipation by antisemites throughout Europe. Thus the nationalist revivals Jews observed around them did not give birth to a significant parallel movement of Jewish nationalism. Individual thinkers in the West developed a Jewish nationalist doctrine, and some traditionalists saw messianic portents in the nationalist uprisings of the time, but no historically effective movement arose until disillusionment with gentile liberalism set in among Eastern European modernists. Under Eastern European conditions in the last quarter of the nineteenth century, secular-nationalist views were held not only by individual eccentrics but grew to be broadly characteristic of a definable group, the *maskilim*: traditionally trained young intellectuals living mainly in the Pale of Settlement, who had acquired some general European culture, usually through their own, unaided efforts, and who wrote or read modern Hebrew literature.

Criticism of the traditionalist community by the enlightened Hebraists was savage from the beginning and remained so well into the twentieth century, long after Zionist sentiments dominated Hebrew literature. Eastern European *maskilim* castigated traditionalist superstition and rabbinical tyranny as violently as any Western Jewish modernist had done. In addition, they vehemently condemned oppression of the poor and weak by the rich and powerful in the community—a theme not stressed to the same degree in Western Jewish Enlightenment literature. On the other hand, since the 1870s Eastern European writers had little occasion to paint in glowing Hebrew phrases the benevolence of enlightened monarchs and the amiable disposition of gentile society toward Jews who acquired enlightenment, themes that constantly recurred in the Jewish Enlightenment in the West.

From the early 1870s, some Eastern European *maskilim* not only stressed themes different from those of their counterparts in the West; they also accused their counterparts of undermining Jewish solidarity and threatening Jewish survival by submitting unreservedly to gentile standards. One may cite as an example Moshe Leib Lilienblum, who became a culture hero for Eastern *maskilim* because of his battle with the traditionalists over issues of religious reform during the 1860s. He sharply rejected any comparison of his views with those of American and German Reform Judaism and attacked them for their discarding of the concepts of a personal messiah and the restoration to Zion, for their innovations in the synagogue ritual, and for proposals to abandon the rite of circumcision and shift the sabbath to

Sunday. His contemporary, Peretz Smolenskin—in a short story first published in 1867 concerning enlightened young Jews who fought in the Polish rebellion of 1863—deplored the pointless sacrifice of Jewish lives in other peoples' quarrels. Smolenskin's critical and journalistic essays took on an increasingly sharp tone against Western Jewry for renouncing the hope of a national return to Zion and, above all, for abandoning the Hebrew language and culture.

Opposition to *both* the Western modernists and Eastern traditionalists, the major antagonists in the Jewish debates of their time, gave the *maskilim* of the Pale at least a negative sense of their special group identity; their commitment to modern Hebrew literature gave it a certain positive content. Nevertheless, neither this group nor others who have been described as "proto-Zionists"—for example the sponsors of a movement for Jewish settlement in Palestine in the 1860s—thought of themselves as a tight ideological formation, bound together in a broad opposition to rival viewpoints on the whole range of issues relating to the Jewish problem. But the shock of the pogroms of the 1880s produced just this sort of transformation among many of the *maskilim* of the Pale. Joining those traditionalist and modernist Westerners who remained committed to the project of Jewish settlement in Palestine, they formed a new ideological position in the culture of modern Jewry. The idea of resettlement in Zion as the solution of the Jewish problem remained the central belief of a new, distinct ideological group.

This group united Russian-trained Jewish intellectuals, modernist *maskilim* who combined a self-taught European culture with traditional schooling, and some of the Orthodox laymen and rabbis who had long been involved with the project of resettlement in Zion. For the Russified intellectuals, their conversion to nationalism was an effect of the pogrom trauma, which shattered fully and finally their reliance on gentile liberalism and Russo-Jewish enlightenment. What they felt was, first and foremost, sheer revulsion against attitudes they had previously shared.

The Hebrew *maskilim*, who had distrusted the assimilationist attitude even before the pogroms, also experienced the pogroms as a severe emotional shock; but it produced not so much a conversion as a radicalization and politicization of their previous attitudes. Their views on all the cultural, social, economic, and political issues current among Eastern European Jews were no longer voiced as a form of marginal dissent on particular points but were now expressed as a distinct group identity. Opinions on specific issues therefore had to flow organically from a common nationalist ideology, which remained to be positively articulated.

Traditionalists who became Zionists suffered no trauma because of the pogroms. The direct and empathetic pain experienced was certainly no less for them than for other Jews. But they needed neither intellectual nor emotional reorientation to cope with it, for such trials and troubles were part of the familiar pattern of exile. That modernist Jews now became nationalists gave them new hope, for they saw this shift as a return of the prodigals to positions they themselves had long occupied.

A Zionist grouping thus emerged as a major ideological component of the Jewish community. Not all who joined it shared every position implied or expressed in the common program, as defined at a given moment, and many who would not join nevertheless sympathized with particular Zionist viewpoints. The varied initial composition and leanings of the group were favorable to divergent definitions of the nationalist aims from the outset. Such divergencies, crystallized by the critical experiences of successive Zionist generations, resulted in a variety of ideological factions, each devoted to a particular national purpose it held to be most essential.

II

The essential ideas of practical Zionism (as well as the strategy and tactics of political Zionism) were anticipated by proto-Zionist enthusiasts. However, agricultural settlement in Zion was an issue largely confined to the traditionalist community. The issue was debated in traditional eschatological terms and confined mainly to such questions as the order of messianic events and the role of religious commandments relating to the Holy Land. Non-Orthodox Jews took little or no interest in such esoteric debates, and, even among the Orthodox, these matters did not become an independent axis of ideological division. The traditionalist community, especially in Palestine, was driven by many conflicting attitudes and opposing interests built into its institutional structure: Sephardim and Ashkenazim, *hasidim* and *perushim*, and one *kollel* against another. The question of resettling Jews on farms in Zion was a secondary issue, cutting across these major factional cleavages: one could find supporters and opponents in almost every camp.

At most, one might say that in general the proto-Zionists, of all camps, represented voices of innovation and radicalism in the Old Yishuv, and the representatives of vested interests were generally sensitive to this menace. But the innovators did not become a cohesive, militant group possessed of *esprit de corps*. They usually sought prior authorization from the establishment for their projects. If they adopted a more rebellious tone and were attacked by the dominant clique with the customary polemical zeal, the conflict often reflected older, long-standing rivalries, primarily unrelated to their proto-Zionist position.

Thus, the controversies over proto-Zionist farm projects divided the Old Yishuv along lines of tactical advantage rather than strategic principle. There were, nonetheless, certain contentions, traditionally formulated but objectively related to the nature of the problem, which recurred in the arguments made on either side. Some issues were highly practical. Supporters argued that agricultural settlement would serve to refute charges that the Yishuv was made up of demoralized paupers. Opponents argued that Jews could not succeed as farmers under Palestinian conditions and that the promoters were leading their followers into financial and personal disaster. Other issues were more far-reaching. Supporters held that the restoration of a self-sustaining community in Palestine was a direct religious duty and believed it would rehabilitate the Jewish people, purging the corruption and averting the dangers afflicting them in exile under modern conditions. Opponents held that only the specific commandments tied to the Holy Land— the temple service, agricultural tithes, offerings, sabbatical years, and so on—were religious duties and that it was positively risky to live in Zion because of the inherent difficulties, or the religious disqualification, of the modern Jews for performing these observances. The only safe way was the traditional, total dedication to study and prayer, whose purifying effect was undeniable. Agricultural colonization not only multiplied the risks of transgression, intentional or otherwise, but diverted men and support from the purely devotional life, as already practiced in the Old Yishuv.

From the 1880s on, however, the movement for farm settlement in Palestine was no longer confined to traditionalist circles, though they continued to play a major role. The participation of modernists, even secular nationalists, raised new issues and presented the old ones in a new light. The result was the crystallization of firm ideological positions dividing the Yishuv in new ways.

One problem implicit in this development was the question of pious Jews associating with nonbelievers or religious liberals in the same community. On this issue, some of the traditionalist circles most prominent in the Old Yishuv had already declared themselves decisively in Europe. The *kollelim* of Hungary, Holland, and Germany were recruited in good part from partisans of so-called *Trennungsorthodoxie* (separatist Orthodoxy). Only yesterday they had fought successfully at home for the right to secede from the liberally inclined general Jewish community and set up a separate, officially recognized Orthodox community. The rise of a New Yishuv, led by avowed secular nationalists, evoked the characteristic response of separatism and avoidance and gave a new, more ideological edge to the old arguments against innovators. Under this pressure, traditionalist Zionist settlers had to define their positions on two fronts: they had to defend in the Old Yishuv their collaboration with nonbelievers, and in the New Yishuv they had to fight for the interests of Orthodoxy.

The issues of avoidance or cooperation with nonbelievers in the national movement and of the religious evaluation of their work in the Holy Land— whether one should condemn it as a profanation and menace or praise it as a consecration, a meritorious act of messianic import—continued to be debated among traditionalists. But they matured as fully developed, opposing ideological positions only after the British occupation.

The young Zionist radicals who arrived in Palestine from the 1880s on were few in number and a minor part even of those actively involved in the new movement. Others who were traditionally committed to the maintenance of the Old Yishuv now extended their support to the migrants who wished to go to Palestine in their flight from Russia. A large number of emigrants came, too, from the same pious circles that were the base of the Old Yishuv and were moved by the same sentiments. Others (as in Rumania) simply found in Palestine an accessible haven of refuge from the mounting pressures at home: among them, some were impecunious drifters, and some, individually or by clubbing together, hoped to invest their savings in Palestine and seek their livelihood there.

These were motives not unknown to the Yishuv and its supporters in earlier days. The disputes they gave rise to, however sharp their occasional expression, had been contained within the familiar limits of a pragmatic consensus: quarrels grounded in different versions of common religious principles were not allowed to undermine traditions of mutual aid that enabled one part of the community to expect and another to extend material support in times of hardship and oppression. But the implicit assumptions of the new, secular Zionists, given explicit form in the ideological writings of Moshe Leib Lilienblum, Leon Pinsker, and others, posed a new challenge for both the traditionalist and modernist establishments—a challenge that was accommodated within a pragmatic consensus only after protracted, repeated encounters.

III

The immigrants to Palestine were a mixed company, reflecting the diverse composition of the diaspora movement from which many were drawn. What they had in common, in distinction from their predecessors in the Old Yishuv, was a new perception of the meaning of *aliyah* to Eretz Israel—one in which escape from acute oppression in Russia and Rumania and vague, as yet undefined hopes to rebuild their lives on a new basis, free of the chronic anomalies of diaspora conditions, played a prominent part.

Within this broad area of consensus, a wide variety of divergent ideological leanings characterized the immigrants. These differences, relatively muted among the early Rumanian settlers, began to rise more ominously among those from Russia. Some were simply impoverished refugees who fled from hardship in their homes; they exerted no ideological pressure on communal institutions beyond posing the problem of providing for their support and integration. Others were relatively well-to-do settlers, many of them religiously traditional, particularly close to the modernizing elements in the Old Yishuv. Still others were of a more secular bent. The student-organized Bilu group (very few of whom actually came to Palestine) formed a third element of young radicals who played a significant part in the ideological battles of the First Aliyah.

The pogrom refugees who gathered in the Austrian town of Brody in the summer of 1881 compelled the Jewish public to face the problem of directing, as well as assisting, the flow of migrants. In the following year, continuing pogroms, arson, and anti-Jewish government policies increased the stream of refugees. Some, responding to lively agitation in the Jewish press by pro-Palestine advocates, now pressed on to Odessa, or further to Constantinople and Jaffa. There the penniless among them created a relief problem similar to that of the refugee throng in Brody—which some pro-Palestinians hoped, indeed, would force Western Jewish philanthropists to aid resettlement in Palestine. Those settlers who expected to invest in land or trade and commerce usually made an effort to explore the possibilities before moving from Europe. Others joined the thousands of uprooted Jews wandering aimlessly around the streets of Jaffa.

When a similar mixed multitude had accompanied the sectaries who formed the Old Yishuv in earlier years, the communal leaders could only urge that immigrants lacking a specific religious commitment be discouraged. The early Zionists were no less embarrassed by the uncommitted mass who flocked to Palestine with no clear prospects or objectives, but they could not simply take the position adopted by the traditionalist leadership. They were carrying on a heated debate in the contemporary press with opponents who advocated America rather than Palestine as the preferred haven. Thus the spectacle of a dependent refugee population in Jaffa undercut the philo-Zionists' argument. They had to prove that Jews could be successfully established on the land or in urban trades and industry in Palestine: for them, success or failure was a critical test of an ideological position, not simply a humanitarian issue.

With the founding of Rishon Lezion, two new elements in the Yishuv's institutional history made their appearance: the new settlers were led by nationalist *maskilim*, and their project was based in Jaffa rather than Jerusalem or Safed. They thus detached themselves from the influence of the traditional establishment. Petah Tikva and Rosh Pina, resettled by an infusion of new immigrants in the same year, remained tied to the Old Yishuv in spite of the difficulties of their relationship.

IV

In the Zionist organization reconstituted by the genius of Theodor Herzl, all the old Zionist views, together with the new political Zionist ideology, were brought within the framework of a disciplined body committed to action. In this setting ideological differences, if they survived, had to be organized in the form of factions. Eventually such factions did emerge. The ideological positions by which they were defined often paralleled the alternative positions abstractly outlined during the long, many-sided debate with Ahad Haam.

Hovevei Zionism in 1897 consisted of three elements: first, a dwindling popular base, increasingly traditionalist and conservative in character, still organized in residual groups in Eastern Europe and the immigrant colonies in major cities abroad; second, disgruntled intellectuals, once consolidated to a degree by Ahad Haam but now organized mainly in the form of Eastern European student societies in Western universities; and third, leadership groups in places like Odessa, St. Petersburg, Berlin, London, Paris, and New York, who gave modest support to Palestinian colonization, in cooperation with influential, non-Zionist, Western Jewish philanthropic agencies. Herzl's new organization absorbed all three elements, but not completely, nor all at once, nor without incurring the growth of an internal opposition. The reports of the First Zionist Congress aroused a lively response among the popularly based local organizations. Herzl enjoyed the immediate and lasting support, not to say adulation, of rank-and-file Hovevei Zionists. The rise of political Zionism not only restored the enthusiasm of the existing groups and brought old members back to action, but extended the movement's ranks far beyond the old limits. At the same time, the old societies represented vested interests: even those who did not question the new views and loyally supported the new activities did not so easily submit to the discipline of the new organization in local matters.

Student Zionists were among the most enthusiastic participants in the First Congress. They had been urging the convocation of a new Zionist assembly to revive the movement in the years before Herzl appeared, and some of them took an active part from the beginning in Herzl's preparations for the congress. But they were also fully conscious of their status as veteran Zionists, with a longer, more intimate knowledge of the movement's aims than Herzl possessed. Committed as they were to Herzl's leadership, they were also responsive when Ahad Haam launched a caustic attack upon Herzl's methods. They, too, felt uneasy about Herzl's autocratic and adventurous tactics and his shallow disregard of cultural Zionist concerns. They were increasingly disturbed by the implied total suspension of colonization in Palestine while Turkish authorization and international support by European powers were fruitlessly pursued. They were prominent among the first factional opponents of Herzl, and, before the end of his brief, galvanic leadership, they established a formally organized party of dissent.

The most resistant to the enticement of Herzlian political Zionism were the leadership groups of Hovevei Zion who conducted the movement's Palestine activities and maintained the contact with non-Zionist philanthropic agencies. They had a vested interest in the existing resettlement efforts that Herzl attacked vigorously; they had a vital stake in good relations with the Western philanthropists who, by rejecting Herzl's overtures, had made themselves his most immediate foes. Nevertheless, political Zionism was a direct expression of the mystique of autoemancipation, which had made most of them—especially the Russians—into Zionists in the first place. Eventually many became active in the World Zionist Organization (WZO) and, through their leadership in the local, countrywide organizations, exercised a powerful influence in the congress. At the end of Herzl's career, such men, too, were prominent in the organized opposition to his policies.

Herzl's attitude toward Zionist parliamentary politics was every bit as odd and equivocal as one might expect in the founding father of so improbable a liberation movement. His strategy for securing a Jewish state did not require a parliament as an instrument of policy. His analysis indicated that the keys to success were financial power and imaginative diplomacy: by offering on behalf of a "society of Jews" to solve Turkey's fiscal difficulties, he might obtain a charter for a "Jewish company" to colonize Palestine; by offering to remove excess Jews from areas of severe antisemitism, he might obtain the support of European powers. Both objectives, he at first assumed, could be most effectively pursued if he could persuade the powerful Jewish philanthropists to adopt his plan and establish the necessary instrumentalities. Only when the Rothschilds and Hirschs rebuffed him did he resort to a popular movement. He now regarded the World Zionist Organization as his society of Jews, the platform for his diplomacy, and he expected the WZO to establish the Jewish company in the form of a bank (funded by popular subscription, if wealthy financiers failed him) to serve as his financial instrument.

Herzl was well aware, of course, that constructing the Zionist Congress in the likeness of a Jewish parliament was his decisive historic achievement. But this form of organization presented certain immediate tactical difficulties. He could only build his diplomacy on the base of the congress if it appeared firm, united, powerful, and reasonable in its social as well as its political aims. Herzl could achieve this public effect at the congress only by applying all his skills to control the inherent tendencies of a popular movement toward impulsiveness, factionalism, indecisiveness, and irrationality. His task, as he saw it during the First Congress, was to perform in public "an egg dance" upon the following array of eggs, visible only to himself, the performer:

1. Egg of the *N. Fr. Pr.* [*Neue Freie Presse*, the Viennese newspaper on which he was employed], which I must not compromise or furnish a pretext for easing me out.
2. Egg of the Orthodox.
3. Egg of the Modernists.
4. Egg of Austrian patriotism.
5. Egg of Turkey, of the Sultan.
6. Egg of the Russian government, against which nothing unpleasant may be said, although the deplorable situation of the Russian Jews *will* have to be mentioned.
7. Egg of the Christian denominations, on account of the Holy Places. . . .
   Egg Edmond Rothschild.

Egg Hovevei Zion in Russia.
Egg of the colonists, whose help from Rothschild must not be queried, *tout en considerant leurs miseres*.[1]

With such a view, even while he proclaimed the Zionist Congress a Jewish forum where at last the Jewish problem would be raised for free, frank, and public discussion, Herzl could not welcome unrestricted debate, let alone the organization of factions. He counted it one of the benefits inherent in the Zionist movement that it made room, for the first time, for the whole range of current ideologies within a Jewish consensus; but he was firmly convinced that Zionists should wait until the state was founded before organizing in rival political parties.

Herzl's attitude toward Orthodoxy—in his eyes, the Jewish analogue of clericalism in a Christian state—manifested the same conservatism and aristocratic sophistication. It goes without saying that traditionalist Judaism could make no claim on one's private belief, but it deserved to be publicly respected and cultivated as a bulwark of popular loyalty to the national cause. The power and magnificence of the "courts" of hasidic *zaddikim* fascinated Herzl. His diaries refer repeatedly to the "Wonder Rabbi of Sadgora" as he speculated about the possible uses of the rabbis in creating and sustaining the Jewish state. Herzl was equally interested when he believed he had penetrated behind the pious facade to the shrewdly cynical tactics by which these clerics maintained their power and even when he had to deal with clerical politicians at the Zionist Congress. His comments then show none of the contempt and anger with which he assailed the motives of other Zionists who, at one time or another, obstructed his aims. They reveal instead a tolerant, if amused, appreciation.

Thus, if Herzl would have liked to prevent the emergence of a religious Zionist faction, it was not, as with socialism, because he thought one of the functions of Jewish nationalism was to serve as a substitute for religion. He simply wished to eliminate from the congress debates any issues that could divide the Zionist camp and divert attention from the political objectives he considered primary. This emphasis did not mean, of course, that Herzl ignored political crosscurrents that affected the course of his policy, whether in the Jewish community at large or in the narrower confines of the Zionist movement. He was, in fact, sensitive to the smallest maneuvers of friend and foe alike; and, in his efforts to impose his own view, he frequently found useful allies in the Orthodox Zionists.

Orthodox leaders from Russia and Poland had no reason to share the anti-Zionism of Western "protest rabbis," who feared that a Jewish congress might produce an impression of "dual loyalties" or suggest a "state within a state," thus imperiling civic emancipation. The rabbis from Eastern Europe were no less interested than the secularist Zionists in strengthening the internal discipline and autonomy of the Jewish community—under their own control, of course. They had even less faith in, or desire for, social integration among the gentiles; and they had been lending practical support to Jewish settlement in Zion since long before secular Zionism arose.

Fifteen years of cooperation with secularists in the Hovevei Zion movement had led the rabbis from Eastern Europe to develop new ideological distinctions. They now accepted, and adopted as their own, a "pure Zionism" that went beyond the religious proto-Zionism of the 1860s by seeking both an economic solution for Eastern European Jewish emigrants and the political conditions for such a solution in Palestine. They rejected, on the other hand, the new cultural Zionism represented by Ahad Haam and his followers. These distinctions were sharply focused in the preliminary conference held in Warsaw by the large Russian delegation on its way to the Second Zionist Congress in Basle.

Despite Herzl's reluctance, the cultural question continued to be discussed at the Zionist congresses and regularly produced disputes between the Orthodox and cultural Zionists. As nothing significant was done by the world Zionist movement in spite of the resolutions adopted, the Orthodox Zionists remained reasonably satisfied with the situation. But proponents of Zionist cultural programs were seriously discontented, and their position was an important factor in the growing opposition to Herzl.

As the diaspora conducted an ideological debate over the issue of culture and religion, significant developments of immediate practical effect took place in Palestine. Local needs and local initiatives rather than the policy of nationalist leaders abroad brought about a critical advance in the revival of spoken Hebrew and a major development of secular Hebrew education under the direction of nationalist pedagogues.

Despite the restricted Jewish influx from Europe in the later 1890s, internal growth and new settlers from other Ottoman regions and Muslim areas, together with travelers who overstayed the legal term, continued to expand the Yishuv's institutional structure. The old-style schools among the Ashkenazi and Sephardi establishments expanded, and immigrants from North Africa, Syria, Yemen, and remoter Asian territories set up their communities and schools on traditional lines. Access to the modernizing influence of Western Jewish philanthropists was available in schools maintained by the Alliance Israélite Universelle, the Austrian Israelitische Allianz, and the Anglo-Jewish Association. After the Hilfsverein der deutschen Juden was founded in 1901, it embarked on a vigorous campaign to rival the French Alliance Israélite Universelle as a sponsor of Jewish education in Palestine. In the Western-supported schools, foreign languages and other secular studies supplemented the core curriculum of traditional Jewish religious studies; in most cases, the schooling provided was limited to the elementary requirements for self-support as an artisan or trader at the existing stage of economic development in Palestine. These schools provided an opening for some nationally minded, Hebraist teachers, especially in the Hilfsverein schools.

Zionism implied a commitment to broader, more ambitious objectives. In the absence of responsibility for institutions comparable in scale to those of the Old Yishuv or the Western philanthropists, proponents of cultural Zionism were free to develop far-reaching plans for education in the spirit of secular nationalism. Their militant activists insisted on Hebrew as the language of instruction not simply in Jewish studies but in all subjects, including the most technical—a proposal that implied an extraordinary, deliberately accelerated development of a language that had been confined to very narrow uses for centuries. They envisaged a program of retraining in the schools that aimed not only to make self-supporting artisans or tradesmen out of indigent, dependent Jews but to transform every aspect of their character and lives, which were held to be degraded by centuries of oppression in exile. The new Hebrew-speaking Yishuv was to be based on productive working farmer families rooted in the soil. They were to be free and proud soldiers if need be and possess a broad liberal culture as well as an intimate understanding and creative mastery of the Hebrew heritage. Eretz Israel was to be transformed socially as well as economically by their dedicated labors.

Steps to implement this secular national vision aggravated existing tensions and provoked the protagonists of traditional Judaism, especially among educators and rabbis, not only to sharper opposition but also to rivalry by emulation.

A hard line of total avoidance and excommunication was the primary and most salient but not the exclusive response of the traditionalist Ashkenazi establishment to the challenge of modernist education. In one sector of the growing Yishuv—the new rural settlements—they undertook to compete with the modernists on the same ground. As a consequence of this rivalry, there were recurrent clashes between protagonists of secular, nationalist schooling and the conservative adherents of the old ways of Ashkenazi religious education in the villages. Younger settlers often welcomed the free spirit introduced by Zionist schoolteachers, forming social bonds with them and looking to them for what they felt was needed for their children as they began to form families. Among the older settlers, who considered the lifestyle that attracted the young to be libertine and impious, the radical Zionist teachers and young workers were seen both as dangerous to religious tradition and provocative to the Ottoman authorities and the Arab milieu. They looked to the Old Yishuv for the kind of elementary instruction that would implant traditional culture and loyalty in the settlements. Jerusalem supplied rabbinical support, including *halukah* grants to a small number of settlers, and provided the teachers for such settlements as Petah Tikva and Ekron as well as for the conservative faction in other settlements. Old-style classes were maintained in such villages in competition with the secular-nationalist schooling that was being slowly and persistently developed by Zionist teachers.

The area of competitive struggle spread to those sectors in the cities where a growing middle class included some who desired for their children the advantages of modern schooling in a developing market economy but feared the seduction of religious license. The issue was forced by the rise of secondary schools in Jaffa, Jerusalem, and Haifa in the early twentieth century—particularly by the foundation in 1906 of the Hebrew *gymnasium* (or as it was later called, the Gymnasia Herzliya) in Jaffa.

Postelementary education, primarily oriented toward vocational training, had earlier been provided by Western-sponsored schools in Jerusalem. These institutions were avoided by the Jerusalem Ashkenazim and served primarily the needy among Sephardi boys and girls in the city. Modern-minded, Zionist-inclined teachers on the staff of Western-supported schools successfully urged the German Hilsverein to build a teacher's seminary in Jerusalem when it began its work in Palestine in 1903. By that time, tolerance for such schools within recognized limits was accepted throughout the diverse Jerusalem community.

V

The Old Yishuv, which had maintained its opposition to the First Aliyah, had little if any connection with the Second, whose radical secularism was utterly repellent. Even so, modernization encroached even on traditionalism, and these extremes of Palestine Jewry came into occasional contact. The rapid growth of the Old Yishuv in Jerusalem severely strained the resources of the *halukah*, and the establishment, as well as the populace, had to seek other ways for sustaining the community. There was a large expansion of building, in which *halukah* funds as well as private capital were invested. There were traditionalist rabbis who encouraged young men to learn artisan crafts or settle on the land. The Bezalel School turned out skilled craftsmen, especially among the Sephardi and Yemenite communities, and stonecutters and other construction workers were recruited from the Old as well as the New Yishuv. There was also a flow of migrants from Jerusalem to Jaffa or the colonies, where they came into the orbit of the New Yishuv.

At these margins of growth, Second Aliyah workers, as well as others in the New Yishuv, came into limited—and often problematic—contact with the traditionalist community. The Poalei Zion in Jerusalem organized a printers' union in 1908, which went out on strike for better wages and conditions. It met not only with a rabbinical ban, due to its antireligious stance, but with opposition from both the Jerusalem intelligentsia and the Jaffa leaders of the New Yishuv. The strike ended without success after eleven days. There were somewhat more effective points of contact of the Second Aliyah activists with some Sephardim and Yemenites. The Sephardi upper class, from the beginning, had cooperated with Ashkenazi modernists, both philanthropic and nationalist, and was also a major liaison between them and the Ottoman authorities. Both native-born Sephardim and Sephardi immigrants could be found among all urban and rural work sites of the Second Aliyah. They were valued as an element adapted to Ottoman and Palestinian practices and thus more likely than the young Ashkenazi "idealists" to persist as laborers in the villages. The Yemenites, who began to arrive in larger numbers at the beginning of the Second Aliyah, were held in special regard for the same reason.

The extension of effective Ottoman control into Yemen at this time gave Zionists an opening to encourage a larger worker immigration from this region. In 1911, the WZO Palestine Office and Hapoel Hazair sent Shmuel Yavneeli to Yemen, posing as an emissary of the *halukah* and equipped with recommendations from the Jaffa rabbi, Abraham Hacohen Kook. The sharp increase of immigration that he stimulated was settled with official Zionist and Hapoel Hazair help in the plantation villages, where it became a permanent part of the work force.

VI

The new dominance of Zionist agencies in the postwar Yishuv, like the Palestine Executive of the WZO, presented a special problem to the leaders of the Old Yishuv, especially the Ashkenazi traditionalists. Instead of repressing the modernists who dissented from or disregarded their long-standing authority, the Zionist agencies now had to cope with modernists who were successfully exercising their authority over the Yishuv. The war, in the meantime, had greatly altered the terms in which they could respond to this scandalous challenge. The community in the Holy Land and the Eastern European traditionalist Jewries were left broken and weakened, but now channels of influence and power were opened to traditionalists in the West. These developments encouraged new methods for resisting the modernist threat.

Within the traditionalist ranks, German and Hungarian Orthodox leaders rose to the fore, bringing with them their doctrine of Orthodox separatism. Implied in such a policy was always a separate, direct relationship to gentile authorities distinct from that of other Jews. This arrangement could easily lead to rivalry for political precedence—a competition in which German Orthodox leaders had considerable success in relation to their country's occupation policy in Eastern Europe during World War I—or to a claim to be the exclusive legitimate representative of all Jews.

German-Hungarian modern Orthodoxy involved two attitudes quite foreign to Eastern Europe. It combined separation from the liberal-dominated Jewish religious community and acculturation to secular gentile standards of legitimacy. Eastern European Orthodoxy, by contrast, re-garded the whole Jewish community, its sinners as well as its pious, as an in-tegral whole—one, to be sure, in which traditionalists were accustomed to exercise dominant authority. The notion of Orthodox separatism was in-herently repellent to the Eastern European traditionalists even though their involvement in the Zionist movement, through Mizrahi, had introduced them to a similar notion of parallel religious and secular organization in the limited field of culture and education. As for the contacts of Jews with gen-tile authorities, Eastern European Ashkenazim traditionally preferred to keep these to a minimum.

The new situation in Palestine, however, with secular Zionists asserting communal authority under sanction of the government, required new, mod-ern tactics, and the German-Hungarian Orthodox provided both leaders and the tradition of an active, separatist political approach. The Old Yishuv's Ashkenazim split under these pressures. A right wing, mustered under the banner of Agudat Israel, which took up the battle with Zionism along the entire ideological front, eventually plunged into conflict on the central, constitutional issues. This change in the political constellation arose and gradually developed out of clashes concerning the organization of the rabbinate and the whole communal structure of the Jews in Palestine in-spired by the new political situation and legal institutions introduced by the British.

No matter how modestly formulated, the essential Zionist political ideal involved establishing a self-governing community of all Jews in Palestine. To build toward this end from the existing forms of communal autonomy was always feasible as an immediate Zionist objective, under Ottoman as well as British rule. One method of approaching this task would be to unite the congregations, the *kehillot* and *kollelim*, which, as already noted, had splintered the traditional community. With so large a proportion living in the holy cities as an act of devotion, the communal organization of much of the Old Yishuv was strongly related to ritual functions. This connection meant far greater weight for rabbinical than lay authorities and far less im-portance for officers in contact with gentile authorities than was required in the diaspora. As a result, the inherent antihierarchical tendency of Jewish tradition was driven to manifestly unreasonable lengths, or so it seemed to those responsible for contacts with the non-Jewish administration. Accord-ingly, in Ottoman times several abortive attempts were made to unite the main Jewish religious communities, often on the initiative of Sephardim. Zionists, especially those of Ahad Haam's circle who laid such stress on communal consensus, naturally took the same attitude; from 1913 to 1915, successive attempts, initiated by Menahem Ussishkin's visit to Jerusalem, were made to unite the congregations in the holy city.

These efforts were taken up again when Chaim Weizmann arrived in 1918 as chair of the Zionist Commission and, with considerably greater authority, by Sir Herbert Samuel, upon assuming the office of high commissioner. Under the pressure of the Palestine administration and its new Jewish officials, a rabbinical assembly was convened in 1921, which elected a rabbinical council with lay participants. The new council assumed the official responsibilities granted to the Jewish millet in Ottoman times: exclusive jurisdiction "in matters of marriage and divorce, alimony and confirmation of wills of members of their community other than foreigners"; jurisdiction in other matters of personal status, if all parties to an action consented to it; and jurisdiction in regard to "the constitution or internal administration" of charitable foundations established under Jewish law before rabbinical courts. The council exercised its power as a court of appeal superior to local rabbinical courts, and the government undertook to enforce such rabbinical judgments with respect to "members of their community." At the rabbinical assembly, too, the office of Haham Bashi, a Sephardi monopoly in Ottoman times, was superseded by electing two Palestine chief rabbis, one Sephardi and the other Ashkenazi.

These innovations were not adopted without opposition. Some Ashkenazi traditionalists in Jerusalem boycotted the rabbinical assembly, refusing to accept any hierarchical principle and subordinate their own courts to the judgments of a rabbinical court of appeal. It should be noted moreover, that unlike the Muslim courts, which retained from Ottoman times their jurisdiction over all Palestine Muslims, the official rabbinical authorities were granted jurisdiction only over "members of their community," adherence to which was voluntary. The Ultra-Orthodox, in rejecting the rabbinical council's appellate jurisdiction, thus implicitly opted out of this community. This dispute soon became involved with a larger quarrel over the creation of a general Jewish community organization, in which rabbinical courts were only one major function. The implicit separatism of the traditionalist right wing became in this context an explicit separation.

In Ottoman times, Zionists made repeated attempts to unite the Yishuv in a country-wide secular organization. Ahad Haam worked toward this end during the crisis years of 1899–1900, leading to a general conference of the new settlements. In 1903 Ussishkin organized the enrollment of two thousand Jews in the towns and villages and convened an elected assembly. When this body collapsed owing to the Uganda conflict, the main Zionist and professional organizations of the New Yishuv established a self-appointed council. All these efforts, as well as subordinate activities (like the network of Jewish arbitration courts) or partial organizations (like the regional federations of villages and the agricultural unions) that developed in the Second Aliyah had one common characteristic: they were essentially confined to the New Yishuv or to parts of it. The new postwar situation produced a radical change: Zionists now approached the task of country-wide community organization as self-evidently including the entire Jewish population of Palestine, old and new settlers alike.

Conferences were convened in November 1917, as soon as the British had successfully occupied areas of Jewish settlement, in order to organize the Yishuv and prepare its postwar demands. But it was intended to create a body of elected representatives of the entire Yishuv, in the whole area of Palestine; and the British did not renew their offensive and occupy the areas of the northern settlements until a year later. Further delay was caused by the long process of peace negotiation, upon which the definition of the Jewish position depended. Hence, elections for the Yishuv's constituent assembly were not held until April 19, 1920 (except in Jerusalem, where communal riots caused further delay), that is, on the eve of the San Remo agreement to allocate the Palestine mandate to Britain. The elected assembly finally convened only in October 1920, after the new civilian high commissioner, Sir Herbert Samuel, was well settled in the country.

During this period immediate issues were dealt with, in the name of the whole Yishuv, by preliminary conferences, assemblies, and a provisional council. The questions that arose, like the political structure of the community and its share in the British military effort and security arrangements in Palestine, were treated as matters of more than local concern. Postwar demands advanced by the Yishuv's spokesmen included far-reaching authority claimed for the Jewish people as a whole, not only in the development of the national home but in the current administration of the country.

Demands like these were dropped by the WZO leadership upon the insistence of the British; as a result, the competencies of various bodies concerned with the Jewish national home had to be separated. Zionists were explicitly denied any share in the Palestine administration. The WZO, recognized as representing world Jewry, was authorized to cooperate with the administration primarily in regard to the development of the national home. Under the circumstances the proposed general organization of the Yishuv, in spite of a continuing major interest in broad political issues, had to find its specific functions in the remaining open field: the administration of essentially local concerns.

But this, too, was a matter conceived by the mandate government far differently from the pattern envisaged by leaders of the New Yishuv. The latter thought in terms of a community organization that would be a nucleus of national autonomy even when the Yishuv represented a small minority. It would function on the same federal principle of the Austrian Social Democratic nationalities theory, which was adopted by Jewish nationalists in Eastern Europe, with the difference that in Palestine the Jewish community came to desire not merely "personal" (exterritorial) but "territorial" autonomy. Their scheme envisaged a general organization to which all Jews belonged and paid taxes compulsorily and that undertook "municipal" responsibilities like defense and economic welfare as well as specifically cultural functions. The British, on the other hand, were predisposed to favor a form of voluntary religious association for Jews, with restricted ritual and charitable activities, as in England. British Jews like Herbert Samuel understood, of course, that under the rubric of a voluntary religious community Jewish tradition included a far wider range of functions than did a Protestant tradition, even in episcopal England. Moreover, they took as their guide the status of an Ottoman millet enjoyed by Jews and other sects before British occupation; this model provided greater, more extensive authority for the proposed communal organization than it had in England. Nevertheless, their conception was fundamentally different from the Yishuv's idea of a proto-national organization, since it built the community primarily on the base of its religious activities and, hence, of clerical authority.

In view of these differing conceptions, it took seven years before regulations for the Jewish community were adopted in a form acceptable to both the Yishuv and the government. In February 1926 the Palestine *Official Gazette* published an ordinance, called the Religious Communities Organisation Ordinance, 1926, permitting "each Religious Community recognised by the Government," in the exercise of its autonomy for internal affairs, to "make, vary or revoke" its own regulations, which, with the approval of the Colonial Office, would be recognized by the Palestine government. At the end of 1927, such regulations were gazetted for the Jewish community.

While general in its terms, the Religious Communities Organisation Ordinance was applied by Jews alone and to some extent reflected their demands. The community organization, though based on voluntary membership, unlike the Palestine Muslim community, was nonetheless conceded a juridical personality and the right to levy enforceable direct "contributions" on its members. There was a considerable reduction of the clerical dominance characteristic of the millet, the model initially favored by the Palestine administration. The original proposals of the New Yishuv leadership had entirely neglected religious functions of the community, thus evoking indignant protest from the already established rabbinical council. In the gazetted regulations the rabbinical council and local rabbinates were incorporated into the general community structure, and the articles relating to them were granted pride of place, preceding other items in the document. One result was to raise questions of general community authority in regard to the election and budgets of religious officers.

Dissatisfaction with such newfangled arrangements had already been manifested by traditionalists during the organization of the rabbinical council. Even more rancor was aroused by the regulations for the new general community organization. Some who had accepted the reorganized rabbinical institutions now opted out. The major source of irritation for them, as for other groups whose interests were affected, were the proposed methods of election to the new governing bodies.

With their political background of Eastern European radicalism, the radical Zionist leaders could think of none but the most uncompromisingly democratic procedures as appropriate for electing the Yishuv's representative institutions. It was obvious to them that elections should be "general, direct, equal, secret, and proportional." Moreover, recent experience, not only in the Zionist organization and the community organizations of Central and Eastern Europe but in some local communities of the Old Yishuv, proved that most of these principles had wide acceptance. "Equal" electoral rights, however, were a subject of dispute among traditionalists in every Jewish community, as they raised the issue of woman suffrage.

The exclusive prerogatives of men in the synagogue and their unquestioned dominance in community affairs were grounded in scriptural and rabbinic texts as well as in traditional practice. But there was, as always, ample room for differences of interpretation; and there were traditional scholars who argued in 1920 that woman suffrage was not only permissible but commanded in the Torah. The Ashkenazi right wing in the Yishuv arose in passionate indignation against such ideas. It was mainly this issue that crystallized their opposition, to the point that they made common cause with Agudat Israel in an outright attack on the legitimacy of the new community in formation.

The proposal of woman suffrage had been raised as early as 1902 in Ussishkin's attempt to organize the community and was then dropped in the name of unity. It was pressed after the war by newly founded women's organizations and by liberal and left Zionists. By successive stages, the emerging community approved, first, women's right to vote and, then, their right to be elected. On this basis the first elected assembly of Palestine Jewry, including women delegates, was eventually chosen by equal franchise in April and May 1920. But during two years of debate preceding this conclusion the issue had opened ideological fissures that threatened to separate traditionalists from other Jews and Orthodox Jews of various degrees of rigor among themselves.

Among the Orthodox Zionists of Mizrahi, opinion was divided on the questions of principle: some favored woman suffrage without reservation, a few were totally opposed, and an intermediate opinion thought tradition sanctioned women's voting but not holding office. Apart from principle, Mizrahi had to consider its role as representative and protagonist of traditional Jewry. This role required a united front of all Orthodox Jews *within* the emerging general Jewish community. In Jerusalem, at any rate, the Agudat Israel, under the leadership of Hungarian Rabbi Isaac Sonnenfeld, had already adopted a position of principled separatism; when the Jerusalem community united and elected a local committee, the Agudah position had attracted a part of the Ultra-Orthodox Ashkenazim, who joined in their dissident congregation. Mizrahi's position on the issue of suffrage had to consider the likelihood of similar developments in regard to the emerging country-wide Jewish communal organization.

Orthodox attempts to reverse the decision in favor of woman suffrage began in 1919, as soon as it was made. The Ultra-Orthodox Jerusalem

Ashkenazi faction ran separate elections, excluding women, for the first elected assembly and obtained validation of the results at a ratio of delegates to voters double that in the general election. The Ashkenazim then demanded that the assembly take up as its first order of business the repudiation of woman suffrage and, when this demand was rejected, suspended their participation.

Thereafter complicated negotiations took place over the participation of the Orthodox in subsequent assembly sessions, with Mizrahi seeking to gain concessions on both sides. Having succeeded at any rate in making woman suffrage problematic through negotiation, they sought in vain to persuade the ultras to continue the fight within the communal organization. By 1925, the community leadership bowed to the Orthodox demand that the abolition of woman suffrage be taken up by secret vote as the first business at the next session. The assembly, however, indignantly repudiated its chair's agreement, and Mizrahi was sharply attacked as hypocritical in view of its present support of women's voting rights and its participation in the WZO, where woman suffrage was fully accepted.

Mizrahi at this point withdrew and set up a separatist community, with the participation of rightist Ashkenazi Orthodox groups and some Sephardi and Yemenite groups, but, upon the refusal of the Palestine Zionist Executive to grant recognition to the new body, it was abandoned. Nevertheless, the community leadership again had to yield to one of Mizrahi's demands, and approval was gained for a referendum on the woman suffrage issue, though not, to be sure, a referendum of men alone, as Mizrahi had proposed. This victory, however, was rejected by the Orthodox ultras, who refused to participate in any referendum. The elections for the second assembly were soon to be held, and Mizrahi had to make its decision. On November 1, 1925, it announced its unqualified participation in the community elections and stated that its aim in proposing a referendum had been solely to keep other Orthodox Jews in the community, as Mizrahi itself had always taken part in conferences with women delegates participating.

Such a positive position on a controversial question crystallized an ideological division among Orthodox Jews whose lines, in any case, had been firmly drawn on the other side by the Agudat Israel. When the draft regulations of the Jewish community were published in 1922, the Agudah had written to the high commissioner refusing "to be subjected in any way . . . to the Jewish National Council." Their consistent separatism, already evidenced in the refusal to be part of the united Jerusalem community or the new rabbinical council, was put on a precise ideological basis: the draft regulations were unacceptable because they were "a solemn proclamation of the deposition of God and the Torah as sovereigns of the Jewish Nation." Failing to persuade the high commissioner or the Colonial Office to reject the proposed regulations and replace them with a substitute draft recognizing the Torah, interpreted in standard rabbinical codes, as the community's fundamental law, Agudat Israel took other measures. It appealed, together with other Ashkenazi ultras, to the League of Nations, claiming that the draft regulations of the Jewish community violated the freedom of conscience of its members and demanding recognition as a separate community. This request was denied them by the British, but the Orthodox right wing continued as an organized separatist entity outside the community. It maintained a direct opposition to the community's claims of legitimacy, in spite of occasional cooperation in specific matters of common concern. Mizrahi, within the general Jewish community, had to develop its policies under constant pressure and criticism from these Orthodox rivals on the outside.

VII

The history of the Yishuv stood in an odd, inverse relation to that of Jews in Europe during the interwar period. The political revolution and economic turmoil that followed World War I produced an immediate upsurge in the resettlement of the Yishuv.

After World War I Palestine became a major destination, and in the early Hitler years, the foremost destination of Jewish emigrants; the Yishuv steadily rose to the proportions of a major Jewish community. Solid Zionist traditions and a strong Hehalutz organization remained important factors in the disproportionate share of Poland and Russia (so long as emigration was permitted) in the influx to Zion. Upon Adolf Hitler's rise to power, Zionists responded to the challenge with a rapid, massive expansion of their organized activities in Germany, too. But the movement to Palestine during the interwar years was also based firmly on the general, unorganized stream of Jews ejected by oppressive local conditions.

With such massive immigration, in which young age groups and unmarried males were disproportionately represented, the Yishuv as a whole was strongly weighted in the young, economically productive, child-bearing population strata. Also owing to immigration, which came primarily from Europe and the Americas rather than Africa and Asia in the interwar period, the preponderant Ashkenazi section of the Yishuv rose on the whole; and among Ashkenazim those elements constituting the New Yishuv greatly outgrew the Old.

But, of course, the New Yishuv itself was far from uniform. The proportion of newcomers drawn respectively to the cities, plantation villages, and labor settlements, or representing various specific diaspora backgrounds, generations, and political leanings, was not necessarily the same as in the already settled Yishuv. The difference challenged the absorptive capacity of the Yishuv's already established institutions and produced pressures for innovation and change.

The institutions created by European Jews in Palestine had from the beginning developed in relative isolation from the local environment. Protection by European consuls had enabled the Ashkenazim of the Old Yishuv to live detached from the Ottoman regime. The settlers of the New Yishuv developed their colonies by avoidance of the Turkish government; and their relations with older communities in Palestine, not only Arabs but Old Yishuv Jews, ranged from remote neighborliness to guarded hostility. Even the various different types of Zionist settlers pursued their several paths in diverging directions, so that the New Yishuv, too, grew up as a set of compartments, separated and considerably insulated from one another.

By the 1930s the trend had turned to much interaction of the sections of the Yishuv, Old and New alike. The overarching institutions sponsored by the mandate regime and by the Jewish Agency, the sheer growth of the Yishuv, and the common problems of contact with Arabs forced greater integration of the distinct communities inspired by partisan ideologies. The Yishuv, still wrestling with the problem of coordinating its contending established elements, had simultaneously to fit into its emerging pattern the flood of immigrants or revise the pattern to fit their divergent needs.

The Zionists of the New Yishuv gradually absorbed and unified diverse, independently sponsored services in the course of developing a general Jewish community. At the same time Zionist parties based on divergent social ideologies gained new scope for expression. Partisan political ideas and interests were pursued not only through the governing councils of the community but in the whole construction and functions of its service institutions.

The earliest source of such division was Mizrahi. The major condition demanded by the religious Zionists for working within the WZO was support for autonomous Orthodox cultural institutions, at least until the whole movement could be won over to full acceptance of Orthodoxy. In 1914, when Zionists took on major responsibilities for education in the wake of the language dispute with the Hilfsverein, the Mizrahi school, Tahkemoni, was also brought into the network of Zionist-supported schools. Mizrahi education expanded together with other Zionist schools under the mandate; continuing on the lines established before the war, religious Zionist schools formed a largely autonomous section under the general supervision of the Vaad Leumi's education department. Moreover, all the extensive activities of the new Chief Rabbinate became closely associated with the religious Zionist party. Agudat Israel and other ultra-traditionalists boycotted this section of the secularist-dominated Jewish community organization.

The Mizrahi precedent regarding education was followed after World War I by the Labor Zionist movement. Labor Zionists, too, created autonomous institutions within the Zionist-supported school system supervised by the Vaad Leumi's education department. Like Mizrahi, the Zionist workers accepted curricular standards set by the general Zionist educational program for general studies and Hebrew culture but added special requirements of their own: Mizrahi schools devoted a fourth of their hours to the traditional rabbinic texts in addition to intensive study of the Bible required by the general curriculum. Labor schools devoted the same proportion to scientific and vocational training for labor and the development of attitudes and indoctrination of ideas appropriate to workers, according to the version of socialism favored in one or another workers' settlement. Commitment to the special purposes of Mizrahi and Labor schools was further strengthened by party control over the administration and teaching staff of the respective schools. Supervision by the nominally superior central body was mainly indirect and limited to general subjects in the curriculum.

The Labor Zionists were motivated in part by the same considerations that made Mizrahi insist on autonomy. Their ideological position, going to issues of basic social philosophy, seemed to them to require freedom to determine their own subjects and methods of study and to maintain a staff committed to their point of view; subordination to the general system had to be limited to matters of general Zionist consensus. But there was in addition a special motivation that activated the Labor drive toward autonomy. In their schools, and in all other aspects of their broad-gauge activity, the Zionist workers believed themselves to be building a new, organized society. What primarily concerned Mizrahi was the need to protect children from demoralization by a secular, general education. The socialist workers had similar apprehensions about bourgeois values in the general schools, but this concern was secondary. They were mainly motivated by their commitment to start afresh, autonomously, in every sphere of human activity.

What was equally characteristic of all Zionist factions that shared in the work of Palestine was the concentration on a particular function, or approach, which each, according to ideology, singled out as centrally important to the success of the entire Zionist enterprise. Religious Zionists devoted themselves to the regeneration of traditional Judaism through the creation of a self-regeneration of traditional Judaism through the creation of a self-sustaining Orthodox settlement of pious Jews in Zion. Cultural Zionists hoped for a revival of the national ethos through Hebrew language and literature, based on a solid Jewish society in Zion and constituting a value system that would restore Jewish creativity and active solidarity throughout the diaspora. Labor Zionists hoped, in two different versions, for a revolutionary restoration of the Jewish people as an active historic entity: Hapoel Hazair, through the construction of a Hebraic, populist, cooperative farmer-worker society, healing the corruption of the Jewish urban ghetto by striking new roots in the ancestral soil; the Poalei Zion, and especially Ahdut Haavodah and the dominant Histadrut leadership, through the concerted, centrally directed, voluntary commitment of all workers in Palestine to the creation of a new Jewish nation out of the constructive achievements of the new Jewish working class. All of them—Mizrahi, Hebraists, populists, and socialists alike—were convinced that the functions they alone were carrying out were the key element of the solution of the Jewish problem for all Jews, and all expected that the social forms and institutions they were creating as partisan ideologies would ultimately encompass the entire, redeemed Jewish people in Zion.

What emerged from these diversely single-minded, ardent efforts was a highly pluralistic society. The Jewish people in Palestine shared a common ultimate perspective only because and insofar as it was not clearly focused. Only by concentrating their rival, absolute ideological claims on limited, immediate tasks that could be pursued side by side were the jostling parties saved from frontal clashes.

The decade of the 1930s brought Hitler and the unspeakable tragedies of European Jewry, which placed Palestine under a pressure of Jewish immigration beyond anything imagined before. The Yishuv and the WZO faced political, social, fiscal, and technical tasks incomparably greater than anything in their earlier experience and unprecedented anywhere. The political trials that accompanied these challenges were an even greater strain, under which the established structure of the national home cracked, buckled, and shifted, but held firm and found new strength.

Notes

1. Theodor Herzl, diary, August 24, 1897, *The Complete Diaries of Theodor Herzl*, ed. Raphael Patai, trans. Harry Zohn (New York and London, 1960), 2:578–79.

Zionism and Its Religious Critics in Fin-de-Siècle Vienna

In the spring of 1882 a fascinating encounter took place in Vienna between the leading spiritual authority of Austrian Jewry, the Moravian-born Adolf Jellinek, and his Russian-Jewish visitor, Leon Pinsker, one of the chief leaders of Hibbat Zion (Love of Zion). Their dialogue, first published by Jellinek in three installments in *Die Neuzeit*, the communal organ of the Viennese *Kultusgemeinde* (religious community), delineates many of the core issues that would divide Zionists from anti-Zionists at the turn of the century as well as the gulf separating Central European from Russian Jewry.[1] Its importance as a historical document derives not only from the stature of the protagonists but also from the lively directness of the repartee and the unimpeded view it permits us of different Jewish responses to the Russian pogroms of 1881—that watershed in European Jewish history which first set the Eastern Jewish masses in motion. Although religion, as we shall see, was only one (and by no means the most important) component in the opposition that Jellinek manifests toward Pinsker's Jewish nationalism, it undoubtedly provided a legitimating framework on which later critics in the *fin-de-siècle* period could build.

Dr. Adolf Jellinek was the leading *Prediger* (preacher) in Vienna during the era of liberal emancipation and assimilation, which in 1882 had reached its peak and (unknown to most of its leading protagonists) would soon begin a slow but steady decline. Almost everything in Jellinek's background might be said to have predisposed him to reject the philosophy and practice of modern Zionism. Since the 1840s he had espoused a liberal, universalist interpretation of Judaism under the influence of the *Wissenschaft des Judentums* (Science of Judaism), one that led him to favor assimilation as a natural and positive corollary of the fight for Jewish emancipation. Moreover, as his passionate articles during the 1848 revolution in Austria reveal, he had a long-standing, powerful identification with German cultural nationalism.[2] For Jellinek as for many acculturated Austrian Jews of his generation, it was axiomatic that freedom and progress for Jews were identical with the freedom and cultural-political hegemony of *Deutschtum* (Germanness) within the Hapsburg Empire.[3]

At the same time Jellinek believed in something very close to the notion of a Jewish messianic mission as it was propagated by German Reform Judaism. In the spirit of the Mendelssohnian Enlightenment, he glorified Judaism as a beacon of intellectual progress and moral elevation for the nations. Despite, or perhaps because of, its dispersion, Israel continued to proclaim, in his eyes, the unity of humankind and of creation on the foundation of morality, justice, and truth. The monotheistic faith of Judaism was destined to be the religion of the future, the new *Weltreligion* (world religion) with its tidings of peace and reconciliation to all of humanity. It proposed a cosmopolitan vision of the Third Temple, beyond divisive confessionalism and open to all races and social classes.[4]

Despite this universalist world view, Jellinek did not deny the importance of *Stammesbewusstsein* (tribal consciousness) or of a halakhically based particularism in Jewish life. Nor did he favor the striking out of all reference to Zion in the prayer book as advocated by the more radical Reform Jews in Hungary or the German-speaking lands. He preferred instead a classically Viennese form of compromise between the exclusivist insularity of Eastern European Orthodoxy and the somewhat bloodless universalism of Westernized Reform Judaism. While eager to acknowledge the "tribal peculiarities" and the genius of the Jewish *Volksgeist* (national spirit), Jellinek was careful to emphasize, as early as 1869, that Jews did *not* have any national characteristics as such but "thanks to their universalism they adapt and absorb qualities from the nations in whose midst they are born and educated."[5]

By the early 1880s, Jellinek and the lay leaders of Viennese Jewry had, however, to face two major challenges to their faith in liberal emancipation—first secured in Austria under the *Grundgesetz* (fundamental law) of 1867. The immediate domestic threat was the rise of a new racial antisemitism that had come to Vienna from Berlin—previously the fountainhead for Austrian Jews of *Aufklärung* (enlightenment), *Wissenschaft* (scholarship), and high culture. It coincided, moreover, with the Russian pogroms of 1881, provoking a massive migration of Jews from the East to the West, which passed across the Austrian border and necessitated the cooperation of many international Jewish philanthropic organizations. This exodus inspired the rise of the Russian Hibbat Zion movement, advocating emigration to Palestine, and a new Jewish nationalism that soon found an echo in Vienna among Jewish university students.

Pinsker's *Autoemanzipation!* (1882), written in German as "an appeal to his People by a Russian Jew" was the ideological crystallization of this profound crisis in Russian Jewry. The pogroms had turned Pinsker away from his earlier faith in assimilation toward the view that Jews must acquire an independent territory and emancipate themselves *politically* as a nation. In his revolutionary pamphlet, Pinsker provided a stark, pitilessly clinical examination of the Jewish condition, emphasizing both the failure of liberal emancipation and the intractable nature of Jewish homelessness in the *galut* (exile). The Jews, he insisted, had become the target of universal hatred. They were eternal aliens "who can have no representatives because they have no fatherland." Furthermore, Pinsker stressed that legal equality should not be confused with *social* emancipation. Even in the West, he observed, "the Jews are far from being emancipated from their exceptional social position." Pinsker's pessimistic conclusion was that not humanity nor enlightenment nor civic emancipation would raise the Jews in the esteem of the nations until they had acquired a home of their own, on their own soil and under their own sovereignty.[6]

Such conclusions could not fail to shock Jellinek and other representative figures of liberal Western Jewry bent on social integration. Yet they were already evident in Pinsker's dialogue with Jellinek in Vienna, which occurred several months *before* the actual publication of *Autoemanzipation!* and clearly made a considerable impression on the Viennese rabbi. The explicit aim of his middle-aged Russian visitor as reported by Jellinek was to create the nucleus for a Jewish political nation—"a fatherland, a homeland, a small piece of earth on which we can live like human beings!" The Jews must have a commonwealth to free themselves from the torment and persecution of the Russian Pale and also to show the nations that "we have not degenerated but that we are a race of indestructible vitality, gifted and capable of founding a state, not matter how small."[7]

Jellinek emphasized that Pinsker had completely lost faith in the victory of liberty, fraternity, and equality, the ruling ideas of the Enlightenment. He expected nothing from the Teutons, the Slavs, or the Latin peoples. His doctrine, thus he told Jellinek, was based on "our great teacher Moses" and on his exodus from Egypt to prepare the newly liberated people for the conquest of a land where they would become a free and independent nation. This was the only dignified reply to the enforced vagrancy imposed by the European nations and their rulers, especially the Russian tsar. Needless to say, Jellinek was astonished that "the same man who studied in Leipzig and lived in Heidelberg and Berlin" should now promote such outlandish ideas, at least from the standpoint of an emancipated, cosmopolitan Viennese Jew. To accept Pinsker's propositions would be to deny his [Jellinek's] entire past and to retract all the sermons he had delivered over more than three decades. "Since the days of Moses Mendelssohn and particularly since the great historic revolution in France," Jellinek began his reply,

the Jews have sent out their best men to fight for their recognition and equality in the European states, and they have marshaled their intellectual resources in numerous writings, on the speaker's platform, and in the pulpit for the lofty goal of emancipation. Have they done all this in order to abandon, in this year of 1882, everything they have achieved, to give up all they have fought for and won, to declare that they are aliens, people without a homeland or a fatherland—or, as you put it, vagrants—and, the wanderer's staff in hand, to set out for an uncertain new fatherland? No! That would mean to accept the view of our implacable foes who deny that we have any true patriotic feelings for Europe. In fact, we are not even capable of doing this. We are at home in Europe and regard ourselves as children of the lands in which we were born and raised, whose languages we speak, and whose cultures make up our intellectual substance. We are Germans, Frenchmen, Magyars, Italians, and so forth, with every fiber of our being. We have long ceased to be true, thoroughbred Semites, and we have long ago lost the sense of Hebrew nationality.[8]

Jellinek pursued his argument by counseling patience. Jews could not reasonably expect to "conquer within a single century the prejudice against their faith and their descent that has been harbored and fostered for such a long time." Not even a century would suffice to gain full civil rights in all European states. Concerning Pinsker's theory of Judeophobia as a hereditary disease of the gentiles, Jellinek retorted that a child of Russian parents born and raised in London was "more likely to become a member of the Mansion House Committee" [i.e., to protest against the pogroms] than an admirer of Jew-baiting Russian Cossacks. Whereas Pinsker pointed to the ravages of the "scientific" antisemitism disseminated by the highly civilized German nation on the Russian people and its national spirit, Jellinek overconfidently declared that "this poisonous plant that has sprouted on the banks of the Spree will wither away more rapidly than you assume, because it has no roots in history."[9]

Jellinek insisted that he has been deeply distressed by the sight of Russian Jewish children on their way to Jaffa by way of Vienna.[10] But for him this was no reason for the Jews to "establish a small state outside Europe *à la* Serbia or Rumania, whose existence would be [dependent upon] a strategic move by one great power against another and whose future would be very uncertain." He preferred to place his trust in the feminine compassion of "the Danish princess who is occupying the throne of Russia" and of the crown princess of Prussia, who "has not disowned her English homeland." The Jewish problem in Russia was admittedly a serious one. But its roots lay in the excessive Jewish concentration in certain provinces, districts, cities, and towns and their imposed lack of social and professional mobility. Large-scale, prudently planned, and well-organized emigration was the answer, but to a free country rather than to Turkish Palestine—described as "an oriental semi-Russia, where the open hands of the pashas smell of Russian leather, where property is rendered insecure by brutal hordes, and religious fanaticism is heated up by the rays of an oriental sun."[11]

Interestingly enough, nowhere in this dialogue did Jellinek use specifically *religious* arguments to invalidate Zionism. He did not criticize the purely *secular* character of Pinsker's proposals, nor did he claim that they are contrary to the essence of the Jewish religion. There was no suggestion that Zionism contradicted the messianic promises of divine redemption, although there was an implication that it conflicted with the loyalty of the Jews to their adopted European fatherlands. On the other hand, it was self-evident for Jellinek (as it was for liberal rabbis in Austria, Hungary, and Germany) that Jewry was a *religious* and not a national community and that any self-conscious mode of Jewish nationalism would constitute a parochial retreat from the universalist Jewish mission of *Weltbürgertum* (world citizenship).

Not surprisingly, the reaction of Jellinek and other Viennese rabbis to the activities of Kadima, the first Jewish nationalist students' fraternity, founded in the Austrian capital in 1883, was particularly sharp. The students of Kadima fully identified with Pinsker's argument that Jews were organically incapable of assimilation, that their efforts at fusion were in vain, and that only the creation of a Jewish nation on Jewish soil would bring antisemitism to an end.[12] Indeed, along with Peretz Smolenskin, Leon Pinsker can be considered as the chief ideological inspiration of Kadima and was elected as an honorary member at its first official meeting on May 5, 1883.[13]

The Jewish religious establishment was particularly offended by the open appeal of Kadima students for the "regeneration of the Jewish nation" and by the patriotic cult of the Maccabees that constituted the annual climax of fraternity meetings at the end of each year. The Maccabees were celebrated for having conducted a liberation struggle against foreign oppression and for their military valor, their self-sacrificing idealism, and their uncompromising defense of Jewish national identity.[14] For Jellinek, this nationalistic reinterpretation of the ancient religious festival of Hanukah was unacceptable and obnoxious. Judaism, he emphasized, did not celebrate the deeds of individual heroes, nor did it idolatrize prowess in war.[15] The cult of military glory and victory in battle were profoundly un-Jewish—arguments that would be used by Jellinek's successor, Rabbi Moritz Guedemann, at the end of the century in his polemics against Theodor Herzl's political Zionism. According to Jellinek, the students of Kadima had introduced a "neo-pagan" element into Judaism, distorting its pure ethical monotheism in the spirit of secular nationalism. He distrusted the militant "love of Zion" and the new gospel of self-reliance for its exaggerated emphases on the primacy of the Jewish *Volk* as the true subject of history. Jellinek was not without sympathy for efforts to revive the glories of the Jewish past in order to strengthen Jewish self-respect in the present, but he did not accept the activist, *this-worldly* interpretation of the messianic hopes of Jewry adopted by the Zionists.[16]

Nor could Jellinek regard the Zionist interpretation of antisemitism as anything but a counsel of black despair. Pinsker's ideology was above all a symptom "of the pathological conditions in Russia" and could have no universal lessons for Western Jewry.[17] Though Jellinek was by no means complacent about the dangers of the new racial antisemitism that was developing in Germany, Austria, and Hungary (indeed some of his analyses were most perceptive), he did not believe in the militant response of the students of Kadima and continued to have faith in the protective hand of the Habsburg state. Jews were "Austrians through and through," dynastic patriots who believed in the integrity of the empire, in the firm rule of Kaiser Franz Joseph and his ministers, and in the black-and-yellow national flag "that extends over all the kingdoms and lands, tribes, and nations" that made up the Danubian monarchy.[18] Within this multinational mosaic, all forms of national chauvinism were detrimental to Jewish interests, including a self-assertive form of Jewish nationalism.

The Maccabean celebrations of Kadima held in Vienna in December 1891 inspired Jellinek to make his position on this issue even more explicit:

There is no Jewish nation. The Jews form, it is true, a separate stock [*Stamm*], a special religious community. They should cultivate the ancient Hebrew language, study their rich literature, know their history, cherish their faith, and make the greatest sacrifices for it; they should hope and trust in the wisdom of divine providence, the promises of their prophets, and the development of humankind so that the sublime ideas and truths of Judaism may gain the day. But for the rest, they should amalgamate with the nations whose citizens they are, fight in their battles, and promote their institutions for the welfare of the whole.[19]

Jellinek could not, of course, deny that the return to Zion was also a "sublime" Jewish ideal and that Palestine had always enjoyed a special place in Jewish religious history. Nor did he dispute its emotional attraction for the persecuted Jewish masses in the Russian Pale of Settlement. But in the language of the Hebrew prophets, the return to the land of the fathers belonged to the end of history, to *ahrit hayamim*, to the coming of the messiah and the establishment on earth of the kingdom of God. Not even a million Maccabean warriors could bring its fulfillment any closer![20] The final dispensation of Jerusalem and of the Holy Land must be left to the advent of a messianic age of universal peace.

On the other hand, this view did not preclude Jews being permitted to settle in Zion to buy land and engage in agriculture or trade. The agricultural nature of the settlements in Palestine might even exercise a beneficial effect by helping to make the Jews productive. But such settlement activity must be purely *philanthropic* and humanitarian in its motivation, declared Jellinek, devoid of any national or messianic dimensions. Otherwise the "romantic enthusiasts of New Judea" with their "mindless phrases about a Jewish nationality" would merely provide new pretexts for antisemites to brand Western Jews as "aliens" in their own fatherlands.[21] In this context it might be recalled that since 1878, when he delivered a speech in the Hungarian parliament in favor of restoring a Jewish state in Palestine, one of the most fervent apostles of "Zionism" in Central Europe was the leading Hungarian antisemitic political Győző von Istóczy.[22] Thus fear of encouraging the antisemites was understandably to be an important factor in the anti-Zionism of Jewish religious leaders in Central Europe, at least until the outbreak of the First World War.[23]

Moreover, fantasies of a Jewish restoration to Zion by force ignored the realities of Ottoman Palestine in the late nineteenth century. This land was, by Central European standards, a provincial Middle Eastern backwater lacking the basic infrastructure of modern civilization, elemental physical security, and human rights and personal freedoms. It was seen, not without cause, as a country dominated by the arbitrary whims of Turkish *pashas* and marauding Bedouin robbers, in the thrall of bizarre superstition and religious fanatacism. Jellinek, who had waged a long battle against Hasidism and Jewish Orthodoxy in economically backward Galicia, was scarcely enamored by the influence of Ultra-Orthodoxy in Palestine, which he denounced as a "demonic force hostile to civilization" and which in his eyes constituted a great obstacle to a prosperous and successful colonizing effort.[24]

The Orthodox leadership in Vienna, on the other hand, did not greatly differ in its attitude to Palestinian settlement from the liberal current represented by Jellinek and his followers. The theological premises were, however, rather different, and they did have some practical consequences. Thus the Hungarian-born leader of the Viennese Orthodox, Salomon Spitzer (son-in-law of the Hatam Sofer, the Ultra-Orthodox spiritual guide of Hungarian Jewry), had vigorously fought the radical reforms that the *Kultusgemeinde* tried to introduce into the synagogue services in 1871. These included the use of the organ and the elimination of all references in the prayer books to an ultimate return to Zion, to belief in the messiah, and to the reinstitution of sacrifices. Unlike the Viennese reformers, the *Altgläubige* (old believers) did not view such changes as an appropriate adaptation to full emancipation and the liberal ideology of the new era. On the contrary, Spitzer mobilized the Orthodox rabbis and called for secession from the community, regarding any deviation from the Shulhan Arukh as a travesty of Judaism.[25] Though the unity of the community was preserved by a characteristically Viennese compromise, Spitzer resigned from the rabbinate of the *Kultusgemeinde*.[26] A decade later, however, he helped to found the Viennese chapter of the Ahavat Zion (Love of Zion) society for the colonization of Eretz Israel, together with the Lemberg physician and Hovevei Zion activist, Reuben Bierer, one of the founders of Kadima.[27] This activity was essentially philanthropic, but it did testify to a closer spiritual and material attachment to the Holy Land than that prevalent in the more liberal Jewish establishment.

The same might be said of the conservative Rabbi Guedemann, who, like Spitzer, was supportive of Hovevei Zion circles and in the communal crisis of 1872 had also adamantly opposed any tampering with the Torah—especially attempts to excise prayers for a return to Zion or references to sacrifices. In neither case did this view imply support for the ideas of political Zionism, but it did reflect a different scale of values in which Torah, tradition, and knowledge of the sacred tongue (Hebrew) retained their centrality.[28]

For many Orthodox Austrian Jews, Reform Judaism was indeed a greater heresy than Zionism, at least in its minimalist definition of settling the land of the fathers and establishing a refuge for persecuted or destitute Jews. Moreover, on the question of antisemitism, Orthodox Jews often tended to be closer to the Zionist view concerning the *futility* of Jewish self-defense, though their explanation was different. For Orthodoxy, Jew-hatred was essentially a divine chastisement for Israel's sins; its more proximate causes were secular enlightenment, assimilation, and the progressive abandonment of Torah Judaism.[29] Nevertheless, Orthodox Jews were sensitive to attacks on Judaism that besmirched its honor and good name. Indeed, one of their criticisms of liberal-minded Reform Jews was that by throwing off their Judaism so eagerly they had encouraged and aggravated gentile contempt for the Torah and the Jewish people in general. (Interestingly enough, Zionists often tended to argue in similar fashion about the adverse consequences of assimilation.) Orthodox spokesmen also saw the growing religious indifference among Viennese Jews as a logical consequence of the "de-Judaized" humanism, which to their minds lay at the core of the Reform program.[30] The Hungarian and Polish Orthodoxy, whose demographic strength even in Vienna had steadily grown since the massive internal migration to the Austrian capital that began in the 1860s, openly despised Jellinek's "universalist" ideals as a formula for self-dissolution, *Konfessionslosigkeit* (being without a denomination), Jewish self-hatred, and ultimately conversion.[31] From this perspective, the Hovevei Zion mode of Zionism might appear to some Orthodox Jews as a last flight from the ravages of reform.

Nevertheless, Austrian Jewish Orthodoxy did share with the liberal camp a common denominator of dynastic patriotism, loyalist *Oesterreichertum* (Austrianness), commitment to reconciliation among the nationalities, and absolute trust in the Emperor Franz Joseph's promise to preserve Jewish equality before the law. Where they differed in their political orientation, at least in the Austrian half of the empire, it was essentially in their coolness and even hostility to the Germanocentrism of the liberal Viennese Jews. Thus the Orthodox camp supported the Slav-clerical-conservative coalition that ruled Austria under Count Eduard Taaffe's premiership between 1879 and 1893.[32] In Galicia it tended to side with the ruling Polish *szlachta* (nobility) who were a pillar of the conservative Habsburg system and to emphasize the relative tolerance of Poles toward the Jews as against the consistent Germanic record of *Judenhetze*[33] (Jew-baiting). Galician Jewish Orthodoxy was on the whole content with a system of government, which however reactionary it might be in economic or political terms, guaranteed Jews their religious rights, their security under the law, and their separate group identity. The last point, in particular, with its rejection of the liberal philosophy of integrationism, gave Orthodoxy a point of contact with the Zionist movement.

The Galician-born Rabbi Joseph Samuel Bloch, perhaps the foremost defender of Jewish rights in the Austrian Reichsrat (parliament) at the end of the nineteenth century, in his own maverick way reflected this Orthodox world view while combining it with a pugnacious political militancy and astute sense of public relations. Bloch came from the Austrian provinces to the Viennese industrial suburb of Florisdorf at the end of 1870s and from the outset challenged the social and political philosophy of the Viennese liberal establishment. He won popularity among working-class gentiles by lecturing to them about the advanced social doctrines in the Hebrew Bible and respect among traditional Jews by his vigorous defense of the Talmud. Above all, he became a popular Jewish hero and parliamentary candidate through his vitriolic onslaught on the Catholic antisemite, Canon August Rohling, whose scurrilous *Talmudjude* (The Talmud Jew) had left the official Viennese Jewish leadership, both lay and religious, floundering in impotent silence and embarrassment.[34]

Like many other Orthodox Galician Jews, Rabbi Bloch aligned himself politically with the Polish Club in the Austrian Reichsrat and with Count Taaffe's conservative ruling coalition. A Habsburg dynastic patriot, he constantly warned the Austrian Jews to remain neutral in the nationalities' conflict and on no account to identify themselves with German, Czech, Magyar, or any other form of national chauvinism.[35] At the same time, he argued that militant Jewish self-defense was necessary to counteract the threat of organized political antisemitism—a point on which he differed from other Orthodox rabbis as well as from most liberal establishment Jews. Indeed, in his aggressively political stance and with his proud, self-assertive Jewish *ethnic* consciousness, Rabbi Bloch in the early 1880s seemed closer to the students of Kadima than any other prominent Jewish public figure in Austria.[36] The journal he founded—the *Oesterreichische Wochenschrift*—for all its conservative, Austrian dynastic loyalism, was also infused with a Jewish national spirit that seemed radical and even populist at the time. Not surprisingly, Rabbi Bloch was a guest of honor in December 1884 at the Maccabean dinner held by Kadima students, though significantly he warned against misinterpreting the message of the Maccabees in a nationalistic warlike spirit.[37] But he shared with the early Zionists the same consciousness of the common fate of the Jews, the same determination to fight against apostasy and self-hatred within Jewish ranks, the same rejection of assimilation and reassertion of Jewish honor and self-respect.

Yet Rabbi Bloch's attitude to the political Zionism that emerged in the 1890s was clearly ambiguous. He had always been sympathetic, like Spitzer and Guedemann, to the moderate, practical colonization efforts of the Hovevei Zion.[38] In 1896 he had even encouraged Herzl's first efforts to publicize his Zionist ideas and introduced him to the Austrian finance minister, Leon Ritter von Bilinski, a Catholic of Jewish origin and a leading member of the Polish Club. Like Bilinski, Bloch had been impressed by Herzl's magnetic personality and by his vision and political insight but remained highly skeptical about his nationalist ideology and its long-term implications for Jewry.[39] He had been pleasantly surprised (like the chief rabbi of Vienna, Moritz Guedemann) that a witty feuilletonist and literary editor of the

Neue Freie Presse should suddenly become passionately interested in Jewish affairs. At a private reading of what would later become known as *Der Judenstaat*, Rabbi Bloch had, moreover, liked its literary style and was relieved that there was no mention of Palestine as the future location of the Jewish state.

When Herzl subsequently evoked the historic Jewish claim to Palestine, Bloch's reaction was, however, sharply disapproving. Recalling the disastrous episode of the "false messiah," Shabbetai Zevi, Rabbi Bloch advised Herzl of the history of the Holy Land and its exposed geo-political position. He also lent to Herzl two addresses on the Talmud given by Dr. Jellinek nearly thirty years earlier, which reflected the prophetic supranational spirit of Judaism and which warned against attempts to rebuild the Temple.[40] He even recounted to Herzl the historic encounter of 1882 in Vienna between Jellinek and Leon Pinsker. This time, however, he sided with the recently deceased liberal rabbi despite the fact that Jellinek had been his *bête noire* for many years and had helped to block his appointment to the chair of Hebrew antiquities at the University of Vienna. Rabbi Bloch explained to Herzl that, though residence in the Land of Israel was considered a great virtue in the Talmud, Judaism forbade a *mass* return to Palestine and a restoration of the Jewish state before the advent of the messiah.[41]

Bloch, like his close friend and ally Rabbi Moritz Guedemann, favored, then, a philanthropic Zionism along the lines of the agricultural settlements encouraged by Sir Moses Montefiore, Baron Maurice de Hirsch, and Baron Edmond de Rothschild. But he objected to Herzl's insistence on defining Jewry as a secular *political* nation, holding the view that this definition would undoubtedly endanger the status of Jews in Austria at a time of rampant antisemitic propaganda calling for their disfranchisement. For his part, Herzl was arrogantly dismissive of Bloch's "medieval, theological tussle with the antisemites," which to his mind suffered from all the familiar illusions of Jewish self-defense activity.[42] When Herzl founded *Die Welt*, a rival journal to Dr. Bloch's well-established *Wochenschrift*, relations deteriorated still further. By the turn of the century, Bloch's weekly was publishing articles sharply critical of Herzl's artificial *Regierungs-Zionismus* (governmental Zionism), his reliance on high diplomacy and his ignorance of Jewish history and of the Jewish masses in Russia and Galicia. The official line of the weekly was to support a practical emigration policy that included Palestine as one of its goals but to reject the diplomatic *Kunststücken* (artifices) and utopian fantasies behind the idea of the Jewish state.[43]

After Herzl's death in 1904, the Austrian Zionists began to engage more openly in *Landespolitik* (regional politics), and the rivalry between them and the Austrian Israelite Union—which Rabbi Bloch had done so much to found in 1886—grew more intense. Bloch resented Zionist politicking in Austrian parliamentary elections, though he chose to see the election of four Jewish national deputies to the Reichsrat in 1907 as a victory for his own credit of vigorous Jewish political representation.[44] For Rabbi Bloch, the Jews had to defend their ethno-religious interests while remaining a *supra-national*, mediating element within the multinational state, but they should on no account be defined as a separate political nation.

Bloch's antipathy to political Zionism appears to have grown with the years. According to one source—though the authenticity of the claim has been challenged—he had received some 250 negative written opinions on Herzlian Zionism from prominent Orthodox rabbis in the period between 1897 and 1913.[45] The successes of the Zionist movement after 1917 in the sphere of international diplomacy did not diminish his conviction that political Zionism was a great danger to the Jews, that it was playing with fire and would only serve to inflame antisemitism. Indeed, in a letter written shortly before his death at the end of 1923 to Rabbi Chaim Bloch, Joseph Samuel Bloch urged his namesake to work for the creation of an "anti-nationalist movement within Jewry" to contain the threat posed by political Zionism.[46]

One of Bloch's closest allies in the Jewish anti-Zionist struggle was, of course, Moritz Guedemann, chief rabbi of Vienna and Herzl's most important religious critic in *fin-de-siècle* Vienna. The Prussian-born Guedemann, a classic product of the *Wissenschaft des Judentums* and an outstanding Jewish scholar in his own right, had been brought to Vienna in 1866 to officiate at the Leopoldstadt synagogue.[47] The conservative factions in the *Gemeinde* (community) looked to his stricter stance on matters of Jewish law to offset the liberalizing influence of Jellinek. Indeed, as we have seen, Guedemann rejected any Reform-tinged innovations to the liturgy, including attempts to tamper with prayers relating to the return to Zion. Yet, in some respects, the Orthodox Guedemann's understanding of the term "Zion" was no less spiritualized than that of nineteenth-century Reform, to the almost complete exclusion of political reality.[48] At the same time, like the Reformers whom he detested, he also saw the Jews as messengers of humanity, as a spiritual and model people charged with the task of disseminating justice among the peoples of the earth and in this way preparing for the messianic age.

Moreover, for all his disagreements with Jellinek over halakhic and other matters, the premises that determined Gudemann's view of political Zionism were remarkably similar. Like Jellinek he believed passionately in the ideology of emancipation, in acculturation, in the superiority of German culture, and in the benevolent, paternalistic character of the multinational Habsburg state. He, too, emphasized the humanism and universal character of Hebraic monotheism—playing down the elements of particularism and ethnic self-assertion. Guedemann, like his predecessor, also insisted that Judaism was not a national religion in the modern sense. Israel had always been a religious community *(Religionsgemeinschaft)*, not a nation *(Volk)* as the antisemites constantly maintained. From this perspective,

Zionism obviously stood in contradiction to Guedemann's idealized and *anational* interpretation of the Torah, which stripped it of any particularist, ethnic, or historical character, let alone any physical link to the Promised Land of Israel. In his treatise, *Jüdische Apologetik* (Jewish Apologetics, 1906), he saw the national history of Israel as having meaning in itself. It is simply a prelude to the recognition by the gentiles (i.e., the nations of the world) of the one true God, a preparation for the reign of universal brotherhood and future divine kingship over all humanity.[49]

Although Guedemann was chief rabbi of Vienna from 1893 to 1918, in one of the politically tensest, most dramatic and creative periods in the history of the Jewish community, he was in fact much less of a political animal than his illustrious predecessors Isaac Noah Mannheimer and Jellinek or his contemporary, Joseph Samuel Bloch. His approach is reflected in his critique of Herzl's Zionism, which is much more "theological" than the kind of reservations and opposition we have hitherto discussed. Guedemann's *Nationaljudentum* (National Jewry, 1897) which was a body blow to Herzl's hopes of winning over rabbinical and lay Jewish leaders to his cause in Central Europe, is essentially written from a *religious* standpoint—combining elements of both the Orthodox and the Reform argument against Zionism.[50] It explicitly rejects any attempt to separate the peoplehood of Israel from its monotheistic faith. Mosaic law is presented as the antithesis of the nativistic ideology of modern nationalism that underpins political Zionism. Indeed, the unique quality of the Torah is said to lie in its independence of territorial, political, or national consideration.[51]

According to Rabbi Guedemann, since the Babylonian exile, the Jewish state had become dissolved into a "church" and the Jewish nation into a "community of faith" *(Glaubensgemeinschaft)*. Its ideals were cosmopolitan and its messianism universalist and future oriented. Jewish nationalism would be a step *backward* in spiritual terms from the sublime vision of the messianic kingdom that diaspora Judaism had developed. The prophetic teachings had preserved the uniqueness and distinctiveness of the Jewish people through centuries of dispersion. To return under modern conditions to an essentially "pagan," exclusivist, or nativist concept of nationality would in effect be a self-destructive form of collective assimilation for the Jews. The Zionists, who blindly attacked the "assimilationist" aspirations of modern Jewry, were thus doubly mistaken. It was they and not the so-called assimilators who contravened the biblical injunction against worshiping false gods. They would end up creating a nationalist Judaism based on cannon and bayonets, which "exchanged the roles of David and Goliath" and could only be a pathetic travesty of that biblical faith which had never glorified wars of conquest or depicted military heroes as divine figures. The biblical Israelites, according to Guedemann, had from the beginning of their history repudiated the "pagan" nationalism of the gentiles—the cult of blood and iron—in favor of divine kingship over heaven and earth. The diaspora had preserved this glorious tradition and "the standard-bearers of Judaism" (philosophers like Philo, Maimonides, and Mendels-sohn) had remained faithful to it while synthesizing Jewish teachings with the highest ideals of the surrounding cultures. Thus there was no basis for the Jewish nationalist claim that "assimilation" would inexorably lead to the "self-dissolution" *(Selbstaufgebung)* of Judaism.[52]

Nor was there any reason for Jews to cease regarding themselves as Germans, Magyars, or Frenchmen of the Mosaic persuasion simply because the antisemites wished to deny them this right. Judaism would long since have perished had it relied for its survival on the definitions of others or if it had tried to imitate gentile nationalism. Austrian Jews, in particular, had excellent grounds for repudiating the "nationality" principle as being contrary both to their fundamental interests and to their entire diaspora heritage. On this point, the chief rabbi's pamphlet *Nationaljudentum* not only echoed the writings of Jellinek and Bloch but also appeal to the conservative Austrian *Biedermeier* poet, Franz Grillparzer—whose epigram "from humanity through nationality to bestiality"—neatly encapsulates the central thrust of Guedemann's anti-Zionist tract.[53]

The chief rabbi sharply dissociated himself from any nationalist interpretation of the biblical promises of redemption. National restoration and independent statehood in Palestine were fundamentally irrelevant to "true Zionism," for the spiritualized biblical Zion that Guedemann had in mind was inseparable from moral perfection and the brotherhood of all humankind.[54] Like so many fin-de-siècle rabbis, whether Orthodox or Reform, Guedemann argued that the attempted conquest of Palestine would be no less than "an encroachment on the leadership of God," a distortion of the teachings of Judaism and of the lessons of Jewish history. Moreover the "profane" Zionism preached by Herzl and Max Nordau was liable to prejudice the civil rights of Jews in their European fatherlands–a key point for Guedemann as it had been for Jellinek and Bloch.[55]

The issue of antisemitism had from the outset played an important role in the complex relations between Herzl and Guedemann, initially as a point of contact and later as a divisive question. The misunderstandings were there from the first approach by Herzl in a letter from Paris in June 1895 that sought to secure the chief rabbi's collaboration in a campaign on behalf of the Jews. Herzl had proposed that Guedemann help draft a memorandum dealing with the situation of the Jews in the world, their occupational distribution, and the problem of antisemitism.[56] Guedemann, pleasantly surprised that such a prestigious and worldly journalist should display so warm an interest in Jewish matters, referred him to Dr. Bloch. Herzl's real goal, however, which he kept secret at this stage, was to secure Guedemann's support as an intermediary to the Viennese Rothschilds. Yet it was the chief rabbi who initially counseled against reliance on rich Jews to support Herzl's plans and who privately decried the spinelessness and passivity of the Viennese liberals, of the Jewish establishment, and the *Neue Freie Presse*.[57] He evidently hoped that Herzl, through his connections with Vienna's great liberal newspaper, would help Rabbi Bloch in his lonely struggle against the massed phalanx of the Austrian antisemites. In other words, Guedemann was for some time under the misapprehension that Herzl's promised solution to the Jewish question was primarily concerned with local conditions in Vienna and the fight against antisemitism.[58]

According to Herzl's account, Guedemann, despite his belief in the universalistic diaspora mission of the Jews, was at first enthralled by his Zionist ideas and even implored him: "Remain as you are! Perhaps you are called of God!"—a statement that Guedemann, in his own memoirs, written in 1913, vehemently denied making.[59] On January 27, 1896, Herzl noted with obvious satisfaction in his diary that Guedemann's conviction that *Der Judenstaat* would "work wonders," and a few days later he recorded that the chief rabbi had read the tract through to the end and found "nothing to criticize."[60] Admittedly, Guedemann had warned him against precipitate action and said that his ideas would be unacceptable to most of Orthodox Jewry. Guedemann had wanted to soften isolated remarks that might be construed as offensive to the rabbis and remove the implication that Jews might somehow be an "unassimilable" minority. But there still seemed to be no hint that the chief rabbi regarded Zionism as incompatible with Jewish religious teachings.

Nevertheless by January 1897, following a chance encounter in Vienna's Schottenring, Herzl, already bitter about Guedemann, described him as an "unctuous creature," without any backbone. He ridiculed Guedemann's notion of the "mission of the Jews" as a piece of self-satisfied complacency.[61] At their last meeting, two months later, Guedemann allegedly rebuked him: "I should go away from here [Vienna], where the name of Jew and all those who bear it are constantly abused and cursed—I should clear the way for our enemies in order to grow vegetables in Palestine? No, not even ten thousand horses could drag me away from here, until I experience my revenge and satisfaction at the downfall of the enemies of the Jews."[62] Herzl contemptuously dismissed this concern and attributed Guedemann's *volte-face* to pressure from the wealthy Jews of Vienna and the anti-Zionist *Kultusgemeinde* leadership.

In reality, Herzl appears to have misread Guedemann no less fundamentally than the chief rabbi misunderstood the Zionist leader's intentions. Both had hoped to use the other for mutually incompatible goals—Herzl to win the Rothschilds over to Zionism and Guedemann to mobilize the *Neue Freie Presse* for the struggle against Viennese antisemitism.[63] Guedemann had seen in Herzl a promising recruit to the cause of local Jewish self-defense, a younger, more energetic, and possibly more influential adjunct to the battle for so long waged by Rabbi Bloch. But in 1895 the latter had been forced by antisemitic pressures to retire from the Austrian Reichsrat, and as a result a vacuum had been created into which Herzl could step. Only Herzl had no inclination whatsoever to combat Austrian antisemitism and least of all to mobilize his employers at the *Neue Freie Presse* for this lost cause.[64]

In any case, however much Guedemann was initially overwhelmed by Herzl's charismatic personality, he had no affinity for the Zionist leader's secular, freethinking approach to Jewish issues. Indeed he had been already taken aback, at the end of 1895, to find a "huge Christmas tree" in Herzl's drawing room.[65] Moreover, he could never really understand how an assimilated Jew like Herzl, thoroughly impregnated with German *Bildung* (education and character formation), should suddenly desire to "uproot himself from his native soil"—thus giving satisfaction to the German and Austrian antisemites.[66] In Guedemann's mind there was never any question of preaching in the Temple in favor of the *political* program of Zionism. Furthermore, like Jellinek before him, he thoroughly disapproved of the noisy antics of the Zionist students of Kadima, who had rallied from the beginning to Herzl's banner. Their nationalist approach was in his eyes a *contradictio in adjecto*: they wanted to be both Jews and freethinkers, that is, to be Jews and non-Jews at the same time.[67] Above all, Guedemann regarded political Zionism as a flight from antisemitism, as a baneful retreat into national separatism. Comments in a letter to the Austrian writer Kamilla Theimer in December 1907 summed up his position on Jewish nationalism: "Would such isolation satisfy their [the Jewish] innate urge and call to influence humanity? For centuries the Christians have accused the Jews of isolating themselves. And suddenly such isolation is to be a panacea? The poison is now to serve as an antidote? That is no sensible cure."[68]

The negative assessment of political Zionism by the leading rabbis of Vienna persisted right up until the end of the Habsburg Empire. Guedemann's death in 1918, which coincided with the disintegration of the Dual Monarchy, brought this era to a close. His successor as chief rabbi, the Galician-born Zwi Perez Chajes, came from a very different background. An ardent Zionist from his youth, he had lectured at the University of Florence since 1904 and from 1912 had been rabbi of the Trieste congregation. He had done much to propagate Zionism in Italy before coming to Vienna in 1918 to serve as Guedmann's deputy. In his first address as chief rabbi of Vienna—the third largest Jewish community in Europe—he openly made a Zionist confession of faith. Despite the unpopularity of these views with the wealthy and comfortable assimilationists, the Orthodox, and the leaders of the *Kultusgemeinde*, Chajes established himself in the 1920s as the undisputed leader of Austrian Jewry with a considerable influence over the younger generation. Chajes attached special importance to the Hebrew language as an essential attribute of Jewish identity and education viewed from a national standpoint.[69] For Chajes the political element in Zionism was a necessary dimension for the renewal of its deeper religious meaning. In his writings and addresses, even before the Balfour Declaration, a mystical, historical, and political messianism oriented toward the Land of Israel did not preclude recognition of the importance of the diaspora for Jewry in the past and present.[70] But Chajes, far more than any of his predecessors, considered the building up of Palestine to become the national and religious center of Jewish life as the major task of world Jewry in the twentieth century. Unlike Guedemann, he combined philanthropic and cultural with *political* Zionism, providing a kind of synthesis of Ahad Haam and Herzl without aligning himself to any particular party within the Zionist movement.[71] Far more than his forerunners in Vienna, Chajes represented a new kind of rabbi, academically trained yet rooted in tradition, uniting East and West, scholarship and political leadership, religion and Zionism in a manner more adapted to the democratization of the Jewish community in the post-1918 era.

But Chajes's synthesis of Zionism and religion did not end the bitter rivalries that continued to exist within the *Israelitische Kultusgemeinde* between Zionists and assimilationists. In the early 1920s, however, the internal balance of power began to change in a more Zionist direction. By 1933 the Zionists had taken over the *Gemeinde*, the first such example in a modern, Westernized Jewish community. From being a vocal minority before the war, in radical opposition to a liberal, integrationist leadership, the Zionists in Vienna had become a significant force in Jewish life, though at the same time also a source of continual acrimony and division. Even the Zionists themselves were split into many factions. But the influx of Jewish refugees during the First World War and immediately after, the rise of a more violent type of antisemitism, and the militancy of the younger generation of Jews in Austria increased the appeal of Zionism in internal Jewish politics. Tragically, these developments did not enhance the capacity of Viennese Jews to unite against the common antisemitic danger. Instead, the prevailing religious class, and political differences among Austrian Jews and the religious-secular divide that Zionism had failed to resolve since the turn of the century continued to fragment Viennese Jewry and weaken its ability to respond to the looming threat that would herald its imminent demise. Both the Zionists and their critics—religious and secular—were swept away in the tidal wave of local antisemitism unleashed by the union of Austria with Nazi Germany.

Notes

1. Adolf Jellinek and Leon Pinsker, "Ein Zwiegespräch," *Die Neuzeit* (Vienna), March 31, April 7 and 14, 1882. See also "Leo Pinskers Begegnung mit Adolf Jellinek: Zur Wiederkehr des 100. Geburtstages Pinskers," *Aus zwei Jahrhunderten,* ed. N. M. Gelber (Vienna, 1924), pp. 193–201. Pinsker was described by *Die Neuzeit* as "the physician Dr. X, from Russia."

2. Adolf Jellinek, "Die Juden in Österreich," *Der Orient,* April 22, 1848, pp. 129ff., is a good example of his Germanocentric credo.

3. See Robert S. Wistrich, *The Jews of Vienna in the Age of Franz Joseph* (Oxford, 1989), esp. chaps. 4 and 5, for an elaboration of this point.

4. Adolf Jellinek, *Schma Jisroel: Fünf Reden über das israelitische Glaubensbekenntnis* (Vienna, 1869). See also Moses Rosenmann, Dr. *Adolf Jellinek: Sein Leben und Schaffen* (Vienna, 1931), pp. 132–40.

5. Adolf Jellinek, *Studien und Skizzen: Der jüdische Stamm: Eine Ethnographische Studie* (Vienna, 1869), pp. 47–48.

6. Leon Pinsker, *Autoemanzipation!* (Berlin, 1882).

7. The dialogue was included a few years later in Adolf Jellinek, *Aus der Zeit: Tagesfragen und Tagesbegenheiten* (Budapest, 1886), pp. 20–81. See also Wistrich, *Jews of Vienna*, p. 462.

8. Jellinek and Pinsker, "Ein Zwiegespräch," reprinted in Jellinek, *Aus der Zeit*, p. 76.

9. Ibid., p. 77.

10. Ibid., p. 78.

11. Ibid., p. 80.

12. See Julius H. Schoeps, "Modern Heirs of the Maccabees: The Beginning of the Vienna Kadimah 1882–1897," *Leo Baeck Institute Yearbook* 27 (1982): 155–70; Wistrich, *Jews of Vienna*, pp. 347–80.

13. On Pinsker's relations with Kadima, see his letters of December 10, 1883, and January 26, 1884, Central Zionist Archives, Jerusalem (hereafter CZA), Z 1/1, A 368/8. See also Wistrich, *Jews of Vienna*, pp. 358–59.

14. Nathan Birnbaum, "Jehuda Makkabi," *Selbstemanzipation* (1885), nos. 21 and 22.

15. Adolf Jellinek, "Weihfest oder Makkabäerfest?" *Die Neuzeit*, December 18, 1891, pp. 491–92.

16. "Kadimah. iv. 1890 bis 1904: Erinnerungen von Ehrrenburschen Medizinal-rat Dr. Isidor Schalit, Wien," in *Festschrift zur Feier des 100. Semesters der akademischen Verbindung Kadimah*, ed. Ludwig Rosenhek (Mölding, 1933), p. 19. In these memoirs Isidor Schalit reports that two of the leaders of Kadimah, Nathan Birnbaum and Moritz Schnirer, were told by Jellinek in 1883 that the Jews would one day regain Zion but that they must wait until the advent of the messiah!

17. Jellinek and Pinsker, "Ein Zwiegespräch," reprinted in Jellinek, *Aus der Zeit.*

18. A. J. [Adolf Jellinek], "Die Juden und die Nationalitäten in Österreich-Ungarn," *Die Neuzeit*, August 22, 1884, pp. 313–14, and February 14, 1890, p. 62.

19. Adolf Jellinek, "Weihfest oder Makkabäerfest," *Die Neuzeit*, December 18, 1891. See also Jellinek, "Das Judenthum—eine Nationalität," *Die Neuzeit*, March 10, 1893, p. 1.

20. Jellinek, "Weihfest oder Makkabäerfest": "Was die Erfüllung der höchsten jüdischen Ideale, die Zukunft des jüdischen Stammes, die Ehrenrettung Zions betrifft, so können auch eine Million Makkabäer nichts dazubeitragen."

21. A. J. [Adolf Jellinek], "Jüdische Colonial-Politik," *Die Neuzeit*, January 9, 1885, p. 12.

22. See Nathaniel Katzburg, *Haantishemiut beHungaryah, 1867–1914* (Tel-Aviv, 1969). See also Andrew Handler, *Dori: The Life and Times of Theodor Herzl in Budapest (1860–1878)* ([Birmingham, Ala.] 1983), p. 115; Wistrich, *Jews of Vienna*, pp. 424–25.

23. Theodor Herzl's *Judenstaat* (Jewish State) was, in fact, enthusiastically received by leading European antisemites like the Hungarian Ivan von Simonyi, the German August Rohling (whose pamphlet *Auf nach Zion* appeared in 1902), and the French Catholic Edouard Drumont. See, for example, Frederick Busi, "Antisemites on Zionism: The Case of Herzl and Drumont," *Midstream* 25, no. 2 (February, 1979): 18–27.

24. [Jellinek], "Jüdische Colonial-Politik," p. 12.

25. Salomon Spitzer, *Rabbinische Gutachten betreffs der vom Vorstande der israelitischen Kultusgemeinden in Wien am 21. Januar gefassten und zur Ausführung gebrachten Reformbeschlüsse* (Vienna, 1872), p. 5.

26. "Die Vorgänge in Wien," *Der Israelit* 6 (February 7, 1872): 107. See also the important article by Wolfgang Häusler, "'Orthodoxie' und 'Reform' im Wiener Judentum in der

Epoche des Hochliberalismus," in *Studia Judaica Austriaca*, vol. 6: *Der Wiener Stadttempel, 1826–1976* (Eisenstadt, 1976), pp. 29–56.

27. Wistrich, *Jews of Vienna*, p. 349.

28. For a more general exploration of Orthodox attitudes to Jewish national identity, modernity, and Zionism, see Jacob Katz, "Orthodoxy in Historical Perspective," *Studies in Contemporary Jewry* 2 (1986): 3–17; Eliezer Goldman, "Responses to Modernity in Orthodox Jewish Thought," *Studies in Contemporary Jewry* 2 (1986): 52–73.

29. "Die Stellung der Juden," *Jüdisches Weltblatt* (Vienna), September 1, 1883.

30. Ibid., December 9, 1885.

31. Ibid., January 8, 1885.

32. Ibid., January 1, 1885.

33. "Das Ministerium Taafe und die Juden," *Jüdisches Weltblatt*, June 1, 1885.

34. Joseph Samuel Bloch, *My Reminiscences* (Vienna, 1923), p. 135; Wistrich, *Jews of Vienna*, pp. 282–83.

35. Joseph Samuel Bloch, *Der Nationale Zwist und die Juden in Österreich* (Vienna, 1886), pp. 28–33, 45–53.

36. Bloch, *My Reminiscences*, pp. 182, 185.

37. Joseph Samuel Bloch to Kadima, May 10, 1883, April 28 and June 5, 1884, CZA, Z 1/1.

38. *Die Neuzeit*, November 19, 1897, p. 474.

39. For an obituary of Theodor Herzl by Joseph Samuel Bloch, see *Österreichische Wochenschrift*, 1904, p. 455. See also Chaim Bloch, "Theodor Herzl and Joseph S. Bloch," *Herzl Yearbook* 1 (New York, 1958), pp. 154–64; N. M. Gelber, "Herzl's Polish Contacts," ibid., pp. 211–19.

40. Wistrich, *Jews of Vienna*, p. 306.

41. Chaim Bloch, "Herzl and Bloch," pp. 158–61.

42. See Theodor Herzl's diary entry of August 6, 1895, in *The Diaries of Theodor Herzl*, ed. and trans. Marvin Lowenthal (London, 1958), p. 58.

43. See "Emigrations-Politik," *Österreichische Wochenschrift*, May 5, 1899, pp. 337–38; "Der Zionismus am Scheideweg," *Österreichische Wochenschrift*, May 12, 1899. See also the articles and reports in this weekly on May 19, 26, June 2, July 7, 1899.

44. *Österreichische Wochenschrift*, February 22, 1906, pp. 121–27; March 29, 1907, pp. 213–17; June 21, 1907, pp. 405–6.

45. Chaim Bloch, *Mi natan leYaakov lemishisah veIsrael levozezim* (Bronx, N.Y., n.d.). The author denounced Zionism from Herzl to Jacob Klatzkin for destroying Judaism and endangering Israel's existence among the nations. The book is based on opinions in German, Yiddish, and above all Hebrew, from learned Torah sages, Orthodox rabbis, politicians, and others, about Jewish nationalism, allegedly sent to Rabbi Joseph Samuel Bloch before the First World War. Shmuel Hacohen Winegarten, *Mikhtavim mezuyafim neged hazionut* (Jerusalem, 1981), claims that these rabbinical opinions are forgeries, but in my opinion at least some must be considered as authentic.

46. The letter, written by Joseph Samuel Bloch in Vienna on the notepaper of the *Österreichische Wochenschrift* and dated September 15, 1923, reads like a testament. Specifically it instructs Chaim Bloch: "Es soll Ihre Aufgabe sein, namhafte Persönlichkeiten für die Schaffung einer antinationalistischen Bewegung innerhalb des Judentums zu gewinnen."

47. See Ismar Schorsch, "Moritz Güdemann: Rabbi, Historian, Apologist," *Leo Baeck Yearbook* 11 (1966): 42–66; Wistrich, *Jews of Vienna*, pp. 122–30.

48. Jacob Allerhand, "Die Rabbiner des Stadttempels von J. N. Mannheimer bis Z. P. Chajes," *Studia Judaica Austriaca* 6 (Eisenstadt, 1973): 6–28.

49. Moritz Guedemann, *Jüdische Apologetik* (Glogau, 1906), pp. 88–90.

50. See Josef Fraenkel, "Bein Herzl veGüdemann" *Shivat Zion* 4 (1956–57): 100–113, and the English version, "Between Herzl and Güdemann," in *Leo Baeck Institute Yearbook* 11 (1966): 67–82.

51. Mortiz Guedemann, *Nationaljudentum* (Leipzig, 1897), p. 20.

52. Ibid., p. 38, 37.

53. Ibid., p. 54.

54. Ibid., p. 41: "Zion galt und gilt den Juden als das Symbol ihrer eigenen, aber auch die ganze Menschheit umfassenden Zukunft."

55. Ibid.

56. Herzl to Guedemann, June 1895, Herzl Archives, CZA H VIII, 309.

57. Guedemann to Herzl, July 17, 1895, ibid.

58. Wistrich, *Jews of Vienna*, pp. 470–71.

59. See Moritz Guedemann, "Aus meinem Leben," 4 vols. (n.d.) Archives of the Leo Baeck Institute, New York, 2:142, 3:118ff, 128ff, 185–95. The section entitled "Meine Stellung zum Zionismus" is also reproduced by Mordechai Eliav, "Herzl und der Zionismus aus der Sicht Moritz Güdemanns," *Bulletin des Leo Baeck Instituts,* nos. 56–57 (1980): 160–68.

60. Herzl, diary, January 27, February 2, 1896, Herzl Archives, CZA, H VIII 309. Guedemann wrote to Herzl: "Ich habe alles gelesen und finde nichts zu monieren."

61. Herzl, diary, January 1893, *Diaries*, p. 203. On March 26, 1896, Herzl had noted that Guedemann "is afraid of the rich Jews"—who in Vienna, as elsewhere, tended at the time to be opposed to Zionism. There is, in fact, no convincing evidence that this was true of the chief rabbi.

62. Guedemann, "Meine Stellung zum Zionismus," p. 166.

63. Guedemann to Herzl, December 26, 1895, Herzl Archives, CZA, H VIII 309 (20).

64. For Herzl's relationship with his employers at the *Neue Freie Presse* and their attitude to antisemitism, see Wistrich, *Jews of Vienna*, pp. 446–49.

65. Guedemann, "Meine Stellung zum Zionismus," in Eliav, "Herzl und der Zionismus," p. 164.

66. Ibid., p. 166.

67. Ibid., p. 168.

68. "Aus einem Briefe von Sr. Ehrw, Ob-Rabbiner Dr. Güdemann an Frau Kamilla Theimer v. 19 Dezember 1907," Central Archives of the History of the Jewish People, Jerusalem, A/W 731.5.

69. See M. Rosenfeld, *Oberrabbiner H. P. Chajes: Sein Leben und Werke* (Vienna, 1933); Zalman Shazar, "Zwi Perez Chajes," in *Or ishim* (Tel-Aviv, 1949).

70. Rosenfeld, *Chajes*, p. 63. See also A. Manczur, "Tefisato hahistorit-leumit shel Zwi Perez Chajot," in *Sefer hayovel le-N. M. Gelber* (Tel-Aviv, 1962), pp. 105–13.

71. Allerhand, "Rabbiner des Stadttempels," pp. 21–28.

STUART A. COHEN

Religious Motives and Motifs in Anglo-Jewish Opposition to Political Zionism, 1895–1920

As issued in its final form on November 2, 1917, the Balfour Declaration was a deliberately ambivalent document. Although undoubtedly a triumph for Zionist statesmen, it also reflected the British government's sensitivity to the weight of opinion against their case. As Chaim Weizmann immediately appreciated, and as subsequent mandatory administrations were repeatedly to protest, the declaration did not unreservedly promise to underwrite each and every Zionist aim. Its key phrase—"the establishment in Palestine of a national home for the Jewish people"—was vague and open to several interpretations. Its essential clause—which expressed the government's readiness to "use its best endeavors to facilitate the achievement of this object"—was hedged by two substantial provisos. One condition was that "nothing shall be done which may prejudice the civil and religious rights of existing non-Jewish communities in Palestine." The other insisted on the preservation of "the rights and political status enjoyed by Jews in any other country."

During the mandate period, when conflicting Arab and Zionist ambitions in Palestine were expressed in violent form, attention not unexpectedly focused on the first of the declaration's provisos. In 1917, however, the maintenance of the second condition—and hence of *Jewish* civil rights elsewhere—had seemed to be a far more crucial issue. Particularly was this so within the Anglo-Jewish community, where debate on the subject had long been intense. Recognizing the importance of the question, the Zionists had themselves moderated the terminology of their claims (it was they who first suggested the establishment of a "National Home" rather than a "Jewish State" when submitting a draft statement to the government in June 1917). Sensitive to the emotions which even that formula might arouse, the cabinet in October 1917 canvassed a wider spectrum of Anglo-Jewish opinion, inviting nine prominent communal figures to express their private views.[1]

This essay will not recount the history of the negotiations that ensued; nor will it attempt yet another reassessment of the tangled web of motives that eventually led the government to embark upon what has been described as one of the costliest errors in British imperial history. Instead, it will concentrate on the internal Anglo-Jewish communal debate that preceded and accompanied the declaration and, specifically, on the arguments advanced by those who declared themselves opposed to the Jewish national idea. Zionist polemic has conventionally accorded these members of the community a bad press, contending that their sole interest was to prevent Zionism from injuring their social standing and from arresting the process of assimilation upon which they had enthusiastically embarked. Clearly enunciated as early as 1919 in Nahum Sokolow's *History of Zionism*, that accusation became virtually official party doctrine with the appearance of Chaim Weizmann's *Trial and Error* in 1949. Anti-Zionist objections to the Balfour Declaration, he therein charged (repeating a phrase he had employed in 1917), expressed no more than the selfish reactions of a plutocracy that "by education and social connection had lost touch with the real spirit activating the Jewish people as a whole."[2]

I

Consideration suggests that such judgments were too harsh. Admittedly, differences of background, occupation, and status did often distinguish anti-Zionists in Anglo-Jewry from Zionists. But those were not the *only* determinants of their positions. Neither can the rivals in the debate easily be dragooned into conventional categories of religious affiliation. While it is true that in 1917 political Zionism did enjoy the support of prominent figures in the community's spiritual establishment (most notably, the Ashkenazi chief rabbi, Joseph Hertz and his Sephardi counterpart, the Hakham Moses Gaster), the overall clerical alignment was hardly monolithic. If anything, among a significantly wide spectrum of local religious opinion, the Jewish national idea had long generated quite different emotions—reserve at best and antagonism at worst. What is more, for all the diversity of their views on other matters of theological concern, when contesting the Zionist thesis this group of intellectuals and clerics had mustered a remarkably parallel range of arguments. It is these that repay attention. Ultimately, the anti-Zionists sought to be measured by the yardsticks of religious responsibility and ideological respectability no less than did their nationalist opponents. The erudition and cogency with which they advocated their case, it will here be argued, shows that they deserve to be taken seriously.

Certainly, the campaign they launched against the Balfour Declaration was neither novel nor shallow. It possessed a long and intellectually distinguished pedigree that can be traced back to the reception the community accorded to Theodor Herzl's very first pronunciations of his scheme.[3] As far as the anti-Zionists were concerned, the lines of debate then drawn had subsequently remained utterly consistent. Whereas the Zionists, with a frequency that suggested ideological disarray, seemed to chase various hares—some political, as in the case of the British government's suggestions with regard to East Africa: some ideological, as in the case of socialist formulations of the Zionist idea—the positions adopted by anti-Zionists changed hardly at all. Equally persistent was the focus of their interest. Only occasionally did they let themselves be sidetracked into debates on the practicability of some of Zionism's various ancillary enterprises (a category that includes the idea of a Jewish university in Jerusalem as well as the establishment of further colonies elsewhere in Palestine). In the main, they refused to be distracted from what they considered to be the primary—and far more fundamental—issues of ideology and religious beliefs. As far as they were concerned, whether Zionist ambitions were realistic had always been a subsidiary question, far surpassed in importance by whether Zionist aspirations were also, by the terms of Jewish traditions, justifiable. Accordingly, it was on the basic tenets of the nationalist positions that their challenge concentrated, and those which they sought to undermine.

The manner in which they did so belies the contention that the anti-Zionists were, to quote Sokolow again, uniformly "impelled by a desire to destroy the distinctive characteristics which recalled their origins."[4] They cannot, therefore, all be roundly condemned as "assimilationists." That classification does perhaps fit the movement's left wing and anarchist opponents (whose objections were in any case not rooted in religious conviction but in the hypothesis that Zionism had been "engineered by the capitalists in order to draw off the attention of Jews from the general social question");[5] but it is self-evidently fallacious where avowedly Orthodox anti-Zionists are concerned. No less is it misleading when applied to those persons affiliated with the Reform and Liberal wings of Anglo-Jewish religious persuasion who were the *prima facie* targets of Sokolow's and Weizmann's disparaging remarks. True, members of this circle did consider Jewish nationalism an aspersion on the English citizenship by which they set so much store. Sensitive to the charge of "dual loyalty" already being spread abroad by Hilaire Belloc, G. K. Chesterton, and the *Morning Post*, they were certainly anxious to unveil what they thought to be Zionism's threat to the very fabric of assumptions upon which Anglo-Jewish emancipation had originally been won.[6]

But even in such cases, acculturation had its limits. As much is most obviously illustrated by the cases of Claude Montefiore, Israel Abrahams, and Lucien Wolf—the persons most intimately involved in the communal campaign against Zionism. Although proud to be Englishmen, none of these men ever disclaimed a deep emotional concern with "a land and a city in which long ago [their] ancestors lived, where the Prophets spoke, the Psalmist sang, the sages taught."[7] More to the point, none ever attempted to deny their Jewish identity or consciously advocated the dissolution of their Jewish separateness. Their labors on behalf of specifically Jewish cultural, social, and political causes leave no doubt that they sought, not the disappearance of Judaism or the Jews, but the preservation of both the people and its religion in what they considered to be a proper form. They insistently—and, it must be said, not incorrectly—contended that they were probably more attached to the traditional religious customs "on historical, ethical, and religious grounds" than were most of the official Zionist leadership; they claimed to be "quite as good Jews . . . and have as excellent a title to be so regarded."[8]

The essential distinction, these leaders argued, was between "good" and "bad" assimilation. Within the latter category came mixed marriages, the transfer of the Sabbath to Sunday, the reduction of Hebrew studies to the curious dissection of a fossil—in short, all the drastic steps that might have sacrificed Jewish distinctiveness and turned Judaism into "a pale reflection of Christianity." "Good" assimilation, by contrast, consisted of a process whereby Jews might absorb, without coercion or compromise, the beneficial elements and characteristics of the cultures and societies in which they lived. That, posited Montefiore, had indeed always been the Jewish way:

The Babylonian Talmud was not developed on Palestinian soil. It grew up in what is now glibly called an "alien environment." Within the Talmud are elements derived from many cultures. After its close we find Judaism again and again flourishing in non-Jewish countries, assimilating, to some extent at least, the good of those countries, and yet growing fuller, higher, and even more influential, just because of its wider horizon.[9]

The appeal to the bar of Jewish history was the first of several recurring motifs throughout the anti-Zionist campaign, and that reflected the purposes of the protagonists as well as their academic interests. Their object was to enunciate a philosophy of Jewish history that would quicken the antinationalist sensibilities which, they felt, had been numbed by Zionism's tendentious distortions of some of the most glorious pages in Jewry's chronology. Not only were the Zionists promulgating a dangerously perverse reading of their people's most recent past—as was repeatedly argued by Lucien Wolf, the *doyen* of Anglo-Jewry's intercessionaries and the community's most respected historian.[10] By attempting to deflect Jewry's future development into the channels of the Western nation-state, they were also betraying Judaism's unique ethos. After all, few official Zionist spokesmen appeared to be making any provisions to provide the specifically *Jewish* character of their future homeland. To date, their only accomplishment had been a revival of the atavistic slogan that Israel become a nation like all others. As Israel Abrahams, Solomon Schechter's successor as reader in rabbinic and talmudic literature at Cambridge, was later to put it: "This 'modern nationalism' is the most extraordinary instance of assimilation that the Jews have ever experienced."[11] Israel Zangwill, himself a Zionist *manqué*, broadly concurred with that observation. Indeed, and as befitted a man of his literary gifts, he had earlier expressed himself still more tartly: "I cannot too strongly draw your attention to the fact that political Zionism run by freethinkers is *not* what the Jewish people have been dreaming of for 19 centuries."[12]

II

It is a testimony to the intensity of concern which political Zionism aroused in Anglo-Jewry that its opponents were not content merely to score occasional debating points of that sort at the movement's expense. They also attempted to construct a more consolidated critique, one that struck at the very core of the nature of Jewish identity and at what they considered to be the "essence" of Jewish religious teachings.

Speaking for his own brand of "Liberal" Judaism, Montefiore provided an indication of things to come as early as 1896, when he first published *The Bible for Home Reading*, two volumes of text and exegesis that swiftly became remarkably popular.[13] Basic to the thesis there presented was the distinction between two entirely different depictions of Jewry: one—the more primitive—which characterized the Jews as a nation; the other—and more sublime—which acknowledged that they had attained the level of a religious community, distinctive by virtue of their beliefs and practices, not their national or racial characteristics. This argument, it must immediately be said, was not altogether novel. Simultaneously being promulgated in other Jewish communities in the United States as well as on the European continent, it drew on teachings nurtured by the German Reform movement of the 1830s and 1840s and that, in Great Britain itself, had already been clearly enunciated in a celebrated article written by Rabbi (soon to be Chief Rabbi) Hermann Adler in the *Nineteenth Century* as early as 1878.[14] But even when all the necessary parallels have been drawn, Montefiore's exposition of the distinction between Jewry as a nation and Jewry as a religious community remains noteworthy. One reason is the lengths to which Montefiore himself went to develop his thesis, both in his writings and in his activities as longtime president of the Anglo-Jewish Association (1895–1922). Another, more relevant to our present concern, is the extent to which he so pressed his argument into anti-Zionist service that it became a standard plank of that particular platform.

Even during the periods of independent Jewish statehood, Montefiore contended, "the religion, in its deeper essentials," had always been "too universal to be satisfied with or happy in its national institutions." The Davidic era itself had witnessed tendencies that sapped an ordinary, secular nationalism at its roots. "The germs of universalism" apparent in many of the Psalms had then begun to overshadow "the glow of patriotism" induced by the original "lawless disposition" of the land of the Canaanites. Even the festival of Hanukah, which the Zionists regularly sought to invest with explicitly nationalist overtones, was primarily a tribute to the victory of the monotheistic idea. Consciously echoing eminently respectable Jewish traditions, Montefiore insisted that "the mere national aspect of the matter is very small and trivial. . . . Chanukah is a *religious* festival."[15]

Exile, in this scheme of things, could not possibly have been the unmitigated disaster of Zionist polemic. On the contrary, "the religion became in many respects purer and freer when separated from the national soil." In their dispersion the Jews had become purged of the tribal, secular chauvinism that blights the biblical record. Indeed, only in exile were they truly fitted to proclaim the concept of God "as the one . . . Deity of the entire world." This privilege compensated even for the pain that the experience had unfortunately entailed. Necessarily, it also affected perspectives on future action. If Jews cherished hopes of a future restoration, they had in mind the reaffirmation of their religious purity, not the revival of their state. In the words of one early summary of the argument:

Israel's mission, like his election, is purely religious. His is no worldly vocation; he has been called not for empire . . . but to distribute the spiritual riches that have been entrusted to him. . . . Isolation . . . even though it be isolation in Palestine, and accompanied by national independence, would mean failure for Israel's mission.[16]

Here, then, was far more than an optimistic (and, in the event, tragically misguided) expression of faith in the belief that Jews *could* remain Jews in the diaspora. Also articulated was a conviction that they had a moral and religious duty to do just that. The events of 1917—not the Balfour Declaration, but the March Revolution in Petrograd—showed that Herzl had been unduly pessimistic to despair of emancipation in Russia.[17] Similarly, the entire sweep of Jewish development would show that he and his followers had been fundamentally wrong to substitute a mundane project of physical action for the transcendent conception of spiritual glory to which the Jewish religion truly aspired. The contrast with the anti-Zionists' learned description of what they portrayed as Jewry's "advance" toward its "universal mission" could not have been more pronounced. Indeed, Montefiore's exposition of that thesis was long regarded as the most influential of all his contributions to the anti-Zionist case. One of his addresses on the subject became a *locus classicus* of its own brand of anti-Zionist religious thought. Promptly printed in the community's two most prestigious academic journals, it was to be reissued, under various titles, several times.[18] It was also extensively quoted—and maligned—in the "battle of books" that preceded and succeeded the publication of the Balfour Declaration. Among other things, it constituted the ideological backbone of such antinationalist broadsides as the Conjoint Committee's Manifesto, published in the *Times* (London) on May 24, 1917, and the Prospectus that the diehard League of British Jews issued in 1918. By the latter date, even the Zionists had been forced to acknowledge its impact, conceding that:

Of the [anti-Zionist] pamphlets, that of Mr. Claude Montefiore, called "Nation or Religious Community" took up by far the most defensible position since it did not venture to argue that the Jews were merely a religious sect, but that they ought to aim at becoming nothing *but* a religious sect.[19]

III

By and large, the anti-Zionist inferences to be derived from the doctrine of Jewry's universalistic mission were most enthusiastically embraced by Reform and Liberal elements in Anglo-Jewry. Traditional and Orthodox Jews, whose numbers were in any case larger, tended to be more circumspect, perhaps because those who were themselves recent immigrants from Eastern Europe could not yet share Montefiore's faith in the inevitable eradication of antisemitism—from which, indeed, many had recently fled. More particularly, their ambivalence reflected the greater depth of their response to Zionism's purposeful invocation of Jewry's ancient symbols and language. Unlike Reform Jews, the Orthodox could never expunge prayers for the return to Zion from the everyday liturgy. Neither could they deny the divine origin of the duty to settle in Eretz Israel. Prior to the advent of Herzl, Chief Rabbi Adler had cited explicit halakhic authority when professing his religious attachment to the Holy Land—to which he himself made a much-publicized pilgrimage in 1885.[20]

Throughout the period under review, the English Zionist Federation continually attempted to exploit such sentiments. That Herzl "bow diplomatically to the wishes of the conscientiously Orthodox" was, accordingly, an early piece of advice.[21] His local lieutenants themselves invested some energy in the task, sporadically launching "synagogue campaigns" designed to make the pulpit a vehicle for "valuable"—and free—propaganda. "We must," they determined, "have in view a systematic and organized scheme to win over the Synagogue to our cause."[22]

That aim was not fulfilled. Even after proponents of religious Zionism founded a Mizrahi Federation in England in December 1918, Jewish nationalism still attracted only a minority of the country's rabbinate. Thereto, opinion had been even more discouraging. Most obviously was this so in native Orthodox circles, where the tone had at a very early stage been decisively set by Chief Rabbi Adler. Although prepared to discuss Zionism with Herzl in 1895, he had soon aligned himself with the *Protestrabbiner* of Germany, declaring that the national program aroused his "unfeigned concern, because I regard it as opposed to the teachings of Judaism, as impolitic, aye as charged with the greatest peril."[23] True, Adler's was not the only voice to be heard. His vociferous opposition to Zionism was in some part balanced by the equally forthright support constantly expressed by the Hakham Moses Gaster. In October 1917—although, it must be stressed, not before—it was also offset by the pro-Zionist response to the government's questionnaire then submitted by Adler's successor, Chief Rabbi Joseph Herzl.[24] Nevertheless, these remained exceptions to a rule characterized by reserve and doubt. As congregants were informed by A. A. Green and Simeon Singer—the two London "reverends" who most obviously approximated to an Anglo-Jewish clerical ideal—Zionism seemed to be "creating new problems which we shall find it hard to solve and new problems which we shall find it hard to palliate."[25]

Equally marked was the division of opinion among the immigrant rabbis, who ministered to the greater mass of Britain's synagogue-attending public. The generalization that they "supported the Zionist movement"[26] really fits only a limited—albeit articulate—circle of new arrivals, prominent among whom were Sholem Yakov Rabinowitz (1857–1921, who came to Liverpool in 1906); Yitzhak Herzog (1888–1954, who held posts in Belfast and Dublin); and the latter's predecessor as chief rabbi in mandatory Palestine, Abraham Isaac Kook (1865–1935, rabbi of the Mahazikei Hadath [Guardians of the Faith] community in London from 1916 until 1919). But their unconditional sympathy with political Zionism was somewhat idiosyncratic. Self-consciously influenced by the barrage of anti-Zionist polemic emanating from the "sages" of Eastern Europe,[27] most immigrant rabbis chose to toe what was becoming the standard Orthodox line. One indication is provided by the attendance of Yisrael Hayim Daiches (since 1902 of Leeds) and Shemuel Hillman (since 1908 in Glasgow) at the 1912 Katowice Conference that founded the Agudat Israel, whose activities also had the blessing of Meir Jung, appointed *rav* of the Federation of [immigrant London] Synagogues in the same year. Equally significant are the records of discussions at the immigrants' own Agudat Harabbanim Haharedim beAngliah (League of the Orthodox Rabbis in England). Twice during the period under review, in 1902 and 1911, this group convened to discuss questions of common interest. Notwithstanding the protests of a radical minority, participants on both occasions decided to curtail all discussion of Zionism and its program.[28]

IV

It is tempting to attribute Orthodox reservations about political Zionism entirely to an unwillingness to cooperate with the movement's confessedly irreligious leaders. The secular beliefs held by most members of the Zionist Actions Committee necessarily remained an anathema to the strictly Orthodox, who believed that Jewish public affairs ought to be the exclusive purview of persons conforming to the traditional standards of piety and observance. Even Abba Werner, rabbi of the Mahazikei Hadath community, who had originally supported Herzl, admitted in 1911 that "some of the [movement's] leaders have greatly disappointed me in their attitude towards the Jewish religion. Unless the Torah is observed, there is no raison d'etre for Zionism.[29]

Yet that was only one part of the story. Orthodox resistance to political

Zionism (opposition is, in this case, probably too severe a term) here, too, owed more to a clash of philosophies than to personal tensions. As traditionally foreseen, the return to Zion would be synonymous with redemption; since exile had been a punishment for Israel's misdemeanors, it could not be terminated without a definitive sign from heaven that the Jews had indeed earned their passage home. Precipitate communal action, unaccompanied by any such omens, was tantamount to rebellion against the divine plan. From Bar Kokhba to Shabbetai Zevi, Jewish history had witnessed a serious of pseudomessianic charlatans whose disobedient impatience had brought physical and spiritual catastrophe to their followers. Salvation would come only when the Jews had been cleansed of their sins. Until then, they had lovingly to accept their sentence. It was by their example of piety under duress that they would sanctify the divine name and justify their designation as a "light to the nations."

In several important respects, this Orthodox interpretation of Israel's mission differed markedly from that being preached in Reform circles. For the latter, as we have seen, dispersion marked the fulfillment of Israel's spiritual destiny; for the Orthodox, it was only a way station. A complete meeting of the minds—even had it not been impaired by social and cultural barriers—was thus impossible. Nevertheless, the community's two wings were not entirely apart. On the contrary, where political Zionism was concerned, the similarities in their arguments seemed strong enough to forge a commonly antagonistic response. Thus it was that both sections of Anglo-Jewry employed remarkably similar themes when addressing the topic.

Three specific examples deserve particular mention. The first, thus placed by virtue of its pivotal importance, is the emphasis Orthodox rabbis placed on the classification of Jewry as a "religious community" rather than a "nation." As has already been noted, this was a theme on which Montefiore persistently harped. It was also one with which most Orthodox clergy (immigrant as well as native) entirely sympathized. Jung, for instance, spoke for a wide cross section of clerical opinion when, during the testy days of June 1917, he declared:

Should I be obliged either to consent to our people being a religious society without national characteristics, or to consent to their being a national association without any religious foundations, and should there be no alternative, I frankly confess that I should not hesitate in giving the preference to religion without nationalism.[30]

The second example is somewhat more recondite, consisting of the traditional interpretation the three "oaths" in the Song of Songs that had long been interpreted as warnings against the use of force to reestablish Jewish national sovereignty and against "excessive supplication" to hasten the End of Days.[31] Although often relegated to a parenthesis by some advanced religious Zionists in the community, this text was more generally taken for what it was: an example of a stream of Jewish thought at odds with the rush to statehood advocated by Zionist activism. Indeed, it was within a specifically anti-Zionist context that the three "oaths" were cited by Orthodox rabbis (the range includes Adler as well as immigrants) and thereby even transmitted to such anti-Orthodox—and otherwise anti-Adlerian—audiences as the radical Jewish Religious Union.[32]

Finally, there was Jewish history—a quarry that all sections of the clerical community assiduously mined for homiletic purposes. Within the anti-Zionist context, obviously relevant was the traditional account of the Rabban Yohanan Ben Zakkai's behavior on the eve of the fall of Jerusalem in 70 C.E.[33] Reform preachers were absolutely sure of the moral to be drawn from that ancient sage's feud with the nationalist zealots and his request that the Roman government grant him the academy of Yavneh rather than the relief of the national capital. In so doing, they argued, Ben Zakkai had shown that true Judaism was "independent of the local Zion." Israel's strength lay "not in the attainment of national grandeur, nor even in the restoration of national existence, but the guarding and dissemination of religious truth."[34] Several Orthodox rabbis echoed those sentiments—albeit in a more guarded and arcane fashion. Thus, in the course of an intricate discourse devoted to the theme of national regeneration, Yisrael Hayim Daiches, too, forcibly contrasted Ben Zakkai's preservation of the true spirit of Judaism with his disregard of the less consequential material welfare of the Holy Land.[35] Meir Jung developed the same theme in his induction sermon, as did Aaron Hyman in his more systematic treatment of the incident. Indeed, the latter became the proof text for the statement that: "In the opinion of our venerable Rabbi, the Jewish State was like every other, transitory. The Jewish People, however, was *not* to perish with its existence as a State or Polity. Israel was to be preserved alive . . . with a life even fuller."[36]

V

To show such coalescence of themes and ideas is not to disfigure the plain differences dividing Orthodoxy from Reform within Anglo-Jewry or to fudge the distinctions between the immigrant and native communities. It is, rather, to demonstrate the extent to which opposition to political Zionism, even where exacerbated by social irritants, was ultimately rooted in intellectual and religious objections. It was because they felt the Zionists to be articulating only one interpretation of Jewish eschatological thought—and the wrong one at that—that the community's anti-Zionists were moved to table their objections to the Balfour Declaration as strongly as they did. Precisely the same considerations enabled them to overcome their own inner disagreements and yoke themselves together in what was, by the community's own standards, perhaps a unique harness.

Notes

1. For texts and commentary, see V. D. Lipman, "Anglo-Jewish Leaders and the Balfour Declaration," *Michael* 10 (1986): 153–80, which also includes the now-notorious anti-Zionist memorandum separately submitted by Edwin Montagu, secretary of state of India. There is evidence that Montagu coached the three anti-Zionist respondents (Sir Philip Magnus, L. L. Cohen, and Claude Montefiore) in his letter to the latter, dated October 4 and marked "secret": "I . . . write in order to be able to help you to be in readiness and advised to act." Files of the Board of Deputies of British Jews, London, C11/12/54(ii). On the drafting of the Balfour Declaration," see Ben Halpern, "The Drafting of the Balfour Declaration," *Herzl Year Book* 7 (New York, 1971): 255–84. For a recent interpretation of its origins, see David Vital, *Zionism: The Crucial Phase* (Oxford, 1987), pp. 207–95.

2. Nahum Sokolow, *A History of Zionism, 1600–1918* (London, 1919), p. 194; Chaim Weizmann, *Trial and Error* (London, 1949), pp. 252–62. See also *The Letters and Papers of Chaim Weizmann,* ed. Leonard Stein (London, 1968–), 7:521–22, 526–28, 533–34.

3. It was to Anglo-Jewish audiences that Theodor Herzl first *publicly* aired his notions. He addressed the Maccabean debating society in November 1895 and published "A Solution to the Jewish Problem" in the *Jewish Chronicle,* the community's most influential weekly, on January 17, 1896—a month before the appearance of *Der Judenstaat.* On reactions, see S. A. Cohen, *English Zionists and British Jews: The Communal Politics of Anglo-Jewry, 1895–1920* (Princeton, N.J., 1982), pp. 25–32.

4. Sokolow, *History of Zionism,* p. x.

5. *Arbayter Fraynt,* July 31, 1903, p. 6. This journal was the organ of the London Jewish anarchist circle led by Rudolf Rocker. In general, see William J. Fishman, *East End Jewish Radicals, 1975–1914* (London, 1975).

6. See Montagu's most famous exposition of this case in the memorandum, rebarbatively entitled "The Anti-Semitism of the Present Cabinet," which he submitted on August 23, 1917. Lipman, "Anglo-Jewish Leaders," pp. 158–62. See also his private letter to David Lloyd George of October 4, 1917, quoted in Vital, *Zionism,* pp. 282–83. More restrained, but equally insistent, were the earlier comments in H. S. Q. Henriques, *The Jews and the English Law* (Oxford, 1908), pp. 209ff., and the preface by Israel Abrahams and S. I. Levy to *Macaulay's Essays and Speeches on Jewish Disabilities* (London, 1908). Zionist retorts are in Samuel Daiches, *Zionism and Patriotism* (London, 1909), and Harry Sachar, *Jewish Emancipation: The Contract Myth* (London, 1917). The background is discussed in Colin Holmes, *Anti-Semitism in British Society, 1876–1939* (London, 1979), esp. pp. 130–40.

7. Claude Montefiore, "Liberal Judaism and Jewish Nationalism," *Papers for the Jewish People* (London) 16 (August 1917): 27. Hence most of these men had supported the local wing of the Hovevei Zion Association in its pre-Herzlian days, and few would have anything to do with the Jewish Territorial Organisation (ITO), founded in 1905 by Israel Zangwill when the Zionist Organisation voted to reject the Uganda option.

8. Claude Montefiore to Israel Zangwill, February 18, [1903], Israel Zangwill Papers, Central Zionist Archives (hereafter CZA), Jerusalem, A120/53a.

9. Claude Montefiore, "Assimilation: Good and Bad," *Papers for the Jewish People* 9 (1909): 16.

10. Lucien Wolf, "The Zionist Peril," *Jewish Quarterly Review* 17 (October 1904): 12–13: "The characteristic peril of Zionism is that it is the natural and abiding ally of Anti-Semitism and its most powerful justification. It is an attempt to turn back the course of modern Jewish history, which hitherto, on its political side, has had for its main object to secure for the Jewish people an equal place with their fellow citizens of other creeds in the countries in which they dwell, and a common lot with them in the main stream of human progress." This was a recurring theme. Voiced as early as Wolf's *Aspects of the Jewish Question* (London, 1902)

and—in opposition to the East Africa "offer"—in his letters to the *Times* (London) on July 8, and September 9, 1903, it was repeated in the *Encyclopaedia Britannica,* to the classic 11th edition (1911) of which Wolf contributed the articles on both "Antisemitism" and "Zionism," and in the run of memorandums he presented to the government throughout World War I.

11. Israel Abrahams, "Palestine and Jewish Nationality," *Hibbert Journal* 16 (April 1918): 457.

12. Zangwill went on: "As for the Zionism run by your orthodox gang, it is even a dirtier form of the Messiah." Zangwill to Joseph Cowen, January 10, 1908, Files of the Jewish Territorial Organisation (ITO) CZA, A36/135.

13. Claude Montefiore, *The Bible for Home Reading* (London, 1896). This work had run to seven editions by 1920. On Montefiore's immense influence on an entire generation of acculturated British Jews, see E. C. Black, *The Social Politics of Anglo–Jewry, 1880–1920* (Oxford, 1988), pp. 22–24.

14. "We have ceased to be a body politic; we are citizens of the country in which we dwell. . . . Judaism has no political bearing whatsoever . . . religion is the main bond." Quoted in Isaiah Friedman, *The Question of Palestine, 1914–1918* (London, 1973), p. 29. Still a valuable introduction to the theme and its origins is M. J. Weiner, "The Concept of Mission in Traditional and Modern Judaism," *YIVO Annual of Jewish Social Science* 2–3 (New York, 1947–48): 1–19. For comparable notions elsewhere, see N. W. Cohen, "The Reaction of Reform Judaism in America to Political Zionism (1897–1922)," *Publications of the American Jewish Historical Society* 40 (New York, 1951): 361–94; Jehuda Reinharz, "Consensus and Conflict between Zionists and Liberals in Germany before World War I," in *Texts and Responses: Studies Presented to Nahum A. Glatzer,* ed. Michael A Fishbane and Paul R. Flohr (Leiden, 1975), pp. 226–38.

15. Montefiore, *Bible for Home Reading,* 1:106, 2:740. The traditions echoed are in the Babylonian Talmud, tractate *Shabbat,* fol. 25a.

16. Morris Joseph, *Judaism as Creed and Life* (London, 1903), pp. 158, 170–71. Joseph was the respected minister of the West London (Reform) Congregation of British Jews.

17. "The 'Jewish problem' in Russia has been solved, as so many of us longed and prayed that it would be solved, *in* Russia itself and by the Russians themselves." Claude Montefiore, "Liberal Judaism and Jewish Nationalism," pp. 16–17. See also his "A Diehard's Confession" (1935), in Lucy Cohen, *Some Recollections of Claude Goldsmid Montefiore, 1858–1938* (London, 1940), pp. 226–27.

18. Claude Montefiore, "Nation or Religious Community?" 1899, printed in *Jewish Quarterly Review* 12 (1900), and in *Transactions of the Jewish Historical Society of England* 4 (1904).

19. Note (unsigned, but dated 1919) on the League of British Jews in the files of the Central Zionist Office, London, CZA Z4/5014.

20. Hermann Adler, *A Pilgrimage to Zion* [a sermon preached at the Great Synagogue], (London, 1885).

21. Jacob de Haas to Theodor Herzl, July 15, 1896, "confidential," Theodor Herzl Papers, CZA, HVIII/513.

22. S. B. Lipton, February 3, 1918, memorandum, Files of the Central Zionist Office, London, CZA Z4/692(11).

23. Hermann Adler, speech to the Anglo-Jewish Association, reported in *Jewish Chronicle,* July 8, 1898, pp. 12–14. In general, see Immanuel Jakobovits, "The Attitude to Zionism of Britain's Chief Rabbis as Reflected in Their Writings," in *"If Only My People . . .": Zionism in My Life* (London, 1984), pp. 211–18.

24. Jakobovits, *"If Only My People,"* pp. 220–22. As Jakobovits points out, Rabbi Joseph Hertz's Zionist sympathies were known before his appointment in 1911. Nevertheless, until 1917, he was pointedly (and, to Zionist eyes, discouragingly) reluctant to make much of a show of them. See Cohen, *English Zionists and British Jews,* pp. 190–91. As for Gaster, he

was altogether a doubtful asset. His simmering relations with his own community probably did more harm than good to the Zionist cause; so, too, did his tendency to provoke dissension within Zionist ranks.

25. A. A. Green to Moses Gaster, October 31, 1898, Moses Gaster Papers, CZA, A203/106. These remained constant themes.

26. L. P. Gartner, *The Jewish Immigrant in England,* 2d ed. (London, 1973), p. 250.

27. On this anti-Zionist polemic, see Yosef Salmon, "Emdatah shel hahevrah haharedit beRussyah-Polin lezionut bashanim 1898–1900," *Eshel Beer Sheva* (Beersheba, 1976), pp. 377–438. One of the most comprehensive anti-Zionist compilations, *Sefer or layesharim,* ed. Sh. Z. Landa and Yosef Rabinowitz (Warsaw, 1900), also included Adler's sermon, "Religious versus Political Zionism" (pp. 62–68), as the only contribution by a Western European.

28. *Beit vaad lahakhamim* 2 (February 1903): 3–5; *Hayehudi* March 16, 23, 31, 1911. On the Katowice Conference, see *Hayehudi,* June 13, 1912. The former was a quarterly representing immigrant Orthodox opinion; the latter was a weekly, Anglo-Jewry's only Hebrew newspaper.

29. Interview with Abba Werner in *Jewish Chronicle,* June 8, 1911, p. 20. See similar sentiments of Rabbi Avigdor Schonfield, the leader of German immigrant Orthodoxy in North London, in *Jewish Chronicle,* July 26, 1918, p. 10.

30. Meir Jung, in *Jewish Chronicle,* June 22, 1917, p. 25. See also Yisrael Hayim Daiches, *Derashot meharyah* (Leeds, 1920), nos. 11, 35.

31. See Song of Songs 2:7, 3:5, 8:4, and Babylonian Talmud, tractate *Ketubot* 111a, and comments by Rashi, 1040–1105.

32. Hermann Adler, reported in *Jewish Chronicle,* October 15, 1897, p. 13. See the citation in O. J. Simon, "The Return to Palestine," *Nineteenth Century* (September 1898): 437–47. For immigrant Orthodox interpretations, see, e.g., S. E. Sabel, *Sefer shir hashirim im perush hadash* (London, 1899), pp. 14–21; Yoel Herzog, *Gilyonei yoel* (Vilna, 1913), p. 144; Gedaliah Silverstone, introd. to Hayyim Broda, *Sefer hadash leshir hashirim* (London, 1903).

33. Babylonian Talmud, tractate *Gittin* 59b.

34. Morris Joseph, *Judaism as Creed and Life,* pp. 197–98; Rev. Israel Harris, sermon delivered at West London Synagogue of British Jews, reported in *Jewish Chronicle,* March 24, 1911, p. 30.

35. *Derashot maharyah,* no. 19, on Babylonian Talmud, tractate *Gittin* 56b.

36. Walter Javitz, "Rabbi Jochanon ben Zakkai," *Sinaiist* 1 (1917); 11–14. The source is Aaron Hyman, *Sefer toledot hatannaim vehaamoraim* (London, 1911), 2:674–81. Jung's view are in *Jewish Chronicle,* June 21, 1912, p. 26.

REFORM, CONSERVATIVE, AND ORTHODOX JUDAISM: ZIONISM IN THE UNITED STATES

The Meaning of Zionism and Its Influence among the American Jewish Religious Movements

In Marshall Sklare's *America's Jews* we find the following evaluation of Zionism in the United States: "Whether he was a pushcart peddler or a justice of the Supreme Court, the role of the American Jews in the Zionist movement was not decisive. The impetus for the establishment of a new Jewish commonwealth derived from the position that Jews occupied in 19th and 20th century European society rather than in the American nation."[1]

Sklare may have been correct in his assertion that international, European-centered Zionism was based on premises and historical developments that were quite different from the political values Jews had adopted while becoming American citizens. Nevertheless, it is the contention of the present essay that during the twentieth century a unique type of Zionism did arise in America. The Jewish religious movements in the United States were a major vehicle in the creation of that new kind of Zionism, which was the result of ideological and social adaptation to American Jewish conditions, and this kind of religious-related Zionism fulfilled an important role in the overall development of contemporary Jewish consciousness. Indeed, the character of Jewish religious life itself in America was significantly influenced by the Zionist idea.[2]

We have to explain how the penetration of Zionism into American Jewry, through the vehicle of the religious movements, took place. Regarding religion itself, today its centrality in American Jewish life and its importance as a focus for the identification of American Jews seem obvious. It should be remembered, however, that there were times when the predominance of religion as a factor in American Jewish life, or at least the ability of religion to withstand the trials of acculturation and adaptation to American conditions, were not taken for granted by all observers of the community. For instance, Chaim Zhitlowsky, one of the important ideologists of Jewish autonomism and a man familiar with American Jewish conditions, was convinced, back in 1915, that the Jewish religion had no future in America and that American Jewry would survive only on the basis of Jewish nationality.[3] Even Solomon Schechter had his moments of doubt about the future of Jewish religion in America. Explaining his adoption of Zionism in 1906, he wrote: "After long hesitation and careful watching, Zionism [i.e., not religion] recommended itself as the great bulwark against assimilation."[4]

That the Jewish religion remained at the heart of Jewish life and organization in the United States was due, in part, to the very significant role which religion in general has played in the United States and the allowances American society gives for religious diversity. Religion in America also fulfilled important tasks of a fundamentally social character, something that squared well with Jewish traditions of European origin. It was in the first years of the century, during that important period of self-definition and organization of the diverse Jewish religious tendencies in America, that their contact with Zionist ideas was established. It may be that one of the characteristics—and perhaps even one of the conditions—of the cross-fertilization between Zionism and Jewish religion in the United States was that both were in a state of flux: both were establishing themselves in the land and adapting to its conditions.

Nevertheless, the encounter between religion and Zionism in America was by no means an easy one. Originally there was strong opposition to Zionism among two of the three main religious trends in American Jewry, Orthodoxy and Reform. The antagonism of the latter had not only religious but also social reasons: it was claimed that Zionism infringed upon the good Americanism of the Jew. Nor should it be ignored that opposition to Zionism existed also in nonreligiously organized sectors of American Jewry. American Jewish socialists, especially those ideologically related to the Bund, were fiercely opposed to Zionism and in the early part of the century they were a force to be reckoned with in the immigrant community. Thus the penetration of Zionist ideas into the mainstream of American Jewish society was a process that evolved over many years.

Throughout this period, Zionism itself did not remain static any more than did the three developing religious tendencies of American Jewry. Today, in the last part of the century, the religious movements in American Jewry are well defined in their diverse religious positions, and Zionism can be said to be among the issues that unite them. We should examine, therefore, the factors in the development of American Jewry, of American Jewish religion, and of Zionism in America, that brought about this present result.

If one begins with the Orthodox movement, it will be found that its attitudes toward Zionism in the United States have not yet been sufficiently researched. As understood now, Orthodoxy was, compared to the other religious trends in American Judaism, less dynamic in its internal development *vis-à-vis* Zionism. In the earlier part of the century there were two Orthodox sectors, both of European origin, one pro-Zionist, the other opposed to it. The pro-Zionists were associated with the Mizrahi movement, established in the United States in 1914. The opposing segment later found its voice, or one of its voices, in Agudat Israel. Between both currents there was a considerable body of Orthodox Jews sentimentally identified with Eretz Israel but politically passive.

Over the next decades there was a sociological shift in American Jewish Orthodoxy, but hardly an ideological one. The anti-Zionist segment, which had always been a minority among the American Orthodox, became even smaller. The central body of the uncommitted became gradually identified with the Mizrahi position even if not necessarily affiliated with the Mizrahi organization. But it is this lack of ideological development that poses questions, especially when compared with the ideological dynamism of the Reform and Conservative movements.

One possible explanation is that for a large part of the present century, Orthodoxy in America was in a defensive position, fighting a losing battle to keep its shrinking ranks together. Such conditions were hardly conducive to the formulation of new and positive attitudes *vis-à-vis* the social and spiritual transformations that American Jewry was experiencing.

It is generally accepted that the Conservative movement, in comparison, was Zionist from its earliest days.[5] Even so, the Zionist orientation of the Conservative movement was a matter of gradual and highly interesting evolution. In its center, as it happened also with so many other central issues of the movement, stood the Jewish Theological Seminary.

Diverse Zionist attitudes were to be found, in the first decade of the century, among the faculty members of the seminary and probably also among the students. But some of the very prestigious lay sponsors of the reorganized seminary were either non-Zionists (Louis Marshall) or anti-Zionists (Jacob H. Schiff), or stood between non- and anti-Zionism (Cyrus Adler, the president of the seminary from 1915). They certainly represented factors of influence to be reckoned with. Solomon Schechter himself hesitated regarding Zionism. He was (and remained) opposed to the idea of Jewish nationalism: "The brutal Thora[Torah]-less nationalism promulgated in certain quarters, would have been to the Rabbis just as hateful as the suicidal Thora-less universalism preached in other quarters." Even after he adopted Zionism in 1906, his position was considered equivocal.[6]

The most clearly defined Zionist position in the early Jewish Theological Seminary faculty was that of Israel Friedlaender. Friedlaender had been active in the movement back in Europe, had participated in the Sixth Zionist Congress, and had developed a personal relationship with Ahad Haam.[7] Friedlaender became one of the outstanding formulators of what later became the Zionist approach of the Conservative movement. It meant, basically, a transformed version of Ahad Haam's spiritual Zionism, into which elements of Simon Dubnov's autonomist approach were integrated. Friedlaender adopted Ahad Haam's concept of the creation of a "spiritual center" in Palestine that would exert a regenerating influence on diaspora Jewry. But his attitude toward the diaspora was quite different from Ahad Haam's.

As it is well known, Ahad Haam explained Jewish life in the *galut* in terms different from those of the political Zionists. The matter, in his view, had a subjective and an objective dimension. Subjectively, he rejected Jewish life in the diaspora. Objectively, he felt himself forced to accept it: whatever solutions Palestine and Zionism may offer to the Jews, still the majority of the Jewish people (and Ahad Haam had in mind the Jewish masses in Eastern Europe) would remain living in the diaspora.[8] In spite of recognizing that reality, Ahad Haam had little faith in, and even less hope for, a Jewish future there.

Friedlaender's geographical focus was different: it was not Jewish circumstances in the diaspora in general he was speaking about, but the Jews in America. And analyzing Jewish life in the United States, he adopted the positive tone that was characteristic of most sectors of American Jewry, the oldtimers of German extraction as well as the Russian newcomers: America was not *galut* in the classic sense: America was the new Jewish center (as in Dubnov's historical structure), *di goldene medine* (the Golden Land) of the masses of Jewish immigrants. From Dubnov, Friedlaender took also another central element: the emphasis on social matters, the communal approach. Ahad Haam cared little for the details of communal life, while for Dubnov they were questions of prime importance. So they were for Friedlaender: the development of the Jewish center in the United States was the issue he concentrated on and participated in with much dedication. Its creation did not exclude the establishment of the Jewish center in Palestine but ran parallel to it. Efforts in both directions were mutually complementary.[9]

Friedlaender's exposition of Zionism differed from Ahad Haam's in other ways. Friedlaender almost ignored antisemitism, which was so central a component in the European movement. Antisemitism was, perhaps, another factor that did not adapt well to the hopes of most American Jews. Friedlaender also ignored the nonreligious foundations of Ahad Haam's position. Friedlaender and most of his colleagues were observant Jews, and the brand of Zionism they advocated was based on some harmonization between Jewish religion and Zionism that was considered obvious, even if left mostly unexplained.

Ideologically close to Friedlaender was Judah L. Magnes. By 1905, Magnes was the secretary of the Federation of American Zionists as well as the assistant rabbi of the most important Reform congregation in New York, Temple Emanu-El, a place hardly congenial for a man of Zionist convictions. But Magnes was moving away from Reform and gradually identifying with the new religious position unfolding at the Jewish Theological Seminary. In 1910, after some fiercely critical sermons at Temple Emanu-El, Magnes resigned. A year before he had become the head of the newly established New York Kehillah. Magnes was a central figure in that group of Jewish intellectuals engaged in developing the new brand of American spiritual Zionism that was to become the position of the Conservative movement.

Perhaps not ideologically profound as Friedlaender, Magnes was as highly articulate and much more influential: his was a voice heard and respected in Jewish circles of diverse religious and ideological persuasions, including among the German Jewish notables.[10]

Friedlaender and his associates thus laid the foundations of an Americanized version of spiritual Zionism that amalgamated his Zionist aspirations and his American hopes. The decisive, creative feature of that combination was that it not only neutralized the potential divergences between Zionism and religion but rendered them mutually supportive: the vision that now evolved was that of an American Judaism made richer by the Zionist influence, squaring also with religious belief. That approach was adopted by the new religious trend, the Conservative movement, growing out of the Jewish Theological Seminary.

Over the next decades, changing Jewish, American Jewish, and Zionist circumstances introduced modifications in the Zionist formulations of the Conservative trend but did not touch its basic assumptions. The basic task—the amalgamation between Zionism and Jewish Americanism—was accomplished in the decade between 1903 and 1914. That amalgamation became a foundation of the Conservative religious position in American Jewry. It would be elaborated later by additional thinkers, among them Mordecai M. Kaplan, the founder of the Reconstructionist movement, who originally was one of the younger members of the Jewish Theological Seminary faculty in Schechter's days.[11]

American cultural Zionism represented one of the original spiritual creations of the developing American Judaism, one that sooner or later would be adopted also by the other Jewish religious movements in the United States. Solomon Schechter, the father of the Conservative movement in American Jewry, had believed that the religious position he proposed would be adopted by the great majority of American Jews. Time proved him wrong. However, the fusion between Zionism and Judaism in America, elaborated in the seminary more by Schechter's collaborators than by Schechter himself, became one of the principles of the American Jewish self-definition accepted by the great majority of American Jews.

Compared to the Conservative movement, the development of the American Reform position *vis-à-vis* Zionism was more radical. Historically considered, the Reform movement in the United States made an almost complete about-turn in its views of Zionism, from general negation at the end of the nineteenth century to wholehearted support in our days. But two qualifications should be made when describing early Reform opposition to Zionism: first, there were always exceptions in the American Reform rabbinate, men who supported the Zionist movement, some of whom enjoyed very high standing; second, support for Jewish life in Palestine (meaning, philanthropic support) struck a responsive chord also among many of the Reform activists who remained ideologically anti-Zionist.[12]

Beyond that, the antagonism to political Zionism was fierce indeed. Few resolutions can compare in succinct extremism to the one adopted by the Montreal Conference of the Central Conference of American Rabbis (CCAR), in 1897, which opened with the sentence: "We totally disapprove of any attempt for the establishment of a Jewish state."[13] The 1897 resolution, sponsored by no less an authority than Isaac M. Wise, became the generally accepted position of the Reform movement for the next decades. The dismissal of three faculty members of the Hebrew Union College in 1907, mainly because of their Zionist ideas (and three, in those days, meant about 30 percent of the faculty), was another milestone in anti-Zionism in the American Reform movement.[14]

A less-known but not insignificant step in Reform anti-Zionism was the call in 1918 for a conference to combat what was seen as the threat of Zionism. It originated in the Chicago CCAR conference of the same year. A committee was formed headed by Rabbi David Philipson; laymen also participated. The forceful opposition of several prestigious figures in American Jewry, such as Jacob H. Schiff, Louis Marshall, and Oscar S. Straus, caused that initiative to collapse.[15] Not until 1943 was an anti-Zionist organization of some significance established—the American Council for Judaism. The council, representing a group of rabbis and laymen connected with the Reform movement, opposed the growing pro-Zionist tendency of their movement and of American Jewry in general. Although active and vocal, it remained marginal in influence, and after 1948 the council faded away.[16]

The resolutions of the Columbus Conference of the CCAR, in 1937, are considered a turning point in the Jewish self-definition of the Reform movement, which also incorporated a new attitude toward Zionism. The Columbus Conference adopted a platform within which a new and more positive attitude toward Jewish peoplehood was formulated, one that went far beyond the positions adopted in the late nineteenth century.[17] One way to explain this change is that by the mid-1930s the social composition of the Reform movement had been drastically transformed, as the majority of its membership became second-generation American Jews of Eastern European origin. Their attitude toward matters such as Jewishness and Zionism was rooted in concepts and traditions different from those of the Jews of German origin, who had been the backbone of the movement earlier in the century.

As stated before, a pro-Zionist tendency had been at work in the Reform movement since the earlier years of the century. At the beginning, its influence was limited, but it increased steadily. The arguments for an understanding between Reform and Zionism were varied. Bernhard Felsenthal, one of the founding fathers of the Reform movement in the United States, explained that it was in the very spirit of the Reform movement to adopt Zionism because both represented progressive and dynamic positions in Jewish life.[18] Gustav Gottheil, Stephen S. Wise, and others formulated these and similar pro-Zionist ideas in various ways.

One argument, less frequently mentioned but surfacing again and again among Reform thinkers, deserves attention: the recognition that Zionism has or will become a central factor in Jewish life and consciousness, combined with a certain apprehension that a non-Zionist Reform movement may end as a marginal element in Jewish life. Much of Bernhard Felsenthal's insistence on the adoption of Zionism was directly or indirectly related to the keeping of the Reform movement in the mainstream of Jewish life.[19] The same reasoning appeared in the first decade of the twentieth century in writings of Maximilian Heller and of Max Schloessinger, who claimed, "Reform Judaism will be Zionistic or it will not be at all."[20] This argument can also be found in Felix A. Levy's utterances in 1943,[21] and it would reemerge with great poignancy in the 1970s and 1980s.

Reform thinkers also discovered Ahad Haam and, like the intellectuals of the Jewish Theological Seminary, stressed the significance of his approach for Jewish life in America. One of the first Reform cultural Zionists was David Neumark, a member of the faculty of the Hebrew Union College. Neumark joined the college in 1907, after (and in a sense, as a result of) the dismissal of the three Zionist members of the faculty.[22]

There were additional reasons for the transformation of the Reform movement, less visible but equally important, resulting from the changing character of the Jewish self-definition in America. No other sector of American Jewry was as sensitive as Reform Jewry (and at so early a stage) to the subtleties of the Jewish-Gentile relationship in the United States; none was more insistent on the "Americanization" of American Jews, meaning the new Jewish immigrants from Eastern Europe. It was an issue in which leading Reform figures related their religious beliefs to certain civil and political principles. The right kind of Jewish religion and the right attitude of loyal citizenship had been interrelated matters in Reform self-consciousness since the Jewish emancipation in Europe in the nineteenth century. For many, Zionism struck a discordant note not so much because it clashed with the religious beliefs of the Reform movement but because of civil and political concerns: Zionism, especially political Zionism, raised the specter of "dual loyalty."

One of the most important debates on Zionism occurred in 1907 between Jacob H. Schiff and Solomon Schechter, because of the latter's ingress in the Zionist movement.[23] This was the year when the three Zionist teachers of the Hebrew Union College were dismissed, and the Reform-Zionist conflict was very much alive in the minds of adherents on both sides of the fence. Schiff, a prominent member of Temple Emanu-El, criticized Schechter sharply, stressing that "speaking as an American, I cannot for a moment concede that one can be, at the same time, a true American and an honest adherent of the Zionist movement."[24]

Quite a number of comments were published in the influential journal, *American Hebrew*, commenting on Schechter's decision and Schiff's reaction.

Especially important were two comments, one by Louis Marshall, Schiff's close associate in many Jewish enterprises in the United States, the other by Joseph J. Jacobs, the English-born editor of *American Hebrew*. Although both men (and especially Marshall) shared Schiff's cultural milieu, both were deeply critical about his attitude, and for reasons of principle: there was nothing wrong with the American patriotism of most Zionists, wrote Marshall; and anyway, asked Jacobs, what is patriotism?[25]

The 1907 debate is historically important because it was one of the first occasions when respected spokesmen of "Americanized" American Jewry publicly criticized the usually accepted views in their circles regarding the implications of being an American. A scrutiny of the content of Americanization, as preached at the time by prominent rabbis and laymen of the Reform movement, raised the question as to whether the ideological concepts behind it were really the result of deep adaptation to the social and political ways of American society. In their utterances, one actually hears an echo of ideas that had been brought over from the Old World and been translated into English.

Marshall's and Jacobs's utterances should not be seen as efforts in ideological analysis, but only as opinions expressed in a public debate. Nevertheless, the unformulated implications of their opinions were of great interest. One was that concepts such as patriotism and political loyalty had a meaning of their own within the American context. In the background hovered a question that was a matter of perennial debate between Zionists and Reform (or Liberal) Jews in Europe: Were the Jews only a religious group, or something more, perhaps a people, or even a nation? In America the issue still remained alive, but much of its European-rooted tension weakened. Almost everybody agreed that Jews were more than just a religious denomination.[26] And last, the debate hinted of an additional implication: that the Reform movement in the United States had itself to undergo a process of Americanization, rather more subtle than the one its leaders were asking from the Eastern European Jewish newcomers, but hardly less significant.

The same questions were addressed also by some Zionist activists: in 1909, both Judah L. Magnes and Louis Lipsky, the emerging leader of the American Zionist movement, spoke and wrote on the issue of patriotism and Zionism.[27] Zionism and citizenship were the main questions dealt with in the public speeches of Louis D. Brandeis upon his becoming the leader of the American Zionist movement in 1914.[28] But most of those utterances had little effect or influence as far as the Reform movement was concerned. It was from the inside that changes in Reform circles were due to happen, and, indeed, much of the 1907 debate was internal. It should, therefore, be considered as the first step leading the Reform movement in a new direction, and it seems that the process then initiated was not without results. In 1917, under the additional influence of the Jewish situation in Europe and of the Balfour Declaration, none other than Jacob H. Schiff accepted Zionism.[29]

Three factors, then, may together explain the change in Reform's attitude to Zionism: first, the change in the social composition of the movement, due to the growing participation of second-generation American Jews of Eastern European origin; second, new ideological arguments, stressing the common points between both positions, with the additional concern over the possible marginalization of a non-Zionist Reform movement. Finally, the foundation of all this was the gradual comprehension that Jewish conditions in America were different from those in Europe: namely, that Jewish "civil" attitudes developed in Europe did not necessarily apply to America, and that Jewish particularism in America, including its adoption of Zionism, was possible and even legitimate in general *American* terms.

There was a fourth factor: the challenge and the attraction of American spiritual Zionism as it was developing in the Conservative movement, with its own positive and constructive view about the future of Jews and Judaism in the United States. American spiritual Zionism had little in it which might disturb Reform Jews; it had much that attracted them.

All together, one of the internal developments that happened in American Jewry during the first half of the present century may be called its "Zionization": the adoption of certain Zionist concepts by a large majority of the Jewish community together with a growing interest in the development of the Jewish national home in Palestine. In the dynamics of that evolution, which were ideological and social, the American Jewish religious movements played an outstanding part.

The roles of each movement were diverse. While the Conservatives contributed mainly to the ideological integration of a certain brand of Zionism in American Jewish life, the social acceptability of that integration was strongly influenced by long-term developments in the Reform movement and in the lay circles close to it. American Reform came largely to accept the Americanized interpretation of Zionism that had evolved in Conservative circles, primarily formulated by intellectuals connected with the Jewish Theological Seminary. On its part, the Conservative movement had no difficulty in accepting the terms of the social legitimacy of Zionism in America, in the way it had mainly been worked out, after much internal debate, in the Reform movement and circles close to it.

One question remaining open is where to localize American Orthodoxy in that process. Most Orthodox Jews in the United States went along with the above-mentioned developments. Most were certainly keen on the success of the Zionist enterprise in Palestine. But the ideological passivity of American Orthodoxy regarding the germination of an American type of Zionism is a phenomenon that has yet to be properly explained.

It seems that Zionism was one of the issues that brought the three main religious trends in American Jewry close to each other, in spite of their continuing religious differences. That process was to continue beyond the period here under consideration and to develop new forms later, in the second half of the twentieth century.

Zionism, in its Americanized version, became then a powerful glue binding American Jewry together. However, it did so laboring under a significant handicap: whatever tasks Zionism came to fulfill in Jewish religious life in America, it was not toward America that the basic aims of the original Zionist idea had been directed but toward the Land of Israel. The ambivalence of American Zionism between America and Zion was apt to limit the effectiveness of American Zionism outside the realm of American Jewry for reasons that were both ideological and practical.

One typical expression of that kind (although not the only one) was what has been called the "Bavel-Yerushalayim equation": the belief that, as in the talmudic period, which had produced both the Babylonian and the Jerusalem Talmud, the Jewish people had now *two* spiritual centers of equal importance, one in the United States, the other in Israel.

Although supported also by American Zionists belonging to other religious tendencies, the Bavel-Yerushalayim equation was rooted in the very beginnings of the Conservatism self-definition.[30] But it was only later, toward mid-century and especially after the creation of Israel that some of its implication were to become fully evident: if there are two spiritual centers of equal standing, and a Zionist happened to live in one of them (the United States, in our case), then it was legitimate for him to apply his interests and energies for the strengthening of that center, in spite of his deep commitment also to the other center (i.e, Israel). As explained by Benzion Bokser, at the time of the establishment of the Jewish state: "We thus visualize a continuing Jewish life in America to parallel the developing Jewish life in Israel. Indeed, we visualize a deepening Jewish life in America as the pressures of those problems to be solved in Israel will be removed, leaving us energies for the positive tasks of building for the American Jewish community."[31]

The consequences of the ambivalence were clear. On one hand, the Bavel-Yerushalayim equation was capable of spurring American Jewish scholars to intellectual activity—in America. On the other hand, it was apt to limit the spiritual participation of American Zionists in Zion.

A parallel result of the American brand of Zionism was that the physical presence of American Jews in Palestine, and later in Israel, was and remained small. Consequently, the lack of American *aliyah* meant that American religious movements acquired little influence on the religious life in Palestine or, for that matter, on most other levels of Jewish life there. The problem of how to influence the content of Jewish religion and how to participate in the religious institutions of the Jewish community in Palestine— and later in Israel—was to trouble the American Jewish religious movements throughout the century.

Notes

Thanks are due to Marianne Sanua for her corrections of the manuscript and her many helpful comments.

1. Marshall Sklare, *America's Jews* (New York, 1971), p. 213.

2. On this topic, see Abraham J. Karp, "Reaction to Zionism and to the State of Israel in the American Jewish Religious Community," *Jewish Journal of Sociology* 8 (1966): 150–74; Naomi W. Cohen, "The Reaction of Reform Judaism in American to Political Zionism, (1897–1922)," *Publications of the American Jewish Historical Society* 40 (1950–51): 361–94; Herbert Parzen, "Conservative Judaism and Zionism, (1896–1922)," *Jewish Social Studies* 23 (1961): 235–64; Michael Meyer, "American Reform Judaism and Zionism: Early Efforts at Ideological Rapprochement," *Studies in Zionism* 7 (Spring, 1983): 51–52.

In my previous work I suggested the following definition, which is used as a point of reference in the present article: "A Zionist is a Jew who believes that Jewish politically independent life in the Land of Israel is an indispensable condition for the existence of the Jewish people in the social and political circumstances of the modern world." That definition falls short of the one favored by most Israeli Jews, who affirm (rather simplistically, in my opinion) that a Zionist is a Jew who settles in Israel. On the other hand, this definition involves more than the one preferred by many diaspora Jews, who consider themselves Zionists, support the existence of Israel, but refrain from defining Jewish statehood as an *indispensable* condition for Jewish life in the modern world.

3. Chaim Zhitlowsky, "Undzer tsukunft do in land," 1915, in his *Gezamlte shriftn* (New York, 1912–31), 10:87–91.

4. Solomon Schechter, "Zionism: A Statement," in *Seminary Addresses,* 2d ed. (New York, 1959), p. 93.

5. See Marc L. Raphael, *Profiles in American Judaism: The Reform, Conservative, Orthodox and Reconstructionist Traditions in Historical Perspective* (San Francisco, 1984), p. 106.

6. Solomon Schechter, *Some Aspects of Rabbinic Theology* (London, 1909), p. 105. See also Solomon Schechter to Herbert Bentwich, November 30, 1904 in *The Wisdom of Solomon Schechter,* ed. B. Mandelbaum (New York, 1963), p. 98. Schechter's position in this matter was not far from Jacob H. Schiff's, although in the latter's case the divergence about Jewish nationalism related also to the so-called dual-loyalty question (see n. 23). Regarding the critique of Schechter's Zionist position, see Shmarya Lewin to the Inner [Smaller] Actions Committee, July 4, 1914, Central Zionist Archives, Jerusalem, Z3/395. Lewin, a member of the [European] Zionist leadership (the Smaller Actions Committee), was the man most familiar there with the conditions of the American movement before World War I.

7. See Baila Round Shargel, *Practical Dreamer: Israel Friedlaender and the Shaping of American Judaism* (New York, 1985), pp. 158–59.

8. Ahad Haam, "The Negation of the Diaspora," in *The Zionist Idea,* ed. Arthur Hertzberg (Garden City, N.Y., 1959), pp. 270–77.

9. See Israel Friedlaender, "The Problem of Judaism in America" (1907), in *Past and Present: Selected Essays,* 2d ed. (New York, 1961) pp. 179–80; Evyatar Friesel, "Ahad-Haamism in American Zionist Thought," in *Ahad Haam: At the Crossroads,* ed. Jacques Kornberg (Albany, N.Y., 1983), pp. 133–41.

10. See Judah L. Magnes, "The Melting Pot," in *Dissenter in Zion: From the Writings of Judah L. Magnes,* ed. Arthur A. Goren (Cambridge, Mass., 1982), pp. 101–6; Magnes, *What Zionism Has Given the Jews* (New York, 1911); Evyatar Friesel, "Zionism in Judah L. Magnes' Conception of Judaism," in *Like All the Nations? The Life and Legacy of Judah L. Magnes,* ed. W. M. Brinner and Moses M. Rischin (Albany, N.Y., 1987), pp. 69–81. See also

Moshe Davis, "Israel Friedlaender's Minute Book of the Achavah Club (1909–1912)," in *M. M. Kaplan Jubilee Volume* (New York, 1953), pp. 157–13.

11. The most developed exposition of Kaplan's Zionist ideas is in his *A New Zionism*, 2d ed. (New York, 1959).

12. Meyer, "American Reform Judaism and Zionism," pp. 51–52.

13. The resolution asserted: "Resolved that we totally disapprove of any attempt for the establishment of a Jewish state. Such attempts show a misunderstanding of Israel's mission which from the narrow political and national field has been expanded to the promotion among the whole human race of the broad and universalistic religion first proclaimed by the Jewish prophets. Such attempts do not benefit, but infinitely harm our Jewish brethren where they are still persecuted, by confirming the assertion of their enemies that the Jews are foreigners in the countries in which they are at home, and of which they are everywhere the most loyal and patriotic citizens.

We reaffirm that the object of Judaism is not political nor national, but spiritual, and addresses itself to the continuous growth of peace, justice and love of the human race, to a messianic time when all men will recognize that they form 'one great brotherhood' for the establishment of God's kingdom on earth." *Central Conference of American Rabbis* (1897): LI.

14. See Herbert Parzen, "The Purge of the Dissidents, Hebrew Union College and Zionism, 1903–1907," *Jewish Social Studies* 37 (1975): 291–322.

15. See *Correspondence on the Advisability of Calling a Conference for the Purpose of Combating Zionism* (New York, 1918), pubished by the Zionist Organization of America.

16. See Howard R. Greenstein, *Turning Point: Zionism and Reform Judaism* (Chico, Calif., 1981), esp. chaps. 4, 5.

17. Ibid., chap. 1.

18. See Bernhard Felsenthal, "The Jew as Politician," 1899, *Bernard Felsenthal: Teacher in Israel,* ed. Emma Felsenthal (New York, 1924), pp. 256–59; Bernhard Felsenthal, *Fundamental Principles of Judaism* (1901; reprint, New York, 1918).

19. Felsenthal's perceptiveness about that question is found in many of his writings from 1897 until the end of his life, in 1908. In those years, Zionism and the relationship between Zionism and Reform became one of his major interests. See his diverse statements on Zionism, collected in *Bernhard Felsenthal,* esp. pp. 256–264; also, his theses presented at the 1907 conference of the CCAR, *CCAR Yearbook* 17 (1908): 31–34.

20. Max Schloessinger, *Reform Judaism and Zionism* (Baltimore 1907), p. 14. See also Maximilian Heller, "The Rationale of Modern Judaism," *Maccabaean* 5, no. 1, July 1903, 32–34.

21. Felix A. Levy, *Are Zionism and Reform Judaism Incompatible?* (New York, 1943), p. 18. "By cutting the latter [Palestine] out of their purview, some liberals have severed connection with the main body of Jewish tradition and people, have become a class movement, a 'landless aristocracy,' with no inner resources to renew the failing Jewish strength;" see also p. 28.

22. See Meyer, "American Reform Judaism and Zionism."

23. Solomon Schechter, "Zionism: A Statement," *American Hebrew,* December 28, 1906, pp. 191–94.

24. Jacob H. Schiff to Solomon Schechter, August 8, 1907, *American Hebrew,* August 23, 1907, p. 385.

25. Louis Marshall to the editor of *American Israelite,* September 1, 1907, in *American Hebrew,* September 20, 1907, p. 488; Marshallik [Joseph J. Jacobs], "Zionism, Patriotism and Other 'Isms,'" *American Hebrew,* October 4, 1907, p. 533. See also Judah L. Magnes, "A Republic of Nationalities," *Emanuel Pulpit,* February 13, 1909.

26. Meyer, "American Reform Judaism and Zionism," p. 53.

27. Magnes, "Melting Pot;" Magnes, "Republic of Nationalities;" Louis Lipsky, "The Duty of American Jews," *Maccabaean,* February 1909, pp. 41–46.

28. Louis D. Brandeis, "The Jewish Problem: How to Solve It," 1915, in Jacob de Haas, *Louis D. Brandeis* (New York, 1929), pp. 170–90.

29. See Evyatar Friesel, "Jacob H. Schiff Becomes a Zionist: A Chapter in American-Jewish Self-Definition," *Studies in Zionism* 5 (1982): 55–99.

30. See Friedlaender, "Problem of Judaism"; Magnes, "Melting Pot."

31. Ben Zion Bokser, "Israel and the American Synagogue," 1950, in *Roads to Jewish Survival,* ed. Milton Berger et al. (New York, 1967), pp. 295–98.

Converts to Zionism in the American Reform Movement

In 1869, Rabbi Bernhard Felsenthal of Chicago protested efforts aimed at Jewish colonization of Palestine and supported the resolution of the Philadelphia Conference of Reform Rabbis declaring that "the Messianic goal of Israel is not the restoration of the old Jewish state under a descendant of David, involving a second separation from the nations of the earth, but the union of all men as the children of God."[1] In 1907, the same Rabbi Felsenthal, now a committed Zionist, declared it his conviction that "Zionism alone will be the savior of our Nation and its religion, and save it from death and disappearance."[2]

In 1893, Rabbi Gustav Gottheil of Temple Emanu-El of New York told delegates assembled at the World Parliament of Religion that Palestine "is no longer our country . . . that title appertains to the land of our birth or adoption; and 'our nation' is that nation of which we form a part, and with the destinies of which we are identified, to the exclusion of all others." Just four years later, Gottheil changed his mind and became vice-president of the Federation of American Zionists as well as a staunch supporter of Theodor Herzl.[3]

In 1899, Rabbi Max Heller of New Orleans preached in opposition to Zionism, characterizing the movement as "a product of despair." He argued that the Jew had a lesson to teach in the diaspora, and declared the very idea of a Jewish state to be totally impractical. Two years later he had begun to rethink his position, and by 1903 he proudly labeled himself "a convinced Zionist." He was now persuaded that anti-Zionists, in his words, "misunderstand Jewish history, misinterpret Judaism and do injustice to the cultural functions of nationalism."[4]

All three of these leading Reform rabbis—Felsenthal, Gottheil, and Heller—were known in their day as "converts to Zionism." They were not alone. The *Maccabaean*, in March 1907, devoted a whole editorial to what it called "Reform converts" and rejoiced that "the Zionistic infection of the Hebrew Union College seems to be spreading" and that more than a score of Reform rabbis had become "workers in the Zionist movement."[5] Yet, this phenomenon of Reform converts to American Zionism has until now received little scholarly attention. For all that has been written on Reform Judaism and Zionism,[6] we know almost nothing about what motivated these converts, why they converted when they did, and what impact they subsequently made. In this essay I shall focus on these questions, emphasizing converts to Zionism among Reform rabbis, although I shall draw in a few cases from the testimonies of lay converts as well. I stress the years prior to 1920, for that is the period when Reform Judaism and Zionism seemed least compatible, and conversions entailed the greatest social risk. Besides seeking to explain these individual conversions, I shall argue that they reflect a development of great importance in the history of American Judaism: an awakening that transformed American Jewish life and produced a new synthesis that permitted Reform Judaism and Zionism to co-exist.

Any discussion of American Reform Judaism and Zionism properly begins with the Reform movement's well-known institutional opposition (prior to the Columbus Platform of 1937) both to the very idea that Jews are a nation and to the corollary that they should return to their ancestral home. At the 1869 Philadelphia Rabbinical Conference, the 1885 Pittsburgh Rabbinical Conference, the 1897 meeting of the Central Conference of American Rabbis (CCAR), the 1898 meeting of the Union of American Hebrew Congregations (UAHC), and on countless other occasions, resolutions against restoration and Zionism won broad approval. The UAHC Resolution, signed by David Philipson, Simon Wolf, and Joseph Krauskopf and adopted unanimously, summarized with particular acuity the major arguments that opponents of Zionism advanced:

We are opposed to political Zionism. The Jews are not a nation but a religious community. Zion was a precious possession of the past, the early home of our faith, where our prophets uttered their world-subduing thoughts, and our psalmists sang their world-enchanting hymns. As such it is a holy memory, but it is not our hope of the future. America is our Zion. Here, in the home of religious liberty, we have aided in founding this new Zion, the fruition of the beginning laid in the old. The mission of Judaism is spiritual, not political. Its aim is not to establish a state, but to spread the truths of religion and humanity throughout the world.[7]

Despite this and other resolutions, however, it is clear that the leaders of Reform Judaism remained divided over the Zionism issue. A careful student of the debates published through the years in the *Central Conference of American Rabbis Yearbook* reminds us, as Arthur J. Lelyveld has concluded, that "the CCAR was never a monolith—never totally anti-Zionist, never totally Zionist. . . . Generalizations or stereotypes as to what constitutes a Zionist or an anti-Zionist point of view are invariably inadequate when one considers the full body of utterances of any individual Conference leader."[8] Similar divisions were evident among the students at the Hebrew Union College and among the faculty as well.[9] What is nevertheless significant is that these disagreements, fundamental as they were, did not lead to a schism within the Reform movement. To the contrary, as Michael Meyer has shown in a seminal article, the basis for ideological rapprochement between Zionism and Reform Judaism took shape during the very period when "to the majority on both sides the two movements seemed to be mortal enemies."[10]

Against this background, we may begin to examine somewhat more closely the whole phenomenon of Reform Jewish conversions to the Zionist cause. The term "conversion," understood in its broadest sense, refers to a "dynamic, multifaceted process of change." William James defined the term psychologically as "a process, gradual or sudden, by which a self, hitherto divided and consciously wrong, inferior, and unhappy, becomes unified and consciously right, superior, and happy in consequence of its firmer hold upon religious realities." More recently, Richard Travisano, seeking to distinguish conversions from other kinds of transformations, has described the process as "a radical reorganization of identity, meaning life."[11] The word "conversion" is most frequently employed within a religious context, which makes its use here in connection with Zionism of some interest. The fact that classical religious terminology was used to describe someone who embraced Zionism reminds us that the movement displayed many characteristic features of a religion, including sacred persons, events, beliefs, rituals, and symbols.[12] Stephen Wise once actually stated that "Zionism is my religion."[13] Conversion to Zionism, then, meant much more than simply an ideological commitment to the movement's mission; it also involved some degree of participation in its broader cult.

Obviously, not all Reform Zionists underwent conversion. "There are those," Alice Seligsberg recognized back in 1917, "to whom Zionism has always been in harmony with their religious traditions, who, therefore, required no argument to convince them of its truth."[14] Reform Jews of this kind had been Zionists (or proto-Zionists) all along, in some cases even before they were Reform Jews. Stephen Wise, for one, imbibed love of Zion from his parents and grandparents. His grandmother settled in Jerusalem and died there, his father was "an ardent Zionist from the pre-Herzlian days," and Stephen Wise himself, as a child, collected funds for Palestine. By the time of the First Zionist Congress in 1897, Wise already identified as a Zionist; meeting Theodor Herzl simply intensified a preexisting emotional tie and commitment.[15] Another early Reform Zionist, Rabbi Max Raisin, identified with Zionism as a young teenager on the Lower East Side of New York and even corresponded with Ahad Haam. He entered Hebrew Union College already committed to the movement and may have influenced some of his fellow students.[16] As time went on, there would be an increasing number of Hebrew Union College students who, like Raisin, entered rabbinical school after having grown up in the Zionist movement. For them, the question was not whether to convert to Zionism but whether to maintain their affiliation in the face of anti-Zionist pressure.[17]

A number of rabbis and about-to-be rabbis did, however, convert to Zionism, and the question remains why. Those who study conversion professionally suggest that one should search, in all cases, for an antecedent crisis:

Virtually all students of conversion agree that some kind of crisis precedes conversion. The crisis may be religious, political, psychological, or cultural, or it may be a life situation that opens people to new options. During the crisis, myths, rituals, symbols, goals, and standards cease to function well for the individual or culture, thus creating great disturbance in the individual's life. According to social scientists, who often work on the assumptions of psychopathology, a conversion in this situation can be seen as a coping mechanism.[18]

In attempting to ferret out these crises, I began by searching for personal psychological factors: underlying reasons that might explain why a disproportionate number of conversions to Zionism seem to have taken place at critical turning points in the life cycle, either at the onset of a career—for example, while studying at the Hebrew Union College—or just after retirement. Judah Magnes, for example, published his first pro-Zionist statement ("Palestine—or Death") during his second year at Hebrew Union College, in 1896. By 1901, when he was studying in Berlin, he considered himself "a warm Zionist"; his conversion was complete.[19] Another student, Harvey E. Wessel, published an article in his senior year (1920) entitled "How I Became a Zionist at the Hebrew Union College." According to Wessel's account, his interest was sparked in his very first year at the college by his study of Jewish liturgy. Thereafter his Zionism was nurtured both by what he learned about Jews as a distinct people and by the "new signs of life" he saw emerging within the Jewish world.[20] Zionism seems to have provided him, as it did Magnes, with a sense of larger meaning, a vision inspiring enough to help him overcome the crisis of self-doubt that so often accompanies rabbinic training. Wessel was not alone in his commitment to Zionism: there were no fewer than seven professing Zionists in his graduating class of ten, as well as "two sympathizers and one anti."[21]

Rabbi Joseph Silverman, by contrast, converted to Zionism at the other end of the adult life cycle, in retirement. Just a year after Wessel's conversion, he "surprised almost 1300 guests at a dinner at the Hotel Astor . . . by declaring himself in favor of upbuilding of Palestine and the establishment there of a republic patterned after the democracy of the United States." Silverman, rabbi emeritus of Temple Emanu-El, had long been known as an anti-Zionist. He helped word the anti-Zionist resolution of the Central Conference of American Rabbis in 1897, delivered a controversial sermon in 1902 in which he lambasted Zionism as unpatriotic and "based on a feigned, fictitious and imaginary love of Zion," and later went so far as to accuse Zionists of financial improprieties and of being land speculators "who seek their own ends." But now, in his retirement, he changed his mind and became "an active propagandist" for Zionism. In 1924 he toured Palestine for the Zionist movement and promised to dedicate the rest of his life "to the great work that lies before us." Privately, according to his former classmate, Joseph Stolz, he confessed that "it afforded him an ineffable joy and satisfaction in his old age to work with almost youthful enthusiasm for the re-establishment of the Jewish National Home in Palestine."[22]

Other rabbis who converted to Zionism in retirement include Gustav Gottheil, Bernhard Felsenthal, and Samuel Sale. Joseph Krauskopf, although not officially retired, also became a Zionist at the end of his career.[23] In all these cases we can, unfortunately, only speculate as to the personal and psychological factors involved. But the reference to "youthful enthusiasm" in the case of Silverman—or a parallel reference to "youthful ardor" in the case of Felsenthal[24]—suggests some effort to, in the words of the psychologist Daniel J. Levinson, "sustain . . . youthfulness in a new form appropriate to late adulthood."[25] Through Zionism these rabbis seem to have recaptured some of that powerful sense of mission that had so inspired them in former days.

Suggestive as these case studies may be, I am now persuaded that it would be a mistake to understand conversions to Zionism in purely personal or psychological terms. Such explanations, even if partially true, are much too limited and reductionist to be wholly satisfying, and they break down when applied to Reform converts as a group. Moreover, like so many psychological explanations, they tempt us, as Charles Hoyd Cohen has suggested, "to esteem the latent content of human production over the manifest and to slight the reasons people advance for their [own] behavior."[26] It is more illuminating, I think, to view conversions in broader cultural terms. Seen from this perspective, Reform conversions to Zionism become part of a larger phenomenon that contemporaries described as nothing less than an American Jewish awakening; we might call it, using the language of anthropology, a period of Jewish cultural revitalization. It began late in the nineteenth century in a general crisis of beliefs and values and extended over several decades, during which a profound reorientation in American Jewish beliefs and values took place. Reform Jewish conversions were symptomatic of this crisis and help us to understand what people thought to be wrong. Zionism responded to this crisis and played an integral role in bringing about the reorientation that transformed not only Reform Judaism but all of American Judaism.[27]

The roots of American Jewry's cultural crisis go back to the late 1870s. Antisemitism explains part of what happened. The rise of racially based Jew-hatred in Germany, a land that many young American Jews (and their parents) had previously revered for its liberal spirit and cultural advancement, challenged a host of Jewish assumptions about emancipation, universalism, and future religious rapprochement.

The growth of social discrimination against American Jews had an equally significant impact. While such discrimination was not new, Jews had not expected that discrimination would grow. The fact that it did grow and, with the development of racial thought, even became respectable in some circles again challenged Jewish liberal assumptions. Where in the

1860s and early 1870s many Jews had confidently looked forward to a coming "new era" of interfaith harmony and religious equality, now these assumptions were shaken.[28]

Developments within American Protestantism added yet another dimension to the mood of uneasiness that one senses in the American Jewish community of this period. The spiritual crisis and internal divisions that plagued Protestant America as it faced the staggering implications of Darwinism and biblical criticism drove evangelicals and liberals alike to renew their particularistic calls for a "Christian America." Visions of a liberal religious alliance and of close cooperation with Jews and Unitarians gradually evaporated. Although interfaith exchanges continued, Jews came to realize that many of their Christian friends continued to harbor hopes that one day Jews would "see the light." Much to the embarrassment of Jewish leaders, some Christian liberals looked to Felix Adler's de-Judaized Ethical Culture movement as a harbinger of Judaism's future course.[29]

On the Jewish side, this period witnessed a comparable crisis of the spirit. Alarmed at religious "indifference," Jewish ignorance, and "Adlerism's success," many began to question old assumptions regarding the direction of American Judaism. A movement of young Jews back toward tradition was evident as early as 1879. By 1884, according to Rabbi David Stern, the religious agenda of the day was "entirely different" from what it had been before. "Then the struggle was to remove the dross; to-day it is to conserve the pearl beneath."[30]

Massive Eastern European Jewish immigration, coming on the heels of all of these developments, added a great deal of fuel to this crisis of confidence. The problem was not simply one of numbers nor was it confined to the fact that in Russia, as in Germany, liberalism had been tested and found wanting. Instead American Jews began to realize that their vision of the future was built on false premises. The optimistic prophecies of the 1860s and 1870s had failed, the hoped-for "new era" had not materialized, and conditions for Jews in America and around the world had grown worse instead of better. This situation posed a cultural crisis of the highest order and precipitated the many and varied changes, particularly Zionism, that took place in succeeding decades.

Admittedly, no Reform converts to Zionism mentioned all of these factors in explaining why they had abandoned earlier beliefs and joined the Zionist movement. But key components of this crisis turn up over and over again in their testimonies. As early as 1875, Bernhard Felsenthal warned that "the very existence of Israel is greatly endangered in America." He worried that "hundreds of individuals and of families are getting estranged, and are gradually melting away from Judaism. . . . A great part of the rising generation is growing up in total ignorance of the religion of their fathers." "In a time not very distant," he darkly predicted, "very many of our descendants will not know whether they are Jews or not."[31] These concerns led

Felsenthal to reevaluate his views on Jewish peoplehood and ultimately propelled him toward support for the Zionist cause.

The pogroms of the 1880s and 1890s led to a period of soul searching on the part of a larger number of Reform Jews. By the late 1890s, several—including up to a dozen students at Hebrew Union College[32]—had come to see Zionism as the only practical solution to ongoing persecutions. They looked to Zion as a potential refuge for Jews seeking to flee.[33] Again, Bernhard Felsenthal's writings expressed this argument with particular force and candor:

I feel deeply with the sufferings of the larger majority of my Jewish brethren, with the Jews in Russia, Roumania, Persia, Arabia, Morocco and elsewhere, and it is my decided conviction that the best method and the most rational way to help them would consist in aiding them to emigrate from their country in which they happen to live and to settle in Palestine and to colonize there and in the adjacent countries of Syria, etc. In America they are not wanted. . . . Neither are the doors wide open for them in Austria, Germany, France, England, or elsewhere in Europe. Where then can the unfortunate people, of whom we speak here, find a quiet and undisturbed home?[34]

The Kishinev pogrom in 1903 intensified these concerns and drew new converts to Zionism. Rabbi Adolph Radin, for example, announced that he had converted, "after much thinking and doubting and listening to arguments pro and con." The "massacre of our brethren in Kishineff [*sic*]," he explained, along with Russian reactions to it "have cured me, radically and totally, from the sweet hope that our modern civilization, based upon egotism and selfishness, will put a stop to Anti-Semitism and its brutalities." Radin found that he no longer believed in universalism and the "Jewish mission" as expounded in the ideology of classical Reform Judaism. "Our mission," he wrote bitterly, "is not to be pillaged and robbed and slaughtered and butchered by drunken beasts."[35] According to a no doubt exaggerated account in the *Maccabaean*, "thousands" of others had come to similar conclusions: "Men to whom all has been darkness," it wrote, "have, through an electric spark, beheld the light. What else but Zionism? What other solution is possible?"[36]

Continuing domestic antisemitism also played a significant role in fomenting the crisis that turned Reform Jews toward Zionism. This influence is, however, harder to document. American Jews were most reluctant to discuss antisemitism in their own country and certainly did not want Zionism to be associated in the popular mind with any lack of faith in American ideals.[37] When, on one occasion, the issue was raised publicly, "the Zionist movement," according to Louis Lipsky, "was reproached with being meddlesome, impertinent and a source of danger to the Jewish people."[38] Still, one can find occasional intimations of this theme, particularly at the turn of the century. The most remarkable one I know by a Reform Jew was made by Richard Gottheil in his celebrated 1897 defense of Zionism delivered at a private meeting of the Judaeans, the cultural society of New York's Jewish elite:

I hesitate to speak of our own country; but I feel that we are amongst ourselves and that I can speak with freedom and with full liberty. Where do *we* stand to-day? Are *we* on the road to the much-vaunted assimilation? I am free to say that we are much further from that goal than we were when I came here 25 years ago. Gradually, but surely, we are being forced back into a physical and moral ghetto. Private schools are being closed against our children one by one; we are practically boycotted from all summer hotels—and our social lines run as far apart from those of our neighbors as they did in the worst days of our European degradation. . . . It is here that modern Zionism steps in. It recognizes the fact, which is so plain yet we refuse to see it, that the attempt at assimilation has been unsuccessful; and that there is absolutely no prospect of similar attempts being more successful in the future. For the world asks too much from us; it demands that we assimilate in reality and completely, and that we do not stop half-way.[39]

Writing a year later in the student paper of the Hebrew Union College, William H. Fineshriber advocated Zionism on similar grounds. "We are strangers in a strange land," he wrote. "Like the negro, the Jew is an alien, with a difference only of degree."[40] The "growing prejudice of Western nations" was likewise one of the factors that, in 1901, led Max Heller to convert to Zionism, after he had initially come out against it.[41]

Yet the key to understanding Reform conversions is neither antisemitism nor the persecution of Eastern European Jewry but rather, as I have suggested, the larger cultural crisis to which both contributed. Events at the turn of the century had outpaced ideology, and, as we have seen, many of the basic assumptions upon which nineteenth-century American Reform Judaism rested had proved false. Zionism, as Max Heller understood sooner than almost anybody else, was a means of revitalizing Reform so that it could meet the crisis of the day:

The Zionist is needed in Reform ranks to protest. . . . He must refuse to join in the noisy acclaim which hails our age and our country as, respectively, the millenium [*sic*] and the paradise of Judaism; he sees religious desolation where the idolater of occidentalism brags of his monumental temples; he observes steady, unhindered growth of prejudice and intolerance, where the worshipper of "up-to-date" is exulting over empty phrases and ineffective resolutions; and, above all else, he preserves a warm fellow-feeling for those bonds of Jewishness . . . which make the Jew kin the world over.[42]

The choice as Heller and other early twentieth-century American Zionists perceived it was between Zionism and the end—the end not just of Reform Judaism but of the Jewish people itself. Zionism alone, they felt, held the capacity to revitalize Jewry by reshaping its goals to meet the desperate needs of contemporary Jews. No wonder Bernhard Felsenthal felt that in time "all would become Zionists";[43] there was, to his mind, no other viable alternative. Henrietta Szold, in a private letter written at about this same time, agreed: "I am more than ever convinced," she wrote, "that if not Zionism, then nothing—then extinction for the Jew."[44]

It comes as no surprise, then, that some Reform converts to Zionism experienced a sense of rebirth, a feeling that through Zionism their lives had at last become meaningful and whole.[45] Julian Leon Magnes—whose "born again" experience with Zionism was symbolized by the fact that he Hebraized his name to Judah Leib—described in a letter to his parents how Zionism transformed not only his intellectual and spiritual interests but his whole "mode of life." "Since I have become a Zionist," he explained, "my view of life has changed; my view as to my calling has changed; my view as to my future has changed; my hopes, my prayers have changed."[46] Harvey Wessel, the Reform rabbinical student who converted while at Hebrew Union College, likewise testified "to the change wrought in my ideas by the adoption of the Zionist point of view." He now viewed Judaism "as a continuum" and felt connected to Jews of the past. Where before he had lacked enthusiasm for the pulpit, now, thanks to Zionism, he pronounced himself ready to embark on his career with "zeal and earnestness."[47]

Having been reborn into Zionism, however, Reform converts still faced the vexing question of whether they could legitimately remain Reform Jews. Leading Zionists, after all, doubted that a true Zionist could be a believing Reform Jew, just as leading Reform Jews doubted whether a believing Reform Jew could be a true Zionist.[48] As a result, some converts slid back. Max Heller observed as early as 1918 that "numbers" of Hebrew Union College students "abandon their Zionist ideals after the rude contact with the world of matter-of-fact people and of ruthless competition."[49]

Those who did remain resolute, however, played an important role in shaping the new synthesis that arose to replace the optimistic, universalistic nineteenth-century American Jewish faith that had now lost credibility in so many circles. While a full description of this new synthesis would take us far afield, two key ideas command attention, for they demonstrate how, in the twentieth century, Reform Zionists (both born Zionists and "born again" Zionists) mediated between Reform Judaism and Zionism, with the results that each movement came to influence the other and both moved toward rapprochement.

We can see this process at work first in the much-discussed "mission motif," the idea that Jews had a mission to serve society at large and a religious and moral message to bring to the world.[50] For nineteenth century Reform Jews this "mission of Israel" was a prime justification for diaspora Jewish life. It transvalued the diaspora, so that far from being a punishment and curse, it became instead a divine blessing for Jews and for all humankind. Early Zionists found this whole idea ridiculous and absurd. They spoke condescendingly of "mission-Jews" and pointed out, as Michael Meyer observes, "that the average American Jew scarcely acted like a missionary for Jewish ideals."[51] Nevertheless, a great many American Jews, and not just Reform Jews,[52] continued to find the idea highly attractive. It effectively countered the Christian explanation of why Jews languished in the diaspora and nicely dovetailed with America's own grandiose sense of mission, rooted in Puritanism.

The great intellectual achievement of American Reform Zionists, beginning with Bernhard Felsenthal and Richard Gottheil in 1897, was to reinterpret this mission idea so that it not only became thoroughly compatible with Zionism but that Zionism itself became, in effect, a Jewish missionary movement. They taught, in other words, that the mission of Israel could best be carried out by Jews living at the very heart of Jewry, in Eretz Israel, and that Zion, in turn, had a special mission to benefit world Jewry and humanity at large. As Allon Gal has shown, this "mission motif," influenced by the cultural Zionism of Ahad Haam and later elaborated upon in different ways by Stephen Wise, Israel Friedlaender, Louis Brandeis, Henrietta Szold, and others, became central to American Zionist ideology.[53]

A second area in which Reform Zionists helped to mediate and then to produce a new synthesis concerned the sensitive question of Zionism's relationship to Americanism.[54] Nineteenth-century American Jews believed that America differed from other lands where Jews resided and that Americanism and Judaism were basically congruent. "This country," Isaac Mayer Wise once wrote, "approaches nearest the Mosaic state among all countries known in history." Taught by Oscar Straus that "the form of government outlined by Moses and practically developed under Joshua and his successors" actually shaped the American republic, Jews concluded that "Judaism is in perfect harmony with the law of the land." Indeed, David Philipson went so far as to claim that "Judaism is so thoroughly in accord with republicanism that it deserves all its adherents to become imbued as soon as possible with free republican ideas."[55] All of this was anathema to European Zionists, who spoke of *shlilat hagalut* (negation of the diaspora) and considered American Jews to be unduly sanguine. Some American Zionists, including Max Heller, agreed; he characterized the Judaism-equals-Americanism equation as "an immature conceit."[56] But he was in the minority. More commonly, American Jews characterized their country in the most laudatory of terms. Furthermore, within the context of early twentieth-century American history, with the specter of immigration restriction, widespread concern over the so-called alien menace, and nagging questions about immigrant loyalties, public displays of patriotic piety made good sense. Zionism thus had to be reconciled with Americanism if it was to have any chance of success.

Once again, it was the achievement of Reform Zionists to help bring such a reconciliation about. Using three different arguments, they played a major role in formulating a definition of Zionism that could be defended in staunchly American terms. First, Caspar Levias and Richard Gottheil explained that Zionism was in harmony with well-established American precedents. They pointed out that many Americans, including the Irish, the Germans, and the Scandinavians, had long maintained ties to "their kinsfolk and co-religionists [who] have a home of their own across the Atlantic," and they implied that Zionism would be no different. Levias went further, suggesting that the whole loyalty question was only raised by frightened rabbis of German background who had been unduly influenced by European conditions. "To us Americans," he smugly declared, "this may remain a subject of little concern. Our population consists of various elements."[57]

A second approach, championed by Bernhard Felsenthal, was to define Zionism as a form of philanthropy, a burden voluntarily assumed by American Jews to help their persecuted brethren overseas. This view again was well within American tradition, as Felsenthal made clear: "There is no conflict," he wrote, "between American patriotism and the endeavors to help poor people and to try to better their bitter lot."[58]

A third and somewhat later approach, which I have not yet found in pre-Brandeis Reform Zionist sources, was essentially to stand the traditional Reform synthesis of America-is-Zion on its head and to argue that Zion was America *redivivus*. Louis Lipsky employed this argument in 1909, pointing to a variety of analogies between Zionism's present and America's past. He compared, for example, the "impulse which animates Zionists" to the "migration of the Pilgrim fathers" and the Zionist ambition to the American Revolution. His conclusion was inevitable: that Zionist ideals were thoroughly "compatible with American tradition, with democratic principles, [and] with present American citizenship."[59]

Subsequently, of course, Louis Brandeis, drawing from all three of these arguments, formulated what became the classic synthesis between Zionism and Americanism in his address entitled "The Jewish Problem: How to Solve It." Here he directly compared the Zionists to the "Pilgrim Fathers" and uttered the lines that would, in his name, be quoted over and over: "Let no American imagine that Zionism is inconsistent with Patriotism. Multiple loyalties are objectionable only if they are inconsistent."[60]

Brandeis delivered his celebrated address on April 25, 1915,[61] before the Eastern Council of the Central Conference of Reform Rabbis. He was himself at that time a fairly recent convert to the Zionist cause and so, apparently, were many of the Reform rabbis in his audience. Another speaker that day, Rabbi Maurice H. Harris, president of the Eastern Council and not an identifying Zionist, commented on this. "Many of the rabbis of the Liberal School," he noted, "have modified their views on Zionism. . . . We cannot be indifferent to a movement that has made so strong an appeal to so large a number of our brethren, many of whom had become estranged from the synagogue."[62] An informal 1915 survey of the Reform rabbinate by Max Heller confirmed that a significant change had taken place. It found "about as many declared Zionists, among our Reform Rabbis, as outspoken Anti-Zionists," with a much larger number who either "see a great deal of good in Zionism, but shrink from its political aspects," or who "are 'on the fence' being unable to make up their minds."[63]

Over the next five years the effects of World War I, the Balfour Declaration, immigration restriction, and Henry Ford's antisemitism added new converts to Reform Zionism's ranks. These converts remained in the minority; well into the 1930s the majority of Reform Jews, and certainly their rabbis, preferred to associate themselves with an ambivalent non-Zionism. But whatever their numbers, Reform Zionists had helped to bring about a major ideological revolution. The new religious synthesis that they formulated, yoking together the mission of Israel, cultural Zionism, and Americanism, became, in time, the dominant faith of twentieth-century American Jews.

Notes

1. *The New World of Reform*, ed. Sefton D. Temkin (London, 1971), pp. 38–39. A decade earlier, Bernhard Felsenthal had supported the removal of prayers "for Israel's return to Palestine" from the prayer book of Chicago Sinai Congregation. See Bernard Felsenthal, *The Beginnings of the Chicago Sinai Congregation* (Chicago, 1898), p. 25.

2. *Maccabaean* 12 (1907): 202.

3. Richard Gottheil, *The Life of Gustav Gottheil: Memoir of a Priest in Israel* (Williamsport, Pa., 1936), pp. 477–7, see also pp. 190–95, 303.

4. *New Orleans Daily Picayune*, November 18, 1899; "An Utopian Dream or a Practical Solution?" *New Orleans Times-Democrat*, December 12, 1901; "A Nation Awakening," *New Orleans Times-Democrat*, September 27, 1903, all clippings in Max Heller Papers, box 15, American Jewish Archives, Cincinnati, Ohio. Gary P. Zola, "Reform Judaism's Pioneer Zionist: Maximilian Heller," *American Jewish History* 73 (June 1984): 379–80, points out that Heller's criticism was less than fervid, suggesting that he was already on the road to conversion. Heller himself, however, characterized his earlier stance as being in "opposition to the movement." See now Bobbie Malone, *Rabbi Max Heller* (Tuscaloosa, 1997).

5. *Maccabaean* 12 (March 1907): 158; see also 30 (May 1917): 223, 257, 267; *American Jewish Chronicle* 3 (September 14, 1917), p. 499, for a report that "several of the most prominent Reform rabbis" had declared themselves "ardent Zionists," including Joseph Krauskopf, Morris Lazaron, and Edgar Magnin.

6. Michael A. Meyer, "American Reform Judaism and Zionism: Early Efforts at Ideological Rapprochement," *Studies in Zionism* 7 (Spring 1983): 49–64, is the most important article on the subject. Other studies include David Polish, *Renew Our Days: The Zionist Issue in Reform Judaism* (Jerusalem, 1976); Cyrus Arfa, *Reforming Reform Judaism: Zionism and the Reform Rabbinate, 1885–1948* (Tel-Aviv, 1985); Howard R. Greenstein, *Turning Point: Zionism and Reform Judaism* (Chico, Calif., 1981); Alfred Gottschalk, "Israel and Reform Judaism," *Forum*, no. 36 (Fall/Winter 1979): 143–60; Harold Floyd Caminker, "Reform Judaism in the United States and Its Relationship to Zionism as Reflected Primarily in Sources Heretofore Not Researched, 1889–1948" (rabbinic thesis, Hebrew Union College–Jewish Institute of Religion, 1978); Stuart E. Knee, "From Controversy to Conversion: Liberal Judaism in America and the Zionist Movement, 1917–1941," *YIVO Annual of Jewish Social Science* 17 (1978); 260–89; Evyatar Friesel, *Hatenuah hazionit bearzot haberit bashanim 1897–1914* (Tel-Aviv, 1970), pp. 90–108; Arthur J. Lelyveld, "The Conference View of the Position of the Jew in the Modern World," in *Retrospect and Prospect*, ed. Bertram W. Korn (New York,

1965), pp. 129–80; Joseph P. Sternstein, "Reform Judaism and Zionism, 1895–1904," *Herzl Year Book* 5 (1963): 11–31; Herschel Levin, "The Other Side of the Coin," *Herzl Year Book* 5 (1963): 33–56; Samuel Halperin, *The Political World of American Zionism* (1961; reprint New York, 1985), pp. 71–101; Naomi W. Cohen, "The Reaction of Reform Judaism in America to Political Zionism (1897–1922)," *Publications of the American Jewish Historical Society* 40 (1951): 361–94.

7. *Proceedings of the Union of American Hebrew Congregations* 5 (1893): 4002. David Philipson was "largely responsible" for the resolution's wording. See his *My Life as an American Jew* (Cincinnati, Ohio, 1941), p. 137.

8. Lelyveld, "Conference View of the Position of the Jew in the Modern World," pp. 130–31.

9. See, for example, the files of the *HUC Journal,* edited by the rabbinical students. The December 1899 (4, no. 3) special issue devoted to Zionism was well balanced, and a subsequent editorial (February 1900, p. 114) reported that "there are Zionists on the Editorial Board and in the College at large . . . but for the cause of truth, and for the information of future generations of historians who may happen to look through our file and find a Zionistic issue, it must be stated that this band of Zionists is in the minority." See also Michael A. Meyer, "A Centennial History," *Hebrew Union College–Jewish Institute of Religion at One Hundred Years,* ed. Samuel E. Karff (Cincinnati, Ohio, 1976), pp. 44–46, 62–69.

10. Meyer, "American Reform Judaism and Zionism," p. 50. See also Michael A. Meyer, *Response to Modernity: A History of the Reform Movement in Judaism* (New York, 1988), pp. 293–95.

11. Lewis R. Rambo, "Conversion," *The Encyclopedia of Religion* 4 (New York, 1987): pp. 73–79; William James, *The Varieties of Religious Experience* (1902; reprint, New York, 1958), p. 157; Richard Travisano, "Alteration and Conversion as Qualitatively Different Transformations," in *Social Psychology through Symbolic Interaction,* ed. B. P. Stone and Harvey A. Farberman (Waltham, Mass., 1970), p. 594, quoted in John Lofland and Norman Skonovd, "Conversion Motifs," *Journal for the Scientific Study of Religion* 20 (1981): 375. For a broad survey of current research on religious conversion, see Lewis Rambo's bibliography in *Religious Studies Review* 8 (April 1982): 146–59.

12. My thinking here has been influenced by the literature on "civil religion." See Russell E. Richey and Donald G. Jones, eds., *American Civil Religion* (New York, 1974); Charles S. Liebman and Eliezer Don-Yehiya, *Civil Religion in Israel: Traditional Judaism and Political Culture in the Jewish State* (Berkeley, 1983); Jonathan S. Woocher, *Sacred Survival: The Civil Religion of American Jews* (Bloomington, Ind., 1986).

13. *Maccabaean* 27 (August 1915): 54.

14. Alice L. Seligsberg, "In the Search for Wisdom," *Maccabaean* 30 (June/July 1917): 267; see also 29 (February 1917): 151–54. This remarkable autobiographical essay, in which Seligsberg recounts her conversion from Ethical Culture to Zionism, is a revealing case study, albeit somewhat outside the scope of our subject.

15. Robert D. Shapiro, *A Reform Rabbi in the Progressive Era: The Early Career of Stephen S. Wise* (New York, 1988), pp. 30, 46. See p. 39 n. 69, where Shapiro effectively refutes contrary claims by previous scholars.

16. Max Raisin, *Misefer hayai: Zikhronot vereshimot otobiografiim* (New York, 1956), p. 45. See also Rachel Hertzman, "An American Rabbi: A Translation of Four Essays from Max Raisin's *Dapim mipinkaso shel rabi"* (ordination thesis, Hebrew Union College–Jewish Institute of Religion, 1985), p. 4. Raisin's older brother, Jacob Raisin, was also a Zionist when he entered Hebrew Union College.

17. Examples include Abba Hillel Silver, Abraham J. Feldman, Joseph Baron, and Barnett Brickner. On their participation while still young boys in the Dr. Herzl Zion Club of New York's Lower East Side, founded at the Silver home in 1904, see Marc Lee Raphael, *Abba Hillel Silver: A Profile in American Judaism* (New York, 1989), p. 4.

18. Rambo, "Conversion," p. 75. Compare John Lofland and Rodney Stark, "Becoming a World-Saver: A Theory of Conversion to a Deviant Perspective," *American Sociological Review* 30 (1965): 864–67, esp. p. 874: "For conversion a person must . . . experience enduring, acutely felt tensions."

19. Yohai Goell, *"Aliya* in the Zionism of an American *Oleh:* Judah L. Magnes," *American Jewish Historical Quarterly* 65 (1975): 100–101; *Like All the Nations: The Life and Legacy of Judah L. Magnes,* ed. William M. Brinner and Moses Rischin (Albany, N.Y., 1987), pp. 5–6, 25, 29–37, 69–70; Judah L. Magnes, *Dissenter in Zion: From the Writings of Judah L. Magnes,* ed. Arthur A. Goren (Cambridge, Mass.: 1982), pp. 7–10.

20. Harvey E. Wessel, "How I Became a Zionist at the Hebrew Union College," *Hebrew Union College Monthly* 6 (May/June 1920): 186–190.

21. According to Max Heller in the *Maccabaean* 34 (August, 1920): 40. Wessel ("How I Became a Zionist," p. 20) quotes a prominent anti-Zionist rabbi, doubtless David Philipson, as asking, "Are there any students at the Hebrew Union College who are *not* Zionists?" Four years earlier, the *Maccabaean* 28 (May 1916): 113, reported the pro-Zionist awakening of another Hebrew Union College student, Harry R. Richmond, which it took as evidence of "how the Zionist ideal is gradually increasing its hold upon the educated Jewish Youth in America."

22. *New York Times,* November 14, 1921, p. 15; *Maccabaean* 3 (1902): 323, 13 (1907): 143; Joseph Silverman, *Pen Picture of the New Palestine* (New York [1924–25], in SC, box/A-78/109, Klau Library, Hebrew Union College, Cincinnati, Ohio; Joseph Stolz, "Joseph Silverman," *Central Conference of American Rabbis Yearbook* 41 (1931); 235. See also Marnin Feinstein, *Amerian Zionism, 1884–1904* (New York, 1965), pp. 218–21. The *American Jewish Chronicle* 3 (September 14, 1917): 499, reported that Silverman had purchased a *shekel,* thus acquiring membership in the organization and attended a Zionist dinner, perhaps as a prelude to his subsequent full-scale conversion.

23. Stolz, "Joseph Silverman," p. 234; Martin P. Beifield, "Joseph Krauskopf and Zionism: Partners in Change," *American Jewish History* 75 (1985): 48–60.

24. *Bernhard Felsenthal: Teacher in Israel,* ed. Emma Felsenthal (New York, 1924), p. 81.

25. Daniel J. Levinson, *The Seasons of a Man's Life* (New York, 1978), p. 35.

26. Charles Lloyd Cohen, *God's Caress: The Psychology of Puritan Religious Experience* (New York, 1986), p. 19.

27. For the beginnings of this awakening, see Jonathan D. Sarna, *JPS: The Americanization of Jewish Culture, 1888–1988* (Philadelphia, 1989), pp. 13–16, and the literature cited therein. Some of what follows has been drawn from that account. My understanding of these phenomena has been shaped by William G. McLoughlin, *Revivals, Awakenings, and Reform* (Chicago, 1978), and Anthony F. C. Wallace's classic essay, "Revitalization Movements," *American Anthropology* 58 (1956): 264–81. See now Jonathan D. Sarna, "The Late Nineteenth-Century American Jewish Awakening," *Religious Diversity and American Religious History,* ed. W. H. Conser and S. B. Twiss (Athens, Ga., 1997), pp. 1–25.

28. Naomi W. Cohen, "Anti-Semitism in the Gilded Age: The Jewish View," *Jewish Social Studies* 41 (1979): 187–210; John Higham, *Send These to Me* (New York, 1975): 116–95.

29. Paul A. Carter, *The Spiritual Crisis of the Gilded Age* (DeKalb, Ill., 1971); Naomi W. Cohen, "The Challenges of Darwinism and Biblical Criticism to American Judaism," *Modern Judaism* 4 (May 1984): 121–57; Benny Kraut, "Judaism Triumphant: Isaac Mayer Wise on Unitarianism and Liberal Christianity," *AJS Review* 7–8 (1982–83): esp. 202–25.

30. David Stern to Bernhard Felsenthal, April 24, 1884, Bernhard Felsenthal Papers, American Jewish Historical Society, Waltham, Mass.

31. *Jewish Times,* January 22, 1875, p. 760.

32. In a letter to Theodor Herzl, March 28, 1899, Richard Gottheil reported on a visit to Hebrew Union College, where he met "at least ten or twelve students who are ardent Zionists and good workers in the local Zionist society." Cited in Feinstein, *American Zionism,* p. 175. See also n. 9, above.

33. Theodor Herzl himself wrote that "American Jews would show the greatest patriotic devotion to America by helping us." He explained that "the aid offered by Zionism is the diversion of the stream of persecuted immigrants." See *Maccabaean* 5 (August 1903): 121; 9 (November 1905): 243. Max Margolis admitted that his early aversion to Zionism stemmed from precisely this point: "I believed that American Zionists were actuated by what I considered an ignoble motive, namely the desire of diverting immigration." *Maccabaean* 12 (March 1907): 97.

34. *American Hebrew* 61 (May 7, 1897): 18. See also Victor L. Ludlow, "Bernhard Felsenthal: Quest for Zion" (Ph.D. diss., Brandeis University, 1979), esp. pp. 236ff. Felsenthal had expressed similar views as early as 1891. See Anita L. Lebeson, "Zionism Comes to Chicago," in *Early History of Zionism in America,* ed. Isidore S. Meyer (New York, 1958), p. 173.

35. *Maccabaean* 5 (July 1903): 15. See Zvi Hirsch Masliansky's description of Rabbi Adolph Radin's conversion in Gary P. Zola, "The People's Preacher: A Study of the Life and Writings of Zvi Hirsch Masliansky (1856–1943)" (ordination thesis, Hebrew Union College–Jewish Institute of Religion, 1982), p. 176, translation of Masliansky's memoirs (New York, 1929), p. 201.

36. *Maccabaean* 4 (June 1903): 340. See also Philip E. Schoenberg, "The American Reaction to the Kishinev Pogrom of 1903," *American Jewish Historical Quarterly* 63 (March 1974): esp. 267–68. Emil G. Hirsch also became more positively inclined toward Zionism in the wake of the pogrom. See Moshe Davis, "Jewish Religious Life and Institutions in America," in *The Jews,* ed. Louis Finkelstein, 3d ed. (New York, 1960), p. 543; and Hirsch's own comments in *Russia at the Bar of the American People,* ed. Isidore Singer (New York, 1904), p. xxvi. But compare *Maccabaean* 31 (June 1918): 145.

37. See Friesel, *Hatenuah hazionit,* p. 63.

38. *Maccabaean* 2 (1905): 62.

39. *American Hebrew* 62 (December 10, 1897): 163. Yonathan Shapiro, *Leadership of the American Zionist Organization, 1897–1930* (Urbana, Ill., 1971), mistakenly attributes this address to Rabbi Gustav Gottheil, Richard's father.

40. *HUC Journal* 3 (December 1898): 61. As Michael Meyer notes, William H. Fineshriber later became "one of the severest critics of Political Zionism." "A Centennial History," p. 45.

41. *New Orleans Times-Democrat,* December 12, 1901. See also Shapiro, *Leadership of the American Zionist Organization,* p. 30; Zola, "Reform Judaism's Premier Zionist," pp. 380–81; Max Heller, "Our Spiritual Golus," *Maccabaean* 30 (August 1917): 314–15.

42. Max Heller, "Zionism as the Leaven," *Maccabaean* 20 (March/April 1911): 95–96.

43. *Bernhard Felsenthal,* ed. Emma Felsenthal, p. 79.

44. Henrietta Szold to Elvira N. Solis, December 12, 1909, in Marvin Lowenthal, *Henrietta Szold: Life and Letters* (New York, 1942), p. 67.

45. Years later, Horace Kallen made the same claim regarding Zionism's effect upon him. Asked what role Zionism had played in his life, he explained that it "was a channel in which I became again a whole person." Sarah Schmidt, "A Conversation with Horace M. Kallen: The Zionist Chapter of His Life," *Reconstructionist* 41 (November 1975): 33.

46. *Dissenter in Zion,* ed. Goren, p. 65; see also *Like All the Nations,* ed. Brinner and Rischin, pp. 6, 70.

47. Wessel, "How I Became a Zionist at the Hebrew Union College," p. 186.

48. Meyer, "American Reform Judaism and Zionism," p. 50.

49. *Maccabaean* 31 (July 1918): 180.

50. See Arnold M. Eisen, *The Chosen People in America* (Bloomington, Ind., 1983), esp. pp. 19–21, 53–72.

51. Meyer, "American Reform Judaism and Zionism," pp. 54–55. See also Naomi W. Cohen, "*The Maccabaean*'s Message: A Study in American Zionism until World War I," *Jewish Social Studies* 18 (1956): 165–66.

52. See, for example, Leo Jung, *Faith* (New York, 1968), pp. 19, 61. See also Michael

Meyer's comments in *Zion* 46 (1981): 56; Max Wiener, "The Concept of Mission in Traditional and Modern Judaism," *YIVO Annual* 2–3 (1947–48): 23–24.

53. Allon Gal, "The Mission Motif in American Zionism, 1898–1948," *American Jewish History* 75 (June 1986): 363–85; Gal, "Independence and Universal Mission in Modern Jewish Nationalism: A Comparative Analysis of European and American Zionism (1897–1948)," *Studies in Contemporary Jewry* 5 (1989): 242–55, esp. the comments of Arthur A. Goren, pp. 261–62. For other early efforts to reconcile "Israel's mission" and Zionism, see Bernhard Felsenthal, "Israel's Mission," *Maccabaean* 4 (March 1903): 135; and see esp. Max Heller, "Zionism and the Mission," *Maccabaean* 20 (July 1911): 232–33, which won editorial endorsement, in advance, as a "new interpretation . . . with which Zionists will agree without condition or qualifications." 19 (January 1911): 255. By 1917, the new synthesis was already fully articulated. See Martin A. Meyer, "Zionism and Reform Judaism," *Maccabaean* 30 (January 1917): 130: "Zionism holds that the mission of Israel . . . can only be realized by the creation of a Jewish center in which Jews will live so normal a life, so complete a Jewish life that the force of this example will influence not only all Jews, both those of the Homeland and of the Diaspora, but also all the peoples of the world." For Rabbi Abba Hillel Silver's role in spreading this new gospel, see Leon Feuer, "The Influence of Abba Hillel Silver on the Evolution of Reform Judaism," in *Rational Faith: Essays in Honor of Rabbi Levi A. Olan*, ed. Jack Bemporad (New York, 1977), pp. 80–87. See now *Abba Hillel Silver and American Zionism*, ed. Mark Raider, Jonathan D. Sarna, and Ronald W. Zweig (London, 1997).

54. See Evyatar Friesel, "American Zionism and American Jewry: An Ideological and Communal Encounter," *American Jewish Archives* 40 (April 1988): esp. 7–9; Melvin I. Urofsky, "Zionism: An American Experience," *American Jewish Historical Quarterly* 63 (March 1974): 261–82.

55. *American Israelite,* December 29, 1898, quoted in Dena Wilansky, *Sinai to Cincinnati* (Cincinnati, Ohio, 1937), p. 127; Oscar S. Straus, *The Origin of Republican Form of Government* (1885; reprint New York, 1901), p. 101; David Philipson, "Judaism and the Republican Form of Government," *Central Conference of American Rabbis Yearbook* 2 (1892): 53, 55. See also Ben Halpern, *The American Jew: A Zionist Analysis* (New York, 1956), pp. 11–33.

56. *Maccabaean* 20 (March/April 1911): 96.

57. Caspar Levias, "The Justification of Zionism," *HUC Journal* 3 (April 1899): 174. See also Richard Gottheil, *The Aims of Zionism* (New York, 1899), pp. 18–19, quoted in Friesel, *Hatenuah hazionit*, pp. 256–57.

58. *HUC Journal* 5 (October 1900): 27.

59. Louis Lipsky, "The Duty of American Jews," reprinted in Friesel, *Hatenuah hazionit*, p. 205. For a brief comparison of Puritans and Zionists, see Feinstein, *American Zionism*, p. 220.

60. Louis D. Brandeis, *The Jewish Problem: How To Solve It*, new ed. (Cleveland, 1934), pp. 21–22. See now Jonathan D. Sarna, "'The Greatest Jew in the World Since Jesus Christ': The Jewish Legacy of Louis D. Brandeis," *American Jewish History* 81 (1994): 346–64.

61. The lecture is frequently misdated. In fact, it was delivered on April 25 and released in printed form in late June. See Brandeis to Louis Lipsky, June 1, 1915, in *Letters of Louis D. Brandeis*, ed. Melvin I. Urofsky and David W. Levy (Albany, N.Y. 1971–), 3:525.

62. *Maccabaean* 26 (May 1915): 95. See also Maurice H. Harris, "Zionism: An Appreciation from a Non-Zionist," *American Hebrew* 98 (March 17, 1916): 530–31.

63. Max Heller, "Zionism and Our Reform Rabbinate," *Maccabaean* 31 (July 1918): 190. Of seventy-eight who responded, Heller classified twenty as Zionists, eighteen as anti-Zionists, twenty-seven as sympathizers, and thirteen as "non-descripts (betwixt and between)."

Conservative Judaism and Zionism

Scholars, Preachers, and Philanthropists

Conservative Judaism, as a Jewish religious movement, must obviously take an attitude to Zionism that is shaped by religious concerns.[1] This essay explains the view which Conservative Judaism held of Zionism as an expression of Judaism. What place did Zionism occupy in the religious ideology of Conservative Judaism, especially before 1948?

A few observations about Conservative Judaism itself are in order. As a religious movement it exists mainly among American Jews. Since it professes to accept the Oral as well as the Written Torah as binding, it regards the Halakhah as binding and obligatory for the Jew. But precisely at this point Conservative Judaism differs from Orthodoxy, since Conservatism argues that the Halakhah has been, and must continue to be, flexible and adaptive to the needs of the time. This principle has its basis in a lengthy array of scholarly studies in Talmud and Jewish history from the days of Zacharias Frankel and the positive-historical school. Halakhic decisions among the Conservatives are collective, although not necessarily binding on individuals, and there have always been disputes over the decisions themselves, both as to their scope and as to their conclusions. Conservative halakhic decisions deal with such areas as *kashrut* (dietary laws), Sabbath observance, conception and birth, burial, and above all marital status. However, the particular style of Conservative Jewish worship has been shaped by the congregations themselves, acting independently but drawing usually on the prayer book published by the Rabbinical Assembly, the association of Conservative rabbis.

When Solomon Schechter (1847–1915) arrived in the United States in 1902, perhaps twenty congregations could be called Conservative, with a membership between one and two thousand families. Today, the Conservative movement has about 825 affiliated congregations, to which about 225,000 families belong, representing about 750,000 individuals. Yet these impressive numbers have always contained an inner weakness, since they give additional prominence to the broad gulf between the religious and halakhic thought of the movement's leaders and the daily lives of the great majority of the members, who are remote from religious observance. The number of Jews affiliated with Conservative congregations who maintain Jewish tradition is small. It was probably higher fifty to eighty years ago. We have no statistics, but the rabbis of those 825 congregations will testify that they can hardly find a significant number of members who observe *kashrut* and the Sabbath. More and more, the main effort of the Conservatives has been to take these Jews, who quite readily became affiliated, and convert them so far as possible, or convert their children, into observant Jews.[2]

The Conservative movement has benefited from general religious trends in America. It is customary and proper to join some place of worship, and so, too, among the Jews. This tendency was strengthened among the white middle class when it moved from large cities to suburbs, especially after 1945. Conservative Judaism struggled to establish among its easily acquired membership a Judaism possessing depth and seriousness. From Orthodoxy it inherited the popular religiosity of the Jewish plebs of the days of mass immigration and dense urban Jewish neighborhoods during the first half of the present century.

Zionism, as expounded in the United States and as understood by members of the movement itself, is another foundation stone of Conservative Judaism. As was not the case with religious observance, here there has been agreement between the sentiment of the Conservative membership and the thought of three generations of leaders. Popular though Zionism has been, what Zionism meant within Conservative Jewry bears closer attention. The typically forceful words of Solomon Schechter in 1907 laid down the line that has always characterized the Conservative view of Zionism:

I belong to that class of Zionists that lay more stress on the religious-national aspects of Zionism than on any other feature peculiar to it. The rebirth of Israel's national consciousness, and the revival of Israel's religion, or, to use a shorter term, the revival of Judaism, are inseparable.[3]

Schechter expected that, "If Zionism cannot identify itself with conservative [i.e., traditional] Judaism, it should attempt, at least in its official organ [*Haolam*], to remain neutral, and give no cause for schisms and protests." This was said when Rabbi Isaac J. Reines complained that the central Zionist office in Cologne was open, though unofficially, on the Sabbath, and that *Haolam*, the Zionist organ, published antireligious articles. Schechter agreed that it "contains articles of a destructive nature, attacking both the Bible and the Talmud." He insisted that "the great majority of Zionists . . . have joined the movement in the hope that it will prove a force for strengthening the cause of Judaism. . . . They resent very deeply to see Zionistic organs criticizing all that is dear and sacred to them under the pretence of free discussion." Like Reines in Russia, Schechter in America was highly sensitive to "this reproach made by many that we represent a cause hostile to religion."[4] His opposition came from the American Jewish leaders who sat on the board of the Jewish Theological Seminary, while the faculty he appointed and the rabbis he trained were strongly Zionist.

One decade later, shortly before the Balfour Declaration was issued, one of these rabbis, Abraham M. Hershman (1880–1959) of Detroit declared, "Let but Israel return to Zion and he will attain the acme and pinnacle of spiritual life, and the world will resound with prophetic messages."[5]

The opening of the Hebrew University in 1925 inspired another prominent Conservative rabbi, Israel Herbert Levinthal (1888–1982) of Brooklyn, to call out in Schechter's spirit, "What we desire is not only the revival of the Jewish *Soil* but the renaissance of the Jewish *Soul!*"[6]

These and other statements no less fervent could be heard in hundreds of the modernized traditional synagogues of the Conservative movement decades before the State of Israel was established. Some have been preserved, edited, in printed collections of sermons.[7] They struck sympathetic chords among the businessmen, lawyers, and accountants who constituted these synagogues' backbone. Yet, as we shall see, Zionism was, for them, not without its perplexities.

At the Jewish Theological Seminary, the Zionist idea held the potential for conflict. This central institution occupied a position of dominance within Conservative Judaism that was without parallel among Jewish religious movements, and it was established and maintained financially by men who were hostile to Zionism. The lay leaders who reestablished the seminary between 1898 and 1901 and brought in Solomon Schechter as its head in 1902 intended an American institution for training rabbis who would teach and exemplify traditional Judaism in America. The beneficiaries were to be mainly the children of immigrants. It was feared they were leaving their inherited Orthodoxy *en masse* for careerism and hedonism and being influenced by undesirable ideologies such as assimilationism and socialism. These leaders were against Zionism, which appeared to them a secular nationalism foreign to Judaism. To them, Zionist leaders like Theodor Herzl and Max Nordau and, later on, Louis D. Brandeis possessed dubious qualifications to head a Jewish movement.

Reform Jews such as Jacob H. Schiff (1847–1920) and Louis Marshall (1856–1929) were not the only ones to oppose Zionism; so was Judge Mayer Sulzberger (1843–1923). As large-spirited men, they tolerated the Zionism that was rife in the institution. But Schechter's statement on Zionism, quoted in part above, irritated Schiff, and he issued a sharp rejoinder. An endorsement of Zionism by the president of the Jewish Theological Seminary differed from the expressions of students and professors because it appeared to challenge, as did the movement itself, the communal leadership of Schiff and his associates. But Schiff's wrath subsided. Sulzberger also cared little for Zionism, and he was a learned, traditionally observant Jew whose private book collection constituted the basis of the seminary's great library. Shortly before the Balfour Declaration was promulgated, Sulzberger, who had regarded with disdainful dismay the intense Zionist politicking to establish the American Jewish Congress, called Zionism "a reversion to a stage of nationalism which ought to be past." Given freedom of emigration, which the war should accomplish, "any Jew in all the world will be free to settle in Palestine. . . . If enough Jews settle there to be the enormous majority, their opinion will doubtless influence the laws."[8] Not Zionist ideology but massive free immigration would make Palestine the Jewish land. .

Mayer Sulzberger's younger relative Cyrus Adler (1863–1940) gave fuller expression to the dissent from Zionism, as his published letters abundantly illustrate.[9] Adler, who was interested in the Mesopotamian territorial project, thought little of Herzl, whom he dubbed "the moshiach [messiah] of Vienna," as a diplomat or a Jewish leader. Adler dissented in principle from the Basle Program's failure to include Judaism together with the national home for the Jewish people. "Offhand," Adler thought that if those active in the Zionist movement would

modify their phrase and indicate that the object of this movement is to secure an opportunity for the cultivation of Judaism upon the historical soil of Palestine, and that the religion as well as the people is a part of the whole programme, the principal objection to Zionism, that is an expression of mere material nationalism will fall to the ground and the united support of all the Jews who are worth considering as Jews would be secured.[10]

Eight months later, just after the Balfour Declaration, he wanted to rally "those like ourselves who are profoundly interested in Palestine and believe that the emphasis must be laid upon Judaism as against Nationalism."[11] In a memorandum at the time, Adler again emphasized that his interest in restoring the Holy Land was the cultivation of Judaism: "The main object is the Judaism of which the Jews are but the vehicles. While it is true that we shall not have Judaism without the Jews, it would be a more profound misfortune to have Jews without Judaism."[12] Cyrus Adler and his non-Zionist colleagues could not accept sympathetically the sudden eruption of Louis D. Brandeis (1856–1941) as the Zionist leader. Brandeis's declaration that every Jew must aid in regaining Palestine and join the Zionist movement, or be shamed as a "slacker," elicited a scathing comment: "This seems rather tall talk for a Jew who turned his back on the Jewish people until he was 57 or 58 years of age and was unmoved by the 35 years' misery of the Jews of Russia before we Jews attracted his august and interested attention."[13] Adler was second to Marshall as a non-Zionist leader, and he inherited the leadership after Marshall's death in 1929. Adler was becoming increasingly isolated at the seminary, however. His views on Zionism coincided with those of the American Jewish Committee, where he also succeeded Marshall as president. But the caliber of the new non-Zionists was much beneath that of their predecessors, while the Zionists were becoming more challenging.

Within the Jewish Theological Seminary, the most active Zionist was the Bible and Semitics scholar Israel Friedlaender (1876–1920). His manifold activity as a public man, lecturer, and writer came at the expense of his scholarly career.[14] The strongest intellectual influences on Friedlaender were Simon Dubnov (1860–1941) and Ahad Haam (1856–1927), although he rejected their secularism. Friedlaender foresaw a brilliant Jewish future in America, which was bound to become the new Jewish center in the historic succession of Jewish centers, as set forth by the diaspora nationalist Dubnov. Friedlaender followed Ahad Haam in expecting the new Palestine to be a cultural center and as such the beacon for the Jews everywhere. He did not follow the sage of Odessa's doctrine that the *galut* (exile) would be dependent on Palestine for its cultural and spiritual sustenance. It was during these pre–World War I years that Mordecai Menahem Kaplan (1881–1983) imbibed the Zionist and other influences that he synthesized in the Reconstructionist philosophy, set forth during nearly three generations of his teaching, preaching, and writing. More systematically than any contemporary, Kaplan in his Reconstructionism placed Palestine at the center of Jewish civilization.[15]

Zionism thus enjoyed the support of Conservative Jewry, notwithstanding the opposition of influential individuals on the board of the Jewish Theological Seminary. Zionism was an idea that could unite the membership of the Conservative synagogues. Conservative rabbis and synagogue officers were frequently presidents and officials of Zionist districts, and Zionist meetings were often held on synagogue premises. Only the adamant opposition of Adler, with his threat to resign as its president and his appeal to the provisions of the United Synagogue constitution, prevented that Conservative organization from officially endorsing the Balfour Declaration.[16]

Why did Zionism prove so attractive to the rabbis and laymen of Conservative Jewry? Orthodoxy, out of which Conservative Judaism emerged, remained the ideological touchstone for Conservative ideology. The Orthodox were, however, generally hostile to Zionism, although less so in America than in Europe, and the masses of poor immigrant Orthodox were preoccupied with eking out a living and establishing the local institutions of religious life. Conservative Jewry possessed reasonably well-financed synagogues and other institutions, and Conservative Jews were consciously American in culture and mores. Many had been immigrants, but that period in their lives lay in their past. Conservative synagogues were not situated in immigrant neighborhoods but in areas of second- and third-generation settlement.[17] Social mobility figured prominently in the passage from immigrant Orthodoxy to Conservatism. To be sure, the number of Eastern European immigrants' children who entered the ranks of Reform Judaism also increased steadily. However, before the 1930s at the earliest, these newcomers were overshadowed by the old-time "classical Reform" laymen, most of whom were anti-Zionist.

Both Conservative Judaism and Zionism had significant precursors during the nineteenth century and came to active life in 1902 and 1897 respectively.

They shared the sense of reacting against false turns in Jewish life. Zionism turned against the certitudes of rational, enlightened, redemptive Jewish emancipation as the sure and sufficient goal of Jewish life. Conservative Judaism turned against rationalist, optimistic, antitraditional Reform. Both movement endorsed Jewish tradition selectively.

What was attractive about Zionism was what had been expressed by the great historian Heinrich Graetz, Zacharias Fränkel's colleague at the Breslau rabbinical seminary. They maintained that the content of Judaism was not restricted to abstract principles of faith and that it possessed a sociopolitical dimension—meaning that after the travail of *galut* and its lessons a Jewish society would arise again in the ancestral land on the basis of Jewish tradition. Thus the Conservative movement and Zionism clearly possess as a common basis the unavoidable encounter between Jewish tradition and the modern world of science, historicism, and nationalism and the synthesis that each movement effected between the old and the new. There was no question but that the Conservative movement would take part in the general historical process. The movement had been born by such participation and by conscious desire dwelled in the modern world. The Zionist conception of a renewed Jewish society was the antithesis of the metaphysical speculation of Israel's return to its land as formulated, for example, by the Orthodox chief rabbinates of France and England and in fullest form by Rabbi Samson Raphael Hirsch.

In the early twentieth century, before *aliyah* was deemed the basis of Zionism and political and philanthropic support did not exhaust its content, the future links between the restored homeland and the dispersion were defined in Ahad Haamian terms. The fresh, replenished Jewish culture would radiate outward to the scattered House of Israel. The content of the culture was not stressed, if only because it had hardly yet come into being. Mutual influence was not thought of. The psychological dimension of Zionism was emphasized. Schechter and Friedlaender saw Zionism as a bastion against radical assimilation and as a means for strengthening Jewish identity, which was becoming infirm from lack of Jewish self-respect. They frequently praised Zionist youth, whose Jewish fervor and self-sacrificing adherence to a Jewish cause were held up as an example. The fine psychological results of Jewish education in a Zionist spirit encouraged the anti-Zionist community leaders to support Hebrew education generously under the auspices of the Kehillah of New York City. Again with their support, in 1909 the Jewish Theological Seminary opened a Teachers' Institute for Hebrew teachers, thereby adopting the new philosophy that revived Jewish education and removed it from Sunday school and the *heder*. The Teachers' Institute, headed by Mordecai M. Kaplan, was by its nature a Hebraic, Zionist institution. Hebrew was the language of instruction, and its teachers were learned Hebraists. Many of its graduates and a significant number among those educated at similar Hebraic institutions enrolled in the rabbinical school and in time were ordained as Conservative rabbis. Thus a thread of Hebraism and Zionism passed through the central Conservative institution.[18]

As the Zionist idea advanced in the still small Conservative movement during the 1920s, it placed the emphasis on the benefits reborn Eretz Israel would bring to the oppressed bodies of Jews in Europe and to their spirits in America. Rabbis such as Israel Herbert Levinthal and Abraham M. Hershman often returned to this point, as did Mordecai M. Kaplan. With the homiletic skill that gained him fame and, by report, the repetition of his sermons in other synagogues, Levinthal noted that Moses' first task as liberator was to prove to the Jews that they were meant to be free (Exod. 3:16–20):

Even so, today there are some of our people who would tell us that the day of the Jew's emancipation has not yet come, that he must remain in slavery. But the signs of the time show that God wills it otherwise. We have our choice either to win our freedom ourselves or to have our freedom thrust upon us.[19]

Referring to the slave who refused freedom at the end of his term of bondage (Exod. 21:5–6):

If the Jew today permits his promised emancipation to slip by, he will be forever marked and degraded in the eyes of his fellow-men, even as was the slave of old who was contented in his bondage.[20]

In 1917, six years before Levinthal's sermon, Hershman used a term that came into vogue almost a half century afterward. He described Zionism as "essentially a liberation movement . . . to emancipate the spirit of the Jewish people."[21] Rabbi Simon Greenberg (b. 1901), addressing his Philadelphia congregation early in 1939, likewise saw in Palestine "the opportunity for the salvation and redemption of the soul of the Jew." Success in Palestine "would create for our people throughout the world a reservoir of spiritual and physical strength which would assure their existence for untold millennia."[22] And Rabbi Abraham M. Heller (1896–1975), speaking at his Brooklyn synagogue in 1937, declared that "Zionism appears and spells for us the confidence we need for our own survival. How many lost Jewish souls have been reborn Jewishly because of the ideal of Zion rebuilt?"[23] Hershman's words of 1938, "The fate and spiritual destiny of Israel the world over are intimately bound up with the fate and destiny of Palestine,"[24] echoed in many pulpits.

What prominent rabbis said to middle-class congregations indicates how much the Zionist ideal was supporting the shaky morale of American Jewry. The threat from antisemitism was all too clear, as the triumph of Nazism in Germany was watched with incredulous horror. The Conservative rabbis showed special sensitivity to the frightened and reluctant Jewishness of a large part of American Jewry. Palestine, they said, would "redeem" Jewish souls, bring about their rebirth, and provide a reservoir of psychic strength. "It will give them a new dignity, a new status. It will beget in them the desire to familiarize themselves with the sources of Judaism."[25] Rabbi Levinthal articulated the widespread belief that the development of Eretz Israel Jewry meant the awakening of Judaism in America. In 1932 or 1933, deep in the Great Depression, he drew on mystical traditions connecting God and His land:

Not only the Jew but the *Shekhinah*, too, is coming back to its own. Judaism, the product of the Jewish soul, is destined again to blossom and to enrich the world. Palestine is becoming once more the Arzot ha-Hayyim . . . the land where Judaism shall be a reality, a living thing with a heart at its old-new center to drive the life-giving blood to every corner of the Dispersion and restore to the worn limbs beauty, freshness and youth.[26]

And in more direct fashion:

With a Jewish life on Jewish soil, in which Jewish culture with its deeply God-conscious character shall be dominant, Judaism will not have to struggle for a bare existence as it does in the Diaspora. . . . The living waters of Jewish inspiration, so long pent in by the unfavorable conditions of the Galut, shall be given in Zion a natural outlet. [They will] irrigate the barren region of our Diaspora Judaism, waking to new life whatever seeds of spiritual interest still remain hidden in the Jewish heart![27]

During more optimistic days fifteen years earlier, Rabbi Hershman did "not hesitate to say that a full Jewish life, a normal development of Israel, is possible only in Palestine."[28] But he and his colleagues in the pulpit shied away from negating the exile. "I do not mean to say," Hershman continued, "that Judaism outside Palestine is doomed, has no future."[29] But Palestine was indispensable. Most of them would have agreed with Kaplan that,

If it were not for the fructifying effect of the interest in the upbuilding of Palestine, the work of the communal centers, synagogues, philanthropic and educational institutions might have gone on, but it would have become soulless and spiritless. . . . Palestine should serve as the symbol of the Jewish renascence and the center of Jewish civilization. . . . Judaism cannot maintain its character as a civilization without a national home in Palestine. There essential Jewish creativity will express itself in Hebraic forms not so easily developed in other lands.[30]

In 1941, early in his long and eminent career, Rabbi Robert Gordis (b. 1908) epitomized the meaning of Zionism for Conservative Judaism. He emphasized the influence of Ahad Haam's thinking, by which Palestine's

central value would reside in its being the spiritual center of the Jewish people. . . . This conception of *the interaction between Palestine and the Diaspora, which gave a significant role in Jewish destiny to both spheres* remains his most fundamental contribution to Jewish thought. This position Conservative Judaism has adopted wholeheartedly.[31]

And in yet broader terms:

Palestine, as the center of the Jewish people, must be the living center of Judaism. Zionism is integral and basic, a central article of faith in the creed of modern Judaism.[32]

As a summary of the Zionist views that had been held within Conservative Judaism since Schechter's time, Gordis's ringing declaration is almost definitive.

But there were also other views. As Cyrus Adler aged and his health declined and other responsibilities pressed hard, Rabbi Louis Finkelstein (b. 1895) became Adler's deputy and heir apparent at the Jewish Theological Seminary. We do not know how this son of an immigrant Lithuanian rabbi—Lithuanian rabbis contributed not a few of its sons to the Conservative rabbinate—arrived at a position far distant from that of Hapoel Hamizrahi to which he had once belonged and which continued the old non-Zionism. Rabbi Finkelstein, gifted with learning and eloquence, served as president (later chancellor) of the seminary from 1940 to 1972 and as such stood *de facto* at the head of Conservative Judaism. He was obviously aware of student and faculty Zionism, while he also had to reckon with the seminary's board of directors. These laymen, who maintained the institution, were still composed of non-Zionists and included a few anti-Zionists.

Rabbi Finkelstein stated his position in "Reflections on Judaism, Zionism and Enduring Peace," which was published in 1943 in the Zionist Organization of America's weekly, the *New Palestine*.[33] There were five sections to the "Reflections." In the first two, "The Place of Palestine in Judaism" and "Palestine in the World Peace," Finkelstein reviewed the religious reverence for the Holy Land: "Even when it is not his temporal dwelling, Palestine is his House of God, the spiritual home for all Israel."[34] To be sure, "the Jew regards his native land, wherever that may be, as his hearth and home, to be loved, to be defended with his life."[35] Finkelstein emphasized the universalist possibilities of the Holy Land, "potentially a unifying medium for all mankind. . . . The restoration of Judaism to Palestine is essential for this task."[36] Otherwise, "Judaism without Palestine is spiritually retarded. Palestine without Judaism is spiritually inert."[37] Proceeding to the section on "The Prophetic and Rabbinic Formula for World Peace," the seminary's president believed that "the men seeking to restore a Jewish homeland are today, as in the past, instruments of a destiny beyond the full comprehension either of themselves or their contemporaries."[38] The obligation exists "to rebuild the Holy Land as a religious community. . . . The establishment of Judaism in Palestine and the understanding of its role in civilized life, will signal the spiritual recovery of mankind."[39] Finkelstein pressed ahead with this depoliticized, religious Ahad Haamism: "The secular view [is] at variance with the Zionist ideal properly conceived, that Judaism is a secular phenomenon."[40]

The last two sections, "The Prophetic and Rabbinic Formula for World Peace" and "The False Doctrines of Racism and Jewish Secular Nationalism," fitted Finkelstein's interpretation of Zionism into his conception of world peace and harmony as taught by Judaism:

The concept of a Palestinian Jewish homeland in a world association of peoples loses all meaning unless it is accompanied by an affirmation of equal rights of Jews—as of members of all other faiths—in the lands of their election.

The creation of an enduring peace presupposes an active cooperative relationship among nations and peoples, which makes the question of statehood less and less relevant; while emphasis on national sovereignty anywhere can be fatal to civilization.[41]

This article must be placed within the larger framework of Finkelstein's religious views. He believed that Judaism had a profound contribution to make to humankind's spiritual needs, expressed not in the customary biblical terms but in terms of Rabbinic Judaism. Universal peace based on human brotherhood was the Rabbinic ideal. Finkelstein wrote two important works of learning in this vein: *Akiba* and *The Pharisees*.[42] Both attempted to show that the Pharisees, as the fathers of Rabbinic Judaism, adopted and extended biblical conceptions of peace and human equality. The Institute for Religious and Social Studies was established at the Jewish Theological Seminary to bring together Christian and Jewish scholars, theologians, educators, and philosophers to consider how the world's religions could aid in grasping and solving the world's underlying problems. These activities projected the seminary into an international prominence that went far beyond that of an institution of Jewish learning. In his "Reflections," Finkelstein was applying his intellectual and rhetorical powers to fitting Zionism within the framework of postwar idealistic internationalism as expounded by the Jewish sages whom he interpreted. The fit was less than perfect. He could not state a position that was acceptable to Zionist sentiment and also to the non-Zionists of his board. Political Zionism based on the Biltmore Program of 1942 was on the march, while many of the seminary's board were moving with the American Jewish Committee into anti-Zionism.

Rabbi Finkelstein was seeking to universalize the rebuilding of Palestine, which all Jews were bound to support, and to make it a center and symbol of the religious and spiritual well-being of humankind. Such an ideal transcended political aspirations. Indeed, "national sovereignty," meaning a Jewish Commonwealth, was undesirable and could be "fatal to civilization." When he turned to the nettling issues of dual loyalty and the destination of uprooted Jews once the war ended, his answers, grounded in religious idealism, did not contradict the American Jewish Committee's "Statement of Views," adopted earlier that year.[43] Finkelstein defined the Jews in the same apolitical fashion:

Conceived as a unit, the Jews are neither a race, nor a political group. They are tied to one another with no distinctive bonds of blood kinship. . . . World Jewry constitutes, of course, no political group; it is rather a "kingdom of priests."[44]

Rabbi Finkelstein was clearly anti-Zionist when he addressed the executive committee of the American Jewish Committee in October 1943.[45] His leanings, and those of board members, brought strains within the seminary.

When the faculty held a dinner for Stephen S. Wise as president of the Jewish Institute of Religion on his seventieth birthday in the spring of 1944, that famous old Zionist used the occasion to chide Finkelstein openly. Wise said that there were no longer non-Zionists but only anti-Zionists, and Finkelstein had no business with them. Around 1946, a few seminary board members, disturbed by signs of the American Jewish Committee's compromising attitude toward Zionism, sought to recruit Finkelstein as the religious ideologist of a very tentative new organization that would continue traditional non-Zionism. Finkelstein avoided the offer and in any event the organization did not come into existence.[46]

The Jewish Theological Seminary thus went through the 1940s in a state of tense division between its faculty and students on one hand and the administration and board of directors on the other. Outside, almost all Conservative congregations were firmly aligned with Zionism. Only the establishment of the State of Israel neutralized Zionism as an issue.

Within the leadership of the Conservative movement and also in its affiliated synagogues, several attempts were made to deal with the exciting but somewhat perplexing reality of the Zionist state, not just the Zionist movement. For example, could a flag that was now that of a sovereign state be raised on an American flagpole? But the attempt to replace the blue-and-white flag with that of the Jewish chaplaincy of the United States Armed Forces, displaying the tablets of the Ten Commandments, won no favor. "Hatikvah" continued to be sung.

After World War II financial support for the seminary began to come from a new source as the older members of the board left the scene. The masses of new Conservative synagogue members, who benefited from the prosperity that began in the United States in 1941 and continued until about 1975, made their contributions to the seminary. Practically all were Zionists or pro-Zionists.

After 1948, Conservative rabbis and some laymen sought more than ever to give religious significance to their Zionist affiliation. Gordis, describing himself as a Zionist from childhood, but a "homeless Zionist," had found American Zionism lacking in Jewish content and practice. He was a perfunctory member of the Zionist Organization of America. Deeply moved by the social justice and mutual responsibility within the *kibbutz* movement, he had joined the League for Labor Palestine. "My happiness, however, was less than complete, for I was aware of the general indifference, if not hostility, to Jewish religious faith and practice within Labor Zionist circles." He had been friendly with the Mizrahi leader Rabbi Meir Berlin (Bar-Ilan), who long urged him to join Hapoel Hamizrahi. Finally, after 1948 Gordis did so in company with Rabbis Simon Greenberg and Benzion Bokser. These prominent Conservative rabbis were welcome as individuals in Hapoel Hamizrahi, but their intention to establish a separate branch caused controversy and was vetoed; the rabbis withdrew.[47]

The Conservatives somewhat hesitantly sought to mention Israel in the prayer book. More consequential for the movement was the state of religious life in Israel and the refusal of its religious establishment to recognize Conservative Judaism. Israeli secularism was a pervasive concern. Rabbi Hershman exemplified the broad view, that "much of the irreligion in Israel is but a reaction from what passes for religion." He was sure that Israel would rear "a new type of Jew . . . a normal and healthy Judaism . . . not a mere topic for discussion, but a life that will be lived."[48] His colleagues were less sanguine and insisted that the religious establishment repelled and possibly stirred hatred for Jewish religion among the masses of nonreligious and secularist Israelis.

The Conservative presence in Israel remained small and diffident while Louis Finkelstein continued as head of the movement. Conflict with Israeli Orthodoxy and its religious establishment was sedulously avoided. During the 1970s and 1980s the movement became more visible and assertive and built its own institutional network.

Changes in the Conservatives' thinking about Israel's relation to the diaspora are typified by Rabbi Judah Naiditch's presidential address to the Rabbinical Assembly in the spring of 1973. While proclaiming American Jewry's full, unhesitating support for Israel, he declared that there was a need for friendly mutual criticism. "Such a relationship is predicated on the assumption that Jewish life in the *Golah* of America is *viable*."[49]

In 1988, an official "Statement of Principles of Conservative Judaism," entitled *Emet veemunah* was produced for the first time. It included a chapter about Israel as a Jewish state and its religion and another chapter about Israel-diaspora relations. Preceding these chapters was "Eschatology: Our Vision of the Future," which bespoke universalist social idealism. The eschatology chapter did not refer to Israel, while those dealing with Israel made no reference to eschatology—a sign that Conservative Judaism did not follow powerful Orthodox currents in tying the Land of Israel to a messianic future. Still, the State of Israel, "a unique phenomenon in history,"[50] is not viewed "just in political or military terms; rather we consider it to be a miracle, reflecting Divine Providence in human affairs."[51] The "Statement" emphasizes the need for religion within Israel, claiming equal rights for all versions of Judaism and deploring religious coercion and the political use of religion. Pride in the existence of Israel and support for its needs are set apart, however, from agreement with every policy adopted by its government.[52] Above all, the existence of the diaspora is unequivocally affirmed:

Both the State of Israel and Diaspora Jewry have roles to fill; each can and must enrich the other in every possible way; each needs the other. It is our fervent hope that Zion will indeed be the center of Torah and Jerusalem a beacon lighting the way for the Jewish people and for humanity.[53]

Thus Conservative Judaism has discarded the conception prevalent in its early days, when Ahad Haam denied the secure existence of the diaspora and saw in the rebuilt homeland a one-sided source of influence for the diaspora. The first Conservatives sought the Jewish homeland in order to strengthen American Jewish identity. To a greater or lesser extent, Conservative Judaism constantly absorbed influence from Israel. Now it appears to be advocating mutual influence and partnership. It remains to be seen whether spiritual resources capable of substantially influencing the State of Israel exist within Conservative Judaism.

Notes

1. See, in general, Melvin I. Urofsky, *American Zionism from Herzl to the Holocaust* (Garden City, N.Y., 1975); Naomi W. Cohen, *American Jews and the Zionist Idea* (N.p., 1975); Yonathan Shapiro, *Leadership of the American Zionist Organization, 1897–1930* (Urbana, Ill., 1971); Evyatar Friesel, *Hatenuah hazionit bearzot haberit bashanim 1897–1914* (Tel Aviv, 1970); Herbert Parzen, "Conservative Judaism and Zionism (1896–1922)," *Jewish Social Studies* 23, no. 4 (October 1961): 235–64. This essay was written well before the publication of *Tradition Renewed: A History of the Jewish Theological Seminary of America,* ed. Jack Wertheimer (2 vols., New York, 1997) which has much to add to our subject, particularly the chapters by Naomi W. Cohen and Eli Lederhendler.

2. Marshall Sklare, *Conservative Judaism: An American Religious Movement,* new ed. (Lanham, Md., 1972), pp. 43–82; Jack Wertheimer, "The Conservative Synagogue," in *The American Synagogue: A Sanctuary Transformed,* ed. Jack Wertheimer (Cambridge, England, 1987), pp. 111–49.

3. Solomon Schechter, "Zionism: A Statement," in *The Zionist Idea,* ed. Arthur Hertzberg (New York, 1960), pp. 504–13. See also Friesel, *Hatenuah hazionit,* pp. 77–80.

4. Solomon Schechter to David Wolfsohn, New York, June 17, 1908, Wolfsohn to Schechter, Cologne, July 1, 1908, Central Zionist Archives, Jerusalem, Z 2/303. I thank Dr. Michael Heymann, director of the Archives, for bringing these letters to my attention.

5. Abraham M. Hershman, *Israel's Fate and Faith* (New York, 1952); *Encyclopedia Judaica,* s.v. "Hershman, Abraham, M."; Rabbinical Assembly, *Proceedings* (1959): 103–5; Robert A. Rockaway, *The Jews of Detroit: From the Beginning, 1762–1914* (Detroit, 1986), pp. 75–77, 80. Since Hershman's sermons were published only many years after they were delivered, their influence beyond the congregation was limited.

6. Israel Herbert Levinthal, *Steering or Drifting—Which? Sermons and Discourses* (New York, 1928), p. 289. See *Encyclopedia Judaica,* s.v. "Levinthal, Israel H."; Deborah Dash Moore, "A Synagogue Center Grows in Brooklyn," in *American Synagogue,* ed. Wertheimer, pp. 297–326. Levinthal's sermons appeared in contemporary publications and were widely read, particularly by other rabbis.

7. There are substantial methodological questions regarding the use of sermons as historical sources. However, the questions relate to their use as a source for contemporary conditions. See Benzion Dinur, "Reshitah shel hahasidut veyesodoteiha hasozialiyim vehameshihiyim," in *Bemifneh hadorot* (Jerusalem, 1955), p. 87, 97–100; Mendel Piekarz, *Bimei zemihat hahasidut* (Jerusalem, 1978), pp. 11–15, 98–104. Here I use sermons to demonstrate a point of view that the preacher sought to persuade his congregation to adopt or when he sought to reinforce an existing point of view. That each rabbi quoted here served one large congregation for many years suggests a basic ideological concord.

8. *Philadelphia North American,* quoted in *Jewish Exponent,* July 13, 1917, reproduced in *American Jewish Ephemera: A Bicentennial Exhibition from the Judaica Collection of the*

Harvard College Library, ed. Charles Berlin (Cambridge, Mass., 1977), no. 44a; Urofsky, *American Zionism*, p. 190, quoting *American Hebrew*, July 21, 1916; Moshe Davis, *The Emergence of Conservative Judaism* (Philadelphia, 1963), pp. 362–65; *Encyclopedia Judaica*, s.v. "Sulzberger, Mayer."

9. Cyrus Adler, *Selected Letters*, ed. Ira Robinson, 2 vols. (Philadelphia, 1985). See my review in *Jewish Social Studies* 48, nos. 3–4 (Summer/Fall, 1986): 334–37.

10. Cyrus Adler to Judah L. Magnes, April 5, 1917, *Selected Letters*, 1:330.

11. Cyrus Adler to Louis Marshall, December 28, 1917, ibid., p. 344.

12. Ibid., pp. 339–40.

13. Cyrus Adler to Louis Marshall, September 7, 1919, ibid., p. 392.

14. A useful study is Baila Round Shargel, *Practical Dreamer: Israel Friedlaender and the Shaping of American Judaism* (New York, 1985).

15. The basic work of Reconstructionism is Mordecai Menahem Kaplan, *Judaism as a Civilization* (New York, 1934).

16. Parzen, "Conservative Judaism and Zionism," pp. 239–42.

17. Sklare, *Conservative Judaism*; Michael A. Meyer, *Response to Modernism: A History of the Reform Movement in Judaism* (New York, 1988), p. 306.

18. Arthur Goren, *New York Jews and the Quest for Community: The Kehillah Experiment, 1908–1922* (New York, 1970), pp. 110–33; Lloyd P. Gartner, *Jewish Education in the United States: A Documentary History* (New York, 1970), pp. 13–23, 118–48.

19. Levinthal, *Steering or Drifting*, p. 188.

20. Ibid.

21. Hershman, *Israel's Fate and Faith*, p. 259.

22. Simon Greenberg, *Living as a Jew Today* (New York, 1940), p. 88.

23. Abraham M. Heller, *Jewish Survival: Sermons and Addresses* (New York, 1939), p. 188.

24. Hershman, *Israel's Fate and Faith*, p. 266.

25. Ibid., p. 16.

26. Israel Herbert Levinthal, *Judaism: An Analysis and an Interpretation* (New York, 1935), p. 254.

27. Ibid., p. 256.

28. Hershman, *Israel's Fate and Faith*, p. 262.

29. Ibid.

30. Kaplan, *Judaism as a Civilization*, pp. 66, 515, 516.

31. Robert Gordis, *The Jew Faces a New World* (New York, 1941), p. 207, italics in original.

32. Ibid., p. 212.

33. Louis Finkelstein, "Reflections on Judaism, Zionism and Enduring Peace," *New Palestine*, May 21, 1943, also published as a brochure from which citations are taken. See also Finkelstein, "Zionism and World Culture," *New Palestine*, September 15, 1944, which Alon Gal kindly brought to my attention.

34. "Reflections," p. 2.

35. Ibid.

36. Ibid., p. 3.

37. Ibid., p. 5.

38. Ibid., p. 5–6.

39. Ibid., p. 6.

40. Ibid., p. 7.

41. Ibid., p. 8.

42. Louis Finkelstein, *Akiba: Scholar, Saint and Martyr* (New York, 1936); Finkelstein, *The Pharisees: The Sociological Background of Their Faith*, 2 vols. (Philadelphia, 1938). *Akiba* was subjected to a lengthy, severe review by Gedalia Allon in *Tarbiz* 10 (1939): 241–82,

reprinted in his *Mehkarim betoldot Israel* (Tel Aviv, 1958), 2:181–27, esp. pp. 182–85, 200–202. *The Pharisees,* and particularly its sociological conceptualization, received penetrating dissenting reviews by Salo W. Baron in *Journal of Biblical Literature* 69, no. 1 (March 1940): 60–67, and in *Review of Religion* 4, no. 2 (January 1940): 196–99. A second edition appeared in 1940 and a third in 1962, each adding extensive introductory material and bibliographies. The sociological argument was first set forth by Finkelstein in *Harvard Theological Review* 22 (1929): 185–261; the universalist aspects evidently were added later.

43. *American Jewish Year Book* 45 (1943–44): 608–10, quoted in Naomi W. Cohen, *Not Free to Desist: The American Jewish Committee, 1906–1966* (Philadelphia, 1966), pp. 253–55.

44. Finkelstein, "Reflections," p. 7. See also Exodus 19:6.

45. Morris D. Waldman, *Nor by Power* (New York, 1953), pp. 268–70, provides a transcript.

46. The account of the dinner came from one who was present. Private correspondence refers to the proposed organization. Indicative of the strains are two wrathful poems by Hillel Bavli, who taught modern Hebrew literature at the seminary: "Leahim nidahim," 1943, and "Geim vearirim," 1945, in *Aderet hashanim* (The Mantle of Years) (Jerusalem, 1955), pp. 68–69, 72–73.

47. Robert Gordis, *Understanding Conservative Judaism,* ed. Max Gelb (New York, 1978), p. 119; the matter of the separate branch was related by individuals prominent in Hapoel Hamizrahi.

48. Hershman, *Israel's Fate and Faith,* pp. 256–57.

49. Rabbinical Assembly, *Proceedings* (1973): 13.

50. *Emet veemunah: Statement of Principles of Conservative Judaism* (New York, 1988), p. 34.

51. Ibid., p. 37.

52. Ibid., p. 38.

53. Ibid., p. 40.

American Orthodox Organizations in Support of Zionism, 1880–1930

A casual remark by the man considered the first American Zionist, dutifully recorded and amplified upon by both the earliest and more recent historians of Zionism, has been widely accepted as capsulizing the attitude of the most Orthodox of American Jews toward the Jewish national movement. In an 1889 article in the *Shulamit*, the short-lived Yiddish language organ of the early Hovevei Zion (Lovers of Zion) of New York, Isaac Jacob Bluestone wrote of opponents to his cause, "The very religious consider us heretics, who wish to bring redemption before its time."[1]

Bluestone's first biographer, Hyman B. Grinstein, drawing on both the *Shulamit* article and passing remarks in his subject's unpublished memoirs, accepted this complaint at face value:

> The history of *Hibat Zion* [sic] in the next decade [early 1880s–1890s] is vividly described in these memoirs. Difficulties beset the movement from the start. The ultra-Orthodox Jews would have nothing to do with what seemed to them an attempt to negate Messiahism [sic].[2]

Marnin Feinstein reiterated this theme of the ultra-Orthodox versus incipient Zionism in America in his focused study of early Zionism in America. He attributed the "slow progress" of the movement to, among other factors, the "opposition of Reform and Orthodox leaders" and wrote matter-of-factly of "the ultra-Orthodox Jewish elements bitter [opposition] to the resettlement of Zion."[3] Similar are the sentiments of Melvin Urofsky, author of a general history of Zionism in America. According to him, in 1897 "opposition of both Orthodox and Reform" stifled growth of Zionist clubs in Chicago and Philadelphia. He offered evidence of staunch Orthodox antipathy to Zionism when he noted that in 1904, while world Jewry mourned Theodor Herzl's death, "at a meeting of rabbis in a small East Side synagogue, Rabbi Samuel Jaffe, leader of an ultra-Orthodox group prayed, 'Blessed is the Lord who struck him down.'"[4]

To be sure, these scholars have been quick to note that not all Orthodox Jews shared this uncompromising view. Urofsky, for one, in discussing the founding of the Federation of American Zionists in 1898, has pointed out that while "the alleged secularism of the Federation also upset many Orthodox Jews who held themselves aloof from the movement on the traditional religious grounds that restoration could not be man's work but God's alone," there were "many Orthodox Jews [who] did not object to man's efforts to save himself." The latters' problems were with the "secular emphasis of Herzlian Zionism." Urofsky locates these more modern Orthodox Jews within the nascent Orthodox Union, formed just a year before the federation, and chronicles their shift from cooperation with the federation toward an independent Mizrahi movement (a process completed finally in 1914) while deftly suggesting important differences on this issue between them and the ultra-Orthodox. In short, extant scholarship has two basic themes: the existence of profound ultra-Orthodox opposition to Zionism, and significant differences of opinion between the ultras and moderns on this highly charged issue.[5]

A closer look at the pronouncements and activities of Orthodox Jewish leaders during the first fifty years of Zionism's slow emergence in America (1889–1930) suggests very different stances and relationships. Both the Eastern European rabbinate, first as individuals (until 1902) and then as an organized group through the Agudat Harabbanim (Union of Orthodox Rabbis of the United States and Canada), as well as the Union of Orthodox Jewish Congregations, the organization of the Americanized Orthodox rabbinate and their lay supporters, largely supported Zionism. Moreover, support for Zionism—always in its religious incarnation and sometimes also in its secular form—was the one area in which there was consistent intra-Orthodox unity of opinion. Among the ultras, resistance to American ways and rejection of accommodationist means did not usually carry over to vocal opposition to the modern Jewish national movement. Divergence from this unified view and profound differences of opinion would come after 1930.

The Agudat Harabbanim was the seat of Eastern European–born opposition to American modernity. The ultras organized this bastion in 1902 to resist the impact of secularism and Americanism on traditional observance. These transplanted Old World rabbis had learned from the sad experience of earlier critics of America—individuals like their revered Rabbi Jacob Joseph, late chief rabbi of New York City—that acculturation was too great a force for any one rabbi to battle. Still, they believed that together they could do much to re-create in America the religious world they remembered from Russia.[6]

Were the ultra-Orthodox fully resolute in their world view and campaign? Certainly their inaugural charter (of 1902) implicitly identified, for example, the undermining influence of free public education on the next generation's allegiance to Judaism. For them the ideal solution was the building of Eastern European *yeshivot* in America, where boys instructed in Yiddish and Hebrew would be taught the lessons of the past and surely socialized into a reconstructed world fundamentally different from the rest of American society. At the same time they were very realistic about what could be accomplished within a society already so secularized that Jews had to be called back to traditional behavior. Thus, in their charter they said that "the *yeshivah* committee should also supervise the secular subjects [albeit only "necessary subjects"] taught in the *yeshivot*." In their recent Eastern European experience, the questions of if, when, and how vernaculars or secular subjects would be taught in a *yeshivah* were hotly debated.[7]

Such pragmatism about what could be achieved here and how it could be done appears again when the Agudat Harabbanim conceded that although "teachers are to translate [Hebrew texts] into Yiddish . . . when necessary the teachers may also utilize English." And, "in areas where only English is spoken, it may be the basic tongue." While it felt that a strong *yeshivah* education was necessary for all boys, it realized that most "youth work or attend secular schools by day." Accordingly, the Agudat Harabbanim called for the building of evening schools with an admittedly watered down curriculum of "Torah, ethical instruction, and the basic history of the Jewish people."[8]

Notwithstanding the Agudat Harabbanim's less than full rejection of modern American ways (the resistance to change of ultras in the United States certainly pales in comparison to that of their European counterparts, and after all they had already broken with their past by immigrating to America), its continual active support of Zionism is still remarkable. Advocacy of the Jewish national cause, particularly, as it moved from its earliest Hibbat Zion phase in the 1880s to a full-blown political and cultural movement in the 1890s, was modernism incarnate, a fundamental break with the view held by the clear majority of Eastern European religious authorities.[9]

For evidence of the proximity of the Agudat Harabbanim to Zionism in America, one has only to look at the time and place of the meeting that called the rabbis' organization into being. According to the Agudat Harabbanim's chroniclers, the meeting of the nine rabbis who determined that the time had come "to raise the standard of Judaism in general and of Torah specifically . . . through the organizing of Orthodox Jewry," took place in May 1902 in the home of Rabbi Moses Sebulun Margolies (Ramaz) in Boston during the Federation of American Zionists Conference (FAZ). Five of these Eastern European–trained rabbis—including their host—were either delegates to the conference or, even more impressively, members of the FAZ Executive Committee. Five other charter members or early affiliates of the Agudat Harabbanim were also delegates or early leaders of the FAZ. In Boston and in other American cities, they deliberated with such seemingly unlikely colleagues as the Reform rabbis Richard Gottheil, Stephen S. Wise, and Abraham Radin and other non-Orthodox Jews as Rabbi Marcus Jastrow and Henrietta Szold, as well as secular Zionists.

Quite early in its history the Agudat Harabbanim indicated its thinking was in line with that of other American Zionists. At its second annual conference, 1903, "Zionism was unanimously accepted as part of the conference program, albeit with the unexplained proviso that the Zionist society in America hold its meetings as literary and religious bodies and not as social clubs." The Agudat Harabbanim also publicly mourned Herzl's death. Notwithstanding the joy expressed by Rabbi Samuel Jaffe and his rabbis "in an East Side synagogue," the organization of Eastern European rabbis in America, upon "receipt of the news of Herzl's death," adopted a "resolution of respect," properly eulogized the fallen leader, and on the last evening of their meeting conducted "memorial services under the auspices of the Mizrahi wing of the Zionist organization."[10]

Remarkably, in each of these early expressions and activities—and particularly in its association with others of very different religious views—the Agudat Harabbanim deviated significantly from its own expressed policies of not recognizing liberal rabbis and not cooperating with their American Orthodox colleagues. To the Agudat Harabbanim, rabbis of the Central Conference of American Rabbis, who embraced Americanization, and rabbis of the Union of Orthodox Jewish Congregation, who made their own social accommodations with this new land, were to different degrees misleading the people. Their stances had to be opposed, and they should not be associated with. But their allegiance to Zionism, born, as we will presently see, primarily out of their continued allegiance to a particular brand of Eastern European religious Zionist thought, was so strong that they were willing to work with others.[11]

Whatever their motivation, the immigrant rabbis' supportive position was, understandably, applauded by American Zionists. As Richard Gottheil proudly said in 1901, the "mere fact that we have among the Zionists Orthodox, good men [and] leading reformers . . . would be a sufficient refutation of all charges against Zionism." But the Agudat Harabbanim's cooperation was probably most appreciated by the rabbis and lay leaders of the Union of Orthodox Jewish Congregations of America (OU). During the years that its President (and FAZ honorary vice-president) Rabbi Henry P. Mendes, outspoken lay leaders like Lewis Dembitz, E. W. Lewin-Epstein (FAZ Executive Committee members) and Harry Friedenwald (future FAZ president and long-time OU vice-president) witnessed the Agudat Harabbanim openly question their authority to represent Orthodoxy in America, it was undoubtedly warming to them to be recognized as equals and worthy co-workers by the Eastern European sages.[12]

If Rabbi Mendes and the others were surprised by this comradeship, they could have been reminded that such understandings were not unprecedented within the Eastern European rabbinic world Agudat Harabbanim members had left behind. Such contemporaneous Torah scholars like Rabbis Isaac Elchanan Spektor, Naphtali Zevi Judah Berlin, and Samuel Mohilever were all publicly identified with the incipient Hibbat Zion movement in Russia. All argued the appropriateness of all Jews laboring together in the national rebirth, and they acted on their beliefs by attending important

Hibbat Zion conferences, such as those at Katowice in 1884 and Druzgenike in 1887. At Katowice they met with and gained the respect of Leon Pinsker, a man far removed from tradition but who appreciated the support emanating from those Orthodox authorities.[13]

The Agudat Harabbanim members who staunchly advocated Zionism in America were keenly aware of the teachings of Spektor, Berlin, and Mohilever, since many were literally their students. The younger America-based Eastern European rabbis, the Agudat Harabbanim members, were the generation that studied with the immediate spiritual predecessors of the Mizrahi, the religious Zionist movement.

The views of Spektor, Berlin, and particularly Mohilever, though the minority opinion among the rabbis of Eastern Europe, became the unquestioned majority view among the most Orthodox Jews in America, as it was the students of the early Hibbat Zion sympathizers Spektor and Berlin and the religious Zionist Mohilever's students who first made the trip to America and then, within the generation of their teachers' deaths, formed the Agudat Harabbanim. At least seven of the founders or early members of the Agudat Harabbanim who were also either honorary vice-presidents, members of the Executive Committee, or delegates to meetings of the FAZ between 1900 and 1906 were students of, or ordained by, Spektor, Berlin or Mohilever. Two America-based students of that illustrious triumvirate, who were also important leaders in the FAZ, did not join the Agudat Harabbanim. Understandably, Rabbis Shepsel Schaeffer and Zvi Hirsch Masliansky, the famous Eastern European rabbi-as-Americanizer, both of whose general orientation beyond Zionism itself was more modern than the Agudat Harabbanim, had even less difficulty cooperating with FAZ members. Rabbi Abraham Ashinsky of Pittsburgh shared their views and their affinity for the FAZ. A disciple of Rabbi Eliezer Rabinowich and Hayyim Rottenberg, who were trained in Kovno, Ashinsky was both a member of the Agudat Harabbanim and an early supporter of the Orthodox Union, putting him also squarely in the promodernity and Americanization camp.[14]

For itself, in cooperating with the FAZ, the Agudat Harabbanim could also draw upon the precedent set locally just a few years earlier by Rabbi Jacob Joseph. Although the chief rabbi had his difficulties with the non-Orthodox character of early constituent organizations of the FAZ, in 1897 he was willing to help organize a pro-Zionist rabbinical conference in New York attended by score of colleagues. That same year witnessed the founding of the Knesset Zion Hamezuyenet by local Orthodox rabbis "to strengthen the position of the Zionist movement among Orthodox Jews."[15] Thus in the decade before there was a Mizrahi, a cadre of rabbis sympathetic to the ideals the Mizrahi would soon stand for settled in the United States, and, while most Eastern Europeans resisted Americanization, these rabbis set a modernist tone within their community on the question of the Jewish national revival.[16]

As a Mizrahi party formed in Russia in the first decade of the twentieth century, Agudat Harabbanim rabbis followed the lead of that minority Eastern European religious authority and founded the American Mizrahi movement as an independent vehicle for expressing their nationalist sentiments. But they trailed their parent organization in their evolution by about a decade.

Initially, the American Mizrahi was, in fact, a creation of the FAZ and was publicly described in 1904 as "the conservative wing of the Zionist organization (FAZ)."[17] It was first set up, primarily through the efforts of Jacob De Haas, to undermine an incipient, competitive group, the United Zionists. This predominantly Orthodox and Eastern European faction was headed by Rabbi Philip Hillel Klein. But interestingly enough, despite Klein, an early important leader of the Agudat Harabbanim, the rabbinic organization did not rally to the United Zionist's banner. And when that ephemeral organization waned in 1905, Rabbi Klein was playing an essential role within the FAZ's Mizrahi. He became president of the early Mizrahi, and five of the seven directors were Agudat Harabbanim members. Moreover, the true split with the FAZ, at the beginning of the 1910s, was neither sudden nor dramatic. Significantly, Klein and member Rabbi Ashinsky served together on the FAZ Executive Committee along with Rabbi Bernard Levinthal, another leading Agudat Harabbanim spokesman throughout that decade. Indeed, until the formal founding of the independent American Mizrahi in 1912, there was a Mizrahi-wing and/or Agudat Harabbanim member in a leadership position in an organization that was, and would always remain, predominantly nonreligious, non-Orthodox, and certainly non–Eastern European Orthodox. For himself, Zvi Hirsch Masliansky, that Eastern European–born rabbinic gadfly, also a frequent member of the FAZ Executive Committee, remained with that organization through its transformation into the Zionist Organization of America in 1917.[18] And the Orthodox Union through Friedenwald, Lewin-Epstein, Harry Fischel, and, later on, Rabbi David De Sola Pool—maintained a tradition of American Orthodox participation within the general Zionist movement that would continue for another generation.[19]

During the succeeding decade and a half, Agudat Harabbanim support and affinity for the Mizrahi were strong and resolute. On an organizational level their missions were intertwined in 1921 under Rabbi Meyer Berlin when the Agudat Harabbanim's favored institution, New York's Rabbi Isaac Elchanan Theological Seminary, incorporated the Mizrahi's fledgling Teachers Institute. In a move somewhat parallel but unequalled in Eastern Europe (significantly in Isaac Jacob Reines's own Lida *yeshivah*), a traditional transplanted *yeshivah* on American soil supported—albeit with some carping by *roshei yeshivot* (teachers of Talmud)—a teacher-training program with a diverse Torah and *Jüdische Wissenschaft* curriculum and a strong Zionist orientation.[20]

The Agudat Harabbanim's consistent cooperation with the world Zionist movement underscored how aligned it was with the Mizrahi world view. Its rabbis bristled at charges that they were not outspoken enough in support of the larger movement. The Presidium member Rabbi Israel Halevi Rosenberg of Paterson, New Jersey, wrote for his group in 1914: "It is self-evident that support for the return to the land of Israel is one of the pillars upon which Orthodox Judaism rests. Asking the Agudat Harabbanim to vote in favor of the return is like asking them to vote for such basics as the Sabbath and other *mitzvot*." For him, human efforts to actualize the Jews' traditional yearning for the ingathering of the exiles was a fundamental article of faith. And he perceived and demanded an essential role for his rabbinical colleagues in advancing the modern national movement. [If only] "the influence of the Agudat Harabbanim would increase," he declared, "they would be more influential in moving forward the work of Zionism, since most of the rabbis are its supporters."[21]

Thus it was totally in character for the Agudat Harabbanim to receive news of the Balfour Declaration "with great joy and enthusiasm" and to react to the San Remo Mandate Conference of 1920 by sponsoring a parade in New York that attracted ten thousand marchers. "How beautiful a sight," one observer remarked, "rabbis, the shepherds of Israel leading a parade with [Zionist] flags at their heads."[22]

When the Agudat Harabbanim supported the return to Zion, it did not mean only the religious institutions of the Old Yishuv. Its organizational historians claimed:

If indeed the Agudat Harabbanim expended most of its energies on behalf of the Old Yishuv, the truth is that we were among the first supporters of the national movement. The rabbis were among the first workers for the Keren Hayesod and other institutions whose goal is the upbuilding of the land.

To take but one example, in 1925 every member rabbi was requested to devote at least one public appeal a year on behalf of the Jewish National Fund. In so doing, the Agudat Harabbanim was reportedly willing to put aside its "unhappiness with the behavior of the Histadrut both here and in Palestine . . . [and to work] with individuals who on other issues were far removed from its position."[23]

If anything, the Agudat Harabbanim's major complaint against rank-and-file Zionist and Palestine relief groups was that the secular Zionists did not do their fair share for religious institutions. Such was their complaint during World War I when the Temporary Organization for Support of the Yishuv designed to support, among other Zionist needs, the educational institutions in Palestine, ignored requests from the Old Yishuv. Apparently, the Joint Distribution Committee (JDC) did the same, causing the Agudat Harabbanim to turn to the Central Relief Committee (the American Orthodox and predominantly OU component in the JDC) with the demand that it work more strongly from within that umbrella organization for the survival of *yeshivot* and synagogues in Palestine.[24]

The Agudat Harabbanim probably demonstrated its staunchest support for Mizrahi by its lack of enthusiasm for the ideology and political agenda of Agudat Israel. America's Eastern European rabbis were not unmindful of the alliance back home of Lithuanian *roshei yeshivot*, hasidic *rebbes*, and German Neo-Orthodox followers of Samson Raphael Hirsch in protesting the Zionist movement and showing profound disdain for Mizrahi policies of cooperation. Indeed, in 1913, a year after the Agudat Israel's formal founding in Katowice, America's Agudat Harabbanim, at its own eleventh annual meeting, voted "to establish branches of Agudat Israel in the United States wherever possible" and to "request that members travel to nearby cities to promote Agudat Israel." But the Agudat Israel that the American-based rabbis were advocating resembled the European parent organization in only one aspect: promoting the growth and fate of holy institutions within Palestine. Their toned-down articulation of the Agudat Israel mission may have had much to do with the American-based rabbis' long-standing desire to maintain the approbation and support of the Eastern European Orthodox rabbinate. The dilemma was how to do so without abandoning their own legitimate principles. To address that question, the Agudat Harabbanim, accordingly, not only projected the Agudat Israel as an organization that shared Mizrahi goals and objectives but also tried to convince European leadership of the value of worldwide unity of purpose.[25]

Let us examine, for example, the resolution adopted by the Agudat Harabbanim on Zionism at its annual meeting of May 1923. The positions reported by Rabbi Joseph Konvitz, chair of the Eretz Israel Committee, extended a "blessing upon God-fearing individuals who work together for the sake of heaven, particularly the organizations of Mizrahi and Agudat Israel, whose common goal is the building up of the land with the spirit of Torah and *mitzvot*" and opposed those who in building up Zion were acting contrary to the Torah. Specifically, the committee set as a goal pressuring the World Zionist Organization to increase support to Mizrahi institutions to improve the level of Sabbath observance. And they called upon both Mizrahi and Agudat Israel "to find means—to the extent that it is possible—to unify themselves and put their strength together to build up the land." To press their point, the Agudat Harabbanim delegated three of its members to attend both the 1923 Zionist Congress and the First World Congress of the Agudat Israel. At the former, secular gathering they were to urge officials to adopt legislation to curb the public desecration of the Sabbath in Tel-Aviv. At the religious gathering they were to appeal for unity between Agudists and Mizrahiites, in essence for the curtailing of attacks against the religious Zionists. The Agudat Israel would not hear of this call for moderation.[26]

Summing up its achievements in the area of Zionism and the Yishuv, the Agudat Harabbanim would boast in 1926 that if the Old Yishuv has survived until now, credit must go to [our] rabbis. . . . We have also done much for the rise of the New Yishuv. When the announcement came from San Remo, we joined the entire people in its joy, tears welled up in our eyes. In our midst may be found both Mizrahi and Agudat Israel supporters, but the Agudat Harabbanim does not interfere in political matters. For us, it is clear: If we are to have a Land of Israel, we must have the Torah of Israel, if we have a Jewish people, we must have a God of Israel.[27]

With all that has been said here of American Orthodox affinity for much of the Zionist cause through the 1920s, can we not find anywhere a dissenting anti-Zionist opinion? In fact, there were individual Orthodox rabbis throughout this period who articulated strong theological reservations. Gershon Greenberg has identified men like the Lithuanian-born Rabbi Shalom Isaacson and the Hungarian immigrant Rabbi Baruch Meir Levin who questioned the theological right of Jews to return to Zion in a nonmessianic context and the fate of Torah within the Zionist movement. Baruch Klein, probably the most outspoken of these rabbis, saved his harshest words for the Mizrahi, who "are used as pious fronts by the secularists." But his strident words, as we have seen, had little effect on the policies of the Agudat Harabbanim, of which he was a longtime, minority opinion member.[28]

Klein's views might have received a somewhat better hearing, beginning in 1920, within the Knesset Harabbonim Haortodoksim beAmerica, a rival in many areas and causes to the Agudat Harabbanim. This other organization of Eastern European–trained rabbis was founded as an extension of the views and work of Rabbi Gavriel Zev Margolis (Reb Velvele).

Reb Velvele was born in 1847 and educated in *yeshivot* in Vilna and Volozhin, receiving ordination from Rabbi Yaacov Beirat of Vilna. He arrived in the United States in 1907 after a distinguished twenty-seven years as a rabbi in Grodno. He became chief rabbi of Boston, a position just vacated by Ramaz, who had moved to New York. Four years later, Reb Velvele would become rabbi of the Adath Israel Society (United Hebrew Community of New York), an organization that had begun, just a few years earlier, as a burial society and was then expanding into the areas of free loans, sick benefits, and, most important for the subject of this paper, *shehitah* and *kashrut* supervision. Almost immediately, Reb Velvele clashed with Ramaz, Klein, and the other Agudat Harabbanim figures over their organization's manifest monopolies and alleged malfeasances in the area of *kashrut*. Often asserting his greater knowledge in Torah and Halakhah, he spent the next decade or more battling the Eastern European rabbinic establishment for control of that lucrative industry.[29]

Reb Velvele's extensive difficulties with the Agudat Harabbanim went deeper, however, than religious and monetary competition over *kashrut*. In the early 1920s he strongly questioned the Agudat Harabbanim's continued support for its favorite institution, the Rabbi Isaac Elchanan Theological Seminary. Representing himself as a true opponent of secularism and modernization, he was appalled to hear that under its president, Dr. Bernard Revel, plans were being made to attach a college to the traditional *yeshivah*. How could Ramaz, Klein, Levinthal, and others, he asked, support a school where philosophy and biblical criticism would be taught? At best, these studies would take young men away from the sacred books and produce religiously ignorant rabbis unable to aid the religiously barren American Jewish community. Even worse was the possibility that these studies would destroy traditional faith at the *yeshivah*, making it but another version of the hated Jewish Theological Seminary of America. Didn't his colleagues understand, Reb Velvele cried, that the *yeshivah*'s proposed move out of the Lower East Side was but an attempt to hide its activities from the traditional immigrant community?[30]

Finally, as the self-claimed upholder of tradition—the quintessential ultra-Orthodox Jew of the 1920s, Reb Velvele had much to say about Zionism and American Orthodox support for the movement.[31]

Actually, as Joshua Hoffman's comprehensive study of Margolis has pointed out, Reb Velvele, a product of the Volozhin *yeshivah*, was a supporter of early Hibbat Zion. Margolis would later write that at the time he had thought that the influence of rabbis like himself would be beneficial to the movement, undermining the power of the antireligious, and he had faith that Zionism would aid the persecuted Jews of Eastern Europe. Consequently, this self-described friend of Rabbi Samuel Mohilever attended the Second Zionist Congress in Basle in 1898. As an incipient Mizrahiite, he believed that while Zionism was not the true redemption, its potential power to help unify the Jewish people could bring a positive response from God. He would also argue the permissibility of cooperating with the nonreligious in the building of the land. However, as the nonreligious viewpoint continued to dominate the Zionist cultural revolution in the early years of this century, Reb Velvele became increasingly disenchanted with the movement.[32]

To be sure, Reb Velvele continued to allow that there were religious Jews who sincerely, if erroneously, supported the movement, hoping their work would aid the condition of their fellow Jews. He could respect their motives. He came, however, to have nothing but contempt for those seemingly religious ones (Mizrahiites?) who backed this irreligious and destructive movement for personal gain. Given the references to self-gain and the rhetoric during his later battles in New York with the *kashrut* establishment, it is not surprising that his differences with religious Zionists became another front in his ongoing war with the Agudat Harabbanim.[33]

It is not known exactly when Reb Velvele accepted the Agudat Israel position. Indeed, Hoffman has shown that as late as 1913 he was still able to say, as the Mizrahi might have, that cooperation with the nonreligious on issues like antisemitism was possible and praiseworthy. It is clear, however, that by the early 1920s, Reb Velvele was theologically opposed to the Zionist cause. Zionists, he argued, should be seen as false messiahs. They were violating talmudic dicta of not rising up against the nations of the world, and they had increased antisemitism, threatening Jewish survival. By then he was firmly proclaiming that "God will send at the end of days his redeemer to those who wait for him. For him and for no one else. And as he took us out of Egypt, so he will show us miracles soon and in our day."[34]

Predictably, Reb Velvele attempted to direct American Orthodox funds and support solely to the religious institutions of the Old Yishuv and not to the Zionist settlement in Palestine. The Agudat Harabbanim had itself frequently pointed out that often the most religious did not receive Zionist funds. Such was the stance on Palestinian activities that Reb Velvele proposed for his Knesset Harabbonim in 1921 at its first convention.

Reb Velvele wanted the Knesset Harabbonim to stand for the many causes he held dear. It was also to express his dismay over the low-caliber and corrupt rabbis who dominated the Agudat Harabbanim, offering an alternative to the truly religious Jew. Among other things, it was

to avoid all forms of unpleasant publicity in sanctioning the marketing of kosher products and to prevent the dealers in such products from encouraging the services of rabbis to advertise their products, and to that end every community is appealed to and urged to support the Orthodox rabbis and to pay them living salaries so that they will not find it necessary to receive remuneration for sanctioning articles as kosher and be obliged to accept perquisites of a questionable source.

It would also "strengthen Jewish education in every city throughout the United States and Canada and extend every effort to have public funds collected for the cause of Jewish education expended on Talmud Torahs and *yeshivot*." On the foreign scene, of greatest interest here, the Knesset was

to help the government in Palestine which is working to establish a new community, but at the same time to leave rabbis of Palestine the work of establishing Judaism and culture . . . to support the old institutions . . . and to bring order out of the chaotic disorder among the various representatives who come to America to solicit funds for the old institutions in Palestine.

And through all its work the Knesset was "to bring about harmony and unity among the different elements which are working for Orthodox Judaism." Such at least were Reb Velvele's draft resolutions for the 1921 convention.[35]

The convention delegates were evidently not as compliant as Reb Velvele might have anticipated. As Hoffman has shown, on the issue of Palestine, they changed the wording in the resolution from "to help the government in Palestine which is working to establish a new community" to read "to assist the British High Commissioner and [unnamed] Zionist authorities in Palestine." Unlike their leader Reb Velvele, who was, predictably, concerned most with the old religious community, the majority of delegates, at this juncture, were equally concerned with the development of the New Yishuv. Interestingly enough, Hoffman has further discovered that two years later the Knesset seemingly had a change of heart when it expressed support for the Agudat Israel positions. Apparently, they reiterated that stance again in 1925. But then, in 1925, the Knesset, possibly for reasons not related to Zionism, sounded again very much like their Agudat Harabbanim counterparts when, at their convention in Lackawaxen, Pennsylvania, they sent greetings to the Zionist Congress in Vienna. Such, then, was the position of a non-Mizrahi American Orthodox group in the mid-1920s.[36]

The true beginning of strong, organized Orthodox opposition to Zionism in America is beyond the scope of this study. Well into the 1930s, and despite the fact that the leader of the Agudat Harabbanim, Rabbi Eliezer Silver of Cincinnati, was himself personally an Agudist, the organized Eastern European rabbinate in the United States still advocated cooperation and unity among Mizrahi and Agudat Israel forces worldwide. In 1933, for example, Silver called for a "meeting in Eretz Israel of all heads of world orthodoxy [to] unify the Mizrahi and Agudat Israel. We must no longer, suffer from disunity."[37]

Silver's efforts went unrewarded. From Europe he heard Agudat Israel leaders insist that "the Mizrahi leave the World Zionist Organization." In America he listened to the fears of Agudat Harabbanim colleagues that their organization's pro-Mizrahi position was being undone.[38]

In 1939, the first permanent American branch of Agudat Israel was organized. Under Silver's presidency the new group closely aligned with its world movement. Efforts were made to move the indigenous Eastern European Orthodox rabbinate into its ranks, and many did become Agudists in the 1940s. Most important, Agudat Israel's ranks were swelled by the arrival in the United States of refugee rabbis and lay Orthodox Jews fleeing Adolf Hitler and World War II. They would bring their own perspectives on modernity, secularism, and Zionism and open a new chapter in the history of Orthodoxy in the United States.[39]

Notes

1. Shlomo Noble,"Pre-Herzlian Zionism in America as Reflected in the Yiddish Press," in *Early Zionism in America*, ed. Isidor S. Meyer (New York, 1958), p. 39.

2. Hyman B. Grinstein, "The Memoirs and Scrapbooks of the Late Dr. Joseph Isaac Bluestone of New York City," *Publications of the American Jewish Historical Society* (hereafter *PAJHS*) 35 (1939), p. 55.

3. Marnin Feinstein, *American Zionism, 1884–1904* (New York, 1965), pp. 19, 42–43.

4. Melvin I. Urofsky, *American Zionism from Herzl to the Holocaust* (Garden City, N.Y., 1976), pp. 76–79, 84.

5. Urofsky, *American Zionism*, pp. 93–94. Grinstein and Feinstein record the diversity of Orthodox approaches to Zionism but do not make clear the difference between the groups. See Feinstein, *American Zionism*, pp. 31, 43, 54–55, 97, 127, 245–48, 268–69; Grinstein, "Memoirs and Scrapbooks of Bluestone," pp. 57–62. See also Hyman B. Grinstein, "Orthodox Judaism and Early Zionism in America" in *Early Zionism in America*, ed. Meyer, pp. 219–24. Unique among the general histories of Zionism in America, Evyatar Friesel, *Hatenuah hazionit*

beArzot Habrit, 1897–1914 (Tel-Aviv, 1970), p. 90, does not make a strong statement about Orthodox opposition to Zionism in America. He does, however, allow that "in the Jewish street during this time period [circa 1897] there were extremist Orthodox organizations that opposed Zionism no less and possibly more than the Reform."

6. On the founding of the Agudat Harabbanim see, Jeffrey S. Gurock, "Resisters and Accommodators: Varieties of Orthodox Rabbis in America, 1886–1983," in *The American Rabbinate: A Century of Continuity and Change,* ed. Jacob Rader Marcus and Abraham J. Peck (Hoboken, N.J., 1985), pp. 19–21.

7. For the text of the Agudat Harabbanim's inaugural charter, see *Sefer hayovel shel Agudat Harabbanim Haortodoksim deArtzot Habrit veCanada* (New York, 1928), pp. 25–26. For a taste of the controversies that surrounded the question of introducing vernaculars and secular subjects in Eastern European *yeshivot,* with a particular focus on the Volozhin *yeshivah,* see Meier Berlin, *MiVolozhin ad Yerushalayim* (Tel-Aviv, 1939), pp. 88–101; Moshe Tzenovitz, *Ez hayim: Toldot yeshivat Volozhin* (Tel-Aviv, 1972), pp. 317–44, Shaul Stampfer, "Three Lithuanian Yeshivas in the Nineteenth Century" (PhD. diss., Hebrew University, Jerusalem, 1981), pp. 79–80, 120–21.

8. *Sefer hayovel,* pp. 25–26.

9. Although, as Ehud Luz points out, "few Mitnaggedic rabbis in Lithuania . . . were attracted to Hibbat Zion" and "the movement faced wall-to-wall opposition from Hasidic *rebbes,*" the intensity of opposition to the nationalist movement clearly increased over time. In the early 1880s, some Lithuanian rabbis were not put off by Zionism's attempt to move the Jewish people away from the tradition of national passivity and thus supported the Hibbat Zion as they had supported the Old Yishuv. By the 1890s, however, as the movement grew and Orthodoxy did not predominate, issues surrounding the background, life-styles, and orientations of leadership put off additional Orthodox rabbis. By the turn of the century, full-scale opposition was articulated as the concerns transcended issues of life-style and the Orthodox felt that Zionism intended to replace traditional Judaism with secular nationalism as the ideology to be followed by the masses of Jews. This opposition led to the founding of the Agudat Israel, and by the 1910s there were two Orthodox camps—the Mizrahi and the Agudat Israel. See Ehud Luz, *Parallels Meet: Religion and Nationalism in the Early Zionist Movement (1882–1904)* (Philadelphia, 1988), pp. 30, 45, 48–49, 65–66, 114–15, 211, 225–26, 286. For contemporaneous polemics against Zionism from Orthodox figures, see Avraham Baruch Steinberg, *Sefer daat harabbanim* (Warsaw, 1902); Shlomo Zalman Landa and Yosef Rabinowitz, *Sefer or leyesharim* (Warsaw, 1900).

10. *Sefer hayovel,* pp. 21–22; *American Jewish Year Book* 5663 (1902–03): 102, 5664 (1903–04): 124; 5665 (1904–05): 240, 282, 5666 (1905–06): pp. 133–24, 5670 (1909–10): 150; "Minutes of the Fourth Annual Convention of the Federation of American Zionists," *Maccabaean* 1, no. 1 (June 1901): ix, xxx; "List of Delegates," *Maccabaean* 2, no. 1 (June 1902): 337–38.

11. For a discussion of the Agudat Harabbanim's negative views of Reform rabbis and its policy of noncooperation with American Orthodox colleagues, see Gurock, "Resisters and Accommodators," pp. 21–29 and passim.

12. *American Hebrew,* July 8, 1904, p. 204; July 30, 1904, p. 282; *Maccabaean* 1, no. 31 (June 1901): xxii–xxiii; *American Jewish Year Book* 5663 (1902–03): 102, 5664 (1903–04): 124, 159, 161, 5665 (1904–05): 240, 5666 (1905–06): 133–34, 5667 (1906–07): 109, 5670 (1909–10): 150. To be sure, the influence of Rabbis Philip Hillel Klein, Shepsel Schaeffer, and Abraham Ashinsky cannot be minimized in understanding the partial rapprochement. They were the three Agudat Harabbanim leaders and members who also held memberships in the Americanized Union of Orthodox Jewish Congregations of America.

13. Ephraim Shimoff, *Rabbi Isaac Elchanan Spektor: Life and Letters* (Jerusalem, 1961), pp. 122, 126–28, 144–45; Judah Appel, *Betokh reshit hatehiya* (Tel-Aviv, 1935); Samuel K. Mirsky, "Isaac Elchanan Spektor," in *Guardians of Our Heritage (1724–1953),* ed. Leo Jung

(New York, 1958), pp. 311–12; Yitzhak Rivkind, *HaNeziv veyihuso leHibbat Zion* (Łódź, 1919), pp. 8–10; Joseph Litvin, "Naphtali Tzevi Berlin (the Neziv)," in *Men of the Spirit,* ed. Leo Jung (New York, 1963), pp. 294–95; Y. Nissenbaum, *Hadat vehatehiyah haleumit* (Warsaw, 1919–20), pp. 92–118; E. M. Genechovsky, "Samuel Mohilever," in *Men of the Spirit,* ed. Jung, pp. 423–32.

14. The other two founders or early members of the Agudat Harabbanim who were also either honorary vice-presidents, members of the Executive Committee, or delegates to the 1900 meetings of the FAZ were Rabbi Moses Sebulun Margolies (Ramaz) and Dr. Philip Hillel Klein. These men were not trained or ordained by the three luminaries. Klein was trained in West Central Europe, and Margolies in Białystok. Their actions and pronouncements reveal them as clearly sympathetic to the world views of Spektor, Berlin, and Mohilever. For more on Klein and Margolies, see Gurock, "Resisters and Accommodators," pp. 30–40. Finally, four other founders and early members of the Agudat Harabbanim were among the founders of Mizrahi in America, a logical step given that at least two of them, I. L. Levin of Detroit and Isaak Ginsburg of Rochester, were disciples of Spektor and Berlin. That these rabbis constituted a next generation of leaders is evidenced from the fact that seventeen of the rabbis about whom we have biographical information (of nineteen) were born within twenty years of one another, and nine of the seventeen attended *yeshivot* in the 1860s. The basic biographical information is from "Minutes of the Fourth Annual Convention of the Federation of American Zionists," pp. ix, xxx; "List of Delegates," pp. 337–38; *Sefer hayovel,* pp. 138, 140–42, 151, 161; *American Jewish Year Book* 5663 (1902–03): 102, 5664 (1903–04): 124, 5665 (1904–05): 240, 282, 5666 (1905–06): 133–34, 149, 5670 (1909–10): 150. For more on Zvi Hirsh Masliansky, see Gurock, "Resisters and Accommodators," pp. 34–35; Moses Rischin, *The Promised City: New York's Jews, 1870–1914* (Cambridge, Mass., 1962), pp. 103, 239–40.

15. *Die Welt,* December 31, 1897, pp. 10–11; Friesel, *Hatenuah hazionit,* p. 30.

16. These rabbis who supported Zionism were trained in Europe and departed for America at a point in the early history of Zionism when levels of opposition to the movement within Orthodoxy were relatively low. See n. 9, above, for the chronology on the evolution of anti-Zionism among Eastern European rabbis. Of course, one must clearly calibrate their degree of Zionism. The message of European religious Zionism heard by these rabbis did not include a commitment to *aliyah.* As noted above, they departed for America and not Palestine in the decade from 1880–1890. Ironically, they were much akin not only to the masses of nonideologically committed immigrant Jews who voted with their feet for America, and not for Zion, but also to their liberal American Jewish religious counterparts and the secular American Zionists who would come to support an American form of Zionism that did not include personal commitment to migration. Few of the Agudat Harabbanim worthies ever left America. Their support was largely in the realm of positive exhortations for the movement, fund raising, and calls for unity among differing Orthodox elements on this crucial question. It may be suggested that here, too, we see a subtle Americanization operating on the most Orthodox of Jews in the United States.

17. *American Jewish Year Book,* 5666 (1905–06): 134.

18. Friesel, *Hatenuah hazionit,* pp. 246–47; Urofsky, *American Zionism,* pp. 92–93; Yonathan Shapiro, *Leadership of American Zionist Organization, 1897–1930* (Urbana, Ill., 1971), pp. 25–28, Grinstein, "Memoirs and Scrapbooks of Bluestone," pp. 58–60. For background information on rabbis and lay people who were leaders of the FAZ, OU, and the Agudat Harabbanim, see *American Jewish Year Book* 5663 (1902–03): 102, 5664 (1903–04): 124, 5665 (1904–05): 240, 282, 5666 (1905–06): 133–34, 149, 5667 (1906–07): 109, 5669 (1908–09): 23, 41, 5670 (1909–1910): 150, 168–69, 5671 (1910–11): 223, 252, 5672 (1911–12): 220, 241, 5673 (1912–13): 222, 245, 5674 (1913–14): 366, 5675 (1914–15): 282, 298, 310, 5676 (1915–16): 293, 310, 5677 (1916–17): pp. 227, 245, 258, 5678 (1917–18): 336, 347, 354, 5679 (1918–19): 316, 324, 5680 (1919–20): 318, 325, 327.

19. Urofsky, *American Zionism,* p. 94, sees the OU as the incipient Orthodox liaison with

the FAZ that went its own way into the Mizrahi. In reality, OU leaders were long-term constituents of the FAZ, while Agudat Harabbanim members moved slowly toward separatist religious Zionism.

20. Whatever problems *roshei yeshivot*—many of whom were good Agudat Harabbanim members—had with the Teachers Institute, they were not caused by the Zionist orientation of the school but the *Wissenschaft* aspects and the religious reliability of some of the teachers. See Jeffrey Gurock, *The Men and Women of Yeshiva: Higher Education, Orthodoxy and American Judaism* (New York, 1988), pp. 78–81. On Reines' Lida *yeshivah*, see Geulah Bat-Yehuda, *Ish hameorot: Rabbi Yitzhak Yaacov Reines* (Jerusalem, 1988), chap. 43.

21. Israel Halevi Rosenberg, "Gilui Daat," *Morgen Zhurnal,* trans. in *Sefer hayovel,* pp. 57–58.

22. *Sefer hayovel,* pp. 81–82.

23. Ibid., pp. 78–79.

24. Ibid., pp. 71–75.

25. Ibid., pp. 76–77. On the founding and structure of the Agudat Israel, see Gershon Chaim Bacon, "Agudat Israel in Poland, 1916–1939: An Orthodox Jewish Response to the Challenge of Modernity" (Ph.d. diss., Columbia University, 1979), pp. 41–43. See also Isaac Lewin, *Unto the Mountains* (New York, 1975), pp. 71–74.

26. *Sefer hayovel,* pp. 76–77.

27. Ibid., p. 110.

28. Gershon Greenberg, "Separation and Reconciliation: American Orthodoxy and the Concept of Zion," *Proceedings on the Ninth World Congress of Jewish Studies* (Jerusalem, 1986), pp. 127–29.

29. On Gavriel Zev Margolis in Boston and in conflict with rabbis in New York, see Harold Gastwirt, *Fraud, Holiness and Corruption* (Port Washington, N.Y., 1974), pp. 92–93, 119–22, and passim. For a comprehensive examination of many aspects of Margolis's career and ideas, see Joshua Hoffman, "The American Rabbinic Career of Rabbi Gavriel Zev Margolis" (M.A. thesis, Bernard Revel Graduate School, Yeshiva University, 1992).

30. For Margolis's view of Rabbi Isaac Elchanan Theological Seminary, see *Haruzei margoliot,* vol. 2 (New York, 1918), pp. 394, 225–402; *Sefer Knesset Harabbonim,* vol. 2 (New York, 1924), pp. 44–45. For more on Margolis's attitude towards RIETS, see Gurock, "Resisters and Accommodators," p. 58.

31. Once again, the description of Margolis as an ultra is mediated by an understanding of what that term means in the American context. As Hoffman's study indicates, like the Agudat Harabbanim that he opposed, Margolis, for example, did not take a totally unyielding position against secular studies *per se.* He was knowledgeable of military and political history among other non-Jewish disciplines. He apparently agreed that English was appropriate in Talmud Torah schools. He also supported the Rabbi Jacob Joseph School in the early 1910s and was a signatory to a fund-raising letter stating that students from that American *yeshivah* could qualify for college entrance. See Hoffman, "Career of Margolis," pp. 80, 124.

32. *Hapeles* (Berlin, 1903), pp. 330–36, discussed in ibid., pp. 5, 9.

33. On Margolis's tolerant, Mizrahi-like attitude, see *Haruzei margoliot,* 2:363, quoted in an earlier version of Hoffman's work, "Rabbi Gavriel Zev Margolis and the Knesset Harabbonim" (unpublished seminar paper, Bernard Revel Graduate School, Yeshiva University, 1989), p. 41.

34. For Margolis's views on Zionism in 1920s, see *Sefer Knesset Harabbonim,* 2:11–21, 22–23, noted in Hoffman, "Rabbi Gavriel Zev Margolis," p. 37. See also Gurock, "Resisters and Accommodators," p. 58.

35. On Margolis's intentions in founding the Knesset Harabbonim, see *Sefer Knesset Harabbonim Haortodoksim beAmerica,* vol. 1 (New York, 1921), p. 2, see p. 9 for Margolis's draft resolutions. See also Hoffman, "Career of Margolis," pp. 87, 101–5.

36. The convention resolutions that differ from Margolis's drafts were published in the

Kansas City Jewish Chronicle, March 4, 1921, pp. 1, 4. See *Jewish Daily Bulletin,* September 3, 1925, p. 8, for the 1925 convention greeting. On these documents, see Hoffman, "Career of Margolis," pp. 105–8. Hoffman hypothesizes that the 1925 greeting to the Zionist Congress reflected Margolis's group's being in agreement with the secular Zionists in opposing a plan to colonize Jews in the Crimea that had been advocated by the Joint Distribution Committee and the Knesset's greatest rival, the Agudat Harabbanim.

37. For Rabbi Eliezer Silver's remarks, see *Hapardes,* December 1933, quoted in Aaron Rakeffet-Rothkoff, *The Silver Era in American Jewish Orthodoxy* (Jerusalem, 1981), p. 156.

38. Rakeffet-Rothkoff, *Silver Era,* pp. 156–57.

39. Ibid., pp. 161–64.

TRADITION AND ZIONISM IN THE YISHUV

The Role of Religious Values in the Second Aliyah

The Second Aliyah marks the beginning of a new era in the history of Zionism and in the colonization of Palestine. It began during the 1903–05 pogroms in Russia and lasted until the First World War, or rather until a new wave of immigrants arrived after the war. It was a spontaneous phenomenon, unorganized and quite individualistic. Yet this movement laid the foundation for a collective way of life inspired by Zionist and socialist ideas.

The pioneers of the Second Aliyah were a motley assemblage, defying standard definitions. One of their outstanding qualities was creativity, an inclination to reject ready-made systems and try out things for themselves. They were, all the same, an ideological generation that strove to realize certain ideals in the making of a new Jewish society.

These pioneers were imbued with an activism that was the ultimate touchstone of all their values. It implied a certain self-reliance that precluded any obedience to authority, whether temporal or spiritual. Theirs was a defiant spirit that aspired to manifest itself in an *ex nihilo* creation while maintaining a delicate link with an ancient tradition. This apparent contradiction was, however, merely a reenactment of a well-known pattern that had existed in Zionism before.[1]

The pioneers accomplished much, but they were imbued with an acute sense of despair that prevailed throughout their endeavors. They came as young people to the Land of Israel, having lost confidence in the Zionist leadership after the Uganda crisis. They struggled hard to become manual laborers and settle on the land, despite socialist theory and official party lines. They adopted Hebraic culture as a negation of their own past and previous identity. In all, they feared a relapse into what they regarded disparagingly as the "diaspora mentality." The despair they constantly referred to[2] apparently served as an incentive to trying out new forms of social organization. They felt that they had nothing to lose but their ghetto shackles, as it were. On the whole, they struck a happy balance between the liberty to forge their own future and a sense of obligation toward a historic mission.

The mixture of despair and great expectations became the dominant tone of a whole counterculture. Its bare essentials were simple and tangible rules, not unlike Jewish religious precepts, stressing day-to-day behavior: physical labor, agricultural settlement, self-defense, Hebrew culture and language.

Naturally not everybody adhered to these tenets in the strictest manner, but they were generally accepted norms of behavior, meant to be shared by all. The main point remained, above all, solidarity in action.[3] Sharing a real life experience and working together were in themselves redeeming.

Social and Cultural Features

I tried so far to sketch an overall picture as a general framework for the subject at hand. But there is one more facet to be mentioned here, even though only summarily—namely the social and cultural makeup of the Second Aliyah.

Who were the pioneers, where did they come from, what was their station in life?

Most of the pioneers came from Russia but this generalization requires some elaboration. At the height of the Second Aliyah in 1910, there were almost 6 million Jews living in Greater Russia.[4] The Russian empire had then the largest Jewish community in the world, and it was naturally far from being uniform. Although Jews were confined mainly to the Pale of Settlement, local varieties were of great importance. Their differing exposure to modernization resulted in a division of Russian Jews into numerous categories: traditionalists and assimilationists, Yiddish- and Russian-cultured, bourgeois and paupers, revolutionaries, nationalists, and others.

Among the young people arriving in Palestine at the beginning of the twentieth century were determined Zionists and radicals of all sorts, as well as dropouts from rabbinic schools, deserters from the Russian army, young ladies from respectable households, and lost souls of all kinds. These newcomers were often in their late teens or early twenties, mostly unattached, without any trade or means of livelihood. Many came from a traditional background, even from Zionist homes, in the smaller towns. They spoke mostly Yiddish with a sprinkling of Hebrew. Others were well versed in Russian culture with almost no grounding in Jewish matters.[5] Among the large number of nonobservant pioneers, the small number of those who remained faithful to religious observance stood out.

The second largest segment of pioneers came from impoverished Galicia, then relatively peaceful under Austrian rule.[6] In addition, there were also some scattered individuals from other parts of the world. However, the Russian element was predominant throughout the Second Aliyah. Ideas that were, so to speak, in the air in Russia filtered through and contributed to the shaping of the pioneers' outlook.[7] Early twentieth-century Russia had an enormous impact on the Second Aliyah. Suffice it to mention that the newcomers were known to the local population in Palestine as the "Moscovites."

Yet many of these newcomers were far from being Russian. They grew up speaking Yiddish: their non-Jewish neighbors were Poles, Ukrainians, Lithuanians, or White Russians. The Russian language belonged to official-dom, to the larger cities and higher culture. Educated young Jews had to master it, and it often served as the first step to entering European culture. Russian was not their natural tongue but a hard-won acquisition.[8] Thus, despite the enormous energy that the pioneers invested in Hebrew, Russian retained its prestige among them as a vehicle of high-culture.

Moreover, one may well remember that Russian classical literature was not regarded as mere *belles lettres*. The arts fulfilled in autocratic Russia a social and political role far beyond the esthetic realm. Literature tended to carry a message and evoked a strongly felt resonance. The great Russian writers, such as Leo Tolstoy and Fyodor Dostoyevski, exerted an enormous influence as critics and mentors. Although their approach was different from that of the positivist and populist social critics, they may have had similar concerns at heart.[9] Thus, a claim was made that they all had an underlying spirituality in common and that Russian literature drew its in-spiration from religious sources.[10]

Such spiritual undertones were not lost on young Jews who fell under the spell of Russian culture. These included the young Zionists emigrating to Palestine,[11] although they showed a strong anticlerical, agnostic, or athe-istic strain. The antireligious trend may be attributed to numerous sources in various degrees: to the militant tone adopted by the Enlightenment in Eastern Europe, to the anticlerical stance of the Jewish labor movement, or even to the positivist and materialist strands of Russian radicalism.[12] It is evident, however, that the secular impetus was brought in with the new-comers from Europe and did not emanate from their encounter with the new environment.

Furthermore, the atmosphere that reigned among the pioneers could be described as a hotbed of defiance toward all conventions and particularly against established religion. The experience of leaving home and trying to fend for oneself in a strange and exotic land, side by side with other up-rooted young people and in the face of adversity and misunderstanding, heightened their sense of alienation. Their clash with the farmers of the old colonies, who had lost some of their original idealism, often concerned re-ligious issues but focused on behavior rather than faith or religious feeling. Religion was to the pioneers one of numerous outdated conventions that was shed on becoming a pioneer in Palestine.[13]

A New Approach to Christianity

One of the leading lights of the Second Aliyah was the Hebrew modernist Micha Yosef Berdichevsky, whose pungent writings introduced the ideas of Friedrich Nietzsche to the Jewish intelligentsia. Berdichevsky's followers were set on reevaluating all values and remolding their attitude toward Judaism.[14] Although this could hardly be owing directly to Nietzsche's influence, they even dared to break the traditional Jewish bias toward Christianity.

Here was no doubt one of the most sensitive points in the emotional equipment of European Jews. Jews living in Christendom as an alien minority must have always felt the brunt of the controversy between the mother religion and its offspring and contender, Christianity. The Christian teaching of contempt with regard to Jews and Judaism had permeated European civilization to the full.[15] Jews, who for ages were unable to respond in kind, harbored a deep resentment toward the dominant religion. True, Christian attitudes had undergone far-reaching changes in the modern period, yet a certain bitterness and distrust could hardly be eradicated from the minds of many Jews.

Modernity brought with it closer and better relations between Jew and gentile, but both preferred to meet each other on religiously neutral ground. Jews and Christians alike were well aware of their common heritage, overlaid as it was with suspicion and apologetics. The history of the relationship was hardly conducive to a candid exchange of views on religious matters, yet Jewish intellectuals were at the same time engaged in revising their approach to Christianity and to Jesus Christ.[16] Unlike their predecessors of old, they could voice their opinions from a *Jewish* point of view: a more favorable attitude to Christianity no longer entailed, perforce, apostasy or disloyalty toward the Jewish fold.

It is within this context that a famous controversy on Christianity took place in 1910, launched by the Second Aliyah writer Yosef Hayim Brenner. The great iconoclast arrived in Palestine at the beginning of 1909. After a brief and painful attempt at becoming a simple laborer, he resorted to writing, editing, and teaching. In one of his early articles in Palestine, Brenner criticized the new craze that imitated, according to him, the then-fashionable "God seekers" in Russia.[17] This trend was part of a cultural blooming, called the "Russian renaissance," that made an enormous impact.[18] Although tinged with Russian Orthodox coloring, it attracted Jews and, among them, Hebrew literati. Thus, Brenner charged Jewish intellectuals, and most of all the historian and editor Joseph Klausner, with an attempt to follow this superficial and pretentious fashion.[19]

Brenner appreciated the religious feelings of the ignorant Russian masses, but he would not tolerate "God seeking" on the part of the seemingly decadent intellectuals. A few months later he again heaped scorn on some Jewish writers who had advocated a more positive attitude toward religion. To him any dogma—be it Jewish or Christian—smacked of "religious fiction" and should be rejected.[20] His emphasis on plain living, on work and productivity, seemed to exclude anything spiritual. Yet Brenner was not indifferent to religion. On the contrary, he was rather attracted to it in his own way. Nevertheless, he discarded it on the public level as a diversion from the more important tasks in life.

After a short while Brenner once again wrote on religious matters. This time he made light of the overseas Jewish press's concern over the growing number of apostates from Judaism.[21] The article started a stormy public debate, and Brenner was attacked and vilified. His detractors went so far as to accuse him of having been in the pay of a Christian mission in London some years earlier.[22] The Odessa Hovevei Zion withdrew its subsidy from the paper that had published Brenner's article, causing local writers and leading pioneers to protest the act of censorship. They thus gave support to Brenner, although not necessarily sharing his views or their acerbity.

During the debate Brenner said some harsh words that had a lasting effect on public opinion. He maintained, for example, that "free" Jews had no need for Judaism and that Jewish religion had become lifeless. Even when religion was still at its best, it incurred, according to him, an act of self-abasement before "some father in heaven, so that he might grant you a living."[23] The reference to prayer as a means for securing a livelihood alludes to the notion that Jews shun physical labor; thus they beseech God to help them.

The main argument, though, centered upon renegades from Judaism. Brenner did not legitimate apostasy, yet he stated that conversion to Christianity was merely the finishing touch to a long process of assimilation and estrangement from Judaism. This process seemed to him almost inevitable, but he did not discuss it in religious terms. While acknowledging the existence of a spiritual void, Brenner rejected the conventional religious response to it. He made a distinction between various components of religion. In his somewhat elliptic style, Brenner seemed to refer to the sometimes contradictory elements within religion, such as history and dogma, tradition and belief, theology and faith, eventually reaching the slippery ground that lies between Judaism and Christianity.

Brenner abhorred pretentiousness and was suspicious of pomp and ceremony. He hated the pagan ritual of the Russian Orthodox Church and its pontifical discourse, yet he had very warm feelings for Christ and the New Testament.[24] Although Brenner professed to be antireligious, he accepted pristine Christianity as part of his Jewish heritage. There lay the main difficulty: like some other contemporaries, Brenner gave expression to a new approach to Christianity, yet at the same time he remained highly critical of religion as such.

In his extreme sensitivity Brenner detected a false note in the then-fashionable religious revival, be it Russian Orthodox or Jewish. He thus seemed to favor some aspects of Christianity that were taboo in the eyes of many Jews, while rejecting Judaism out of hand, as it were. If one considers the pent up Jewish feelings toward Christianity, it is easy to understand the violent reaction against Brenner. Only his personal integrity stood above suspicion and enabled his well wishers to support him in public.[25]

Existential Judaism

Brenner would sometimes be carried away by his obsessive candor. But for all his individualism and radicalism, he remained in close touch with the pioneers. It was to them that he addressed himself in his articles. He did not live in splendid isolation, and the feelings he expressed were part of an ongoing relationship with the Second Aliyah people. Brenner acted in a sense as spokesman for his generation, while exerting at the same time, without professing to do so, a subtle influence on others. Thus one may look in his writings for a broader climate of opinion.[26]

Beyond Brenner's idiosyncrasy, one could detect in his writings a viewpoint that was shared by many of his contemporaries. Brenner basically held that being Jewish was not a matter of personal choice or of religious beliefs and practices. To him, being Jewish merely meant that one must accept the fact of life and knowingly play a historically determined role. To him Judaism transcended the sphere of the individual and constituted an existential community.[27] Nevertheless, although he allocated a dominant part to history and ethnicity, other facets, such as the spiritual and cultural heritage, were also incorporated in his Jewishness.

As befits an estranged *yeshivah* student, Brenner carried his Jewishness as a heavy yoke that was never to be alleviated. To him the Jews who tried to change their way of life and create a working community in Palestine were never the new and proud breed of people that they appeared to be in the vision of more sanguine Zionists.[28] Note that the tragic sense of life and a sense of imminent failure were hardly ever absent.[29] The fateful link with the Jews of Berdichev or Whitechapel and with a long and painful history were always there, too. Not only could one not escape one's Jewishness; one should not even be tempted to try, for escape was futile. Anything done by Jews, any thought or feeling, would always be Jewish. Thus the new life created by the pioneers was Jewish by definition, beyond good or evil, beyond spirituality or ritual.

This kind of approach to Judaism played a most prominent role in the self-perception of the Second Aliyah. It would be difficult to trace its origins, as it appeared throughout in various manifestations. Brenner himself did not simply repeat an established commonplace, for he deviated from the typical antidiaspora stance of the time. The Second Aliyah pioneers tended on the whole to distinguish between themselves, torchbearers of the new "Hebraic" entity, and the old Judaism. This distinction was made in the boldest fashion by another influential writer, Micha Yosef Berdichevsky, who had referred to the choice as between "the last Jews or the first Hebrews."[30] Unlike Brenner, the innovators rejected the designation "Jew" (which also smacked of the Russian derogatory *Zhid*) and chose the term

"Hebrew" instead. Their self-identity was based on the negation of the diaspora and what it stood for.[31]

The basic common tenet, though, was a *de facto* Judaism that manifested itself in an existential manner. Despite the opprobrium incurred by diaspora Jews, there was no thoroughgoing break with Judaism in its entirety. Surely, there was anger and bitterness and even shame, but all these feelings stemmed from an underlying recognition of a common destiny. The pioneers saw themselves in a sense as better Jews than their diaspora brethren. Whereas many diaspora Jews clung to the external trappings of Judaism while defiling its true essence, the pioneers claimed to lead a pure and productive life that constituted a cleansed Jewishness.

This postulate led in different directions and eventually formed a cluster of ideas. Some strands were congruent with each other, some were mere variations of the same theme, while others were diametrically opposed to each other. Thus four different approaches can be distinguished: (1) an empirical stance maintaining Judaism or Jewishness to be basically a reflection of what the Jews do and implying that whether or not Judaism bears any intrinsic values, such values are irrelevant to the issues at hand; (2) a humanistic view that wishes to discard the metaphysical dimension of Judaism and replace it by "here and now" Jewish values; (3) a dialectic approach that sees some "cunning of reason"[32] at work, which in turn attaches spiritual significance to even the pioneers' menial tasks; (4) a mystic trait that enhances the significance of the above dialectic approach by bestowing on it a religious sense.[33]

I must reiterate that this rather formal division of opinion is retrospective; it was not a conscious and clear-cut pattern existent at the time. There were no schools of thought that embraced any systematic philosophies, nor were there ideological camps that arranged themselves according to such criteria. People may have given expression to different shades of opinion under certain circumstances, in reaction to a particular situation or following their varying moods. The distrust toward formal organization left such ideas to the individual; nor did the pioneers flock round religious issues in the first place. The distinctions made here among various attitudes toward Judaism are, to my mind, a mental substratum that gives meaning to the more explicit responses to current issues in the public realm.[34]

The primary attitudes taken by the Second Aliyah as regards religion could be exemplified by the discourse of some leading personalities. These were obviously no philosophers or theologians, nor were they professional writers or scholars. The greatest influence belonged to political and ideological leaders. Here a word of explanation on leadership is appropriate.

These leaders had still very little political power to wield, and their primary task was to lay the foundations for society and establish a new hierarchy of values. These tasks were accomplished in the framework of a voluntary association, and they required some special skills. Only exemplary figures who could move their followers were capable of mustering the necessary force to create new communal forms.[35] Although the Second Aliyah was influenced, *inter alia*, by the established leaders of Zionism and socialism, the lion's share fell to indigenous leaders. These came up from the ranks; they did their apprenticeship as agricultural laborers and for a long time retained close relationships with their peers. Their leadership mirrored the extraordinary conditions of the time, coupled with the human qualities of the pioneering community.

The innovative constructivism of the Second Aliyah required a leadership of its own that would be all-embracing and not just fragmentary. The political leader, the economic manager, and the ideological mentor were often one and the same person. He might pass judgment on literature and art or comment on entertainment and life-style. In fact, he would be expected to voice an authoritative opinion on everything under the sun. It is from this quarter that we can gather the most relevant information on the attitude to religion as well. The leaders sometimes reflected what others had in mind, too, but more often than not their views served as guidelines for the group, notwithstanding the much-emphasized individualism of its members.[36]

A Superior Jewish Life

The different approaches to religion that were evolved by the Second Aliyah leadership have been described as a cluster. There was an assumption that the pioneer could attain a superior Jewish way of life, as compared to other Jews, particularly those living in the diaspora. This cluster of ideas spread out in four different directions: empirical, humanistic, dialectic, and mystic.

A prominent exponent of the empirical direction at the time was Jacob Vitkin, better known as Zerubavel (1886–1967). He had been one of the Poalei Zion leaders in Russia, and he arrived in Palestine in 1910. There he joined the party leadership and left his particular mark on its writings. He gave expression to the idea that the young generation in Palestine was, *ipso facto*, living a Jewish way of life. Zerubavel was never a negator of the diaspora, but he viewed the life of the pioneers as diametrically opposed to that of the *galut* Jews, who, imbued with the foreign spirit of their environment, were apprehensive of the pioneers' "non-kosher Judaism."[37]

Zerubavel expressed this stance, for example, in polemics against a conciliatory approach to Arab aggressors following the appearance of a book commemorating their Jewish victims. He spoke of the "tragedy of passivity" that had characterized the history of the Jews. He scorned Jewish martyrology and rejected the traditional image of the Maccabees, interpreting them not as religious martyrs but as active heroes. The modern pioneers were, he believed, heirs to an ancient heroic tradition.[38]

Zerubavel further elaborated this theme when he joined others in publishing a Yiddish book in memory of the fallen heroes in Palestine. Here he
was even more outspoken in rejecting the "lofty," spiritual character of the
diaspora-type Judaism. He stated that after the Bar Kokhba revolt against
the Romans (135 C.E.), Judaism degenerated in the hands of idle "Torah
Jews." Judaism, according to Zerubavel, lost touch with reality, with the
productive forces, and was stultified to the point of lifelessness.[39]

Zerubavel also praised the act of collective suicide at Masada after the
destruction of Jerusalem by the Romans.[40] Here was a new approach to
human life and dignity that brazenly deviated from Jewish—or, for that
matter, Judeo-Christian—norms, preferring classical (that is, pagan) models
instead. This opinion was more than an expression of individual taste, for it
augured the future Masada cult in Israel.[41] In that same vein, his paper had
much sympathy with the theories of the French socialist leader Paul Lafargue, who, with his wife Laura (neé Marx), committed suicide in 1911 to
escape old age.[42]

The upshot of all this is not in the attitude to religion as such but in the
role allocated to religion in Jewish history and as a living force in Jewish
life. Religion, to Zerubavel and his colleagues, was of little importance; it
was seemingly doomed in the long run, anyway. Unlike the rival labor party
Hapoel Hazair, the Zionist Marxists rarely felt the need to contend with religion on a theoretical level. In the spirit of previous Zionist thinkers, they
were prone to detect the national essence behind the religions forms.[43] In
view of the evolution now taking place, they had much confidence that the
objective historical process would bring about a change for the better. Their
aim was to reconstruct Jewish life and turn the Jews, a religious minority
that fulfilled a peculiar socioeconomic function, into a "normal" nation.

It was perhaps no coincidence that Zerubavel, despite his pioneering pa-
thos, eventually became a leading figure of the strongly Marxist Poalei Zion
Left. They characteristically relied mainly on the objective forces of history
with the concomitants of a diaspora-oriented Zionism as well as emphasis
on Yiddish culture.

Rather surprising, though, was the contribution of the Marxist theoretician Ber Borochov, a subtle and sophisticated thinker. He would not be
satisfied with a mere matter-of-fact accommodation to the realities of Jewish existence. In 1912 Borochov published an essay on the First of May celebrations. He rejected the notion that socialism was solely a materialistic
system and emphasized its spiritual underpinnings. Borochov thought that
socialism could satisfy the religious quest of humankind through humanistic measures.[44] He subsequently spoke of the connection between progress
and tradition, positing this link as essential for the Jewish labor movement
in particular.[45] Though Borochov deviated from the orthodox Marxism attributed to him, these views were published by his colleagues in the United
States and later in Palestine, too.

Here was a notion that humanism should replace Jewish religion, not just declare it redundant, as the empiricists would have it. This idea went hand in hand with the need to establish a link with the Jewish past, as did the pioneers in fact when they settled in the Land of Israel and cultivated the Hebrew language. This tone was also dominant in the discourse of Yitzhak Tabenkin, a founding father of the *kibbutz* movement; the revolt against religion was to him a necessary step toward Jewish liberation.[46]

A New Religious Life

So much for the secular approaches to religion in the Second Aliyah. Now two more strands can be distinguished, noticeable for their particular use of religious rhetoric. Unlike Marxists, whose relation to religion extended from a militant to a tolerant position, populists often displayed a more complex attitude to religion, Marxist theory relegated religion to a marginal status, while non-Marxists were much more preoccupied with religious issues.[47] They may have demonstrated a more combative mood concerning religion, but they were hardly ever indifferent to it. Thus they tended to use religious language in a new sense.

Take the testimony of a young girl, whose father had left the country in despair. She criticized the *galut* atmosphere that reigned, to her mind, in Palestine: the party politics and bureaucracy, the low level of education, and so forth. However, she bewailed most bitterly the lack of faith; not *religion*, she emphasized, but *religiosity*.[48] Her attitude could be placed in the same context perhaps as the affirmative statement by Shlomo Lavi, a *kibbutz* leader, who said: "We have a God, he who ordains an equitable life, work, creativity, the commune. This is the God we would like to bequeath to our descendants."[49]

Here a whole range of quasi-religious ideas seemed to fill the void that had opened up before them when the pioneers left their homes in Eastern Europe. New ideas replaced the religious norms; more important, a hard pioneering life supplanted the minutiae that had been the daily routine of the observant Jew. Pioneering was the new religious life that demanded devotion and self-sacrifice to the point of martyrdom, when necessary. Here was a way of life that made an absolute claim on the individual but gave him or her the satisfaction of doing the right thing, together with the promise of terrestrial salvation.

The exponents of the dialectic direction rejected the normative Jewish religion in its conventional form.[50] They were critical of the religious establishment and could not identify with conventional religion in any given sense. They even sought to replace religion by their own brand of spirituality, which sometimes amounted to the glorification of the pioneering life in Eretz Israel. The most important spokesman of this direction was probably

Berl Katznelson, who is regarded as the spiritual leader of the labor movement inasmuch as David Ben-Gurion was its political leader.[51]

To mention Katznelson in this context requires some qualification. Most
of the texts quoted here had a double function: they reflected a certain attitude, while at the same time trying to influence the pattern of behavior in
general. Berl Katznelson was to many a source of inspiration: his writings
are less indicative of the spirit of the time than an indication as to what
ought to be. His respect for tradition, for instance, was an encouragement,
even admonition, to others. One could have classified him almost as an
intermediary between the dialectic and the mystic approaches, were it not
for his rather functional attitude to religion. In this he resembled Ahad
Haam, who also made use of religion in order to fortify the collective consciousness of the Jews.[52]

Katznelson had a very keen sense of history, and he emphasized the links
with the Jewish past. Since the history of the Jews is so thoroughly intercon-
nected with religion, his position evinced a more positive evaluation of Jewish tradition than was customary. He had a gift for evoking traditional images, symbols, and locutions in reference to the new pioneering life-style.
He also appreciated the role of the Jewish holidays in the creation of the
new Hebraic culture.[53] It seems that he had a gradually growing influence
on the pioneering community. He was the model charismatic leader, always
an outstanding individual, foreshadowing the shape of things to come.[54]
His preoccupation with Jewishness undoubtedly left its imprint on the new
society.

Let us now consider the fourth direction, which tried to arrive at a religious expression of its own. The major proponent of this approach was Aharon David Gordon, a singular figure whose contribution to the new society
in Palestine is well known. Gordon came to Palestine at the age of forty-
eight and worked as an agricultural laborer for the rest of his life. His exemplary idealism coupled with a warm personality and a patriarchal appearance made him almost the patron saint of the Second Aliyah. His admirers
did not always understand the depth of his philosophy, published occasionally in essay form.

Gordon's name is often mentioned as the originator of a "Religion of
Labor" theology, a term he did not endorse himself. He was an Orthodox
Jew, but gradually turned away from strict observance, though never to relinquish his faith entirely. It developed, though, and had a pantheistic bent
that smacked somewhat of Zen Buddhism.[55] His thinking combined the individual, Jewish, and even cosmic aspects of life into an organic whole, vi-
brating through physical labor. His ideas pulsate a mystic air that turn the
pioneering life into a religious ritual.[56]

In the same vein, Gordon not only espoused tolerance but believed that
religious and nonreligious Jews really complemented each other, particularly in Palestine.[57] He considered his approach as life affirming, yet he per-

sonified an ascetic quality that befitted the material shortcomings of the time. In the atmosphere of early twentieth-century Palestine, Gordon's was not an abstract, but a life-enhancing, influence. Gordon's theology reminds one also of Rabbi Kook's impact on the pioneers, which was profound even though it did not actually affect their practices in the religious sphere.[58]

The religious quality of the pioneering life was apparent to many visitors from abroad. Moshe Calvary noted in 1915, for example, that, sacrilegious verbiage to the contrary, the pioneers led a life of strenuous dedication and self-denial. He then asked: "Is this not religion?"[59] In a similar manner Joseph Klausner stated some time earlier: "Work has become really sacred to them and they devote themselves to it in purity and reverence, as did the Jew of old to Torah and prayer."[60]

Summing Up

This essay has described a counterculture in which religious values were undergoing a thorough transformation. The major change was existential, from a traditional Jewish way of life in Eastern Europe to the pioneering life in Palestine. Concurrently, values also changed: physical work, agricultural settlement, self-defense, and Hebrew replaced the daily routine of Jewish religion and even acquired a sacred aura.

Within this context, attitudes toward religion varied extensively. Nevertheless, the Second Aliyah people had a common belief that their own evolving society should be Jewishly superior to any other community elsewhere. From there onward, the different approaches to religion were classified into four categories: empirical, humanistic, dialectic, and mystic.

The first assumed that religion was outdated and its influence on the wane. It was indifferent to metaphysics and the supernatural but adamant about the religious establishment, past and present. It saw the essence of Jewishness in the deeds of the Jews. The second category was intent on replacing religious values with humanistic ones. These secular categories also prompted, among other things, a revised Jewish attitude to Christ and Christianity.

The two opposing categories took a religious approach to the interpretation of Judaism, or at least used religious metaphors to define their own values. The dialectic category made do with a spiritual quality that had manifested itself within the pioneering life, whereas the mystic category attached a higher meaning, or a religious connotation, to the new way of life.

Notes

1. See my *Zionism and History: The Rise of a New Jewish Consciousness* (New York, 1987), pp. 12–14.

2. Berl Katznelson to Haim Katznelson, 13 Av 1910, *Igerot,* vol. 1, ed. Yehuda Sharett (Tel Aviv, 1961), p. 159.

3. David Ben-Gurion, "Hazeadim harishonim," *Haahdut* 46 (September 15, 1911): 8.

4. Salo W. Baron, *The Russian Jews Under Tsars and Soviets* (New York, 1987), p. 64.

5. Nora Levin, *While Messiah Tarried: Jewish Social Movements 1871–1917* (New York, 1977), p. 402; Yosef Gorni, "Hashinuim bamivneh hahevrati vehapoliti shel haaliyah hashniyah bashanim 1904-1940," *Hazionut* (1970), 1:204–28.

6. Nathan Melzer, "Prakim letoldot tenuat havodah beGalizya hamizrahit," in *Pirkei Galizyah,* ed. Israel Cohen and Dov Sadan (Tel Aviv, 1957), pp. 112–13.

7. Shlomo Tzemakh, *Shanah rishonah* (Tel Aviv, 1965), p. 85.

8. Robert J. Brym, *The Jewish Intelligentsia and Russian Marxism* (New York, 1978), pp. 43–46.

9. Aileen Kelly, introd. to Isaiah Berlin, *Russian Thinkers* (Harmondsworth, England, 1981), p. xx.

10. Nicolas Berdiaev, *Les Sources et le sens du communisme russe* (Paris, 1951), p. 146.

11. Moshe Smilansky, *Zikhronot* (Tel Aviv, 1924–28), 1:1–3.

12. David Knaani, *Haaliyah hashniyah haovedet veyahasah ladat velamasoret* (Tel Aviv, 1976), pp. 36–45. See also Richard Pipes, *Russia under the Old Regime* (Harmondsworth, England, 1979), pp. 271–73.

13. Jonathan Frankel, *Prophecy and Politics: Socialism, Nationalism and the Russian Jews, 1862–1917* (Cambridge, England, 1981), pp. 405–6.

14. Almog, *Zionism and History,* pp. 118–21.

15. Jules Isaac, *Genèse de l'antisémitisme: Essai historique* (Paris, 1956), pp. 159–72.

16. See, for example, Fritz Kahn, *Die Juden als Rasse und Kulturvolk* (Berlin, 1921), pp. 187–93.

17. Yosef Hayim Brenner, "Regashim vehirhurim," *Hapoel Hazair* 17 (July 1, 1909): 3–5.

18. James H. Billington, *The Icon and the Axe: An Interpretative History of Russian Culture* (New York, 1970), pp. 479–89; Eugene Lampert, "Modernism in Russia 1893–1917," in *Modernism,* ed. Malcolm Bradbury and James McFarlane (Harmondsworth, England, 1978), pp. 146–47.

19. Brenner, "Regashim vehirhurim."

20. Brenner, *Ketavim,* ed. Yitzhak Kafkafi (Tel Aviv, 1985), 3:392–402.

21. Brenner, "Baitonut ubasifrut," *Hapoel Hazair* 3 (November 24, 1910): 6–8.

22. Nurit Govrin, "Meora Brenner," in *Hamaavak al hofesh habitui* (Jerusalem, 1985), pp. 24–25; Jonah Spivak, "BeLondon," in *Joseph Haim Brenner: Mivhar divrei zikhronot,* ed. Mordecai Snir (Kushnir) (Tel Aviv, 1971), pp. 66–77.

23. Brenner, "Baitonut ubasifrut." See also Leonard Shapiro, *Russian Studies* (London, 1986), p. 348.

24. Brenner, "Baitonut ubasifrut."

25. Govrin, "Meora Brenner," pp. 98–99.

26. Dan Miron, *Bodedim bemoadam: Ledyokanah shel harepublikah hasifrutit haivrit betehilat hameah haesrim* (Tel Aviv, 1987), pp. 270–71.

27. Menahem Brinker, "Brenner's Jewishness," *Studies in Contemporary Jewry* 4 (1988): 243–44.

28. Walter A. Ackerman, "Religion in the Schools of Eretz-Yisrael, 1904–1914," *Studies in Zionism* 11 (Spring 1985): 13.

29. See Miguel de Unamuno, *The Tragic Sense of Life* (London, 1921).

30. Micha Yosef Berdichevsky, quoted in Almog, *Zionism and History,* p. 120.

31. Charles S. Liebman and Eliezer Don-Yehiya, *Civil Religion in Israel: Traditional Judaism and Political Culture in the Jewish State* (Berkeley, Calif., 1983), p. 37.

32. The phrase is Georg Wilhelm Friedrich Hegel's. See *The Philosophy of History* (New York, 1956), p. 33.

33. See Jaroslav Pelikan, *The Melody of Theology* (Cambridge, Mass., 1988), p. 221.

34. Fernand Braudel, *Écrits sur l'histoire* (Paris, 1977), pp. 62–63.

35. Robert C. Tucker, "The Theory of Charismatic Leadership," in *Philosophers and Kings: Studies in Leadership,* ed. Dankwart A. Rustow (New York, 1970), pp. 74–76.

36. Karl Mannheim, *Ideology and Utopia: An Introduction to the Sociology of Knowledge* (New York, n.d.), p. 207.

37. Zerubavel [Jacob Vitkin], "Haraayon vehamaaseh," *Haahdut* 24 (March 22, 1912), p. 5.

38. Zerubavel [Jacob Vitkin], "Yizkor," *Haahdut* 11–12 (January 2, 1912): 30–33, 13 (January 9, 1912): 17–18.

39. Zerubavel [Jacob Vitkin], Y. Ben Zvi, A. Khashin, *Yizkor tsum ondenken fun di gefalene vekhter un arbeter in Eretz Israel* (New York, 1916), p. 9; Jonathan Frankel, "The Yizkor Book of 1911," in *Religion, Ideology and Nationalism: Essays Presented in Honor of Yehoshua Arieli,* ed. H. Ben Israel et al. (Jerusalem, 1986), pp. 355–84.

40. Flavius Josephus, *The Wars of the Jews,* vol. 7, chaps. 8–9.

41. Bernard Lewis, *History: Remembered, Recovered, Invented* (Princeton, N.J., 1975), pp. 6–9.

42. Liebman and Don-Yehiya, *Civil Religion,* pp. 42–43, 149–50.

43. Almog, *Zionism and History,* pp. 165–68.

44. Ber Borochov, "Mahi hag rishon lemai?" *Haahdut* 29–30 (May 10, 1912): 16.

45. Ber Borochov, "Masoret vehitkadmut bitenuat hapoalim haivrit," *Haahdut* 32 (May 24, 1912): p. 8.

46. Knaani, *Haaliyah hashniyah,* pp. 44–45.

47. Ibid., pp. 48–49.

48. Joshua Barzilay, "Ayelet hashahar: Sefer zikhronot," *Hashiloah* 27 (1912): 147–48.

49. Shlomo Lavi, *Ketavin nivharim* (Tel Aviv, 1954), 2:88. Although this statement dates from a later period, it is still representative.

50. See, for example, Gideon Aran, "From Religious Zionism to Zionist Religion," *Studies in Contemporary Jewry* 2 (1986): 121–23.

51. Anita Shapira, *Berl, The Biography of a Socialist-Zionist: Berl Katznelson, 1887–1944* (Cambridge, 1984). I am very grateful to Shapira for drawing my attention to the gradual development of Berl Katznelson's attitude to tradition, which came to fruition in the 1930s rather than during the Second Aliyah years.

52. Liebman and Don-Yehiya, *Civil Religion,* pp. 232–33; Avraham Tsivion, *Dyokano hayehudi shel Berl Katznelson* (Tel Aviv, 1984), pp. 139, 245–52.

53. *The Zionist Idea,* ed. Arthur Hertzberg (New York, 1981), pp. 393–95.

54. Barry D. Karl, "The Power of the Intellect and the Politics of Ideas," in *Philosophers and Kings,* p. 452.

55. Aharon David Gordon, *Mikhtavim vereshimot* (Jerusalem, 1954), pp. 200–201.

56. *Zionist Idea,* Hertzberg, ed., pp. 370–71.

57. Aharon David Gordon, *Haumah vehavodah* (Jerusalem, 1952), p. 209.

58. Rabbi Kook's role has been well researched in recent years and is amply dealt with in the relevant literature.

59. Moshe Calvary, "Behevlei kismah shel haivrit," in *Sefer haaliyah hashniyah,* ed. Brakha Habas and Eliezer Shokhat (Tel Aviv, 1947), p. 678.

60. Joseph Klausner, "Olam mithaveh," *Hashiloah* 29 (1913): 209.

The Religious Motifs of the Labor Movement

Do not hear, my son, the instruction of your father
And to your mother's teachings do not lend an ear,
For your father's instruction says: "patiently, patiently . . ."
And your mother's teaching: "slowly, slowly . . ."
And the spring storm speaks:
"Listen, man, to the voice of the son!"

This famous poem by David Shimonovitz, published in 1922 by a Hash-omer Hazair youth movement journal in Warsaw, caused a furor. Printed in letters and a graphic setting traditionally reserved for a page of the Bible, it made use of a biblical literary model, "Hear, my son, the instruction of your father, and forsake not the teaching of your mother" (Prov. 1:8). But it turned its meaning the other way round: the son, originally the object of parental exhortations, becomes the subject, carrier of the new truth. The use of the traditional graphic form for this revolutionary manifesto served to emphasize its aggressive message. By the same token, it also serves to suggest some of the ambiguities inherent in the attitude of the Zionist labor movement toward religion. In a wider context, ambivalence toward religion was part of the very complex attitude of that movement to Jewish history and tradition and, consequently, to the educational values it strove to impart to the younger generation.

The Palestinian labor movement inherited two antireligious traditions: that of the Haskalah (Jewish Enlightenment) and that of the socialist movement. The Enlightenment's criticism of Jewish society encompassed all aspects of a Jew's life: worldview, education, occupation, appearance, behavior, relations with non-Jews, and relations within the Jewish family and the community. Struggling to reform Jewish life, the proponents of the Enlightenment clashed constantly with Jewish Orthodox circles, who viewed any change in the old order as a threat to the entire structure of traditional Jewish society. This struggle took on the dimensions of a *Kulturkampf*. It was fought with a vehemence that sometimes contradicted the religious tolerance esteemed by the Enlightenment. Abraham Mapu, Yehuda Leib Gordon, Moshe Leib Lilienblum, Micha Yosef Berdichevsky, Mendele Mokher Seforim, Yosef Hayyim Brenner, and even Ahad Haam, in his own way, imbued their teachings with a secular approach. They viewed Jewish religion, in its present state, as an unfortunate obstacle in the way of the Jews, preventing them from joining the universal march of progress. It is true that among the *maskilim* were others whose approach to religion was less harsh, but on the whole one can describe the heritage of the Enlightenment as basically antireligious.

The socialist movement accepted Karl Marx's dictum about religion being the opiate of the masses. Gentiles occasionally attempted to combine a religious and a socialist outlook, but not Jews. The Jewish socialist movement, which began to emerge in Russia in the late nineteenth century, was marked by a strong antireligious streak. The Bund adopted an anticlerical platform and campaigned against religion and the religious establishment. So did the Jewish labor movement in the United States. Abe Cahan, the famous editor of the largest Jewish newspaper, *Forverts* (Forward), promoted the same fierce antireligious spirit.

Apparently, the anticlericalism of the Palestinian labor movement owed more to the tradition of the Enlightenment than to that of the Bund, as most Bundists and their descendants never reached the shores of Palestine. Those who did settle there had usually grown up in families that embraced the spirit of the Hibbat Zion movement (Love of Zion), and they were educated on its journals and literary periodicals. The secular principle—namely, the denial of the existence of divine providence and the rejection of the predominance of the religious system over all other systems—was an essential element of this education. Ahad Haam was one of its main proponents.

When these young socialists arrived in Palestine, two groups they encountered there confirmed the antireligious stance. The Orthodox Jews in Jerusalem epitomized all that they found repulsive in the Jewish religion in its present condition: poor, uneducated, superstitious, cowardly, zealous, lacking in self-respect, living on the *halukah* (charitable funds received from abroad by Jews in Palestine for distribution among the needy). Ahad Haam's words about a people destroyed came naturally to mind.[1]

The Old Yishuv, however, was marginal from the point of view of the Second Aliyah; the traumatic encounter was with the colonists. The deeply religious colonists in Petah Tikva demanded that all Jews maintain a religious way of life. They refused to hire the young socialist workers on religious, cultural, and economic grounds, employing Arab laborers in their fields instead. The young socialists, in turn, regarded these Orthodox Jews as the epitome of hypocrisy, disguising class interests and prejudice by sanctimonious piety. David Ben-Gurion described the farmers of Petah Tikva as having installed an idol in the Temple and desecrated the land by idolatry.[2] His imagery captures the young socialist view of traditional society: religion came to be identified with all that was abhorred. The struggles within the Jewish community in Palestine over such issues as the *shmitah* (sabbatical year) or the effects by Rabbi Abraham Isaac Kook to compel the workers to observe the religious commandments heightened the tension and sharpened the antireligious convictions of the youth in the labor movement.

Like almost any statement concerning the Palestine labor movement, this one has to be qualified. Most of the immigrants of the Second Aliyah, and even of the Third and the Fourth, came from traditional households. They rebelled against the authority of religion, but they were not cut off from traditional Jewish culture. Seculiarization was a gradual process, the pace of which was not necessarily determined by conviction. A person tended to observe the religious commandments as long as he or she lived in the home of his parents. Sometimes a young man would maintain a kosher kitchen in his own home, so that his parents could eat at his table, but he would smoke secretly on the Sabbath. On the other hand, those who left the village and moved to the city soon found themselves drawn to a way of life in which religious practice gradually became dispensable. This process was particularly manifest among those who went to Palestine. Palestine was not conducive to a religious way of life; there was something in the atmosphere that promoted breaking away from old traditions and customs. The parental home was far away, and society did not frown upon those who neglected to adhere to religious precepts. The departure from religious practice happened almost imperceptibly. Shmuel Yosef Agnon described it as follows:

In other things he behaved like most of our comrades. He did not go to the synagogue, and did not wear phylacteries, and did not observe the Sabbath and did not respect the holidays. At first he differentiated between positive and negative commandments . . . but in the end he stopped making the distinction. And if he happened to have an opportunity to transgress, he would not hesitate.[3]

As to matters of faith, Agnon remarked ironically, "Rabinovitz has nothing in favor of his Creator, nor against him. From the day Rabinovitz left his hometown, it is doubtful whether he remembered Him. A person has many affairs, and does not have time to remember everything."[4]

Distinguishing three terms used by adherents of the labor movement—religion, tradition, and *Yiddishkeyt*—will help to explicate the attitude a Jew might have to Judaism. Religion relates to a system of faith and beliefs, and the laws deriving from them, that prescribe a particular way of life. Tradition relates to the external aspects of the customs, rooted in religion. While religion views the commandments as immutable, to be neither altered nor debated for they were revealed by God to Moses at Sinai, tradition entails a fundamentally secular approach. It implies that religious law was not divinely imposed but developed from habits and customs adopted over the course of time and sanctified by long practice. Moreover, tradition lacks the force of obligation inherent in religion: practices are no longer compulsory but optional; one can choose those one likes and practice them while disregarding others. The third term, *Yiddishkeyt*, relates to a body of ethnocultural traits connected with the habits of a Jewish household and relations within the family and between people. While tradition focuses mainly on cultural and spiritual matters, *Yiddishkeyt* centers on daily life, folklore, and humor. *Yiddishkeyt* is interested in the Jew as a human being, not as the object of divine will, and tends toward Jewish popular culture.

These terms constitute a declining scale of commitment toward Judaism. For young socialists, attraction increased as obligations decreased. Thus they adopted a negative approach toward religion, a semipositive one toward tradition, and an even more positive one toward *Yiddishkeyt. Yiddishkeyt* provided ideological legitimacy for their longings for the Sabbath and holidays in the homes of their parents, the aromas of mother's cooking, and the whole way of life in a Jewish household in the diaspora. The concrete expressions of their ethnic and cultural identity were inevitably tied to religion. Youths who abandoned religion but wanted to maintain ties to the Jewish people through symbolic or ritualistic expression were bound to borrow religious symbols and rituals. These practices were usually adopted instinctively, with little acknowledgment of their religious sources. The decision as to what constituted tradition and what *Yiddishkeyt* was personal: some maintained very few customs; others observed the dietary laws and even studied Talmud.

It is generally accepted that the socialist movement emerged within the framework of European rationalism. But the Palestine labor movement stands as an exception. Marked by an especially strong ethnic identity and a dominant national sentiment, this movement was rooted as much in instincts and mysticism as in the rule of reason and logic. The Zionist and socialist tenets of the labor movement in Palestine were shaped by the world of Jewish myth. Woven into its emotional and ideological fabric were the dreams of redemption, messianism, the ancestral home, and the realization of God's kingdom on earth. Marxist ideology was superimposed on this layer of secret, irrational yearnings.

Basically, the Palestine labor movement was a religious movement. It might be called a "secular religion" or "political messianism," to use terms current in modern historiography, but it stands as a religious movement even without the secular modifiers. Its inner character was religious and it parallels the millenarian sects in Christianity and the mystical movements that had accompanied normative Judaism. It was first and foremost a great fraternity of believers—people whose lives were directed by an all-consuming faith. This faith had many shades and was variously perceived by different groups, but it had a common denominator: the belief that the end of days was within sight, that the realization of the Zionist idea was immanent. The belief in the coming of the messiah, or the realization of the Zionist idea, or the approaching socialist revolution, endowed every day and every deed with special meaning.[5] Beyond disagreements and internal fights, there existed a silent, secret consensus, not to be expressed orally or in writing, that molded daily behavior, the relationship between individuals, and the relationship between the individual and society. The concept of self-sacrifice—"the love of self-sacrifice" was the phrase—stemmed from the Russian revolutionary movement. Its implementation depended on the existence of a constant religious fervor that was nurtured by demonstrations of zeal in the private domain and in public intercourse. It was by virtue of this hushed fervor, which endowed the daily sufferings and hardships with special meaning, that generations of pioneers could continue to bear the burden of the socialist Zionist enterprise.

Religiosity was especially manifest in the rites of simplicity adopted by the *kvutzot* (agricultural communes) and the *kibbutzim*, the youth movements, and the Halutz (Pioneer) movement. Simple attire, the avoidance of pomposity and hypocrisy, forthrightness and absolute honesty heralded a new, pristine quality in human relations, hitherto jeopardized by civilization. The community was accorded precedence over the individual, who stood subject to the judgment of his peers.

The traces of this hidden fabric were rarely exposed. Berl Katznelson revealed a little of this emotional frame of mind in his letter to "My Friends in the Ohel Theater." He talked about it as

another link in the magic chain, whose existence we do not recognize only because we live in its midst, and it resides in our own "flesh and blood." And we do not sense that it is the sublime mystery of all time whose name is Eretz Israel. And blessed be every moment which enhances and strengthens this feeling.

The play that prompted this comment was *Hamekubalim* (The Mystics). In the same letter Katznelson used the following expressions: "the holy spirit of the generation"; "The divine presence did not forsake us"; "seeing the public in its ascension." He defined the qualities characterizing this public: "an atmosphere of communality, of devoutness, of true enthusiasm and self-sacrifice, of patriotism, of social idealism, of yearning for cultural roots."[6]

The religious layer undergirding the labor movement tended to emerge in periods of special significance. When, during World War I, the British captured Palestine with the help of the Jewish Legion, there was an outburst of messianic hope. The expressions "redemption," "the end of days," "forcing the end," and "the coming of the messiah" appeared frequently in the labor periodicals.[7] In a short passage (four and one-half lines) Berl Katznelson used the following idioms:

hazon haam (vision of the nation)
gilui shekhinah (epiphany)
shavrirei nitzotzot (fragments of divine light)
hitgalut (revelation)
negohot (splendor)
tsafrirei geulah (winds of redemption)
tsofim umevasrim (scouts and heralds)
nevi emet (true prophet).[8]

The use of kabbalistic and messianic terminology is not accidental; it reflects the emotional and psychological sources from which this movement drew its inspiration.

The poets of the era, Abraham Shlonsky and Uri Zvi Greenberg, openly expressed the religiosity of the labor movement. Shlonsky opens his book of poems *Bagalgal* (In the Wheel) with a poem called "Hitgalut" (Revelation) describing God's revelation to Samuel in the presence of Eli. The poem is imbued with a deep sense of God's presence and proximity. This feeling recurs in other poems in the same volume.[9] An amazing example is the following:

Make us suffer, God
unleash your anger on the entire universe
only do not keep silent any longer
only do not cover up your face
my Lord, my Lord.[10]

In one of his famous passages in the poem "Toil," Shlonsky uses the prayer shawl and phylacteries as metaphors to describe the emotions of the pioneer building the roads:

Dress me, good mother, in a glorious robe of many colors, and at dawn lead me to [my] toil.
My land is wrapped in light as in a prayer shawl. The houses stand forth like frontlets; and the roads paved by hand, stream down like phylactery straps.
Here the lovely city says the morning prayer to its Creator. And among the creators is your son Abraham, a road-building bard of Israel.[11]

The poem "Ohalenu" (Our Tent) is suffused with religious motifs such as the *mezuzah* (parchment scroll affixed to the doorposts of Jewish homes) and the *menorah* (candelabra). One passage begins:

God, please wrap my soul in the prayer shawl
and sing aloud: Come my bride!
My beautiful wife, light the candles
and prepare the Sabbath bread.[12]

The poet unlocks the meaning of another poem, "Ad halom" (Up to Here) in a single phrase:

We are worthy of sitting up front
at the feast of your great Sabbath.

The building up of the land is comparable with the work of God and preferable to the observance of the commandments. Reacting to the Palestinian landscape, Shlonsky writes,

Like the Name of God, will I whisper now "Gilboa."[13]

In "Beein elohim" (Without God), he continues to search for the sacred in everyday life. When he despairs of finding it, he writes,

O, how will we wrap our shrinking body in the prayer shawl?
How will we put phylacteries on our head?
when our calendar is blackened by
365 days, 365 nights of profanity.

But soon he retreats:

Look
whence comes the prayer shawl which covers the shoulders of the mornings?
who tied the sun's frontlets to the morning star?
by my blood
the nights here weave their silk into a curtain of the ark
to wrap my body in prayer
for I am as tall as a Torah scroll.[14]

The fact that Shlonsky uses religious metaphors is not surprising: coming from a religious home, he longed for the holiness of a Sabbath night, for the look on his mother's face when she lit the candles, the spirit of the weekday still present inside her wrinkles. Overwhelmed by the new world, he invests it with the symbols and values of the old. Once endowed with holiness, the daily experiences became more bearable; toil is transcended; the encounter with the land becomes a revelation. Thus Shlonsky was able to overcome his yearnings for the lost world of yesteryear, for mother and father never to be seen again. In an indirect way, he legitimized the old world by infusing its symbols with new meaning and relevance.

Uri Zvi Greenberg also attributed holiness to the upbuilding of the land. He refers to Jezreel Valley, the symbol of the Third Aliyah, the kingdom of toil, as "the earthly Jerusalem."[15] In another poem he describes Jerusalem as the phylacteries worn on the head and the Jezreel Valley as the phylacteries worn on the hand.[16] Elsewhere he likens the steamroller used in road construction to the carriage of the messiah.[17] Even without using explicitly religious symbols, he conveys the religious spirit of the workers' communities he came across in the valley:

A patchy garment, no socks, no roof, blood to soil,
rejoicing and poverty, a savage dance
quiet-quiet-quiet hunger; and in every bone a feverish wine like the hope of the scar-
    let string to the toenails
would rise from every stone, every piece of wood, from every utensil, till red
    morning rises.[18]

He calls the bread eaten by the pioneers *lekhem hapanim* (shew bread).[19]

Generally, Greenberg's metaphors and symbols are drawn from ancient Hebrew myth, not from the Halakhah. He refers to Jerusalem, its holiness and its landscape; the kingdom of David; the Temple, priests, and zealots. Scenes from the Roman era are joined with scenes from British rule. Describing conflicts between Jews and gentiles, he creates a world view in which past and present, myth and reality, are intertwined, and he mythologizes the present by using religious-nationalist symbols. This blending of symbols is vividly seen in the following passage, written during the 1929 Arab riots against Jews, which erupted after eight years of peace:

> Tonight they are shooting in your gates, my holy city!
> A Jewish soldier is praying for your health with a gun,
> let the gun please you more than a playing organ![20]

The leadership of this "holy community" was based in the hidden religious layer and frequently marked by its charismatic qualities. Yitzhak Tabenkin and Meir Yaari, for example, were frequently compared to hasidic rabbis and their disciples, a comparison not entirely unfounded. These leaders, and to some extent Berl Katznelson, were authoritarian; they rejected criticism, demanded complete loyalty and total submission, and appealed to the emotions of their followers. Meir Yaari, who came from a hasidic family, was famous for the special power he exercised over his followers. Some described it as magic, others as demonic. The case of Bitanyah, a commune of Hashomer Hazair whose members staged public confessions in the dead of night, is understandable only as a community living on the edge of religious frenzy.[21] The initiation rites in the Hashomer Hazair youth movement, which were modeled after the ritual of Bitanyah, included complete spiritual exposure of the individual before his peers. One cannot appreciate the nature of the Kibbutz Meuhad movement without taking into account the impact of Tabenkin's personality and the irrational reverence he engendered in his followers. Tabenkin, who could trace his ancestry to a rabbinic dynasty, was not renowned for the logic of his arguments; he did, however, have a gift for firing up the imaginations of those who responded to his philosophical outlook. These people followed him even when they could not accept his views. Ostensibly, Katznelson always appealed to reason, basing his views on well-founded, rational arguments. But actually he had, as well, a deep-seated power through which he did not so much convince people as "conquer" them. During the 1920s, these leaders, with their dedication to a life of toil and poverty, were not unlike leaders of a religious sect.

This sacred congregation had its own rituals. The participants in *kibbutz* assemblies or the great political conventions of the Second Aliyah and of the 1920s and 1930s experienced a deep sense of catharsis. These conventions were not intended to be intellectual discussions but rather processes through which the community was to attain purification and reach the spiritual elevation needed for its cohesiveness. Such was the character of the memorable convention in Petah Tikva in 1918 that eventually led to the establishment of the Ahdut Haavodah Party in 1919. The same was true for the first convention of the Histadrut. Eventually, the heart-felt unity evaporated, as the intimacy on which it depended slowly dissipated with the expansion and politicization of the movement. From the 1930s on the disappointment expressed by the veterans in their political organizations, especially by members of Mapai, stemmed largely from the fact that the sacred congregation had become a political party and along the way had lost that special quality of religious exaltation typical of the cadre of believers.

Thus from its very beginning, the labor movement was marked by a duality—a rejection of religion and even to a certain degree of tradition on the one hand, and its own brand of religiosity, rooted in Jewish sources, on the other.

Quite early on, the leaders of the labor movement faced the problem of historical continuity. Their attitude to the Jewish past was ambiguous. On the one hand, they rebelled against the Jewish way of life in the diaspora. They viewed the era of exile as lost time in Jewish history, not to be emulated or learned from. On the other hand, they were keenly aware of the importance of imbuing the young with a sense of Jewish continuity. Always a small minority within the Jewish labor movement, not to mention the Jewish people as a whole, the founders of the Palestine labor movement attached great importance to instilling in the young generation clear, unquestionable national convictions. The components of this nationalism were rooted in the Jewish religion: the age-old ties of the Jews to the Holy Land; the historical right to the land; the attempts of Jews all through the centuries to resettle in Palestine as manifested by the messianic movements. These leaders taught the young that the present Jewish distress was additional justification for a Jewish state. However, "in the face of the many entanglements awaiting us in the unknown future, it is incumbent upon us to provide our young with a deeply emotional education, which will stir their souls."[22] This statement by Berl Katznelson, indisputably the greatest teacher of that generation, revealed the main thrust of the movement's educational approach: to mobilize the spiritual resources of its disciples by inculcating historical values that can arouse the emotions and the senses. Historical memories, symbols, and rituals play a crucial role in this kind of education. While the efficacy of socialist symbols was doubtful, the symbols of Jewish identity could call forth the patriotism of the youth. But how does one adopt these symbols while rebelling against the entire Jewish experience for the last millennium? How is one to preserve religious symbols and rituals and at the same time reject their theological content? In short, how was the atheistic character of the socialist movement to be maintained even as its proponents strove to inculcate a sense of historical continuity?

This problem was linked with another: the 1920s and early 1930s also witnessed an attempt by the labor movement to create an independent workers' society. It was to be an autonomous entity, with its own life-style and behavioral norms, a special attire and decorative style in the communal and private rooms in the kibbutzim, a separate educational system, a program for leisure, and the development of reading habits. In essence, the labor leaders aspired to establish a separate branch of the national culture. The Soviet model was a source of inspiration, but it was not applicable to

Palestine. The best model was a workers' society in a capitalist regime in Vienna. There the Social Democratic Party, which controlled the city government, had built special workers' quarters, in which proletarian culture could develop and thrive. It had its own literature, theater, and unique life-style. Parallels could be found in labor Palestine: a labor-directed educational system; the Ohel Theater; and the emergence of proletarian writers and poets, including Shlonsky, Alexander Penn, Yitzhak Lamdan, and for some time Uri Zvi Greenberg, who, in addition to their political identification with the Left, dedicated most of their works to the barefoot workers. Rahel Blaustein, known simply by her first name and the poet most closely identified with labor Palestine, made her literary debut at this time. The crown of this culture was the special atmosphere and life-style that developed in the *kibbutzim*. Expressions of this unique culture were thought to be indicative of the emerging "alternative society" that signified the independence of the working class within the capitalist society.

The emerging workers' culture of necessity had to grapple with the national culture and the Jewish heritage. What symbols could the workers adopt from the so-called national culture that would neither jeopardize their cultural independence on the one hand or, on the other undermine their proclaimed atheism?

The secularization of religious symbols and the infusion of new meaning into religious constructs were the subject of much deliberation within the Zionist movement from its inception. Educators in the New Yishuv faced the question of how to strike a balance between modernization and the preservation of traditional symbols and rituals. The Orthodox who launched an attack on the Gymnasia Herzliya correctly understood its program to be antireligious and conducive to secularism.[23] The school did its best to promote a secular spirit. Courses in Hebrew language and literature and in the Bible were designated to transmit Jewish tradition in a secular vein. Insignificant in the curriculum of traditional Jewish education, these subjects had a special status in the secular study plan.

The founders of the labor movement believed that one of its most important achievements was the revival of Hebrew as the language of the Jewish national renaissance. The secularization of the holy tongue was part of the maskilic (enlightened) tradition. Their adoption of the Sephardi pronunciation may be understood as in keeping with efforts to cut ties with the Eastern European Ashkenazi tradition. Hebrew had its own logic, however. Its idioms, modes of expression, ways of thinking, and syntax were linked to the world of tradition. As much as some of the socialists strove to escape tradition, the language they used inevitably attached them to it.[24]

Although until recently considered inferior to the Talmud, with "rejection of the *galut*" (negation of exile) the Bible became central to the Zionist educational system. In fact, the Talmud and the entire body of religious literature were removed from the curriculum. To be sure, the Bible was no longer perceived as the revelation of divine truth but rather as a work of literature and history, subject to scholarly criticism. The founders of the Gymnasia Herzliya adopted this approach. Portions of the Bible dealing with the commandments were treated as marginal. On the other hand, those chapters that described the life of the Jews in their ancient land were emphasized in the belief that the students would be attracted by its vigor. They would, it was hoped, be aroused by a "tremendous desire to renew our days as of old. The teaching of the Bible should be geared towards this end."[25] The Bible not only strengthened the "rejection of the *galut*" concept; it also served as a link to ancient Jewish history and the Jewish cultural heritage without demanding religious commitment. One could be a Jew of national convictions, with an attachment to Jewish heritage, without observing the commandments.

The Bible was read as a great literary work, revealing human nature in all its strengths and weaknesses. It also served as the history book of the Jewish people. The settlement of the tribes, the tales of heroism and defeat, the stories of a people living on the land—all these added up to a great saga, the theme of which was the emergence of the Hebrew nation. At the same time, the Bible was also the guidebook to the flora and fauna as well as to the landscape of Palestine. Through it youngsters were inspired with feelings of attachment to the land and feelings of ownership.

The Bible was, in fact, woven into the emotional and cultural fabric of the Second Aliyah. It was found in the rooms of the workers, and passages from it decorated every youth convention, every camp or celebration.[26] Almost all the labor leaders admitted its enormous impact. Through the stories of the Bible, Palestine came to life as a tangible reality. Upon arrival in Palestine, these immigrants traced the footsteps of their heroes and searched for Jewish settlements of old or places of special significance in Jewish history. The Bible helped create an emotional bond between the newcomer and the land. Tabenkin remarked:

The Bible was a kind of birth certificate to the newcomer, helping to erase the estrangement between man and land and cultivate a "feeling of homeland." These ties elicited the human forces that enabled the newcomer to strike roots and attach himself to a land so different in climate, nature, and landscape from the land of his childhood.[27]

Finally, the Bible served to legitimate socialist education. Since the early days of the Jewish labor movement in Eastern Europe it had been used to promote the socialist message. A. S. Liebermann had already cited the biblical laws regarding the Sabbath, the care for the stranger, the orphan, and the widow, and especially the laws of the jubilee and the sabbatical years as evidence that socialism was rooted in the Jewish tradition. The socialists read the teachings of the prophets, particularly those of Micah, Amos, Isaiah, and Jeremiah, as clearly socialistic. Many acknowledged the link between the spirit of their early Jewish education and their aspirations for justice, equality, and universal redemption.[28] These impulses were also strong among the workers in Palestine. Those branches of the labor movement that rejected ties to the world socialist movement claimed the Bible as the source of their socialist theories. A. D. Gordon, for example, who all his life vehemently denied being a socialist, cited the Bible as the inspiration for his calls for social justice, equality, and a life of toil. The members of Hapoel Hatzair, who claimed to be nationalists and not socialists, adopted the same position. Actually all the non-Marxists viewed the Bible's laws as evidence of the Jewish sources of socialist ideas and on this basis were able to make the case that the socialist credo was compatible with Jewish nationalism. Thus Nahman Syrkin, the socialist Zionist theoretician brutally attacked the Jewish religion, quoting Heinrich Heine's epigraph, that it was nothing other than a disaster. At the same time, he saw the Bible, and especially the prophets, as initiating a tradition of exemplary men who strove to change the world through moral wholesomeness.[29] Like others who preceded him, Syrkin attributed the adherence of Jews to movements seeking universal salvation to the Jewish tradition passed down since biblical times. Katznelson, too, who did not hesitate to acknowledge his affinity to the socialist tradition, credited the Bible with attracting Jews to socialist teachings. Thus the Bible gave a kind of national legitimization to socialism.

The secularization of literary models, symbols, and rituals involved retaining the traditional framework while changing its contents. This practice dated back to the very beginning of the Jewish workers' movement. The first Jewish socialists copied literary models from Midrash and Talmud, and also from the liturgy, through which they hoped to infuse the Jewish masses with socialist ideas. For instance, Morris Winschewsky, a disciple of A. S. Liebermann, published a modern version of the prayer "Let it be His Will," in which he asked for "life without exploitation and mistreatment of the poor; a life without spiritual speculation and empty affairs."[30] Winschewsky imitated the teachings of the prophets, and even printed his paper employing the traditional setting of a biblical passage, only its contents dealt with those who "are devouring my people and sucking its blood." He also published an essay by Moshe Leib Lilienblum, imitating the design of a page of Talmud, with the text in the center surrounded by commentaries. In his memoirs, Winschewsky described his method of smuggling in socialist ideas under religious cover "as do those who smuggle diamonds inside Dutch cheese." The same technique was used by Abe Cahan, editor of *Forverts*. He wrote his articles on socialist beliefs as sermons on weekly Bible readings adopting the familiar style of preachers in the synagogues. His conclusions recast the traditional form "and a redeemer will come to Zion" to "and a redeemer will come to the proletarians."[31]

Other early examples of the labor movement's recasting a ritual form for secular purposes occurred in the *yizkor* (memorial) book, published in 1912 by members of the Second Aliyah and in Katznelson's famous poem "Yizkor," written in memory of the workers and guardsmen who perished in Tel Hai. The traditional *yizkor* prayer asks God to preserve the memory of the deceased; it does not identify the cause of death—natural causes, a pogrom, or martyrdom. Katznelson's "Yizkor" addresses not God but the Jewish people, exhorting them to remember the heroes "who gave their lives for Israel's dignity and for Israel's land."[32] The indeterminate death in the traditional *yizkor* becomes, in the modern version, a heroic death for a national cause. The memory of the dead heroes becomes a tool in the struggle for the revival of Jewish sovereignty in its land.

The use of religious imagery and forms to express secular ideas was important in the work of Shlonsky and Greenberg and especially in David Shimonovitz's famous poem "Do not hear, my son," quoted at the beginning of this essay. But it is important to remember that this usage did not originate with the Jews. As secularization made its impact on life throughout Europe, the transfer of symbols and literary models from the religious to the secular sphere became an integral aspect of European culture. One cannot, for example, imagine romanticism without Christian symbols. But where Jewish socialist practice stands out as different from European secularization as a whole is in the matter of rituals. The Palestinian labor movement did not give much thought to the three basic life-cycle rituals—birth, marriage, and burial. It seems that practically everyone observed the rites of circumcision. Devoted atheists would not invite a traditional circumciser to perform the surgical procedure, but nonetheless would see to it that the baby was circumcised, justifying the practice by pointing to its important medical benefits. Dispensing with the religious ceremony that traditionally accompanied the circumcision made it acceptable to the young parents who, on the one hand, refused to initiate their son into the Covenant of Abraham but, on the other hand, felt uneasy about letting their offspring go uncircumcised, as circumcision was a common indicator of Jewish identity.

The wedding ceremony was not accorded any greater significance. On the whole, the institution of marriage was viewed with little enthusiasm, as it was the product of formal vows rather than an expression of free will. The religious sanction was thought to be meaningless, even hypocritical, and informal attachments were considered as binding as those sanctified by a rabbi. Still, most couples had a religious ceremony, all the while apologizing that it had been categorically demanded by their parents and showing their disdain by refusing the special wedding feast and honeymoon. To further diminish the significance of the ceremony, some couples arranged for their weddings to take place on the same day, all using the same ring. As far as I know, no serious attempt was made to devise a secular ceremony. When the political atmosphere changed in the mid-1950s, socialists simply returned to traditional weddings.

Burials were also treated matter of factly. The comrades would accompany the dead body to a cemetery, usually located on the outskirts of the small community and lovingly decorated with shrubs and trees. The observance of the religious components of the ritual depended on the measure of atheistic zeal practiced by the community. In most cases, someone would recite the "El male rahamin" (God of mercy) prayer. The *kaddish* (prayer for the dead) posed more of a problem, for it expressed the acceptance of divine judgment. In any event, the religious ritual was strictly observed during the public funerals of the leaders of the movement such as Chaim Arlosoroff and Katznelson.

It seems that while very little attention was paid to private rituals, a great deal of energy went into the reformulation of the traditional public rituals. These were mostly communal rituals, aimed at mobilizing individuals to identify with the community. Holiday observance, once a family affair, now became a collective festivity, an occasion for reaffirming communal goals. Eliezer Livenstein of Ein Harod remarked that the holidays "sometimes mark the beginning of the feeling of attachment of the individual worker to his community, intensify his readiness to serve it, his faith in the value of unity and in the inevitability of the forthcoming victory." It is then that "the communal soul of all the workers" emerged.[33]

The tendency to infuse the traditional frameworks of the holidays with new content again did not originate with the labor movement. The Zionist movement as a whole attached much greater significance to Hanukah than it had merited in the past. The focus of the holiday changed: the miracle of the cruse of oil, which had been its central theme, now yielded to the heroism of the Maccabees. A good illustration of the change is found in two songs—"Maoz tzur yeshuati!" (Mighty Rock of My Salvation) and the more modern "Mi ymalel gevurot Israel" (Praise the Heroes of Israel). The first deals with God's wonders and miracles for His people and culminates with the rededication of the Temple. The authors of the second recast a passage from Psalms—"Who will tell of the heroic deeds of God, and who will pronounce all His glory"—to glorify the exploits of Israel instead. Here redemption loses its transcendent character: it is the people, who will arise to redeem itself, not through an act of God but through the sheer force of human will. This motif recurs in another Hanukah song, "A miracle did not happen to us, a cruse of oil we did not find." Lag baOmer underwent a similar transformation: traditionally a holiday celebrating the feast of Bar Yohai and centered on the temporary relief from the mourning period during the counting of the Omer, it turned into a holiday of heroism whose symbol was Bar Kokhba. Another holiday thus transformed was Tu biShvat: in the diaspora it was dedicated to the seven kinds of fruits that blessed Palestine, expressing the longing of a people for a different country, with different fruits and climate. In its new guise it became the holiday of tree planting, in keeping with scriptural injunction, "When you come to the land, you will plant there a tree." This children's holiday was, perhaps, the most "Zionist" one of all, symbolizing the rejuvenation of the land.[34]

During the 1920s, when the pioneers in the Jezreel Valley wanted to create their own version of the holidays according to their needs, they found patterns to learn from and to emulate. Apart from the early trend to infuse the holidays with national meaning, people sought to highlight the centrality of agriculture in their lives. The first holidays to be invested with new content were those that could be connected to the agricultural cycle. The focus of Shavuot changed from a celebration of the giving of the Torah to a celebration of the first crops. Everyone took part in the ceremonies, which emulated the ancient custom of a pilgrimage to Jerusalem to offer the first crops to God in the Temple. *Kibbutz* members used songs, meditations, and greenery, as well as the first crops of the fields and the firstborn of the livestock, to signify the recent achievements of their community and to express their hope for a bountiful year. Sukkot, a holiday that traditionally focused on the four species, was turned into a harvest festival in keeping with the agricultural calendar. Attempts were made to give new meaning to the water-drawing festival of Sukkot, mentioned in the Midrash. Simhat Torah, a festival that celebrates the reading of the Torah, was completely ignored.[35]

One might have expected Passover to be the first holiday to be secularized, but it was not. For many years the holiday simply went unobserved. At the very beginning at Umm Djuni (1909), the night of Passover was the occasion for a special gathering. It culminated in wild dancing, and A. D. Gordon joined hands with young Yosef Bussel to give a rousing rendition of "Off to Work in the Morning."[36] But for many years no ritual *seder* (feast) was arranged in the *kibbutzim*. The *seder* was replaced by a festive evening of eating, singing, and dancing. In some places people read a humorous parody of the traditional *Haggadah* (book prescribing the Passover service), sometimes designed as a kind of local newsletter, relating to current events.[37] It was only at the beginning of the 1930s that new Passover ceremonies appeared, with modern *haggadot*, most of them produced locally and of passing value. In 1934 for the first time a new *haggadah* was printed, and from then until 1944, several hundred more were published. From 1944 on a process of institutionalization took place: each *kibbutz* movement published a *haggadah* of its own, reflecting its sensibilities and peculiarities. The local one-of-a-kind *haggadah* disappeared.

Why it took so long for the labor movement to respond to the challenge of remodeling Passover is an intriguing question. Azaria Allon attributed it simply to the prevalent atheism of the time.[38] This explanation is not satisfactory: by the same token, the socialists should have refrained from reformulating Shavuot or Sukkot. The Sabbath was also endowed with new content and dedicated to sports, neighborly visits, cultural activities, or communal gatherings.[39] The initiators of the independent workers' culture claimed that leisure hours and the celebration of the holidays should reflect the new needs and life-style of the worker in Palestine. The festivals and rituals should be relevant to the people, the socialists argued; otherwise they lacked authenticity and were hypocritical.[40]

This attitude only complicates the question of Passover. On the face of it, there was no other holiday so well suited for secular reformulation as Passover. As a festival of freedom, it had a clear universal message with socialist connotations. It also had a very strong nationalist message—the story of the emergence of a nation. And it also had an agricultural aspect, coinciding with spring and the beginning of the harvest season. Yet despite all these potential applications, something stood in the way. It is possible that memories of the traditional Passover *seder* in the parental home in the diaspora were too cherished to be subjected to the early, coarse experimentation in creating a secular alternative. Most of the holidays were traditionally centered in the synagogue, in the public domain. Passover, however, had always been a family affair, stressing the continuity of the generations. Perhaps the socialists, determined to separate themselves from the recent historical past on the one hand, and harboring the pain of leaving an old home behind on the other, found it difficult to create new Passover rituals. The population in the *kibbutzim* during the 1920s was still young; without children present to hear the recitation of the *Haggadah* according to the ancient command, "and you will tell your son," the celebration seemed pointless. Moreover, the attraction of the *Haggadah* stemmed from age-old music. How could these youngsters create something that would even approximate it? For a long time they could not cope with the question of the new materials and contents to be incorporated into a new *haggadah*.[41]

Consequently, instead of coming to grips with Passover, the socialists treated it almost disdainfully: a parody on the *Haggadah*, which did not pretend to be the real thing, was tolerable. The hasidic songs, which were sung in public with great devotion and even served as the musical background to the *horah* (folk circle dance), expressed their hidden yearning as well as the poverty of the alternatives.

By the mid-1930s a new factor had emerged: a Palestinian-educated generation. While their parents had come from traditional homes and were, as a consequence, deeply aware of Jewish culture, these youngsters had very little Jewish education. They absorbed the antireligious stance of the socialist movement without the mitigating effects of personal knowledge. In this new generation, the inherent ambivalence of the labor movement toward tradition came to the fore. In 1934 Berl Katznelson twice made it a point to elaborate on the importance of preserving ancient symbols sanctified by the people over the course of time:

A modern and creative generation does not throw onto the garbage heap the heritage of generations. It ought to examine that heritage, expand upon it and draw it near. Sometimes it adopts an existing tradition, and expands upon it. And sometimes it pokes into junk heaps, to uncover forgotten traditions, cleanses them of their rust, thereby reviving an ancient tradition to nourish the soul of the modern generation.[42]

This statement was recited time and again during youth movement celebrations, and it was hung on the walls of youth clubs as a slogan. It bestowed ideological legitimacy on the use of traditional Jewish symbols while asserting their national and secular meaning. Katznelson also made clear his disapproval of the desire of the pioneers of the Third, Fourth, and Fifth Aliyah to break completely with the past. He viewed the new symbols, adopted from the revolutionary lore and fashion, as far inferior to the traditional ones, and the most important historical symbol, ever fresh through the ages, was Passover.

From fathers to sons, through all the generations, the story of the Exodus was relayed as a personal memory, which does not pale and does not fade. . . . No more elevating peak of historical consciousness, and no greater molding together of [the fate of] individual and community, can be found in the whole world and through the ages, than in this ancient pedagogic command.[43]

For Katznelson, Passover epitomized the collective memory of national redemption, in its annual repetition always evoking new hope. His words became a staple in the new *haggadot* and in the youth movement rituals; they were reprinted endlessly in holiday supplements to movement newspapers.

In the mid-1930s, the *kibbutzim* began to celebrate the Passover *seder*, and modern *haggadot* were printed in a solemn vein. One cannot tell whether the renewal of Passover was the result of Katznelson's teaching, or the fruition of a long process, or the manifestation of longings formerly concealed by the generation now in their forties who had grown discontented with a *seder* celebration devoid of spirituality. An incident recalled by Shlomo Lavi is revealing. In Ein Harod, he participated in a *seder* for the first time since his arrival in Palestine, seventeen years before. He saw the whitewashed dining hall, brightly lit, and the comrades, in white shirts, sitting at tables covered with white linen, and on them white *matzot*. Every now and then he had to go outside to wipe off the tears from his face, tears of joy at having at long last participated in a real *seder*.[44]

The modern *haggadot* focused on Passover as a holiday of freedom and as a festival of spring. The passages of the original *Haggadah*, derived from *midrashim* and rabbinic lore, were eliminated; they were considered the spiritual creation of the diaspora and therefore unfit for the modern Hebrew nation. In their place were biblical passages on the Exodus story, as well as modern poems, the themes of which were spring, harvest, growth, and prosperity. In addition to the agricultural symbolism, the *haggadot* were meant to transmit a clear Zionist message. Thus, literary passages, such as "Metei midbar" (The Desert Dead) by H. N. Bialik could be found next to a modern *haggadah* story, of little literary value, retelling the history of the Jewish resettlement of Palestine. The socialists did their best to preserve the structure of the *Haggadah*, while changing the contents. For instance, the pattern of the four questions was retained, but new, momentous questions were asked: "Why do people all over the world hate Jews? When will the Jewish people return to its land? When will our land become as bountiful as a garden? When will peace and fraternity reign supreme?"[45] Usually the *haggadah* was laced with references to current events, and in 1936–39 the *haggadot* expressed the tension in the Yishuv arising from the Arab Rebellion. During the years of the Second World War, the *haggadot* grew increasingly somber as the horror of the Holocaust became known: The slogan, "If ever I forget thee, O diaspora!" replaced the spring songs.[46] Appropriate passages from Ezekiel or from Isaiah were cited to express the hope for swift redemption.

A *haggadah*, printed in stencil by the Shekhunat Borochov branch of Hanoar Haoved youth movement in 1941, can serve as a model of the kind of *haggadot* used by the youth movements at the time. The *haggadah* was almost completely devoid of its original content. Only "Ha lahma ania" (The Bread of Affliction) and some passages from Exodus were retained. A few passages from the Bible were added, with certain emendations; references to the almighty God were deleted or transformed as the Hanukah songs had been: "Our movement did not experience the revelation of the Torah, we did not receive any Holy Scriptures. It is from our daily existence . . . that our living Torah was molded."[47] Katznelson's words about Passover and preserving the chain of the generations were included in the *haggadah* as a matter of course. In actuality, however, members of the youth movement viewed themselves not as a link in the chain but rather as the innovators of a new tradition. They resisted traditional patterns, and consequently, their reliance on the traditional structure of the *haggadah* was largely superficial.

In 1931 the Hanoar Haoved youth movement published an instruction booklet for youth group leaders called *Anu vehadat (Religion and Us)*. Noting that there were many religions, the group leader was expected to impress upon his disciples "the relativeness of the term 'religion.'" As to the Jewish religion, its "present form was the product of diaspora conditions." On the question whether God exists, the sixteen-year-old leader was instructed to answer directly: "There are some people who believed in His existence, and others, who do not. I myself do not believe." Jewish education in the youth movement focused on the holiday cycle. As in the Hebrew school, the holidays served as the vehicle for acquainting youngsters with tradition and its symbols and were explained in rational and functional terms. This was the period of the *haggadah* parodies, and the instructor was obliged to organize a *seder* in that spirit. Shavuot, a festival of the first crops, was the occasion for a lesson in agriculture. The book of Ruth was presented as an illustration of the social laws in the Bible, such as gleanings, the forgotten sheaf, and the poor man's tithe. Other holidays mentioned in the booklet included Lag baOmer, Tisha beAv, Hanukah, Tu biShvat, and

Purim. The explanations followed the same guidelines. The emphasis was on learning Jewish folklore as it related to the holidays—special customs, foods, games. The explanations were accompanied by literary illustrations, including works by I. L. Peretz, Sholem Aleichem, H. N. Bialik's *Sefer Haaggadah* (Book of Legends), and stories by David Frischmann.

Two new holidays were added to the list: Tel Hai Day and May Day. While the traditional holidays were summarily dealt with, these two were treated lovingly; their meanings, as well as the customs linked with them, were more expansively explained. In theory, they added one ritual dedicated to Zionism, and one to socialism, but in actuality the distinction between the two was not so clear-cut. Yosef Trumpeldor, the legendary hero of the Tel Hai confrontation, was presented as a socialist no less than as a Zionist hero. By the same token May Day was celebrated as the holiday of the working class all over the world and also as the holiday of the worker in Palestine who struggled for Zionist goals, such as the immigration of Jewish workers.[48]

The old rituals, remolded according to the needs of the movement, symbolized the past and were aimed at strengthening the attachment to the land. The new rituals, on the other hand, expressed the ideals of the present and were future oriented. The workers' holidays were vital to the formation of a unique, independent workers' society. They emphasized its separateness from the general society, as they created a powerful focus for identity. At the same time, they inspired that collective "soul lifting" which turns a group of individuals into a single body. The religious character of the May Day celebration was manifested in many characteristic details: the widespread use of red flags instead of national flags; the singing of "The International" and "Tehezaknah" (Onward to Strength, the anthem of the Palestinian labor movement), instead of "Hatikvah"; the white shirt worn by everyone; the processions and the public gatherings; and speeches by prominent public figures. One of the participants in such a celebration in the Jordan Valley described the faces of the people gathered as "lit up by a precious light" and "the inner joy which flooded the depth of the soul."[49]

In the instruction booklet mentioned above no reference was made to the high holidays—Rosh Hashanah and Yom Kippur. This was not an oversight but willful omission. It is interesting to note the change that occurred in the attitude toward these holidays: today participation in high holiday services has come to symbolize minimal attachment to Judaism. During the Yishuv period, however, these holidays received no attention from the labor movement. Their exclusively religious character, and the lack of some other rationale, prevented them from being adapted to the secular arena, as the other holidays had been. The personal reckoning between humankind and their creator did not fit into any philosophical system of the movement and was consequently dismissed from the educational program. This fact did not escape the attention of leading educators of that generation. During a discussion on educational matters, Tabenkin stated his desire that the children of the *kibbutz* be acquainted with the tune of "Kol Nidrei" (All Vows), the twelve-hundred-year-old prayer said on the eve of Yom Kippur, the holiest day of the Jewish calendar.[50] But this all-embracing approach to the national cultural heritage, typical of many of the Second Aliyah pioneers, was seldom found among those of the Third and Fourth Aliyah and virtually nonexistent among the Palestine-educated youth.

Since the late 1940s, and mostly since the 1950s, the trend toward secularizing religious symbols slowed, and signs appeared of a return to the traditional religious format. It seems that this process was the result of several factors. One effect of the Holocaust was to reassert Jewish identity through traditional symbols and contents. "The world turned its back on us": this slogan was frequently pronounced at the central committee of Hamahanot Haolim youth movement in 1945, during a crucial debate on education. It expressed the tendency of a large sector of the labor movement to distance itself from the socialist world movement and to seek spiritual guidance and inspiration within Jewish history and culture.[51] The leftist minority in the labor movement still looked to the Soviet Union for guidance and remained faithful to socialist symbols. But the anti-Soviet majority emphasized specifically Jewish symbols and downplayed socialist ones.

These processes were associated with the retreat from an independent workers' society that began in the late 1930s and in time became more prominent. "Class Independence," during the 1920s the accepted slogan and philosophy of mainstream Labor Zionists, became more and more identified with the extreme Left. During the 1930s Ben-Gurion formulated the slogan "From Class to Nation." After the emergence of the State of Israel, this slogan was succeeded by the slogan of "statehood." Both assumed the existence of an identity between class and nation, between class interests and national interests. Accordingly, no difference should exist between national and labor culture. In addition, the mass immigration during the 1950s included Jews who had not experienced secularization. Their sheer numbers and presence had an impact on the national culture and likewise affected labor leadership and policy. Spiritual phenomena often experience florescence just before their decline. It was during the 1950s that the cultural traditions and forms of holiday rituals of the 1930s became institutionalized, but the time of creativity had passed. Slowly the old *Haggadah* was reinstated, at first with only some of the passages from the *midrashim* and the *aggadot* (legends) excised and later in its entirety. The old rituals were reestablished in the birth, wedding, and funeral ceremonies. The appearance of synagogues in most of the *kibbutzim* of the Ihud Hakvutzot Vehakibbutzim movement symbolized the change.

It would not be far-fetched to claim that the decline of the labor movement as a political-religious movement, which had been said to offer total solutions to the Jewish plight on the individual and national level, was accompanied by the disappearance of its rituals and a return to the old religious rituals. This shift did not herald the return to religion but rather to the nebulous cultural notion of "tradition." The process did not stem from a quest for a new religion but for collective identity symbols. The failure of the socialist Zionist symbols to meet this need resulted in the return to the age-old Jewish ones. The change occurred almost imperceptibly, as several factors converged: the aging of the founding generation, coupled with fatigue and loss of zeal; the disappointment, then disillusionment with the Russian Revolution; the loss of self-confidence and a sense of mission. The return to tradition did not inspire people to the same enthusiastic creativity as did the trend toward secularization. More than anything, it expressed the disappearance of the "holy spirit" of the labor movement and the onset of emotional indifference toward any religion.

Notes

This paper was written during my stay as fellow at the Annenberg Research Institute, Philadelphia. I am greatly indebted to my colleague David Berger, another fellow at the institute, who germinated some of the ideas developed in this paper. He also read the manuscript and made very useful comments. Furthermore, he was a great help in translating traditional terms from Hebrew into English. I also want to thank Gabriel Warburg, also a fellow at the institute, who read the manuscript and gave me some good advice.

1. Ahad Haam, "Emet meEretz Israel," in *Al parashat derakhim* (Berlin, 1921), 1:43.

2. David Ben-Gurion, "BiYehudah uvaGalil," in *Luah ahiever* (New York, 1921).

3. Shmuel Yosef Agnon, *Tmol shilshom* (Jerusalem and Tel Aviv, 1947), p. 82.

4. Ibid., p. 450. See also David Cnaani, *Haaliyah hashniyah haovedet veyahasah ladat velamasoret* (Tel-Aviv, 1976), p. 28.

5. See, for instance, the quotation from Ferdinand Lassalle that Berl Katznelson used as a motto to his speech "Likrat hayamim habaim" (Toward the Forthcoming Days), *Kol kitvei*, 2d ed. (Tel-Aviv, n.d.), 1:60–61.

6. Berl Katznelson, "Lehaverai baOhel'" (My Friends in the Ohel Theater), *Kol kitvei*, vol. 2 (Tel-Aviv, 1946), pp. 201–5.

7. See, Shmuel Yavneeli, *Yalkut ahdut haavodah*, vol. 1 (Tel-Aviv, 1929), pp. 155–60.

8. Berl Katznelson, "Likrat hayamim habaim," in *Kol kitvei*, 2:p. 67.

9. See Abraham Shlonsky, "Hitgalut" (Revelation) in *Bagalgal* (Tel-Aviv, 1927), pp. 5–6, see also "Taatuim" (Phantoms), pp. 168–71, and untitled poem, p. 179.

10. Shlonsky, "Beein elohim" (Without God), in ibid., p. 192.

11. Shlonsky "Amal" (Toil), in ibid., p. 98, translation from *The Penguin Book of Hebrew Verse*, ed. and trans. T. Carmi (New York, 1981), p. 534.

12. Shlonsky, "Ohalenu" (Our Tent), in *Bagalgal*, p. 138.

13. Shlonsky, "Ad halom" (Up to Here), in ibid., p. 137.

14. Shlonsky, "Beein elohim" (Without God), in ibid., pp. 189–190.

15. Uri Zvi Greenberg, *Beemza haolam uveemza hazmanim* (Tel Aviv, 1979), p. 34.

16. Greenberg, "Hizdaharut" (Radiance), in ibid., p. 52.

17. Greenberg, "Hazon ehad haligyonot" (The Vision of One of the Legions), in ibid., p. 85.

18. Greenberg, "Hitnazlut" (Apology), in ibid., p. 25.

19. Greenberg, "Lemargloteikha" (At Your Feet), in ibid., p. 33.

20. Greenberg, "Ezor magen" (Defense Zone), in ibid., pp. 112–13.

21. David Horowitz, *Haetmol sheli* (Tel-Aviv, 1970), pp. 105–12.

22. Berl Katznelson, "Bamivhan" (On Trial), in *Kol kitvei*, vol. 6 (Tel-Aviv, 1947), p. 387.

23. Zalman Epstein, "Hagimnazyah haivrit beYafo," *Hashiloah* 25 (1911–12): 150–58.

24. On this point, see Gershom Sholem to Franz Rosenzweig, December 26, 1926, in *Od davar*, ed. Avraham Shapira (Tel-Aviv, 1989), pp. 59–60.

25. Ben-Zion Mossinson, quoted in Ahad Haam, "Hagimnazyah haivrit," *Al parashat derakhim*, 1:152.

26. See, for instance, *Bivritekh: Hoveret lesikum makhaneh hashikhvah habogeret shel hamakhanot haolim biGvat* (Summer 1937): 37ff.

27. Yitzhak Tabenkin, "Mekoroteiha haraayoniim shel haaliyah hashniyah," *Devarim*, 2:25.

28. Yehuda Erez, "Tanakh umasoret bitnuat hapoalim hayehudit," *Niv hakvutzah* (September 1954).

29. Ibid.

30. Ibid.

31. Ibid.

32. Berl Katznelson, "Yizkor," in *Kol kitvei*, vol. 1, p. 202.

33. Eliezer Livenstein, "Hagei avodah umasoret datit," *Kuntres* 375 (Sivan 5, 1929).

34. Ibid. The transformation in the song "Mi ymalel" was brought to my attention by Professor David Berger of Brooklyn College, to whom I am grateful. He also referred me to the verse in Psalms 106:2.

35. Ibid.

36. Josef Sprinzak, cited in Aryeh Ben-Gurion, "Seder pesah, haggadah shel pesah vetekes haomer beEin Harod," *Mibifnim* (Spring 1984).

37. Ibid.; Azaria Allon, "Al hahaggadot shel pesah shel hakibbutzim," *Lamerhav*, April 4, 1967; Getzel Kressel, "Hahaggadot lepesah shel yeshuvei haovdim," in *Sefer Hamoadim*, (1961), ed. Yom Tov Levinsky, vol. 2, pp. 161–69.

38. Allon, "Al hahaggadot."

39. Livenstein, "Hagei avodah."

40. Ibid.

41. Livenstein hinted at the difficulties that accompanied the formulation of the new contents of the holidays. Ibid.

42. Katznelson, "Bamivhan," p. 390. For a reference to the issue of Tisha Beav, see his "Hurban utelishut," in *Kol kitvei*, 6:365–67.

43. Katznelson, "Bamivhan," p. 390.

44. The incident is recorded in Aryeh Ben-Gurion, "Seder pesah."

45. Ibid.

46. Kressel, "Hahaggadot shel pesah."

47. Hanoar Haoved Archives, Kibbutz Hameuhad Archives (KMA), Efal, div. 8, ser. 3, sec. A, file 6.

48. *Kuntresim lashikhvah habogeret*, no. 1, 1937, KMA, div. 8, container 6, ser. 5, sec. A.

49. David Ben-Zvi, "Ehad bemai beEmek Hayarden," *Kuntres* 375 (Sivan 5, 1929).

50. *Protokol moetzet hakibbutz hameuhad beYagur*, April 27–29, 1944, 6th sess., KMA, div. 5, container 8, file 1.

51. *Bamivhan* (February 1945).

Religion, Society, and State during the Period of the National Home

The history of the relationship among religion, state, and society in Palestine during the period of the British mandate and the national home reflects several significant developments, including the institutionalization of ideological trends that emerged in the Zionist movement and the testing of that ideology in the life of a community.

Historically, different solutions evolved in different Jewish settings to the problem of religion and community in the modern era. In Germany and Hungary, some Ultra-Orthodox communities isolated themselves from the general community. In early twentieth-century Eastern Europe, the Jewish communal organization split along religious and national lines. There was also division between Zionists and non-Zionists. While these divisions were related, they did not necessarily overlap.

Religion was a more acute issue for the Yishuv than for the Zionist Organization. The Jewish community in Palestine was unique: it reflected the entire gamut of Jewish attitudes toward religion and included Ultra-Orthodox elements who immigrated in the nineteenth century, traditional Jews who identified with Zionist ideals, as well as Zionist pioneers and intelligentsia who opposed all forms of institutionalized religion, and even elements that rejected religion itself. Moreover, the vision of Eretz Israel as both a holy land and projected national homeland meant that the community had to provide not only for present needs but also to strive to respond to each group's aspirations.

The constitutional solution to the status of religion in Palestine reached toward the end of the mandatory period is known as the *status quo* agreement. It established minimal standards for the Jewish character of the public sphere such as Sabbath observance and *kashrut* (dietary laws), placed matters of personal status such as marriage and divorce under rabbinical law, and awarded autonomy to a separate sector for religious education.

The *status quo* agreement may be examined on different levels. On one level, we may inquire if and to what extent it laid the foundation for a spiritual renewal that stressed the common Jewish denominator over and above regulation of conflict. On another level, the agreement served to facilitate co-existence among the deeply divided, even irreconcilable, segments of the Jewish community. Nonetheless, its status was precarious; by its very nature it was doomed to recurring crises and deadlocks. More substantively, we may claim that the *status quo* agreement violated the rights of men, and especially women, as well as restricting Jewish religious life and renewal to an Orthodox halakhic interpretation.

The concrete solutions set forth in the *status quo* agreement do not exhaust the possible responses to the thorny relationship among religion, state, and society in the Yishuv. Essential issues beyond questions of Sabbath observance and dietary laws, the nature of public life, and the status of the rabbinate were at stake, brought to the fore by the shift from diaspora settings to an emerging political entity in Palestine. The practical nature of the solution bears witness to the Yishuv's inability to address the fundamental issue of the role of religion in society. Rather, compromise was a means of enabling various sectors to cooperate in establishing a new order. The fact that a majority of the religious sector in Palestine accepted these compromises illustrates the primacy awarded to shared political goals over religious tradition or adherence to Jewish law.

In and of itself the Zionist territorial and political solution to the Jewish question was not inimical to religion and could be implemented without impairing the religious way of life. Nonetheless, *de facto*, Zionism established a new national priority in Jewish life. Religion became secondary to national existence; at the same time, nationalism absorbed and transformed religious symbols. This shift permitted, or at least facilitated, maintenance of a Jewish identity that did not require an explicit commitment to the Jewish religion. We must note, however, that this new definition of Jewish identity denied the option of conversion to another religion.

The shift to nationalism as the basis for Jewish life raised fundamental questions regarding the role of religion despite the traditional bond between religion and nationalism. For Jews, Zionism contributed to the process of secularization. Although religious Zionists asserted that the "return to the land" had the potential to retard secularization, in actuality the realization of Jewish national aspirations, with the renewed exposure to nature, life, and secular scholarship, could distance Jews from religion.

The secularization of European society in general was influenced by the rise of values that superseded, but did not necessarily negate, religion, in a process whereby the material world took precedence over the spiritual realm. For many Jews, Zionism, with its stress on productivity, literary creativity, political organization, and defense, filled the role of the primacy of the material world as opposed to the traditional "ghetto" image. In their conflict with the Jewish religious mores, nationalistic circles were influenced by elements of a general European critique of religion based upon a negative assessment of religion's role in history. The historian Edward Gibbon and the anthropologist John Frazer blamed Christianity for the fall of the Greek city-states and the Roman Empire. In their view, by substituting individual redemption for communal responsibility, Christianity undermined the foundation of political and social involvement. As a result, contemplation took precedence over fulfillment of civic responsibilities.

This critique was not fully applicable to Judaism. Unlike Christianity, Judaism is a this-worldly religion that does not focus upon the inner life of the individual. Nonetheless, the opposition to historical activism and the shift in emphasis from national building to Torah study could be interpreted as a stumbling block to renewed national existence. A long line of critics, ranging from Yehuda Leib Gordon to Saul Tchernikhovsky, condemned traditional Judaism for abandoning the political and economic spheres. In general, Jewish life in Eastern Europe was regarded as the epitome of *galut* (exile) existence, defined not only politically as dispersion, subjection, and persecution but as withdrawal from active involvement in this-worldly life in favor of Torah study and petty commerce. Secular proponents of Zionism blamed religion for this retreat from "life." From a religious viewpoint this trend could be attributed to historical circumstances that should be altered for the sake of religion.

Thus the image of Jewish religion as antagonistic to historical activism often prevented secular Zionists from seeing it as a potential partner in the national rebirth, despite Judaism's quasi-national liturgical themes and the religious nature of the bond to the land. Unlike other national colonizing movements, in which religion sometimes served as an energizing factor, in the Jewish case, religion was seen as engendering passivity and lack of progress toward modernization.

Having briefly surveyed the encounter between Zionism and religion from the nationalistic viewpoint, we must now examine nationalism from the point of view of religion. From the late eighteenth century, Judaism and the religious Jewish community faced a series of upheavals that called their beliefs, historiosophical outlook, and the halakhic system into question. Religious toleration and civil equality, the open society (economic, intellectual, and artistic), the processes of modernization, and contact with other cultures necessitated a Jewish response.

It is well known that the Jewish response ranged from isolationist tendencies at one extreme to assimilation or reduction of Judaism to a creed at the other. The potential contribution of the Zionist movement to solving the dilemma of Judaism in the modern world was controversial. Many religious Jews rejected Zionism's historical activism, fearing the deleterious effects on the sacred Jewish community of active messianism, cooperation with nonreligious Jews, and attainment of political power. Alternately, it was possible to view Zionism as a vehicle for Jewish religious revival. The return to Palestine and the restoration of the national communal structure were believed by some to have the potential to spark a Jewish religious renaissance.

Religious thinkers like Yehiel Michal Pines and Rabbi Abraham Isaac Kook frequently criticized Jewish diaspora existence on a religious basis, attributing Judaism's loss of contact with the diverse spheres of human activity to the exilic condition. In their view, the detachment from the land and from a broad spectrum of professions and activities not only weakened the Jewish social fabric but impoverished Judaism itself. According to the historian of religion Max Wiener, in the modern era the Jewish community lost its integrative, all-embracing function for both the Orthodox and Reform denominations, becoming in most areas part of general society. Only the specifically religious domain remained Jewish. In effect, the Zionist idea offered the option of restoring the total communality that had characterized traditional Jewish society.[1]

A different viewpoint tested the role of Eretz Israel in determining the vitality of Judaism in contrast to other religions, especially Christianity. Martin Buber, for example, did not see the era as one of religious decline. Nonetheless, he feared that at present Judaism could not meet the challenge of other religions and argued that the path to renewed Jewish creativity lay in the formation of a new Jewish community in Palestine. On the other hand, Buber also saw transcendental values as essential to cultural growth, and in this respect Jewish culture could not develop in Israel without such values.[2]

I

The problematical nature of the relationship between religion and the national Yishuv was the result of the nature of Jewish religion on the one hand and social and historical preconditions on the other. Judaism does not stress individual commitment to theological content; rather, it emphasizes the strong individual-communal bond as expressed through Halakhah. An essential part of the faith is belief in the divine covenant and identification with the shared history of the Jewish people. The halakhic precept binds the individual to the people and renders the community as a whole sacred. This is the source for the overwhelming importance of the public domain in Jewish life.

The composition of the Zionist movement and the social origins of the immigrants also played a role in the question of religion's status in the Yishuv. In the Zionist movement, as well as among the immigrants, the majority espoused a secular outlook. Those traditional Jewish groups that joined the Yishuv were characterized by isolationist tendencies, by strict adherence to Halakhah. Thus, at this juncture a revolutionary movement—Zionism—confronted a conservative stage of religion. By and large, both Zionist and non-Zionist religious Jews were influenced by the Eastern European brand of Orthodoxy. Neither the German modern Orthodox *Torah vederekh eretz* movement, nor certainly, the Reform and Conservative movements, had any sway.

The Zionist movement was ideologically unprepared to deal with the knotty problems raised by the relationship among religion, state, and society in the Yishuv during the mandatory period. From its inception the Zionist movement skirted essential questions of Jewish existence. Political partnership became the answer to the question of Jewish identity, thereby enabling religious Jews to maintain their belief in the divine covenant and secular Jews to believe in a nation united by territorial, linguistic, and historical links. But ideological definitions aside, the public sphere became the test case for the nature of the Jewish community. A public domain in which essential precepts like the Sabbath or Jewish dietary laws were deliberately abrogated could lead only to an open break with the religious community.

Conversely, the nonobservant Eastern European immigrants were extreme in their opposition to institutionalized religion. In their eyes, adherence to Halakhah retarded both individual and communal development and represented the negative aspect of *galut* society. Among the Eastern European immigrants who set the intellectual tone in the Yishuv, literature—not theology—was considered a supreme spiritual achievement, the guide to a renewed, full Jewish existence. The theological speculation characteristic of German Jewry played a minor role in the Yishuv. In general, the members of the Yishuv viewed religion as an impediment to economic activity and modernization.

Religion was not a new issue in the Zionist movement, nor did it relate solely to the nature of Jewish organization in the diaspora or to the question of Jewish society in the Yishuv and the future Jewish state. Essentially, from the first Zionist Congresses the debate centered on the legitimization of a secular Jewish nationalism characterized by secular culture and education. In the post-Herzl era this debate intensified, with the augmented involvement of the Zionist Organization in the educational and cultural activity of the Yishuv.

This involvement aroused opposition among the religious Zionists, the Mizrahi in particular. Its position was that the Zionist Organization should restrict its activities solely to the political sphere and refrain from direct involvement in educational activity. Nonetheless, the majority of Mizrahi members chose not to break with the Zionist Organization over this issue at the Tenth Congress (1911). Instead, they later opted for a semi-autonomous religious educational sector in the Yishuv.[3] However, although Mizrahi reluctantly complied with the existence of secular Jewish education and culture in the Yishuv, it found public violation of the precepts of Jewish law untenable. Even prior to World War I Mizrahi spokesmen demanded that the Sabbath be observed in settlements on National Fund land. Rabbi Meir Berlin formulated a statement of the principle that was to guide his party in the postwar period: "The private sphere is not our concern, but rather the public violation of religious precepts."[4] While the Mizrahi cooperated with nonreligious Zionists and gave *de facto* recognition to a secular society, it could not tolerate a public domain that denied essential precepts of Judaism, just as it could not recognize a Jewish Christian or a Jewish Muslim.

Rabbi Berlin's statements reflected Mizrah's tactical dilemma: it was caught in the cross-fire of the Ultra-Orthodox Agudat Israel (founded in 1912) and the secular Zionists. The response of the secular spokesmen at the congress was characteristic and a precursor of future developments, that is, the total rejection of imposition of religious precepts by the Zionist Organization. For secular Zionists, self-sacrifice for the national cause became the defining Jewish characteristic, not adherence to Jewish law. For his part, Rabbi Berlin argued that neglect of traditional Jewish values could endanger the transmission of national loyalty to succeeding generations.

Within the Yishuv both the Zionist intelligentsia and the labor movement contributed to the increased secularization of the new settlements. However, different trends existed within the labor camp. Anticlerical and even antireligious attitudes met with yearnings for a spiritual revival inspired by quasi-religious themes. Characteristically radical tendencies stressing individual liberty and rational thought prevalent in European labor movements were mitigated by the aspiration to create a new Jew through productive labor on the land.

The growing labor movement in Palestine also mitigated the more extreme elements of its European background. The Bund's extreme rationalistic and materialistic ideology for example, with its aggressively antireligious attitude, which viewed religion as contradictory to knowledge, freedom, and historical activity, was seen as detrimental not only to Jewish religion but to Zionist nationalism on account of its implicit and explicit rejection of the Jewish historical heritage and bond to the Land of Israel. Within the Zionist and Palestine labor movement, new ideas current in turn-of-the-century Hebrew literature stressing "inner personal truth" gained the upper hand. While the labor pioneers rejected halakhic Judaism as such, yet the encounter with the land, the Bible, and Jewish history had elements of a quasi-religious experience. Although the spiritual nature of this experience prevented the predominance of radical rationalism and atheism, it also enhanced the rejection of formal institutionalized religion.[5]

For laborites the decisive plane for communal partnership was not religious faith but rather the united effort to build an independent productive Jewish commonwealth based on "liberated labor." Religious partnership was regarded as secondary or even irrelevant in this venture.

As previously noted, within the labor movement itself no consensus on the role of religion in the new society existed. The attitudes of Ber Borochov, on the one hand, and of Berl Katznelson on the other, are indicative. Borochov, the founder and mentor of Poalei Zion, considered the socialist idea an all-embracing expression of the lofty human motives that once belonged to the religious sphere. However, Borochov's definition of socialism as a comprehensive set of philosophical beliefs did not gain total acceptance. At the other end of the spectrum we find Berl Katznelson, who claimed that socialism was not a set of philosophical and religious beliefs.

He regarded religion as a personal matter. Katznelson was willing to tolerate and even sympathize with religious belief, and he did not support waging an active campaign against religion. Nonetheless he opposed the compulsory enforcement of religious precepts.[6]

Thus Zionism was nourished by two contradictory hopes: first that it would provide the conditions for a secular Jewish existence, and second that it would spark a spiritual and/or religious revival. Due to this lack of internal ideological unity, the public sphere became the main bone of contention in the issue of the relationship between religion and society in the Yishuv.

II

The crucial period in the self-definition of the Jewish community was the years following the First World War. Prior to the war the so-called Old Yishuv in Palestine lacked a unified comprehensive organization. Under Ottoman rule the various religious communities enjoyed extensive autonomy in matters of religion and personal status. Although the Jewish community was officially represented by the Sephardi chief rabbi, the Hakham Bashi, due to internal divisions within the Sephardi community his status had declined. The Ultra-Orthodox Ashkenazi sector was self-regulating. In general, the various ethnic communities were only loosely bound under the aegis of the official representation. At the same time, the settlers, workers, and intelligentsia of the New Yishuv were engaged in building their own forms of organization—local communities, cultural associations, and political organizations. However, these forms did not reach national unity prior to 1914.

The need to organize the divided Jewish community and the predominant influence of the Zionist organization in the Yishuv's life in the wake of the British conquest and the arrival of the Zionist Commission put the basic ideological factors in the diverse Jewish community to the test. Following the British conquest in 1917–18, the Zionist elements in the Jewish community attempted to organize the Yishuv along national and democratic lines. This trend was enhanced by the need to present the Jews as a united nation *vis-à-vis* the new dominant power in Palestine.[7]

At that time the Old Yishuv constituted a significant portion of the Jewish community. Three factors distinguished the Orthodox community from the national idea of organization: religion, inner ethnic and collegiate divisions, and undemocratic communal rule. The conflicting principles were expressed on three planes: the general organization of the Yishuv, the local communal organization, and the institution of the Chief Rabbinate.

However, the predominant role of the Zionist representatives during the first period of British rule drove even the Ultra-Orthodox sections to consent to a common structure for the Yishuv. From the religious point of view, there were two alternatives to such an arrangement. The first was to confine it to secular affairs and to exclude any spiritual matters, a line initially followed by the Mizrahi in the Zionist movement. But this option was inapplicable to communal life in Palestine. The second option was to base the organization on Orthodox lines. Whereas the idea of a national democratic organization envisaged a new secular Jewish law, distinct from religious law, as well as a new national educational system, the conception of the Ultra-Orthodox and even Orthodox Jews of the Mizrahi type was totally different.[8] In the proposals presented to the Second Constituent Assembly in July 1918, they stated their conditions for the organization of the Yishuv.

These proposals outlined a community that would adopt the law of the Torah as binding in all spheres of life—agriculture, industry, and education. The community would be governed by halakhic law as set forth in the Shulhan Arukh and not by secular Jewish law. Moreover, they insisted that public officials not descecrate the sancta of the nation.[9]

This was a far cry from the national democratic idea. The following story illustrates the encounter between these conflicting concepts and its results.

The endeavors to organize the Yishuv and the qualified readiness of the Orthodox wing to cooperate in this effort brought about the politicization of both the Mizrahi in Palestine and sections of the Old Yishuv. Mizrahi was well established in the Zionist Organization, but almost nonexistent in the Yishuv. The Old Yishuv, which comprised a significant part of the Jews in Palestine, was not represented in the Zionist Organization.

The nucleus of Mizrahi in Palestine grew out of an Orthodox school network. This origin signaled in a certain sense a change in the orientation of Mizrahi in general. It no longer opposed the inclusion of cultural work in the agenda of the Zionist Organization; rather, it now opted for an autonomous sector in the general Zionist educational system. In 1920 the Zionist Actions Committee in London approved a separate religious trend in the general framework of the Zionist education system, and Mizrahi in Palestine worked to implement this decision.[10]

In spite of the far-reaching differences on the very basis of the Jewish community, during the formative years 1918–20 there was a certain readiness on the part of the Orthodox camp to accept an operational partnership with the secularists and to take part in the organization of the whole community. The stumbling block was woman suffrage. The Ultra-Orthodox wing refused to acknowledge the right of women to vote, while in the New Yishuv women were considered equal partners in the building of a pioneering society. In the first elections to the Assembly of the Yishuv (1920), a compromise solution accorded the Ultra-Orthodox a double vote as compensation for the abstention of women in this constituency. This compromise did not last beyond the elections to the First Assembly. In 1925 the Ultra-Orthodox seceded from the Elected Assembly, and in 1928 they did not join the official Jewish community recognized by the mandatory authorities.

Woman suffrage was not the only obstacle to unification of the Jewish community in Palestine. Problems existed on the local plane and in the sphere of the Rabbinate as well. On the local plane the community of Jerusalem became the test case for the possibility of uniting the varied elements in the Jewish population.[11]

In March 1918 the Zionist representation initiated a joint communal committee in Jerusalem in order to unite the New and Old Yishuv, the Ultra-Orthodox, Orthodox, and secularists in addition to the various ethnic groups. Here not only basic principles but tangible interests were at stake. The Old Yishuv as well as the ethnic groups controlled both educational and welfare institutions. An attempt to secure satisfactory representation for all the segments of this society by means of a complicated electoral system was only partially successful. The Ashkenazi colleges refused to join the general community. This refusal laid the foundation for a separate Ashkenazi community that later became the Ultra-Orthodox sector.

A similar phenomenon occurred in the field of the Rabbinate. For national reasons the Zionist Organization was interested in a united Rabbinate; thus the Zionist faction became a unifying factor in the rabbinical field as well.[12]

In April 1918 the traditional elements in Jerusalem made an attempt to establish a Jerusalem Rabbinate Committee that would unite Ashkenazim as well as Sephardim. Such a committee could have been considered a supreme religious authority in a wide sense and, more narrowly, a supreme court of appeals. Due to differences of opinion, which were only partially related to the problem of cooperation with the Zionist elements, this committee disintegrated. Clearly, the traditional communities and institutions lacked the capacity to form a united religious authority even when Zionism was not directly concerned.

In late 1918 the Zionist Commission established a Rabbinical Office in Jerusalem that should have constituted a united religious authority, but its authority was limited. The initiative to establish the Chief Rabbinate came from the British mandatory government and stemmed from the needs of the British mandatory authorities.

Under the Ottoman constitution the non-Muslim minorities enjoyed certain cultural-religious autonomous rights subject to the supreme authority of Muslim law. The new administration had to determine the status and rights of the various communities within the new constitutional framework. In the case of the Jewish community, the problem was twofold: it was not only a question of the country's general constitution but of the inner structure of the community as well. The chief rabbi, the Hakham Bashi, was still the officially recognized religious head of the community. But the Sephardi community that elected him was in disarray, and the numerous Ashkenazi communities of various religious shades did not accept his authority.

The mandatory government established two committees to advise on the organization of the religious communities in the country in general and the Jewish community in particular. The initiative to establish a Chief Rabbinate as a central religious authority sparked a debate within the Jewish community.

In the early 1920s the Jewish community was polychromatic and even polarized. The Ultra-Orthodox on the one hand and the freethinkers on the other did not support a Chief Rabbinate. The Ultra-Orthodox preferred autonomous communities and voluntary courts without a supreme authority or court of appeals, while the freethinkers endeavored to establish a secular legal system. The only public factor that found the establishment of a Chief Rabbinate compatible with its ideological premises was the Mizrahi, which at that time constituted a small minority within the Jewish community.[13]

The national intelligentsia faced a grave dilemma. The only way to establish a legally sanctioned Jewish authority was to accept the official Rabbinate. But that also meant that in the land of Jewish rebirth and revival, traditional Jewish law and the traditional authorities would be vested with a power they did not possess in the diaspora. Not only would "meaningless" precepts be imposed on the individual, not only would women be discriminated against, but the community by and large might be removed from productive work and from the whole gamut of life and human experience.[14]

The inner debate brought the problem of the role of the Rabbinate in Jewish history to the fore: Was it a domineering "clerical" power that restricted the rights of the individual and prevented freethinking? At the opposite ends of the political spectrum, both Rabbi Moses Ostrovsky (Hameiri) and A. D. Gordon defended traditional Jewish authority. Let me quote Rabbi Ostrovsky, who tried to differentiate between the battle against clericalism in France and the situation in Palestine: "Are the children of Israel like the French? They [the French] knew and felt that religion chained their hands and feet, their freedom and liberty; whereas the religion of Israel is not opposed to life and liberty—only he who studies Torah is free."[15]

Rabbi Ostrovsky objected to the secessionist trend espoused by Rabbi Samson Raphael Hirsch in Germany, which advocated the withdrawal of the pious from the general community. Rabbi Ostrovsky opposed such a trend in Palestine, inferring instead from the common affiliation with the Zionist Organization the necessity for a united Jewish religious community. Surprisingly, Rabbi Ostrovsky found a "partner" in the labor camp. A. D. Gordon likewise pleaded for the tolerant nature of the traditional Jewish authorities. Like Ostrovsky he praised the Jewish religion for not having governing institutions and disclaimed any resemblance between Judaism and the Christian churches.[16]

The differences of opinion among the Jews themselves on the status of the Rabbinate were reflected in their appearance before the committee of inquiry on the status of the communal religious courts. The options were many: a civil court or a Jewish secular court, plural Jewish religious courts, or a centralized religious system of law. Out of its own considerations the mandatory government opted for the continued existence of religious courts. The Muslims and Christians supported a pluralistic system, and since there was no civil legal system in matters of personal status it was convenient to adopt the existing structure.

The decision to submit matters of personal status to denominational Muslim, Christian, and Jewish courts implied the establishment of a Jewish legal authority. The Jewish representatives were divided on this issue as well. The Sephardi community favored the renewal of the post of the Hakham Bashi; the Ultra-Orthodox favored a plural system comprised of various Jewish courts without a supreme authority. Most of the Jewish representatives recommended the establishment of a supreme Rabbinical Council but felt that its authority should be confined solely to religious matters and that it should avoid interference in secular affairs. The council was envisioned as including an equal number of Ashkenazi and Sephardi Jews and would have two chairmen: an Ashkenazi and a Sephardi.

The Norman Bentwich Committee that recommended the establishment of the Rabbinical Council invested the Jewish community with the right to elect the council and its chairmen; this step gave rise to problems of principle as well as of procedure, as the electoral college was supposed to include laymen as well as rabbis. The proportion between the clerical and lay elements, the nature of the electoral body of the laymen, and the character of these laymen (traditional or not) were controversial points. Another problem may be defined as "Who is a rabbi?" Is ordination alone sufficient, or must he hold a rabbinical post?

On February 23, 1921, sixty-eight rabbis and thirty-four lay representatives of local communities convened in Jerusalem. The Ultra-Orthodox Jews of Jerusalem did not participate, as they refused to accept the authority of the Rabbinical Council as a supreme court of appeals for the various rabbinical courts in the country. This assembly elected a Rabbinical Council composed of six rabbis, three Ashkenazi and three Sephardi. Two chief rabbis, Rabbi Abraham Isaac Kook (Ashkenazi) and Rabbi Yaakov Meir (Sephardi) were elected as chairmen of the Council.

On April 1, 1921, the government officially announced the establishment of the council. Upon its establishment, a sharp argument ensued regarding the status of the three lay counselors to be elected (in accordance with the government's demand) to the Rabbinical Council in addition to eight rabbis. Finally a compromise proposal suggested by Rabbi Kook was adopted. Three laymen "versed in Torah and religiously observant" were to form the council attached to the Chief Rabbinate.[17]

Upon the Rabbinate's establishment, the government insisted that not only should the new religious authority impose the "fundamental principles of the Jewish religion" and bring unity to the Jewish camp, but it should also act in "accordance with the demands of justice and equality of the present era."[18] This demand was made to placate the national intelligentsia, but in reality the government did not interfere in the proceedings of the Rabbinate.

Thus the constitutional framework for Jewish religious life stemmed neither from the Zionist idea nor from the social structure of the Yishuv in 1921. The character of the Rabbinate only partially reflected the social forces and ideological tendencies predominant in the Jewish community. The mandatory regime imposed the mold upon Jewish religious life, a mold that shapes religious life in Israel today. We may speculate about the possible development of religious life in the Yishuv had the government not taken this course. For example, religious institutions might be voluntary in nature, and a separation between religious and secular law might have been effected. Alternately, the inherent logic of the Zionist idea might have led to a liaison between religious and national institutions.[19]

Here the personality of Rabbi Kook played a significant role. Rabbi Kook envisioned the Rabbinate not as institution restricted to Halakhah but as the spiritual mentor of the nation. As such, he conceived it as independent of a secular body like the Zionist Organization. From his point of view, the Chief Rabbinate should lead the nation—and not the religious parties or even the religious pioneers.[20]

Rabbi Kook's attitudes were open to diverse interpretations. He certainly wished to open the Orthodox world to the whole gamut of human experience and to renew Judaism; he believed in a dialectical process that would revitalize tradition on the one hand and sanctify the secular world on the other. This process might have meant the sanctification of national unity and the secular pioneers, but also the domination of Halakhah in all spheres of life.

Rabbi Kook objected to woman suffrage, differing on this point with the leader of Mizrahi, Rabbi Y. L. Fishman (Maimon). The latter was prepared to accept woman suffrage *post factum* and even rejected the idea of rabbinical authority in the political sphere.

The national intelligentsia's opposition to Rabbi Kook was expressed by Joseph Klausner in the electoral college of the Chief Rabbinate. He accused Rabbi Kook of wishing to dominate all views and opinions in the Jewish community. He rejected Rabbi Kook's claim that there is no secular domain in Judaism, that everything is holy. "We—the moderate left wing—wish the revival of Judaism—but by no means the patronage of Judaism on life," said Klausner.[21]

The constitution of the Chief Rabbinate was only one layer in the structure of the Jewish community under the mandatory regime. This layer took precedence due to the government's interest in forming a Jewish legal authority. The fact that the Rabbinate preceded the official organization of the Jewish community made it neither a supreme mentor of the Yishuv nor a political leader. Its status was precarious for several reasons: lack of independent financial resources, controversies between Ashkenazi and Sephardi Jews, disobedience of local courts, and mainly the tense relations between the Rabbinate and the then still unofficial but representative organs of the Yishuv. Moreover, the Rabbinical Council was elected for a period of only three years; it was assumed that once the general organization was established, permanent procedures might be formulated for the election of the Rabbinical Assembly and chief rabbis. But formal procedures were not approved until 1936. Actually the Chief Rabbinate's status could not be determined prior to the establishment of the general organization of the Yishuv, a process that was in its formative stage during the 1920–28 period.

In 1925 the Ultra-Orthodox finally seceded from the Elected Assembly over the issue of woman suffrage. But even before that they expressed their objections to the suggested communal organization presented by the Jewish authorities to the government. The organized Yishuv acted to achieve governmental recognition for a network of local communities united on a national basis, a network to be included in the general national organization. The proposed Jewish national community was supposed to be responsible for a wide area of activities, including education, health, and welfare. The specific nature of the communal organization in Palestine was to be territorial, namely, the municipal unit where Jews constituted a majority was to be identical with the Jewish community.[22]

The internal debate within the Jewish community in the wake of the establishment of the Chief Rabbinate and toward the formulation of the regulations of the official Jewish community clarified the positions of the various factions in the Yishuv—each party's "red lines." The Mizrahi were convinced that the secularists would make no concessions on woman suffrage. The secularists were certain that the Orthodox would make no concessions regarding religious marriages or the rule of rabbinical law in matters of personal status. At a certain point, in 1922, labor representatives David Ben-Gurion and Solomon Schiller suggested civil marriage for those who refused to accept religious law, but they later sacrificed this demand to the need for unity.[23]

The constitution of the Jewish community as approved by the British government in 1927–28 differed considerably from that conceived by the Jewish Elected Assembly and National Council. The Jewish Community (Knesset Israel) was recognized as a religious, not a national, community. The government recognized a pluralistic religious structure in the country that included Jews, Muslims, and Christians and refused to define the Jewish community as a national one. This character did not determine the internal structure of the Yishuv, nor did it grant the Chief Rabbinate a leading role in the community. Supreme authority was vested in the Elected Assembly and the National Council, not in the Rabbinate.

The local Jewish community was officially religious in character but national in fact. The Zionist Organization and the Yishuv authorities obtained the right that only *one* Jewish community be recognized in each settlement, thereby assuring the recognition of Jewish unity. However, the Ultra-Orthodox and Agudat Israel obtained the right to secede from the general community and to establish a separate community on a voluntary basis. Thus the secessionist trend from Germany and Hungary found parallel expression in Palestine.

The Chief Rabbinate was incorporated into the Jewish community approved by the mandatory authorities in 1927–28. This integration presented practical as well as essential problems. First of all, the Rabbinate was financially dependent on the general organization. Moreover, the Jewish communities, which were sometimes identical with the municipal bodies, were authorized to appoint members to the electoral body of the Rabbinate as well as to the local religious councils. Thus nonobservant laymen might be entitled to interfere in the religious establishment. On the other hand, the members of the religious councils had to belong to the authorized Jewish community and thus were under the national body's authority.

This complicated relationship between the Rabbinate and the national organization was prone to tension. An elaborate mechanism of checks and balances was established in order to settle the relations between the two. In case of a disagreement, the Zionist Executive and the Jewish Agency were to arbitrate.

The regulation of the Jewish community put the relation between national loyalty and religious-ethnic loyalty to the test. The attitudes of the two chief rabbis were not identical on this point. Rabbi Kook gave priority to the principle of the basic unity of the Jewish people *(klal Israel)* and maintained his allegiance to the general organization despite his opposition to woman suffrage. Rabbi Yaakov Meir had greater reservations regarding the dependence of the Rabbinate upon the general organization and did not oppose ethnic secessionist tendencies.[24]

This structure could be interpreted in various ways: by secularists as the supremacy of a national organization over a religious establishment, and by the Mizrahi as proof that religion is not a private matter in the Jewish community but an integral part of it, that religious authorities can acquire official and obligatory status. Mizrahi spokesmen could view this outcome as a triumph over the two dichotomous poles that strove to separate religion from the state and the nascent national society. The Ultra-Orthodox strove to achieve separation in order to assure the independence of their courts, schools, and other institutions. The secularists sought a national secular legal system in order to withhold dominion from religious authorities.[25]

Not only was the Rabbinate unsettled institutionally and legally, but its real status remained labile. Its spiritual impact as well as its representative nature remained undefined as well. It was the personality of the chief rabbi and the degree of his cooperation with the Jewish Agency that determined his real status. The chief rabbis were generally Zionists and supported the Zionist political positions versus the British government. On certain occasions, the rabbis expressed their views on the moral aspects of the use of force. One area of friction between the institutions of the Yishuv and those of the Rabbinate was the conflict over the mode of education for children saved from the Holocaust (the "Teheran Children" 1943).[26]

III

Just after the establishment of the Chief Rabbinate and the Jewish communal organization in the late 1920s, at the time of the rapid growth of the Yishuv and the formation of its society and culture in the 1930s, a confrontation occurred on the social level. The Chief Rabbinate had become neither the spiritual mentor of the community as expected by Rabbi Kook nor the "inquisition" feared by freethinkers. In the early 1920s the secularists had feared a domineering Rabbinate; in the early 1930s, observant Jews felt as if they were living in a society that had abandoned its religious Jewish character. It was not just the institutional frailty of the Rabbinate that diminished its influence on the religious character of the Yishuv. The new waves of immigration, together with the process of secularization in the *moshavot* (smaller settlements) and the cities, changed the nature of public life. Nationalism did not cultivate a return to religion; rather, it became a substitute for religion. The national pioneer was estranged from the religious legacy.

Of course, the Fourth Aliyah (1924–26) brought with it a more traditional element from the Polish Jewish middle class. There was also a group of intellectuals from Central and Western Europe who gravitated to the Hebrew University. For these individuals—among them Gershom Scholem, S. H. Bergman, and Ernst Simon—Zionism meant a return to Judaism. But their type of Judaism, learned and unorthodox, was confined to a small circle.

The hedonistic character of urban Jewish life could be criticized not only from a religious point of view. It could also be seen as a change in the nature of Jewish life—the loss of its puritanism and frugality in favor of permissiveness and frivolity. In addition to a religiously based critique of the new urban culture, there was a national, moral, and socialist criticism as well.[27]

Faced with these developments, the Zionist religious camp was caught in a dilemma. On the one hand, the importance of Eretz Israel in general Jewish life increased as a result of the mass immigration, and that further accentuated the Jewish nature of the country. On the other hand, its society grew more and more secular.

The secular nature of the Yishuv diminished the influence of the Mizrahi in the religious camp, where it promoted the Zionist idea; the Ultra-Orthodox of Agudat Israel could claim that its opposition to Zionism had proven correct. Concurrently, the extreme wing in Mizrahi itself grew stronger.

These processes occurred during a unique time in the Zionist Organization. Since 1933 the Mizrahi had not been a member of the Zionist coalition. Although Mizrahi spokesmen insisted that there was no connection between fulfillment of their religious demands and their participation in the Zionist coalition, the atmosphere was influenced by this political constellation. Thus a *Kulturkampf* raged in the Jewish community and the Zionist movement from 1933 to 1935; its outcome laid the foundation for the *status quo* agreement.

The Mizrahi itself essayed different strategies for tackling the situation that emerged during the early 1930s. The party moved permanently between two circles—the circle of Torah-observant Jewry all over the world, be it Zionist or not, and the Zionist circle, be it observant or not.

During the 1933 Mizrahi conference in Cracow, on the eve of the Eighteenth Zionist Congress, the party had to admit failure on both fronts.[28] Rabbi Fishman (Maimon) stated that the organization that had been destined to become "a national religious movement" had become a "partisan movement," one factor among others in the Zionist Organization.[29]

The conference's chief spokesman was Rabbi Moshe Avigdor Amiel.[30] He tried to define a specific brand of Jewish nationalism as well as to direct the movement toward enhancement of the Torah worldwide no less than to participation in the construction of the national home in Palestine. Rabbi Amiel spoke in favor of a uniquely Jewish nationalism that was not simply a combination of Jewish religion and general nationalism. It was to be based on "Israel's love for God and for all the beings created in His image." According to Rabbi Amiel, Jewish nationalism was distinct from the European brand; there was no harmony between Judaism and French or German nationalism for example, just as there was no harmony between Judaism and French or German culture. In fact, he gave precedence to the Torah over the Land of Israel, claiming that whereas the observance of the Torah was an absolute demand, settlement in Eretz Israel was contingent upon the fulfillment of the commandments.

At this conference the Mizrahi changed its platform and stated that the party's task was no longer only the construction of Eretz Israel according to the written and oral Torah but also the strengthening of traditional Jewry in Palestine and the enhancement of its influence in the diaspora.[31]

Rabbi Fishman (Maimon), who stood at the forefront of the struggle for Mizrahi's claims in the Zionist movement, was aware of the dangers inherent in Amiel's attitude. The shifting of emphasis from activity in Palestine to general Torah activity might bring non-Zionists into the Mizrahi and thus entirely alter the nature of the movement.[32] Rabbi Fishman's (Maimon) strong Zionist stance did not diminish his zeal for religious claims. He even hinted at the possibility of violent opposition by the Orthodox wing. In spring 1934 the Mizrahi conference in Palestine resolved to leave the National Council, thus bringing about a split in the Mizrahi itself, to be discussed below.

Characteristically, the Mizrahi did not direct its efforts toward a religious revival in the Yishuv but to the regulation of public life. Rabbi Meir Berlin clearly stated its position:

We are not talking about religion, religious feelings, or other lofty sentiments; he for whom labor is holy has created a "religion of labor," like a divinely gifted artist who bows down and prays to creativity and art. We do not mean this. Our intention and claim is not for a religion, whatever it may be, but to the religion of Moses and Israel. We do not mean a "religious feeling." Each individual may feel whatever he likes but must adhere to religious practice.[33]

Rabbi Berlin reiterated this stance in 1937 when the establishment of a Jewish state seemed imminent. "When one speaks of a Jewish state one should preserve first of all the Jewish specificity and not the all-human. It is the Sabbath and *kashrut* that will shape the nature of our state as a Jewish state."[34]

The Mizrahi encountered opposition in the Zionist Congress and the Zionist Executive Committee as well as in the organs of the Yishuv. It tried to force adoption of a resolution on Sabbath observance during Zionist Congresses in the 1920s. Attempts to impose the observance of the Sabbath through municipal ordinances failed, as the government refused to enforce these laws. In 1932 the Elected Assembly of the Jewish community demanded that all the local councils and communal committees "recognize the Sabbath and holidays in life" as public days of rest in all branches of the economy and that the mandatory government be asked to implement this recognition by law.[35]

The Mizrahi had presented religious claims at the Eighteenth Zionist Congress in 1933.[36] Its far-reaching demands, which were rejected for procedural reasons, included not only an absolute prohibition of work on the sabbath on National Fund land and obligatory *kashrut* in public restaurants but also related to use of leisure time by proposing the prohibition of trips and assemblies on the Sabbath and other holidays. In addition, the Mizrahi demanded that the Jewish Agency ask the government to authorize the municipalities to legislate the public nature of the Sabbath and holidays and thus to shape their character.[36]

The Zionist leadership initially tried to ignore the Mizrahi's religious claims by objecting to any form of religious compulsion and by speaking in favor of mutual respect and toleration. Only on the topic of the Sabbath were the Zionist leaders ready to recognize a day of rest as a national value. But the Zionist Executive soon learned that the Sabbath had become a crucial issue. On March 27, 1934, a session of the Zionist Actions Committee became a forum for the discussion of the relation between religion and the emerging society, the most essential debate on this issue in the history of the Yishuv.[37]

Rabbi Berlin presented the Mizrahi position. He complained that the issue was no longer the "desecration of the Sabbath" but the "abolition of the Sabbath." *Kashrut* in public restaurants was the other decisive point. Rabbi Berlin made a connection between the fact that the Mizrahi did not belong to the Zionist coalition and the religious situation. He blamed the secularists, and particularly the labor camp, saying that the exclusion of the Mizrahi from the coalition created a psychological predisposition to the violation of religious precepts.

The leaders of the Mizrahi were not alone in their criticism. Even a devoted Zionist like Menaham Ussishkin thought that the abandonment of the Jewish religious character undermined the very nature of Jewish life in Palestine. In his view, desertion of tradition, schools that eliminated Jewish content, and disrespect for the family diminished the national value of Eretz Israel *vis-à-vis* the diaspora. He objected to the antireligious ideology that prevailed on the fringes of the pioneering camp. But even more, he denounced the hedonistic and frivolous bourgeoisie of Tel-Aviv. In this he agreed with the labor leaders who claimed that the profanation of Jewish life was not class based. But he also maintained that the Zionist Executive was powerless to change the situation, "even if Rabbi Kook were a member." He felt that change might come only through the influence of thinkers.

The response of the labor leaders to the Mizrahi's challenge should be examined on the tactical level as well. Naturally, they needed the support of the religious camp in their struggle against Revisionism; they were aware that the unity of the Jewish community should be maintained. Likewise they had a clear interest in preserving the unity of labor by not alienating the observant workers. But their response emerged from ideological principles as well. In general, but not unanimously, they were sympathetic to religion itself and rejected antireligious activities, but they also objected to any attempt to enforce religious commandments. They conceived of Judaism as a national body, not to be separated from Jewry. This body was in a dynamic process of self-realization that was not directed against religion and religious law but that took precedence over the law. They strove for an open and free Judaism that would not exclude religion but was not solely expressed, let alone exhausted, by religion.

The Jewish character of the laborers' Judaism was clearly expressed by the labor leaders. They defended their rights and status as loyal Jews. For them observance of the law was not a test for their Judaism. Ben-Gurion recast religious values as humanistic and national values, such as justice, honesty, equality, and the love of humanity. Yitzhak Tabenkin, the labor camp's most prominent spokesman, took a historical approach, arguing that *aliyah*, a life of labor, acquisition of the Hebrew language, and the formation of a real bond to the homeland were no less significant than the observance of halakhic tenets. He defined the Jewish identity of the laborers as resting upon "Jewish totality and historical unity." Tabenkin accused the religious spokesmen of stirring up controversy. To him, who claimed to represent the Jewish legacy in its entirety, their objections appeared to defame the nature of the Sabbath in Palestine. In his view, there was no place in the world where the Sabbath was so truly felt as in Tel-Aviv, the *moshavim, kibbutzim*, or the Jewish suburb of Hadar Hacarmel in Haifa. His point could be interpreted as referring to the traditional observance of the Sabbath, stronger in Palestine than in the diaspora, but it could also be understood as noting a new mode of Sabbath observance.

Throughout this debate Berl Katznelson took a position that differentiated between the attitude to religious instruction and religion itself and the attempt to impose obedience to the Halakhah. He repeatedly asserted that there was no link between religion and coercion and that the debate was pernicious to both Zionism and religion. He was ready to refrain from work on Saturdays but rejected any attempt to impose a religious mold on leisure by prohibiting, for example, travel on the Sabbath and holidays. Katznelson was sensitive to the combination of religious and national themes, and thus he was prepared to support legislation prohibiting the sale of pork in the Tel-Aviv area. But he insisted on maintaining the balance between the observance of inherited values and the imposition of religious commandments.

The Actions Committee's resolutions concerning religious demands were soon forthcoming. They confirmed the resolutions adopted by the Elected Assembly of 1932 on the Sabbath as a rest day, adding a resolution prohibiting labor in construction, agriculture, industry, and commerce on Jewish holidays. The Sabbath was proclaimed to have both religious and national value. Although the Mizrahi should have been pleased with this outcome, its adherents claimed that these resolutions were not implemented.

In the 1935 session of the Zionist Actions Committee the representatives of the Mizrahi brought the religious issue to the fore.[38] But they made a tactical error. Rabbi Berlin based his arguments on the importance of religion from the national point of view. He admitted that it was difficult for him to present religion as a means toward a national end; nonetheless, he adopted this line in the hope that it would influence the labor camp. Moshe Shapiro referred to religious yearnings within the labor camp itself. Both spokesmen received a sharp rebuttal from Berl Katznelson. In spite of his sympathetic stance on religion, he refused to allow discussion of these issues in the committee.

Relations between the Mizrahi and the Zionist Executive deteriorated, and at the Nineteenth Zionist Congress in 1935, the Mizrahi seceded from the forum as well as from the presidium and the committees.[39] This time the controversy was resolved on the lines of the 1934 Zionist Actions

Committee resolution by unofficial negotiations and by the force of circumstances in general. At this Congress the Mizrahi joined the Zionist Executive chaired by Ben-Gurion. Moreover, the three preceding years of controversy had demonstrated to both parties the limits of their ability to impose their way of life on each other. The controversy had also made clear that while the Mizrahi was reluctant but willing to cede the total rule of Halakhah, it was not prepared to compromise on the Jewish religious character of public life. This was the "soul of the nation" and must not be violated.

From the late 1920s on, internal divisions within Mizrahi intensified, and support for the struggle inside the Zionist Organization was not unanimous. Some Mizrahi members in Palestine (the "Veteran Mizrahi") as well as some members in Germany objected to the aggressive attack on freethinkers and the rejection of the Yishuv's socialist tendencies. Others recommended integration into the Zionist institutional framework to enhance the Mizrahi's influence in the educational and settlement sectors. To them, the positive impact on society in general seemed more meaningful than imposition of legal prohibitions. In the social sphere, they accepted two sectors—private and labor—and would not reject a life of labor as sacrilegious.[40]

When the Mizrahi conference in Palestine decided to secede from the National Council in spring 1934, this latter group within the Mizrahi declined to go along with the rest. They defined secession as manifesting the erroneous thinking that preferred "accidental political gains" to "permanent and silent work." Participation in the national institutions was a precondition for conducting a whole range of educational work. These differences caused a rift in Mizrahi that was mended only after the Nineteenth Zionist Congress in 1935 and the agreement reached between the Mizrahi and the other parties.[41]

The "Veteran Mizrahi" was an ephemeral phenomenon in the Zionist religious camp. Much more significant was Hapoel Hamizrahi, which was founded in 1922 and became a rising force in the movement. Hapoel Hamizrahi was in accord with the larger Mizrahi movement as far as observance of Halakhah in public life was concerned. But it sought enforcement of the commandments as well as a common spiritual ground for the Yishuv. As an integral part of the labor and pioneering camp it viewed the religious tradition as a shared foundation.[42]

Hapoel Hamizrahi itself was comprised of at least three factions, but the dominant trend interpreted Jewish tradition as a revolt against the conditions of *galut*. *Galut* was comprehended not only as discrimination against Jewish individuals and the Jewish collective but also as an impediment to religious fulfillment. The content of this fulfillment was interpreted in socialist terms. Capitalistic society was criticized according to religious criteria, thus establishing a link between religious observance and social ethics.

Capitalism, living on interest, and speculation were presented as religious offenses. In this Hapoel Hamizrahi followed the thinking of Yehiel Michal

Pines and Rabbi Kook, who wished to expose Judaism to the whole spectrum of human life with religion as the supreme value. But the content of that "life" was socialist. Its adherents considered themselves a movement of religious renewal; and although they adhered to strict obedience to Halakhah, they criticized the Mizrahi for confining itself to its imposition. In their cry for religious renewal they compared themselves to the *hasidim* and explicitly dissociated themselves from any inclination toward Reform.

Thus although they could have served as a bridge between the religious camp and the general society, the Hapoel Hamizrahi succeeded in arousing opposition in the Orthodox religious camp and, to a lesser extent, among the workers. Some feared that its attempt to adhere to the labor camp might dilute its religious allegiance; others feared that the link to the Mizrahi might distance it from the general labor movement. Hapoel Hamizrahi constituted a relatively small faction that tried to identify with the Zionist revolution and give it a religious tinge. The close relations with the general labor movement and the strengthened position of Hapoel Hamizrahi after the 1944 elections to the Elected Assembly enabled it to push forward some restrictions on work on the Sabbath.

IV

Nonpartisan writers and thinkers also faced the problem of the character of Jewish life in the Yishuv, going beyond Halakhah and political alignments. Particularly outstanding was Hayim Nahman Bialik's endeavor to shape the Sabbath in Tel-Aviv. Bialik did not rely upon legal prohibitions; rather, he tried to imbue the Sabbath with positive content. This attitude was integrated with a general view that advocated the encounter of Jewish tradition with the whole range of human life and experience. Unlike religious thinkers, he did not define the tradition in halakhic terms as a predetermined obligatory canon; rather, he considered it a cultural legacy. Its cultural assets could serve as a fountainhead for new Jewish forms of life. The living language, theater, architecture, and even the marketplace should, in Bialik's view, be inspired by the traditional concepts and, at the same time, breathe new life into them.[43]

The mental atmosphere of the Yishuv shifted in the 1940s. At this point it came of age. The Holocaust obligated the Yishuv to consider itself not only as a corrective to *galut* but as responsible for the entire Jewish legacy. Moreover, a new generation was growing up in Palestine, and the content of its Jewish identity was an acute problem for educators. The land, the Hebrew language, and the Bible by themselves no longer could be considered sufficient spiritual basis.

It was not accidental that in August 1943, when information about the Holocaust first reached the Yishuv, a group of writers, scholars, and thinkers

—Orthodox and non-Orthodox—appealed to the Yishuv for the observation of the Sabbath. At that critical moment these intellectuals found devotion to military and political tasks devoid of spiritual content insufficient. The Sabbath came to symbolize spiritual as well as family values. Its religious-national nature was presented as inseparable from its social-humanistic content.[44]

At the same time, small circles of "pathseekers" came into being. They went beyond institutionalized religion, having nothing to do with Mizrahi or even Hapoel Hamizrahi. They did not join in the demands of the religious camp for religious legislation or for benefits for the religious sector. Instead they sought the inner value of religion. At the same time they resisted any attempt to cast them as a brand of religious Reform movement.

The initiators of these circles came from varied social origins. Some came from Germany or Central Europe and were affiliated with Hebrew University. Others came from writers' circles, and still others came from the labor movement, transferring the spiritual experience of renewal from the social-historical plane to the religious one.

A variety of factors motivated those who joined these circles. Some were affected by the times: the events that led to the Second World War brought disillusionment with humanist culture and the idea of progress in history. The capitulation of intellectuals to fascism seemed to indicate the weakness of secular culture. In addition, there was a growing unease with the supreme cultural values of the Yishuv like "nation" and "class." Others confronted the eternal plight of the individual in a godless world, the wasteland of human existence in the face of death. The combination of nation and religion in Judaism directed any religious urge to Jewish sources.

The first conferences of these circles were held in the early 1940s; the most notable was in 1942. Conferences continued in various forms into the 1950s and 1960s.[45]

From its inception the movement was ideologically heterogeneous. In a certain sense, these differences of opinion were characteristic of the internal difficulties faced by every Jewish movement of religious revival. The relation between the personal experience of belief on the one hand and tradition, precepts, institutions, and authority on the other presents obstacles to such movements in the Jewish context. In these circles, some adherents defined themselves as seekers for a "religious experience" and endeavored to build the nation's life on the basis of this experience. Naturally this trend wished to attach the inner experience to Jewish sources but also to preserve freedom of interpretation. Others were in search of Jewish tradition as manifested in Halakhah. Yet, all these pathseekers had to ask themselves whether ritual or social action was the proper outlet for religious feeling.

The differing attitudes of these circles to Martin Buber typify these dilemmas. Buber, who came to Palestine in 1938, could have served as a link to Central European Jewish theological thought; he also sought to endow religion with real significance on the social plane. But Buber rejected obedience to Halakhah in principle as well as in action. Thus the Orthodox circles considered him sacrilegious, while the pathseekers found in his figure and his teaching a superb manifestation of the vitality of Jewish religion.

V

The final stage in the confrontation between the Zionist society and religion occurred in the summer of 1947. This period, which also marks the transition from mandatory rule to an independent state, saw the emergence of the *status quo* agreement. Like the previous arrangements discussed above, the *status quo* agreement was dictated by external and internal political circumstances and contained no definitive exposition of the relationship among the state, society, and religion. Nor was it reached by majority decision; rather each side tried to meet the others' minimum demands, taking its most inflexible positions into consideration.

The *status quo* agreement between the Jewish Agency and Agudat Israel was confirmed in summer 1947. At this juncture a visit from a United Nations Committee (UNSCOP) was in the offing, and the Jewish Agency was interested in presenting a united Jewish front.[46]

Agudat Israel itself belonged neither to the Zionist movement nor to the organized Yishuv. Large sections of its membership supported this separationist trend, advocating dissociation from the community at large due to its nonobservance of Halakhah. Nonetheless, conditions in 1947 created a climate whereby certain elements in Agudat Israel favored political cooperation with the Jewish Agency, and a majority of its membership backed the demand for the founding of a Jewish state. While its support for the Jewish Agency's political aims was surprising, Agudat Israel's position that there should be a connection between the state-to-be and religion was even more so. Although the Agudah had profound reservations regarding a Jewish political entity in the form of a state, it found the idea of such an entity without minimal adherence to halakhic standards wholly unacceptable.

For its part, although the Jewish Agency aspired to attain political unity, it was confined not only by the will of the Jewish majority but also by the external political constraint that required a democratic rather than a theocratic Jewish state.

The final agreement between Agudat Israel and the Jewish Agency took the form of a letter composed by the Jewish Agency Executive. Its signatories were David Ben-Gurion, chairman of the Jewish Agency Executive, Rabbi Y. L. Fishman of the Mizrahi, and Yitzhak Gruenbaum a radical Zionist known for his antireligious views.

In effect, the *status quo* agreement was similar to prior arrangements reached between the Mizrahi and secular elements in the Yishuv. It specified trends and aspirations, not absolute commitments binding the parties. The Sabbath was designated as the official day of rest in the Jewish state, essentially confirming the decision reached at the Nineteenth Zionist Congress in 1935. In addition, Agudat Israel was promised continued autonomy in education, as Mizrahi had enjoyed since 1920 within the frameworks of the Zionist Organization and the National Council. No explicit promises were made for future legislation regarding personal status. However, the enunciation of the following guiding principle—"to prevent the division of the Jewish nation into two nations"—mitigated against the establishment of a nonhalakhic framework for marriage and divorce.

This letter, sent to the world headquarters of Agudat Israel on June 19, 1947 (1 Tammuz 5707), became the basis of the *status quo* agreement on religion in the State of Israel.

Conclusion

Institutionally and constitutionally the period of the Yishuv ended with the *status quo* agreement. We have seen that this agreement, which sanctioned the Chief Rabbinate, set minimal standards for halakhic observance in the public sector, and established a religious sector for education and settlement, emerged from the compelling need for co-existence and as a result of the influence of religious Zionists. We have also noted that for all practical purposes, Agudat Israel also accepted the *status quo* agreement.

This institutionalized arrangement did not reflect the prevailing cultural trends in the Yishuv, and it is doubtful whether it was capable of exercising any substantial influence on them. Cultural pluralism predominated over religion, placing emphases on cooperation in the national venture, opposition to *galut*, the use of Hebrew, the encounter with nature in the land of Israel, and for some, the socialist partnership. Religion lost its absolute authority, and religious loyalties were transferred to the national sphere. On the other hand, there was no active opposition to religious faith *per se* in the Yishuv, and such opposition as existed was marginal in nature.

The institutionalized agreement was primarily the result of a combination of several factors: the need to meet the minimal demands of the religious sector in order to preserve the unity of the Yishuv, the mandatory government's policy, and the bargaining power of the religious Zionist parties. A different balance of power might have led to the development of alternative agreements, perhaps to the creation of two parallel legal systems governing personal status similar to the two sectors in education. Or a different balance might have produced the converse—a unified educational system for both religious and nonreligious students.

As the *status quo* agreement was conditioned by a combination of principled stands and pressing circumstances, in effect it could not answer the essential question of the relationship between religion and society in the Yishuv for either the religious or the secular camps. The *status quo* agreement did not define the essence of Jewish nationhood, nor did it take a decisive stand on the critical dilemma of whether the Jewish people constitute a religious or a national community, although even the national definition held adherence to a different religion untenable. Imposition of halakhic standards in matters of personal status and the insistence on minimal standards of religious observance in Jewish public life enabled the religious Zionists to believe that the national community would not sever itself totally from the traditional concept of *klal Israel*. In its eyes, even if every individual no longer adhered to halakhic precepts, at least the public sphere had not entirely lost its traditional Jewish flavor.

To a certain extent the groundwork for acceptance of individual deviation from Halakhah had already been laid by the process of secularization in the diaspora. With the breakup of the traditional *kehillah* in the European diaspora, it was no longer possible to regulate each individual's behavior. Thus the emphasis shifted to maintaining the religiously identifiable substance of *klal Israel*, the Jewish body-politic as a whole.

The religious Zionists anticipated a change in this state of affairs with the renewal of the settlement in Palestine, to result either from a return to Judaism or from reinstatement of the traditional authority of the *kehillah*. But these hopes never materialized. As we have seen, nationalism did not serve as a bridge to a religious revival; if anything, it had the opposite effect. Moreover, the attempt to invest the local municipal authorities, who represented the *kehillah*, with the power to enforce Sabbath regulations did not meet with success.

The Mizrahi and Hapoel Hamizrahi did not feel compelled to alter their basic ideology despite their recognition of the intrinsically secular nature of Yishuv society. They continued to maintain that legitimate Jewish nationalism could be based only on the Torah and that Zionism was the only legitimate expression of the Jewish religion. This view conflicted with both nonreligious Jewish nationalism and anti-Zionist religious views (like that espoused by Agudat Israel). Nonetheless, proponents of religious Zionism gave precedence to the principle of Jewish unity and a shared Jewish destiny over strict ideological conformity, recognizing the need for joint political action by observant and nonobservant Jews. This priority enabled them to make their peace with both nonreligious nationalistic and non-Zionist religious circles.

The compromises reached during the Yishuv period clearly illustrate the essential dilemma of religious Zionism, shared to a large extent by the non-Zionist religious sector. Forced to accept a Jewish state founded in real and profane historical circumstances, largely by secular Jews inspired by a secular national ideology, they could not grant religious legitimization to either a Yishuv or a state not governed by Halakhah. Certain sectors within the religious Zionist camp adopted an ideological stance legitimating the state as "the beginning of the era of redemption," but this ideology never achieved full consensus. Nevertheless, despite their refusal to sanction a state not governed by Halakhah, neither the religious Zionist camp nor the non-Zionist religious camp of the Agudat Israel type was willing to accept a total separation of church and state in Eretz Israel. In their eyes the state represented the Jewish public sphere and as such had to meet the minimal standards of religious observance stipulated during the period of the Yishuv.

In addition to the institutionalized status of religion in the Yishuv, we must note the existence of the religious political parties. We have already examined the extent to which their existence and influence in the political arena shaped the *status quo* agreement.

The role played by the religious parties in reaching the *status quo* agreement was not determined only by virtue of their political influence or by the weight of their numbers. Nor did it emerge solely from advantages accruing from the existence of a religious establishment on the one hand or from their function as the deciding factor in the composition of the political coalition on the other. The institutional advantages came with the founding of the Rabbinate and the local communal structure, which gave the religious parties control over financial resources and jobs. Their function as the pivotal factor in the political arena dated from the split between Labor and the Revisionists in the 1930s and, with the exception of the late 1950s, continued in the state. We must note that totally different circumstances and needs unrelated to determining the character of the new Yishuv had prompted the founding of the Zionist religious party, Mizrahi. Mizrahi's founders acted on their assessment of the importance of Zionism to Judaism as a social and religious entity. They sought to achieve a dual goal—to spread Zionism among the *haredim* (Ultra-Orthodox) and to prevent the legitimization of a nonreligious Jewish identity. Practically speaking, Mizrahi also attempted to infuse the Zionist movement with religious content to the greatest possible extent.

Upon their realization that they could not prevent the Zionist movement from engaging in cultural and educational activities, the religious Zionists secured an autonomous religious educational sector. At a late date, this demand for a separate sector was extended to other areas, including settlement.

Following the First World War, when building the Yishuv became the focus of the Zionist movement, Mizrahi shifted its attention to shaping the Jewish nature of Yishuv society. Its influence was not only a function of tactical political considerations—in the 1920s Mizrahi had little role in tipping the balance of power on the internal political map. Rather, the religious Jewish camp perceived certain arrangements as crucial if they were to participate in the national venture. No Jewish national body could allow itself to set conditions that would bar participation by the religious parties.

The relationship between religion and society in the Yishuv illustrates two basic dilemmas of the modern Jewish era: first, the co-existence of traditional halakhically bound communities with secular Jews, and second, the transformation of the *kehillah* into a Jewish state. Neither problem permitted a radical solution; thus compromise conditioned by changing social and historical circumstances was sought. Above and beyond the institutional arrangements, the question of the role of religious faith and tradition in general, and of Jewish faith and tradition in particular, within the variegated fabric of the Yishuv, remained open. That the attempts to formulate an answer to this question failed was not simply the result of the multiplicity of trends and influences; the outcome was primarily the consequence of a free Jewish society exposed to independent political life and to non-Jewish cultures.

Notes

1. Max Wiener, *Judische Religion in Zeitalter Der Emanzipation* (Berlin, 1933 [Hebrew ed., Jerusalem, 1974]), pp. 51, 57.

2. Martin Buber, "Yahadut vetarbut," in *Teudah veyiud* (Jerusalem, 1973), 1:226.

3. Y. L. Fishman (Maimon), "Toldot haMizrahi vehitpathuto," in *Sefer Mizrahi* (Jerusalem, 1946), pp. 165–74.

4. See *Haolam shanah hamishit* 5, no. 31 (August 24, 1911): Fifth Congress session.

5. Yehuda Erez, "Tanakh umasoret betenuat hapoalim hayehudit," appended to A. N. Poliak, *Hatanakh vehatenuot hasozialiyot baamim* (Tel-Aviv, 1954).

6. Ber Borochov, "Mah nishtanah proletari," in *Ketavim* (Tel-Aviv, 1966), 3:322–27; Borochov, "Hirhurei pesah shel apikores," in ibid., pp. 328–34.

7. On the organizational efforts of the Yishuv, see *Din veheshbon havaad hazemani leyehudei Eretz Israel, Kislev 1917–Tishri 1921* (Jerusalem, 1921); Moshe Burstein, *Self-Government of the Jews in Palestine since 1900* (Tel-Aviv, 1934); Moshe Attias, ed., *Sefer hateudot shel havaad haleumi likneset Israel, 1918–1948* (Jerusalem, 1963); Attias, *Kneset Israel beEretz Israel: Yisudah veirgunah* (Jerusalem, 1944); Moshe Ostrovsky, *Irgun hayishuv hayehudi beEretz Israel* (Jerusalem, 1942); S. Z. Abramov, *The Perpetual Dilemma* (Cranbury, N.J., 1976), chap. 3; Yitzhak Gilhar, "Hitargenut vehanhagah azmit shel hayishuv beEretz Israel mireshit hashilton habriti ad leishur hamandat (1917–1922)" (Ph.D. diss., Hebrew University, Jerusalem, 1973). For the viewpoint of Agudat Israel and the Orthodox community (*edah haharedit*), see Emile Marmorstein, *Heaven at Bay* (London, 1969), pp. 77–90. For the Orthodox community and the new regime, see Menahem Friedman, *Hevrah vedat* (Jerusalem, 1977), chap. 1.

8. Moshe Ostrovsky, *Toldot haMizrahi beEretz Israel* (Jerusalem, 1944), p. 75; Ostrovsky, "Reshit haMizrahi baaretz," in *Sefer hazionut hadatit*, ed. Yitzhak Rafael and S. Z. Shragai (Jerusalem, 1977), 1:372–87; Geulah Bat Yehuda, *Harav Maimon bedorotav* (Jerusalem, 1979), pp. 245–47; Fishman, "Toldot haMizrahi vehitpathuto," pp. 243–45.

9. Ostrovsky, "Reshit haMizrahi baaretz," p. 373.

10. Ibid., p. 384.

11. Friedman, *Hevrah vedat*, pp. 34–46, 85; Gilhar, "Hitargenut vehanhagah azmit," pp. 250–55; Mordechai Ben-Hillel Hakohen, *Athalta* (Jerusalem, 1931), bk. 1, chap. 10.

12. A. Morgenstern, *Harabanut harashit leEretz Israel* (Jerusalem-Netanyah, 1973), chap. 1; Friedman, *Hevrah vedat*, chap. 2.

13. Attias, *Kneset Israel,* pp. 87–96; Gad Frumkin, *Derekh shofet biYerushalayim* (Tel-Aviv, 1955), pp. 248–49.

14. Geulah Bat Yehudah, "Yisud harabanut harashit vehaMizrahi," in *Sefer hazionut hadatit,* 1:388–431; Burstein, *Self-Government,* chap. 7.

15. Ostrovsky, *Toldot haMizrahi,* p. 33.

16. A. D. Gordon, "Kneset Israel," in *Haumah vehaavodah* (Tel-Aviv, 1957), pp. 209–10.

17. Quoted in Bat Yehudah, "Yisud harabanut harashit," p. 241. See also Frumkin, *Derekh shofet;* Morgenstern, *Harabanut harashit,* chap. 3. For the protocols of the Founding Assembly of the Rabbinate, see Fishman, "Toldot haMizrahi vehitpathuto," pp. 255–90. See, for example, Joseph Klausner's comment, "We cannot allow religion to consume life," ibid., p. 274.

18. Burstein, *Self-Government,* p. 175.

19. See Fishman, "Toldot haMizrahi vehitpathuto," p. 279; Morgenstern, *Harabanut harashit,* chap. 4; Ostrovsky, *Irgun hayishuv,* chap. 1.

20. On Rabbi Kook and the Chief Rabbinate, see Morgenstern, *Harabanut harashit,* chap. 2; Friedman, *Hevrah vedat,* chap. 3; Yossi Avneri, "Degel Yerushalayim," in *Bishvilei hatehiyah: Mehkarim bezionut hadatit,* ed. Mordechai Eliav, vol. 3 (Ramat-Gan, 1988).

21. Quoted in Bat Yehudah, *Yisud harabanut harashit,* p. 413.

22. For the development of the governing rules of Knesset Israel and negotiations with the government, see no. 1, above; and, Leon Stein, "The Development of the Jewish National Home in Palestine," in A. J. Toynbee, "Survey of International Affairs," 1925, in *The Islamic World,* vol. 1 (London, 1927), pp. 376–79; Ostrovsky, *Irgun hayishuv.*

23. For the discussion regarding the authority of the Rabbinate in the National Council on May 22, 1922, see Morgenstern, *Harabanut harashit,* pp. 185–93.

24. On secession from Knesset Israel, see Friedman, *Hevrah vedat,* chap. 8; Abraham Haim, "Hanhagat hasefaradim biYerushalayim veyahaseha im hamosdot hamerkaziim shel hayishuv betekufat hashilton habriti (1917–1948)" (Ph.D. diss., Tel-Aviv University, 1984), chap. 4.

25. Ostrovsky, *Toldot haMizrahi,* chap. 10; *Haveidah hashlishit shel histadrut haMizrahi beEretz Israel* (Jerusalem, Tammuz, 1928).

26. S. Eliash, "Hayahasim bein harabanut harashit leEretz Israel vehashilton hamandatori, 1936–1945" (Ph.D. diss., Bar-Ilan University, 1979).

27. Abramov, *Perpetual Dilemma,* p. 105.

28. Bat Yehudah, *Harav Maimon,* pp. 379–85.

29. See Y. L. Maimon, in *Sefer hazionut hadatit,* 1:12.

30. Rabbi Moshe Avigdor Amiel's speech, "Hayesodot haidiologiim shel haMizrahi," in *Sefer hazionut hadatit,* 1:3–11.

31. See A. Patchenik, "Hatenuah bein shtei milhamot haolam," in *Hazon, torah vezion,* ed. Simon Federbush (Jerusalem and New York, 1960), pp. 204–5.

32. Rabbi Maimon's reply was "Heshbonah shel histadrutenu," *Sefer hazionut hadatit,* 1:12–16.

33. Meir Berlin, speech, in *Haveidah hasheviit shel Hapoel Hamizrahi beEretz Israel, 1935,* ed. Yossi Avneri (Ramat-Gan, 1988), p. 111.

34. See Ostrovsky, *Toldot haMizrahi,* p. 148.

35. See Attias, *Sefer hateudot shel havaad haleumi,* p. 190.

36. The Mizrahi had already presented these demands at the Fifteenth Congress in 1927. See Bat Yehudah, *Harav Maimon,* p. 362. For the debate in the Eighteenth Congress, see *Davar,* January 16, 1934.

37. Hahanhalah hazionit (Zionist Actions Committee), Moshav havaad hapoel hazioni biYerushalayim, 1934.

38. Hahanhalah hazionit, Moshav havaad hapoel hazioni, 1935.

39. Nineteenth Zionist Congress, 20 August–4 September 1935, Lucerne (Jerusalem, 1937), pp. 73ff. See also David Ben-Gurion, *Zikhronot,* vol. 2 (Tel Aviv, 1972), p. 426.

40. Ostrovsky, *Toldot haMizrahi*, chap. 13. See also *Haaretz*, July 15, 1934.

41. Bat Yehudah, *Harav Maimon*, chap. 35, pp. 405–9ff.

42. M. Unna, *Bederakhim nifradot: Hamiflagot hadatiot beIsrael* (Alon Shevut, 1983), chap. 4; Y. Bernstein, "Min hayesod," in *Sefer hazionut hadatit*, ed. Rafael and Shragai, 1:124–35; S. Z. Shragai, "Leheshbonah shel hazionut hadatit vetenuat torah veavodah," ibid., pp. 241:55; A. Fishman, ed., *Hapoel Hamizrahi, 1921–1935* (Tel-Aviv, 1979), introd.; Avneri, ed., *Haveidah hasheviit shel Hapoel Hamizrahi*, introd.; *Diyunei havaad heleumi*, 5 June 1945.

43. Hayim Nahman Bialik, *Devarim shebealpeh* (Tel-Aviv, 1935), bk. 1, *Tehiyat hatarbut beEretz Israel*, pp. 159–165, p. 174.

44. "Kruz hasofrim," *Haaretz*, August 12, 1943.

45. *Hakinus lebeayot hadat* (Haifa, July 1942). The protocol ended with the following decision: "We see the Jewish religion as the foundation for the life of the Israeli nation and for private and social morality." See also D. Sadan, "Mibnei emunah" (about Yitzhak Zimmerman) in *Alufai umeyudaai* (Tel-Aviv, 1974), p. 209. These circles continued their activity in various forms following the founding of the State of Israel. See "Hug amanah upeulotav," *Prozdor* (1963).

46. Jewish Agency Executive meetings, June 16, 1947, and especially June 22, 1947 when Rabbi Fishman (Maimon) tendered his resignation over the issue of mass public desecration of the Sabbath in Dalia M. Friedman, "Veeleh toldot hastatus quo: Dat umedinah beIsrael," in *Hamaavar miyishuv lemedinah*, ed. V. Pilowsky (Haifa, 1990).

Confronting the Religious Question within the Zionist Youth Movement

The first Jewish youth movements, which were established on the model of German youth movements and acquired their ways of thinking, forms of organization, and methods of education, expanded throughout Germany between the two world wars and spread to Austria, Czechoslovakia, and Eastern Europe.[1] The Jewish youth movement was launched in 1907 with the foundation of the first Blau-Weiss (Blue-White) hiking group in Breslau. After World War I the Jewish youth movements in Germany included the Jungjüdischer Wanderbund (JJWB, Young Jewish Hiking Group); the Kameraden (Comrades); the Esra, the Kadima (Forwards); the Werkleute (Artisans); Brit Olim (Association of Immigrants); Zeire Mizrahi (Mizrahi Youth); Hashomer Hazair (Young Guard); and the Jüdischer Pfadfinderbund Makkabi Hazair (Jewish Scouting Group Young Maccabean). These groups are customarily classified as Zionist (Blau-Weiss, JJWB) and non-Zionist (Kameraden), or bourgeois (Blau-Weiss, Kadima, Makkabi Hazair), socialist (JJWB, Kameraden, Brit Olim, Hashomer Hazair), and Orthodox (Esra, Zeire Mizrahi). But despite their ideological divergences, all Jewish youth movements had important structural elements in common. The reasons for this uniformity are to be found in the common problems faced by Jewish youth, in their common social background, and above all in the model of German youth movements, which shaped their attitudes and modes of behavior, characteristic of the youth movement as a whole.

Jewish adolescents who joined the Jewish youth movements in Germany belonged to the third or fourth generation following emancipation and grew up as German citizens, deeply rooted in German culture and the German world of thought. Never before in Jewish history had there been a generation that had moved so far away from the spiritual and intellectual sources of Judaism. Jewish youth in Germany presented a fairly uniform picture of a generation torn by an increasing inner conflict between Jewishness and Germanness. It was the picture of a divided self, beset by mounting tension between the diverging elements of its personality and leading to spiritual insecurity, a crisis of identity, a consciousness afflicted by existential distress. Continuing assimilation and increasingly intimate bonds with German culture, with *Deutschtum*, did not alleviate the distress; if anything, they accentuated the inner cleavage.[2]

Brought together by their common psychological difficulties, Jewish adolescents set up Jewish organizations and movements that represented various sociological types. With a few exceptions, all Jewish youth organizations, driven partly by external circumstances, partly by an inner urge, became involved in a process of gradually turning back to the sources of Judaism, to their own innermost being. In embarking on this course, the young people were as a rule not concerned with politics, let alone with political parties; they had set out on a process of self-discovery in their striving for integrity.

It was only natural that a highly spiritual, emotionally motivated movement of Jewish youngsters, most of who came from assimilated families and were seeking their way back to Judaism, Jewish consciousness and nationality, would be confronted with the religious question. Indeed, in all Jewish youth movements throughout Europe, especially in their initial phases, the question of attitude toward religion and Orthodoxy was raised and discussed.

At the outset, there was a tendency for the movements to maintain certain traditional patterns, such as keeping kosher, giving a certain traditional style to Sabbath eves, and refraining from holding marches on Saturdays and holidays so as not to offend the sensitivities of observant members,[3] and a call was published in the JJWB's periodical for a secondary organization of observant members.[4] Very quickly, however, it became clear that most Western and Zionist youth could not respond to this call for a "return to tradition" literally, in its theological sense.[5] The patterns of traditions, holidays, and prayers were perceived by these youth movements in a wider, nonpersonal context as fulfilling a vital role in creating a national, historical, ethical, and social awareness. A free Jewish national life would lead to Jewish religiosity, not in the patterns of Jewish tradition in the theological sense[6] but as an expression of the people and in service for the people and of its history and Jewish community *(Gemeinschaft)*. This religiosity could not be dissociated from the Jewish people and from the land of the Jews.[7] It was, as a proponent stated, "religion as the guardian force of Judaism."[8]

This instrumental conception of religion as a sustaining and connecting chain of Jewish *Gemeinschaft* was developed especially in the Kameraden movement and afterward in the Werkleute movement. Again, as a proponent expressed, "We do not believe in God or in the giving of the commandments at Sinai, but the commandments are the armor of the Jewish people that has preserved it."[9]

In the pre-Zionist period, religion appeared as a means of tying Jews to their community even if they did not seek the redemption of their souls in Zionism;[10] in later stages, Zionism and the Land of Israel were identified with religion or were considered as the ground from which a new religiosity would sprout. Again in the words of a proponent, "Only through Zionism can the Jewish religiosity become increasingly liberated and free, alive, and

creative." A free national life, free and divinely pleasing labor, would lead
to a revival of the Jewish religiosity, even if not in the patterns of Jewish tradition as the Orthodox might expect for Jewish life in Palestine.[11]

The youth movements seemed to dispute everything that existed, and the
following comment on religion, the Kameraden newspaper typically asserted that there is justification for the outlook that religion is an interest of
the youth movement when the value of religion is seen as ethics only. These
ethics are a subdepartment of the "youth culture"—a conclusion at which
many of the youth have already arrived.[12]

In several youth movements, particularly Kameraden and JJWB, the religious yearning that was not ready to accept Orthodox patterns turned in
the ethical-social direction to the point of complete identification. Yet even
within the ranks of the youth movements, many objected to "seeing a substitute for religion as religion itself."[13] They warned that those who thought
an awareness of togetherness was sufficient "forget that they still have not
gone back to grasp what is most profound and sublime in Judaism—its religious content."[14] Others cautioned against an oversimplification in the
combination of religion and socialism that was harmful to proponents of
each.[15] This combination satisfied neither the Jews for whom faith in the divine source of the commandments was lost nor the Jew who believed that
the commandments fulfilled the divine will and were not intended to preserve mere by-products such as the nation.[16]

While these opinions were repeatedly raised at almost all levels of Jewish
public life—in the parties, the communities, organizations, schools, and
adult education institutions—there was among the youth movements an increasing crystallization of a unique approach that constituted, in effect, a
basic principle of youth movements.[17] Two features in particular brought
the youth movements into direct confrontation with the principles of religion: the concept of "inner truth" as an ontological criterion and the idea
that convictions and attitudes could be molded.[18] The endeavor to fashion
life in the spirit of inner truth—to reject externally established and imposed
norms that were regarded as ossified traditions—was common among all
youth movements.[19] This "inner truth" was regarded as the truth in its pur-
est form, indivisible and exempt from compromise with other "truths,"
such as those of positive and codified religions.

Moreover, youth movements held that human reactions and modes of
behavior are determined by psychological predispositions, classified as *Ge-
sinnung* (convictions) and *Haltung* (bearings), which in turn are derived
from certain value judgments. Therefore, there appeared to be little point in
attempting to influence modes of behavior and to exert external pressure directly, as religious commandments did. Instead, convictions and bearings
resulting from the "inner truth" should predominate. These would spontaneously and without any further outside intervention direct behavior in the
desired channels. In place of direct influence, the youth movements sought

to affect the attitudes of its followers indirectly: not by preaching the word, but through the mysterious workings of symbols and, above all, through the participation in experiences charged with emotion. This approach depended not on outside influences but on the inward force of moved hearts and souls.

More than anything else, these features influenced the relationship between youth movements and religion.[20] Proponents wrote:

It is a pity that for so many religion is merely something external. It is up against ignorance. Despite this, a mostly unconscious yearning has been passing over our youth movement, but one that is deeply felt within, for something internal, something more sublime, spiritual—for religion.[21]

Religious education cannot be directed so as to implant religion, but only to preserve the internal readiness to experience (erleben) the religion or, where it no longer exists, to aid in its coming into being, to add what is missing; to be a religious person, then, is the completely private matter of the individual.[22]

Similar reasoning was heard in the JJWB:

Religion today is a very broad concept. First and foremost, it should not be something external. . . . Religion needs to constitute the experience of human beings. It must be felt through experience just like youth. Therefore, we have to deepen and develop the religiosity within us, the sense of God. . . . First of all, the internalization of our individual selves, the push for truths, for the divine within us; then beyond that—the religion.[23]

The same in Kadima:

It seems to me that even the return to tradition does not constitute a road for us. No goals from the outside; they can only arise from within ourselves.[24]

In this approach the Jewish youth movements could also rely on the words of their great teacher, Martin Buber, who pointed out that "religious truth is not conceptual but vital." Accordingly the task was not "to impose religion upon youth . . . but to awaken the religion lying dormant within youth."[25] "Truth" said Buber, "is the soul of religion."[26]

The principle of fashioning life with inner truth, determined, too, the relationship between the religious sense and its manifestations and forms, which the youth movements wanted to mold for themselves at certain stages of their history. This principle was propounded by the German youth movements as well,[27] and it was a leading motif among all the Jewish youth movements in Western Europe that were influenced by them. In an essay on the principles of education in Blau-Weiss, a proponent pointed to the obvious way Judaism relates to the traditional world of forms as a hindrance to positive Jewish values:

It certainly may occur to one that the will to live, the life that is lived, is what creates and bears the forms, rather than the forms being the bearers of the will to live. The forms are no more and no less than an expression of life, and from this point of view an end in and of themselves—never a means to support something that would not stand up on its own. Every attempt to transfer through the forms the spirit that created those forms is therefore doomed to fail.[28]

In thinking about the nature of the relationship between the religious sensibility and its expressions and forms, a member of Kameraden juxtaposed two outlooks: the religious form as an expression or symbol of the sense that creates it, as an elementary expression of a sense of self, and the form as a check on feelings, having an educational value in and of itself. There is no doubt, he declared, that the youth movements, without distinction of *Weltanschauung*, favor the first concept. Holidays are not to be celebrated according to the calendar but according to the heart, with no conscious tie to the religion. We will be deceived if we believe that we can renew our religion by stamping our feelings with strange forms.[29]

Even the religious youth movement, Esra, following the example of its Catholic and evangelical counterparts in the German youth movement, experienced a tension between its principles and the opposite principles of Orthodoxy. From the religious viewpoint, Esra did not deviate from the Ultra-Orthodox Agudah line, from which it originated and to whose council of sages it was subject even after parting from it. Yet its nature as a youth movement shaped the original forms and, to a great extent, determined the orientation of the movement among the various religious streams in the Orthodox camp. Moreover, the members of Esra used the youth movement mechanism in the process of transformation to achieve, in their opinion, a fuller, more truthful Judaism. Just as in the German youth movement a yearning was expressed for extrication from "soulless" religious conventions to soul-pulsating life fashioned from self-responsibility,[30] so Esra held that "soulless" Judaism had become, for its proponents, a system of routine habits, while what was needed was a return to a renewed faith having internal and binding significance.[31] Esra's objection was directed at

that outlook that attempts to restrict the living Judaism, for which our forefathers went to the stake, to a certain summary of legal paragraphs and legalistic equations in order to adjust Judaism somehow to our convenience (and in so doing) it is stripped of its religiosity, the essence of life drained from it, and what remains is but a dead skeleton.[32]

This religious criticism was also bound with social criticism.

The argument over "clarity or harmony,"[33] which continued for a long time in Ezra, was merely a transmigration of the youth movement's vintage argument over a way of recognizing the truth: rationally-intellectually vs. intuitively-internally (by means of feelings). Those members who accepted the second position, characteristic of youth movements,[34] faced the question of how to compromise between the contradiction that existed between, on the one hand, internal recognition of the truth and a life design on the basis of self-responsibility and, on the other hand, acceptance of the yoke of

Torah as the complete and binding truth, imposed as it is from the outside and directing the life of the believer. Most of the discussions on religious matters in the movement were devoted to the search for a synthesis between these two understandings of cognition. In this, too, Esra tended to follow in the track of Samson Raphael Hirsch, who wrote:

Life as lived should be the flower of knowledge: but in order that life may blossom out of knowledge, knowledge alone is not enough. The knowledge with which you have enriched your mind must be applied to yourself; you must recognize what you know as appertaining to you; you must transfer it from the mind to the heart, which decides your course of action; it must penetrate you through and through, it must become part of yourself. Then only will it become the basis of your activity. It will become life.[35]

Because of its emphasis on anticipating the deed and molding it, Esra took a clear, decisive line on the issue of "commandments require devotion." It was difficult for members of this organization to come to terms with the opinions of sages who argued that mere fulfillment of the commandments obviated any need for devotion, in that the very act was the determinant. The movement, therefore, inclined toward Hirsch's approach on the matter of the symbolic meaning of the commandments and the eternal mutual effect between the deed on its doer and the doer on the deed.[36]

Isaac Breuer argued that "the fulfilling of the deed does not adjust itself according to how one is convinced. The law subdues the will, but leaves the personality its freedom."[37] Taking the opposite view was Buber, who rejected the very principle of this dialectic and argued that

Whoever fulfills the commandments from true certainty, that and only that is informed with a religious value; whereas in the absence of that certainty, his willingness to sacrifice, whether this is in consequence of piety or habit, loses its religious significance and thereby its overwhelming sacredness.[38]

Most members of Esra apparently supported Buber on this point.

The Zionist youth movements in Eastern Europe—Hashomer Hazair, Dror, Bnei Akiva, Zionist Youth, Gordonia, Beitar, Hashomer Hadati, Young Pioneers, and others—were distinguished from those in Western Europe in their world outlook, political orientation, social composition, extent of Jewish identification or assimilation, as well as in the various ways they wanted to realize their ideas on their way to and once in Palestine. While the origins of most of the Jewish youth organizations in Western Europe lay in the classical German youth movement, which started with *Wandervogel*, the origin of most Jewish youth movements in Eastern Europe is found in the political parties and ideological camps whose outlooks the youth groups reflected—even in coping with the religious question. Only in a movement like Hashomer Hazair, especially in Galicia and in countries bordering German-speaking territory, such as Rumania, and to a lesser extent like Gordonia, was the influence of the classic German-style youth movement felt from the outset. Youth movements joined the Hehalutz Organization but kept their autonomy in educational and ideological matters. Despite the fact that most members of Hehalutz (Pioneer) and Hehalutz Hazair (Young Pioneer) and the young guard of the political parties were also members of youth movements, there were fundamental differences between those organizations and the youth movement during the entire period of their close collaboration.[39]

The most profound differences between these two groups were intellectual, residing in their distinct perceptions of both Zionism and socialism, in their differing understandings of the essential nature of youth and its social function, in their wholly antithetical attitudes toward the significance of the idea of "vocation," and in the value they attached to the half-playful symbolism of the various "scouting methods." The Zionism and socialism of the youth movements in Germany were, at least in their initial stages, essentially ethical, nonpolitical and fundamentally opposed to political parties.

Another difference had to do with the role of youth in society. The thinking of the German youth movement was rooted, on the one hand, in the Kantian tradition, in which man was regarded as an end in himself, and on the other hand in the tradition of educational reform in Germany represented by Gustav Syneken, according to which youth was an end in its own right. This outlook was being challenged by a functional sociological outlook characteristic of the sort of Marxist dialectic being practiced in Eastern Europe. Thus the youth movements in Western Europe believed that its members should be allowed to choose their profession freely and receive extensive and thorough vocational training that fit their personal inclinations and talents—a kind of self-realization in accordance with "inner truths."

For Hehalutz and most youth movements in Eastern Europe, this view represented a survival of bourgeois distinctions that had to be rooted out completely, since it suited neither *halutz* socialism nor the needs of Palestine. The members of the youth movements in Eastern Europe, upon joining, had already reached a stage of Jewish identity at which their Western comrades hoped to arrive when leaving the movement. The sense of Jewish identity and social and national affiliation with which the movements in Western Europe sought to imbue their troubled and irresolute members by means of a drawn-out process of indirect education and influence on their attitudes, convictions, and bearing, was something that was taken for granted and that constituted a primary state of mind among the youth movements in Eastern Europe. Here, instead, the various ideologies of the political parties were directly adapted. This also holds true for their confronting of the religious question. In Eastern Europe, most Zionist youth movements belonged to the Left and were entirely politically orientated, rejecting religion as such for ideological and political reasons and without any inner longing for religiosity. This was also the message that reached the Zionist youth movements in Germany through emissaries from Palestine, where the political-ideological line of the Eastern European movements was dominant among the pioneers and the *kibbutz* movements.

"Our times are a period of the complete undermining of the concepts of family, religion, holidays, divinity," wrote an emissary of the United Kibbutz Movement, Abraham Tarshish.

The illusion of *geborgensein* [security] has disappeared, the solid ground has given way under our feet, and the sure God has slipped away from above us. We find ourselves in a class war, that of socialism with capitalism and with reactionism. It was only natural that in moments of weakness, despondency, and powerlessness, the yearning rose for mystic worlds, causing in turn the yearning and clinging to the past. Our movement however was founded on the destruction of the poor and humiliating Jewish existence of diaspora Jewry. Above the ruins, we are forced to go and conquer a desolate land; much mental energy has been invested in building and establishing new forms.

In the yearning for the Jewish *shtetl*, Tarshish saw a process of idealization that is unfounded. Our productive work in Palestine, he claimed, stems from a denial of the past and utter rejection of the life forms in the diaspora: "We will not fashion the new holidays with the artificial glue of old forms; rather we must fill them with new content, free of the chains of tradition."[40]

These ideas were in the air in Palestine, and thus encountered by members of the Zionist youth movements when they arrived. Naturally a clash ensued, felt especially in the Werkleute movement, which perhaps struggled most deeply and seriously with the question of the attitude toward religion.

As Elijah Maoz (Mosbacher), a former member of the movement, pointed out, the reality in Eretz Israel was very different: on the one hand, a very militant Orthodoxy that did not endeavor to convince those who held other opinions but wanted to force them to obey religious laws with or without conviction; on the other side, the camp of the *halutzim*, who had by and large found their way to Zionism and physical labor in the struggle against the Orthodox past. The *mitzvot*, which in the diaspora separated Jew from gentile, here divided Jews from Jew; and the Jews who followed the *mitzvot* were not those with whom Werkleute wished to be identified.

Perhaps the most decisive factor for their alienation from religion was the new insight into the depths of the human soul as it was revealed in fascist barbarism. The Holocaust caused a mistrust of every irrational and metaphysical trend. The belief of the Werkleute had not been received from authority but had grown from inner (irrational) experiences; these could no longer be regarded as a source of objective truth.[41]

Herman Gerson, a leader of the movement, reported a tension between him and members who had preceded him to Palestine, particularly in the matter of giving a certain tone to the Sabbath and, in general, the spiritual tie with tradition. Collectively the newcomers met with sharp, rationalistic criticism and came to feel that previously they had made things easy for themselves and had accepted things without thinking them through. "Our

Jewish stance is entirely the point at which we meet the greatest opposition from all sides. This is a very complex situation for our movement."[42]

With the adjustment of Zionist youth to the reality of Palestine and the loss of their identity as youth movements, they also reached the end of their attempts to cope with the religious question.

Notes

1. On the Jewish youth movements, see Herman Meier-Cronemeyer, "Jüdische Jugendbewegung," in *Germania Judaica,* Kölner Bibliothek zur Geschichte des deutschen Judentums, n.s. 27–28, vol. 8, nos. 1–4 (1969); Chanoch Rinott, "Major Trends in Jewish Youth Movements in Germany," *Leo Baeck Institute Year Book* 19 (1974); Jehuda Reinharz, "Hashomer Hazair in Germany," *Leo Baeck Institute Year Book* 31 (1986), and 32 (1987); Reinharz, *Hashomer Hazair beGermanyah, 1931–1939* (Tel-Aviv, 1987); Chaim Schatzker, "Die jüdische Jugendbewegung in Deutschland," in *Die deutsche Jugendbewegung, 1921–1933: Die bundische Zeit,* III (1975); Schatzker, "Buber's Influence on the Jewish Youth Movement," *Leo Baeck Institute Year Book* 33 (1988); Schatzker, "The Jewish Youth Movement in Germany in the Holocaust Period," in *Leo Baeck Institute Year Book* 32 (1987), and 33 (1988); "Toldot Ha 'Blau-Weiss': Darka shel tenuat hanoar hayehudit harishonah beGermanyah el hazionut," *Zion* (Jerusalem), 38 (1973): 137–68; "Toldot ha'Kameraden': Gilgula shel tenuat noar yehudit beGermanyah," *Proceedings of the Sixth World Congress of Jewish Studies,* vol. 2 (Jerusalem, 1975); "Makabi Hazair: Tenuat hanoar hayehudit haahronah beGermanyah" in *Tenuat hanoar hazionit bashoah,* ed. Yehoyakim Kochavy (Haifa, 1989), pp. 82–103.

2. See Chaim Schatzker, *Jüdische Jugend im zweiten Kaiserreich* (Frankfurt, 1988), pp. 11–24.

3. See "Wanderpflichten," *Blau-Weiss Blätter,* September 1913, p. 2; "Mitteilungen der Bundesleitung," *Blau-Weiss Blätter,* July 1914, p. 16; "Kameraden," *Deutsch-Jüdischer Wanderbund,* September 1924, pp. 1–21; *Mitteilungen des Jung-Jüdischen Wanderbundes,* December 1924, p. 2.

4. *Jung Jüdischer Wanderbund* (Bundestag, 1927), p. 23.

5. Siegfried Kanowitz, "Zionistische Jugendbewegung," in *Die neue Jugend,* vol. 4 of *Forschungen zur Völkerpsychologie und Soziologie,* ed. Richard Thurnwald (Leipzig, 1927), p. 25.

6. Ibid.

7. Arthur Seelig, "Ein Wort an unsere Chaluzim," *JJWB Führerblätter,* May 16, 1924, p. 17.

8. Heinz Lichtenstein, "Die Religion als erhaltende Kraft im Judentum," *Kameraden,* December 1920, p. 16.

9. Herman Gerson, "Werkleute," *Bundesblatt,* March 1934, p. 7.

10. Georg Beer, "Unser Gemeinschaftsglaube," *Kameraden,* October/November 1920, p. 16.

11. Dr. Noack, "Zionismus als Kulturbewegung," *Jungjüdischer Wanderer Fahrtenblaetter,* August 5, 1923, p. 16.

12. Siegfried Kanowitz, "Zionistische Judgendbewegung," p. 25.

13. *Führerblatt des Jüdischen Jugendbundes "Kameraden,"* July 1921, p. 4.

14. Fritz Kronenberger, "Judentum," *Kameraden,* September 1924, p. 30.

15. Blanca Straus, "Nation oder Religion," *Blätter des Jung-Jüdischen Wanderbundes,* August 1924, p. 12.

16. George Lubinski, "Religion and Sozialismus," *JJWB choser Teth,* October 1, 1926, p. 1.

17. Ernst Bauer, "Zur Traditionsfrage," *Werkleute Bundesblatt,* October 1934, pp. 9–10.

18. On the fundamental features of the youth movement, see Schatzker, "Buber's Influence."

19. In 1913, at a national meeting of the Freideutsche Jugend held on the Hohe Meissner,

at which representatives of most of the youth movements in Germany participated, a declaration of intents was drafted to serve as a beacon to all youth movements. Later known as the Hohe Meissner Formula, it stated: "The Freideutsche Jugend is resolved to fashion its existence according to its own lights, on its own responsibility and in the spirit of inner truth. It will stand up for this inner freedom in solid unity under any circumstances." See *Der Meissnertag, 1963: Reden und Geleitworte im Auftrage des Hauptausschusses für die Durchführung des Meissnertages,* ed. Werner Kindt and Karl Vogt (Düsseldorf and Cologne, 1964), p. 43.

20. Kronenberger, "Judentum."

21. *Kameraden,* December 1920, p. 13.

22. Erich Hirschberg, "Gedanken über die Stellung der 'Kameraden' zum Judentum," *Kameraden,* June 1921, p. 4.

23. *Mitteilungen des Verbandes der jüdischen Jugendvereine Deutschlands,* June 1920, p. 31.

24. "Kadima, Bund jüdischer Jugend": *Älterenrundbrief,* February 1932, p. 2.

25. Martin Buber, *Cheruth: Eine Rede über Jugend und Religion* (Vienna and Berlin, 1919), pp. 18, 5.

26. Martin Buber, "Was ist zu tun: Einige Bemerkungen zu den "Antworten der Jugend," in *Jüdische Renaissance,* vol. of *Die jüdische Bewegung: Gesammelte Aufsätze und Ansprachen, 1900–1915* (Berlin, 1916), pp. 123–26.

27. Helmut Gollwitzer, "Festansprache," in *Der Meissnertag, 1963* ed. Kindt and Vogt, p. 60.

28. *Blau-Weiss Blätter,* January 1919, p. 109.

29. Julius Freund, "Erziehung durch die Form," *Kameraden,* September 1924, pp. 5–30.

30. Gollwitzer, "Festansprache."

31. Rudi Herz, in *Führer-Blätter des Esra* (Marcheschwan-Kislev 5690/1930), p. 9.

32. Benno Zimmer, *Führerschafts-blätter des Esra* (Aw 5688/1928), p. 12.

33. Felix Munk, "Esra: Klarheit oder Harmonie," *Führerschafts-Blätter des Esra* (Schewath 5687/1927), pp. 29–32.

34. Ernst Freimann, "Über das Intuitive und Rationale in unserer Erziehung," *Führerschafts-Blätter des Esra* (Schewath 5687/1927), 32–37.

35. *Esra Führer Blätter* (Nissan 2, 1926), p. 15.

36. Carl Hamburger, in *Esra Führer-Blätter* (Tamus 1925), pp. 4–6.

37. Isaac Breuer, *Judenproblem,* p. 126, see also p. 8.

38. Buber, "Cheruth."

39. See Chaim Schatzker, "The Relations between the Youth Movement and Hechalutz," *Leo Baeck Institute Year Book* 33 (1988).

40. Abraham Tarshish, "Sehnsucht zum Geborgenen Sein"; Aus der Zeitschrift des Kibbuz Hameuchad, Mibifnim, *Der Junge Jude* (July/August 1930), pp. 135–39.

41. Elijah Maoz (Mosbacher), "The Werkleute," *Leo Baeck Institute Year Book* 4 (1953): 179–80.

42. Werkleute, 6, Verbindungs-Rundbrief, August 1934, Aus Palaestina, Bericht, July 1934, pp. 5–6.

The Religious Factor in the Encounter between Zionism and the Rural Atlas Jews

In the early 1950s the rural parts of the Moroccan High Atlas still preserved their traditional character almost intact. The status of the small Jewish minority in local Berber society was typical of such preindustrial Islamic societies. Jews were *a priori* seen as inferior, in need of a Berber patron, and they were subject to discriminatory laws and customs that emphasized their lower status, such as restrictions on the colors of clothing. There were about 3,500–4,000 Jews scattered in no fewer than ninety separate quarters *(mellahs)* in proximity to Berber villages. This extreme dispersal reflected their economic role as artisans—shoemakers, saddlers, dressmakers, blacksmiths, and so forth—who gave exclusive services to the Berber farmers and shepherds. Indeed, some of them, including many artisans, were engaged in local commerce and moneylending, but their main economic function, which determined their dwelling patterns, was their craftsmanship. Among the ninety rural *mellahs*, twelve were exceptional: their inhabitants farmed plots of land—the main occupation of their Muslim neighbors. In the other *mellahs* there also were some Jews engaged in agriculture, who usually came from the poorest families of the community.[1]

The famous British anthropologist, Ernest Gellner, conducted some of his studies in the central High Atlas, not far from the main Jewish concentrations in the area. Some of his research dealt with the penetration of Moroccan nationalism into the Atlas hinterland.[2] It should be emphasized that the Jewish minority was a minor issue for Moroccan nationalists in comparison with the Berber problem. Ethnically and culturally, the Berbers differed from the Arab majority, and for a long time their adherence to Arab nationalism was tenuous. French colonialism was constantly trying to benefit from the ethnic rifts in local Muslim society, and the last French effort to oppress Moroccan nationalism, the deposition of King Muhammad V in August 1953, involved the help of a Berber coalition headed by Glaoui Pasha, the Muslim governor and patron of Marakesh and its Atlas hinterland.[3]

Gellner followed the process by which the modern Moroccan state imposed its rule in the Berber areas and offered enlightening explanations for its relative success. He later developed a general theory on nationalism in which Zionism is mentioned as a successful example of "diaspora nationalism"—one of the three archetypes of nationalism in his thesis.[4] Diaspora nationalism, according to Gellner, develops among communities of originally foreign status, scattered, and lacking their own agrarian stratum. In preindustrial society their members have "pariah" status, are totally dependent on the local rulers, and can therefore fulfill functions that are too dangerous to be assigned to members of the dominant society, such as guarding the palace and moneylending. Such specializations were generally profitable and could compensate for the pariah status. However, the advent of the modernizing processes, or industrialization, undermined the arrangements that had perpetuated this situation for generations. The majority began competing for the economic functions of the diaspora minority, and conflict started between the two. Such conflict led to persecutions on the one hand and efforts at assimilation on the other. On occasion it also engendered the rise of nationalist sentiment among the diaspora minority.[5]

Apparently Gellner was not thinking of the Atlas Jews but of European Jewry when he wrote of diaspora nationalism. Still, as Arab nationalism penetrated the Atlas region, so did Zionism. Practically the whole local Jewish population was caught up in the process and ultimately immigrated to Israel. Gellner's theory raises the question of how to account for the Atlas Jews' response to Zionism. As the description of their economic condition indicates, Gellner's assumptions about the occupations and economic status of diaspora minorities does not necessarily correspond to the very diversified profile of the Jewish populations around the world. More essential to this thesis, however, is the competition between members of such minorities and members of the dominant society in the process of industrialization. Industrialization, then, offers the clue to the emergence of diaspora nationalism (and to every archetype of nationalism, according to Gellner's theory). As we will see below, the Atlas region (with the exception of its strictly rural parts) did not escape the effects of industrialization. Was the exodus of the Atlas Jews primarily motivated by the changing economic and social conditions, or was it a product of other factors, specific to Jewish diaspora nationalism?

Indeed, the encounter between Zionism and the Atlas Jews seems to raise a fundamental problem inherent to diaspora nationalism: How does it appeal to the scattered segments composing a "diaspora society"? After all, Jews were—and still are—scattered all over the globe. Political, cultural, and economic conditions prevailing in Europe did not necessarily apply in Asia and Africa. How could Zionism affect and unite such divergent Jews as, for instance, individuals from England and from the Moroccan Atlas? What elements of the present reality—or of the diaspora heritage—facilitated the proliferation and spread of Zionist activities all over the Jewish world?

In the present article an attempt will be made to demonstrate the crucial role of the religious factor in the encounter between Zionism and the rural

Atlas Jews. We shall first describe the path of Zionism to the Atlas region and then concentrate on the initial stage—in the summer and autumn of 1954—of the encounter between Zionism and the local Jewish communities.

I

Prior to the establishment of Israel, the Zionist movement was not especially interested in the Jews of Morocco. Zionism is indeed a nationalism of a diaspora population scattered all over the world, but at its pre-independence stage—apart from limited periods and affairs, in connection for instance with the Yemenite Jews in 1911–12 or Zionist work when faced with the consequences of the Holocaust in 1943–44—it was not especially oriented toward Afro-Asian Jewish populations outside the Land of Israel. Numerically, these communities did not exceed 8 percent of the Jewish population worldwide, so that they did not seem to constitute a main human reservoir for Jewish nationalism. Moreover, the condition of the European diaspora seemed—and indeed was—the most acute source of anxiety impelling the nationalist renaissance. Europe and America with large Jewish concentrations were the more important sources for Zionist leadership, manpower, and funds, and these were channeled to the New Yishuv in Palestine, strengthening it and eventually resulting in the establishment of Israel. Finally, Zionism could not escape the effects of the colonial era in which it developed. In a world divided in colonial parlance into "Europeans," and African and Asian "natives," Zionism was the only nationalism that united both of these categories in a single nationalist movement. Both "Europeans" and "natives" (provided they were Jews), were called upon to join the Jewish national movement. Still, even Zionism could not be totally detached from the widespread attitudes and stereotypes stemming from the real and imaginary gaps between Europeans and non-Europeans. Thus the Asian and African Jews were generally looked down upon by the European Zionists, and the Zionist Organization did not expect much from its "oriental" branches without the help and guidance of special envoys.[6]

This macroproblem of Jewish nationalism appeared at a microlevel in many of its oriental branches, especially in the colonial areas. In contrast to their homogeneous stereotype of a primitive and ignorant Jewish diaspora, many oriental communities, especially in the cities, included a European-like elite and an ever-growing Westernized middle class. No general research has yet been done on the effects of Western colonialism on the Jewish diaspora in the colonized areas. But partial studies suggest that the local Jewish populations did not escape colonial hierarchization, being subdivided into "Europeans," "natives" in various states of Westernization, and "natives" who retained their formal traditional state. Thus, in Morocco, for instance, the rural Jews of the High Atlas, who were—by Western standards—the most backward Jews in the country, were indeed treated by their Moroccan co-religionists in the developing cities as the lowest local Jewish subgroup. This treatment was not unique to Jewish society, as all the inhabitants—Muslims and Jews—of the High Atlas, who were nicknamed "Chleuhs," were looked down on by Moroccan town dwellers. Still, there are signs to indicate the deteriorating status of the Jewish Chleuhs under colonial rule. Their reaction, according to Pierre Flamand, is quite interesting: rather than defend themselves, they attacked the other people's easy inclination to sway with the new winds.[7]

Let us return, however, to the Israeli angle. Under the British mandate, in the Yishuv the real and imagined gaps between European and non-European (Ashkenazim and Mizrahim) had created socioeconomic and cultural tensions. These, in turn, generated a major internal problem, which was clearly sensed and was given several names, such as the "communal" or "ethnic" problem. However, as long as the demographic balance between the European and non-European elements was heavily in favor of the former, the communal problem did not spill over into open conflict.

The first waves of mass immigration to Israel changed the whole profile of the European, elitist, veteran Yishuv. They consisted mainly of Jewish refugees from Europe, along with whole populations from different Muslim countries such as Yemen, Iran, Iraq, and Libya and other North African countries. One consequence of this change was an aggravation of the relations between Europeans and non-Europeans in the vastly changed host society, Israel. Of the Asian and African immigrants, the Moroccans gained the most problematic reputation.[8] An attempt was made by several senior Israeli officials responsible for immigrant absorption and health to initiate a restrictive policy toward future immigration, especially from North Africa. The aim of this policy, known as the "selection regulations," was to diminish the general number of old, unproductive, and sick immigrants and those from particular regions. The "selection regulations" began to be implemented in 1951 but were strongly criticized by many politicians and civil servants of almost all parties. In connection with their fight for the North African immigration, the critics took two routes: they attempted to represent this Jewish diaspora, or some parts of it, as threatened by immediate danger. The North African Jews had to be "rescued." This attitude probably stemmed from the impact of the Holocaust on the Yishuv and was the most frequent argument for abolishing the restrictions. Second, the critics tried to counter the image often projected of the Moroccans as primitive, immoral, unhealthy, and unproductive Jews.[9]

Circumstances in Israel and Morocco in 1953–54 were conducive to both efforts. In the first place, the Moroccan struggle for independence had entered its final stages. The general state of security in the country started to deteriorate, and it became easy to alarm both the Israeli public and the authorities to the situation of Jews in Morocco. As for the Moroccan immigrant's image, a change at this stage in Zionist ideology prepared the groundwork for greater receptivity toward those who were culturally different from the veteran population of Israel. This change related to what was perhaps the most central theme of Zionism—the notion of returning to the land and "redeeming" it. Until 1948 the role of reconstituting the regular relations of a people with its land through settlement, agriculture, and fighting had been assigned to the young Zionist elite of *halutzim* (pioneers). In a process that was originally initiated by Levy Eshkol to solve the acute housing problem of the immigrants, Zionism started to foster the idea that nonelitist newcomers could also serve as a colonizing element. This orientation apparently helped solve two of the country's most acute problems: the integration of mass waves of immigrants with no solid nationalist training and with a low image in the veteran Yishuv, and the overconcentration of the Jewish population of Israel in a narrow coastal strip along the Mediterranean. The ideology now assigned immigrants an active role as settlers of the uninhabited Negev and border areas, thus putting them on a par with the veteran *halutzim*. Economically they were also given the highest rank in the Zionist "hierarchy" of professions, as workers, farmers, and defenders of the land.[10]

This dramatic turn in Zionist ideology crystallized in summer 1954, when Eshkol's group laid the foundations for the newly planned settlement areas of Lakhish in the Negev and the Taanachim in the lower Galilee.[11] At the same time, a green light was given to the different settlement agencies of the Zionist parties to send emissaries to Morocco and enlist the best potential Jewish populations for the new *moshavim* (cooperative smallholders' settlements).

II

Among the many Zionist emissaries who went to Morocco during those turbulent days was Yehuda Grinker, who gained a reputation as the first Israeli envoy to introduce Zionism to the rural Jews of the High Atlas. Grinker (1897–1972), a native of Yesod Hamaala in the northern Galilee, was a member of Nahalal, the first Zionist *moshav* and symbol of the whole *moshav* movement (Tenuat Hamoshavim).[12] He was sent by Tenuat Hamoshavim, a branch of the socialist Histadrut (Federation of Labor), to organize *garinim* (nucleus groups) for future settlements planned for his movement. His mission to Morocco is interesting from many points of view, but we will concentrate here only on his initial encounter with the rural Jews of the central High Atlas.

To understand the special character of this encounter, we shall, however, first examine the relations that developed between Grinker and Jews from a different corner of Morocco. His first attempt to organize a *garin* involved a Jewish group from Mazagan, a town on the Atlantic shore of central Morocco. It was not Grinker who first formed the group. It had taken shape before he came to Morocco and was composed of a few dozen families, mostly middle-aged and young clerks, of modest means. They were religious, as were most members of the Jewish communities in similar urban centers. In the local Zionist chapter, they were supposed to be under the influence and guidance of the nationalist religious party, Hapoel Hamizrahi. Apparently their first attempts to organize came under the auspices of Hamizrahi's envoys to Morocco, but they soon realized that the *moshav* movement of Mapai, the ruling socialist party in Israel, would be in a better position to assist with their immigration and settlement. This was probably the reason why they initiated the contact with Grinker.[13]

This independent move of the Zionist group from Mazagan is in keeping with its general contacts with Grinker. Several times he traveled from Kadima, the Zionist headquarters in Casablanca, to meet them and answer their questions about the location of their future *moshav*, the dwelling conditions, the communal regulations, the quantities of water to be assigned to them, and so forth. They also required information on their rights to transfer their belongings, few though these were, and wanted to know about the policy concerning importation of agricultural machinery for individual use and small weapons for self-defence. Grinker described them as having fine potential—an appraisal borne out in the screening process. When a location in Israel with a bad reputation was suggested to him for their settlement, he objected. He did not feel that this group of people should be manipulated to suit his movement's needs and convenience. On the contrary, he was afraid that unless they were treated efficiently and properly, they would disband or be lost to a competing settlement movement.[14]

The religious factor did not seem to play a central role in the group's activities or in its relations with Grinker. Whatever spontaneous growth occurred in the community's nationalist sentiments had nothing to do with religion or religious feelings. In August 1954, the time of Grinker's arrival in Morocco, most Jews who held posts in the colonial administration or business were worried. France's prime minister, Pierre Mendès-France, had already given autonomy to Tunisia; Morocco would probably be next. Their jobs did not seem secure, and their whole economic future was vague. That very month, Muslim signs of rebellion grew worse, and for the first time, the population began to turn against Jews.[15] Within about a year Mazagan itself would become the scene of the greatest act of violence against Jews during the Moroccan struggle for independence.[16] The concrete social, economic, and political background for the spontaneous self-organization and activities of the Mazagan group was clear. Religious feelings, if they played any role in the turn of these Jews to nationalism, were secondary.

Nor did religion play any significant role in the Mazagan group's communications with Grinker. Although they were perfectly aware that they were expected to adhere to a religious Zionist movement, this did not prevent them from trying their chances with the nonobservant socialist Grinker. They invited the Israeli envoy to attend their prayers and to preach Zionism to the audience. But Grinker accepted their invitation halfheartedly and in his letters to Israel did not conceal his displeasure with those Jews who wasted his time and theirs in synagogues.[17]

III

Let us now examine Grinker's encounter with the rural Jews of the central High Atlas. Until the early 1950s it is impossible to point to manifestations of Zionist sentiments among the local Jews. They did not spontaneously start any activity of a nationalist character, nor did they simply follow the Zionist movement or join the first waves of immigration to Israel in significant numbers.[18] Indirect as well as tangible signs of Zionism—like the famous Keren Kayemet leIsrael (Jewish National Fund) box—that reached them, one way or another, seem to be incorporated into their traditional religious heritage.[19] In short, there were no signs of a turn to nationalism in their culture prior to the first visits of Israeli envoys like Yehuda Grinker in the High Atlas region.

Why and how did Grinker go to meet the High Atlas Jews? As emphasized above, his mission was actually a by-product of an ideological change relating to the role of nonelitist immigrants in Israel. Zionist militants who were conscious of the hard life of the pioneers in the Land of Israel were skeptical about the feasibility of such a shift. Accordingly, Zionist envoys went to great lengths to locate groups of future immigrants with the best prospects of succeeding in their new role. Grinker's first impressions of the urban Jewish populations of Morocco were rather negative and roughly correspond to the stereotype of Moroccan Jews in Israel.[20] The Mazagan group was an exception. However, in the midst of the Jewish proletariat of Salé, another city on the Atlantic shore, Grinker met a few Jews who seemed to him to have an agricultural background. They told him they had come from the Atlas. Back in Casablanca he discovered that rumors about the existence of Jewish farmers in the Atlas region had already reached Kadima, the headquarters of Zionist activity in Morocco. This news stirred the imagination of the Israeli envoys, and a small expedition was then organized to go to the Atlas mountains. Its main mission—at least in Grinker's eyes—was to discover whether Jewish farmers did indeed exist there.[21]

According to Grinker's book—which contains diary notes and letters from his mission—this first expedition, which took place in September 1954, was a failure.[22] Still, toward its end he met two local Jews who confirmed that they belonged to a *mellah*, Ait Rabaa, the inhabitants of which were all *harattin-qassabin* (plowers and reapers).[23] This news kept his hopes up, and he soon made a second journey, to see Ait Rabaa with his own eyes. The *mellah* was indeed an agricultural one. Its Jewish inhabitants gave Grinker a very warm welcome and were apparently prepared to register *en masse* for *aliyah* (immigration to Israel) at once. But Grinker had to obey the selection regulations. As some heads of families were away, tending their flocks, he could register only fifteen families. He asked the Jews of Ait Rabaa whether they knew of other villages like theirs. They answered in the affirmative and gave him the names of no fewer than twenty-six *mellahs* and their estimated populations. Grinker felt as if he had discovered a precious new field for Zionist work and a completely new type of Moroccan Jew. Though the day was a Jewish holiday, a messenger was sent to the nearest *mellah*, Isseres, to announce the coming of the Zionist envoy the following day.[24]

From Ait Rabaa, Grinker initiated a series of tours in which he visited practically every Jewish village of the High Atlas. As news of his mission spread throughout the region, the Jewish populations waited for him and, as far as we know, manifested the same feelings as had their co-religionists in Ait Rabaa.[25] The rural Jews were all prepared to register for *aliyah*. Thus, by November 1954, less than two months after he started to work in the region, Grinker could already submit a list of four *garinim* of rural Jews. This was the result of his visits in thirty-nine villages in four different districts. They consisted of about six hundred families (about 3,200 people).[26] While the Atlas Jews seemed prepared to leave their *mellahs* at once, the selection regulations, absorption possibilities in Israel, opposition of the French colonial administration, and transportation difficulties prevented the Zionist agencies in Morocco from moving them too fast. However, beginning in winter 1955, the rural Jews of the High Atlas evacuated one *mellah* after another, leaving the region where they had lived for centuries. By the time Morocco turned independent, in March 1956, there were very few Jews left in the area.[27]

IV

Let us now try to analyze the role of religion in the Atlas Jews' response to Grinker's mission. The rural Atlas Jews practiced a characteristic variant of traditional Judaism. The Ait Bouli district was one of the most important concentrations of Atlas *mellahs*. Assamer was the most significant Jewish village in this district. In his study of a *moshav* inhabited by immigrants from Assamer, Israeli anthropologist Moshe Shokeid wrote the following about their religious tradition:

In their geographical isolation [in Morocco], they were only loosely connected with world Jewry at large and even with their own cultural centres, which had, in any case, declined in recent centuries. Despite these difficulties, they lived within the fold of Jewish culture which they had inherited and kept alive largely by oral tradition handed down from generation to generation, but owing to their isolation it had not been influenced by the mainstream of Jewish cultural development. They spoke Judeo-Arabic and the holy books and prayers, written in Hebrew, were no longer understood by most of the community members although they could technically read Hebrew. The later literature, especially the Talmud, which since the early Middle Ages had been the main subject of scholarship in Jewish centres, was generally beyond their reach. Judaism meant mainly the strict adherence to the old commandments and the code of behavior with respect to food sanctions, everyday prayers, the regulations for the Sabbath and festivals, marriage, and sexual norms.[28]

Typical of the Jews of Assamer, then—according to Shokeid—was a mixture of rather poor religious learning and strict reverence for all elements of the Jewish religious code and faith as they knew them. Another characteristic of their religious culture was their strong belief in kabbalist and occultist activities.[29] For instance, reciting the Zohar (the basic book of Jewish mysticism) played a major role in their daily rites, even though the book's words were utterly meaningless to them. Finally, Shokeid stresses their messianic fervor and finds the clue to their immigration to Israel in their unsophisticated and living faith in the redemption of Israel.[30]

Shokeid, who observed the rural Atlas Jews several years after their immigration to Israel, tended then to attribute the Atlas exodus primarily to religious factors. Do the historical facts pertaining to those Jews while still in their Atlas villages support Shokeid's conclusion? We have at our disposal a doctoral thesis on the Jewish communities of southern Morocco, the field study for which was apparently completed around 1954. Its writer, Pierre Flamand, found that the relations between the rural Jews of the High Atlas and their Berber neighbors were fairly sound and that in contrast to other sectors of southern Morocco's Jewish population they had not been the victims of economic straits. He was especially impressed by the conditions in the agricultural *mellahs*, where he found an atypical degree of intimacy and reciprocity between Muslim and Jew.[31] The impressions of anthropologists who questioned the rural Atlas immigrants in Israel about their former economic conditions and Berber-Jewish relationships correspond to Flamand's observations in Morocco.[32] Small wonder then that Flamand did not find it difficult to explain why the rural Atlas Jews had not tended to leave their region *en masse* either to Morocco's big cities or for Israel.[33] However, when he heard of the sudden departure of the Jews of Ait Bouli—where some *mellahs*, like that of Assamer, had an important farming element—he started wondering whether he might have underestimated the religious element in their life.[34]

Grinker's own descriptions of his first visits in the rural *mellahs* leave no doubt that he understood the local Jews' response to this message as stemming from a spiritual source. His reports in fact offer no account of the immediate and sweeping response of the local Jews to his call. We know that he had not anticipated such a reaction and must therefore been surprised.[35] Yet he does talk explicitly of the mystical atmosphere he sensed among the Jews who welcomed him, and one gets the impression that no special explanation seemed necessary in the case of those Jews to account for their immediate response when called on to take part in the redemption of Israel.

Indeed it seems that Grinker himself was, in a way, swept up by the special religious atmosphere that surrounded him. His nonobservant orientation—which had been so prominent in his contacts with the Mazagan *garin*—was toned down. Instead of trying to avoid religious rites—as he had done in Mazagan—we find him directing his plans according to their possible religious impact and participating willingly in Jewish festivals.[36] Jews and the Jewish ways of life he encountered in the Atlas reminded him of religious aspects in his personal education and of the Bible. Thus, for instance, his own perception of the local Jews had been strongly influenced by biblical images. Ait Rabaa may represent an especially interesting example of this inclination. In the book he published many years after his mission, the original name of this locality is not mentioned. Grinker talks only of Ait Arbaa, which—he said—reminded him of Kiryat Arba, the biblical name of Hebron. He first heard this name uttered by local Jews whose descriptions by him remind us of biblical stereotypes.[37]

The belief in the redemption of Israel is closely connected with the messianic belief. But the hasty way in which the rural Jews left their *mellahs* was not accompanied by rumors of the arrival of the messiah or of his messenger. As far as we know, Grinker was never seen by the Atlas Jews as a mystical figure. It was the rebuilding of the Jewish state and the mass return of Jews to the ancestral homeland that were apparently conceived by them in religious and spiritual terms.

If Grinker was neither the messiah nor his messenger—why the haste? The Atlas Jews' quick departure for Israel may also be explained in part by their religious culture. Our knowledge of the local variant of messianism is negligible, and further research may shed new light on this subject.[38] But the religious factor was by no means the only one to play a role in the Atlas exodus and to contribute to the haste with which it occurred. Other factors—social, political, and especially economic—were also involved, and a brief discussion of their role will take us back to our questions about Gellner's theory of diaspora nationalism.

V

It is quite obvious that processes connected with industrialization had not changed or even shaken the traditional structures in the rural and mountainous area. However, an accurate analysis of Grinker's mission should not overlook Flamand's findings concerning changes that had been taking place in the surrounding area at that time. Clearly, industrialization had begun to penetrate the Atlas region and to bring about changes in a different type of Jewish settlement in the Atlas—the piedmont *mellahs*, such as Demnate or Amizmiz. These big *mellahs*, located at crossroads and market-places, were much more exposed to the new, modern forces coming from Morocco's Atlantic coast. In such localities unprecedented competition with local Muslims, on the one hand, and with outside wholesale companies—most of them of urban Jews—on the other seriously hurt the local Jews' monopoly on trade and craftsmanship. Unable to hold their own in this competition, more and more Jews began leaving these Atlas commercial centers for the big cities, mainly Marakesh and Casablanca.[39] In Casablanca the Atlas Jews joined other poor Jewish immigrants from southern Morocco, creating a high social burden for the local Jewish communities. This situation was, by the way, the background for a plan—drawn up as far back as 1951–52 between the AJDC and the Immigration Department of the Jewish Agency—to transfer the nonurban Jewish population from southern Morocco to Israel (the "village evacuation plan").[40]

Thus, though not yet directly affected by the harmful effects of industrialization, the rural Atlas Jews could feel them approaching. Furthermore, the introduction in the piedmont *mellahs* of such modern facilities as schools and hospitals, coupled with modern transportation and means of communication (including printed matter in Hebrew), confronted rural Jews with alternative models of living, different from their primitive existence. In a letter of thanks written by Moshe Asoulin of Ait Bougmez on behalf of his community's members after their immigration to Israel, this aspect of "redemption" is emphasized:

Gentlemen—We the people of Bougmez extend blessings and wishes of success to the founders of KKL [the Jewish National Fund] and to their leader Mr. Grinker, who did all he could to assist us and to overcome the countless obstacles, sparing neither effort nor means. . . . Our feet have not crossed the threshold of a school, there are no cars in our village. All we have is the mountain. . . . And now our thanks to the Almighty and our thanks to the people of KKL who gave us of themselves and of their worldly goods until they brought us out of our slumber. They have led us from darkness to light and have redeemed us from exile. A magnificent redemption did they bestow on us. And they fed us, and to children who had not known speech they gave schooling and brought a doctor to treat the ailing. Blessed be the Almighty who has not deprived the Jewish people of a redeemer.[41]

Asoulin's letter also sheds light on the local Jews' attitude toward the principle of subordination *vis-à-vis* their Berber neighbors:

Our culture has become that of the Ashdodites [the Biblical term used by the Atlas Jews in describing Berbers], and we have become enslaved to them. We have assimilated among them and have become dependent on their support. We live in sorrow, submitting to them like mules and eating whatever bread they deign to give us. . . . I recall well the day when Mr. Grinker arrived in the village to register us. How we

looked forward to seeing him approach. And the Ashdodites would encircle his vehicle. They would enclose us in the village and bar us from meeting with him.

We still remember the day when we rode forth to greet him. We arrived on mules
over mountain passes and ditches. Old and young alike, frightened though we were
of the cruel Ashdodites lurking in the mountains. A book would not suffice to recount all we felt.[42]

Within the terms of their traditional status, the Jews of Bougmez might
have had bearable or even sound relationships with their Muslim neighbors. However, redemption primarily meant breaking the yoke of inequity
and hard labor—the essence of *galut* (life in exile). Furthermore, Asoulin's
evidence on Berber-Jewish relations might also point to an important cause
for the hasty departure of the local Jews. It is worth noting his reference to
an incident in which pressure was exercised on the Jews in connection with
Grinker's first visit to the village. From Grinker we know that the local Berber population wanted to bar him from meeting the village Jews by actually
blocking his way to Ait Bougmez.[43] This action apparently had to do with
the fact that the economic services of the Jews, including various fees and
taxes, were considered vital for the well-being of the village and of its chief.
Interestingly enough, evidence from the Ait Bouli district seems to contradict this. There, we are told, the Berbers actually expelled the Jews, declaring Jewish rights to their property null and void and forcing them to leave
as quickly as possible.[44] The two, however, only seem contradictory at first
sight; they actually represent two different phases of the process of the exodus. The Ait Bougmez incident relates to the initial encounter of the local
Jews with a Zionist emissary; the Berbers seemed aware of the excitement
among their artisans, merchants, and fellow farmers and tried to avoid any
threat to the long-standing local order. The Ait Bouli case, on the other
hand, shows the local attitude toward the Jews more than seven months
after Grinker's initial visit.[45] By then it had become clear that the Jews were
determined to leave—as did most, if not all of their fellow Jews in the region. By then it was also time to covet their property. One would even find
easy pretext for pushing out the *dhimis* (the Islamic term indicating pro-
tected Jews or Christians). Their behavior could be judged harmful and in-
jurious if not an outright act of revolt that called for punishment.[46]

The change in the Berber attitude toward the Jews in 1955 was not only
a result of Zionist activity in the area. It probably had more to do with the
indirect effects of the spreading Arab nationalism. We have limited our description to the initial encounter between Grinker and the Atlas Jews that
took place in October–November 1954. In the course of the following
months, however, the Berber populations of the Atlas were changing their
attitude toward Moroccan nationalism and starting to take part in terrorist
activities.[47] Instability was now rampant in the area. Effective protection became rare, and the *dhimis*' property and security were in danger. This was

not an unfamiliar situation, and in the preindustrial environment it might have been a key factor in the crisis in majority-minority relationships.[48]

One may finally add that the different phases and the nature of reactions among the Berbers to the Jewish exodus demonstrates the initial impact of industrialization on this process as well. In the Ait Bougmez case we probably see how the still traditional phase of the local economy conditioned the Berbers' first reaction to the idea of the departure of the Jews. However, the attitude of Ait Bouli indicates that the local inhabitants reasoned it would be possible, after all, to survive without the services of the Jews. This attitude is understandable considering the growing impact of industrialization on nearby markets, if not on the mountain villages themselves. These industrial developments made the departure of artisans and merchants less painful than in the past.

It would seem, therefore, that the exodus of the Atlas Jews was due to a combination of religious, economic, social, and political factors more than to a sudden rise in religious fervor. How, then, can we assess the role religion played in the Atlas Jews' encounter with Zionism? And what can this unique event teach us about diaspora nationalism?

Before the first Zionist emissaries came on the scene it was not possible to discern any national activity or Zionist sentiments in the modern sense among the Atlas Jews. Contrary to his public image, Grinker was not the first Israeli official to visit the remote *mellahs* of the Atlas. The Atlas Jews were first discovered in 1952 in connection with the "village evacuation plan" and the earliest efforts to oppose the "selection regulations."[49] An investigation committee of officials from both the Joint Distribution Committee and the State of Israel was created to look into the qualifications of the village Jews and explore their willingness to emigrate to Israel. The members of the committee visited at least four *mellahs* in the central High Atlas (Ouled Mansour, Tamazert, Tazert, and Hamadna) and registered a "100 percent" in the slot indicating the willingness of the *mellah* inhabitants to leave their homes and go to Israel.[50]

How may we explain the consistently uniform response of the Atlas rural Jews—artisans, small merchants, and farmers alike—to the call of modern Zionism? As Flamand's survey and other evidence clearly shows, the economic effects, which had transformed the traditional profile and functioning of other sectors of Moroccan Jewry, had as yet but a weak impact on the lives of the rural Atlas Jews. They did not push these Jews to move to nearby cities, let alone abroad. The political and cultural effects associated with modernization seem to have played a greater role in the Atlas exodus. Among these, the Moroccan national struggle seems to have been a decisive factor, as periods of political disorder and general insecurity were traditionally considered dangerous for the Jews and had in the past involved inner migrations.[51] However, the local Jews' enthusiastic reaction to the prospects of immigrating to Israel had been clearly sensed even before security conditions deteriorated in Morocco. There is, furthermore, no evidence that Grinker's initial activities in the autumn of 1954 were crowned with success because of the rural Jews' fear of their neighbors. In fact, acute friction between Muslims and Jews seems to have first manifested itself exactly at that time, as a direct result not of purely local circumstances but of the external influence of both Jewish and Arab nationalism.

The fact that both nationalisms, Moroccan and Zionist, penetrated the Atlas preindustrial hinterland from the outside underlines an important similarity between them. Moroccan nationalism, like all third world national movements, did not necessarily require an industrialized environment to spread. It was enough that part of Moroccan society—namely certain elite groups—were industrialized sufficiently to establish a modern national movement. They could serve as a modernizing and national leadership with the potential to reach out to the traditional elements of the society. At the right moment, they could mobilize a national turnabout. Zionism, as demonstrated, also had the ability to enlist preindustrial segments of the Jewish diaspora to the national enterprise. This similarity reflects the extreme dispersal of Jews, including in Afro-Asian areas, and the need for the Jewish diaspora nationalism to struggle with problems that characterize third world national movements.

It remains to be seen, however, what allowed militants of such movements to succeed among the non-Westernized elements of their nation-to-be. Gellner tried to answer this question with respect to the Berber population of the Atlas.[52] As to the Jewish communities, it seems that the historical evidence supports Shokeid's observation that the clue to this success lies in the Jewish religion. As we have tried to show, not only are the other factors insufficient to account for the overwhelmingly positive response to Grinker's mission, but the records are unanimous in pointing to the religious factor as dominating the encounter between the Zionist emissary and the Atlas Jews. Messianic expectations and the vision of redemption were certainly not the only causes motivating the Atlas exodus and determining its speed and form, but they may be defined as the trigger to the whole process, without which Grinker's mission to the area would probably have passed unnoticed.

Similar cases of response to Zionism by Afro-Asian Jewish traditional populations were often termed "messianic Zionism." The use of this term in such cases (in contrast with other contexts) warrants clarification. Modern Zionism is based on the idea of a return to the land of the ancestors. Traditional Judaism includes the belief in the redemption of Israel, which may assume a concrete political meaning. Religion then supplies modern Zionism with a preindustrial quasi-national counterpart to its basic theme. However, as shown above, nationalism did not evolve independently among the Atlas Jews. They needed the outside intervention of people like Grinker, representing Westernized parts of the Jewish diaspora society, to manifest their basically traditional response to modern Zionism. In such cases, messianic Zionism was a response to Zionism, not a special variant of the modern national movement.

The relationship revealed here—in which participation of preindustrial groups in national activities is totally dependent on the work of Westernized members of the nation's elite—again reminds us of the usual situation in third world national movements. As seen above, the unusual attempt of Zionism to unite both European and non-European populations into a single nation created an especially grave inner problem in Israel. Judging by Grinker's mission, religion could play a role not only in bridging the gaps that separated the Atlas Jews from the modern national movement but also in helping people like Grinker, representing the Israeli European elite, to overcome the distance between themselves and the preindustrial "native" Jews. Grinker's first steps in the direction of the rural Atlas Jews were motivated by a shift in Zionist ideology. But once he had met the Atlas Jews, his perception started to be affected by elements of the old religion, which in his eyes turned the locally disregarded Chleuhs into virtual heroes of ancient Israel. Here again the quasi-national elements of traditional Judaism are very clear. An ancient heritage, of a basically political nature but embodied in the Holy Scriptures, is easily and probably unconsciously manipulated by the Zionist militant.[53]

In Grinker's encounters with other parts of the Moroccan diaspora religion did not play such an impressive role. We have seen it in the case of the Mazagan *garin*. There the rise of Zionism was basically a product of modern causes. The people who composed the local *garin* were fairly Westernized and basically resembled groups of *halutzim* in Europe. Neither Grinker nor the *garin* members felt the need to give religion a prominent place in their contacts. It seems that the deeper the gaps between the Israeli envoy and the local Jews, the more the religious and biblical layers of the Jewish heritage were harnessed toward creating the necessary link between the two parties. If diaspora nationalism may have to bridge real and imaginary gaps of unusual width and depth, it could do so by using elements of the diaspora's religion and of its past, the nature of which is spiritual, and sometimes unrealistic and imaginary.

The use of such tools had clear advantages for Jewish diaspora nationalism, as seen in the case of the Atlas Jews, but it also posed risks for the different and far-flung diaspora populations. Thus the economic difficulties encountered by the Atlas Jews in Israel did not at all correspond to their concepts of redemption. They quickly had to renounce their messianic fervor.[54] Modern Jewish nationalism, too, encountered disillusionment in the absorption of the Atlas Jews in Israel. Grinker had been searching for Jewish farmers in the Atlas region. As emphasized in the beginning of the article, farming was only a marginal Jewish occupation in this area. However, oriented by Zionist lay ideology and quasi-biblical perceptions, he portrayed all the local Jews as farmers and had a central role in persuading both the authorities and the public in Israel of the authenticity of this image.[55] Grinker's orientations and inclinations in this case were totally motivated by his devotion to Zionism. But the artisans and merchants did not easily turn into farmers, and for many years both his Atlas immigrants and the settlement authorities of Israel had to cope with the consequences of his rather unrealistic vision.[56]

Notes

1. Overall there were some 7,000–8,000 Jews in the Atlas, but about half of them lived in five big piedmont *mellahs* that resembled small towns, and the encounter of their inhabitants with Zionism is not discussed in the present article. A detailed and documented description of the rural Jewish population of the central High Atlas is found in Pierre Flamand, *Diaspora en terre d'Islam: Les communautés israelités du sud marocain* (Casablanca, 1959), pp. 67–106. For further information gathered from the Atlas immigrants in Israel, especially concerning their internal life and Berber-Jewish relations, see Dorothy Willner and Margot Kohls, "Jews in the High Atlas Mountains of Morocco: A Partial Reconstruction," *Jewish Journal of Sociology* 4 (1962): 207–41; Moshe Shokeid, *The Dual Heritage: Immigrants from the Atlas Mountains in an Israeli Village* (Manchester, England, 1971), pp. 15–33. On farming among the local Jews, see Willner and Kohls, "Jews in the High Atlas Mountains," p. 208; Flamand, *Diaspora en terre d'Islam,* pp. 84–95, 105.

2. For information on Ernest Gellner's studies on the area, see P. Shinar, *Essai de Bibliographie sélective et annotée sur l'Islam maghrébin contemporain: Maroc, Algérie, Tunisie, Libye (1830–1978)* (Paris, 1983), detail nos. 572, 858, 860–62.

3. For a bibliography on the French "Politique bèrbère," see ibid., pp. 169–74; Ch.-A. Julian, *Le maroc face aux imperialismes, 1415–1956* (Paris, 1978), passim.

4. Ernest Gellner, *Nations and Nationalism* (Oxford, England, 1983), pp. 101–9. See also the classification of Zionism as diaspora nationalism from a different point of view in A. D. Smith, "The Formation of Nationalist Movements," in *Nationalist Movements,* ed. A. D. Smith (London and Basingstoke, 1976), p. 4.

5. Gellner, *Nations and Nationalism,* pp. 104–6.

6. I have examined the relations between the Zionist centers and the non-European communities and Zionist branches in *Kehillah Kruah: Yehudei Maroko, haleumiut vehaaliyah, 1943–1945* (forthcoming), translated into French as *Les Juifs du Maroc, le nationalisme et la Aliyah, 1943–1945* (forthcoming).

7. Flamand, *Diaspora en terre d'Islam,* pp. 97–98.

8. Yaron Tsur, "Carnival Fears: The Moroccans and the Ethnic Problem in Young Israel," *Journal of Israeli History* (forthcoming).

9. A full study of this affair has yet to be written. A general sketch of its development in connection with the Moroccan immigration can be found in Shmuel Segev, *Mivzah-yakhin: Aliyatam hahashait shel yehudei Marocco leIsrael* (N.p., 1984), pp. 40–53.

10. Alex Bein, *Aliyah vehityashvut bemedinat Israel* (N.p., 1982), pp. 79ff.; Yishai Geva, "Yishuv haaretz bereshit yemei hamedinah: Bein hityashvut halutzit lehityashvut hamonit," *Yaad* 3 (1989): 97–104.

11. Bein, *Aliyah vehityashvut bemedinat Israel,* pp. 134–42. For more on the relations between the settlement plans and the Moroccan *aliyah,* see Tsur, *Kehillah Kruah,* chap. 3.

12. For more biographical details, see Yehuda Grinker, *Aliyatam shel yehudei haAtlas* (Tel-Aviv, 1973), pp. 17–20.

13. Grinker to the director of the Settlement Department of the Jewish Agency in the northern district [of Israel], October 7, 1954, copy in Archives of the Jewish Labor Movement (AJLM), Tel-Aviv, IV, 307-1-277; Grinker to Tenuat Hamoshavim (TM) secretariat, n.d. [November 20, 1954], ibid. See also Grinker to Z. Shragai, head of the Immigration Department of the Jewish Agency, February 7, 1955, Central Zionist Archives (CZA), Jerusalem, S6/6245; Julien, *Le maroc face aux imperialismes,* p. 369.

14. See the correspondence cited in note 13, above.

15. Julien, *Le maroc face aux imperialismes,* p. 369.

16. On the general background of Mazagan incidents, see ibid., p. 434. Somewhat exaggerated reports on the Jewish losses are to be found in "Immenses incendies au Mellah de Mazagan," *Petit Maroc,* August 22, 1955; "Mille quatre cents refugées israélites à Mazagan," *La vigie Marocain,* August 25, 1955.

17. Grinker to Tenuat Hamoshavim, September 2, 1954, AJLM, IV, 307-1-277.

18. Flamand, *Diaspora en terre d'Islam,* p. 103.

19. Report of Z. Haklai cited in Segev, *Mivzah-yakhin,* p. 57. See also the central role of Keren Kayemet LeIsrael in the Atlas Jews' conception of Zionist work, in a letter by Moshe Asoulin cited in note 41, below.

20. Grinker, *Aliyatam shel yehudei haAtlas,* p. 37.

21. Ibid., p. 22.

22. Ibid.

23. Ibid., pp. 22–23.

24. Ibid., pp. 25–26; Grinker to TM's secretariat, October 29, 1954, AJLM, IV, 307-1-277.

25. Grinker, *Aliyatam shel yehudei haAtlas,* passim. See also Asoulin's letter cited in note 41, below.

26. Grinker, *Aliyatam shel yehudei haAtlas,* p. 44. I have not been able to find the detailed list. I assume it contained people of other sectors of the Jewish population of the Atlas region, apart from the rural one.

27. Ibid., passim. But systematic and more detailed information on the pace of the Atlas immigration is to be found in files S6/6002 and S6/6245 of CZA.

28. Shokeid, *Dual Heritage,* pp. 28–29.

29. Ibid. See also Willner and Kohls, "Jews in the High Atlas Mountains," pp. 214–19.

30. Shokeid, *Dual Heritage,* pp. 32–33; Shokeid, "Jewish Existence in a Berber Environment," in *Le relations entre juifs et musulmans en Afrique du nord XIXe–XXe siècles* (Paris, 1980), p. 66.

31. Flamand, *Diaspora en terre d'Islam,* pp. 98–99, 102–3.

32. Shokeid, *Dual Heritage,* passim; Shokeid, "Jewish Existence," passim; Willner and Kohls, "Jews in the High Atlas Mountains," passim.

33. Flamand, *Diaspora en terre d'Islam,* pp. 102–3.

34. Pierre Flamand, *Quelques manifestations de l'espirit populaire dans les juiveries du Sud-Marocain* (N.p., n.d.), p. 67.

35. From his first and unsuccessful expedition, Grinker was convinced that economic considerations of the rural Jews would disturb his mission. Grinker to TM secretariat, October 14, 1954, AJLM, IV, 307-1-277.

36. Grinker, *Aliyatam shel yehudei haAtlas,* pp. 24–26, 56.

37. Ibid., pp. 22–23. It is worth mentioning that in his original letter to TM, dated October 29, 1954, where he first described this meeting, Grinker used the correct name of the village. AJLM, IV, 307-1-277.

38. The messianic idea in the writings of important rabbis, mainly in the urban centers of Moroccan Jewry, has already been studied by several scholars, notably by Professor Haim Zafrani and Dan Manor. Still, the same belief could assume some special characteristics in the remote, Judeo-Berber areas. Professor Y. Shitrit is now studying the epic and popular poetry of Moroccan Jewry, which contains messianic themes.

39. Flamand, *Diaspora en terre d'Islam,* p. 79; Flamand, *Un mellah en pays bèrbère: Demnate* (Paris, 1952), p. 139; Flamand, "Quelques reseignements statistiques sur la population israelite du Sud marocain," *Hespéris* 37 (1950): 393ff.; André Adam, *Casablanca* (Paris, 1968), pp. 198–201.

40. See correspondence on this project in file S6/6008, CZA; see also "Sikumei hasihah im baei koah haJoint bidvar hishtatfutam betakziv Maroko," n.d. [end 1951?], and Z. Haklai to Y. Raphael, March 4, 1952, CZA, S6/6162. The Joint Distribution Committee was interested in the project not because of Israeli interests but primarily because of Moroccan Jewish ones. See Conseil des communautés israélites du Maroc, *Congres 1953: Motions* (N.p., n.d.), chap. 2 (7), where the evacuation idea (without specification of its destination) is strongly advocated by the Moroccan Jewish leadership. For more on the village evacuation plan, see Tsur, *Kehillah Kruah,* chap. 3.

41. A photocopy of the original letter by Moshe Asoulin is reproduced in the collection of pictures in Segev, *Mivzah-yakhin,* between pp. 128–29.

42. Ibid.

43. Grinker, *Aliyatam shel yehudei haAtlas,* p. 40.

44. Note from June 7, 1955, ibid., p. 50.

45. Grinker started his activity in this district by the first week of November 1954, immediately after discovering that his way to Ait Bougmez was blocked. Ibid., p. 40.

46. On such interpretations and reactions in traditional Muslim-Jewish relationships in Tunisia and Zeidite Yemen, see Yaron Tsur, "France and the Jews of Tunisia: The Policy of the French Authorities toward the Jews and the Activities of the Jewish Elites during the Period of Transition from Muslim Independant State to Colonial Rule, 1873–1888 (Ph.D. diss., Hebrew University, Jerusalem, 1988), p. 57 and n. 10.

47. Julien, *Le maroc face aux imperialismes,* pp. 361ff. See also Grinker, *Aliyatam shel yehudei haAtlas,* pp. 62–63.

48. See Flamand, *Diaspora en terre d'Islam,* p. 106 (the author's remarks on the possible effects of Arab nationalism on the area, before it actually manifested itself); Yaron Tsur, "Hahaapalah uvinyan hahevrah haleumit: Hashpaat haaliyah hahashait al hazikah bein Israel veyehudei Maroko," *Hazionut* 15 (1990): 152–53, 160–61.

49. American Jewish Joint Distribution Committee (AJDC) correspondence enclosed to H. Shiba (director of the Health Ministry, who headed the "proselection" campaign) to David Ben-Gurion and others, July 2, 1952, CZA, S6/6008; Z. Haklay, "Yehudim beharei haAtlas," in Grinker, *Aliyatam shel yehudei haAtlas,* pp. 122–30 (selection of Haklay's references to the Atlas Jews in his series of articles on Moroccan Jewry, *Davar,* June 1955).

50. Investigation Report, enclosed with a letter from W. Bein (AJDC Casablanca) to B. Katzki (AJDC Paris), May 30, 1952, copies in CZA S6/6008.

51. The last such period preceded the French occupation and involved large-scale demographic changes. See, for instance, M. Laskier, *The Alliance Israélite Universelle and the Jewish Communities of Morocco, 1862–1962* (Albany, N.Y., 1983), pp. 124–26.

52. See Shinar, *Essai de Bibliographie,* detail nos. 572, 858, 860–62.

53. See. A. D. Smith, *The Ethnic Origins of Nations* (Oxford, England, 1986), pp. 212–14.

54. Shokeid, *Dual Heritage,* pp. 36–39.

55. Grinker was not the first to contribute to the favorable stereotype of the Atlas Jews at this stage. Their stereotyping in official circles started earlier, but crystallized with his intensive and fruitful labors, which were rather widely publicized. See, for instance, Shabtai Tevet's reports from Morocco, *Haaretz,* February 1955.

56. See the reciprocal disillusionment as reflected in the case of the Assamer Jews' first encounter with their *moshav.* Shokeid, *Dual Heritage,* p. 36.

Contributors

SHMUEL ALMOG is Professor Emeritus at the Institute of Contemporary Jewry at the Hebrew University of Jerusalem, Israel. His publications include *Zionism and History: The Rise of a New Jewish Consciousness* (1987) and *Nationalism and Antisemitism in Modern Europe, 1815–1945* (1990).

SHLOMO AVINERI is Professor of Political Science at the Hebrew University of Jerusalem, Israel. He is the author of *Hegel's Theory of the Modern State* (1974) and *The Making of Modern Zionism* (1981).

ISRAEL BARTAL is Professor of Jewish History at the Hebrew University of Jerusalem, Israel. His publications include *Poles and Jews: A Failed Brotherhood* (1993) and *Galut baaretz* (1995).

STUART A. COHEN is Professor of Political Studies at Bar-Ilan University, Ramat Gan, Israel. He has written *The Three Crowns: Structures of Communal Politics in Early Rabbinic Jewry* (1991) and *The Scroll or the Sword? Dilemmas of Religion and Military Service in Israel* (1997).

EVYATAR FRIESEL is Professor of Jewish History at the Hebrew University of Jerusalem, Israel, and Israel State Archivist. His publications include *The Zionist Policy after the Balfour Declaration, 1917–1922* (1977) and *Atlas of Modern Jewish History* (1990).

LLOYD P. GARTNER is Professor of European Jewish History at Tel-Aviv University, Israel. He has written *The Jewish Immigrant in England, 1870–1914* (1973) and *Hayishuv hayehudi beArzot haBerit* (1988).

JEFFREY S. GUROCK is Libby M. Klaperman Professor of Jewish History at Yeshiva University, New York. He is the author of *American Jewish Orthodoxy in Historical Perspective* (1996) and co-author, with Jacob J. Schacter, of *A Modern Heretic and a Traditional Community: Mordecai M. Kaplan, Orthodoxy and American Judaism* (1997).

ISRAEL KOLATT is Dr. Israel Goldstein Professor of the History of Zionism and the New Yishuv at the Hebrew University of Jerusalem, Israel. His publications include *Avot umeyasdim* (1975) and *Haam hayehudi verayon hayishuv haleumi beEretz Israel* (1990).

EHUD LUZ is Senior Lecturer in Jewish History at Haifa University, Israel. He is the author of *Parallels Meet* (1988) and the forthcoming *Power, Morality and Jewish Identity*.

MICHAEL A. MEYER is Professor of Jewish History at Hebrew Union College—Jewish Institute of Religion, Cincinnati, Ohio. His publications include *Response to Modernity: A History of the Reform Movement in Judaism* (1988) and *German-Jewish History in Modern Times* (1996–98).

AVIEZER RAVITZKY is Sol Rosenblum Professor of Jewish Thought at the Hebrew

University of Jerusalem, Israel. His publications include *Messianism, Zionism and Jewish Religious Radicalism* (1996) and *Faith and History: Studies in Jewish Philosophy* (1996).

JEHUDA REINHARZ is Richard Koret Professor of Modern Jewish History and President of Brandeis University, Waltham, Massachusetts. He is the author of *Chaim Weizmann: The Making of a Zionist Statesman* (1993) and co-author, with Ben Halpern, of *Zionism and the Creation of a New Society* (1998).

YOSEF SALMON is Professor of Jewish History at Ben-Gurion University, Beer Sheva, Israel. He has written *Zionut vedat* (1990) and *Shivat Zion: Mahadurah madait* (1998).

JONATHAN D. SARNA is the Joseph H. and Belle R. Braun Professor of American Jewish History at Brandeis University, Waltham, Massachusetts. His publications include *JPS: The Americanization of Jewish Culture (1888–1988)* (1989) and *The American Jewish Experience* (1997).

CHAIM SCHATZKER is Professor of Jewish History at Haifa University, Israel. He is the author of *Die Juden in den deutschen Geschichtsbuchern: Schulbuchanalyse zur Darstellung der Juden, des Judentums und des Staates Israel* (1998) and *Noar yehudi beGermanyah ben yahadut legermaniyut, 1870–1945* (1998).

ANITA SHAPIRA is Ruben Merenfeld Professor on the Study of Zionism at Tel-Aviv University, Israel. Her publications include *Berl Katznelson: A Biography of a Socialist Zionist* (1985) and *Land and Power: The Zionist Resort to Force, 1881–1948* (1992).

YARON TSUR is Senior Lecturer in Jewish History at Tel-Aviv University, Israel. He has written *Yehudim beidan shel temurot* (1978) and the forthcoming *Une communaute dechirée: Les Juifs du Maroc, le nationalisme et la Aliyah, 1943–1954.*

ROBERT S. WISTRICH is Professor of Jewish History at the Hebrew University of Jerusalem, Israel. His publications include *The Jews of Vienna in the Age of Franz Joseph* (1989) and *Antisemitism: The Longest Hatred* (1992).

STEVEN J. ZIPPERSTEIN is Daniel E. Koshland Professor in Jewish Culture and History at Stanford University, California. He is the author of *Elusive Prophet: Ahad Ha'am and the Origins of Zionism* (1993) and the forthcoming *Imagining Russian Jewry: Memory, History, Identity.*

YAAKOV ZUR is Professor of Jewish History at Bar-Ilan University, Ramat Gan, Israel. He has written *Haortodoksyah hayehudit beGermanyah veyahasah lehitargenut yehudit velazionut, 1896–1911* (1982) and "Hayahadut haharedit beGermanyah bimei hashilton hanazi," in *Toldot Hashoah—Germanyah* (1998), edited by Abraham Margaliot and Yehoyakim Kochavy.

Index

Aaron, 79

Abrahams, Israel, 161–62

Adath Israel Society (United Hebrew Community of New York), 227

"Ad halom" (Shlonsky), 256

Adler, Cyrus: Balfour Declaration opposed by, 208; dissent from Zionism, 207; Finkelstein as successor to, 212; as between non-Zionism and anti-Zionism, 177

Adler, Felix, 193

Adler, Hermann, 32, 163, 165, 168

Agnon, Shmuel Yosef, 67, 253

Agudat Haelef, 34

Agudat Harabbanim, 220–30; and Agudat Israel, 226, 230; on Balfour Declaration, 225; conflict with Reb Velvele, 227–29; cooperation with American Orthodox colleagues, 222–23; Eastern European influence in, 220–21; founding of, 221; members as staying in America, 232n.16; and Mizrahi movement, 223, 224–26, 230; on Old Yishuv, 225, 227; resolution on Zionism of 1923, 226

Agudat Harabbanim Haharedim beAngliah (League of Orthodox Rabbis in England), 166

Agudat Israel: and Agudat Harabbanim, 226, 230; Alfandari on, 82; in *Austrittsgemeinde* in Frankfurt, 110; Breuer on, 113; British rabbis in founding of, 166; draft regulations of Jewish community rejected by, 135–36; Esra youth movement originating in, 306; and Mizrahi movement, 112, 278; Mizrahi split in formation of, 31; Reb Velvele accepting position of, 228; right to secede from general community, 286; right-wing Ashkenazim in, 130; and secular nature of the Yishuv, 288; separatist tendency in, 135, 295; Shapira of Munkács's opposition to, 70–74; *status quo* agreement between Jewish Agency and, 295–96; on woman suffrage, 134

Ahad Haam, 55–66; American Reform thinkers on, 181; American Zionist ideology influenced by, 197; becomes Bnei Moshe leader, 63; cultural Zionism of rejected, 126; Dawidowicz on, 59–60, 66n.17; distances himself from Bnei Moshe, 55; distinguishing characteristics of, 58; Friedlaender compared with, 177–78, 208; on the *galut*, 178; Gordis on, 211; hasidic background of, 62; and Herzl, 5, 123; Katznelson compared with, 247; "Ketavim balim," 63, 64, 65; "Lo zeh haderekh," 57, 58–59, 66n.17; on modernization as precondition of Zionism, 50; on national spirit, 51; in Odessa, 63; pen name of, 61; on religion and national identity, 29; secular approach of, 251, 252; as secularizing hasidic leadership patterns, 56; self-discipline of, 58; on spirituality, 64; on virtue of toleration, 29–30, 50–51; Yishuv unification attempt, 131. *See also* Bnei Moshe

Ahavat Zion, 35–36, 146

Ahdut Haavodah Party, 138, 258

Ait Bougmez (Morocco), 322–24

Ait Bouli district (Morocco), 319–20, 323, 324

Ait Rabaa (Morocco), 319, 321

Akiba (Finkelstein), 213, 217n.42

Alexander II (emperor of Russia), 16, 22

Alfandari, Solomon Eliezer, 82–83, 88nn. 66, 67

Aliyah: First, 122, 128; Fourth, 270, 287; Third, 257, 270. *See also* Second Aliyah

Alkalai, Judah Solomon Hai, 3–4

Alliance Israélite Universelle, 126

Allon, Azaria, 265

Altneuland (Herzl), 5, 31

America. *See* United States

American Council for Judaism, 180

American Hebrew (journal), 181–82

American Hebrew Congregations, Union of (UAHC), 189

Americanization, 181, 182
American Jewish Committee, 207, 213
American Jewish Congress, 206
American Jewish Joint Distribution Committee (JDC), 225, 322, 324
America's Jews (Sklare), 175
Amiel, Moshe Avigdor, 288
Amir, Aharon, 7
Amizmiz (Morocco), 322
Amos, 261
Anglo-Jewish Association, 126, 163
Antisemitism: American Jewry affected by, 210; in Austria after First World War, 155; Bloch on defense against, 148; in crisis in American Jewry, 192, 194; of Ford, 199; Friedlaender as ignoring, 178; in Guedemann and Herzl's relations, 152–54; and Herzl's *Judenstaat,* 156n.23; Orthodox interpretation of, 146–47; Pinsker on German "scientific," 143, 144; to Vienna from Berlin, 141; Zionism alleged to incite, 94, 107–8, 117, 145, 169n.10. *See also* Pogroms
Anti-Zionism: in American Conservative Judaism, 177, 206; in American Orthodoxy, 227; of American Reform movement, 180; Anglo-Jewish opposition to political Zionism, 159–71; of Shapira of Munkács, 67–89; of Ultra-Orthodox in America, 219–21; and Zionism in traditional Judaism in Eastern Europe, 25–43; and Zionism in Vienna, 140–58
Anti-Zionist Committee (Antizionistisches Komitee), 95, 97–98, 102n.6
Anu vehadat (instruction booklet), 268–69
Arab nationalism, 2, 312–13, 323
Arlosoroff, Chaim, 264
Ashinsky, Abraham, 223, 224, 231n.12
Ashkenazim: in Chief Rabbinate, 131; Hakham Bashi's authority rejected by, 282; in New Yishuv, 136; in Old Yishuv, 77, 129, 130, 137; under Ottoman rule, 279; on Rabbinical Council, 283; and Sephardim in Palestine, 129; in unification of the Yishuv under British rule, 281; on woman suffrage, 134–35
Asoulin, Moshe, 322–23
Assamer (Morocco), 319–20
Assembly of the Yishuv, 280
Assimilation: Anglo-Jewry as seeking, 160, 161; distress associated with, 302; "good" versus "bad," 162; Guedemann on, 151, 152; Jellinek as supporter of,

140; nationalism as antithesis of, 27; Pinsker's rejection of, 141–42; Preil on Jews' refusal of, 30; Schechter on Zionism as bulwark against, 175–76, 209; Zionists on, 147
Association for Liberal Judaism in Germany (Vereinigung für das liberale Judentum in Deutschland), 99, 102n.6
Atlas, Eleazer, 32
Atlas Mountains: exodus of Jews from, 313, 314–15, 319, 321, 323–24; Glinker's mission to, 316–27; industrialization in, 321–22; Jewish population in, 312, 327n.1; Zionism and rural Atlas Jews, 312–29
Austria: Franz Joseph, 144, 147; *Grundgesetz* of 1867, 141; Jews as patriots in, 144; Taaffe, 147, 148. *See also* Vienna
Austrian Israelite Union, 149
Austrittsgemeinde, 108, 114n.5
Autoemanzipation! (Pinsker), 141
Avardam, Zechariah Mendel, 35
Avraham of Sochaczew, 84n.14
Avraham Yaakov ben haZaddik miRuzhin, 62
Azariah of Pano, 86n.36

Babylonian Talmud, 162, 184
Baden (Germany), 112
Baeck, Leo, 94, 100, 101, 105nn. 35, 37
Bagalgal (Shlonsky), 256
Balfour Declaration: Agudat Harabbanim on, 225; "battle of books" surrounding, 164; Conservatives fail to endorse, 208; as deliberately ambivalent, 159; Schiff influenced by, 182; Shapira of Munkács on, 69; Weizmann on opposition to, 160
Bar-Ilan, Meir. *See* Berlin, Meir
Bar Kokhba, 167, 245, 264
Baron, Joseph, 200n.17
Bartal, Israel, 1
Bar Yohai, 264
Barzilai, Yehoshua, 56
Basle Program, 30, 207
Bat-Yehudah, Geulah, 41n.31
Baumgardt, David, 105n.35
Bavel-Yerushalayim equation, 184
Bavli, Hillel, 218n.46
"Beein elohim" (Shlonsky), 256–57
Beirat, Yaacov, 227
Beitar youth movement, 307
Beit vaad lahakhamim (newspaper), 171n.28
Belloc, Hilaire, 161

Belorussia, 14
Ben-Avigdor (Abraham Leib Shalkovich), 56
Ben-Baruch of Rothenburg, Meir, 68, 84n.4
Ben David (Jehuda Leib Dawidowicz), 59–
60, 66n.17
Ben-Gurion, David: civil marriage proposal
of, 285; "From Class to Nation" slogan,
270; on Petah Tikva farmers, 252; as po-
litical leader of labor movement, 247; on
religious values as national values, 290; in
status quo agreement, 295
Benjamin, Walter, 1
Bentwich, Norman, 283
Ben-Yehuda, Eliezer, 20, 66n.17
Ben Zakkai, Yohanan, 168
Berbers, 312, 322–24
Berdichevsky, Micha Yosef, 239–40, 242,
251
Bergman, S. H., 287
Berlin (Germany): antisemitism radiating
from, 141; Cohn affair, 96; Jewish intel-
lectuals in, 18; Lehranstalt für die Wis-
senschaft des Judentums, 96, 98
Berlin, Meir (Bar-Ilan): and Gordis, 214; on
Mizrahi position on religion in the Yishuv,
289, 290; on public observance of relig-
ious precepts, 277, 278; on religion and
nationalism, 291
Berlin, Meyer, 224
Berlin, Naphtali Zevi Judah (the Neziv), 27,
46, 222–23, 232n.14
Bernstein, Béla, 104n.25
Bezalel School, 128
Bialik, Hayim Nahman, 267, 269, 293
Bible, the: and Labor Zionism, 6; Ruth, 268;
in Second Aliyah's cultural fabric, 261; so-
cialism compared with, 261–62; Song of
Songs, 167–68; in Zionist education,
260–61
Bible for Home Reading, The (Montefiore),
163
Bierer, Reuben, 146
Biltmore Program, 213
Biluim: as ancestor of Second Aliyah, 55; as
nonobservant, 27, 33; in Palestinian mi-
gration of 1880s, 121–22
Birnbaum, Nathan, 156n.16
Bitanyah, 258
Blau, Amram, 77
Blaustein, Rahel, 260
Blau-Weiss (Blue-White) hiking group, 302,
305–6
Bloch, Chaim, 150

Bloch, Joseph Samuel: and Herzl, 148–49;
and Jellinek, 149; and Kadima, 148; Orthodox militancy of, 147–48; political
Zionism opposed by, 148–50
Bluestone, Isaac Jacob, 219
Blumenfeld, Kurt, 100
Bnei Akiva youth movement, 307
Bnei Moshe: Ahad Haam becomes leader of,
63; Ahad Haam distances himself from,
55; Ahad Haam's purpose in founding,
60–61; attempt to revive, 55; attempt to
take over Odessa Committee, 29; as bizarre interlude, 55–56, 65n.1; core membership of, 57; failure of, 64–65; failure
to reach consensus with the observant, 50,
51; as Garden of Eden, 64; Masonic influences in, 61–62; Mendele on, 58; observant and nonobservant sought by, 56–57
Bokser, Benzion, 184, 214
Bornstein, Abraham, 34, 39
Borochov, Ber: secularized background of, 3;
on socialism and religion, 245–46, 278–
79
Brainin, Reuven, 59
Brandeis, Louis D.: Conservative attitude to-
ward, 206, 207; "The Jewish Problem:
How to Solve It," 198; mission motif in,
197; synthesis of Zionism and American-
ism, 198; on Zionism and citizenship, 182
Brenner, Yosef Hayim, 240–42, 251
Breuer, Isaac, 109, 111, 113, 307
Brickner, Barnett, 200n.17
Britain. See Great Britain
British Jews, League of, 164
British mandate. See Mandate period
Brit Olim (Association of Immigrants) youth
movement, 302
Brody (Poland), 13, 122
Buber, Martin: on Eretz Israel and Judaism,
276; on fulfilling the law, 307; as "path-
seeker," 294–95; on religious truth, 305;
and Seligmann, 95; in symposium on Lib-
eral Judaism and Zionism, 105n.35
Bund, the, 176, 252, 278
Bunem, Simhah, 41n.46
Burial, 264
Bussel, Yosef, 265

Cahan, Abe, 252, 262
Calvary, Moshe, 248
Canaanite movement, 7
Capitalism, Hapoel Hamizrahi on, 292
Catherine the Great (empress of Russia), 14

Central Conference of American Rabbis
(CCAR), 180, 186n.13, 189, 191, 222
Central Conference of Reform Rabbis, 198
Central Europe: fear of antisemitism in anti-
Zionism in, 145; leadership's response to
modernization in, 45; "pathseekers" originating in, 294; Russian Jewry compared
with that of, 140. *See also countries by
name*
Central Relief Committee, 225
Centralverein deutscher Staatsbürger
jüdischen Glaubens, 93
Chajes, Zwi Perez, 154–55
Chesterton, G. K., 161
Chief Rabbinate: incorporation into Jewish
community, 286; institutional frailty of,
287; Kook's conception of, 284; and reli-
gious Zionists, 137; Sephardi and Ashke-
nazi rabbis, 131; in *status quo* agreement,
296; in unification of the Yishuv under
British rule, 281–87
Christianity: civic responsibility as secondary
to contemplation in, 274–75; Protestant
calls for Christian America, 193; Second
Aliyah's new approach to, 239–41
Circumcision, 263
Civil marriage, 285
"Class Independence," 270
Cohen, Charles Hoyd, 192
Cohen, Hermann, 95, 100
Cohn, Emil, 95–96, 103nn. 13, 15, 16
Columbus Platform of 1937, 189
Conjoint Committee, 164
Conservative Judaism: approach to Zionism,
177–79; *Emet veemunah,* 215; Ortho-
doxy compared with, 204, 208; Rabbini-
cal Assembly, 204; spiritual Zionism of,
178, 179, 183; and Zionism, 204–18
Conversion, 190–91
Cracow (Poland), 35, 38, 288
Cultural Zionism: American, 179; in
American Jewish ideology, 197, 199; East-
ern European rabbis rejecting, 126; at
First Zionist Congress, 31; goal of, 138;
of Neumark, 181
Czech nationalism, 2

Daat rabbanim (anti-Zionist book), 33
Daiches, Yisrael Hayim, 166, 168
Dawidowicz, Jehuda Leib (Ben David), 59–
60, 66n.17
Declaration of the Rights of Man and the
Citizen, 5

De Haas, Jacob, 224
Dembitz, Lewis, 222
Demnate (Morocco), 322
De Sola Pool, David, 224
Deutschtum, 140, 302
"Diaspora mentality," 237
Diaspora nationalism, 313, 324–26
Dienemann, Max, 101
Dietary laws. See *Kashrut*
Divorce, 273, 296
Dizengoff, Meir, 28
Dr. Herzl Zion Club (New York City),
200n.17
Doresh Zion, 36
Dostoyevski, Fyodor, 239
Dror youth movement, 307
Drumont, Edouard, 156n.23
Druzkieniki Conference, 27, 223
"Dual loyalty," 107, 111, 125, 161, 185n.6
Dubnov, Simon, 58, 177, 178, 208

East Africa, 161
Eastern Europe: Ahad Haam and the Bnei
Moshe, 55–66; cooperation between observant and nonobservant during Hibbat
Zion period, 44–54; as epitome of *galut*
existence, 275; German-Hungarian Orthodoxy compared with that of, 129–30;
Haskalah in, 13–24, 117–18; immigrants
from setting tone in Yishuv, 277; Jewish
population in, 15–16; Jewish youth
movements in, 302, 307–8; Jews emigrating to United States from, 193; late disintegration of traditional Jewish society in,
22; "pure Zionism" of rabbis of, 126; responses to modernity, 13–24; Shapira of
Munkács, 67–89; split in Jewish communal organization in, 273; tradition and
modernity in, 11–89; Zionism and anti-
Zionism in traditional Judaism in, 25–43.
See also Pale of Settlement; *and countries
by name*
Edah Haredit, 77, 78
Education: the Bible in Zionist, 260–61;
Jewish schools established in Palestine,
126–28; labor movement approach to,
259; Labor Zionist schools, 137–38;
Minsk Conference on, 52; Mizrahi
schools, 137–38; Teachers' Institute,
209–10; Zionist/traditionalist conflict
over, 47. *See also* Religious education
Eibeschütz, Jonathan, 69–70
Eighteenth Zionist Congress, 289

Ein Harod, 264, 267
Einheitsgemeinden, 108, 114n.8
Ekron (Palestine), 127
Elbogen, Ismar, 100, 105n.35
Elected Assembly, 281, 285, 286, 289, 291
Eliasberg, Jonathan, 30
Eliasberg, Mordecai, 27, 46
Elijah Hayim of Łódź, 27
Elk, Max, 101, 105n.35
Emancipation: assimilation as corollary of for Jellinek, 140; the messiah as realized in, 4–5; Pinsker contrasting legal equality with, 142
Emden, Jacob, 81
Emet veemunah (Conservative statement of principles), 215
English language, 221, 233n.31
English Zionist Federation, 165
Enlightenment, European: confessional separated from political in, 15; Jewish heritage and, 13
Enlightenment, Jewish. See Haskalah
Eretz Israel (Land of Israel): Amiel on Torah and, 288; as arena of conflict, 76; for Hasidism, 33; as holy land and projected national homeland, 273; moderate Haskalah on, 21; Mohilever on settlement of, 28, 35–36; mystical belief in therapeutic power of, 53; Orthodox versus Zionist understandings of, 111; paradox of redemption of, 48–49; religious demands of, 68–69; Shapira of Munkács on settlement in, 68–70; Shapira of Munkács's demonization of, 74–76. See also Palestine
Eshkol, Levy, 316
Esra youth movement, 302, 306–7
Ethical Culture, 193, 200n.14
Exile. See Galut
Existential Judaism, 242–44
Ezra, 46, 109

Fallow (sabbatical) year, 6, 28, 48, 252
Federation of American Zionists (FAZ): Agudat Harabbanim cooperation with, 223; in American Mizrahi, 224; in founding of Agudat Harabbanim, 221; Magnes as secretary of, 178; secularism alleged of, 219–20
Feigenbaum, Isaac, 34–35
Feinstein, Marnin, 219, 230n.5
Feldman, Abraham J., 200n.17
Felsenthal, Bernhard: on all becoming Zionists, 195; on American Jews as endangered, 193–94; conversion to Zionism, 192; Jewish colonization of Palestine opposed by, 188, 199n.1; on Zionism and Reform, 180, 181; Zionism as missionary movement for, 197; on Zionism as philanthropy, 198
Fineshriber, William H., 195, 202n.40
Finkelstein, Louis, 212–14, 215
First Aliyah: Bilu group in, 122; Old Yishuv opposition to, 128
First Zionist Congress: Basle Program, 30, 207; cultural issues at, 31; German Orthodoxy influenced by, 109; German rabbinical opposition to, 94; Herzl's "egg dance" at, 124–25; students at, 123
Fischel, Harry, 224
Fishman, Y. L. (Maimon), 284, 288–89, 295, 301n.46
Flamand, Pierre, 315, 320, 324
Ford, Henry, 199
Forverts (newspaper), 252, 262
Fourth Aliyah, 270, 287
Fränkel, Zacharias: on Halakhah as flexible, 204; Jewish religion redefined in context of emancipation, 5; on sociopolitical dimension of Judaism, 209
Frankfurt am Main (Germany), 108, 109, 110
Franz Joseph (emperor of Austria), 144, 147
Frazer, John, 274
Free Association of Orthodox Rabbis (Freie Vereinigung für die Interessen des Orthodoxen Judentums), 109
Freideutsche Jugend, 310n.18
Freie Vereinigung für die Interessen des Orthodoxen Judentums (Free Association of Orthodox Rabbis), 109
Friedenwald, Harry, 222, 224
Friedlaender, Israel: Ahad Haam compared with, 177–78, 208; Conservative approach to Zionism, 177, 207–8; mission motif in, 197; on Zionism as bulwark against assimilation, 209
Friedman, David, 27
Friedman, David Moses: and Ahavat Zion, 35; Herzl appeals for support from, 30, 37; and Lipschitz's anti-Zionist organization, 39; pro-Zionist views of, 34, 36–37
Friedman, Isaac, 28, 36
Friedman, Israel, 37, 42n.66
Friedman, Jacob, 36
Friesel, Evyatar, 230n.5
Frischmann, David, 269

Frumkin, J. D., 32
Funerals, 264
Furet, François, 2

Gal, Allon, 197
Galicia: Brody, 13, 122; Cracow, 35, 38, 288; government schools for Jews in, 16; Hashomer Hazair youth movement in, 307; Hasidism in, 33, 35; Haskalah in, 13; Hovevei Zion in, 35; Jellinek's opposition to Orthodoxy in, 146; Mahzikei Hadas in, 38; Orthodoxy in, 147; Second Aliyah pioneers coming from, 238
Galut (exile): Ahad Haam on, 178, 208; in America, 178; condition of the Jewish people in, 45–46; Eastern Europe as epitome of existence in, 275; Graetz on, 209; Hapoel Hamizrahi on, 292; labor movement on, 259; Montefiore on, 164; "rejection of" in Zionist education, 260, 261; shlilat hagalut, 197
Garinim, 316
Gaster, Moses, 160, 165
Gederah (Palestine), 28
Geiger, Abraham, 94, 99
Geiger, Ludwig, 102n.3
Gellner, Ernest, 312–13, 325
Gemeindeorthodoxie, 108
General Zionism, Labor Zionism contrasted with, 7
German Nationalist Jews, League of (Verband nationaldeutscher Juden), 98
Germany: Baden, 112; emigration after Hitler's rise, 136; Frankfurt am Main, 108, 109, 110; German nationalism, 2, 140; Haskalah in, 18; Jewish youth movements in, 302, 307–8; Liberal Judaism and Zionism in, 93–106; Orthodoxy in, 18–19; Orthodoxy's attitude toward Zionism in, 107–15; Ultra-Orthodox separatism in, 273. See also Berlin
German Zionist Association (Zionistische Vereinigung für Deutschland), 93, 99
Gerson, Herman, 309
Geulat haaretz, 6
Gibbon, Edward, 274
Ginsburg, Isaak, 232n.14
Ginzberg, Asher. See Ahad Haam
Ginzberg, Isaiah, 62
Glaoui Pasha, 312
"God seekers," 240
Goldmann, Felix, 94–95, 98, 102nn. 5, 8, 104n.26

Goldstein, Moshe, 87n.45
Goldstein, Yossi, 55
Gordis, Robert, 211–12, 214
Gordon, Aharon David: the Bible as inspiration of, 262; dancing and singing at Passover, 265; "religion of labor" of, 6, 247–48; on status of the Rabbinate, 282
Gordon, Eliezer, 27
Gordon, Yehuda Leib, 26, 251, 275
Gordonia youth movement, 307
Gottheil, Gustav, 180, 188, 192
Gottheil, Richard: and Agudat Harabbanim, 221; defense of Zionism, 195, 197; on Orthodox Zionists, 222; on Zionists at Hebrew Union College, 201n.32
Gottlober, Abraham Dov, 19, 21
Graetz, Heinrich, 209
Great Britain: Anglo-Jewish Association, 126, 163; Anglo-Jewish opposition to political Zionism, 159–71; conquest of Palestine, 279. See also Balfour Declaration; Mandate period
Greek nationalism, 2
Green, A. A., 165
Greenberg, Gershon, 227
Greenberg, Simon, 210, 214
Greenberg, Uri Zvi, 256, 257–58, 260, 263
Grillparzer, Franz, 152
Grinker, Yehuda, 316–27
Grinstein, Hyman B., 219, 230n.5
Gronemann, Selig, 102n.1
Gruenbaum, Yitzhak, 295
Grundgesetz (Austria), 141
Grünwald, Max, 105n.35
Guedemann, Moritz: on assimilation, 151, 152; and Herzl, 148, 151, 152–54, 158n.61; on Kadima, 154; Nationaljudentum, 151, 152; political Zionism opposed by, 144, 150–54; on tradition, 146
Gymnasia Herzliya (Jaffa), 128, 260, 261

Haggadah, 265, 266, 267, 268
Haifa (Palestine), 101, 128
Hakham Bashi, 131, 279, 281–82, 283
Hakibbutz Hadati, 114
Halakhah: Buber on, 295; Central European leadership on role of, 45; Conservative Judaism on, 204; on deviation from the Torah, 48; Hapoel Hamizrahi on, 292, 293; individual-communal bond expressed in, 276; Katznelson on imposing obedience to, 291; Kook on role of, 284; the nonobservant on, 277; Orthodox

interpretation of, 110; in *status quo* agreement, 296

Halberstam, Ezekiel Schraga, 35–36

Halukah grants, 127, 128, 252

Hamahanot Haolim youth movement, 270

Hamelitz (periodical), 33

Hanoar Haoved youth movement, 268

Hanoch Henich of Alexander, 34

Hanukah: Bnei Moshe's resurrection of, 65; Jellinek on nationalist reinterpretation of, 144; labor movement observance of, 264, 268; and Labor Zionism, 6; Montefiore on, 163

Haolam (newspaper), 205

Hapeles (periodical), 39

Hapoel Hamizrahi, 214, 292–93, 297, 317

Hapoel Hazair, 129, 138, 245, 262

Haredim. See Ultra-Orthodoxy

Harris, Maurice H., 198

Hashomer Hadati youth movement, 307

Hashomer Hazair youth movement, 251, 258, 302, 307

Hasidism: Ahad Haam influenced by, 62; growing influence in Eastern Europe, 17; Haskalah opposing, 15; Jellinek's opposition to, 146; and Mahzikei Hadas, 38; traditional Jewish life preserved by, 14; on Zionism, 33–37

Haskalah: as anachronistic, 20; in Eastern Europe, 13–24, 117–18; German contrasted with Eastern European, 19; in Germany, 18; Hasidism opposed by, 15; Hovevei Zion associated with, 35; Orthodoxy as reaction to, 18; versus Orthodoxy in preserving Jewish identity, 19–24; in Palestinian labor movement, 251–52; radical, 19, 20–21

Hatam Sofer, 146

Hataot neurim (Lilienblum), 58

"Hatikvah" (anthem), 214, 269

Hayehudi (periodical), 171n.28

Hebrew language: Alkalai's argument for, 3; Chajes on, 154; cultural Zionism on, 138; in culture of the Yishuv, 296; in education, 127; Jellinek on, 145; labor movement's secularization of, 260; Labor Zionism on, 5–6; moderate Haskalah on, 21; in Orthodox American *yeshivot*, 220, 221; Orthodox versus Zionist understandings of, 111; revival in Palestine, 126; in Second Aliyah, 237; Teachers' Institute, 209–10

Hebrew Union College: as divided over Zionism, 189, 200n.9; Zionist faculty dismissed from, 180, 181; "Zionistic infection of," 188; Zionist students at, 190, 191, 194, 201nn. 21, 32

Hebrew University (Jerusalem), 287, 294

Hehalutz Hazair (Young Pioneer) youth movement, 308

Hehalutz Organization, 136, 308

Hehalutz (Pioneer) youth movement, 255, 308

Heine, Heinrich, 262

Heller, Abraham M., 210

Heller, James, 97

Heller, Maximilian: conversion to Zionism, 188, 195; German Liberal Jewry compared with, 97; on Judaism-equals-Americanism equation, 197; mission motif in, 203n.53; on students abandoning their Zionism, 196; survey of Reformed rabbinate on Zionism, 198–99, 203n.63; on Zionism and Reform, 181, 195; on Zionism as product of despair, 188, 199n.4

Hershman, Abraham M., 206, 210, 211, 215

Hertz, Joseph, 160, 165, 170n.24

Herzl, Theodor: Cyrus Adler on, 207; and Ahad Haam, 5, 123; *Altneuland*, 5, 31; on American Jews and Zionism, 201n.33; and Anglo-Jewry, 160, 169n.3; and Bloch, 148–49; Breuer on, 113; "conquer the communities" call, 31; Conservative attitude toward, 206; "egg dance" at First Zionist Congress, 124–25; English Zionists' advice to, 165; and Friedman, 30, 37; and Guedemann, 148, 151, 152–54, 158n.61; and Hovevei Zion, 123; Mahzikei Hadas as opposed to, 38; on the Orthodox in Zionism, 50, 125–26; secularization in Zionist vision of, 5; secularized background of, 3; "A Solution to the Jewish Problem," 169n.3; Ultra-Orthodox response to death of, 219, 222; Western-liberal inclinations of, 31; Zionism shifted from culture to politics by, 30; on Zionist parliamentary politics, 124. *See also Judenstaat, Der*

Herzog, Yitzhak, 166

Hess, Moses: on Jewish religious tradition, 7–8; *Rome and Jerusalem*, 8; secularized background of, 3

Hevrat Marbei Haskalah (Society for the Promotion of Enlightenment among the Jews), 17

Hibbat Zion. *See* Hovevei Zion
High holidays, 269–70
Hildesheimer, Azriel, 26, 108
Hilfsverein der deutschen Juden, 126, 128, 137
Hillman, Shemuel, 166
Hirsch, Emil G., 202n.36
Hirsch, Maurice de, 149
Hirsch, Mendel, 113
Hirsch, Samson Raphael: anti-Zionist arguments presented to, 26; attitude toward Reform, 108; Esra youth movement influenced by, 307; on Jewish nationalism, 110–11; Jewish religion redefined in context of emancipation, 5; Ostrovsky on secessionism of, 282; Zionism contrasted with, 209
History of Zionism (Sokolow), 160
Histadrut, 138, 225, 258, 316
"Hitgalut" (Shlonsky), 256
Hoffman, Joshua, 228, 229, 233n.31
Hohe Meissner Formula, 311n.18
Holidays: high holidays, 269–70; labor movement observance of, 264–70; youth movement on celebration of, 306. *See also* Hanukah; Passover; *and other holidays by name*
Holocaust, the: Jewish youth movement affected by, 309; and rescue of North African Jews, 315; the Teheran Children, 287; Teitelbaum on, 73; traditional symbols after, 270; the Yishuv affected by, 293–94
Horovitz, Mordechai Halevi, 108
Horowitz, Asher Isaiah, 35
Hovevei Zion (Hibbat Zion): and Agudat Harabbanim rabbis, 223; Ahad Haam on executive of, 58; Anglo-Jewish support for, 169n.7; and Bnei Moshe, 29; Brenner censored by, 241; controversy regarding, 25, 27–29; cooperation between observant and nonobservant during period of, 44–54; Druzkieniki Conference, 27, 223; Feigenbaum's support for, 34; in Galicia, 35, 38; hasidic opposition to, 33; Haskalah associated with, 35; Herzl's organization absorbing, 123; Hildesheimer on Orthodox cooperation with, 108; Jewish migration in rise of, 141; Katowice Conference, 27, 223; and Lithuanian rabbis, 231n.9; nationalism and religion in, 22, 23; Odessa Committee, 28, 29; Reb Velvele as supporter of, 228; Vilna Conference, 28
Hungary: Hasidism in, 33; Hatam Sofer, 146; Hungarian nationalism, 2; Shapira of Munkács, 68; Ultra-Orthodox separatism in, 273
Hyman, Aaron, 168

Ihud Hakvutzot Vehakibbutzim movement, 270
Inner truth, 304–5, 311n.18
Institute for Religious and Social Studies (Jewish Theological Seminary), 213
Irish nationalism, 2
Isaac Meir of Gur, 34
Isaacson, Shalom, 227
Isaac Zelig of Sokołów, 34
Isaiah, 261
Israel, Land of. *See* Eretz Israel
Israel, State of: American Jews in, 184; Conservative attitude toward, 215–16; Teitelbaum on establishment of, 73; transition from mandate period to, 295. *See also* Palestine
Israelit, Der (periodical), 26, 107
Israelitische Allianz, 126
Israel Joshua of Kutno, 34

Jabotinsky, Vladimir, 3, 7
Jacobs, Joseph J., 182
Jaffa (Palestine), 122, 128
Jaffa School, 23, 47
Jaffe, Samuel, 219, 222
James, William, 190
Jampel, Sigmund, 104n.25
Jastrow, Marcus, 221
Jawitz, Zeev, 20
Jellinek, Adolf: Bloch opposed by, 149; on the Kadima, 144; liberal, universalist interpretation of Judaism, 140; on messianic mission of Judaism, 140–41; and Pinsker, 140, 142–43, 149; on settlement in Palestine, 145
Jeremiah, 261
Jerusalem: Edah Haredit, 77, 78; German Liberal congregation in, 101; Natorei Karta, 77, 78; Orthodox versus Zionist understandings of, 111; secondary schools in, 128; Shapira of Munkács's warning to denizens of, 75; zealots of, 77–82. *See also* Old Yishuv
Jerusalem Rabbinate Committee, 281
Jerusalem Talmud, 184
Jewish Agency, 137, 286, 289, 295–96
Jewish National Fund (Keren Kayemet leIsrael), 6, 225, 318

Jewish nationalism: Ahad Haam on, 51; Amiel on, 288; as basis for toleration, 45–46; of Bloch, 148; diaspora nationalism, 313, 324–26; in Eastern Europe, 21–24; in English rabbinate, 165; factions within, 116; in labor movement education, 259; and Liberal Judaism, 94–95, 97, 99; Mizrahi movement on, 297; moderate Haskalah connected with, 19; Montefiore on, 163–64; Orthodox interpretation of, 110–11; religion as secondary to in Zionism, 274; Schechter on, 177, 185n.6; as substitute for religion, 287; traditionalist opposition to, 117–18. *See also* Zionism

Jewish press: in Eastern Europe, 17, 27; pro-Palestine advocates in, 122. *See also publications by name*

"Jewish Problem, The: How to Solve It" (Brandeis), 198

Jewish Territorial Organization (ITO), 169n.7

Jewish Theological Seminary (New York City): as divided over Zionism, 177, 205, 206, 208, 214; Finkelstein as head of, 212; Institute for Religious and Social Studies, 213; Kaplan as faculty member, 179; Schechter as head of, 206; Teachers' Institute, 209–10

Jezreel Valley, 257, 265

Joint Distribution Committee (JDC), 225, 322, 324

Joseph, Jacob, 220, 223, 233n.31

Joseph, Max, 96–97, 98, 103nn. 17, 19, 104n.25, 105n.35

Joseph, Morris, 170n.16

Joshua, 197

Joshua of Belz, 35, 38

Judaeans (cultural society), 195

Judah Leib of Gur, 34

Judaism: Americanism and, 197; as covenant of fate, 45; as dialectic of religion and nation, 46, 143, 163, 167, 182; existential Judaism, 242–44; as this-worldly religion, 275; "who is a Jew," 52; as world religion for Jellinek, 141. *See also* Conservative Judaism; Liberal Judaism; Orthodox Judaism; Reform Judaism

Judenstaat, Der (Herzl): antisemites on, 156n.23; Bloch on, 149; Guedemann on, 153; Herzl's conception of a Jewish state in, 31; in shift in Zionist rationale, 30

Judentum am Scheidewege, Das (Joseph), 96, 103nn. 17, 19

Jüdischer Pfadfinderbund Makkabi Hazair (Jewish Scouting Group Young Maccabean), 302

Jung, Meir, 166, 167, 168

Jungjüdischer Wanderbund (Young Jewish Hiking Group; JJWB), 302, 304, 305

Kaatz, Saul, 94

Kadima: Bloch supporting, 148; founding of, 144; Guedemann on, 154; in Jewish youth movement, 302, 305; Maccabean cult of, 144; Pinsker as inspiration of, 144

Kafka, Franz, 1

Kahal: abolition of, 14; associations and societies taking over role of, 15; as "invisible," 16

Kalischer, Zvi Hirsch: anti-Zionist arguments presented to, 26; gradual stages theory, 35; secular influences on, 3, 4

Kallen, Horace M., 202n.45

Kameraden (Comrades) youth movement, 302, 303, 304, 306

Kaplan, Mordecai Menahem: amalgamation of Zionism and Americanism in, 179; on benefits of reborn Eretz Israel, 210; on Palestine as symbol of Judaism, 211; Reconstructionist movement, 179, 208; as Teachers' Institute head, 209

Karaites, 26, 48

Karo, Joseph, 74

Kashrut (dietary laws): in Conservative Judaism, 204, 205; Katznelson on pork, 6, 291; Mizrahi on observance of, 289, 290; observance and social intercourse with gentiles, 110; Reb Velvele and Agudat Harabbanim clashing over, 227; in *status quo* agreement, 273

Katowice Conference (1884), 27, 223

Katowice Conference (1912), 166

Katz, Jacob, 1

Katzenellenbogen, Aharon, 77

Katznelson, Berl: on ancient symbols, 266–67; as authoritarian, 258; on the Bible and socialism, 262; on communality, 255; on emotional education, 259; funeral of, 264; on imposing obedience to Halakhah, 291; on messianic hope in labor movement, 255; and Mizrahi at Zionist Actions Committee's 1935 session, 291; on Passover, 267, 268; on pork, 6, 291; on socialism and religion, 278–79; as spiritual leader of labor movement, 247; "Yizkor Am Israel," 6, 263

Kehillah (New York), 178, 209
Keren Hayesod (Palestine Foundation Fund), 98, 101
Keren Kayemet leIsrael (Jewish National Fund), 6, 225, 318
"Ketavim balim" (Ahad Haam), 63, 64, 65
Kibbutz galuyot, 7
Kibbutzim: culture of, 260; Eastern European youth movement ideology in, 309; German Orthodox youth in, 114; holidays as observed by, 265; oneg shabbat in, 6; Passover as observed by, 265, 266, 267; simplicity in, 255; in workers' society, 259
Kibbutz Meuhad, 258
Kishinev (Moldavia), 194
Klal Israel, 45–46, 49, 53n.2, 112, 286, 297
Klatzkin, Elijah, 43n.84
Klausner, Joseph, 240, 248, 284
Klee, Alfred, 98, 104n.25
Klein, Baruch, 227
Klein, Philip Hillel, 224, 231n.12, 232n.14
Knesset Harabbonim Haortodoksim be-America, 227, 229–30
Knesset Israel, 285
Knesset Zion Hamezuyenet, 223
Kohn, Hans, 1, 99, 104n.33
Kol Nidrei prayer, 270
Konvitz, Joseph, 226
Kook, Abraham Isaac Hacohen: Alfandari on, 88n.67; on the Chief Rabbinate, 284; compelling workers to observe commandments, 252; diaspora existence criticized on religious basis, 275–76; and Hapoel Hamizrahi, 292; on klal Israel, 49, 53n.2, 286; Klausner's criticism of, 284; Margolis on, 81–82; Mohilever compared with, 4; as Rabbinical Council chair, 283; as rabbi of Mahazikei Hadath community, 166; Second Aliyah influenced by, 248; woman suffrage opposed by, 284; and Yavneeli's mission to Yemen, 129
Kovner, Abraham Uri, 19
Krauskopf, Joseph, 189, 192, 199n.5
Kulturkampf: and Ahad Haam, 30; struggle between labor movement and Orthodox as, 251; in 1930s, 288
Kvutzot, 255

Labor movement: anticlericalism of, 252; antireligious traditions in, 251–52; Berlin blaming for Mizrahi exclusion, 290; differing trends within, 278; distancing itself

from socialism, 270; duality of, 259; educational approach of, 259; ethnic identity in socialism of, 254; Hapoel Hamizrahi, 214, 292–93, 297, 317; Hapoel Hazair, 129, 138, 245, 262; historical continuity as problem of, 259; holiday observance, 264–70; on Jewish character of laborers' Judaism, 290–91; Katznelson as spiritual leader of, 247; life-cycle rituals in, 263–64; on Old Yishuv, 252; religious motifs of, 251–72; as religious movement, 254–56; secularization of religious symbols by, 260–70; self-sacrifice in, 254–55; split with Revisionists, 298; workers' society as goal of, 259–70
Labor Palestine, League for, 214
Labor Party, decline of, 7
Labor Zionism: "Class Independence" slogan, 270; goal of, 138; National Religious Party alliance, 7; religious language in, 5–7; social origins of, 7. See also Labor movement; Poalei Zion
Lafargue, Paul and Laura Marx, 245
Lag baOmer, 264, 268
Lakhish (Negev), 316
Lamdan, Yitzhak, 260
Landa, Shlomo Zalman, 171n.27, 231n.9
Land of Israel. See Eretz Israel
Lapidot, Alexander Moses, 25, 46
Laqueur, Walter, 65n.1
Lavi, Shlomo, 246, 267
Lazaron, Morris, 199n.5
Lazarus, Paul, 101
League for Labor Palestine, 214
League of British Jews, 164
League of German Nationalist Jews (Verband nationaldeutscher Juden), 98
League of Orthodox Rabbis in England (Agudat Harabbanim Haharedim beAngliah), 166
Lehmann, Marcus, 26
Lehranstalt für die Wissenschaft des Judentums (Berlin), 96, 98
Leib, Moshe, 83
Leibush Mendel of Botosani, 37
Lelyveld, Arthur J., 189
Leo Baeck School (Haifa), 101
Levi, tribe of, 79
Levias, Caspar, 197
Levin, Baruch Meir, 227
Levin, Hayim Meir Noah, 43n.84
Levin, I. L., 232n.14
Levin, Judah Leib, 20

Levinger, Jacob, 113
Levinson, Daniel, 192
Levinthal, Israel Herbert, 206, 210, 211
Levy, Felix A., 181, 186n.21
Lewin, Shmarya, 185n.6
Lewin-Epstein, E. W., 222, 224
Liberal Judaism: of Montefiore, 163; and
    Zionism in Germany, 93–106
"Liberal Judaism" (Kohn), 99, 104n.33
Liberal Judaism in Germany, Association for
    (Vereinigung für das liberale Judentum in
    Deutschland), 99, 102n.6
Liberal Rabbis in Germany, Association of
    (Vereinigung der Liberalen Rabbiner
    Deutschlands), 98, 104n.28
Liebermann, A. S., 16, 261, 262
Liebes, Yehuda, 81
Lilienblum, Moshe Leib: Hataot neurim, 58;
    in Hovevei Zion leadership, 27; maskilic
    circle of, 57–58; on nonobservant settling
    in Palestine, 46; on the observant in Zion-
    ism, 50; on reform, 20, 26, 117; secular
    approach of, 251
Lipschitz, Jacob, 32, 39
Lipsky, Louis, 182, 194, 198
Lithuania: Haskalah in, 13; Jews and the
    aristocracy in, 14; Orthodoxy in, 20; rab-
    binical response to Zionism in, 231n.9;
    sages of, 15
Livenstein, Eliezer, 264
Love of Zion. See Hovevei Zion
"Lo zeh haderekh" (Ahad Haam), 57, 58–
    59, 66n.17
Lubarsky, Abraham Elijah, 58, 66n.25
Luz, Ehud, 1, 56, 231n.9

Maccabaean (periodical), 188, 194, 203n.53
Maccabees, 144, 148, 244, 264
Magnes, Judah L.: conversion to Zionism,
    191, 196; identifying with Conservatism,
    178–79; on patriotism and Zionism, 182
Magnin, Edgar, 199n.5
Mahanayim (Palestine), 36
Mahazikei Hadath community (London),
    166
Mahzikei Hadas, 35, 37–38
Maimon, Y. L. (Fishman), 284, 288–89,
    295, 301n.46
Mandate period: civil rights of non-Jewish
    communities in, 159; gap between Euro-
    pean and non-European Jews in, 315; re-
    ligion, state, and society during, 273;
    transition to independent state, 295

Mannheimer, Isaac Noah, 151
Maoz, Elijah (Mosbacher), 309
Mapai, 259, 317
Mapu, Abraham, 19, 21, 251
Marcus, Aaron, 35, 37
Margolies, Moses Zebulun (Ramaz): in
    founding of Agudat Harabbanim, 221,
    232n.14; Reb Velvele as successor in Bos-
    ton, 227; Reb Velvele's criticism of, 227,
    228
Margolis, Gavriel Zev (Reb Velvele), 227–
    29, 233n.31
Margolis, Max, 202n.33
Margolis, Yeshayahu Asher Zelig, 78–82
Marriage: civil marriage proposal of 1922,
    285; mixed marriages, 110, 162; in status
    quo agreement, 273, 296; wedding cere-
    monies, 263
Marshall, Louis, 177, 180, 182, 206
Marx, Karl, 252
Marx, Laura, 245
Masada, 245
Maskilim. See Haskalah
Masliansky, Zvi Hirsch, 223, 224
Maybaum, Sigmund, 93–94
May Day, 269
Mazagan (Morocco), 317–18, 321, 326
Meir, Yaakov, 283, 286
Meisel, Elijah Hayyim, 39
Menahem Mendel of Rymanów, 83
Mendele Mokher Seforim, 57, 58, 251
Mendelssohn, Moses, 142
Mendes, Henry, 222
Mendès-France, Pierre, 317
Menuhah Venahalah, 35
Messiah, the: Agudat Israel on, 72; Alkalai's
    interpretation of, 3–4; Atlas Jews' mes-
    sianism, 321, 325, 328n.38; emancipation
    as modern realization of, 4–5; messianic
    hope in labor movement, 255; Zionism as
    conflicting with messianism, 32, 69, 81,
    228
Messianic Zionism, 325
Meyer, Michael, 189–90, 196–97
Micah, 261
Minhat Elazar (Shapira), 70
Minsk Conference (1902), 31, 52
Mitnagdim, 32, 33
Mixed marriages, 110, 162
Mizrahi movement: and Agudat Harabba-
    nim, 223, 224–26, 230; and Agudat Is-
    rael, 112, 278; Alfandari on, 82; on Chief
    Rabbinate, 282; Cracow conference of

Mizrahi movement (*continued*)
  1933, 288; dual goal of, 298; on education, 52; in England, 165; extreme wing's
  growth, 288; German Orthodox collaboration with, 109, 110; Hapoel Hamizrahi,
  214, 292–93, 297, 317; internal divisions
  within, 292; on Jewish nationalism, 297;
  Jewish unity given precedence by, 297;
  Mahzikei Hadas contrasted with, 37–38;
  at Nineteenth Zionist Congress, 291–92;
  Orthodox opposition to, 136; and Orthodox Union, 220; Palestine conference of
  1934, 289, 292; political emphasis of, 31;
  Pressburg Convention, 109; proposed
  Liberal version of, 101; on religion's role
  in the Yishuv, 287–93; religious demands
  at Eighteenth Zionist Congress, 289; on
  Sabbath observance, 289; schools of,
  137–38; secession from National Council, 289, 292; as source of division in Palestine, 137; and unification of the Yishuv
  under British rule, 280, 285; in the United
  States, 176; on woman suffrage, 134,
  135; at Zionist Actions Committee's 1935
  session, 291; on Zionist Organization's
  role in Yishuv, 277–78
Modernity: bringing better relations between
  Jews and Christians, 240; Eastern European responses to, 13–24; and tradition
  in Eastern Europe, 11–89
Modernization, 44–45, 50, 238, 260, 324
Mohilever, Samuel: address to First Zionist
  Congress, 4; and Agudat Harabbanim
  rabbis, 222–23, 232n.14; on Eretz Israel
  settlement, 29, 35–36; and Katowice
  Conference, 27; as neo-*haredim* leader,
  26; on Torah as foundation of Zionism,
  31; at Vilna Conference, 28
Montagu, Edwin, 169nn. 1, 6
Montagu, Lily H., 105n.39
Montefiore, Claude: on Babylonian Talmud,
  162; *The Bible for Home Reading*, 163;
  on Jewish identity, 161–62; on Jewish na-
  tionalism, 163–64; Weltsch on, 100
Montefiore, Moses, 149
Morgenstern, Israel, 34, 41n.46
Morocco: independence struggle in, 315–16;
  Jews in administrative posts in, 317; Mazagan, 317–18, 321, 326; nationalism in,
  325; problematic reputation of Jews of,
  315; Zionism and rural Atlas Jews, 312–
  29
Mosbacher, Elijah (Maoz), 309

"Moscovites," 238
Moses, 56, 79, 142, 197, 210
Moshav movement, 316
Motzkin, Leo, 55

Nahalal (Palestine), 316
Nahmanides, 74
Naiditch, Judah, 215
Napoleon, 5
National Council: Mizrahi's secession from,
  289, 292; supreme authority vested in,
  286
National Home: in Balfour Declaration, 159;
  religion, society, and state during period
  of, 273–301
Nationalism: as antithesis of reform and as-
  similation, 27; and Eastern European
  Jews, 16; secularization at root of, 1–3.
  See also Jewish nationalism
Nationaljudentum (Guedemann), 151, 152
National Religious Party, 7
Natorei Karta, 77, 78
Naumann, Max, 98
Negev, the, 316
Nehemiah, 109
Neo-*haredim*, 26
Neo-Orthodoxy: and Haskalah, 18; univer-
  salistic elements in, 5; Zionism opposed
  by, 26
Netter, Charles, 62
Neue Freie Presse (newspaper), 153, 154
Neumark, David, 181
Neuzeit, Die (periodical), 140
New Palestine (periodical), 212
New Yishuv: Ashkenazim in, 136; balancing
  tradition and modernization, 260; diver-
  sity in, 136; Hebrew use by, 127; Jewish
  characteristics of, 52; under Ottoman
  rule, 279; relations with their neighbors,
  137; and Second Aliyah, 128, 131; secu-
  larism of, 48, 120; and the "third
  Yishuv," 113; in unification of the Yishuv,
  131, 132, 133; women's role in, 280
New York Kehillah, 178, 209
Neziv, the (Naphtali Zevi Judah Berlin), 27,
  46, 222–23, 232n.14
Nicholas I (emperor of Russia), 16
Nietzsche, Friedrich, 239, 240
Nineteenth Zionist Congress, 291–92, 296
Ninio, Yaakov Shealtiel, 86n.36
Noar Agudati, 113
Nonobservant, the: Bnei Moshe recruiting
  from, 56–57; collaboration with obser-

vant in Germany, 108–10; cooperation with the observant during Hibbat Zion period, 44–54; focuses of conflict with the observant, 47–48; on Halakhah, 277; on *klal Israel*, 46; movement's leadership in hands of, 48; and observant as complementing each other, 247; Orthodox attitude toward nonobservant Zionists, 46; in Palestine, 23, 27, 35, 120; position of, 50–52; theological function of nonobservance, 49

Nordau, Max: Conservative attitude toward, 206; Guedemann on Zionism of, 152; secularized background of, 3

Norden, Hans, 103n.19

Norden, Joseph, 103n.19

Nussbaum, Max, 101

Observant, the: adapting themselves to democratic principles, 52; Bnei Moshe recruiting from, 56–57; collaboration with nonobservant in Germany, 108–10; cooperation with the nonobservant during Hibbat Zion period, 44–54; focuses of conflict with the nonobservant, 47–48; on *klal Israel*, 46; and nonobservant as complementing each other, 247; position of, 48–50; secession from Zionism, 50, 52

Odessa (Ukraine): Ahad Haam in, 63; Bnei Moshe's core membership from, 57; Jewish community emerging in, 17; pogrom of 1871, 20

Odessa Committee, 28, 29

Oesterreichertum, 147

Oesterreichische Wochenschrift (journal), 148, 149

"Ohalenu" (Shlonsky), 256

Ohel Theater, 255, 260

Old Yishuv: Agudat Harabbanim on, 225, 227; communal organization of, 130; detachment from Ottomans, 137; in education, 127; First Aliyah opposed by, 128; and Hovevei Zion, 28; labor movement on, 252; and organization of the Yishuv under British rule, 280; in *Or layesharim,* 32; under Ottoman rule, 279; Reb Velvele on directing funds to, 229; and Second Aliyah, 128; and Shapira of Munkács's anti-Zionism, 77; and the "third Yishuv," 113; and traditionalist agricultural settlements in Palestine, 119–22; Zionist dominance presenting problems to, 129

Oneg shabbat, 6

Orah leZion (anti-Zionist book), 33

Or layesharim (anti-Zionist anthology), 31, 37, 39

Orthodox Jewish Congregations of America, Union of (OU), 220, 222, 231n.12

Orthodox Judaism: American Orthodox organizations in support of Zionism, 219–34; American Orthodoxy's attitude toward Zionism, 176–77, 183; as anachronistic, 20; British Orthodoxy's attitude toward Zionism, 165–68; collaboration with non-Orthodox in Germany, 108–10; Conservative Judaism compared with, 204, 208; elements of, 18; German Orthodoxy's attitude toward Reform, 108–9; German Orthodoxy's attitude toward Zionism, 107–15; in Germany, 18–19, 107; versus Haskalah in preserving Jewish identity, 19–24; Herzl's attitude toward, 50, 125–26; isolation of, 110; Jellinek's opposition to, 146; on Jewish nationalism, 110–11; linking with Zionism against Reform, 112; nationalist, 21; on nonobservant Zionists, 46; as reaction to Haskalah, 18; on Reform, 46, 112; secession from Zionism, 50, 52; *status quo* agreement restricting Jewish life to, 274; *Trennungsorthodoxie,* 120; two types of Eastern European, 25–26; and unification of the Yishuv under British rule, 279–87; in Vienna, 146–47; youth movements confronting in Palestine, 309; youth movements of, 302; and Zionism, 116–39. *See also* Neo-Orthodoxy; Ultra-Orthodoxy

Orthodox Rabbis, Free Association of (Freie Vereinigung für die Interessen des Orthodoxen Judentums), 109

Orthodox Rabbis in England, League of (Agudat Harabbanim Haharedim beAngliah), 166

Orthodox Rabbis of the United States and Canada, Union of. *See* Agudat Harabbanim

Ostjuden. See Eastern Europe

Ostrovsky, Moses, 282

Ozar Hahityashvut, 37

Pale of Settlement: diversity within, 238; government schools for Jews in, 16; Haskalah in, 117; Pinsker on Jews freeing themselves from, 142

Palestine: Adler's visit to, 165; versus America as a haven, 122; American Jews in,
184; American Reform supporting Jewish
life in, 179; Balfour Declaration on, 159;
Bloch on settlement in, 149; British conquest of, 279; campaign against new settlers, 28; Conservative rabbis on, 210–
12; control of colonists' life in, 47–48;
German Liberal Judaism in, 101; for Hasidism, 33; interwar immigration to, 136;
Jellinek on settlement in, 145; Jewish
schools established in, 126–28; labor
movement in, 251–72; nonobservant immigrants to, 23, 27, 35, 120; as Ottoman
backwater, 145–46; Ottoman restrictions
on entering, 28, 34; Sulzberger on free immigration to, 207; traditionalist agricultural settlements in, 119–22; uniting Jewish
communities in, 130–36. See also Aliyah;
Chief Rabbinate; Eretz Israel; Mandate
period; Jerusalem; Yishuv
Palestine Foundation Fund (Keren Hayesod),
98, 101
Passover: Katznelson on, 267, 268; labor
movement secularizing, 265, 266–68;
and Labor Zionism, 6
"Pathseekers," 294–95
Patriotism, 182
Penn, Alexander, 260
Peretz, I. L., 269
Perlow, Aaron, 33
Perlzweig, Maurice L., 105n.35
Personal status, 273, 283, 285, 296
Perushim, 33
Petah Tikva (Palestine), 122, 127, 252, 258
Pharisees, The (Finkelstein), 213, 218n.42
Philadelphia Rabbinical Conference (1869),
189
Philipson, David, 180, 189, 197, 201n.21
Phinehas Ben Eleazer, 79
Pines, Yehiel Michal, 20, 27, 51–52, 275,
292–93
Pinsker, Leon: Ahad Haam on, 62; assimila-
tion rejected by, 141–42; Autoemanzipa-
tion!, 141; Jellinek on, 140, 142–43, 149;
Kadima inspired by, 144; leadership of
Hovevei Zion, 27; on the Orthodox in
Zionism, 50; secularized background of, 3
Pittsburgh Rabbinical Conference (1885), 189
Pluralism: in communal religious courts,
283; cultural pluralism of the Yishuv, 296;
as outcome of modernization and secular-
ization, 44

Poalei Agudat Israel, 114
Poalei Zion: Labor Zionism of, 138;
printers' union in Jerusalem, 128; Zerubavel as leader of, 244, 245
Pogroms: Jewish migration caused by, 122,
140, 141; in Odessa in 1871, 20; Reform
conversions resulting from, 194; Zionism
strengthened by, 27, 118
Poland: Brody, 13, 122; Cracow, 35, 38,
288; in Fourth Aliyah, 287; Hasidism in,
33; Haskalah in, 13, 14; interwar emigration to Palestine, 136; Polish nationalism,
2, 19. See also Warsaw
Political Zionism: American Reform opposing, 180, 189; Anglo-Jewish opposition
to, 159–71; Biltmore Program, 213;
Bloch's opposition to, 148–50; Chajes on,
154–55; Guedemann's opposition to,
144, 150–54; movement expanded by,
123; mystique of autoemancipation in,
124; rabbinical opposition to, 38; Reines's
initiative on, 31; as unfeasible, 41n.31
Pork, Katznelson on, 6, 291
Practical Zionism, 119
Prayer book, 112
Preil, Joshua Joseph, 30
Press, the. See Jewish press
Pressburg Convention, 109
Prinz, Joachim, 101, 105n.42
Protestantism, 193
Purim, 269

Rabbi Isaac Elchanan Theological Seminary
(New York City), 224, 227–28
Rabbi Jacob Joseph School, 233n.31
Rabbinate, Chief. See Chief Rabbinate
Rabbiner-Verband in Deutschland, 94
Rabbinical Assembly (Conservative Judaism),
204
Rabbinical Council, 131, 283, 285
Rabbinical Office (Jerusalem), 281
Rabinovich, Isaac Jacob, 43n.84
Rabinowich, Eliezer, 223
Rabinowitz, Baruch, 83
Rabinowitz, Elijah Akiva, 31, 39
Rabinowitz, Jacob Samuel, 31
Rabinowitz, Sholem Yakov, 166
Rabinowitz, Yosef, 171n.27, 231n.9
Radim, Abraham, 221
Radin, Adolph, 194
Rahner, Karl, 54n.10
Raisin, Jacob, 200n.16
Raisin, Max, 190, 200n.16

Ramaz. *See* Margolies, Moses Zebulun
Ratosh, Yonatan, 7
Rawnitzky, Yehoshua Hana, 57
Reb Velvele (Gavriel Zev Margolis), 227–29, 233n.31
Reconstructionist movement, 179, 208
"Reflections on Judaism, Zionism and Enduring Peace" (Finkelstein), 212
Reform Judaism: American Reform conversions to Zionism, 188–203; American Reform's attitude toward Zionism, 179–83; British Reform's attitude toward Zionism, 167; emancipation interpreted in messianic terms by, 5; German Orthodox attitudes toward, 108–9; Hess on, 8; Kook on, 53n.2; Lilienblum on, 117; Orthodox attitude toward, 46, 112; Orthodoxy linking with Zionism against, 112; in Vienna, 146–47
Rehovot (Palestine), 35
Reines, Isaac Jacob: on irreligion in Zionism, 205; Lida *yeshivah* of, 224; on nonobservance, 49; on old religious community in Palestine, 85n.21; on political Zionism, 31, 41n.31
Religion: in America, 176; as factor in encounter between Zionism and rural Atlas Jews, 312–29; Judaism as dialectic of nation and, 46, 143, 163, 167, 182; religious motifs in the labor movement, 251–72; religious question in the Zionist youth movement, 302–11; religious values in the Second Aliyah, 237–50; separation of state and, 2, 51, 298; and society and the state during National Home period, 273–301. *See also* Judaism
Religion and Us (instruction booklet), 268–69
Religious Communities Organisation Ordinance (1926), 133
Religious education: Mizrahi accepting equal rights for secular and, 52, 277, 298; of the Old Yishuv, 127; Rabbi Isaac Elchanan Theological Seminary, 224, 227–28; Shapira of Munkács's criticism of Agudat Israel's, 70–71; in *status quo* agreement, 273; youth movements on, 305. *See also* Hebrew Union College; Jewish Theological Seminary; *Yeshivot*
Religious Zionism: American spiritual Zionism, 178, 179, 183; condition for participating in WZO, 137; in Frankfurt Jewish community, 110; goal of, 138;

Herzl on, 125; Jewish unity given precedence by, 297; and Labor Zionism, 7; Margolis on Kook's, 81; of Mohilever, 29; Pines's call for, 51; and secular nature of the Yishuv, 287–88; on Zionist Organization's role in Yishuv, 277. *See also* Mizrahi movement
Remnant of Israel, 80
Return to Zion (prayer), 112
Revel, Bernard, 228
Revisionist movement: Labor Zionism contrasted with, 7; Mizrahi opposition to, 290; split with Labor, 298
Richmond, Harry R., 201n.21
Rishon Lezion (Palestine), 122
Rohling, August, 148, 156n.23
Rome and Jerusalem (Hess), 8
Rosenberg, Israel Halevi, 225
Rosenheim, Jacob, 111, 112
Rosenzweig, Franz, 103n.16
Roshei yeshivot, 224, 226, 233n.20
Rosh Hashanah, 269
Rosh Pina (Palestine), 36, 122
Rothschild, Edmond de, 149
Rottenberg, Hayyim, 223
Rumania, 36, 121, 307
Russia: Alexander II, 16, 22; Catherine the Great, 14; integration of Jews in, 14; interwar emigration to Palestine, 136; Jellinek on Jewish problem in, 143; Jewish migration to Palestine from, 121; Jewish population in 1910, 238; Montefiore on Revolution in, 164, 170n.17; Nicholas I, 16; Russian nationalism, 2; Second Aliyah pioneers coming from, 238–39. *See also* Pale of Settlement
Russian language, 239
Russian literature, 239
Russian renaissance, 240
Russification, 22
Ruth, book of, 268
Ruzhin, Israel, 62

Sabbath, the: Bialik and Tel-Aviv observance of, 293; in Conservative Judaism, 204, 205; Elected Assembly resolutions on, 291; labor movement secularization of, 265; and Labor Zionism, 6; Mizrahi on observance of, 289, 290; observance and social intercourse with gentiles, 110; in *status quo* agreement, 273, 296; as symbolizing spiritual values, 294; Tabenkin on observance of, 291; transferring to

Sabbath (*continued*)
Sunday, 162; youth movement's observance of, 303
Sabbatical (fallow) year, 6, 28, 48, 252
Sacrifices, Hess on, 8
Sale, Samuel, 192
Salmon, Yosef, 1
Samaritans, 109
Samuel, Sir Herbert, 131, 132, 133
Samuel of Słonim, 39
San Remo Conference, 132, 225, 227
Schaeffer, Shepsel, 223, 231n.12
Schalit, Isidor, 156n.16
Schama, Simon, 2
Schechter, Solomon: on adoption of Conservatism, 179; on Jewish nationalism, 177, 185n.6; on religious-national aspects of Zionism, 205; Schiff debate, 181–82, 206; on Zionism as bulwark against assimilation, 175–76, 209
Schiff, Jacob H.: as anti-Zionist, 177, 206; anti-Zionist organization opposed by, 180; on Jewish nationalism, 185n.6; Schechter debate, 181–82, 206; Zionism accepted by, 182
Schiller, Solomon, 285
Schlesinger, Abraham, 104n.25
Schloessinger, Max, 181
Schmelkes, Isaac, 35
Schneersohn, Joseph Isaac, 69
Schneersohn, Shalom Dov-Baer, 32, 39, 47
Schneersohn, Zalman, 28
Schnirer, Moritz, 156n.16
Scholem, Gershom, 1, 287
Schonfield, Avigdor, 171n.29
Schools. *See* Education
Second Aliyah: the Bible in cultural fabric of, 261; Biluim as ancestors of, 55; existential Judaism of, 242–44; Kook as influence on, 248; as a motley assemblage, 237; new approach to Christianity of, 239–41; new religious life of, 246–48; and New Yishuv, 128, 131; and Old Yishuv, 128; political conventions of, 258; religious values in, 237–50; Russian background of, 238–39; and Sephardim and Yemenites, 128–29; social and cultural features of, 238–39; superior Jewish life sought by, 244–46; traditional background of, 253
Second Constituent Assembly, 280
Second Zionist Congress, 31
Secularization: exile as cause of Jewish, 49; as gradual process, 253; in Herzl's Zionist vision, 5; in the *moshavot*, 287; in nationalism, 1–3; of religious symbols by labor movement, 260–70; among settlers in Palestine, 28; toleration and pluralism as outcome of, 44; Zionism as secularizing force, 32, 52, 274
Seder, 265, 266, 267, 268
Sefer or layesharim (Landa and Rabinowitz), 171n.27, 231n.9
Selection regulations, 315, 319
Seligmann, Caesar, 95, 101, 102n.10
Seligsberg, Alice L., 190, 200n.14
Separatism: in Agudat Israel, 135, 295; in Margolis's ideology, 78, 82; Orthodoxy on, 109, 129–30; Shapira as separatist, 72; *Trennungsorthodoxie,* 120; of the Ultra-Orthodox, 273
Sephardim: in Chief Rabbinate, 131; Hakham Bashi, 131, 279, 281–82, 283; on Rabbinical Council, 283; and Second Aliyah, 128–29; in unification of Jerusalem congregations, 130; in unification of the Yishuv under British rule, 281
Shabbetai Zevi, 149, 167
Shalkovich, Abraham Leib (Ben-Avigdor), 56
Shapira, Hayim Elazar, of Munkács, 67–89; Agudat Israel opposed by, 70–74; and Alfandari, 82–83; death of, 83; Land of Israel demonized by, 74–76; *Minhat Elazar,* 70; on settlement of Land of Israel, 68–70; Teitelbaum influenced by, 72–74; visit to Jerusalem, 78, 82–83, 89nn. 70, 75
Shapiro, Moshe, 291
Shavuot, 265, 268
Shelom Yerushalayim (Morgenstern), 34, 41n.46
Shimonovitz, David, 251, 261
Shlilat hagalut, 197; in Zionist education, 260, 261
Shlonsky, Abraham, 256–57, 260, 263
Shokeid, Moshe, 319–20
Sholem Aleichem, 269
Shomer Israel, 38
Shreier, Feibush, 35
Shulamit (periodical), 219
Shulhan Arukh, 146, 280
Silver, Abba Hillel, 97, 200n.17, 203n.53
Silver, Eliezer, 230
Silverman, Joseph, 191–92, 201n.22
Simon, Ernst, 105n.35, 287
Simon, Leon, 65n.1
Singer, Simeon, 165

Sklare, Marshall, 175
Smolenskin, Peretz, 20, 118, 144
Socialism: antireligious attitude of, 252; the
  Bible compared with, 261–62; Borochov
  and Katznelson on religion and, 278–79;
  Borochov's spiritual interpretation of, 245;
  the Bund, 176, 252, 278; ethnic identity in
  Palestine labor movement's, 254; of Ha-
  poel Hamizrahi, 292; Jewish youth move-
  ments of, 302, 304, 308; labor movement
  distancing itself from, 270; on Old Yishuv,
  252; socialist formulations of Zionism,
  161; Zionism opposed by Jewish, 176
Society for the Promotion of Enlightenment
  among the Jews (Hevrat Marbei Haska-
  lah), 17
Sofer, Simon, 35, 38
Sokolow, Nahum, 160, 161
Soloveichik, Hayim, 26
Soloveichik, Joseph Dov-Baer, 27
"Solution to the Jewish Problem, A" (Herzl),
  169n.3
Song of Songs, 167–68
Sonnenfeld, Isaac, 134
Sonnenfeld, Joseph Hayim, 77
Spektor, Isaac Elchanan, 27, 34, 222–23,
  232n.14
Spitzer, Salomon, 146
State and religion, separation of, 2, 51, 298
State of Israel. See Israel, State of
"State within a state," 125
Status quo agreement, 273–74; emergence
  of, 295–96; and Kulturkampf of 1930s,
  288; as not answering essential question
  of religion and society, 296–97; religious
  parties' role in, 298; rights violated in,
  274
Steinberg, Avraham Baruch, 231n.9
Stern, David, 193
Stern, Heinrich, 101
Stolz, Joseph, 191
Straus, Oscar S., 180, 197
Suffrage for women, 134–35, 280–81, 284,
  285
Sukkot, 265
Sulzberger, Mayer, 206–7
Syrkin, Nahman, 262
Szold, Henrietta, 196, 197, 221

Taaffe, Eduard, 147, 148
Taanachim (Galilee), 316
Tabenkin, Yitzhak, 246, 258, 261, 270,
  290–91

Talmud: Babylonian Talmud, 162, 184; Jeru-
  salem Talmud, 184; removed from Zionist
  curriculum, 260
Talmudjude (Rohling), 148
Tarshish, Abraham, 309
Tchernikhovsky, Saul, 275
Tchernowitz, Chaim, 57, 58
Teachers' Institute (Jewish Theological Semi-
  nary), 209–10
Teachers Institute (Mizrahi), 224, 233n.20
Teheran Children, 287
Teichtal, Issakhar Shlomo, 85n.25
Teitelbaum, Yoel, 72–74, 76, 77–78, 85n.26
Tel-Aviv (Palestine), 55, 101, 290, 293
Tel Hai Memorial Day, 6, 269
Temple Emanu-El (New York City), 178,
  181, 188, 191
Temporary Organization for Support of the
  Yishuv, 225
Tenth Zionist Congress, 31, 277
Tenuat Hamoshavim, 316
Theimer, Kamilla, 154
Third Aliyah, 257, 270
"Third Yishuv," 113–14
Tinok shenishbah, 54n.8
Tisha beAv, 268
"Toil" (Shlonsky), 256
Toleration: Ahad Haam on virtue of, 29–30,
  50–51; Jewish nationalism as basis for,
  45–46; of the nonobservant as condi-
  tional, 49; as outcome of modernization
  and secularization, 44; Rahner's theory of,
  54n.10
Tolstoy, Leo, 239
Torah: Agudat Israel on role of, 135; Amiel
  giving precedence over Eretz Israel, 288;
  as basis for Jewish nationalism for Mizrahi, 297; in Breuer's denunciation of
  Zionism, 112; as foundation of Zionism
  for Mohilever, 31; in Mizrahi proposals
  to Second Constituent Assembly, 280; Orthodoxy on the state existing for, 111
Torah vederekh eretz movement, 114, 276
Tradition: in Conservative Judaism, 205,
  209; Herzl on, 125; for labor movement,
  253, 254; and modernity in Eastern Europe, 11–89; modernization's impact on,
  44–45; traditionalist agricultural settlements in Palestine, 119–22; traditionalist
  opposition to nationalism, 117–18; youth
  movements on, 303; Zionism and anti-
  Zionism in traditional Judaism in Eastern
  Europe, 25–43; Zionism and Jewish

Tradition (*continued*)
  religious, 1–9; Zionism as challenge to,
  25; and Zionism in the Yishuv, 235–329.
  See also Orthodox Judaism
Travisano, Richard, 190
Trennungsorthodoxie, 120
Trial and Error (Weizmann), 160
Trumpeldor, Yosef, 269
Tu biShvat, 264–65, 268

Uganda, 131, 237
Ukraine: Hasidism in, 36. *See also* Odessa
Ultra-Orthodoxy: anti-Zionism of, 25–43;
  Chief Rabbinate opposed by, 282; on plural system of religious courts, 283; Rabbinical Council of 1921 rejected by, 283;
  on Rabbinical Council, 131; Reb Velvele
  as quintessential Ultra-Orthodox Jew,
  228, 233n.31; right to secede from gen-
  eral community, 286; separatism in, 273;
  and unification of the Yishuv under Brit-
  ish rule, 279–87; woman suffrage re-
  jected by, 134–35, 280–81, 285; Zion-
  ism and Agudaism opposed by, 67–89;
  Zionism opposed in America by, 219–21.
  See also Agudat Israel; Hasidism; Old
  Yishuv
Union of American Hebrew Congregations
  (UAHC), 189
Union of Orthodox Jewish Congregations of
  America (OU), 220, 222, 231n.12
Union of Orthodox Rabbis of the United
  States and Canada. *See* Agudat Harabba-
  nim
United Hebrew Community of New York
  (Adath Israel Society), 227
United Kingdom. *See* Great Britain
United States: American Jewish movements
  as influenced by Zionism, 175–87;
  American Reform conversions to Zion-
  ism, 188–203; Conservative Judaism and
  Zionism, 204–18; crisis in American
  Jewry, 192–95; Eastern European Jews
  immigrating to, 193; Orthodox organiza-
  tions in support of Zionism, 219–34; ver-
  sus Palestine as haven, 122; Protestant
  calls for Christian America, 193; religion's
  role in, 176; Zionism in, 173–234; Zionization of American Jewry, 183–84
Universalism: Finkelstein on, 212; in
  Jellinek's interpretation of Judaism, 140,
  141; Montefiore on, 163; in Neo-
  Orthodoxy, 5; Schechter on, 177

Urofsky, Melvin, 219–20
Ussishkin, Menaham Mendel: attempt to attract followers to Hovevei Zion, 28; attempt to unite Jerusalem congregations,
  130, 131; in Bnei Moshe, 55; on religion
  in Jewish life in Palestine, 290; on woman
  suffrage, 134

Vayoel Moshe (Teitelbaum), 78
Verband nationaldeutscher Juden (League of
  German Nationalist Jews), 98
Vereinigung der Liberalen Rabbiner Deutsch-
  lands (Association of Liberal Rabbis in
  Germany), 98, 104n.28
Vereinigung für das liberale Judentum in
  Deutschland (Association for Liberal Ju-
  daism in Germany), 99, 102n.6
Veteran Mizrahi, 292
Vienna (Austria), 140–58; antisemitism
  coming to, 141; as workers' society, 260
Village evacuation plan, 322, 324
Vilna (Lithuania), 13
Vilna Conference (1889), 28
Vitkin, Jacob (Zerubavel), 244–45
Vogelstein, Heinemann, 93–94, 104n.24
Volozhin (Lithuania), 15
Von Bilinski, Leon Ritter, 148
Von Istóczy, Gyözö, 145
Von Simonyi, Ivan, 156n.23

Waks, Eleazer, 27
Warsaw (Poland): Bnei Moshe membership
  from, 57; Jewish community emerging in,
  17; *yeshivah* in, 71
Warschauer, Malwin, 100–101, 105n.35
Wedding ceremony, 263
Weil, A. Leo, 105n.39
Weiss, Benjamin, 37
Weizmann, Chaim: on anti-Zionist objec-
  tions to Balfour Declaration, 160; attempt
  to unite Jerusalem congregations, 130; on
  Balfour Declaration's ambivalence, 159;
  in Bnei Moshe, 55; *Trial and Error,* 160
Welt, Die (journal), 149
Weltsch, Felix, 105n.35
Weltsch, Robert, 100, 105nn. 35, 36
Werkleute (Artisans) youth movement, 302,
  303, 309–10
Werner, Abba, 166
Wessel, Harvey E., 191, 196, 201n.21
Wessely, Naftali Herz, 18
Western Europe: Anglo-Jewish opposition to
  political Zionism, 159–71; German

Orthodoxy's attitude toward Zionism, 107–15; Liberal Judaism and Zionism in Germany, 93–106; Orthodoxy, Liberalism, and Zionism in, 91–171; Zionism and its religious critics in Vienna, 140–58. *See also countries by name*

Wiener, Max, 100, 105nn. 35, 38, 276

Winschewsky, Morris, 262

Wise, Isaac Mayer, 180, 197

Wise, Stephen S.: and Agudat Harabbanim, 221; Finkelstein criticized by, 214; German Liberal Jewry compared with, 97; mission motif of, 197; and World Union for Progressive Judaism, 105n.39; on Zionism and Reform, 180; Zionist background of, 190

Wissenschaft des Judentums, 140, 150

Wolf, Lucien, 161–62, 169n.10

Wolf, Simon, 189

Wolfsberg, Oscar, 105n.36

Women: *status quo* agreement violating rights of, 274; suffrage controversy, 134–35, 280–81, 284, 285

World Union for Progressive Judaism, 100, 105n.39

World Zionist Organization. *See* Zionist Organization

Yaari, Meir, 258

Yavneeli, Shmuel, 129

Yemen, 129

Yemenites, 128, 129, 314

Yeshivot: for America, 220–21; growth of, 17; *roshei yeshivot,* 224, 226, 233n.20; traditional Jewish life preserved by, 15

Yiddish, 220, 221, 238, 239

Yiddishkeyt, 253–54

Yishuv, the: Eastern European immigrants setting tone of, 277; gap between European and non-European Jews in, 315; hedonism in urban life in, 287; the Holocaust affecting, 293–94; religion, society, and state during National Home period, 273–301; religious values of the Second Aliyah, 237–50; "third Yishuv," 113–14; tradition and Zionism in, 235–329; unification attempts after British conquest, 279–87; unification attempts in Ottoman times, 131–33. *See also* New Yishuv; Old Yishuv

Yizkor, 262–63

"Yizkor Am Israel" (Katznelson), 6, 263

Yom Kippur, 269, 270

Youth movements, Zionist. *See* Zionist youth movements

Zangwill, Israel, 162, 169n.7, 170n.12

Zederbaum, Alexander, 58–59

Zeire Mizrahi (Mizrahi Youth) youth movement, 302

Zerubavel (Jacob Vitkin), 244–45

Zevi, Shabbatai. *See* Shabbatai Zevi

Zhitlowsky, Chaim, 175

Ziegler, Ignaz, 105n.35

Zionism: American Jewish movements as influenced by, 175–87; American Orthodox organizations in support of, 219–34; American Reform conversions to, 188–203; antisemitism allegedly incited by, 94, 107–8, 117, 145, 169n.10; and anti-Zionism in traditional Judaism in Eastern Europe, 25–43; competing ideologies within, 116; Conservative Judaism and, 204–18; cooperation with non-Zionists, 116; dissemination of, 47; German Orthodoxy's attitude toward, 107–15; historical activism of, 275; and Jewish religious tradition, 1–9; left wing criticism of, 161; and Liberal Judaism in Germany, 93–106; as liberation movement, 210; messianic Zionism, 325; as missionary movement, 197; modernization as precondition of, 50; Orthodox attitude toward nonobservant, 46; and Orthodoxy, 116–39; and patriotism, 182; Pilgrims compared with, 198; practical Zionism, 119; religion as secondary to nationalism in, 274; and rural Atlas Jews, 312–29; secular character of nationalism of, 110–12; as secularizing force, 32, 52, 274; traditional Judaism challenged by, 25; and tradition in the Yishuv, 235–329; truisms about, 3; turning point in Jewish attitude toward, 32–33; in the United States, 173–234; utopian nature of, 53; in Vienna, 140–58. *See also* Cultural Zionism; Labor Zionism; Political Zionism; Religious Zionism; Revisionist movement

Zionist Actions Committee: debate on religion and society of 1934, 290; Mizrahi bring religious issue to fore of 1935 session, 291; and rabbinical committee proposal, 31; Russian and Galician rabbis demand clarification from, 37; secular beliefs of members of, 166; on separate religious education, 280

Zionist Commission, 279, 281

Zionist Executive, 286, 289, 291–92

Zionistische Vereinigung für Deutschland (German Zionist Association), 93, 99

Zionist Organization: Agudat Harabbanim pressure on, 226; and the British administration, 132; in educational and cultural activities of Yishuv, 277; establishment of, 30; as Herzl's "society of Jews," 124; and Mizrahi movement, 288; Old Yishuv as not represented in, 280; rabbinical opposition to, 31; religious Zionists' condition for participation in, 137; on woman suffrage, 135

Zionist youth movements: Buber's influence on, 305; in Eastern Europe, 302, 307–8; in Germany, 302, 307–8; inner truth concept in, 304–5; the religious question within, 302–11

Zionist Youth youth movement, 307

Zirelson, Judah, 31

UNIVERSITY PRESS OF NEW ENGLAND
publishes books under its own imprint and is the publisher for Brandeis University Press, Dartmouth College, Middlebury College Press, University of New Hampshire, Tufts University, and Wesleyan University Press.

Library of Congress Cataloging-in-Publication Data

Tsiyonut ve-dat. English.
    Zionism and religion / Shmuel Almog, Jehuda Reinharz, and Anita Shapira, editors.
      p.   cm. — (The Tauber Institute for the Study of European Jewry series ; 30)
    Papers from an international conference on Zionism and religion.
    Includes bibliographical references and index.
    ISBN 0–87451–882–2 (hardcover : alk. paper)
    1. Zionism and Judaism—Congresses. I. Almog, S. II. Reinharz, Jehuda. III. Shapira, Anita. IV. Title. V. Series.
DS149.T86413 1998
320.54'095694—dc21   98–22925